# THE GODS IN EPIC

# THE
# GODS IN EPIC

*Poets and Critics of the Classical Tradition*

D. C. FEENEY

CLARENDON PRESS · OXFORD

*This book has been printed digitally and produced in a standard specification*
*in order to ensure its continuing availability*

# OXFORD
UNIVERSITY PRESS

Great Clarendon Street, Oxford OX2 6DP

Oxford University Press is a department of the University of Oxford.
It furthers the University's objective of excellence in research, scholarship,
and education by publishing worldwide in

Oxford New York

Auckland Bangkok Buenos Aires Cape Town Chennai
Dar es Salaam Delhi Hong Kong Istanbul Karachi Kolkata
Kuala Lumþur Madrid Melbourne Mexico City Mumbai Nairobi
São Paulo Shanghai Taipei Tokyo Toronto

Oxford is a registered trade mark of Oxford University Press
in the UK and in certain other countries

Published in the United States
by Oxford University Press Inc., New York

ISBN 0-19-814938-7

For Jude
Matthew, and Peter

# Preface

The subject of this book is the role of the gods in the ancient world's literary epic tradition. The book begins, not with Homer, but with the reception of Homer, and with the evolution of diverse ways of understanding the gods in epic; it then goes on to trace the interaction between those diverse traditions and the epics which were created by poets of later generations. The book attempts, then, to view the classical literary tradition as a whole, and to provide a context for reading poems which are often treated in isolation not only from each other, but also from the intellectual and critical traditions which were so important in shaping their creation and their reception. The gods in epic are a problem into which most classicists run at one time or another, but one of the classicist's main prefatory topoi is the hope that one's work will be useful to students of other literatures. I have, accordingly, translated all but a very few scraps of the original Greek and Latin; in a few places, as indicated, I have given the translations of others.

An ideal book on such a large and manifold subject would require an ideal author, with a range of competence beyond anything to which the present author may lay claim. I have, however, profited very much from the conversations or communications of many friends, students, and colleagues (beginning with the Press Readers): E. K. Borthwick, W. Burkert, E. P. Garrison, S. J. Harrison, H. M. Hine, A. B. E. Hood, N. M. Horsfall, J. G. Howie, R. L. Hunter, H. D. Jocelyn, A. A. Long, J. C. McKeown, T. B. McKiernan, W. G. Moon, W. S. M. Nicoll, R. G. M. Nisbet, B. B. Powell, J. S. Richardson, N. J. Richardson, J. S. Rusten, N. K. Rutter, R. Wardy, and J. E. Wills. My greatest debt is a joint one, to A. J. Woodman, who read most of the book in draft, and to S. E. Hinds, who read all of it; their help and encouragement have been invaluable to me. Whatever all these people may have done to remedy my deficiencies, they cannot, of course, be held responsible for the use I have made of their generosity with their scholarship. I am, further, conscious of a more general obligation to my teachers at Auckland, and especially to W. R. Barnes, with whom I first read Homer, Apollonius, and Vergil, and who taught me much of what I now take for granted about the workings of ancient epic.

I have incurred debts also to institutions. I first began background reading for the book as a Junior Fellow in the Harvard University Society of Fellows in 1982–3; I am deeply grateful to the Chairman and Senior Fellows for electing me to a position in which I could enjoy the precious luxury of undisturbed months in the company of A, b, T, D, M, Q, and the rest. Interrupted and delayed by the demands of a peripatetic career, the work was completed at the end of two very happy years in Madison; I must acknowledge the support given me in the summer of 1989 by the Graduate School of the University of Wisconsin–Madison. Hirmer Verlag provided the photograph of Jupiter of Otricoli which is on the jacket. Finally, I thank the editors of *Classical Quarterly* and *Proceedings of the Virgil Society* for permission to use portions of articles published in their journals, which appear in the bibliography as Feeney (1984) and (1986a).

*Madison, Wisconsin*                                                    D.C.F.
*Anzac Day, 1990*

The appearance of a paperback edition has enabled me to make a few corrections (some supplied to me by D. West). It also makes a little updating possible. A. A. Long's essay on 'Stoic Readings of Homer' (pp. 32–3) has now been published (with seven other valuable papers) in R. Lamberton and J. J. Keaney (edd.), *Homer's Ancient Readers: The Hermeneutics of Greek Epic's Earliest Exegetes* (Princeton, 1992), 41–66; note also D. Dawson, *Allegorical Readers and Cultural revision in Ancient Alexandria* (Berkeley and Los Angeles, 1992). On the problem of fiction, see now T. P. Wiseman and C. Gill (edd.), *Lies and Fiction in the Ancient World*, (Exeter, 1993); in the 'Epilogue', I follow up some of the issues of *The Gods in Epic*.

*October, 1992*                                                         D.C.F.

# Contents

# Abbreviations

Periodicals are abbreviated according to the system of *L'Année philologique*. References to ancient authors follow the abbreviations of *The Oxford Classical Dictionary*², with occasional expansion for clarity.

| | |
|---|---|
| Bowra | C. M. Bowra, *Pindari Carmina cum Fragmentis*² (Oxford, 1947) |
| CAF | T. Kock, *Comicorum Atticorum Fragmenta* (Leipzig, 1880–8) |
| CHCL | *The Cambridge History of Classical Literature*, Vol. 1 *Greek Literature*, ed. P. E. Easterling and W. B. M. Knox (Cambridge, 1985); Vol. 2 *Latin Literature*, ed. E. J. Kenney and W. V. Clausen (Cambridge, 1982) |
| DK | H. Diels, *Die Fragmente der Vorsokratiker*⁶, ed. W. Kranz (Berlin, 1951–2) |
| EGF | M. Davies, *Epicorum Graecorum Fragmenta* (Göttingen, 1988) |
| Geo | H. Georgii, *Ti. Claudii Donati Interpretationes Vergilianae* (Leipzig, 1905–6) |
| GGM | C. Müller, *Geographici Graeci Minores* (Paris, 1855–61) |
| GLP | D. L. Page, *Select Papyri* III. *Literary Papyri: Poetry* (Cambridge, Mass., 1942) |
| H.–Sz. | J. B. Hofmann, *Lateinische Syntax und Stylistik*, rev. A. Szantyr (Munich, 1965) |
| Jacoby | F. Jacoby, *Die Fragmente der griechischen Historiker* (Berlin and Leiden, 1923–58) |
| Lex. Icon. Myth. | *Lexicon Iconographicum Mythologiae Classicae* (Zurich, 1981– ) |
| OLD | *The Oxford Latin Dictionary* (Oxford, 1968–82) |

| | |
|---|---|
| P. Oxy. | *The Oxyrhynchus Papyri* (London, 1898– ) |
| Pack | R. A. Pack, *The Greek and Latin Literary Texts from Greco-Roman Egypt*² (Ann Arbor, 1967) |
| *PLF* | E. Lobel and D. L. Page, *Poetarum Lesbiorum Fragmenta* (Oxford, 1955) |
| *PMG* | D. L. Page, *Poetae Melici Graeci* (Oxford, 1962) |
| Powell | J. U. Powell, *Collectanea Alexandrina* (Oxford, 1925) |
| *RE* | *Real-Encyclopädie der classischen Altertumswissenschaft* (Stuttgart, 1893–1978) |
| Roscher | W. H. Roscher, *Ausführliches Lexicon der griechischen und römischen Mythologie* (Leipzig, 1884–1937) |
| Schanz–Hosius | M. Schanz and C. Hosius, *Geschichte der römischen Literatur* (Munich, 1914–35) |
| Schmid–Stählin | W. Schmid and O. Stählin, *Geschichte der griechischen Literatur* (Munich, 1929–48) |
| *SH* | H. Lloyd-Jones and P. J. Parsons, *Supplementum Hellenisticum* (Berlin and New York, 1983) |
| Snell | B. Snell, *Bacchylidis Carmina cum Fragmentis*⁵ (Leipzig, 1934) |
| *SVF* | H. von Arnim, *Stoicorum Veterum Fragmenta* (Leipzig, 1902–5) |
| Thilo–Hagen | G. Thilo and H. Hagen, *Servii in Vergilii Carmina Commentarii* (Leipzig, 1881–1902) |
| *TLL* | *Thesaurus Linguae Latinae* (Leipzig, 1900– ) |
| Vahlen | I. Vahlen, *Ennianae Poesis Reliquiae*² (Leipzig, 1903) |
| Warmington | E. H. Warmington, *The Remains of Old Latin*² (Cambridge, Mass., 1956–7) |
| Wehrli | F. Wehrli, *Die Schule des Aristoteles*² (Basel, 1967–9) |

# Introduction

*Aud.* I do not know what poetical is: is it honest in deed and
word? is it a true thing?
*Touch.* No, truly: for the truest poetry is the most feigning.

Shakespeare, *As You Like It,* Act 3, Scene 3

The activities which we now label 'theology' and 'criticism' were
originally the preserve of the poets. Speaking about the gods was
something reserved for special occasions, an act performed in a
unique, 'marked', language;[1] and the masters of this craft reflected
upon the unique nature of their task in highly self-conscious
ways.[2] Then, in a profound and prolonged cultural shift, beginning in the sixth century BCE, the poets' monopoly on speaking
about the gods was broken, and 'theology' became the defined domain of intellectuals writing in prose. Although the poets never
surrendered the field altogether, they had to live with the knowledge that they had been displaced from the centre. The first critics
of the poets' forms of speech were hostile, denying any truth-value
to poetic depiction of the gods, and this tradition of hostility never
died out. Other traditions of criticism, however, building on the
poets' own insights, evolved sophisticated theories of fiction and
poetics which were more accommodating to the unique forms of
expression encountered in poetry.

The first chapter of this book is devoted to exploring the critical
attitudes which were formulated in response to these dramatic cultural transformations. The study of these traditions of criticism is
useful in various ways to the modern student of the surviving epics
of the literary tradition. Most obviously, it can help us recapture
something of the interpretative conventions of the original reading
community. Further, the poets themselves were, of course, part of

[1] Burkert (1985), 125; Nagy (1989), 3–4.
[2] Thalmann (1984); Walsh (1984).

this reading community, and they were inheritors of the critical tradition as well as the poetic. Indeed, the critical tradition was, inextricably, the medium through which each poet apprehended his poetic tradition. Each of the poets covered in this book demonstrates an intimate acquaintance with contemporary conventions of exegesis and scholarship. The representation of the divine in post-Homeric epic was not and could not be an unmediated response to earlier poetry, but found its forms within a rich and complex intellectual environment.

An acquaintance with ancient interpretative traditions can, moreover, provide invaluable historical perspective for the modern critic, engaged with an alien convention which is deceptively familiar. If we gain some insight into the reading conventions of the epics' reading communities, we give ourselves another view of familiar problems: the main example in this book is the ancient critics' attitude to the levels of naturalism and verisimilitude to be expected in epic. Even when they appear most obtuse, the critics may provide insight in very unexpected places. The ancient critics' pronouncements on Lucan's *Bellum Ciuile*, for example, may strike us as jejune and beside the point, yet I could not have arrived at my own conclusions about Lucan's strategies if I had not taken very seriously the categorizations and assumptions behind the critics' pronouncements.

The frustration evidently felt by many modern readers of epic shows that classicists' prevalent reading habits are not doing their job. Classicists tend to be the (unwitting) victims of realistic—indeed, novelistic—conventions of reading. One often hears professional classicists describing the gods in epic as a literary device: and this is usually meant as a criticism. But criticizing the gods in epic as a literary device is like criticizing the carburettors or pistons in a car as an engineering device. 'Of course they are', and 'What else can they be?' are the only replies possible. Such language betrays an attitude which one may most economically describe as novelistic prejudice, and it issues almost inevitably in readings which gloss over the gods as a more or less lame shorthand which the poets must perforce employ in order to achieve effects more satisfyingly achieved by novelistic naturalism. Although there are various ways of arguing against such approaches, a powerful one is available to us in the ancient critics' well-developed theories of epic fantasy and generic classification, as the first chapter will show in detail.

The ancients' traditions of criticism have been pressed into service by a number of recent studies of ancient literature. Since my own exploitation of ancient criticism may be open to misinterpretation, it is important for me to state that the ancient critics are used in this book as an aid, even a guide, but not as a prescription, or a straitjacket. It is no part of my brief to disqualify any readings on the grounds that they do not square with what an ancient critic might conceivably have thought. I am interested in opening up ways of interpreting these poems, not closing them down. If we refuse to countenance any interpretation which was unavailable to an ancient critic, we will be doing these poems a profound disservice. I do not, in other words, believe, as some of my contemporaries appear to believe, that the ideal reading of an ancient epic would be one achieved by necromancy with the shade of Servius— or even Aristarchus—or even Aristotle. The critical techniques of the ancient world should enlighten, not constrain, us. Modern linguists or philologists would never dream of allowing the boundaries of their discipline to be marked out by the interests or competence of a Servius—no more should modern critics.

The problem of how to read the gods in epic is a problem of fiction before anything else, and here too the ancient critical tradition has much to teach us. Poets and critics were closely engaged with the issues of what kind of meaning poetry creates, what kind of truth it achieves, as it works its deceitful way upon the audience, generating falsehoods which gesture towards truths not apprehensible in any other medium; the gods, inevitably, were at the cutting edge of this problem of the truth-value of epic fiction. One of the book's main themes is therefore the problem of the poet's authority, of what kind of belief it is that poetry generates. It is, of course, often assumed that there was a golden age when poet and audience, poetry and religion, art and experience were all in seamless accord. Yet belief, and the authority of the poet, were always potentially problematic, not least because the contexts in which people apprehended the gods varied so widely. Listening to Homer, Aeschylus, or Pindar—these were all discrete varieties of experience,[3] and none of them was an experience which made unmediated sense to the audience in terms which applied directly

---

[3] A point excellently made by Lamberton (1986), 11, speaking of 'the period previous to the fourth century B.C.' (10).

to other aspects of their lives.[4] As Mikalson's study of Athenian popular religion in the fourth century BCE shows, the picture of religious experience which emerges from the fourth-century sources (oratory and inscriptions) is very different from that which emerges from the fifth-century sources (tragedy and lyric). Yet, as he cautiously observes: 'This difference between the highly detailed and fully anthropomorphic conception of the gods seen in the poets of the fifth century and the collective, generalized conception of the gods found in the fourth-century sources is primarily, I think, a difference of genre and does not reflect a change in religious conceptions.'[5] Epic's unique way of depicting the gods deserves to be studied as a unique phenomenon—not something divorced from its religious and cultural context, but a form of speech with its own definitive and characteristic modes.

These issues will be discussed in detail in the first chapter, after which the surviving epics themselves become the subject. A number of themes recur throughout the book, and it has seemed convenient to give the main discussion of each in the context of the poem which most explicitly or interestingly engages with it. Fiction, then, receives its main discussion with Apollonius, belief with Vergil, allegory with Statius, anthropomorphism with Ovid, and so on. Some readers may be surprised at the amount of attention devoted to the Silver Latin epics. I make no apology, since I hope that the prominence they have in this book may play some part in contributing to the rehabilitation which three of them, at any rate, so richly merit, and which one of them is now at last receiving.

---

[4] The study of Homer's gods by Erbse (1986) is the most extreme statement of this position. One may criticize his book in detail, especially for the view that Homer invented the apparatus of his poetry, rather than inheriting it from his tradition (307); but his fundamental point, that the experience of Homer's poetry is not simply commensurate with the experience of religion, is theoretically irrefutable.

[5] Mikalson (1983), 114.

# 1

## The Critics: Beginnings, and a Synthesis

---

### I

> The prologues are over. It is a question, now,
> Of final belief. So, say that final belief
> Must be in a fiction. It is time to choose.
>
> Wallace Stevens, 'Asides on the Oboe'

The aim of the first chapter is to give a picture of the intellectual environment inhabited by the epic poets of the classical tradition, and their readers, as they confronted the problems of the gods in epic. The task is rendered difficult by the obvious fact that this was no homogeneous environment, but a contested and evolving one, of extreme complexity, itself always being transformed by the contribution of each successive poet. It is, further, practically impossible to establish any very firm boundaries around the environment we are trying to recover, so pervasive was the presence of the epic gods in antiquity. We cannot here, for example, treat the subject of how dramatic poets responded to the gods of epic, although the responses of the dramatic poets will feature incidentally throughout the book. The problem of the gods in epic is large enough as it is without involving yet another distinctive set of problems; the argument of this first chapter will, I trust, establish the justification for taking one literary mode at a time. It will be necessary to be selective to the point of curtness, yet even a selective introductory chapter, by charting the main critical responses to the gods of Homer, and by setting out the cardinal ancient attitudes towards fiction, will lay enough of a foundation to help the subsequent readings of the post-Homeric epics.

This first Section in particular is meant to assist those who are not familiar with the basic history of ancient criticism, and the bulk of it will therefore be quite familiar to professional classicists, who may feel well advised to move on and begin at Section II

(p. 33). In Section I, with all allowable concision, the story will be taken down to Hellenistic times, introducing the two intertwined themes which Section II will develop in detail: first, the principal techniques which successive generations of increasingly professionalized critics developed for reading the gods of epic; second, the attitudes towards fiction which the poets entertained, and which the critics, in their turn, distilled from the poets.[1]

Xenophanes' truculent voice is the first heard raised against the gods of epic.[2] His criticisms are famous. Justly, for not only are they excitingly vigorous and compelling in themselves, but they have a considerable historical significance, establishing, or first embodying, many important lines of argument. Behind much of Xenophanes' varied output lies the popular epic tradition, the tradition of Homer and Hesiod, which conditioned his ideas of what was important, and provided a first principle for his originality to react against.[3] Mulling over the nature of the divine, he was inevitably engaged with Hesiod, and with Homer, from whom, in Xenophanes' own words, 'everyone had learnt from the start' (B 10). He energetically set about attacking the epic picture of the gods, in verses that are still superbly effective and intelligent. As a first point, these gods are quite immoral:

πάντα θεοῖς ἀνέθηκαν Ὅμηρός θ' Ἡσίοδός τε
ὅσσα παρ' ἀνθρώποισιν ὀνείδεα καὶ ψόγος ἐστίν,
κλέπτειν μοιχεύειν τε καὶ ἀλλήλους ἀπατεύειν.

Homer and Hesiod attributed to the gods everything which in mankind is disgrace and reproach: stealing, committing adultery, deceiving one another. (B 11)

Since Xenophanes explicitly says that humans conceive of the gods as resembling men and women, in clothing, speech, and body (B 14), it is a reasonable inference that he saw the gods' immoral behaviour in epic as a consequence of their anthropomorphism.

[1] If professional readers do peruse this section, and wonder where my discussions of Heraclitus, or Parmenides, or Empedocles have vanished to, I can only ask their indulgence; a number of books could grow out of this first Section, and I can do no more than stress again the strictly introductory function of the following pages.
[2] Fragments in DK 21; Untersteiner (1955); Kirk, Raven, and Schofield (1983), 163–80. Xenophanes was active from the mid-550s BCE until around 478, according to Steinmetz (1966), 13–34.
[3] Havelock (1966), 51–4.

Xenophanes brings out formidable weapons of comparative ethnography to show that the Greeks are no more correct in this regard than anyone else: Thracians and Ethiopians have gods that look like Thracians and Ethiopians, and if cattle and horses and lions had gods and images of gods, then cattle and horses and lions is what they would look like (B 15, 16). The conventional, epic, picture of the gods is shown to be false, a thing made up by men thinking on false premises. In another context, Xenophanes introduces to describe this 'making up' a word that is to be of crucial and various significance for later discussion. In setting the scene for a symposium, and discussing the appropriate type of poetry, he rejects that kind of poetry which deals with the battles of Titans, Giants, and Centaurs, describing such compositions as πλάσματα τῶν προτέρων, 'things "moulded", "formed", by men of earlier times' (B 1. 21–2). Xenophanes' main concern is ostensibly to declare that tales of strife are not fitting for the scene, but his choice of the word πλάσματα constitutes a glancing disparagement by a further criterion: these stories are not only out of place, they are made up.[4] This type of poetry is a πλάσμα, depicting not something real or actual, but something fabricated.

The first critic of epic displays another important concept, with an even more potent afterlife. Describing his supreme deity, he says:

αἰεὶ δ' ἐν ταὐτῷ μίμνει κινούμενος οὐδέν
οὐδὲ μετέρχεσθαί μιν ἐπιπρέπει ἄλλοτε ἄλλῃ,
ἀλλ' ἀπάνευθε πόνοιο νόου φρενὶ πάντα κραδαίνει.

Always he remains in the same place, moving not at all; nor is it fitting for him to go to different places at different times, but without toil he shakes all things by the thought of his mind. (B 26 and 25, Kirk's trans.)

This picture is likewise a reaction against the epic account of the modes of divine operation, as Havelock has shown,[5] and exhibits already a style of thought which is completely characteristic of much later argument, from both critics and philosophers. As Hussey puts it, 'Xenophanes . . . relies entirely on certain general principles—certain conceptions of what it is reasonable or fitting

---

[4] Fränkel (1975), 328; Havelock (1966), 52.

[5] Havelock (1966), 53–4. One should perhaps stress (as Havelock does) that this is a reaction against the *Hesiodic* account; see Lloyd-Jones (1971), 81–2, for a reading of Xenophanes' words which sees them as consonant with certain aspects of Homer's Zeus.

that a god should be.'[6] Violations of these general conceptions of what is πρέπον ('fitting' or 'seemly') constitute anomalies which must be explained away, in one fashion or another. To Xenophanes, the violations embodied in epic are only inventions of men who are mistaken; they could be dismissed as having nothing to do with the true nature of the divine. And here we touch upon a third line of development, undeveloped (so far as we can now tell) in Xenophanes, which needed only activation and exploitation, namely, the notion that there was a necessary divorce between true or philosophical theology and the theology of the poets.[7] A blade with two edges, this, for use in polemic or defence—to impugn the authority of the poets, or to claim for them exemption from the criteria appropriate to another form of speech and apprehension.

At the death of Xenophanes, such claims, together with the critical apparatus necessary to beget them, lay far in the future. But the sage from Colophon had left his mark. The gods we see in epic are immoral. They are fabrications of poets. They do not correspond to what it is seemly for the divine to be. They are a way of looking at the divine which has no contact with the way a wise man should look at the divine.

Xenophanes' attacks on the gods of the epic tradition were occasioned by the tradition's pervasive cultural influence and prestige, and it was the very prestige of the tradition which made it inevitable that others would take it upon themselves to provide a defence. The person whom later tradition remembered as the first to do so was one Theagenes, from the city of Rhegium in Magna Graecia.[8] Although there is no explicit evidence that Theagenes was reacting to Xenophanes, the assumption is widely made.[9] Nothing of his writings survives, and the only evidence we have for what he said about the gods in Homer comes from a scholion on the Battle of the Gods in *Iliad* 20—a discussion which was in all probability written some eight hundred years later.[10] The scholion does not purport to give us details of Theagenes' doctrine

---

[6] Hussey (1972), 14; cf. Untersteiner (1955), pp. clxxxvii–clxxxviii. On τὸ πρέπον, the fundamental discussion is Pohlenz (1933).

[7] Jaeger (1947), 50.

[8] DK 8; Buffière (1956), 103–5; Pépin (1958), 97–8.

[9] Decharme (1904), 273; Pépin (1958), 98; Griffiths (1967), 79.

[10] Schrader (1880–2), 403.

as such. It reports, rather, that some people reply to attacks on Homer's stories about the gods as 'unseemly' by explaining them 'on the basis of the form of expression used' (ἀπὸ τῆς λέξεως).[11] The commentator goes on to give examples: these people see the battle of the gods as being really a description of the fight in nature between the dry and the wet, the hot and the cold, the light and the heavy. The same people (continues the scholion) consider that Homer also gives the names of the gods to human qualities: he gives the name Athene to φρόνησις ('wisdom'), Ares to ἀφροσύνη ('folly'), and so on. Such a defence, then, consists in interpreting the names of the gods as referring to something other than what the words ostensibly refer to; and this sort of defence, says our commentator, the defence 'on the basis of the form of expression used', is 'really old, and goes back to Theagenes of Rhegium, the first man to write about Homer'.[12]

It is plain that the author of this passage knows nothing at first hand of Theagenes' writings, and is aware only of a tradition that he was the first to use 'this sort of defence'. If it is possible to attribute any precision to the words of the scholion, when it describes Theagenes as using the defence which took the form of expression as its base, then it is very probable that he discussed the *names* of the gods, attempting to show that these names referred to something other than their first apparent reference. As we shall see, there was later (and not very much later at that) a positive industry of such identifications, many of them founded on etymologies. It all had to start somewhere. All someone like Theagenes had to do to get going was to follow the lead of Hesiod, who shows that Zeus' very name reveals his power as the one *through whom* things happen (Δί' ἐννέπετε ... ὅν τε διὰ βροτοί ... κτλ., *Op.* 2–3).[13] Or he could consider *Iliad* 21. 6–7, where Hera spreads out a thick mist to keep the Trojans back: ἠέρα δ' "Ηρη / πίτνα πρόσθε βαθεῖαν ἐρυκέμεν. The identification of the goddess (HPA) with the middle air (AHP) is one of the earliest, most popular, and durable of such cases.[14] Or else he could have observed Homer's plays on the very name for 'god', which align it with 'rapidity'.[15]

---

[11] On this critical term, see Carroll (1895), 40–55; Combellack (1987).
[12] Schrader (1880–2), 241. 10–12.
[13] See West (1978) ad loc.; Fraenkel (1950) on Aesch. *Ag.* 1485–6.
[14] Buffière (1956), 106–10.
[15] Haywood (1983); cf. Lamberton (1986), 38, on how the roots of the technique are 'demonstrably Homeric'.

'Allegory' is the word which the modern reader will have been instinctively assuming throughout this discussion, and it is the word which the scholiast uses of this kind of defence: 'everything is said by allegory for the nature of the elements.'[16] Yet the word ἀλληγορία was not used in this sense until the first century BCE, while the earliest evidence for the word which ἀλληγορία superseded (ὑπόνοια, 'hidden meaning'), occurs something like a hundred years after Theagenes.[17] Theagenes' own terminology is irrecoverable, along with his motives and rationale; yet, whatever his procedures may have been, it appears tolerably certain that he was not presenting his own vision of the nature of things, but expounding a text.[18] He was remembered not only as the first man to use the λύσις ἐκ τῆς λέξεως for the Theomachy in the *Iliad*, but also as the first man to 'search after Homer's poetry and birth and date', and as the man who began the study of 'Homer's correct usage of the Greek language'; there is even a variant reading in the text of the *Iliad* attributed to him.[19] It is very difficult to know what to make of all this. Claims have been made for Theagenes as a 'grammarian', and even as the 'editor' of a text of Homer.[20] This is anachronistic, to say the least, but it is crucial to see him as someone interested in writing about Homer's life, language, and meaning, and hence as the first identifiable member of a race which was to breed and flourish for centuries.

It is in the highest degree unlikely that Theagenes devised the full panoply of allegorical technique which we see exemplified in the scholion on the Battle of the Gods, with its twin techniques of explaining the gods as elements of nature (the so-called 'physical' allegory), or as qualities ('moral' allegory).[21] Tate was right to stress the gradual development of this 'allegorical' way of reading

[16] Schrader (1880–2), 240. 17–18.

[17] Pépin (1958), 85–8; Richardson (1975), 66–7; Whitman (1987), 263–8 ('On the History of the Term "Allegory"').

[18] A point put most strongly by Decharme (1904), 275; Detienne (1962), 65–7.

[19] I give DK 8. 1a in the translation of Pfeiffer (1968), 11. Theagenes' variant is recorded by A on *Il.* 1. 381.

[20] Detienne (1962), 65–7 ('grammarian'); Mosino (1961), 78 ('editor').

[21] Tate (1927); Detienne (1962), 67; Lamberton (1986), 32. On ancient allegory, Hersman (1906); Tate (1927), (1929), (1930), (1934); Wehrli (1928); Buffière (1956); Pépin (1958); Lévêque (1959); Rollinson (1981); Nugent (1985); Hardie (1986), esp. 5–29; Lamberton (1986); Whitman (1987), 1–57. Modern studies include Fletcher (1964); Murrin (1969) and (1980); Quilligan (1979); van Dyke (1985).

and discussing Homer;[22] and we must bear in mind the variety of motives which may have been behind such techniques, since some proponents will have been attempting to use Homer's authority to bolster their own speculations about the world.[23] None the less, for whatever reason, Theagenes' contribution was distinctive or authoritative enough to guarantee the survival, if not of his works, at least of his name, as the first person to interpret the gods of Homer as being something other than what a surface reading would suggest. The quasi-scholarly investigations which formed part of the same enterprise marked the beginning of a great industry.

The development of such allegorical interpretations, and their potent influence on the epic poets who followed, will be an important sub-theme in this book. Other responses to the problems of the gods in epic became available, however, although less preoccupied with defending the poets' style of myth, and more with saving the phenomena. Not many years after Theagenes, the writings of Hecataeus of Miletus already exhibit a 'rationalizing' approach.[24] As this enquiring traveller sifted through the many items of tradition, he would sometimes rescue from myth a kernel of what might be salvaged as historical fact.[25] The hound of Hell, accordingly, carried off by Heracles from the Underworld, becomes in Hecataeus a terrible snake, called the dog of Hades because anyone it bit died immediately from its poison (fr. 27 Jacoby). Similarly, the spectacular exploits of Heracles in Spain are circumscribed by the logographer: Geryon, the cattle-rancher king, lived merely on the shores of the gulf of Ambracia, no more than 125 miles from the hero's birthplace (fr. 26 Jacoby). Such treatments of myth flourished, and not only in the writings of historians and scholars: as we shall see, poets also could exploit the material and the approach.

It is commonly maintained that such were the two reactions available

---

[22] Tate (1927), 215; but see Griffiths (1967), 79–80, for some caution over Tate's sweeping demotion of Theagenes.

[23] Tate (1930) and (1934).

[24] On ancient rationalism, see Wipprecht (1902); Nestle (1942), 132–52; Wardman (1960), 408–11; Walbank (1960), 226–7; Wiseman (1979), 49, 146–7, 158–9; Veyne (1983).

[25] We return below, in the first Section of Chapter 6, to the highly controversial question of what passed in the ancient world for 'historical'.

to those who were loath to jettison outright the epics' picture of the gods.[26] One could, on either count, redeem the data of the poems by revealing a kernel of fact: 'philosophical' fact in camouflage, or 'historical' fact preserved behind a smokescreen of mythological irrelevancies. Both approaches are historically significant, and the scholarly tradition behind both is of the highest importance for later composers of epic, for whom these methods of interpretation were a basic part of their intellectual equipment. Yet the prominence of allegorical and rationalizing interpretation can be distorting, for their very reductionism was liable to disqualify them from the task of explaining how meanings generated by poetic forms of speech differed from meanings generated by other forms. The gods, of course, are only one of the problems in the way of any such account, even if they were, to the Greeks, the biggest one. Before any other methods of reading the gods could be established, some attempt was necessary at understanding the way in which poetry achieves the significances it does achieve. The scholars were a long time in coming up with any such understanding, and when they did, they got there by following the leads given by the poets themselves.[27]

When looking at the 'fictions' (πλάσματα) of the poets, the critics might scoff, like Xenophanes; they might plead or salvage, like Theagenes or Hecataeus. For the composers themselves, when standing up to sing, or ordering the chorus, the problem was of quite a different order. From the beginning of the surviving poetic tradition, the artists show themselves to be much preoccupied with the nature of poetic representation, with the kind of truth or reality that poetry depicts, or creates, or achieves. The issues here, and the key texts, are well known;[28] it is worth considering a few major passages in order to allow the main points to emerge.

The earliest pronouncement on the truth-value of poetic lan-

[26] Wipprecht (1902), 8–11; Nestle (1942), 126–52.

[27] Cf. Richardson (1985), 398–9, on the decisive insights of Pfeiffer (1968): 'it was the poets themselves who led the way in the development of literary and rhetorical theory, just as they did also in the field of scholarship'.

[28] On early Greek poetics, see the collection of Lanata (1963); then Maehler (1963); Detienne (1967); Harriott (1969); Pucci (1977); Walsh (1984); Thalmann (1984); Nagy (1989). The truth value of poetic and fictional statements has received extensive modern discussion: Ruthven (1979), 164–80; Waugh (1984), 87–114; Pavel (1986); Bruner (1986); further bibliography in the important article of Rösler (1980), 283–5.

guage—and in many ways the most potent—is given by Hesiod, who tells us that he met the Muses when he was shepherding on Mt. Helicon, and that they told him this:

ἴδμεν ψεύδεα πολλὰ λέγειν ἐτύμοισιν ὁμοῖα,
ἴδμεν δ᾽ εὖτ᾽ ἐθέλωμεν ἀληθέα γηρύσασθαι.

We know how to say many lies that are similar to true things, and we know how to speak true things, when we wish. (*Th.* 27–8)[29]

It is up to the Muses, in characteristic divine manner, to bestow on the poet true song or misleading song 'as they wish', and therefore 'there is no way of knowing whether the song with which the Muses inspire him is authentic truth or falsehood that simulates it'.[30] What Hesiod is recognizing when he gives these words to his goddesses is the inherently unstable nature of the craft. However much Hesiod may himself wish to tell the truth (at the beginning of the *Works and Days* he declares that he 'would say true things to Perses', 10),[31] the positive side of his craft is always implicated in the devices of convincing deception which mark the negative side. The very power of language, working upon its audience with Peitho ('persuasion'), is represented by Hesiod as something that works obliquely, and approximates to the modes of deceit, even when it is beneficent.[32]

The poets' awareness of the plasticity and fictive power of their medium is nowhere more dramatically shown than in their acutely self-conscious attitudes towards their tradition, and their control over that tradition. Already Homer altered stories he inherited,[33] but he did not call the audience to take stock of the fact of alteration. Later poets do precisely this, however, as they select, reject, adapt, and innovate.[34] The composer of the *Hymn to Dionysus*,

[29] On these much-discussed lines, see Lanata (1963), 22–6; Pucci (1977); Walsh (1984), 26–33; Thalmann (1984), 143–56. My brief account glides over the controversial nature of the discussion.
[30] Thalmann (1984), 148; cf. Pucci (1977), esp. 1; Walsh (1984), 33. See West (1966) ad loc. for expressions such as 'when we wish', a token of the gods' unaccountability to man.
[31] Cf. Walsh (1984), 33.
[32] Detienne (1967), 62–8; Buxton (1982), 62–6; Thalmann (1984), 148–9. Blunter statements on the language of poets are notorious. Solon's assertion became proverbial: πολλὰ ψεύδονται ἀοιδοί, 'bards tell many lies' (fr. 29). Still, the man who said this was a poet, and his assertion was part of a poem. He may have gone on to claim that his poetry had a 'truth' that other poetry did not have.
[33] Willcock (1964); Braswell (1971).
[34] The best general account of this phenomenon is now March (1987).

for example, passes in review alternative versions of the god's birth, rejects the authors of those versions as 'liars', and puts forward his own account (*Hymn. Hom.* 1. 1–7). In order to illustrate the poets' command over tradition, and its implications for the nature of their fiction, two cases may be treated here in moderate detail: Stesichorus on Helen, and Pindar on Pelops.

By the traditional poetic account, as seen in Homer and the Epic Cycle, Helen left her husband, Menelaus, and journeyed with Paris to Troy, where she remained during the ten years of siege, as the wife first of Paris, then of Deiphobus, finally to be reunited with Menelaus after, or even during, the sack.[35] According to Plato's Socrates (*Phdr.* 243 a), Stesichorus wrote a poem which followed this traditional version of Helen's story, but he was then struck blind. Recognizing that the anger of Helen was the cause of his blindness, he forthwith composed another poem, attempting to redeem himself by setting the record straight with a 'palinode' or 'recantation':

> οὐκ ἔστ' ἔτυμος λόγος οὗτος,
> οὐδ' ἔβας ἐν νηυσὶν εὐσέλμοις
> οὐδ' ἵκεο πέργαμα Τροίας.

That story is not true, you did not go in the well-decked ships, nor did you come to the citadel of Troy. (fr. 192 PMG)

The problems of interpretation are legion, especially since we now know, from a papyrus published in 1963, that Stesichorus actually wrote not one, but two palinodes, one attacking the version of the Helen story to be found in Homer, the other attacking the version of Hesiod.[36] It is not now possible to tell what part of the poet's words gave rise to the detached anecdote about the blindness, nor is an occasion for the composition of the later poems recoverable. What we can recognize, however, even in our shattered evidence, is a remarkable orientation of the poet towards his matter.

The first time Stesichorus dealt with Helen, it appears that she

---

[35] Helen is a most controversial figure in early Greek poetry and poetics: Schmid (1982); Zagagi (1985).

[36] P. Oxy. 29 fr. 26 col. i (193 PMG). I am most grateful to Malcolm Davies for permission to consult and refer to his (as yet unpublished) Oxford thesis (1979). He has a full discussion and bibliography of the issues involved in the reconstruction of these poems.

was the adulteress and 'husband-deserter' of the popular tradition (fr. 223 *PMG*). When, for whatever reason, he wanted to treat of her again, he turned against that tradition, and told of how an 'image' (εἴδωλον) of Helen was in fact responsible, the woman herself staying in Sparta the whole time, or else accompanying Paris only so far as Egypt, where she stayed with King Proteus. Although he must have done something new with the εἴδωλον, it is almost certain that he did not invent it altogether, for it appears that Hesiod was the first to introduce the εἴδωλον into the story of Helen (fr. 358), and it is difficult to see what else Stesichorus may have criticized Hesiod for in his anti-Hesiodic Palinode, if not for an inept or unsatisfactory exploitation of this device.[37] Stesichorus, then, surveys his (already multivocal) tradition, and not only dissociates himself from this tradition, but also from an earlier production of his own which the tradition had led him to compose. He explicitly denounces that 'version' or 'story' (λόγος) as not 'true' (ἔτυμος), thereby implicitly asserting that his new version *is* 'true' (in the lost portions of the poem this claim may have become explicit). For a composer freely and self-consciously innovating, this is an arresting stance, testimony to a striking self-assurance about the malleability of mythic, poetic matter. If, as has been suggested, the two palinodes told different stories, this pose is even more striking.[38]

Even the Muse, patroness of poets' tradition, may be involved. The papyrus now reveals that the οὐκ ἔστιν palinode began with the following line,[39] which looks very much like an address to the Muse: δεῦρ' αὖτε θεὰ φιλόμολπε ('Hither, again, goddess, lover of song', fr. 193. 9–10 *PMG*). The epithet is appropriate for a Muse, and the use of δεῦρο ('hither') also suits such a context.[40] The intriguing word is αὖτε, 'again'. It may mean no more than 'again, as many times before'.[41] Yet it may be that we have here an allusion to a specific earlier poem, and the obvious candidate is the original *Helen*.[42] If this is the case (and we have no means of knowing), then Stesichorus is indulging in a feat of tremendous

[37] Davies (1979), 469–72.
[38] Segal (1985), 191.
[39] Davison (1966), 84.
[40] Elsewhere Stesichorus calls a Muse ἀρχεσίμολπον ('beginner of song', fr. 250 *PMG*); for δεῦρο, cf. frr. 240, 935. 2 *PMG*; fr. 127 *PLF*.
[41] Cf. Sappho, fr. 127 *PLF*.
[42] Bowra (1963), 246.

panache, calling upon the Muse, the guarantor of poets' 'truth', to collaborate with him in setting right the version which the two of them had earlier given the world. The 'truth' of the Muses and their poets is indeed a protean thing.

The plasticity of Greek myth has been often remarked upon. Amongst the scattered, locally-based cults, there was no possibility of 'orthodoxy', nor any vested interest in it. There was no authority over the speech about the gods and the myths which was the special prerogative of the poets; the poet remade tradition (the 'truth') every time he sang. There were books but no Book; even Homer's and Hesiod's prestige as the great systematizers did not carry them into being, in a strict sense, canonical.[43] A frame of mind which arranged belief according to occasion or setting is exceedingly difficult for inheritors of a revealed, Church tradition to recapture; yet our problem is a rather different one when we face the pronouncements of a Stesichorus. Here the very problems of acceptance and belief are placed in the foreground—almost revelled in. There is no question of 'How do you know this is true?'; the new story is just said to be true, is *made* to be 'true'.

What is at issue is the authenticating power of the poet's language, and our second example of a poet's control over his tradition will focus explicitly on the qualities of poetic language which give poetry that authenticating power. It is being increasingly recognized that Pindar's pronouncements on poetry anticipate the attitudes adopted by the men who, shortly after his death, began for the first time to produce in prose what we might call criticism.[44] Yet, as Pindar's more modest contemporary, Bacchylides, was prepared to admit, ἕτερος ἐξ ἑτέρου σοφός / τό τε πάλαι τό τε νῦν ('one man gets wisdom and skill from another, now as in the old days', fr. 5. 1–2 Snell); and Pindar's poetics, bold as they are, are firmly grounded in his tradition—indeed, the very manner of his reference to these concerns shows that such topics were 'things expected and well understood'.[45]

At the beginning of the First *Olympian*, Pindar is praising Hieron, tyrant of Syracuse, for his victory in the horse-race at Olympia in 476 BCE, and one of his devices of praise is to produce

[43] Gould (1985), 6–8; Burkert (1985), 119–25.
[44] Young (1983); Richardson (1985).
[45] Russell (1981), 19.

a new version of the myth of Pelops, the 'patron-hero' of the
Olympic Games, so that Hieron may share as closely as possible in
the hero's great glory. He no more than touches on the myth, with
a mention of Poseidon's love for Pelops, when he checks, and reflects on the transformations he is about to achieve:

ἦ θαυματὰ πολλά, καί πού τι καὶ βροτῶν
φάτις ὑπὲρ τὸν ἀλαθῆ λόγον
δεδαιδαλμένοι ψεύδεσι ποικίλοις ἐξαπατῶντι μῦθοι.

Χάρις δ', ἅπερ ἅπαντα τεύχει τὰ μείλιχα θνατοῖς,
ἐπιφέροισα τιμὰν καὶ ἄπιστον ἐμήσατο πιστὸν
ἔμμεναι τὸ πολλάκις·
ἀμέραι δ' ἐπίλοιποι
μάρτυρες σοφώτατοι.
ἔστι δ' ἀνδρὶ φάμεν ἐοικὸς
ἀμφὶ δαιμόνων καλά· μείων γὰρ αἰτία.
υἱὲ Ταντάλου, σὲ δ' ἀντία προτέρων φθέγξομαι ...

Indeed, wonders are many, and, methinks, what men say deceives—
stories embellished with intricate lies, beyond true speech. But Grace of
song, which makes for mortals all soothing joys, if she adds her honour,
often makes believed even what is not to be believed; but the days to
come are the wisest witnesses. It is seemly for man to say fine things
about the gods; for then there is less reproach. Son of Tantalus, contrary
to earlier men, I will say of you that ... (Ol. 1. 27–36)

The preoccupation with 'deceit' and 'lies' will by now be familiar. Further, Pindar speaks of the 'true story' being exceeded,
implying that he will give the ἀλαθὴς λόγος, going against the
version of 'earlier men' (36). Pindar's innovations in the Pelops
story are every bit as self-conscious and dramatic as those of
Stesichorus in the Helen story. Certainly Pindar presents his
changes in the story as being the result of moral decisions, as he is
reluctant to speak evil of the gods; but it is possible to be misled
by the proclamation of religious fastidiousness into overlooking
the fact that Pindar tells the repulsive traditional tale at some
length (48–51).[46] It is not altogether, or even primarily, a question
of religious taste and scruple, for Pindar's changes are consistently
dictated by his particular rhetorical and poetic needs.[47] It matters
that Pindar gives an ethical colour to the changes which he is imposing according to the criteria of praise-poetry, but they remain

[46] Köhnken (1974), 200–1; Stinton (1976), 67–8.
[47] Köhnken (1974), 203–4, 206; Gerber (1982), 69–70.

# 18                    *The Critics*

the criteria of praise-poetry for all that. Pindar knew, and his audience knew (if they cared to think like this), that his story was
'novel', and 'without authority'. That is not the point. Only poetic
power makes the other story believed, and Pindar's poetic power
can supplant it, to offer a story more worth accepting, more
'true'.[48]

Pindar is not being complimentary here in speaking of the
power of poetry to deceive. Yet the apparent stability of this position is disturbed when he describes the deceitful stories as
δεδαιδαλμένοι ψεύδεσι ποικίλοις ('embellished with intricate lies',
29), for these epithets of intricacy and embellishment are also applied by Pindar elsewhere, in terms of full approbation, to his own
poetry.[49] A similar two-sidedness is seen when Pindar goes on to
speak of Charis ('Grace of song'), as being the power which gives
τιμά ('honour', almost 'authority') to this false story, making
credible even what is incredible. Charis achieves this by her power
to charm, and the conditional force of the participle ἐπιφέροισα
must be stressed; *if* she adds authority by her charm, she makes
even the unbelievable believable. This divine caprice recalls the
Muses of Hesiod, with their εὖτ' ἐθέλωμεν ('when we wish', *Th.*
28).[50] Grace by herself, or else the three Graces together, have a
very important role in Pindar's poetics.[51] Overwhelmingly, it is a
favourable role, yet the attributes of Pindar's own 'good' Charis
cohere with those of the Charis in *Olympian* 1. The Charites are
the givers of pleasure and delight, especially in poetry, just like the
Charis of *Olympian* 1.[52] Although Pindar in our poem appears to
claim that the power of Charis will not prevail against the passage
of time, elsewhere he says that it is the Charites who will ensure
the survival of true fame.[53] In fact, in *Olympian* 1, as Kirkwood
observes, the 'statement about the power of Charis is ambiguous',
for Pindar's new version will succeed by virtue of the same Charis
which perpetuated the old version.[54]

---

[48] Gianotti (1975), 62. Generally, on Pindar's manipulation of truth, see now
Segal (1986).
[49] *Nem.* 8. 15; fr. 94b. 44 Snell; see Kahn (1978), 132; Young (1983), 168–9.
[50] Lanata (1963), 91 refers the problems of Pindar's Charis to the Hesiod passage.
[51] Duchemin (1955), 54–94.
[52] *Ol.* 9. 26–8; 14. 3–12; cf. Duchemin, loc. cit.
[53] *Ol.* 4. 8–10; *Nem.* 4. 6–8.
[54] Kirkwood (1982), on *Ol.* 1. 30; cf. Duchemin (1955), 61–2; Lanata (1963),
91.

Pindar's 'Hesiodic' awareness of the inextricably complex sources of poetic authority is perhaps best shown in a fragment of a Maidens' Song, where there is a prayer to personified Truth not to make good faith stumble against rough falsehood (fr. 194 Bowra). In *Olympian* 1, however, the credibility of the incredible represents a stage further than Hesiod's 'lies similar to true things'. In Pindar, the problem of 'true' and 'false' is verging into the problem of 'believable' and 'unbelievable', as he reflects upon the power of his craft to make credible that which should not be so, and, likewise, to make incredible that which should not be so.

Simonides, a poet born a generation before Pindar, had made the point as trenchantly as possible: τὸ δοκεῖν καὶ τὰν ἀλάθειαν βιᾶται ('appearance forces even truth', fr. 598 *PMG*). This 'appearance' is the quintessential effect of poetry; if any reliance may be placed in an anecdote told by Plutarch, Simonides will have described ἀπάτη ('deception') as the agent by which 'appearance' was created and the truth 'forced'.[55]

Pindar does not gloat over the polyvalency of poetry, as Simonides may have done; he is too intent upon validating his own productions. Yet he does revel in his innovative control over myth as he produces his own 'truth'—a 'truth' which has its roots in the weird authenticating power of the poet's language. As Richardson points out, it is very striking how Pindar anticipates later criticism in pinpointing the marvellous, the elevated, and the charming as the decisive forces in achieving the eerily irresistible πιθανότης of poetry, its persuasive convincingness.[56] We shall shortly be examining the critics' attempts to capture and define these poetic pronouncements on the fictive power of poetry.

Here we take leave of the poets until the next chapter, where we shall see our first epic composer, Apollonius, deeply engaged with his tradition's complex attitudes towards the fiction and truth of the poet. It is time to return to the critics, and complete the setting of the scene for the synthesis of Section II.

We may first note the continuing development of critical and

---

[55] Plut. *Quomodo adul.* 15 d. It is very probable that this deception was the common element dominating the image when Simonides described painting as silent poetry and poetry as speaking painting (Plut. *Mor.* 346 f); both 'deceive' as they create an 'appearance'.
[56] Richardson (1985), 386.

scholarly techniques for the analysis of poetry.[57] Theagenes was in
all probability still alive when Pindar was born in 518 BCE, and
during the eighty years of Pindar's lifetime, people in various parts
of Hellas were busy at the sort of activity which had engaged
Theagenes. Although Homer was not the sole subject (lives of
other poets were also investigated, as Theagenes had investigated
Homer's), the poems of Homer were the principal focus, if only
because those poems were the principal focus of such education as
there was;[58] it remained vitally important to make sense of
Homer, and to accommodate him to the new modes of thinking
which the times were producing. Homer's diction, antique and sui
generis, was puzzling; many words (the so-called 'glosses',
γλῶσσαι), were a mystery, and invited attempts at elucidation, of
which traces survive at least from the time of Theagenes.[59] Glosses
were not the only difficulty, for other 'problems' existed in
Homer, even when the words were familiar, and these too attracted solvers and solutions.[60] Theagenes' allegorical approach
is likewise not without exponents, although the evidence is decidedly unsatisfactory.[61] Attempts at rationalizing the myths continued as well; their currency is attested by Plato's Socrates (*Phdr.*
229 c–e).

These and similar investigations were pursued by the itinerant
wise men and educators who became known as the Sophists. Their
interests were very varied, and only a couple of them can be seen
as 'scholarly' in any sense at all, but an interest in poetry was general amongst them: the greatest of their number, Protagoras
(*c.*490–420 BCE), is said to have asserted that the most important
part of a man's education was being skilled in the subject of poetry.[62] As part of a newly self-conscious interest in the nature and
history of language, the inveterate Greek fascination with etymology flourished. In enquiries that overlapped with allegory, sophists and non-sophists alike investigated the names from the myths
in order to discover what their true moral or physical significance

[57] Fundamental here is the extremely valuable article of Richardson (1975);
Pfeiffer (1968), 16–56, is of course indispensable.
[58] On Homer as the focus of education, see Jaeger (1939), 34–54; Marrou
(1948), 34–6. Investigation of other poets' lives, Tsirimbas (1936), 45–7.
[59] Latte (1925).
[60] On λύσεις ('solutions'), see *RE* 13. 2. 2511–29.
[61] Richardson (1975).
[62] Pl. *Prt.* 338 e. On the literary work of the Sophists and their contemporaries,
see Pohlenz (1920); Kranz (1933), 5–7; Tsirimbas (1936); Rostagni (1955), 1–59;
Pfeiffer (1968), 16–56; Richardson (1975); Kennedy (1989), 82–9.

might be—or might be represented as being.[63] According to a scholion on *Il*. 8. 39, for example, the philosopher Democritus etymologized Athene's epithet Τριτογένεια ('Trito-born') as being really Wisdom (φρόνησις), for wisdom has three ('tria') consequences: to reason well, to speak finely, and to do what is necessary. A show-piece display of the science is to be found in Plato's *Cratylus*. Many of the explanations of divine names given here, such as those of Zeus and Hera, are quite standard,[64] and Socrates implies the existence of a veritable industry when he speaks of how the *majority* of the interpreters of Homer say that the poet represents Athene as mind and intellect (407 a–b). The poets themselves, as ever, are on the cutting edge of such speculation (which they invented, after all). Aeschylus follows Hesiod in playing on the very etymology of Zeus mentioned by Socrates (διαὶ Διός, 'through Zeus', *Ag*. 1485),[65] and he clarifies the allusion immediately afterwards by giving Zeus the epithet παναιτίου ('responsible for everything'). Euripides, finding γῆ in Δη, refers *De-meter* to *Earth* (Δημήτηρ θεά—γῆ δ᾽ ἐστίν, *Bacch*. 275–6).[66]

The sophist Prodicus, active towards the end of the fifth century, was the individual particularly associated with researches into the understanding of religion, undertaken within a wideranging reconstruction of cultural history.[67] Prodicus produced a striking hypothesis to explain the processes by which early man came to worship both beneficent natural forces and beneficent individual humans; his approach appears to have been radically hostile to the conventional religion as exemplified in Homer or Hesiod,[68] and in this regard he will have been, in a very general

[63] Interest in language, Kerferd (1981), 68–77.

[64] Zeus is referred to διά (396 a–b), as already in Hesiod (*Op*. 3), and as in later scholarship (*SVF* 2. 312. 21); Hera is referred to *aer*, the middle air (404 c), as already in Homer (*Il*. 21. 6–7), and as in later scholarship (Buffière (1956), 106–10).

[65] See Fraenkel (1950) ad loc.

[66] See Dodds (1960), on 274–85; and see Pease (1955–8), on Cic. *Nat. D*. 2. 67, for the prevalence of this identification in later scholarship. I often wonder whether the speech of Teiresias, in which these lines appear, is not an extensive parody of the professors' talk on such topics: 286–97, on the etymology behind the story of Dionysus' birth, strike me as particularly technical, prolix, and humorous. Diverse introductions to the problem of Euripides' relationship with these currents of thought and learning: Schmid–Stählin 1. 3. 688–716; Yunis (1988); Lefkowitz (1989).

[67] On Prodicus, see now Henrichs (1975), (1976), (1984).

[68] Henrichs (1975), 111, for a reconstruction of Prodicus' theory; his papers of 1975 and 1976 put the case for Prodicus' 'atheism' on a new footing, and should settle this long-standing debate.

sense, in the tradition of Xenophanes. Very few Sophists, however, seem to have been atheists as such. Protagoras, in particular,
gave memorable expression to a fundamental scepticism concerning the possibility of knowledge about the divine: 'About the gods
I am not in a position to have knowledge, either that they exist or
that they do not, or what they are like; for many things prevent
knowledge, the unclarity of the matter and the shortness of human
life' (DK 80 B 4).

Developing techniques of criticism, interest in religious enquiry
through etymology, exploitation of allegory—all these find
remarkable exemplification in the papyrus found at Derveni in
northern Greece in 1962, to be dated somewhere around the end
of the fifth century.[69] Much of the surviving material takes the
form of a running commentary on a *Theogony* which the author
takes to be by Orpheus.[70] The author wrenches meanings from the
text as he wills, for, so it is claimed, the poem is αἰνιγματώδης
('riddling', i.e. 'allegorical', III. 3–4; the poet αἰνίζεται, IX. 6).
Etymologies are offered (Kronos from κρούω, 'strike', X. 7). Reference is made to the particular name a god may have in the popular
religion, by convention; thus Earth, Mother, Rhea, and Hera are
all the same goddess, but called Earth by convention (νόμῳ), and
Mother because all things come from her (XVIII. 7–8). The author
demonstrates an acquaintance with matters of more philological
import. He speaks of how the poet uses hyperbaton (ὑπερβατόν,
A. 11), and debates what the poetic use of 'Olympus' means,
pointing to poetic usage to reinforce his claim that it cannot refer
to 'Ouranos', 'heaven' (VIII. 3–10). This particular problem becomes something of a chestnut in the later commentators on
Homer,[71] and in fact the papyrus shows many close correspondences in forms of approach and expression with the later scholia.
In the Derveni author, just as in the Homeric scholia, we see various phrases built around the word δηλόω, 'show', 'signify': 'in this
verse it is shown that ...', δεδήλωται ἐν τῶιδε τῶι ἔπει (IV. 1);
'he shows by speaking thus ...', δηλοῖ ὧδε λέγων (IX. 3).[72] Again,

---

[69] Still (1990) not properly published. I refer to the text which appears in *ZPE*
47 (1982), after p. 300. A valuable paper by Burkert (1986) suggests Stesimbrotus
as the author, with a date between 420 and 370 BCE; an account of the find, and
the nature of the text, in West (1983), 75–82.

[70] West (1983), 77–8, and Burkert (1986), 5, stress that the original text was,
almost certainly, not all in the form of a commentary.

[71] Schmidt (1976), 75–105; noted by Burkert (1986), 3–4.

[72] Cf. e.g. b *Il*. 2. 20; A 2. 686; bT 3. 325.

the Derveni papyrus often displays the familiar pattern of later scholia in referring to those whose position is about to be attacked: 'those who think such-and-such are wrong, for they do not realize or know that . . .', οὐ γιγνώσκοντες ὅτι . . .[73] It seems far more likely that the Derveni author is dependent on established ways of treating Homer's text than that later Homeric scholarship should learn its habits from discussions of Orpheus, or else hit upon several normative techniques independently. However bizarre the Derveni papyrus may appear (and it can appear very bizarre indeed), it is very valuable evidence for systematic treatments of poetic text of a nature that many would have considered impossible for a pre-Hellenistic date.

A variety of critical modes are evolving all through the fifth century, together with a variety of ways of looking at the data of myth, but prose writers are late to address themselves systematically to the problem which so exercises the poets themselves, the problem of what it is about poetry that allows it to achieve the kind of creation or depiction that it does achieve. Aristotle will be the goal of this portion of the investigation; we may approach him by looking at the so-called Δισσοὶ λόγοι (*Dissoi Logoi*, 'Contrasting Arguments'), set-piece sophistic arguments which date to around 400 BCE.[74]

These deadpan little treatises are valuable for their very unpretentiousness and commonplace character, which is evidence for the pervasiveness of the viewpoints they embody. They explicitly regard poetry as a form where talk of truth or falsehood is simply beside the point—a position of more potential than might at first appear, in that it made it possible to exempt poetry from irrelevant criticisms relating to other forms of writing or speech. In the set of contrasting arguments on the Just and the Unjust, the author concludes with the argument of those who 'claim that they can demonstrate that the same thing is both just and unjust' (3. 15): 'They adduce as evidence arts in which what is just and what is unjust have no place. And poets compose their poems not with

---

[73] I. 6; V. 2; VIII. 5; XIX. 5; cf. e.g. A *Il.* 1. 197; bT 4. 297–9; A. 15. 626; bT 16. 31. Exactly the same form of expression is found in the Latin commentary of Servius on Vergil (Thilo–Hagen, 1. 4. 17–20); Fraenkel (1964), 2. 388, compares the scholia on Euripides (*Or.* 396, *Phoen.* 267, *Andr.* 32).
[74] DK 90; ed. Robinson (1979), whose translations are given here.

a view to truth but with a view to people's pleasure' (17).[75] By this view, poetry is a form in which such questions do not apply, because what poetry is concerned with is pleasure, and it is therefore exempt from the criteria one would apply to a form concerned with truth. Of course, the notion that poetry gives pleasure is fundamental to any Greek idea of poetics whatever—it was possible to attack poetry on precisely these grounds. At issue here is something rather different, namely, the criteria which it is appropriate to use in assessing or judging poetry.[76]

This embryonic notion of the autonomy of poetry is seen also in another passage of the treatise on the Just and the Unjust, where again the inadmissability of applying such criteria to poetry is stressed: 'I shall turn to the arts—particularly the compositions of poets. For in the writing of tragedies and in painting the best person is the one who deceives the most in creating things that are like the real thing' (ὅστις κα πλεῖστα ἐξαπατῇ ὁμοῖα τοῖς ἀληθινοῖς ποιέων, οὗτος ἄριστος, 3. 10). It is commonly recognized that the paradoxical force of the language here is a token of the writer's indebtedness to the sophist Gorgias, who speaks of the 'deception' of tragedy, 'by which the one who deceives is more just than the one who doesn't, and the one who is deceived is more wise than the one who isn't'.[77] The firm oxymorons highlight the autonomy being accorded to poetry, and the delight in reversal is eminently Gorgianic. Yet both authors depend closely on the notions we have been tracing in the poets, so as to acknowledge the power of deception and illusionism, and even, like Simonides, to use painting as an analogy for the verisimilitudinous appearance that poetry creates. There is no concern here for what sort of truth it might be that poetry achieves; rather, a highly self-conscious refusal to apply moral criteria to poetry, and an assertion that poetry must be judged on its own terms, so that 'justice' in poetry is 'success'—success at achieving what it sets out to achieve.[78] The same approaches may be seen in

---

[75] Exactly the same argument is used in the preceding treatise, on the Shameful and the Fine (2. 28).

[76] Koster (1970), 22; Rösler (1980), 311–12; Häussler (1976), 52. It is interesting that only in the *Laws*, his last work, does Plato actually take cognizance of the idea that pleasure is the criterion by which poetry should be judged (655 c–d; 668 a).

[77] Plut. *Mor.* 348 c; cf. Robinson (1979), 68.

[78] On Gorgias' notion of poetic deception, see Rosenmeyer (1955)—although he

Gorgias' *Encomium of Helen*.[79] Gorgias spends much time on the power of speech in this work; by referring to poetry as 'speech with metre' (9), he is able to appeal to his audience's shared preconceptions about the power of poetry, and then have them see that any speech can partake of that same power.[80] What he says of speech generally, then, must be understood *a fortiori* of poetry. The effectiveness of the power of speech is a function of speech's own nature, not of its relationship to truth, for in most things people rely only on 'belief' (δόξα), and this is the very area where the deceit and illusionism of speech come into their own (11–12). Gorgias gives expression to the same consciousness of the power of the apparent in speech as had moved Simonides and Pindar. He expresses also the same awareness of where the power of the apparent lies, in the action of forcing and charming the listener into seeing as 'clear' what is 'incredible and obscure' (13; cf. 10).[81]

The trends we have been following find their culmination in Aristotle's *Treatment of the Art of Poetry* (Πραγματεία Τέχνης Ποιητικῆς), which we call the *Poetics*. This book was part of a range of works devoted to the study of literature and literary history. Aristotle wrote a dialogue *On the Poets*, which, together with his other dialogues, has not survived. Besides writing such theoretical works, he investigated and 'solved' Homeric problems, producing a book of that title, which, although lost, leaves traces in the *Poetics*, and in a collection of the third-century CE Neoplatonist Porphyry.[82] In large part, Aristotle is reacting against the famous denunciations of poetry produced by his master, Plato.[83] To Plato, poetry is something which issues from the

sets Gorgias in opposition to the poets' insights, instead of in debt to them (see here, rather, Richardson (1985), 386); Lanata (1963), 204–7; de Romilly (1973); Verdenius (1981).

[79] DK 82; ed. MacDowell (1982); bibliography in MacDowell, 7–8, and Classen (1976), 683–9.

[80] The famous phrase 'speech with metre' is not, then, a definition of poetry: Russell (1981), 23.

[81] de Romilly (1973), 160–1; Richardson (1985), 386.

[82] On Porphyry's use of Aristotle, see Erbse (1960), 61–3; on Aristotle's scholarship, see Pfeiffer (1968), 67–84. For the title, see Lucas (1968), xiii. Except in one case (n. 92 below), I give the translation of Margaret Hubbard in Russell and Winterbottom (1972), 85–132.

[83] Halliwell (1986), esp. 331–6. Moravcsik and Temko (1982), Halliwell (1986) and (1989), Else (1986), and Ferrari (1989) are the latest contributions to a vast scholarship.

chimerical world of 'deceit' and 'opinion'. Its falsehood is irre-
deemable, not least when it deals with the divine, since it represents the gods as fallible and immoral; in the passage in the
*Republic* which most systematically develops this point (378 d),
Plato states explicitly that he does not countenance the fashion-
able attempts to defend epic by means of allegorical interpretation. Further, with his description of poetry as an imitation
(*mimesis*) of objects in the world of sensation, Plato had made the
poet inferior even to the craftsman in his fidelity to the 'real', the
world of forms created by god.[84]

To Aristotle, poetry is a human phenomenon in its own right,
with its own τέλος (*telos*, 'end', 'purpose'), to be investigated on
its own terms. This insistent stress on poetry's right to be ex-
empted from inapplicable criteria of judgement is one of the most
remarkable aspects of the *Poetics*.[85] It represents a fundamental
breach with Plato's orientation, and may be seen as a (more sophisticated) statement of the banal or undeveloped intuitions of such
spokesmen as Gorgias and the authors of the *Dissoi Logoi*. Other
elements of the traditions we have been tracing also shape Aristotle's approach to poetry: his recognition of poetry's peculiar
emotional power, and the convincing persuasiveness which that
power creates; his tolerance of poetry's distinctive openness to
myth; and his acceptance of the fact that the poet is moulding and
creating something with its own plausibility and rules of meaning.

Aristotle declares the *telos* of poetry to be 'effecting through
pity and fear the catharsis of those emotions [i.e. pity and fear]'.[86]
Certainly, Aristotle is speaking of tragedy here, but immediately
before this section he says that tragedy is a development of epic,
and has everything that epic has; so that epic, too, effects catharsis
through pity and fear.[87] Poetry attains this end by its mimesis of
an action, and here Aristotle departs from Plato, as clearly stated
by Hubbard: 'Plato had claimed that an instance of mimesis has
less reality than an individual particular, which in turn has less

[84] An introduction to the topic of mimesis in Russell (1981), 99–113; on Plato's
presentation of *mimesis* in *Republic* 10, see Annas (1982).

[85] Halliwell (1986), 3–4, 132–3, 265–6.

[86] 49 b 27–8. Catharsis is itself, of course, a very large topic, which does not
directly concern us here: see Halliwell (1986), 350–6, for an introduction.

[87] 49 b 17–20; cf. 62 a 14–15. Further, the later comments on epic's emotional
effects of surprise, to be considered shortly, must be referred to the presupposition
that what he says here of tragedy is inevitably true also of epic.

reality than the *idea*. Aristotle replies that the statements of the poet, so far from being inferior to statements of particulars, are more comprehensive and more philosophical.'[88] Aristotle's reply is mainly to be found at 51 a 36–51 b 11, a section distinguishing between poetry and history, introduced with the following words: 'the poet's job is saying not what did happen but the sort of thing that would happen, that is, what can happen in a strictly probable or necessary sequence' (οὐ τὸ τὰ γενόμενα λέγειν, τοῦτο ποιητοῦ ἔργον ἐστίν, ἀλλ' οἷα ἂν γένοιτο καὶ τὰ δυνατὰ κατὰ τὸ εἰκὸς ἢ τὸ ἀναγκαῖον, 51 a 36–8). Further, Aristotle greatly expands the range of those things susceptible to the mimesis of the poet, from Plato's 'things in the actual world of phemonena',[89] to the sum, in effect, of human experience and imagination: 'what was or is, what is commonly said and thought to be the case, and what should be the case' (ἢ ... οἷα ἦν ἢ ἔστιν, ἢ οἷά φασιν καὶ δοκεῖ, ἢ οἷα εἶναι δεῖ, 60 b 10–11).

Such is the background to Chapter 25, where Aristotle deals with criticisms of Homer, and how to answer them.[90] Since the chapter is an extreme condensation of his larger work, *Homeric Problems*, the discussion is curt and involved, but a sheet-anchor is there for us if we keep our eyes always on Aristotle's principles of what poetry's *telos* is, and what it 'imitates'. Plato's criticisms are very much at issue here, although his name is never mentioned. The strictures of the master are the object of Aristotle's momentous observation that 'correctness in poetry is not the same thing as correctness in morals, nor yet is it the same as correctness in any other art' (οὐχ ἡ αὐτὴ ὀρθότης ἐστὶν τῆς πολιτικῆς καὶ τῆς ποιητικῆς οὐδὲ ἄλλης τέχνης καὶ ποιητικῆς, 60 b 13–15). The correctness of poetry is not a matter of ethics, and failure to attain its correctness will only come about 'if the poet is incapable of representing what he set out to represent' (60 b 16–17).

Aristotle's concept of mimesis comes into play when defending Homer against the charge that some of the things he says are neither true nor as they should be (60 b 35). One may reply, says Aristotle, that here the poet is 'imitating', as is his right, 'what people say', 'what is commonly said to be the case' (οἷά φασιν,

---

[88] Russell and Winterbottom (1972), 88; see here Rösler (1980), 308–11, and Halliwell (1986), 22, 125.

[89] So put by Grube (1965), 54.

[90] Carroll (1895) is still a very valuable discussion of this chapter, in the light of later Greek criticism; see also Rosenmeyer (1973).

60 b 10): 'an example of this is the treatment of the gods: for this, perhaps, is neither a better thing to say nor a true one, but instead the facts are perhaps as Xenophanes saw them; but anyhow that is what people say' (οἷον τὰ περὶ θεῶν· ἴσως γὰρ οὔτε βέλτιον οὕτω λέγειν οὔτ' ἀληθῆ, ἀλλ' εἰ ἔτυχεν ὥσπερ Ξενοφάνει· ἀλλ' οὖν φασι, 60b 35–7). The response may appear bald (although it would doubtless have been elaborated in the more discursive *Problems*, and even, perhaps, in *On the Poets*). Yet Aristotle is appealing here to an entirely different concept of mimesis from that of Plato, and granting the poet the right to use the stories of myth and tradition as models to work from.

Alternatively, one may look to the *telos* of poetry, to what it aims at, in order to defend the poet. The poem may contain something which is, strictly speaking, impossible: 'that is a fault,' says Aristotle, 'but it is all right if the poem thereby achieves what it aims at (what it aims at I have already discussed [i.e. effecting through pity and fear the catharsis of those emotions]), that is, if in this way the surprise produced either by that particular passage or by another is more striking (ἐκπληκτικώτερον). An example is the pursuit of Hector' (60 b 23–6). Surprise, and the ἔκπληξις ('thrill of shock') which it produces, are especially effective sources of pity and fear (Aristotle states this earlier);[91] and they are especially at home in epic, as he observes just before Chapter 25, using the same example of the pursuit of Hector: 'Though one ought of course to aim at surprise in tragedy too, epic is more tolerant of the prime source of surprise, the irrational, because one is not looking at the person doing the action. For the account of the pursuit of Hector would seem ludicrous on the stage, with the Greeks standing still and not pursuing him, and Achilles refusing their help; but in epic one does not notice it' (60 a 11–17). When Aristotle observes that epic has the advantage over tragedy as far as ἔκπληξις is concerned, in being less representational and more accommodating of the irrational and impossible, he sets in train a most important and fruitful critical tradition, which will concern us in the next Section.

Only a skilled poet can make this sort of thing work, and he makes it work—as Simonides, Pindar, and Gorgias had acknowledged—by achieving the authoritative aura of plausibility. Aristotle makes much of this point. First of all, after his first

[91] 52 a 1–7.

discussion of the pursuit of Hector: 'one ought to prefer likely impossibilities to unconvincing possibilities' (60 a 26–7). He gives another example in that context: 'For it is clear that even the irrationalities in the *Odyssey* about his being put ashore on Ithaca would have been intolerable if produced by a bad poet; but as it is, Homer, by sweetening the absurdity, makes the absurdity disappear with his other good points' (τοῖς ἄλλοις ἀγαθοῖς ὁ ποιητὴς ἀφανίζει ἡδύνων τὸ ἄτοπον, 60 a 35–60 b 2).[92] One is irresistibly reminded of Pindar: 'But Grace of Song, which makes for mortals all soothing joys, if it adds her honour often makes believed even what is not to be believed' (*Ol.* 1. 29–31). Aristotle makes this point about plausibility again when he is summing up at the end of Chapter 25. One may, he says, as in the case of the pursuit of Hector, answer a charge that a thing is impossible by a reference to the nature of poetry; by which (so he explains) 'I mean that a convincing impossibility is preferable to something unconvincing, however possible' (61 b 9–12).

Although Aristotle's particular examples here concern defences against the charge that something is 'impossible' or 'irrational', the same defences can equally well be applied if there is a charge that something is 'morally dangerous, self-contradictory, or contrary to technical correctness [i.e. correctness in some other art, such as zoology or medicine]' (61 b 23–4). It is up to the poet to bring his moulding power to bear on the world of experience and tradition, in order to produce something which functions within a genre that has its own rules of meaning and effect. This is the nearest thing the ancient world ever produced to a theory of fiction.[93] Equipped with it, Aristotle felt no need to fall back on allegory or rationalism to allow for the gods in epic.

Aristotle's insights had a potent after-life in criticism, which may be traced in the Homeric commentaries that will largely concern us in Section II, for they exhibit markedly Aristotelian features in many of their basic aesthetic and critical orientations.[94] Before coming to terms with the commentary tradition itself, we may conclude this Section with a brief continuation of the historical survey.

---

[92] My translation of the portion given in Greek.
[93] On the problems facing Aristotle in evolving a theory of fiction, see esp. Halliwell (1986), 12–13, 21–3, and (1987), 72–4, 172, 177–9.
[94] Carroll (1895), 14–17; Erbse (1960), 61–72; Hintenlang (1961); Gallavotti (1969).

Aristotle's school maintained a high degree of interest in questions of criticism and literary history. His contemporary and pupil, Heraclides of Pontus, together with other followers, continued to produce defences of Homer against those who impugned the poet's craft and moral content.[95] The attacker about whom we know most is Zoilus of Amphipolis, whose carpings brought him fame, and an epithet—'the scourge of Homer' ( Ὁμηρομάστιξ).[96] Everything is grist to this man's mill, including the gods. Criticisms along the lines of Xenophanes' and Plato's are aimed at episodes such as Demodocus' song of Ares and Aphrodite (Od. 8. 266–366), for criteria of moral propriety are the yardstick in such cases: the story is ἄτοπον, 'out of place', i.e. 'morally objectionable'.[97] Elsewhere Zoilus, ever intent on plausibility,[98] stumbles against the actualization of metaphor. When Zeus puts the fates of Achilles and Hector in the scales, 'are they sitting', asks Zoilus, 'or standing?' (fr. 35). Others are in the same business.[99] There were those who answered such attacks, of course. We know of a later reply to Zoilus by a certain Athenodorus, and others will have carried on the λύσεις ('solutions').[100] It may look like a petty environment, but such activity at least reflected and enforced close attention to the text, and to potentially important questions of procedure and technique.

More substantial questions of theory also received attention. Aristotle had regarded epic as being more accommodating of the irrational than tragedy, because it is less mimetic, or mimetic in a different manner: we are not sitting and watching the events in epic; they are further removed from 'reality' (above, pp. 28–9).

---

[95] On Peripatetic poetics, see Rostagni (1955), 76–237; Podlecki (1969). For Heraclides' Homeric work, see Wehrli, vol. 7, frr. 169–70, 171–5; Gottschalk (1980), 133–9.

[96] Fragments and discussion in Friedländer (1895); cf. RE Suppl. 15. 1531–54.

[97] Fr. 38; Friedländer refers to the Platonic criticisms of the same passage (Rep. 389 a, 390 c).

[98] Fr. 39 explicitly uses the criterion of τὸ ἀπίθανον ('implausibility'); similar preconceptions in frr. 26, 34, 36.

[99] Megaclides (RE 2R 15. 124–5) concerned himself with the implausibility of Achilles' pursuit of Hector (an episode treated by Aristotle, Poet. 1460 a 13–17): b Il. 22. 205. Chamaeleon, author of at least five books on the Iliad (RE 3. 2103), took issue with Aristotle's defence of Zeus' laughter at the battle of the gods, according to schol. Ge Il. 21. 390; he used the key language of ἀτοπία ('what is out of place, objectionable').

[100] On Athenodorus, see Friedländer (1895), frr. 23–4; other λύσεις, Lehrs (1882), 200–12; RE 13. 2512.

Such an approach was too promising to lie fallow, and the ideas were soon taken up and elaborated upon, presumably in Aristotle's own school, the Peripatus. In time a triad of levels of narrative became canonical, in which each member is increasingly distant from τὸ ἀληθές, 'actuality': ἱστορία ('history'), πλάσμα ('fictitious story'), μῦθος ('myth').[101] The practical applications of this categorization are discussed below.[102]

The two tools of rationalization and allegorization continued to be available as a means of dealing with the myth of tradition and poetry. Trenchant little demolition works survive, attributed to a Palaephatus (of the late fourth century?), in which the stories of myth are stripped down to a bare kernel of fact.[103] Nothing could have happened in the past, says this hardheaded character, which we do not see still happening today. No Actaeons, therefore, turning into deer (14. 4–10), no Pasiphaes coupling with bulls (6. 1–2). Such stories are ridiculous (γέλοιον, 15. 12, 45. 13); false (ψευδές, 17.9); overly mythical (μυθῶδες ἄγαν, 23.11–12); impossible (ἀδύνατον, 6. 2–3, 11. 4); incredible (ἄπιστος, 11. 4); unlikely (οὐκ εἰκός, 50. 6). The poets elaborate an actual occurrence into myth (8. 8–10, 14. 8–10). So Pasiphae, for example (7. 1–2), did not mate with an actual bull, but with a handsome companion of her husband, called Taurus ('Bull'). It is typical of ancient rationalizing that Palaephatus should generally give a circumstantial and detailed account of what 'really' happened, as he does with Pasiphae and Taurus, rather than jettison the myth altogether. Treatments like this were very common throughout antiquity,[104] and have not altogether lost their vogue even today.

The rationalizer with the greatest eventual fame was Euhemerus, active perhaps around 280 BCE, not long after

---

[101] Rostagni (1955), 207 attributes the theory to Theophrastus, but see Brink (1960), 17 n. 3. Walbank (1960), 227, goes too far in denying Peripatetic interest; the concern with verisimilitude is not that of a rationalizer, but of someone with an Aristotelian preoccupation with genre. Woodman (1988), 24, would see such demarcations already in Thucydides 1. 22. 4.

[102] pp. 42–4.

[103] Ed. Festa (1902), 1–72. References to Palaephatus are by Festa's page and line numbers. Similar accounts by other authors in Festa, 73–99.

[104] See the dissertations on Palaephatus by Wipprecht (1892) and Schrader (1893); cf. Veyne (1983), esp. 26–7, 69–77; further, the first Section of Chapter 6 below.

Palaephatus; his name is still with us as a term for his method.[105] His work was a novel, in which he described how he journeyed to a utopia, and read there a holy inscription (hence the title, Ἱερὰ ἀναγραφή). The pillar told of how the great gods had in fact all once been men, kings and warriors, who had received immortality as a thanksgiving from their grateful people. The motives behind the book remain obscure, but it seems clear that the general thesis is consistent with the approach begun by Prodicus, and continued by such men as Hecataeus of Abdera.[106] Since the time of Prodicus himself, however, the world had been transformed by the spectacular feats and divine pretensions of Alexander and his successors;[107] rulers who were busily instituting cult for themselves and their dynasties were bound to have a ready ear for such accounts of the immortal rewards which awaited those who aided and protected mankind.[108]

The allegorical interpretation of early poetry continued apace— as we shall see shortly, it was such a widespread way of reading Homer that it drew the condemnation of the great Hellenistic scholar, Aristarchus.[109] The best way to gain an impression of this world is to read the so-called *Homeric Questions*, transmitted under the name of 'Heraclitus', which probably dates to the first century CE;[110] according to this work, Homer was a great philosopher, who clothed his learning in poetic form. Although such allegorical interpretation was very common, it has long been traditional to see its main proponents in the Stoic school, founded by Zeno in the last years of the fourth century.[111] The *communis opinio* has, however, been thrown into serious doubt by A. A. Long, in a paper of the highest importance.[112] He makes a subtle but convincing distinction between, on the one hand, the 'intentionalist' allegorical readings practised by 'Heraclitus' and

[105] For the date, *RE* 12. 953; ed. Vallauri (1956); testimonia and bibliography in Pease (1955–8), 517–18; cf. Fraser (1972), 1. 289–95.

[106] So Henrichs (1984), 347–8.

[107] Habicht (1970).

[108] On the fertile environment which the times provided for these doctrines, see Henrichs (1984), 344–5.

[109] Below, pp. 37–8.

[110] Buffière (1962), vii–x.

[111] Pohlenz (1948), 1. 97, 2. 55; De Lacy (1948), esp. 259–62; Buffière (1956), 137–52, 314–17; Pfeiffer (1968), 237–8.

[112] I am very grateful to Professor Long for showing me his paper (unpublished at the time of writing), and for permitting me to refer to his basic approach; the paper is to appear in a volume edited by R. Lamberton.

his ilk, and, on the other hand, a more 'anthropological' approach, which he attributes to the Stoics. According to Long, the Stoics saw Homer and (especially) Hesiod as useful sources for primitive thought, but not as proto-philosophers who deliberately veiled their message in a poetic medium; the Stoics were able to exploit such techniques as etymology in order to recover traces of pristine insights from the poets, without believing that Homer and Hesiod could themselves distinguish between such insights and the myths which they perpetrated in their capacity as poets.

Long's reinterpretation will no doubt trigger a keen debate. Even if one accepts his arguments (and I, for my part, find it very difficult not to), the Stoics' interest in Homer and Hesiod remains striking testimony to the tenacious cultural power of the poets and their myths. Such testimony is provided, likewise, by the work of the greatest Hellenistic scholar of religion, Apollodorus, who wrote twenty-four books Περὶ Θεῶν ('On the Gods').[113] This vast enterprise was 'essentially a work on Homer', which took as its starting-point 'the names of Homeric gods and their etymologies'.[114] The poets' versions of the divine, however contested and impugned, continued to be a central concern of intellectual enquiry. The contrast with the intellectual environment of Rome, when we arrive there in Chapter 3, will be dramatic.

II

Sed haec sic accipias uelim, ut ex commentariis ueterum scias me esse collecturum; antiqua enim et fabulosa ac longinquitatis causa incognita nisi priscorum docente memoria non poterunt explicari.

But I would like you to read my material in the knowledge that I will be gathering it out of the commentaries of men of the past; for the subject-matter—ancient, fabulous, and unfamiliar by virtue of its remoteness—won't be able to be disentangled without the tradition of earlier generations to teach us.

Ti. Claudius Donatus[115]

[113] 2 B 244. frr. 88–153 Jacoby; Münzel (1883); Pfeiffer (1968), 261–3.
[114] Pfeiffer (1968), 261; cf. Jacoby 2 D. 753–6, esp. 756.
[115] 2. 643. 4–7 Geo.

It was among the scholars of Alexandria that the perspectives captured by Aristotle found their inheritors. From the foundation of the Library in Alexandria at the beginning of the third century, down to the time of the greatest of the line, Aristarchus (*c.*216–*c.*144 BCE), there flourished a continuous tradition of scholarship and criticism.[116] For our purposes, what counts is not their work on establishing the texts of the poets—the basis of their achievement and fame—but their critical theories, and their observations on Homer's techniques.

Our knowledge of the work done here comes almost exclusively from a series of marginal comments on the *Iliad* and the *Odyssey* which survive from later periods of antiquity, and which preserve in excerpted form fragments of the lost original Alexandrian commentaries.[117] The history of these marginal comments, 'scholia', is confused, confusing, and controversial. Various traditions are represented, and there is a great deal of material in the scholia which is post-Hellenistic, just as there is some, particularly in the D-scholia, which is pre-Hellenistic.[118] The scholia preserve also excerpts from the *Homeric Problems* of the third-century CE Neoplatonist Porphyry, who in his turn preserves elements of earlier lore, particularly from Aristotle's work of the same title.[119] Finally, a Byzantine bishop of the twelfth century, Eustathius, who put together a prolix commentary on both of the Homeric poems, appears to have had access both to the original Porphyry and to the archetype of what we now call the bT-scholia; so that his comments may at times have independent value as a source for some earlier thinking.[120]

---

[116] The classic account is Pfeiffer (1968), 87–233; see also Fraser (1972), 1. 305–479.

[117] A clear and accessible picture of the sources of our knowledge of the Alexandrian commentaries is now available in Kirk (1985), 38–43; see, further, Erbse (1960), and (1969–88), vol. 1. XLV–LIX. The scholia on the *Iliad* are quoted from Erbse (1969–88); D-scholia must still be consulted in Lascaris (1517), although all the D-scholia which I quote are in Bekker (1825). The *Odyssey* scholia are much thinner; I quote from Dindorf (1855). Since the great bulk of my references are to the *Iliad* scholia, readers should assume that the *Iliad* scholia are being given unless the *Odyssey* is specifically cited.

[118] On the pre-Hellenistic material, see Henrichs (1971), 99–100; Montanari (1979), 13–15, 40. According to the summing-up of Richardson (1980), 265, 'in general they seem to reflect the critical terminology and views of the first century BC and first two centuries AD'.

[119] Ed. Schrader (1880–2); all references to Porphyry are to the page and line numbers of this edition. On Porphyry's relation to Aristotle, see Erbse (1960), 61–3; Hintenlang (1961).

[120] Eustathius' *Iliad* commentary has been edited by van der Valk (1971–87); for

Out of all this material, the most fruitful for the present purpose are generally the so-called 'exegetical', bT-scholia, for, as
their name implies, their authors are principally concerned with
the exegesis of the text, with expounding the poems in the light of
what they took to be basic governing principles of poetics, rhetoric, and composition. It has long been recognized that these
sources, and the bT-scholia in particular, offer a detailed view
onto important currents of ancient literary criticism (the plural in
'currents' is important, because the material is by no means uni-
form, as will become clear).[121] The opportunity the scholia provide
will be exploited here, as a means of providing a framework for
reconstructing the responses to the gods in epic which were formulated by those ancient critics who were actually engaged in the
practice of exegesis. An acquaintance with the scholia is the best
available way of reconstructing the apparatus which informed
Vergil's or Ovid's reading of epic; however widely the discussion
ranges in this section, the scholia will be our Michelin.

However readers and scholars may have reacted to the gods in
epic, it was a datum that the form demanded their presence.[122]
Homer himself offers something of a definition of his form, when
he has Penelope ask the bard Phemius to choose another song:
'You know many other charms for mortals, the deeds of men and
of gods, such as bards make famous' (πολλὰ γὰρ ἄλλα βροτῶν
θελκτήρια οἶδας, / ἔργ᾽ ἀνδρῶν τε θεῶν τε, τά τε κλείουσιν
ἀοιδοί, *Od.* 1. 337–8). So one arrives at definitions such as that
given by Posidonius: 'A poem is poetic diction which has meaning,
containing an imitation of things divine and human' (ποίησις δέ
ἐστι σημαντικὸν ποίημα, μίμησιν περιέχον θείων καὶ
ἀνθρωπείων).[123] The Latin scholarly tradition is perfectly in accord.[124] Servius defines the *Aeneid* as *heroicum*, meaning, as we

his *Odyssey* commentary, one must consult Stallbaum (1825–6). On Eustathius'
sources, see Erbse (1969–88), vol. 1. LI–LII. Van der Valk (1963–4), 1. 86–106,
believes Eustathius had access to no more than the same scholia we have.

[121] Richardson (1980) is an invaluable introduction; see also Griesinger (1907);
von Franz (1943); Roemer (1879) and (1924); but note the cautionary remarks of
Fraser (1972), 2. 669 n. 148, concerning Roemer's zeal in attributing material to
Aristarchus.

[122] For the problem of the exceptions, see Chapter 6.

[123] Diog. Laert. 7. 60, fr. 44 Edelstein and Kidd (1972–88). For a discussion of
these words, see the commentary of Edelstein and Kidd, and Brink (1963), 43–78,
esp. 65–7.

[124] On the close links between the Latin and Greek commentators, see Fraenkel
(1964), 2. 381–90; Mühmelt (1965); Zetzel (1981), 29–30.

would say, 'epic':[125] 'It is heroic because it consists of divine and human characters, containing truth with things made up' (*est autem heroicum quod constat ex diuinis humanisque personis continens uera cum fictis*, 1. 4. 4–6 Thilo–Hagen).[126] To many, if not most, the representation of divine beings in a narrative remained a snare and a scandal. Criticism continued to be aimed at what was regarded as the unseemly and impious misuse which the poets made of the divine. The scholia report charges (which they often attempt to 'solve') that an episode is ἄτοπον ('out of place', i.e. 'objectionable'), or ἀπρεπές ('unseemly'). So, for example, bT *Il*. 22. 231: 'it is objectionable for Athene, who is a god, to trick Hector' (ἄτοπον θεὸν οὖσαν πλανᾶν τὸν Ἕκτορα).[127] Or else, on the most general level: 'It appears unseemly that most of the things against the gods have been said by Homer' (ἀπρεπὲς δὲ δοκεῖ τὸ τῶν παρὰ θεοὺς τὰ πλεῖστα παρ' Ὁμήρῳ λελέχθαι).[128] Allegory was, of course, the basic way around such objections; the rationale is succinctly put by 'Heraclitus', the author of the so-called *Homeric Problems*: 'Everything is impiety if nothing is allegory' (πάντα γὰρ ἠσέβησεν, εἰ μηδὲν ἠλληγόρησεν, 1. 1).[129] The conventional defences, of rationalizing and allegory, are indeed aired in the scholia. The rationalizing angle is only found at all commonly in the *Odyssey* scholia and in Eustathius; in the *Iliad* scholia, it is rare to find b 11. 54, for example, explaining the bloody mist sent by Zeus as being a natural phenomenon, the result of odd rain patterns caused by all the blood in the rivers.[130] Allegorical interpretations are more common throughout, although they are seldom advanced overtly in the role of defence *as such*. Again, Eustathius and the *Odyssey* scholia are more extensive exponents of this line,[131] while the *Iliad* scholia, with the exception of a

---

[125] On the interesting question of the various words for 'epic', see Nadjo (1987).
[126] See, further, Koster (1970), 86–91; Häussler (1978), 226–7.
[127] Cf. e.g. bT 3. 397, 424; T 5. 703.
[128] Porph. 226. 9–10; cf. e.g. A. 3. 423; bT 4. 4; bT 19. 407; bT 24. 23.
[129] Very similar language in 'Longinus', *Subl.* 9. 7.
[130] Representative rationalizing *Odyssey* scholia: B 1. 241; E 4. 456; B 12. 39; BQ 12. 104; HQ 12. 105; Eust. 1414. 38–40; 1709. 35–7. In his introduction to the *Iliad* commentary, Eustathius catalogues the available defences of allegory, convention, and rationalization (3. 26–32).
[131] Representative allegorizing *Odyssey* scholia: E 1. 8, 22, 38; E 3. 372; EM 4. 384; E 5.1; B 12. 353; B 13. 103. Cf. Eust. 512. 23–7; 517. 30–6; 561. 28–36; 1387. 24–6; 1707. 41–50.

plethora of comments on the Battle of the Gods, tend to keep to a number of fixed identifications: Hera stands for the *aer*, Athene for wisdom, Ares for battle-lust and madness, Aphrodite for passion.[132] In cases such as these, the clumsiness of our all-embracing term 'allegory' reveals itself, for a critic who says that Homer uses Athene to represent wisdom is not necessarily involved in the same enterprise as someone who says that the *Iliad* is a quasi- or protophilosophical text, with Athene and other gods being used as covering names for moral or physical truths. The identifications of the scholiasts are not always apologetics; they are rather what would strike a modern reader as a kind of paraphrasing gloss, in the same way as it is common for moderns to speak of how Athene 'stands for' the mental processes of a character. The scholiasts can distinguish, for example, between personifications and gods who are characters. When Ares and Athene lead out the armies in *Iliad* 4, a scholion hesitates as to Ares' status: 'he is the urge for war. Or else the god in bodily form' (ἡ προθυμία τοῦ πολέμου. ἤ ὁ σωματοειδὴς θεός, D 4. 439). In the same company are Terror and Rout (Δειμός and Φόβος). They are not actually present as allies, says the scholiast, but they are invented from our emotions (ἐκ τῶν ἡμετέρων παθῶν, b 4. 440): the gods themselves, by implication, are not.[133]

Allegory and rationalization were used to defend the poet against charges of impropriety, but an alternative tradition followed Aristotle's lead, kept its eyes on the distinctive nature of the form, and insisted that the critic's duty lay in respecting the poet's right to exploit the freedom which went with the distinctive nature of the form. We are told explicitly that Aristarchus dismissed the sort of allegorical defence we have been examining:

Ἀρίσταρχος ἀξιοῖ τὰ φραζόμενα ὑπὸ τοῦ ποιητοῦ μυθικώτερον ἐκδέχεσθαι κατὰ τὴν ποιητικὴν ἐξουσίαν, μηδὲν ἔξω τῶν φραζομένων ὑπὸ τοῦ ποιητοῦ περιεργαζομένους.

Aristarchus thinks that we should take what the poet says in a more

---

[132] Hera is *aer*, bT 1. 53–5; Athene is wisdom, D 1. 195, bT 5. 131–2 (and commonly); Ares is battle-lust, D 4. 439, bT 5. 335–6; Aphrodite is passion, bT 5. 335–6. Exceptional in their intricacy are bT 1. 399–406, bT 5. 392–400.

[133] Similar distinctions in b 4. 441; bT 4. 442–3; bT 20. 48.

mythical sense, according to poetic licence, not going to needless trouble over anything external to what the poet says. (D *Il*. 5. 385)[134]

A scholion on the Battle of the Gods expounds the basic rationale:

ἀπρεπὲς δὲ δοκεῖ τὸ τῶν παρὰ θεοὺς τὰ πλεῖστα παρ' Ὁμήρῳ λελέχθαι. ὧν ἡ λύσις κατὰ τὸ πλεῖστον ἀπὸ ἔθους λαμβάνεται· ἐξ ἔθους γάρ τινος τοῖς ποιηταῖς παρακεχώρηται καὶ τοῖς ζωγράφοις καὶ τοῖς πλάσταις ἀνθρωποπαθείας τῶν θεῶν διατυποῦν καὶ μάχας αὐτῶν πρὸς ἀλλήλους καὶ θητείας καῖ ἀλλοιώσεις διαμυθολογεῖν.

It appears unseemly that most of the things against the gods have been said by Homer. The solution for these things is normally taken from convention; for it is on the basis of a certain convention that it is conceded to poets and painters and sculptors to represent the gods as having human characteristics, and to tell of their battles against each other, their periods of servitude, and their metamorphoses. (Porph. 2. 226. 9–14)[135]

Lurking behind this apparently defensive exposition is the faith in the self-sufficiency of Homer's craft which informed the readings of an Aristotle or an Aristarchus, and which conditioned their hostility to cramping apologetics. A strongly Aristotelian streak is detectable, for example, in the bT-scholion's comment on *Il*. 21. 269, where Achilles seems to be the only person affected by the flooding river: it is implausible (ἀπίθανον), but the listener is not allowed to calculate the truth or falsity of the action; 'it is acceptable as being in a poem' (ὡς δὲ ἐν ποιήσει παραδεκτά). How is it that Homer says in the *Iliad* that the winds live in Thrace, while in the *Odyssey* he says that they live with Aeolus? The fiction is taken up for the purposes of the moment, says the scholiast, so that there is no need to enquire into such things; the data of myth

---

[134] From the context it is quite plain that allegorizing is at issue; there is therefore no reason to insert ἀλληγορικῶς in the last clause, as does Hintenlang (1961), 140. Incidental objections to particular allegorical readings are recorded by bT 8. 192, A 8. 195, T 21. 6–7. Eustathius notes Aristarchus' objection to allegorical interpretation, and protests strongly against it (40. 29–33). For discussions of Alexandrian and Aristarchean hostility to allegorical interpretation, see Roemer (1924), 153–6; Weinstock (1927), 138; Hintenlang (1961), 140; Schmidt (1976), 75–87.

[135] The opposite λύσις to the one from convention is the one ἀπὸ τῆς λέξεως, 'on the basis of the form of expression used', i.e. allegory. The famous Porphyry scholion which mentions Theagenes as the inventor of the solution ἀπὸ τῆς λέξεως lays out the two solutions (2. 240. 14–241. 17). The most extended ancient discussion of what poets and artists in other media have in common (and what differences they have), is to be found in Dio's interesting twelfth oration.

cannot be put to examination (ἀνεύθυνα τὰ τῶν μύθων, T *Od.* 10. 20).[136] As usual, the Latin commentary tradition follows suit: *in carminibus quaedam nec ad subtilitatem nec ad ueritatem exigenda sunt* ('in poems certain things are not to be made to conform with strict interpretation or with truth', Serv. *Aen.* 9. 74).[137] The 'Aristotelian' view of autonomy is definitely a minority trend within ancient literary criticism as a whole.[138] It could perhaps only be comfortably held by those who were more or less 'detached'—the scholars, and the poets. For the majority of the ancient practitioners of criticism, embroiled in education and affairs, the case was different. To a large extent, it depended on what view you took of the ends of poetry, and an educationalist could not afford to take a view that did not hold to an overtly moralistic end. Accordingly, those who stressed the educative function of poetry almost necessarily had recourse to mechanisms of defence,[139] while it was the Alexandrian scholar Eratosthenes who most trenchantly stated the case that niggling enquiry into the details of Homer's history and geography was beside the point, since 'every poet aims at affecting the audience's emotions, not at instruction' (ποιητὴς πᾶς στοχάζεται ψυχαγωγίας, οὐ διδασκαλίας, Str. 1. 1. 10).[140] Such language takes us back to the controversies involving the *Dissoi Logoi* and Gorgias.[141] Aristotle's way of coping with the problem had been, in part, to contend that poetry had a unique function, and was exempt from criticisms that applied to other forms of speech. The complexities of his vision (particularly as regards the audience's emotion) were soon lost, but ultimately his stance is behind the brusque

[136] Similar comments on the futility of enquiring into the data of the poems in A 2. 45, 494; A 4. 491.

[137] Cf. Serv. *Aen.* 12. 725; Ti. Donatus 1. 6. 1–12 Geo.

[138] Pfeiffer (1968), 166–7.

[139] I think especially of 'Longinus' here, but there was little criticism that did not have a public context of the sort which might make moral defence desirable. Plutarch's fascinating essay on 'How the young man should study poetry' does not use allegorical defences, but he shows how important it was to chart the moral pitfalls which faced the reader of poetry, and to guide the young reader around them.

[140] No one can resist quoting Eratosthenes' marvellous jibe against the earnest folk who read Homer for geographical information: 'You'd find where Odysseus wandered when you found the cobbler who stitched together the bag of winds' (Str. 1. 2. 15). The beginning of Strabo's attack on Eratosthenes shows in the clearest possible manner the educational and moral impetus behind the dominant ways of reading poetry (1. 2. 3). On Strabo and Homer, see Schenkeveld (1976); Biraschi (1984).

[141] Above, pp. 23–5.

utterances of an Eratosthenes, and of the sizeable group who voiced similar opinions.[142] Such observers might hold different views on the ends of poetry. Some no doubt enjoyed an iconoclastic pose. Further, a trend is observable towards reconciling the two camps, with compromises which saw the poet as giving entertainment and instruction simultaneously.[143] But whatever the particular motivation in each case, the views of people like Eratosthenes stemmed from a more or less conscious apprehension that poetry had its own rules and functions, and was not to be examined or put to the test according to extraneous canons.[144] Inevitably, such a pose could degenerate into a slack assertion of 'poetic licence' (ποιητικὴ ἐξουσία, poetica licentia).[145]

Some critics, then, were prepared to allow the poet the right to exploit the body of myth for his own purposes, as Aristotle had recommended (*Poet.* 1460 b 10, 35–7). Aristotle had also, it appears, allowed for the poet's right even to innovate in myth.[146] Certainly later writers acknowledge the way in which Homer invents, and changes his inherited material. When Achilles reminds his mother of how she helped Zeus against Hera, Poseidon, and Athene (*Il.* 1. 396–400), the scholiasts recognize that Homer is making up a new story, which best suits the case of Thetis at this point.[147] Similarly, they take it that Homer made up the whole business of the Achaean wall (and that he tried to cover up the

[142] Cf. esp. Agatharcides, *GGM* 1. 117. 8, and Philodemus: see Grube (1965), 195, for a synthesis of Philodemus' hostility to those who require a 'moral and educational purpose from a poet'. Agatharcides and Eratosthenes, in particular, were speaking from a scientific standpoint when they claimed that the poets did not yield defensible data: Pfeiffer (1968), 166. One gains a fairly clear picture of Eratosthenes' attitudes by reading through the diffuse pages of Strabo's attack on him (1. 2. 3–23).

[143] Pfeiffer (1968), 166–7, referring especially to Hor. *Ars* 333–4.

[144] Law-court testimony, and official examinations of magistrates (εὔθυνα), are common metaphors for the canons which do not apply: Cic. *Leg.* 1. 4; Ov. *Am.* 3. 12. 19; Petron. *Sat.* 118; Lucian *Iupp. Trag.* 39 (poets no witnesses); Agatharcides *GGM* 1. 117; T *Od.* 10. 20 (εὔθυνα).

[145] Testimonia on poetic licence in Stroh (1971), 164–6, with 278; Häussler (1978), 29–33; Bömer (1969–86) on Ov. *Met.* 13. 733 f. The most extended meditations on the *licentia* of poetry are *Aetna* 74–93 and (on epic in particular) Dio 12. 64.

[146] This is controversial, but it seems to me to follow from *Poet.* 1453 b 25–6: see Else (1957), 320–1, 416–17.

[147] bT 1. 399–406, 400; see Bachmann (1902), 18; Willcock (1964), 143–4.

fact).[148] Plutarch and Eustathius say that poets take over some
myths from their predecessors, already made up, and invent others
in addition on their own initiative.[149] Cornutus claims that Hesiod
adds his own inventions to the existing stock of myth, while Dio
says that sculptors and painters follow poetic precedent when they
innovate in myth.[150] Rather quaintly, a scholiast on the song of
Demodocus (*Od.* 8. 267), remarking that Demodocus has an
anomalous version of the marriage of Hephaestus, attributes to
the Homeric character the same licence granted to his creator (τῇ
ἰδίᾳ μυθοποιίᾳ, 'by his own invention of myth').

On the whole, however, most writers were happiest when they
could exculpate the poet by claiming that he was following tradition, thereby taking the softer of Aristotle's options. On Homer's
account of the birth of Heracles, for example, a scholion says that
'the whole thing is mythical; for in fact Homer does not say these
things on his own initiative, nor are these actual events he is introducing, but he mentions them as being things handed down concerning the birth of Heracles' (τό μέν οὖν ὅλον μυθῶδες· καί
γὰρ οὐδ' ἀφ' ἑαυτοῦ ταῦτά φησιν Ὅμηρος οὐδὲ γινόμενα
εἰσάγει, ἀλλ' ὡς διαδεδομένων περὶ τὴν Ἡρακλέους γένεσιν
μέμνηται, A *Il.* 19. 108).[151] In such comments, the poet's right to
follow the myths (ἕπεσθαι τοῖς μύθοις) is regarded as a matter
of course, and the Latin commentary tradition follows suit: *in
deorum ratione fabulae sequendae sunt* ('in the system adopted for
the gods, the myths have to be followed', Serv. *Aen.* 1. 297).[152] At
times, however, a more directly apologetic tendency is discernible,
as when the bT-scholia on *Il.* 5. 385 say that Homer's following
of old traditions absolves him from blasphemy, since he is not
innovating; a similar tack is found in Servius' urge to find some
precedent for apparent innovations in Vergil.[153]

[148] bT *Il.* 7. 443, 445.
[149] Plut. *Quomodo adul.* 20 c; Eustat. 1379. 11–12.
[150] Cornutus, *Theol. Graec.* 17 (p. 31. 14–17 Lang (1881) ); Dio 12. 46.
[151] Cf. A 20. 40; T 20. 147; PEQ *Od.* 6. 42; see Kroll (1924), 60. Even the language of παραδεδομένοι μῦθοι goes back to Aristotle (*Poet.* 1451 b 24): Hintenlang
(1961), 44–51.
[152] Servius' standard phrase is *opinionem sequitur*: *Aen.* 1. 15; 3. 119; 5. 527.
The adaptation of the Greek critical term was current in Horace's day: *famam
sequere, Ars* 119.
[153] *Aen.* 3. 46; 9. 81; contrast his comment on 6. 617, that poets frequently vary
myths.

If the gods belonged in epic by virtue of tradition, they were like-wise at home in a genre which was not thought of as aiming at a realistic or naturalistic representation of life in the first place.[154] The point had first been systematically made by Plato's polemic, and countered by Aristotle's redefinition of the range of mimesis.[155] Subsequently, probably in Aristotle's school, there developed the hierarchy of narrative types which became traditional: ἱστορία ('history'), πλάσμα ('fictitious story'), μῦθος ('myth'); in Latin, *historia, argumentum, fabula*.[156] As modern studies of narrative have made us more aware of the artificiality of any narrative forms, even the novelistic forms, with their strenuously achieved 'realism',[157] we ought to be in a receptive frame of mind to contemplate the ancients' approaches to the problem of the verisimilitude of epic. The degrees of verisimilitude felt to be proper to each level of narrative are shown in Quintilian's typically clear-cut formulation:

narrationum ... tris accepimus species, fabulam, quae uersatur in tragoediis atque carminibus non a ueritate modo sed etiam a forma ueritatis remota, argumentum, quod falsum sed uero simile comoediae fingunt, historiam, in qua est gestae rei expositio.

We have three types of narrative: myth, which you get in tragedies and poems, and which is removed not only from truth but even from the appearance of truth; fiction, which comedies invent, false but verisimilitudinous; and history, in which there is an exposition of something which actually happened. (*Inst.* 2. 4. 2)

The preconceptions behind such divisions are very deep-rooted. One may compare the criticisms which Aristophanes levelled against Euripides' overly realistic (technically, quasi-comic) representations of human action.[158] Categorizations of the sort given by Quintilian are quite standard. An extended discussion is available in Sextus Empiricus, who defines ἱστορία as the exposition of true

---

[154] Kroll (1924), 44–63, has a valuable account of epic's essentially 'non-mimetic' character.

[155] Above, pp. 26–8.

[156] Kroll (1924), 60–1; Barwick (1928); Walbank (1960), 225–8; Schmidt (1976), 60–3; Häussler (1978), 212–31; Puglisi (1985).

[157] Barthes (1974) and Genette (1980) have been perhaps the most influential contributions to a large production. Syntheses are available in e.g. Ruthrof (1981), 78–96; Waugh (1984).

[158] Kroll (1924), 48; cf. Russell (1964), 99, on ancient opinions about the difference between the *Iliad* and *Odyssey*: 'there is a positive correlation between realism and lack of seriousness and tension'.

events which actually happened, πλάσμα as the exposition of things which did not happen but which are spoken of in the same way as things which did happen, and μῦθος as the exposition of things which never happened, of lies.[159]

The scholia express this general approach, and it is significant that the most extended comment along these lines is given in response to a criticism made by Plato against the representation of the gods (*Rep.* 390 c).[160] The reply is given that there are three varieties of poetry: one which imitates reality (μιμητικὸς τοῦ ἀληθοῦς), one where reality is imagined (κατὰ φαντασίαν τῆς ἀληθείας), and one which exceeds reality by the process of 'imagination' (καθ' ὑπέρθεσιν τῆς ἀληθείας καὶ φαντασίαν); the gods belong in this last category, along with Cyclopes and Laestrygones.[161] Extraordinary suspensions were expected of readers when they experienced narratives of the third, least verisimilitudinous, category; we shall return shortly to the nature of these suspensions.

A rough analogy with forms in our own culture might suggest itself, if we think of the scale of expectations concerning norms of realism which a modern audience automatically traverses when viewing, successively, an historical drama; a Broadway musical, with 'realistic' dialogue interspersed with song-and-dance routines on the top of taxi-cabs; and an opera, with the Rhine bursting its banks, and the gods in Valhalla being blotted out by flames, as at the end of Wagner's *Ring*; or with the animated statue of the Commendatore, and the Don's engulfment into Hell, as at the end of Mozart's *Don Giovanni*. A special handicap for most moderns as readers of ancient epic is our insensible assumption of the naturalistic novel as the norm for narrative—a norm which itself often remains unexamined, since classicists tend to assume that naturalism is 'natural'. In discussing the epics which follow in the next chapters, I shall be suggesting that we do multiple harm to the ancient epics when we read them as texts of realism; a useful

---

[159] *Math.* 1. 263; cf. Serv. *Aen.* 1. 235; Cic. *Inv.* 1. 27; [Cic.] *Rhet. Her.* 1. 13. See Lewis (1936), 82, for the related Renaissance doctrine of 'the probable, the marvellous-taken-as-fact, the marvellous-known-to-be-fancy'.

[160] The mere presence of the gods can force a redefinition of a genre in which they do not belong: witness Plautus' redefinition of his comedy, *Amphitryo*, as a 'tragi-comedy', because it has gods as characters, who belong in the highest genre of tragedy (51–61).

[161] bT 14. 342–51; a similar formulation in AbT 2. 478–9.

preliminary corrective is at hand in the blunt demarcations of a
Quintilian or a Sextus Empiricus.

Still, if one considers the ancients' hierarchies, a certain confusion
of categories is discernible. A definition such as Quintilian's concentrates on the level of verisimilitude appropriate to an entire
genre, while Sextus Empiricus sees the distinctions in terms of
subject-matter.[162] Aristotle's emphasis had been squarely in the
former camp, as Else shows: 'Aristotle makes no distinction between "myth" and history as poetical subjects, but only between
the ways in which the poet and historian . . . handle their material'.[163] Certainly Homer, the master, was praised as containing all
three levels of narrative (ἅπερ ἅπαντα παρὰ τῷ ποιητῇ ἐστι,
AbT 2. 478–9). It was, in fact, conventional to regard epic as being a mixture of the actual and the invented, or false, and hence as
containing elements of narrative style appropriate to more than
one level: thus Polybius defines Homer's poetic licence as 'a mixture of history, description, and myth' (συνέστηκεν ἐξ ἱστορίας
καὶ διαθέσεως καὶ μύθου, 34. 4. 1).[164]

Epics were regarded in this way because they were thought to
be, ultimately, about something that had happened, something in
the tradition.[165] Even the undupable Eratosthenes took it for
granted that the Trojan war had taken place: he gave it a date
(eighty years before the return of the sons of Heracles).[166] The
result was that myth was often regarded, in a rather blunt fashion,
as the distinctive adornment which a poet used to transform his
kernel of historical raw material into a true epic, with the true epic
qualities of grandeur, emotional impact, and elevation: 'so, taking
the Trojan war, which actually happened, he adorned it with his
manufacturing of myths—and he did the same to the wandering of

---

[162] Though it is highly revealing that even Sextus, who is trying as hard as he can
to set up distinctions in terms of subject-matter, cannot help slipping into language
more appropriate to mode, when he defines πλάσμα as the exposition of things
which did not happen but which are *spoken of* in the same way as things which did
happen (*Math.* 1. 263). The first Section of Chapter 6 will return to the problems
revealed by Sextus' equivocations.

[163] Else (1957), 315–16.

[164] From Strabo, 1. 2. 17. When Servius makes his famous claim that *Aen.* 4 has
'a stylistic level virtually out of a comedy' (*paene comicus stylus*, 4. 1), he is rather
ineptly applying a rule of thumb, and trying to find an example of second level of
narration.

[165] Gomme (1954), 3–4; further, Chapter 6, Section I below.

[166] Pfeiffer (1968), 163–4.

Odysseus' (οὕτω τόν τε Ἰλιακὸν πόλεμον γεγονότα παραλαβὼν
ἐκόσμησε ταῖς μυθοποιίαις, καὶ τὴν Ὀδυσσέως πλάνην
ὡσαύτως, Str. 1. 2. 9).[167] Such an attitude goes back at least to
Thucydides, who speaks of Homer adorning his poetry with a
view to exaggeration as a result of being a poet (1. 10. 3). It is
canonized in the Hellenistic apotheosis of Homer: the relief of
Archelaus of Priene shows the figures of Myth and History sacri-
ficing at an altar before the divine figure of Homer.[168] However inadequate this approach may appear in its text-book form,[169] it is
important to acknowledge that the quintessence of the epic effect
*qua* epic was felt to be located in the mythic elements which were
imposed upon the 'facts' of history and tradition—from which one
receives the first explanation of the paralysis of ancient critics
when faced with the *Bellum Ciuile* of Lucan.[170] It is necessary,
therefore, to appreciate how the ancient critics responded to the
sort of narrative effect they were prepared for in high epic.

Before addressing ourselves to the question of how the gods were
actually read, however, it is worth pausing to mark an important
implication of the categorizations which we have been discussing.
The ancient critics, equipped with a clear notion of a hierarchy of
genres, recognized that the characteristic nature of the narrative in
which the gods figured inevitably entailed a characteristic—
unique—manner of representing those gods. In a fundamental
sense, the gods existed for the ancients according to the rules of
the particular context in which they were encountered, whether
that be epic, lyric, cult, or philosophy. At some level, of course,
this is true of anybody's apprehension of anything. It is, or ought
to be, a truism that our experience of any object or concept is, to
some degree, a function of the medium through which we experience it.[171] Accordingly, it made a difference whether a Greek experienced, let us say, Zeus, as the Zeus enshrined in his own city

[167] The whole context, which is too long to quote here, is very informative; cf. 3.
2. 13; Eust. 1379. 25–7; Serv. *Aen.* 1. 382; 3. 349. See Curtius (1953), 454–5, on
the extensive later Latin tradition of such attitudes.

[168] Pollitt (1986), 16.

[169] Servius in particular insistently tries to find Vergil cloaking 'historical fact' in
cunning ways: *Aen.* 1. 382, 443; 2. 636; 3. 256; see Lazzarini (1984).

[170] In Chapter 6 the problems of 'history' and 'myth' will be discussed in more
detail.

[171] Such is the basic insight of semiotics: introductions in Belsey (1980), 37–47;
Culler (1981), esp. 18–43.

or in another city; as Zeus Soter, Basileus, or Meilichios;[172] as
Zeus in the prose writings of the Stoic Cleanthes, or in the verse
hymn of the same Cleanthes; as Zeus Ammon in Libya, or as
Pheidias' chryselephantine statue at Olympia. Studies of the Greek
gods from Otto to Kahn have tried to capture the essence of what
is distinctive about an individual deity, and their results are
important and illuminating.[173] Once the distinctive nature of
Hermes or Athene has been charted, however, it still remains to
acknowledge that each mode of recognizing what Hermes 'is' cannot help but be in itself a determining factor in the apprehension
of what he 'is'. If a god is a character in an epic, then he or she
cannot exist there as an essence any more than a couch can exist
as a couch in an epic, or a ship as a ship. The deity is, in the last
resort, inseparable from his or her vehicle. Much of the talk of the
gods in epic being 'literary devices'—especially when this is meant
as a criticism—is oddly inconsequential: what else can they be?[174]
The relationship between the ways a god is experienced in an epic
and in any other form of experience remains, of course, problematic, and the readings of the poems offered in the later chapters
will attempt to address that problem. But it is vital to appreciate
the determining force of the medium in this realm, as in any other.

The terms I have been using would no doubt have struck a
Greek or Roman as very alien. In their dogged way, however, the
ancient commentators are fully alive to the fact that the gods in
epic—solely and sufficiently by virtue of the fact that epic presents
them according to its own rules of narrative and characterization—are of a different order from the gods of the philosophers or
the gods of cult. The form of expression is an element—more than
an element—of their meaning and status:

ὅταν εἰς τὴν ἀξίαν ἀτενίσῃ τῶν θεῶν, τότε φησὶν αὐτοὺς μὴ κινεῖσθαι περὶ
θνητῶν, ὡς οὐδὲ ἂν ἡμεῖς περὶ μυρμήκων. ὅταν δὲ ἐπιλογίσηται τὴν
ποιητικήν, ἕπεται τοῖς μύθοις καὶ τὴν ὑπόθεσιν ἐκτραγῳδεῖ, συμμαχίας καὶ
θεομαχίας παράγων.

---

[172] To give the example (which I take from Vernant (1980), 99) of a problem
faced by Xenophon (*An.* 7. 8. 4).

[173] Otto (1954); Kahn (1978). Veyne (1986), 259, has some brief and clear
words on the importance of looking at the experience of the gods as 'relations vari-
ables'.

[174] A point made with such force as to be intemperate by Lynn-George (1982),
242–3.

Whenever the poet looks to the actual status of the gods, he says that they are not moved on account of mortals, just as we wouldn't be on account of ants; but when he takes the genre into consideration, he follows the myths and treats the subject-matter in tragic manner, introducing gods fighting along with mortals and against other gods. (bT 8. 429)

When Zeus, then, is 'moved on account of a mortal' and laments for Sarpedon, a scholiast remarks that the poet is not to be reproved, for he must either drop the kinship between men and gods or else speak consistently with it (οὐ μεμπτέον τὸν ποιητήν· ἢ γὰρ ἀφιέναι δεῖ τὴν συγγένειαν τῶν θεῶν τὴν πρὸς ἀνθρώπους ἢ τὰ ἑπόμενα αὐτῇ λέγειν, T 16. 433–8). Again, when Homer says that Dawn brings light to the immortals, a scholiast comments that since the poet has it that the gods live on Olympus, which is a mountain, it is in consistency with the fiction that he says the gods are in darkness sometimes (ἁρμοδίως τῷ πλάσματί φησιν αὐτοὺς καὶ ἐν σκότῳ ποτὲ εἶναι, bT 11. 2). The pseudo-Plutarchean *Life of Homer* (113) has an extended discussion of the necessary anthropomorphism of epic, in which the author shows that Homer had no other way of making the divine nature accessible to his audience.

Students of Milton will recognize something rather akin to the notion of 'accommodation', according to which post-lapsarian humanity can only gain an idea of God's true nature by the analogy of imperfect anthropomorphic conceptions. The crucial point is that once Milton starts to portray God within the conventions of epic, the very nature of that narrative mode has its own determining power, which may be a disruptive one: Milton's theological discourse is not straightforwardly commensurate with his epic tale.[175] Bloom states the case with characteristic forcefulness in his discussion of Dante: 'Doubtless poetic form and theological significance are inseparable and pragmatically unified in Dante, but they are not and cannot be one and the same entity.'[176]

The recognition that gods are not the same things in epics as gods in temples or philosophers' books was something that tended to be packaged up into another neat tripartite hierarchy (with, naturally, philosophers on top). It was conventional to talk of the 'three theologies': of the poets, of the state, and of the philosophers.

[175] Murrin (1969), 132–4; Kermode (1971), 266–91; Daiches (1984), 32; Damrosch (1985), 75–86.
[176] Bloom (1989), 39.

The first formulation of precisely this stratification is unknown, but it must be Hellenistic, at least;[177] ultimately, of course, it has its roots in the fracturing of the poets' monopoly on speaking about the divine which was begun by those such as Xenophanes. Naturally, many people thought that Homer was telling them important truths from the religion of the philosophers, as we have seen. The scholiasts, too, insistently speak of Homer as 'teaching piety'.[178] Yet anything in the portrayal of the gods which is at odds with the theology of the philosophers may be defended on the grounds that the genre's licence entitles it to these forms of speech: this is how the gods are spoken of when they are in a poem of this kind.

It is here that we may take up discussion of how the gods were read, for being in a poem of this kind entails that they are ἀνθρωποπαθεῖς, subject to the same passions and possessing the same qualities as human beings. It is, of course, precisely this fact to which Xenophanes and Plato had objected, yet for the scholiasts it is a fundamental aspect of Homer's technique (and hence a sufficient defence in itself) that the poet represents the gods' actions as being analogous to human actions. So, for example, when Homer says that Ares, sitting on high Olympus, did not know that his son Ascalaphus had been killed in battle, a scholiast records:

ἐζήτηται δὲ πῶς θεὸς ὢν ὁ Ἄρης οὐκ ᾔδει περὶ τοῦ υἱοῦ. ῥητέον οὖν ὅτι παρὰ τῷ ποιητῇ οἱ θεοὶ σωματικῶς λαμβανόμενοι ἀνθρωποειδῶς ἐφίστανται· ἀθανασίᾳ γὰρ διαφέροντες μόνον ἀνθρώπων τοῖς αὐτοῖς ἐνέχονται πάθεσιν.

The question is asked how Ares, inasmuch as he is a god, didn't know about his son. The answer is that in Homer the gods, being understood in physical terms, appear in human guise; for, differing from men only in their immortality, they are subject to the same passions.[179]

The same norm is appealed to in dismissing Plato's objections (*Rep.* 390 c) to Hera's self-adornment before the seduction of Zeus (bT 14. 176); and the scholiasts often refer to the way in

---

[177] So Lieberg (1973), 107 (the standard study).
[178] e.g. bT 1. 46; bT 2. 169; bT 4. 66, 104; bT 5. 127, 407.
[179] Porph. 2. 186. 9–11, on *Il.* 13. 521; cf. bT ad loc., ἐπειδὴ ἀνθρωποπαθεῖς οἱ Ὁμηρικοὶ θεοί.

which Homer's gods resemble humans in using keys, going home
to bed, valuing gold, talking together in secret, giving and receiving wedding-gifts, and so on.[180] As usual, the Latin commentators
follow suit, so that when the gods escort Jupiter from the 'Senate-
house' at the end of the council in *Aeneid* 10, Servius comments:
*poetice mores hominum ad deos refert: ut magistratum deducunt*
('according to the norms of poetry he applies the customs of men
to the gods: they escort him like a magistrate', 10. 117).

As characters in narrative, the gods should conform to the
norms of narrative, and the commentators, in accordance with
their Aristotelian principles, are eager to discover plausibility in
the descriptions of the gods in action. At times, no more is at issue
here than the recognition that the divine action is more or less
inevitably figured on analogy with human action. The commentators often talk of the gods acting in a 'lifelike' or 'plausible' manner (βιωτικῶς, πιθανῶς). It is lifelike for the gods' quarrel at the
end of *Iliad* 1 to be broken up by everybody laughing at
Hephaestus (bT 1. 571); it is plausible that Hera should anticipate
Aphrodite's objections to helping her by being frank about their
differences (bT 14. 192).[181] Sometimes, however, the commentators are concentrating on how the particularizing of the gods' action is a manner of fixing them in the narrative, meshing them into
the poem's norms, making them believable in the poem's terms.
This is seen most clearly in the comment of the bT-scholion on *Il.*
14. 226–7, where Homer gives a list of the places traversed by
Hera as she goes from Olympus to Lemnos:

ἄκρως κατονομάζει τοὺς τόπους, τὰς ὁμόρους χώρας διεξιών ... τῇ
γὰρ ὀνομασίᾳ τῶν τόπων συμπαραθέουσα ἡ διάνοια τῶν
ἐντυγχανόντων ἐν φαντασίᾳ καὶ ὄψει τῶν τόπων γίνεται. ἅμα οὖν τὸ
ἀργὸν περιέφυγεν, οὐκ εὐθὺς ἀγαγὼν αὐτὴν ἐπὶ τὰ προκείμενα χωρία·
μάρτυρας γοῦν ἐπαγόμενος τοὺς ἀκούοντας πιθανωτάτην καθίστησι
τὴν διήγησιν.

He names the places meticulously, detailing the lands that border on each
other ... For the mind of the audience, as it rushes along in unison with
the naming of the places, is engaged in a process of imagination and
visualization. At the same time Homer avoids being too blunt, by not

---

[180] T 14. 168 (keys); A 1. 606 (bed); bT 4. 2, bT 13. 25–6 (gold); bT 14. 189
(talking); T *Od.* 8. 318 (wedding-gifts). Much material on debates over anthropomorphism in Pease (1955–8), 306–7.
[181] Cf. bT 8. 407, 423–4; T 21. 328.

taking her immediately to the intended destination; so by calling the audience in as witnesses he makes the narrative most plausible.

Similarly, when Athene and Apollo meet on earth in *Iliad* 7, Homer fixes the place of their encounter, by the oak-tree at the Scaean Gate: 'to make it convincing,' says the scholiast, 'he puts the place as well' (ἀξιοπίστως ἔθηκε καὶ τὸν τόπον, AbT 7. 22). The same approach is exemplified in the Latin commentator on Vergil, Ti. Donatus, in discussing Vergil's description of a divine colloquy: *tempus et locum et personas et rem posuit, quibus maximum relationis fidem fecit: tunc enim uerum ostenditur factum, cum dicitur quando exstiterit et ubi et quibus adnitentibus* ('he put down time, place, characters, event, and with all of these he gave the greatest credibility to his narrative; for something is shown to be a true fact when we are told when it happened, and where, and on whose initiative').[182] Again, when Poseidon looks down from on high in Samos, the height is mentioned in the interests of plausibility (πιθανῶς), so that he can look down on everything from above (T 13. 12). As so often, the pithiest expression of the matter is Horace's: *ficta uoluptatis causa sint proxima ueris* ('let things made up for the sake of pleasure be very close to the real', *Ars* 338).[183]

This is, no doubt, a quite basic norm of epic technique—indeed, of any technique which engages with the fantastic.[184] The poet assimilates the strange and the extraordinary to the patterns of human action, making the process work with apparently inconsequential authenticating elements. The first description of divine action in *Iliad* 1 establishes the norm. The priest prays to Apollo, who 'hears' him (ἔκλυε, 43); responds for a reason (χωόμενος κῆρ, 44); moves down from Olympus with his carefully described bow and quiver on his shoulders (44–5), the arrows meticulously

---

[182] 2. 197. 6–9 Geo. Donatus' language lays bare the rhetorical background to such formulations: on the concern of rhetorical theory with creating plausibility through names, places, and events, see Woodman (1988), 85–7.

[183] See Kroll (1924), 52, on the doctrine of πιθανὸν πλάσμα ('plausible fiction'). The doctrine presumably goes back to Aristotle's insight that 'the more realistic details are inserted in an account of an improbable event, the more probable it is made to seem': Lucas (1968), 229. Modern criticism knows this as 'l'effet de réel': Barthes (1968); Martin (1986), 57–80; Genette (1988), 46–7. On the interest of Renaissance poetics in the probability of the fantastic, see Steadman (1985), 143–50.

[184] Brooke-Rose (1981), esp. 72–102. Chapter 2, on Apollonius, will be particularly concerned with this question.

clanking on the shoulders of the angry god when he moves to set off (46–7). He sits down away from the ships and shoots an arrow: the sound, the targets, and the sharpness of the missiles are all there (48–52).

Yet the levels of realism in epic are plastic, to say the least. In the middle of the particularized passage just referred to, we read an unnerving half-line, a gesture away from the anthropomorphized features which make it possible for the god to be a character: ὁ δ' ἤιε νυκτὶ ἐοικώς ('and he went like night', 47). [185] A constant poetic preoccupation in Homer, and in later epic, is the question of how far divine power is susceptible to the narrative accommodations which are the indispensable medium for capturing that power—and this preoccupation mirrors the recurrent pagan insistence on the 'contradiction and ambiguity' which are inherent in the 'predictable and unpredictable, human and non-human' divine.[186] The commentators find it very important to acknowledge not only the anthropomorphism, but also the elements of the fantastic and implausible and bizarre which the poems assert as being inextricably part of the action of the divine.

At a basic level, one often finds them commenting on how Homer catches the effortless power of the gods' action by brusque and swift narrative; it is, of course, a fundamental donnée of Homeric religion that the gods act 'easily', 'effortlessly': ῥεῖα μάλ', ὥς τε θεός.[187] A term one sometimes encounters in this connection is φαντασία (*phantasia*, 'appearance'), a word used to describe the process by which the poet makes something 'appear before the eyes' of the audience, in vivid imaginative actualization.[188] The word is often used of the description of the gods in action, from Aphrodite plucking at Helen's robe, to Athene appearing before Achilles (bT 3. 385, bT 1. 198). Regularly, this usage is a comment on the incorporation of the gods in the narrative, of the sort which we have just been discussing. As the author of *On Sublimity* remarks, however, it is typical of examples of *phantasia* in poetry that they go beyond the visual, and 'have a quality of exaggeration that belongs to fable [myth] and goes far beyond credibil-

---

[185] On the disjunction between the simile and the picture of the god's movement, see Dietrich (1983), 55.

[186] The quotations are from the invaluable paper of Gould (1985), 24, 32.

[187] *Il.* 3. 381, *et saepe*: see T 15. 357; AbT 15. 668; AbT 16. 666; T 21. 235–40.

[188] 'Longinus' *Subl.* 15 is the key text: see Russell (1964), 121.

ity'.[189] Here belong what 'Longinus' calls such 'extraordinary, monstrous imaginings' (ὑπερφυᾶ φαντάσματα) as those introducing the Battle of the Gods in *Iliad* 20.[190] The uncanny and the eery are often labelled with this description of *phantasia*: Thetis 'rises swiftly out of the grey sea like mist' (bT 1. 359); Zeus 'pushes Hector from behind with his huge hand' (bT 15. 695).

When the limits of coherence and credibility are strained to rupture, and epic's latent incommensurability with verisimilitude becomes overt, then even *phantasia* is sometimes felt to be an inadequate term, and the critics speak of τερατεῖαι, *monstra* ('portentous monstrosities'). So, for example, the bloody mist that Zeus sheds on the earth to honour his son Sarpedon is a 'fitting portent' (ἁρμόδιος τερατεία, bT 16. 459).[191] And Eustathius describes as 'completely monstrous' (πάντῃ τερατῶδες) the scene where Hera gives Achilles' horse the power to speak and prophesy (1190. 23, on *Il.* 19. 407).

Such phenomena produce the thrill of shock which the Greeks called ἔκπληξις, an emotional response which Aristotle had recognized as being particularly at home in the less strenuously verisimilitudinous form of epic.[192] It was common dogma (either for praise or blame) that epic was especially concerned with achieving this effect, and especially well suited to attaining it, since the genre was far less representational in nature even than tragedy, with which it shared the category of *fabula*.[193] It is the action of the divine in particular which contributes to the creation of ἔκπληξις,[194] and the commentators regularly call attention to the way in which the introduction of the divine effects an intensification or heightening (αὔξησις) of the narrative.[195] Further, say the scholiasts, Homer's switching of scene from the human to the divine provides variety, and relief from any risk of monotony.[196]

In particular, the intervention of the gods at moments of crisis and deadlock makes it possible for the poet to gear the human

[189] 15. 8 (in the translation of Russell, in Russell and Winterbottom (1972), 479, with my gloss of 'myth').
[190] 9. 5; see Russell (1964), 91, for similar ancient judgements on this passage.
[191] Cf. T 18. 24; Kroll (1924), 54.
[192] *Poet.* 1460 a 11–17.
[193] Polyb. 34. 4. 1; Dio 12. 67; Plut. *Quomodo adul.* 17 f, 20 f, 25 d (a leitmotif throughout the essay); other passages collected by Heinze (1915), 466 n. 1.
[194] Eust. 1379. 14–15; bT 15. 695; T 18. 51; T 20. 62.
[195] AbT 2. 478; bT 4.1; Richardson (1980), 275.
[196] bT 4. 1; bT 7. 17; Richardson (1980), 266.

action up to a pitch of extraordinary tension. The scholiasts regularly comment on how Homer 'brings the turns of events to such a point that they can be put right only by gods' (ἐπὶ τοσοῦτον ἄγει τὰς περιπετείας ὁ ποιητὴς ὡς ἀπὸ μόνων ἰᾶσθαι θεῶν, bT 3. 380).[197] Since it is a given that the gods are capable of virtually anything, the actions they take to cut the knot will have a plausibility that a human resolution would lack. While commenting, then, on how Athene acts like a tragic *deus ex machina* in the assembly scene in *Iliad* 2 (bT 2. 144), the scholiasts claim that her intervention makes the resolution πιθανόν ('plausible', AbT 2. 96, bT 2. 144, bT 2. 278-82); the commotion has been made so vast that it would have been implausible for the human characters to resolve it themselves.[198] However one may now react to their particular examples, their assumption that the gods contribute to the plausibility of the epic action is a useful check on the very common modern assumption that the gods generally undermine the plausibility of the human action. The modern slant originates, I imagine, in the unexamined first principle that the humans are 'really' the only characters in the story; they are the ones the story is about, and the ones on whose terms narrative consistency must be judged. One path away from this one-sidedness is given us by the scholiasts' blunt dogma, according to which plausibility on the gods' terms is something which can be made valid for the general tenor of the action.

A special problem for modern readers, and one which will very much concern us in our readings of the epics in the following chapters, is that posed by the gods' intervention to influence or aid a human character. In general, such participation of a god in the action is seen by the commentators as intensifying the power of the narrative, and as heightening the status of the human character. At *Il.* 15. 637, for example, when the Achaeans are 'routed by Hector and father Zeus', the T-scholion says: 'he magnifies Hector by bracketing him with Zeus' (αὔξει Ἕκτορα συγκαταλέγων αὐτὸν τῷ Διί).[199] On the other hand, the directly opposite view is

[197] Cf. bT 1. 195; Hor. *Ars* 191-2, *nec deus intersit nisi dignus uindice nodus / inciderit*; Griesinger (1907), 55; Richardson (1980), 270.
[198] Similar comments on the gods making impossibilities plausible in T 10. 482; A 18. 204, 217-18; bT 19. 347; Ab 20. 443; Serv. *Aen.* 1. 8; 2. 620; 9. 761 (on each of these three passages, Servius quotes Hor. *Ars* 191-2).
[199] Cf. T 5. 703-4; bT 20. 4; T 21. 385; bT 23. 383.

often taken, that the aid of a god debases the human's achievements, making them 'spurious' (νόθα, b 11. 300). On the very same passage from *Iliad* 15, for example, Eustathius comments that the continual mentioning of Zeus during Hector's *aristeia* reflects badly on the Trojan hero, in that he has to rely on someone other than himself to succeed (1035. 9–11). It is, however, significant that comments of this nature are almost invariably levelled at scenes involving Hector and the Trojans;²⁰⁰ the commentators here are in the grip of their hypothesis that Homer is 'philhellene'.²⁰¹

One also very commonly finds certain stock identifications coming into play when a god or goddess appears to a mortal. Athene, in particular, is said to be the φρόνησις ('wisdom') of whichever character she is aiding or advising.²⁰² According to D 1. 198, for example, the reason that only Achilles sees Athene when she appears to him is that only he can see his own φρόνησις. One may well feel that this does less than justice to Homer's technique,²⁰³ and in fact the commentators can employ other, and less reductionist, approaches. The importance of giving full weight to a god's status as a character is assumed by a commentator on the scene in *Iliad* 3, where Aphrodite forces Helen to join the defeated Paris in his bedroom:

κατηγοροῦσιν ὡς προαγωγὸν εἰσάγοντος αὐτοῦ τὴν θεόν. ἀλλ' ἐπεὶ ὥρμηται γέλωτα μὲν θέσθαι τὸν Πάριν, ἐπαινέσαι δὲ τὴν Ἑλένην, καὶ τοῦ μὲν τὴν ἀκρασίαν, τῆς δὲ τὴν σωφροσύνην ὑπ' ὄψιν ἄγειν, οὐ δύναται δὲ διεστῶτα τὰ πρόσωπα δι' ἑτέρου τινὸς συμβιβάζειν, ἐπίτηδες παρέλαβε τὴν Ἀφροδίτην.

People accuse Homer of bringing on the goddess in the role of a procuress. But since he has set out to make Paris a laughing-stock while still praising Helen, and to depict *his* lack of self-control beside *her* sexual moderation, and since he cannot bring the two characters together, now they are separated, through any other agency, he makes express use of Aphrodite. (bT 3. 383)

---

²⁰⁰ Ge 21. 215 is unusual in that it concerns Achilles (and even there the comment is on what an enemy of Achilles says); otherwise, b 8. 335; b 12. 173; T 12. 437; bT 13. 1; bT 16. 119. Very similar comments in Ti. Donatus on Turnus being aided by Juno: 2. 282. 6–8; 2. 285. 31–286. 4 Geo.

²⁰¹ Richardson (1980), 273–4.

²⁰² e.g. Porph. 1. 71. 3–5; AbT 5. 131–2; E *Od.* 7. 14.

²⁰³ Roemer (1914), 177–8, stresses how the use of Athene is only tangentially a device of revelation; it is also a πιθανόν way of preserving Achilles' ἦθος.

The particular reading given here may, indeed, not convince: to speak of Helen's sexual moderation in antithesis to Paris' lack of self-control is to eclipse the very question which the scene is making problematic. Yet this commentator is at least refusing to gloss the deity as nothing more than an emotion of the humans. He is interested in what the poet achieves by having the goddess as part of the narrative, and it is precisely this angle which may lead to a genuinely fruitful reading, of the sort given by Johnson:

Despite the complexities of Helen's feelings, what she is doing and why she is doing it become fairly clear to us because her action and her motives have been unfolded before us in realistic speech, in economical and graceful pictures, and the divine intervention, fearful as it may be, is ɋo less intelligible than the human action that it influences.... The woman hates and loves, and this is what Homer's picture, mostly because of the divine intervention, is able to show. Something complicated has been rendered intelligible without being simplified.[204]

Related to the approach which sees Athene as a character's own wisdom is the approach which sees the god working on the character's own emotions or resources. When Poseidon aids the Greeks in the battle by the ships, for example, the scholiast comments that 'the divine power assists their zeal' (ταῖς προθυμίαις συλλαμβάνει τὸ θεῖον, bT 13. 678).[205] Plutarch, in, of all places, his life of Coriolanus (32), has a remarkable and extended discussion of this way of reading. For two pages he quotes and analyses Homer to prove that the poet consistently shows gods working on emotions and powers which are already present in the human.[206]

There is no one norm to which Homer's flexible technique can be reduced. Each later poet's exploitation of Homer's examples is so individual that it is necessary here only to register the ways in which such scenes could be read, and wait to see what is made of such readings by Homer's followers, each in his turn.

The followers of Homer were not circumscribed by the interests

---

[204] Johnson (1976), 40–1. Following our preoccupation with the naturalism which makes it possible for the gods to exist in the narrative, Johnson's concentration on the 'economy and realism' of Aphrodite's appearance is also worthy of note, especially with his superb focus on the chair which the goddess places for Helen, which 'leavens the whole passage, naturalizes it, completes its growing plausibility' (40).

[205] Erbse (1969–88) ad loc. compares Aesch. *Pers.* 742.

[206] Wüst (1958), 75; Lesky (1961), 18–22.

and competence of the critics we have been studying here. It goes without saying that Vergil and Ovid, not to mention Apollonius and Statius, were far more canny and insightful readers of epic than were the gentlemen shrouded behind b, T, A, D, or Q. It is a modern cliché—which I am not concerned to dispute—that these critics were not adequate to the masterpieces they were studying. But no critics ever are; and rather than repeat the traditional patronizing judgements on the merits of ancient literary criticism, we may take our leave of the critics with due gratitude for the aid they have given us towards the task which now claims our attention, of reading the epics from Apollonius to Statius.

# 2

# Apollonius' *Argonautica*

## I

Verily thou art a God that hidest thyself.

Isaiah 45: 15

Even if he had never written a line of poetry, Apollonius' name
would still be known to us, for he was one of the leading scholars
of his day, and headed the library at Alexandria for some dozen
years (probably from around 260 to 247 BCE).[1] He published researches on Homer, Hesiod, Archilochus, and Antimachus, and
modern studies have documented the way in which his learning
became part of the fabric of his great epic, the *Argonautica*.[2] If he
was very much in the mainstream of scholarship, he was also a
brilliant reader by any standard, as every page of his poem shows.
It is exceedingly frustrating that we are effectively shut out from
reading much of what was important to him, for only fragments
survive from the epics composed between the Homeric era and the
time of Apollonius. The loss of Antimachus is especially to be re-
gretted; here was an innovative artist who was famous for his
learning, spoken of as the 'editor' of a text of Homer, and a poet
whom Apollonius treated as the object of scholarly study.[3]
   The holes in the tradition are only the first problem for the
reader of Apollonius. The *Argonautica* has begun to come into its

---

[1] Pfeiffer (1968), 140–8. On the gods in the *Argonautica*, see Klein (1931);
Faerber (1932), 79–90; Herter (1944–55), 275–84; Händel (1954), 93–116;
Fränkel (1968), 630–3; Gaunt (1972); Herter (1973), 33–5.
   [2] Bibliography in Herter (1944–55), 315–24; fragments in Michaelis (1875), 17–
56. On Apollonius' incorporation of his scholarship into his poetry, see also Erbse
(1953), with Erbse (1964), 554, an answer to the criticisms of van der Valk (1963–
4), 1. 250–74; Giangrande (1973), and papers on Apollonius in Giangrande
(1980).
   [3] Wyss (1936), pp. XLVIII–IL. On Antimachus' scholarship, see Pfeiffer (1968),
93–4; but note the comments of Wilson (1969), 369.

own in the last thirty years, but it is still held in puzzlingly low regard by many classicists. Part of the explanation lies in the fact that it is a difficult poem to read—opaque, enigmatic, yet with a disconcertingly bland texture, as if the poet is unaware of the ironies and resonances he is setting up. It is hard for a critic to know how to make a way into the poem. Since the gods are our subject, let us begin from Zeus.

When you are five lines into the *Iliad* you read Διὸς δ' ἐτελείετο βουλή ('the plan of Zeus was being fulfilled'), and you know that this poem's action will comprise the will or plan of Zeus. After the first hundred lines of the *Odyssey*, when the council of the gods is over, the same god's guiding dispensation is also in the open. The epic norms are clear. The *Cypria*'s proem has the same line as the *Iliad*'s (F 1. 7 *EGF*), and Hesiod's paraphrase of the story of Medea uses very similar language: μεγάλου δὲ Διὸς νόος ἐξετελεῖτο ('the purpose of great Zeus was fulfilled', *Th*. 1002).[4] As the νόος or βουλή of Zeus reaches its fulfilment (τέλος, *telos*), so does the plot of an epic. As the reader of Apollonius' *Argonautica* moves into the poem, whose will and plan is revealed to be the determinant of the action?

Apollonius' proem has nothing explicit on show. The oracle of Apollo (5) is a catalyst, not an organizing principle. Yet at 13–14 an oblique lead is given us, when we learn that Jason meets King Pelias at 'a feast which the king was performing for his father Poseidon and the other gods; but he paid no attention to Pelasgian Hera'. Apollonius here directs us to the traditional versions of the Argonauts' story, in which the slighted Hera's desire for revenge against Pelias was the motive force for the expedition.[5] No word, however, of Zeus, while the only individual described as planning and ordaining is the mortal, Pelias (3, 15).

The causal power of Hera's wrath will receive further attention, but first Apollonius has some more turns on the apparent absence of Zeus. As the Argonauts make their way through the town to the ship, Apollonius inserts the poem's first direct speech (delivered, most extraordinarily, by no named speaker):[6] 'King Zeus, what is the

---

[4] Further examples collected by Richardson (1974), on *Hymn. Hom. Cer. 9*.

[5] Pherecydes fr. 105 Jacoby; generally on Hera's role in the earlier tradition, Klein (1931), 19–27.

[6] As a cap, the second speech is delivered by an unnamed *woman* (251–9).

purpose of Pelias?' (Ζεῦ ἄνα, τίς Πελίαο νόος;, 242). The fact that the words are addressed to Zeus makes it all the more remarkable that the directing νόος is not his but that of the mortal, Pelias. None of this is haphazard, for straight afterwards the women pray to the gods to provide 'a pleasing fulfilment/end in the form of homecoming' (νόστοιο τέλος θυμηδές, 249). A homecoming may be the τέλος desired by the gods, but certainly it is the opposite of the plan of Pelias, who is sending Jason on the perilous journey in order to cause his death. Even this early the problem is raised of what the τέλος of the poem will be, and it is linked with the problem of the purpose of god and man. In fact, before very long we see how feeble is the νόος of Pelias, when his own son evades him to join the Argonauts, 'contrary to the purpose of Pelias' (Πελίαο παρὲκ νόον, 323). A fog of complexity surrounds the apparently clear dynamism of the beginning: a hint at the directing power of Hera, tokens of the ineffectual plannings of a human agent, and a deft highlighting of the absence of the will of Zeus.

Apollonius' refusal to lay out the divine motivation of his epic at the beginning is thrown into relief by his opposite procedure in the mini-epic of the Lemnian women, which he inserts into the middle of Book 1. At the start of that digression he dwells on the divine wrath of Aphrodite as the motive cause for the catastrophe (614–15), as if to show his awareness of the norms which the reticence of his main narrative is violating. When the Lemnian queen, Hypsipyle, tells Jason the background to the story, she also speaks explicitly of the terrible anger of Aphrodite as the cause of the disaster (802–3). The ancient commentators on Apollonius quote here some lines from his so-called 'first edition' (προέκδοσις), from which it appears that, in one version, Apollonius had made Hypsipyle speak more vaguely, referring to a madness which fell among the people, 'either from god, or from their own folly, I don't know' (οὐκ οἶδ' ἢ θεόθεν ἢ αὐτῶν ἀφροσύνῃσι).[7] In rewriting, Apollonius has (perhaps) taken the opportunity to lay more stress on the open nature of the divine motivation for this self-contained unit of his poem.[8]

---

[7] 804*, quoted by the L scholion, which gives four different lines for 801–4, and says they come from the 'earlier edition', προέκδοσις. One must be cautious at using the 'earlier edition' to bolster any argument, for the whole question is most controversial: see Fränkel (1964b), 7–11. Fränkel (1968), 106 remains uncommitted as to which version of 1. 801–4 was written first.

[8] My caveats about the use of the 'first edition' stand, but while we are referring

The reader's attention is brought brusquely to concentrate on the plan of Zeus when the sea-god Glaucus rears up out of the water at the end of Book 1, to tell the quarrelling Argonauts not to go back in search of Heracles, accidentally marooned on the shore of Mysia. 'Why', he says, 'are you eager, contrary to the plan of great Zeus, to take bold Heracles to the city of Aeetes?' (*Τίπτε παρὲκ μεγάλοιο Διὸς μενεαίνετε βουλήν / Αἰήτεω πτολίεθρον ἄγειν θρασὺν Ἡρακλῆα;* , 1315–16). In this part of the poem Apollonius twice more mentions 'the plan of Zeus' in connection with the abandonment of Heracles, and of his friend Polyphemus (1. 1345, 2. 154), so that we see that Zeus has some sort of plan for some of the characters; but nothing is said of any wider plan for the expedition (or poem) as a whole.

The partial and uncertain nature of any knowledge of the mind of Zeus is given emblematic status in the figure of Phineus, the seer who was blinded by Zeus for revealing the *νόος* of Zeus 'accurately and completely' (*ἀτρεκέως*, 2. 182). Phineus himself explains the implications to the company:

> Κλῦτέ νυν· οὐ μὲν πάντα πέλει θέμις ὔμμι δαῆναι
> ἀτρεκές, ὅσσα δ' ὄρωρε θεοῖς φίλον, οὐκ ἐπικεύσω.
> ἀασάμην καὶ πρόσθε Διὸς νόον ἀφραδίῃσιν
> χρείων ἐξείης τε καὶ ἐς τέλος. ὧδε γὰρ αὐτός
> βούλεται ἀνθρώποις ἐπιδευέα θέσφατα φαίνειν
> μαντοσύνης, ἵνα καί τι θεῶν χατέωσι νόοιο.

Listen now. It is not right for you to know everything accurately and completely, but as much as pleases the gods, I will not hide. Before, in my madness, I foolishly revealed the purpose of Zeus straight through, right to the end. What he wants is that the revelations of prophecy to men should be incomplete, so that men should want knowledge of the purpose of the gods. (2. 311–16)

The necessary fallibility of human prophecy is a topic from Homer on,[9] but Phineus' words have extra power in a poem where the revelation of Zeus' mind and will has been turned into such a problem. The omniscient prophet and the omniscient narrator

to the 'earlier edition', note that it seems to have mentioned Zeus as responsible for a favourable wind at 1. 518*; again, it is possible (and no more) that Apollonius rewrote the lines in order to remove even this much reference to Zeus' guidance.

[9] *Il.* 5. 150; Pind. *Ol.* 12. 7–12; Xen. *Symp.* 4. 5; Ap. Rhod. 4. 1503–4; Verg. *Aen.* 4. 65, 9. 328; Dover (1974), 76.

both appear to have difficulties in communicating the mind of Zeus, and both maintain inscrutability over what the τέλος ('end') of the expedition/poem will be.[10] A vital passage of explication comes towards the end of Book 2, when the Argonauts meet the sons of Phrixus on the island of Ares. Phineus had directed the Argonauts to go to this place, but he had refused to be explicit about why: 'but why should I sin once more by prophesying all the details one after another?' (ἀλλὰ τίη με πάλιν χρειὼ ἀλιτέσθαι / μαντοσύνῃ τὰ ἔκαστα διηνεκὲς ἐξενέποντα;, 2. 390–1). Such language reminds us of Phineus' initial fault, of telling the νόος of Zeus, and this same key word recurs as the Argonauts get to the island, and Apollonius asks: 'What was the νόος of Phineus, telling them to go there?' (2. 1090). It is, then, not too surprising to find, for the first time, Zeus directly taking an active hand in directing an episode, for the νόος of Phineus is a fragment of the νόος of Zeus. Zeus himself, Apollonius tells us, had caused a storm to force the sons of Phrixus, en route from the palace of Aeetes to Greece, onto the island of Ares, so that they could meet the Argonauts.[11] In one of Apollonius' beautifully gentle narrative moves, the rain from Zeus stops with the sunrise and the two groups meet (2. 1120–2). All through this episode, one epithet of Zeus follows another, relatively uncharged at the moment, but eventually, as the story of Jason and Medea works its way to a conclusion, to be fully invested with force: 'He who overlooks' (Ἐπόψιος, 2. 1123); 'He who protects strangers and suppliants' (Ξείνιος, Ἱκέσιος, 1132); 'He who protects exiles' (Φύξιος, 1147).

Apollonius gradually divulges the necessary facts. Phrixus had been marked down to be sacrificed by his own father, at the instigation of a second wife. He had managed to escape on a ram with a golden fleece, which carried him to the land of Aeetes, where he sacrificed it, and hung up its fleece. Jason now tells the sons of Phrixus that he too has a concern in the ram of Phrixus, and at the

[10] Many fine observations on the relationship between Phineus and Apollonius in the (regrettably unpublished) dissertation of Margolies (1981), 46–7, 134–5, 141–3, 188; cf. Beye (1982), 18. We return to Phineus as a model for Apollonius below: p. 94. The question of the telos of the poem is raised early on (1. 249), and maintained as a problem till the last book (4. 1600). The end of the poem is, of course, much discussed: Livrea (1973), 486–7.

[11] 2. 1098. It is typical of Apollonius' sly avoidance of the epically obvious that he should bestow his big set-piece epic storm on these subsidiary characters, and not on the Argonauts themselves.

end of his speech he makes explicit—for the first time—Zeus' interest: 'I am going on this expedition in order to atone for the attempted sacrifice of Phrixus, which has caused Zeus to be angry against the descendants of Aeolus' (Φρίξοιο θυηλάς / στέλλομαι ἀμπλήσων, Ζηνὸς χόλον Αἰολίδῃσιν, 2. 1194–5).[12] Jason is one of the family of Phrixus' father, the Aeolidae, so that Zeus does have a purpose after all, and Jason will atone for the crime—although not in the way he thinks.

Further confirmation of Zeus' moral interest in the expedition comes in Book 3, when one of the sons of Phrixus gives King Aeetes this same explanation of why Pelias has despatched the Argonauts, describing Zeus—uniquely—with the savage epithet ἀμειλίκτοιο ('he who will not be appeased . . .', 3. 337).

Hera's motives have been out of the limelight for some time. Since they will come into catastrophic harmony with Zeus', Apollonius lays them out more fully in Book 3. It is Hera's idea to help Jason by asking Aphrodite to make Medea fall in love with him (3. 25–9), and she explains her reasons to the goddess of love. Hera picks up the hint given in the proem when she says that she wishes to punish Pelias for dishonouring her (64–5), and she also claims to favour Jason for his kindness to her when she was on the earth testing men's piety (68).[13] She too, like Zeus, has a grievance and a plan for its avenging. If it is not immediately plain why Medea should be linked to the punishment of Pelias, Apollonius dwells on the matter again, later in the book, when Medea reacts to Jason's offer of marriage and a home in Greece:

οὐ μὲν δηρὸν ἀπαρνήσεσθαι ἔμελλεν
Ἑλλάδα ναιετάειν· ὣς γὰρ τόγε μήδετο Ἥρη,
ὄφρα κακὸν Πελίῃ ἱερὴν ἐς Ἰωλκὸν ἵκηται
Αἰαίη Μήδεια λιποῦσ' ἀπὸ πατρίδα γαῖαν.

She wasn't going to say no for long to this offer of living in Greece; for this was the plan of Hera, that Medea of Aea should leave her fatherland and come to holy Iolcus as an evil for Pelias. (3. 1133–6)

Medea, of course, will murder Pelias in the boiling pot.[14]

It is, naturally, quite impossible for any reader with a memory

---

[12] Following the interpretation of Fränkel (1968), 304–5.

[13] The version of the Argonaut story known to Homer stresses Hera's kind motive for aiding Jason, 'since he was dear to her' (ἐπεὶ φίλος ἦεν Ἰήσων, *Od.* 12. 72).

[14] Cf. 4. 21, 242–3; Faerber (1932), 82–3; Levin (1971), 15–23.

of Euripides' *Medea* to be heedless of the fact that Medea's murder of Pelias led directly to the couple's move to Corinth, and to
the ensuing murder of their children.[15] When Jason and Medea
talk to each other for the first time, Apollonius points up the
future nightmares. Jason promises that Medea will be his wife,
and that nothing will separate them from their love until the day
of their death (3. 1128–30). As she hears these words, she is
happy, yet shudders with the fear of seeing deeds as yet invisible
(ἔμπης δ᾽ ἔργ᾽ ἀίδηλα κατερρίγησεν ἰδέσθαι, 1132).[16]

If such is the case, what of Hera's other motive, her predilection
for Jason? Does she not know of the evils to come from her relentless insistence that Medea be linked to Jason? Indeed she does, for
in the fourth book she tells Thetis, the mother of Achilles, that her
son will one day marry Medea—and this is before Hera has even
arranged Medea's first marriage, to Jason (4. 814–15). Her desire
for revenge becomes entirely preponderant, and all her active aid
for·the Argonauts as they return home in the fourth book appears
progressively more sinister. In particular, it is in this fourth book
that she fulfils her role as the goddess of marriage (indeed, as we
have seen, she arranges *two* marriages for Medea). Hera is 'consort of Zeus' (Διὸς δάμαρ) when she beautifies Jason on the day
he goes to meet Medea (3. 922). When Jason publicly promises to
take Medea to Greece and marry her, he appeals to 'Hera patroness of marriage, wife of Zeus' (Ἥρη ... Ζυγίη, Διὸς εὐνέτις, 4.
96). Hera is likewise Ζηνὸς ἄκοιτις ('wife of Zeus') as the eery
hymenaeal is sung by the nymphs at the cave where Jason and
Medea finally become man and wife (4. 1152), the cave where
Macris purified Heracles for the murder of *his* children (4. 1139–
41, with 4. 540–1). The very last time Hera is mentioned in the
poem, it is as the instigator of this disaster-laden union (4. 1194–
5); once her instrument of vengeance is safely married to the transport she disappears from the story, now fully assimilated to her
standard pattern of malevolence, with the anomaly of her initial
beneficence removed.[17]

---

[15] See Eichgrün (1961), 93, on the importance of Euripides' *Medea* here.
[16] For a defence of the reading ἀίδηλα, see Vian-Delage (1976–81), vol. 2. 47 n.
4. Note that Jason, too, before he sets off, speaks of pains from the gods that are as
yet ἀίδηλα (1. 298).
[17] On Hera's essential malevolence in myth, see Burkert (1985), 134; it will be a
major theme in this book. Her active aid for the Argonauts in Book 4 is itemized
and discussed by Campbell (1983), 53–5.

Hera's plan of anger against Pelias harmonizes with Zeus' plan of anger against the Aeolidae. Almost half the poem is gone by before, at the island of Ares, we discover the origins of Zeus' motives and responsibility, and the apparent means of appeasing him, by fetching back the fleece. In fact, the Aeolidean Jason will come to disaster despite and yet because of the fact that he succeeds in bringing the fleece back to Greece. The expedition is meant to appease Zeus, but it ends by arousing him to yet another anger, when Jason and Medea incur shameful guilt with the murder of Medea's brother, Absyrtus. Their offence against Zeus Xenios is marked by the fact that they lure Absyrtus to his death with ominous ξεινήια δῶρα ('gifts of guest-friendship', 4. 422),[18] including a cloak given to Jason by the first woman whom he loved and abandoned, Hypsipyle—a cloak used by Dionysus as the 'marriage-bed' for Ariadne, the model for Medea, after she had been deserted by Theseus (4. 430–4).[19] In struggling out of one net of responsibility Jason has enmeshed himself in another, as Zeus' original μῆνις and χόλος ('anger') against his family transmutes into a more personal χόλος.[20] As we finally learn in Book 4, the great anger of Zeus *is* his epic plan (βουλή), so long hidden from us: καὶ τότε βουλάς / ἀμφ' αὐτοῖς Ζηνός τε μέγαν χόλον ἐφράσαθ' Ἥρη ('and then Hera considered the plans of Zeus for Jason and Medea, his great anger', 4. 576–7).[21] The fleece of the refugee Phrixus, marriage-coverlet for the guilty pair, emblematizes jointly the two chains of sin: no surprise, then, that when the Argonauts see it on the ship for the first time, it is λαμπόμενον στεροπῇ ἴκελον Διός ('flashing like lightning of Zeus', 4. 185).

The fitfully partial and shifting emergence of the plans of the gods helps to establish the uncertainties of human responsibilities and initiative.[22] Phineus tells us that no man may speak unerringly

---

[18] Jason's crime is prepared for by his own declarations of the regard due to Zeus Xenios: 3. 192–3, 986.

[19] On the cloak, see Rose (1985), esp. 39–41. Ariadne is Medea's model throughout her meeting with Jason in Book 3: 997–1005, 1074–6, 1096–1101, 1107–8; cf. Hunter (1989), 207–8. The 'marriage-bed' of Ariadne and Dionysus resembles the fleece, 'marriage-bed' of Medea and Jason: cf. 4. 428–9 and 1147–8; Rose (1985), 39–40.

[20] Anger against the family: 2. 1195, 3. 337–8; against Jason and Medea: 4. 557–8, 577, 585.

[21] On the text, Livrea (1973), 177–8.

[22] Cf. Hunter (1987), esp. 135–8.

the mind of Zeus, and the narrator's voice is, as often, Phinean when he introduces the statement of the anger of Zeus with a destabilizing που ('I suppose', 4. 557).[23] We do not know, for example, whether Circe's purification of Jason and Medea will be effective in turning away the anger of Zeus.[24] And there are new offences against Zeus for Jason to commit, after the poem, when he will jettison the wife he claimed with an appeal to Zeus: 'Let Zeus Olympios himself be witness . . .' (Ζεὺς αὐτὸς Ὀλύμπιος ὅρκιος ἔστω, 4. 95). This line anticipates, as it were, the *Medea* of Euripides, which Apollonius fashions into his sequel, so that he has Euripides' Medea appeal to the oaths and witnesses of the *Argonautica*:

> Μήδεια δ' ἡ δύστηνος ἠτιμασμένη
> βοᾷ μὲν ὅρκους, ἀνακαλεῖ δὲ δεξιᾶς
> πίστιν μεγίστην, καὶ θεοὺς μαρτύρεται
> οἵας ἀμοιβῆς ἐξ Ἰάσονος κυρεῖ.

The unhappy Medea, dishonoured, cries on the oaths, calls on the mightiest of pledges, that of the right hand, and calls the gods to witness what sort of return she is getting from Jason. (*Med.* 20–3)

The telos of the *Argonautica* is not the telos of the plan of Zeus.

The uncertainty of the poem, poet, characters, and reader concerning the guiding will of Zeus is compounded by Apollonius' treatment—or non-treatment—of Zeus as a character. The plans of Zeus and Hera run separately but to a common end, yet Hera is as much part of the narrative as any Argonaut, with speech, gesture, and emotion figured in the text, while Zeus, with whose name she is so often linked as consort, is not with her ever, nor once represented in the narrative. At the beginning of Book 3, especially, Hera and Athene are 'apart from Zeus himself and the other immortal gods' (8–9).[25] Apollonius is not only stressing

---

[23] Denniston's remark on Herodotus' use of this particle is, *mutatis mutandis*, most suitable for Apollonius: 'Herodotus is fond of divesting himself of the historian's omniscience, and assuming a winning fallibility': Denniston (1954), 491 n. 1.

[24] The poet does not tell us Zeus' response to the prayer that he should give over his anger (4. 713–17). Besides, the description of Medea as 'defiled by blood from within her own family' (4. 716–17) already points forward to her murder of her children.

[25] The force of the various Iliadic parallels is well brought out by Campbell (1983), 7.

Hera's responsibility for the events of the book; he is also highlighting his refusal to incorporate Zeus as a character. The breaking up of the gods' familial cohesion, a piece of occasional usage in Homer, has here become a standard mode.[26] Zeus' absence from the narrative has been taken as a strategy for preserving his majesty.[27] Yet Apollonius gladly enters controversy when, for example, he describes Ganymede, 'whom Zeus brought to live in heaven, to share the hearth of the immortals', postponing to an enjambed position of surprise the salacious shock of Zeus' motive, 'because he was filled with desire for his beauty' (τόν ῥά ποτε Ζεύς / οὐρανῷ ἐγκατένασσεν ἐφέστιον ἀθανάτοισιν, / κάλλεος ἱμερθείς, 3. 115–17). This version is crucially different from Homer's, as the ancient commentators on Apollonius are keen to point out, for in Homer it was not Zeus, but the other gods, who stole Ganymede, and he was chosen as a wine-pourer, not as a catamite (*Il.* 20. 234–5).[28] The force of Apollonius' change is shown by his retention of Homer's enjambed κάλλεος ('beauty'), now the object of Zeus' desire, not a token of the gods' taste. The Greeks were interested in the fact that homosexuality does not feature in Homer, and the Ganymede text was an element in the debate;[29] so far from avoiding the sort of moral dilemmas which Homer aroused, Apollonius has gone out of his way to create a scandal where there was none in Homer, capitalizing on scholarly interest in these matters in order to do so.

We hear quite a lot about Zeus as the seducer of females as well.[30] In fact, the first time he is mentioned in the poem it is as the father of the Dioscuri by the mortal Leda (1. 150). In Book 2 we hear of how he was tricked by a nymph into granting her eternal virginity (2. 947–51). In Book 4 the heights of impropriety are

---

[26] On the effacement of Zeus, see Klein (1931), 251, 253. Note how, for example, Zeus is not mentioned as sending his Iliadic messenger Iris, when she intervenes at 2. 286, whereas in the anecdote of Aeetes we do get the Homeric norm, when Zeus sends Hermes (3. 587–8).

[27] Vian–Delage (1976–81), vol. 2. 12 n. 2; Hémardinquer (1872), 35–52.

[28] The scholiast (to be found in Wendel (1935)) omits Homer's own reference to the beauty of Ganymede.

[29] The T-scholion on *Il.* 20. 234 makes the same points about Homer's blamelessness as the scholion on Ap. Rhod. 3. 114–17; cf. Dover (1978), 196–7. It also claims that pederasty began only with the Spartans; see here Dover (1978), 185–9.

[30] Xenophanes, of course, the first critic of Homer's picture of the gods, had picked on their adultery (above, p. 2).

scaled when his own consort addresses one of the objects of her husband's lust, congratulating her on resisting, and speaking with the bleak lack of illusion proper to the wife of a philanderer: 'For that's what he's always been interested in, sleeping with ladies, immortal or mortal' (κείνῳ γὰρ ἀεὶ τάδε ἔργα μέμηλεν, / ἠὲ σὺν ἀθανάταις ἠὲ θνητῆσιν ἰαύειν, 4. 794–5).

It is not, then, a matter of τὸ πρέπον ('seemliness'). One enlightening angle on the inscrutable Zeus comes from a pattern of theogonic references which is intricately arranged throughout the poem. Before the Argonauts even set sail, the blustering, blasphemous Idas, who rates his spear above Zeus (1. 467–8), almost causes a quarrel (νεῖκος, 1. 492). He is prevented by the company, and the arch-poet Orpheus sings a miniature cosmogony (1. 496–511). The song, taking its lead from Homer's 'Shield of Achilles',[31] begins with earth, heaven, and sea, and how they took distinct shape out of strife (νεῖκος, 498) amongst the primordial mass. A succession myth follows:[32] first Ophion and Eurynome had power, control (κράτος) over Olympus (503–4), but they yielded to Cronus and Rhea, who in turn ruled over the Titans, while Zeus was still a boy in the cave in Crete, and while the Cyclopes had not yet ensured κράτος for Zeus with thunderbolt, thunder, and lightning (505–11)—the very means by which Zeus will destroy Idas.[33] Births and battles of gods, stressed physicality,[34] struggles for power—Xenophanes and Plato would have recoiled in disdain, while the problematic nature of any discussion of the birth and childhood of Zeus is wittily shown in the opening lines of the *Hymn to Zeus* by Apollonius' contemporary, Callimachus (4–9). Yet Apollonius here is firmly in the Hesiodic tradition, with its series of generations, and its embodiment of Zeus' power in the might of the sky's explosive forces.[35]

[31] Schwabl (1962), 1470.

[32] On Apollonius' sources, see Vian–Delage (1976–81), vol. 1. 253. Note that Orpheus' song begins with νεῖκος, as does Demodocus' first song in the the *Odyssey* (8. 75); and its theme is cosmogony, which was thought to be the (allegorically expressed) theme of Demodocus' second song, with Ares representing νεῖκος in the universe, and Aphrodite φιλία (*Od.* 8. 266–366); see Buffière (1956), 168–72.

[33] So Fränkel (1968), 77–8.

[34] Note βίη καὶ χερσίν ('force and hands'), 505. Apollonius uses this phrase of Ophion yielding to Cronus, but in Hesiod, his source here, it is used of the *next* succession, from Cronus to Zeus (*Th.* 490); Apollonius' 'unchronological' use of the phrase underscores the inevitability of the cycles.

[35] Note esp. *Th.* 504–6.

The song of Orpheus is only the first link in a chain. Orpheus' beginning is from a poem and an artifact (the Shield of the *Iliad*) outside the *Argonautica*; his ending is picked up and carried forward some 230 lines later, in the beginning of another artifact, Jason's cloak, given to him by Athene.[36] The first decoration of the cloak picks up the temporal progression of the song, for on it are the Cyclopes, now manufacturing the thunderbolts for Zeus (1. 730–4). Again, there is much here of Hesiod, for the *Theogony* likewise concentrates strongly on Zeus' babyhood in Crete, and on the Cyclopes' giving him thunder, thunderbolt, and lightning (*Th.* 477–506). At 2. 1211–12, to complete the progression, we are told of Zeus using this power, to defeat the threat of Typhaon.

Zeus, then, is a usurper, and 'every usurper is threatened with the same fate'.[37] Book 4 contains an averted usurpation, when Hera tells Thetis of the prophecy given Zeus, informing him that Thetis was fated to give birth to a son greater than the father (4. 801–2): 'For that reason, although he desired you, he let you go, for fear that some other, just as good as himself, might rule over the immortals; he wanted to keep his own power for ever' (τῶ καί σε λιλαιόμενος μεθέηκεν / δείματι, μή τις ἑοῦ ἀντάξιος ἄλλος ἀνάσσοι / ἀθανάτων, ἀλλ' αἰὲν ἑὸν κράτος εἰρύοιτο, 4. 802–4). This is the same power, κράτος, held by the first generation (1. 504). As the poem has gone on, we have seen a kind of cycle, from the first holders of power, through the maturation of the current holder, with his defence against Typhaon, to the averted possibility of his overthrow by his own son.

The human characters have their ways of talking about Zeus, but the inspired poet Orpheus, the goddess Hera, and the cloak given by the goddess Athene, all tell a story of amoral (or supramoral) power-struggles which determine the way the world is now. The god who looks after suppliants and guests, the guarantor of moral order, is the heir of an apparatus based on might, and a character left carefully unpurged of the flaws exposed by three hundred years of criticism; his power is the same power as that of the old gods, his flaws the same flaws. The conventional criticisms

---

[36] Newman (1986), 77.

[37] Burkert (1985), 127, mentioning a number of stories (among them the story of Thetis, which Apollonius uses at 4. 799–804) where Zeus 'is imperilled by women destined to bear a son who is greater than his father'. So Milton, after retailing the cycles of succession: 'So Jove usurping reigned' (*Paradise Lost* 1. 514).

of Zeus' morality must be seen in this context of succession-struggles over power. The non-philosophical ways of apprehending the gods are always open to this perspective, always capable of acknowledging that the apparent order and serenity of Zeus' dispensation are founded on mere might.[38] Apollonius accentuates this side of Zeus' character by refusing to give any ground to the other aspect of his control which was stressed by early myth—his mastery of intelligence and cunning.[39] Humans have to obey this god's moral laws, and in the *Argonautica* characters are terribly punished if they do not; yet they are laws from which Zeus' own might is exempt.[40] Zeus' oppressive absence makes his unaccountability all the more inscrutable, and absolute.

In looking at Apollonius' presentation of the divine backdrop to the action, we have already touched at times on some problems concerning the gods' modes of operation in the poem, and it is now time to consider the gods' figuring in the narrative. The norms and levels of realism in Homeric epic are, as we saw in the last chapter, problematic, and Apollonius' response is itself artfully and rewardingly problematic.

It is worth noting at the outset that Apollonius for long keeps us in suspense as to how (or even, perhaps, whether) he will represent the gods in the narrative. The gods are referred to by poet and characters in the early part of the poem, but they do not themselves appear as characters in any early scenes, as do the gods in both *Iliad* and *Odyssey*. The prolonged absence of the gods is highlighted by a typical piece of Apollonian wit, when he gives us a stock scene of prayer and sacrifice (1. 411–36). His scene is modelled on the first set-piece sacrifice of the *Iliad* (1. 451–74), where the same god, Apollo, is addressed. In the *Iliad* the god's reactions to the humans' activity are twice described. He hears the prayer (1. 457), and he takes pleasure in the hymn sung after the

---

[38] Clearly stated by Fontenrose (1959), 471–4; cf. Vermeule (1979), 125; Burkert (1985), 128, 'power is latent violence'. The *Prometheus Vinctus* is the most extended exposition of this perspective on Zeus' power; cf. Hes. *Th.* 385–8, on how Power and Force always abide by the side of Zeus.

[39] Symbolized by his swallowing of Metis, 'Wisdom', Hes. *Th.* 886–91: see Detienne and Vernant (1974), 61–124. *Prometheus Vinctus* may itself have been qualified in the other plays of the trilogy, showing a Zeus who came to rely more on wisdom than on might; for a discussion of the issues, see Conacher (1980), 120–37.

[40] Again, Burkert (1985), 130.

sacrifice (1. 474). In the *Argonautica* no reaction from Apollo is described after the prayer, but after the sacrifice we read: 'and he rejoiced, looking at the flame, . . . Idmon' (γήθει δὲ σέλας θηεύμενος Ἴδμων, 1. 436). The poet's refusal to describe Apollo's reaction is made more striking as he brings in the name of the prophet Idmon, a character not mentioned before in this scene, and one whom we do not expect to make this sudden appearance.

Only as Argo sails for the first time does Apollonius introduce gods as characters, telling how they all looked on from heaven at the ship and at their offspring, the crew (1. 547–52). Since the Argonauts are their descendants, the gods naturally take an interest;[41] they are also fascinated by the ship itself, for that was made by one of their own number, Athene. Here, still, the gods are not doing very much, but are the ultimate divine audience.

Before any other divine appearance, we are treated to an extended experiment in alternative techniques of representation, when Apollonius spends nearly forty lines describing the scenes embroidered on Jason's cloak (1. 730–67). Various pictures follow the Cyclopes (730–4), among them two involving gods—Aphrodite (742–6), and Apollo (759–62). It would be too much of a digression to explore fully this highly interesting ecphrasis,[42] but the picture of Aphrodite in particular repays a moment's attention, for it catches a problem which will recur. The goddess is shown looking at herself in the mirror formed by the shield of her lover, Ares. Commentators refer us to famous statues which the description is evoking,[43] and the lines certainly do make us think of statuary. Yet the oddity of Apollonius' procedure must be allowed to register, for here we have, in an epic poem which has not yet embodied a god in action, the first representation of a god. And it is a representation in words of a representation in cloth of a representation in marble of a goddess—and her reflection.[44] The mechanics of capturing these creatures in the mesh of his poem is plainly something of intense interest to the poet.

The first time a divine creature of any sort acts as a character in

---

[41] So noted by the scholion on 1. 547–8.

[42] On the cloak, see Fränkel (1968), 100–3; Shapiro (1980); Newman (1986), 76–9; Zanker (1987), 68–70, 75–6.

[43] Vian–Delage (1976–81), vol. 1. 258 (on 1. 746); Shapiro (1980), 281–2, and see 271–4 on the interests of Hellenistic authors in the aesthetics of other artistic media; cf. here Zanker (1987), 68–70.

[44] Zanker (1987), 69: 'a poetic description of a reflected image in a woven picture'.

the poem is when the nymph sees Hylas, has her wits stunned by Aphrodite, and pulls the boy into her pool (1. 1228–39). She has no name, unlike her counterparts in Theocritus' version (13. 45); she emerges without a word and subsides with her victim. After a coyness lasting almost a quarter of the poem, it seems somehow appropriate that Apollonius' first use of the convention should be in this dreamy, or nightmarish, excursus.

After that, nothing until the shock of Glaucus' eruption from the sea, towering up in the water to take reader and Argonauts by surprise (1. 1310–28). 'Abrupt and mysterious', as Hunter calls it,[45] Glaucus' intervention is odd in a number of ways. Standing there in all his shaggy glory, with his mighty hand on the gunwales, his function is to tell the Argonauts the plan of Zeus for Heracles (or some of Zeus' plan), together with the fates of Polyphemus and Hylas. It is significant that he prophesies only about characters with whom they have lost touch, for it is likely that Apollonius knew of versions where Glaucus foretold the destinies of certain crew-members when they were present;[46] it is more characteristic of this poem for him to keep his addressees in the dark. His appearance looks like a random event—Glaucus is part of no pattern, appearing this once only in the poem—; but is he acting as the mouthpiece of Zeus? We are not told, and there is no conversation between deity and humans.[47] Glaucus' words do, however, fulfil the classic function of a god's intervention, in providing a solution for a crisis which the humans cannot resolve.[48] The sons of Boreas have prevented the ship turning back to pick up their lost comrades (1. 1300–1), and so the immediate decision has been taken, but bitter quarrels are in train, and are only quelled by the god. Yet Apollonius has told us that Heracles will later kill the sons of Boreas for preventing his rescue (1. 1302–9); is it irrelevant to reflect that if Glaucus had intervened seconds earlier he would have saved their lives? It is Apollonius' own timing which has condemned them, for his version of their death is unique.[49]

---

[45] Hunter (1986), 52.

[46] As in Diod. Sic. 4. 48. 6.

[47] We return below (p. 89) to the problem of what may be learnt about Zeus' part in the events surrounding the disappearance of Heracles and the appearance of Glaucus.

[48] Above, pp. 52–3.

[49] Vian–Delage (1976–81), vol. 1. 112 n. 2. Note Apollonius' ironical gesture back to his innovation in the next book, where the sons of Boreas are terribly

72     Apollonius' Argonautica

Nymphs and sea-gods are from the lower echelons of divinity, and we have to wait until well into Book 2 before we see a major god in action, when Athene helps her ship Argo through the Symplegades. The episode is prepared for in Phineus' prophecy, and is an extensive piece; it repays some study. Phineus tells them to send a dove ahead through the rocks as a test; if it passes through, he says,

> μηκέτι δὴν μηδ' αὐτοὶ ἐρητύεσθε κελεύθου,
> ἀλλ' εὖ καρτύναντες ἑαῖς ἐνὶ χερσὶν ἐρετμά
> τέμνεθ' ἁλὸς στεινωπόν, ἐπεὶ φάος οὔ νύ τι τόσσον
> ἔσσετ' ἐν εὐχωλῇσιν ὅσον τ' ἐνὶ κάρτεϊ χειρῶν·
> τῷ καὶ τἆλλα μεθέντας ὀνήιστον πονέεσθαι
> θαρσαλέως· πρὶν δ' οὔ τι θεοὺς λίσσεσθαι ἐρύκω.

Don't hold back for ages from going ahead yourselves, but grab your oars firmly in your hands and cut through the narrow strait; for your salvation will not be so much in your prayers, as in the strength of your hands. So the most useful thing is to drop everything else and exert yourselves boldly (though I don't forbid you to pray to the gods earlier on). (2. 331–6)[50]

It is, therefore, rather odd, once they have made their prayers (2. 531–3), taken the dove on board, and set off (533–6), that the goddess Athene comes directly into the action for the first time: 'Nor did their departure escape Athene's notice' (οὐδ' ἄρ' Ἀθηναίην προτέρω λάθον ὁρμηθέντες, 2. 537). As this first major deity comes into play, her anthropomorphic corporeality receives very disconcerting notice, in a moment of masterful comedy and poise:

> αὐτίκα δ' ἐσσυμένως, νεφέλης ἐπιβᾶσα πόδεσσι
> κούφης, ἥ κε φέροι μιν ἄφαρ βριαρήν περ ἐοῦσαν,
> σεῦατ' ἴμεν Πόντονδε, φίλα φρονέουσ' ἐρέτῃσιν.

Straightaway, in haste, she stepped with her feet onto a cloud, a light one, which could carry her in a moment, despite her weight, and she swept off to the Black Sea, with kindly thoughts for the oarsmen. (2. 538–40)

In the *Iliad*, this same goddess gets into a chariot with Diomedes, 'and the oaken axle gave a loud creak from the weight,

concerned that they may upset a god if they help Phineus by scaring off the Harpies (2. 250–1). By persuading the Argonauts not to go back and pick up Heracles, they have already offended a 'god', and thereby caused their own deaths.

[50] Following the text of Fränkel (1964a) for 335.

for it was carrying an awesome goddess and a man of the first rank' (μέγα δ' ἔβραχε φήγινος ἄξων / βριθοσύνῃ· δεινὴν γὰρ ἄγεν θεὸν ἄνδρα τ' ἄριστον, 5. 838–9). A scholiast registers a reaction characteristically provoked when Homer directs his audience's attention too insistently to the physicality of the gods: 'These two lines are athetized, because they are not necessary, they are ridiculous, and they are self-contradictory; what if the two of them were very bad spiritually, and still well-endowed and of substantial physique?' (ἀθετοῦνται στίχοι δύο, ὅτι οὐκ ἀναγκαῖοι καὶ γελοῖοι καί τι ἐναντίον ἔχοντες· τί γὰρ, εἰ χείριστοι ἦσαν ταῖς ψυχαῖς, εὐειδεῖς δὲ καὶ εὔσαρκοι;, A ad loc.).[51]

Apollonius' Athene is stepping on no chariot, but standing with her particularized feet on a cloud, which enjambment stresses as light, and which none the less carries her despite her weight. The bizarre paradoxes receive extra emphasis in the following simile, describing her movement through the air, where her flight is compared to the quintessentially immaterial movement of thought (2. 541–6). And at the end of the simile, when she lands, Apollonius brings our attention back to those feet: θῆκεν ... πόδας, 548. The simile, with its insistence on the otherness of the gods' means of being and moving, comes from Homer (*Il.* 15. 80–3); likewise from Homer is the god's body and weight, together with the carefully realized travel (*Il.* 13. 17–21; 14. 225–30). Quite novel is the combining of the two ways of conceptualizing divine motion, with the resultant shifting tension between the physicality and the immateriality of the goddess. Going beyond his glance at the strange representation of Aphrodite on Jason's cloak (1. 742–6), Apollonius is now engaging directly with the practical narrative problems of meshing a divinity into the action.

Her decisive intervention is yet to come, for first the heroes follow Phineus' advice, aiming to row through 'relying on their own strength' (κάρτεϊ ᾧ πίσυνοι, 2. 559). But, after all, the peril is beyond their resources (578), and the poet, having screwed the tension to the highest pitch, has Athene prop herself on a rock with her left hand and bat Argo through with her right (2. 598–9). The

---

[51] The scholiast is repelled by the apparent equation between physical mass and pre-eminence of spirit or nature. Although great weight is a conventional attribute of divinity (Bömer (1969–86) on Ov. *Met.* 2. 162, 4. 449–50), it is not a neutral matter, but one which could be turned to irony or ridicule: see Hinds (1988), 27, on the question of Nero's obesity in Lucan, 1. 56–7.

action is even more abrupt and productive of ἔκπληξις than was the appearance of Glaucus,[52] and the power of the marvel is made more complex by the earlier plays on the god's nature: the goddess whose feet stand on a light cloud without it giving way has a right hand that can send a ship and fifty-two warriors flying through the air like an arrow (2. 600). The simile of the arrow is not random, for the heroes eight lines earlier row so hard that their oars bend like curved bows (2. 591–2). It is Athene, and not they themselves, who completes the action of the simile. The effect is to cap the sense of climactic anti-climax which has already been achieved by the deflation of Phineus' solemn words about relying on human strength. Homer, too, brings events to a pitch which only a god can resolve, but he does not announce in advance that the resolution will be a solely human one.

Phineus, of course, cannot say all he knows, and we can reconstruct a divine plot whereby Athene is testing the virtue of the Argonauts, rather as she does with Odysseus and Telemachus in the *Odyssey* (22. 236–8).[53] We are not told any of this, however, and all the marvellous shock and tension of the episode is, as a result, left strangely unintegrated, for the human and the divine experiences are not interlocking. The failure of any such interlocking is followed up very soon, when the reaction of the steersman introduces another twist on Homeric norms. Tiphys reckons that he knows why they got through: 'I think that the ship herself is responsible for our safe escape' (Ἔλπομαι αὐτῇ νηὶ τό γ' ἔμπεδον ἐξαλέασθαι / ἡμέας, 2. 611–12).[54] Not so, as the reader knows. But Tiphys carries on, apparently on the right track: 'and none other is as responsible as Athene' (οὐδέ τις ἄλλος ἐπαίτιος ὅσσον Ἀθήνη, 612). Yet see how he continues: 'inasmuch as she breathed divine power into the ship when Argus was fitting her together with bolts' (613-14). Right goddess, wrong reason. They have not seen Athene, and, unlike many of Homer's characters after a god's intervention, do not recognize what has just happened.[55] The de-

[52] See the comments of Klein (1931), 217–19, and Gaunt (1972), 121, who comments on the 'slightly grotesque' picture, and on the 'suddenness and the unlikeliness of the scene as Apollonius depicts it'. For a favourable appreciation of Apollonius' boldness here, see Lloyd-Jones (1984), 68–9.
[53] Herter (1944–55), 277.
[54] Following the interpretation of Vian (1973), 96–7.
[55] Faerber (1932), 82. On Homer's characters' recognition of the gods, see below, pp. 85–6.

layed revelation of Tiphys' incomprehension serves to highlight the transformations of the Homeric norms.

It will be necessary to pursue further this question of the human characters' knowledge or ignorance of the divine characters' actions. For the moment, let us continue investigating Apollonius' representations of the gods.

If the Argonauts do not see Athene, they shortly afterwards do see a god, and in all his full divine splendour. They arrive at the island of Thunias, just before daybreak (2. 669–70), and there the god Apollo appears to them (ἐξεφάνη, 676). He is described in great detail as he makes his way towards the land of the Hyperboreans (676–9). The passage is one of diverse interest.[56]

First of all, we may note the recurrent preoccupation with the problems of representing divinity. The visual interest, with the god's hair, his bow in his left hand, hanging quiver, and eyes, all fixed in the description, no doubt calls forth the plastic art and painting which were part of the audience's common culture.[57] On the other hand, the archer god's progress cannot help but put the reader in mind of the first divine appearance of the *Iliad*, with the arrows clanking on Apollo's back as he moves (1. 46).[58] We are reminded that representational art depended on literature as much as the other way around—witness the famous story of the sculptor Pheidias, who said that his inspiration for the statue of Zeus at Olympia was Homer's image of the god in *Iliad* 1.[59] The allusion to artistic representations of the god comes with an intimation that these artistic representations are themselves, in some sense, ultimately 'literary', while the literary force of the picture is stressed by the fact that Apollo is present, and effective. The island shakes under his feet, and waves crash on the shore (679–80), before he moves on through the air (684). Apollo is not simply seen,

[56] Herter (1944–55), 281; now Hunter (1986).
[57] Hunter (1986), 51, with reference to Apollo's statue at Delos.
[58] Above, pp. 50–1.
[59] *Il.* 1. 528–30; the anecdote is the basis of a most interesting discussion by Dio Chrysostom of the problems of representing divinity in various media, with Pheidias as spokesman (*Or.* 12, esp. 25–6). On pictorial and plastic art's dependence on epic, see Schefold (1966), 28 and (1975), 3; Dietrich (1985–6), 179: 'this ideal of beauty ultimately was based on the artist's interpretation of epic data rather than on his notion of the probable form in which divine power manifested itself.'

in other words; the reaction of nature shows that he is 'physically' and weightily 'there'.

The reality of the god's presence, within the norms of epic, is a token of Apollonius' determination to maintain the level of reality appropriate to epic. Of course, by one mode of reading, it is possible to see Apollo in his guise as sun-god here, so that Hunter is quite correct to say that 'Apollo's epiphany is at one level a poetic version of sunrise'.[60] Yet Apollonius is making it impossible for us to subscribe straightforwardly to an alternative, 'rationalizing' explanation for the epithet given Apollo in the later cult on the island, Ἑῷος ('of the morning'). When the poet Orpheus proposes that they sacrifice to Apollo of the Morning, because that is when he appeared to them (2. 687–8), Apollonius is shouldering aside a rationalizing account, which attributed the name to the simple fact that the Argonauts arrived in the morning.[61] As a scholar, Apollonius may have been quite happy to give such aetiologies, but as a poet he will adhere to the versions of myth. Elsewhere he goes out of his way to maintain mythic versions of the origins of names and customs,[62] while his rigour in eschewing even the casual metonymic uses of the gods' names is very remarkable; only Ares is used in this way in the poem, so that the gods' names always refer to an individual character.[63]

Of particular importance is the impression of the vast gulf between god and men which the passage conveys, an impression wholly in accord with the poem's usual strategies, as seen already in the section on Athene above. The Argonauts have their experience when they are on a deserted island (2. 672), where there are normally no people, and when they see the god he is on his way to the Hyperboreans, a group, like the Ethiopians, who are able to consort with the gods because they occupy the far margins of the

---

[60] Hunter (1986), 52.

[61] The rationalizing version of Herodorus (fr. 48 Jacoby) is given by the *Argonautica* scholion on 2. 684–7.

[62] So he gives a 'mythical' explanation of the name of the river Parthenius (2. 937–9), against other 'natural' versions (reported by the scholion on 2. 936–9). Another rationalism of Herodorus', on Prometheus (fr. 30 Jacoby), is likewise shunned by the poet at 2. 1248–50 (where see his scholia). Some people rationalized the entire saga, writing out fleece, bulls, dragon, and all, à la Palaephatus: Diod. Sic. 4. 47. 2–6.

[63] This conclusion emerges from the lists of Reichenberger (1891); Ares' metonymic uses are 1. 189, 1024; 2. 797, 870; 3. 183, 1385.

human world.[64] Apollo's journey is a transit, quite unconnected with his observers. Soon after, he provides goats for the Argonauts' sacrifice (2. 698), but only the poet knows this, not the characters, so that the vision remains an experience with no direct consequence or reference point. Certainly, Orpheus is inspired to institute a cult of Homonoia, one of Apollo's greatest blessings,[65] and all the crew swear to help each other for ever, in concord of mind (2. 715–16). Yet, as the reader knows, three of the company are later to die fighting each other.[66] By any reckoning, Apollo's epiphany is an eerily random and puzzling event.

The *Odyssey* opens with a council of the gods, and the *Iliad* has a council at the end of its first book. Those who know the *Argonautica* are so familiar with the elaborately portrayed meeting of the three goddesses at the beginning of Book 3 that they may overlook the great shift in gear which the passage represents. Until half-way through the poem, the scene has not been set in Heaven, nor have we encountered divinities on their own terms and in their own setting, independent of the human action, interacting with each other as characters in a self-contained piece of narrative.[67] The shift is marked by an invocation to a Muse (3. 1), while the oddity of the deities' late appearance is highlighted by the fact that Hera and Athene take over the deliberations which the human character Ancaeus had tried to initiate at the end of Book 2.[68] The wit of Apollonius' transformations of the Homeric Athene, so proud of her gifts for craft, has been well shown by Campbell, who brings out the ironies of the resourceful goddess's aporia when called upon to come up with a plan.[69]

Such learned humour is eminently Apollonian—even 'Alexandrian'.[70] As far as the depiction of the deities is concerned, however, we must not allow our appreciation of such humour to obscure the fact that, when the gods are in their own sphere,

---

[64] In the *Odyssey* (1. 22–5), Poseidon is visiting the Ethiopians, the 'furthest of men' (ἔσχατοι ἀνδρῶν, 23); cf. *Il.* 1. 423–4. On the gulf between gods and men in the *Argonautica*, see Klein (1931), 235; Faerber (1932), 83; Visser (1938), 62.

[65] Hunter (1986), 53–4.

[66] Idas, Lynceus, and Castor, named together in the catalogue (1. 147–51).

[67] Stressed by Gaunt (1972), 124–5.

[68] Cf. 2. 1278–80 and 3. 11–15; Hunter (1989), on 14–15.

[69] Campbell (1983), 8–10; cf. the most perceptive paper of Lennox (1980).

[70] Zanker (1987), 205–6.

Apollonius observes the Homeric norms very closely.[71] Their physical appurtenances (chairs, combs, and so on), their characterful speech, the whole human tone of their interaction— all this is eminently Homeric. Only by glossing over Homer's naturalism can critics acclaim Apollonius' novel capturing of a domestic atmosphere.[72] One need refer only to the easy intimacy with which Charis greets the visiting Thetis in *Iliad* 18 (an important model for Apollonius here),[73] and especially to the casual grace of her call to her husband: 'Hephaestus, come here; Thetis needs your help' (Ἥφαιστε, πρόμολ' ὧδε· Θέτις νύ τι σεῖο χατίζει, 392). The whole scene is a tour-de-force, but it is carried off without the large-scale upsetting of Homer's norms that we observed at work when the gods' actions mesh into the human action. The genuinely un-Homeric innovation comes soon after, when Apollonius introduces the figure of Eros (85), for the child of Aphrodite is not a character in Homer, nor, so far as we can now tell, in any other of the early epics; for Apollonius, he is a creature of lyric, epigram, and other 'minor' genres.[74] The mother, Aphrodite, had been the key figure in earlier versions, and Apollonius gives the reader to understand that he will follow these versions when he has Phineus prophesy explicitly about the help which Aphrodite will give the Argonauts, saying that she will be responsible for the achievement of the task (2. 423–4).[75] His introduction of Eros is, probably, novel, and it is a decisive factor in the power of the crucial scene where Medea falls victim to the gods—a scene which will claim our attention below, at the beginning of Section II.

Apollonius' most extended play on the nature of the gods is his

---

[71] The norms of epic anthropomorphism. Apollonius' observation of Homeric norms of speech is stressed by Ibscher (1939), 53; cf. Lennox (1980), esp. 68–73.

[72] So, rightly, Lennox (1980), and Hunter (1989), 24–5, who stresses how little we know of how Alexandrian ladies of any rank acted when alone.

[73] Lennox (1980), 49; Campbell (1983), 11–12.

[74] On Eros' absence from Homer and the Homeric Hymns, see Lasserre (1946), 18–19; on Apollonius' non-epic sources for Eros, Lasserre (1946), 180–3; Klein (1931), 27–30. Still, despite Klein's confident denial (28), I cannot help feeling that there may well be some poetic model for Euripides at least, when he has Jason speak of Medea being forced to save him by the inescapable arrows of Eros (*Med.* 530–1).

[75] On Aphrodite's key role in earlier versions (e.g. *Naupactia* F 7ᴬ *EGF*; Pind. *Pyth.* 4. 213–19), see Klein (1931), 20–1; Vian–Delage (1976–81), vol. 2. 6–7.

last. Argo is lost in the Tritonian lake in Libya, when the sea-god Triton meets the company, looking like a sturdy man (αἰζηῷ ἐναλίγκιος, 4. 1551). The phrase has Homeric (and Pindaric) associations; Homeric, likewise, are the god's assumption of a human name (4. 1561), his swift subsequent disappearance back into his divinity (1590–1), and the humans' recognition of the fact that they have seen a disguised god (1591–2).[76] Having done the normal thing, Apollonius reintroduces Triton ten lines later, and this time Triton is 'exactly as he really was to look at' (τοῖος ἐὼν οἷος περ ἐτήτυμος ἦεν ἰδέσθαι, 1603). What is that like? A simile immediately follows, comparing Triton to ... a man: 'As when a man ...' (ὡς δ' ὅτ' ἀνήρ ..., 1604). 'His body', then says Apollonius, 'from the top of his head, around his back and waist down to his stomach, was exactly like the immortals in its outstanding nature' (δέμας δέ οἱ ἐξ ὑπάτοιο / κράατος ἀμφί τε νῶτα καὶ ἰξύας ἔστ' ἐπὶ νηδύν / ἀντικρὺ μακάρεσσι φυὴν ἔκπαγλον ἔικτο, 1610–12; he goes on to describe the sea-monster that he was in the lower parts). The last line is a tissue of epic phrases, used to compare a human being to a god, or to compare something divine to a human being.[77] But to say that something divine looks like something else divine, when you have compared it to a man and spent a line detailing its anthropomorphism, is to introduce a remarkable confusion of categories. Small wonder, then, that Apollonius reflects on his creation as an 'extraordinary portent' (τέρας αἰνὸν, 1619).

Gaunt remarks that 'there is an air of unreality about the scene'.[78] Indeed there is, and a very finely realized unreality it is at that. Triton is there to transport the ship through impassable regions, to make the impossible plausible, as an ancient critic would have put it. One may think of Aristotle's comment on the beginning of *Odyssey* 13, of how Homer, 'by sweetening the absurdity, makes the absurdity disappear with his other good points' (*Poet.* 1460 a 35–b 2). Apollonius' scene is certainly sweet, but it serves to accentuate the absurdity, not to make it disappear, for the norms of anthropomorphism are adhered to in order to be destabilized.

[76] Pind. *Pyth.* 4. 21, 28–9; Homeric parallels in Campbell (1981), on the noted lines.
[77] e.g. *Hymn. Hom.* 5. 55; *Od.* 4. 796; see Campbell (1981), and Livrea (1973) ad loc.
[78] Gaunt (1972), 123.

What is happening with Triton and his fellow gods is a highly self-conscious foregrounding of the problems of capturing, representing such a sphere in the fictive narrative world of the epic; and the flaunting of these narrative problems becomes a way of reflecting upon the strange nature of the unassimilable yet familiarized divine. Any attempt to represent a god is going to be potentially unstable, as Gordon remarks, in connection with statues and paintings of gods: 'It is of the essence of representation that it denies in order to assert. It is a sort of logical puzzle. But then, so are gods. They are here and not here, seen and invisible, human and not human, just and unjust, ordered and disorderly, powerful and weak'.[79] It is a commonplace that the Olympian gods, however assiduously their cults were maintained, were felt to be more distant from the people of the Hellenistic world than they had been from their ancestors.[80] This sense of estrangement—most dramatically caught with the absence of Zeus and the tangential epiphany of Apollo—becomes for Apollonius a desperate problem of definition: how may one catch these gods in a narrative, how may one conceptualize them? What can they be made to mean if they cannot be made to appear, or to conform to the poem's necessary narrative sense? On their own ground and on their own terms, as in the beginning of Book 3, the gods are easy to handle. But as soon as they impinge upon the human sphere of the poem, they either resist embodiment altogether, or make themselves exceedingly difficult to assimilate. It becomes necessary to investigate their interaction with humans in more detail.


## II

The ways of God to men.

Milton, *Paradise Lost*

1. 26


When the gods appear, realism and verisimilitude are made acutely problematic, and this is particularly the case when the

---

[79] Gordon (1979), 25.

[80] Walbank (1981), 209–21; cf. Bulloch (1984), esp. 209–14: 'The dislocation of the early Hellenistic world, psychological and spiritual as well as geographical, must have been immense' (214).

gods actually impinge on the psyche of the human characters. Medea's falling in love with Jason is an episode which embodies many of the issues, and has come to be something of a crystallization of the problems for critics.

It is Hera's plan that Eros should make Medea fall in love with Jason, so that her witchcraft may help him get the fleece (3. 85–9). Eros has had his orders from Aphrodite (3. 129–44), and Hera has played her part (3. 250), by keeping Medea in the palace of her father Aeetes, with whom Jason and the sons of Phrixus now seek audience. Jason and his fellow-ambassadors receive hospitality (3. 270–4), but the stock 'hospitality-scene' is interrupted by Eros' intervention (275–98):[81] with meticulous detail, Apollonius has the god fly down, select an arrow, take up position, and shoot Medea (275–84). The effect of the interruption is to make Eros' arrival intrusive in a formal sense before any other, as the epic of diplomacy and martial endeavour is disrupted and put off track, to become an epic of love. The Homeric model (Pandarus' shooting of Menelaus in *Iliad* 3, 105–26) shows the converse movement: the epic of war is going to end prematurely, but Pandarus' bow-shot puts it back on track.[82] Medea, struck by Eros' arrow, is possessed by passion.

Most critics betray considerable frustration over the fact that Apollonius has, in effect, not written a novel. It is conventionally claimed that we can 'read out' Eros, or even, with unwonted frankness, that Apollonius would have done better not to have had the god at all.[83] Such approaches try to rescue matters by salvaging a psychological gloss: Medea saw Jason standing there and fell passionately and instantaneously in love with him. Apollonius, by this reading, is in fact being psychologically acute, and Eros' actions are a form of shorthand for a natural human experience, which we can recover if we do enough whittling away, until we reach a level behind the text which is satisfyingly 'real' or 'natural'. At some level of paraphrase this gloss means something,

---

[81] On the 'hospitality-scene', see Campbell (1983), 24; on its interruption, Hunter (1989), on 270–4.
[82] On Pandarus, Lennox (1980), 62–8. T. B. McKiernan helped me to this point.
[83] Dissatisfaction is general: see e.g. Herter (1944–55), 279, 369; Gaunt (1972), 124, on how, after Eros has left, 'at this point Apollonius really gets into his stride'. Novelistic glosses offered by e.g. Händel (1954), 110; Vian–Delage (1976–81), vol. 2. 6. An important exception to this reductionism is Johnson (1976), 41–5.

but we are not reading a paraphrase, we are reading Book 3 of Apollonius Rhodius' *Argonautica.* No doubt Apollonius could have described Medea falling in love without using Eros. No doubt James Hogg could have described a young man's perversion by a mutant form of Christianity without introducing the devil as a character. But Gil-Martin is *there* in *Confessions and Memoirs of a Justified Sinner,* just as Eros is there in the *Argonautica,* and it would be as well to try and understand the effect of his presence instead of wishing he had never been introduced. As we shall see, Apollonius has an intense interest both in arousing our interest in Medea's psychology, and in investing that psychology with a striking realism; but it is necessary to allow his particular modes to make a precise impact on our reading, for otherwise the precise nature of his interest will be lost.

If Eros flies down and becomes a character in a narrative, it is important to allow the narrative its force. As Eros goes through his routine in Aeetes' palace, creeping and peeping, shooting and flying away, the very discrepancy between the playful zest of the description and the suffering of Medea becomes more and more compelling—especially if we think of the ultimate consequences of what is happening, as we can hardly fail to do, since Eros is the tool of Hera, who has her plan for Medea. This particular use of the convention enables the scene to arouse feelings of misgiving and disquiet even as it charms and delights. Such a mix of responses is, first of all, supremely appropriate to what is taking place—a young woman is falling in love with a total stranger in her father's house. More than this is achieved, however, if we keep our eyes on Eros, and keep thinking of him not only as the tool of Hera, but also as a creature who has dominion over the universe,[84] for Medea's falling in love may then acquire a resonance and a context which only this use of convention makes possible. The disjunction between the kitschy antics of Eros and the suffering of the human is allowed to find its place in the larger disjunction between the inhuman, self-sufficient ease of the gods and the baffled pain of the human experience. Only by giving full weight to Eros' utter frivolity can we avoid trivializing the scene.[85]

---

[84] Hunter (1989), on the crucial passage of the allegorically significant ball which Eros is given by Aphrodite (3. 135).

[85] See here the fine discussion of Zanker (1987), 207, on how Apollonius sets up

Apollonius was of course familiar with the paraphrasing readings of Homer's gods which were discussed in the previous chapter.[86] He also knew that this scene was the beginning of the most
'naturalistic' and 'realistic' piece of epic ever written, and in fact
the progress of the scene reveals interesting movements towards
and away from 'realism'. The vivid actualization of Eros is at odds
with some other strands here. His missile (βέλος) burns like a
flame (3. 286–7)—and then immediately Medea is 'throwing missiles' at Jason, to remind the reader of the metaphor which is
being actualized (ἀντία δ' αἰεί / βάλλεν ἐπ' Αἰσονίδην ἀμαρύγματα,
3. 287–8). Eros leaves, and then, ten lines later, 'there secretly
burned, covered beneath her heart, baneful eros' (ὑπὸ κραδίη
εἰλυμένος αἴθετο λάθρη / οὖλος ἔρως, 3. 297–8). The god's name is
also the name of his effect; in this line the metaphorical force of
'eros' is guaranteed by the passive form of the verb, but the book's
many subsequent references to 'eros' or 'erotes' are not always as
easy to decide on.[87] Modern printing conventions force editors to
choose whether or not to give ἔρως/ἔρωτες a capital letter, but to
Apollonius' audience, without a minuscule script, it was all ΕΡΩΣ,
so that the problem was sharper for each ancient reader, who had
to decide alone, with each occurrence of the word, whether to see
an effect or a character. It is a problem highlighted at the very beginning of the sequence, as Apollonius veers from the creature
who acts in the narrative and causes the passion, towards an available metaphorical range of reference.

It is equally important to take the narrative effect of a deity
seriously later in the book, when, after a long and intricate description of Medea's equivocations (3. 771–816), Hera stops
Medea from deciding to commit suicide (818). Again, as with the
Eros scene earlier in the book, it is conventional to gloss Hera out
of the text, and to regard her as an entirely dispensable apparatus on top of the intrinsically natural human account. Campbell,

---

a humorous atmosphere in the first divine scene of Book 3, and then uses Eros to
'undercut that superficial humour and make a serious thematic point crucial to the
epic'.

[86] Above, pp. 54–5.

[87] On the force of the passive, see the apparatus of Fränkel (1964a) on 3. 297;
the later passages are discussed by Frankel (1968), 367. Campbell (1983), 130–1
would cut the knot by distinguishing between Erotes (plural), Eros before returning
to Olympus, and *eros* after returning. I am not sure that this works; even if it does,
the sudden appearance of a cluster of brothers for our familiar character is in itself
a rewarding problem.

however, has well shown what damage is inflicted by such reductionism.[88] Hera's increasingly sinister interest is a process of real importance in the poem, and this example of it cannot be so blithely written out.[89] Further, only Hera's influence at this point can make possible the acutely realized indecisions of Medea which are to follow when she meets Jason.

Eros, Erotes, and Hera are not discrete factors, but part of a developing series of problems, a series which bears on the question of why Medea acts in the way she does. Hunter has demonstrated for the last book the dominant theme of the helplessness that the characters—including Medea—encounter in attempting to account for her motivations.[90] Medea asks herself already at 3. 464 'What pain is this I am suffering?' (Τίπτε με δειλαίην τόδ' ἔχει ἄχος;), while at 3. 675 her sister asks her 'What has happened to you? What is this terrible pain that has come upon your heart?' (τίπτ' ἔπαθες; τί τοι αἰνὸν ὑπὸ φρένας ἵκετο πένθος;). In the fourth book, Medea herself begins to express a foggy awareness of how the divine is somehow impinging on her life, but she can have no knowledge of the process (4. 413, 1016–17, 1040). Apollonius' charting of Medea's imprecise awareness of what is happening to her is itself an ironic reflection on the splendid new 'realism' he had created in Book 3, and these ironies are achieved by amplifying Book 3's hints about the limits of that realism.[91]

Medea's hunches about the gods' influence are one example of a widespread phenomenon in Apollonius, which we have already touched on in discussing Tiphys' fumbled acknowledgement of Athene's aid at the Symplegades, namely, the inability of the human characters to have the sort of knowledge about the gods' interventions that Homer's characters can often command. Medea does not know that Eros has shot her, and her ignorance is given ironic emphasis when she wishes (3. 773–4) that Artemis had shot

---

[88] Campbell (1983), 50–3. The alternative approach may be exemplified by Vian–Delage (1976–81), vol. 2. 44: 'L'intervention d'Héra (3, 818) n'est là que pour réinsérer l'action dans son contexte légendaire.'

[89] Cf. Hunter (1989), on 476 and 697, for Apollonius' stress on how Hera is also working through Argos and Chalciope.

[90] Hunter (1987).

[91] We return below to the problem of accounting for Medea's motivation: pp. 89–91; and cf. p. 239, on Ovid's exploitation of Apollonius in his version of Medea.

her ('instead'). She never knows what Hera is doing to her, nor why Hera is doing it, nor even that Hera is doing it.

This question of the characters' knowledge of the gods' actions is an important aspect of epic technique. In Homer, human characters very often recognize the divinity of a god. The god may be undisguised, or else the human senses their divinity, or has it announced.[92] Sometimes, however, a disguised god remains unacknowledged as a god by the humans,[93] a usage which is an aspect of the conventional dichotomy between the knowledge of the poet and the knowledge of the human characters. The poet can tell of the gods in their own setting, or in their interaction with humans, because he is the mouthpiece of the Muses, who know all (*Il.* 2. 485–6). The human characters do not have access to this privileged information, and their apprehension of divine operations is consequently imperfect, with proper insight only being vouchsafed if the gods so will.[94] The *Odyssey*'s first interaction of gods and men provides an example, when Athene disguises herself as Mentes in order to visit Telemachus (1. 105–323). As she departs, Telemachus recognizes her divinity (1. 323; cf. 420); it is regularly when the gods return from man's sphere to their own that their nature is revealed.[95] In the next book, when Telemachus wishes to invoke his visitor, Homer says: 'He prayed to Athene: "Hearken to me, you god who came yesterday to our house . . ." ' (εὔχετ' Ἀθήνῃ · / Κλῦθί μοι, ὃ χθιζὸς θεὸς ἤλυθες ἡμέτερον δῶ . . ., 2. 261–2). The scholiast at this point remarks: 'Telemachus invokes a "god", *tout court*, for he does not know which of the gods had appeared to him. The poet, on the other hand, says "he prayed to Athene" ', BQ 2. 262).[96]

This distinction is closely, even meticulously observed in Odysseus' long narrative of his adventures, for he has only his

---

[92] A useful collection and discussion in Kullman (1956), 99–105.

[93] *Il.* 13. 239–40; 16. 715–27; *Od.* 7. 78–82.

[94] The fundamentally important article of Jörgensen (1904) first laid out this convention.

[95] *Il.* 13. 62–72; *Od.* 3. 371–9; cf. Wlosok (1967), 84 n. 4 (on this convention in the *Aeneid*).

[96] The Latin commentary tradition likewise remarks on this convention. When Ilioneus tells Dido that the rise of Orion caused the storm which drove the Trojans to Carthage (*Aen.* 1. 535), Servius censures those who object that Juno was really responsible: *Ilioneus ista non nouit quae a poeta supra dicta sunt, per musam, ut dictum est, cognita* ('Ilioneus does not have knowledge of what was said by the poet above, information which the poet, as I noted, had *via* the Muse').

own viewpoint to speak from, and talks generally of θεός, δαίμων, or Zeus, where the poet would tell of a specific deity. Indeed, at the points where Odysseus' and Homer's narratives overlap, we do find Odysseus speaking of θεός or δαίμων, where the poet stipulates Athene or Poseidon.[97] Odysseus once only tells of a divine scene in Heaven, and then he meticulously gives his authority as the divine Calypso, who said she herself had the information from Hermes (12. 389–90).

Such norms are very important to Apollonius, but they are honoured as much in the breach as in the observance. Apollo's magnificent epiphany is acknowledged for what it is by Orpheus and the Argonauts (2. 686–8); the same god's aid is properly recognized at the end of the poem (4. 1702–30); the Argonauts appear to make the correct identification of Triton, after initial uncertainty (4. 1597–9), for they set up an altar to him after he has led Argo to the sea (4. 1621). On the whole, however, Apollonius' humans are remarkably unsuccessful in recognizing divine action. At the passage of the Symplegades, as we have seen, far from being merely uncertain as to which god has helped them, Tiphys does not even realize that a god has intervened at all. The accessibility of divine appearance to mortals is likewise a problem in the mirror scene in Book 4, the passage of the Planctae (930–63). Do the Argonauts actually see the nymphs who twirl their ship through the rocks? The only sign of a reaction is to be found in the simile which compares the Nymphs to dolphins, who disport themselves around a boat, 'to the delight of the crew' (4. 936).[98]

Another example of incomprehension occurs in Book 3, when Jason goes to meet Medea for the first time. As he sets out, he is beautified by, surprisingly enough, the goddess Hera.[99] He is accompanied by Argus and by the prophet Mopsus, who is, says Apollonius, with another use of that disabling particle που,

[97] Jörgensen (1904), 369; cf. Friedrich (1987), 385–9, and esp. 385 n. 28. The failure to observe this fundamental distinction of 'qui parle?' weakens many generalizations about Homeric practice.

[98] The preceding words of Thetis to her deserted husband Peleus (4. 854–64), which introduce this episode, are fascinating and difficult (besides being the poem's most painful illustration of the distance between mortal and immortal). She tells him not to point out her body to anyone when she later comes with her nymphs (862); but what does νόῳ δ' ἔχε (863) mean?

[99] 919–23. Hera is probably a surprise after the elaborate Medea/Artemis simile of 876–85, for the correspondences there with *Od.* 6. 102–9 might lead us to expect Athene to beautify Jason as she does Odysseus (6. 229–35).

'already, I suppose, foreseeing everything to come' (ἤδη που ὀισσάμενος τὰ ἔκαστα, 926). They pass a tree packed with crows, one of which 'began to mock, according to the plans of Hera' (Ἥρης ἠνίπαπε βουλαῖς, 931).[100] The apparently sighted Mopsus is arraigned by the vocal crow as a seer without fame, a bad seer, for not knowing that in love two's company (932–5); 'Aphrodite and the gentle Erotes do not love or inspire you' (οὐδέ σε Κύπρις / οὔτ' ἀγανοὶ φιλέοντες ἐπιπνείουσιν Ἔρωτες, 936–7). A poor prophet he is indeed, for he is misled by these words, and by his memory of Phineus' prophecy that Aphrodite would be responsible for the success of the expedition (2. 423–4), into fixing on the wrong goddess:

> Τύνη μὲν νηόνδε θεᾶς ἴθι, τῷ ἔνι κούρην
> δήεις, Αἰσονίδη, μάλα δ' ἠπίη ἀντιβολήσεις
> Κύπριδος ἐννεσίης, ἥ τοι συνέριθος ἀέθλων
> ἔσσεται, ὡς δὴ καὶ πρὶν Ἀγηνορίδης φάτο Φινεύς.

You go on to the goddess's temple, where you will find the girl, Jason; you will meet her in a well-disposed frame of mind, by the designs of Aphrodite, who will be your ally in your trials, just as Phineus son of Agenor foretold. (3. 940–3)

The seer's calculation is accurate on a human level, but amiss on the gods' responsibility; one prophet is misled by another.[101]

A related but significantly different phenomenon confronts us elsewhere in Book 3, when the poet uses in his own person language which would be appropriate in the mouth of a Homeric character. Let us note first that Apollonius does regularly have his characters speak with Homeric vagueness, as when Jason says that a δαίμων is making him go on his quest (3. 389); or when Argus says that 'some god saved us' (θεὸς δέ τις ἄμμ' ἐσάωσεν, 3. 323).[102] It is more disconcerting to find the poet using such language.

---

[100] Following Fränkel (1968), 404–7.
[101] Hunter (1989), on 3. 942, takes Aphrodite rather to be at one with Hera in the divine plan for Jason and Medea: 'Aphrodite has given herself over completely into Hera's service, and fine distinctions of responsibility are not maintained.' I none the less feel that Apollonius' general preoccupation with the allocation of divine responsibility, together with his concentration on human fallibility, makes it worthwhile to be meticulous in such matters.
[102] Cf. 1. 820; 2. 146; 3. 691, 776; 4. 1445 (θεός); 1. 443; 2. 249, 421; 3. 539; 4. 1040 (δαίμων).

At 3. 540, for example, after Argus has suggested his plan, and expressed his hope of success with the help of a Homerically unspecific δαίμων (539), an omen is sent: 'The benevolent gods gave them a sign' (τοῖσι δὲ σῆμα θεοὶ δόσαν εὐμενέοντες, 540). Which gods? The human prophet Mopsus, relying once more on the incomplete words of Phineus, seizes on Aphrodite, for her bird, the dove, figured in the sign (548–53). Yet Aphrodite's traditional role in the story has been crowded out by Hera, and Campbell has good grounds for inferring that Hera (and Athene?) sent the sign.[103] But why does Apollonius not say so? In Homer, when a character hopes for a sign and it is given, the narrator specifies the god who responds.[104] Apollonius' general θεοί here is, rather, akin to the vague attributions made by Odysseus when he is narrating; and we have to guess, as we have to guess which gods are behind Odysseus' blanket terms.[105] Again, in Book 1, when the Argonauts are detained at Cyzicus by bad weather, a halcyon descends and announces the end of the gales, whereupon Mopsus recognizes an omen (1078–87). The bird is then moved on by 'a god' (καὶ τὴν μὲν θεὸς αὖτις ἀπέτραπεν, 1088). Which god? Mopsus seems to think it is Rhea (1093–1102), and Vian agrees; to Fränkel, however, it remains uncertain which divinity is meant.[106] When 'a goddess' (θεά) sends a sign at 4. 294, commentators opt for Hera, though Fränkel admits that, in the context, one might think of Hecate.[107] Some cases are easier to judge than others, but the point about all these passages is that Apollonius' narrative is, so to speak, Odyssean rather than Homeric.

The same distinction is to be seen in the many passages where Apollonius speaks of Argo's progress being aided or retarded by good or bad weather.[108] Hera's influence is acknowledged in Book 4,[109] yet nowhere in the first two books does Apollonius commit himself to naming a god as responsible, beyond one case of

[103] Campbell (1983), 36.

[104] *Il.* 17. 645–50; 24. 308–16; *Od.* 20. 98–102; cf. *Od.* 2. 143–7.

[105] Campbell (1983), 36 refers Apollonius' θεοί.to *Od.* 12. 394, but there it is Odysseus who is narrating.

[106] Vian–Delage (1976–81), vol. 1. 37; Fränkel (1968), 132.

[107] Livrea (1973), ad loc.; Fränkel (1968), 475.

[108] Fränkel (1968), 630, section 1,35,3.

[109] 241–2, 578, 646–8. Note in the last two cases Apollonius' allusions to the common *HPA / AHP* equation (above, p. 9); cf. 3. 210–11, with the note of Hunter (1989).

'breezes from Zeus' (2. 993)—this despite the fact that there often appear to be excellent reasons why a deity might be imagined as acting to influence the weather for his or her own purposes.[110] The departure from Homer's practice is particularly clear here, for in the *Iliad* and *Odyssey*, whenever the poet mentions the influence of a wind on a voyage's progress, he *invariably* names the god who is responsible.[111]

One final case, to return us to the specific problem of the gods and human motivation, is the pillow-talk of Queen Arete and her husband Alcinous in Book 4. She wins from him the assurance that he will not hand Medea over to the pursuing Colchians if the fugitive is married to Jason (1107–9). Arete takes his words to heart, gets out of bed, silently summons a herald, and, *in her wisdom* (ᾗσιν ἐπιφροσύνῃσιν, 1115), tells the herald to have Jason marry Medea (1111–16). Some eighty lines later, the goddess Hera is mentioned for the last time, in an address from the poet, and Apollonius lets fall the information that it was in fact Hera who instigated Arete's action: 'For you put it in Arete's mind to divulge the prudent utterance of Alcinous' (σὺ γὰρ καὶ ἐπὶ φρεσὶ θῆκας / Ἀρήτῃ πυκινὸν φάσθαι ἔπος Ἀλκινόοιο, 4. 1199–1200). This jolt is reminiscent, in a way, of Medea's dream in Book 3 (616–32), where Apollonius does everything to make us think that the dream is sent by Hera, except actually saying as much.[112] The last mention of Hera is part and parcel of the strange uses of Eros, Erotes, and Hera in Book 3. The difficulties of understanding which god is acting, or how the gods act, and the difficulties of understanding human motivations all run together. The clammy atmosphere of uncertain confusion thus produced is a major vehicle for many of the poem's central preoccupations, in particular its complex pessimism, to which we return below.

Yet the matter has another dimension, seen most starkly at the beginning of Book 4, where the range of presentations of Medea's

---

[110] See Fränkel's comments on the various passages cited in Fränkel (1968), 630, section 1,35,3; Vian–Delage (1976–81), vol. 1. 77 n. 4; 257 (on 1. 652). A particularly important case is the abandonment of Hylas at the end of Book 1, where it is fairly plain that Zeus causes a favourable wind for them to leave (1. 1274), and then unfavourable winds so that they cannot return to pick up Heracles (1299), since Glaucus says it is against the plan of Zeus for Heracles to go to Colchis (1315–16): see Fränkel (1968), 144 n. 325, 148–50 ('Das Wetter').

[111] *Il.* 1. 479; *Od.* 2. 420–1; 5. 263–8, 382–7; 15. 292.

[112] Campbell (1983), 38.

passions and motivations becomes, explicitly, a problem for the *narrator*. Apollonius actually involves himself in the perplexities of accounting for why Medea acts the way she 'does act' (that is, the way she is represented as acting); he involves himself in asking the same questions as Medea and her sister Chalciope (3. 464, 675). The problems of fiction and realism become acute at this moment of Apollonius' self-consciousness. This is a problem of the authentication of the fictive world of the epic, and it may best be approached through considering how Apollonius treats the traditional authenticators of poetry, the Muses.[113] For it is a Muse to whom Apollonius turns in his crisis at the beginning of Book 4:

> Αὐτὴ νῦν κάματόν γε θεὰ καὶ δήνεα κούρης
> Κολχίδος ἔννεπε Μοῦσα, Διὸς τέκος· ἦ γὰρ ἔμοιγε
> ἀμφασίῃ νόος ἔνδον ἑλίσσεται, ὁρμαίνοντι
> ἠέ μιν ἄτης πῆμα δυσίμερον ἦ τόγ' ἐνίσπω
> φύζαν ἀεικελίην ᾗ κάλλιπεν ἔθνεα Κόλχων.

Do you now yourself, goddess, tell of the toil and plans of the Colchian girl—Muse, child of Zeus; since, for my part, my mind revolves within me in speechlessness, as I ponder whether I should say that it was unlovely misery of infatuation or shameful panic through which she left the nations of the Colchians. (4. 1–5)

Poets invoke the Muses regularly, and for many reasons. In itself, Apollonius' invocation is not necessarily out of place. But Apollonius had started his poem in full and confident control ('Beginning with you, Apollo, I shall make mention of . . .'), using of himself a verb which Homer had used of the Muses;[114] and there his Muses had been—most unepically—relegated to a subordinate position of afterthought, twenty-two lines in, with the relationship between poet and Muses the inverse of what the traditional relationship was: 'let the Muses be the interpreters of the song' (Μοῦσαι δ' ὑποφήτορες εἶεν ἀοιδῆς).[115] There is a process at work here, which repays attention.

---

[113] An interesting account of some of the issues which concern us in Beye (1982), 13–19; cf. Livrea (1973), 388–90.

[114] *Il.* 2. 492. Note how Theocritus explicitly asserts that the praise of the famous deeds of good men is the joint responsibility of Muses and poets (16. 1–2); Apollonius' subject is the famous deeds of men of old (παλαιγενέων κλέα φωτῶν, 1. 1), but it is no joint responsibility.

[115] This is a most contentious point: see Livrea (1973), 389. I trust that the course of my argument will show why my interpretation of 1. 22 follows Paduano Faedo (1970); see also Fusillo (1985), 365–7.

If the poet dominates the Muses as the poem opens, by the half-way stage he is admitting a position of, at least, equality to the Muse Erato: Eros and eros are the issue for the third book, and this conveniently eponymous Muse is required:[116] 'Come now, Erato, *stand beside me* and tell me how Jason brought the fleece from there to Iolcus, thanks to the love of Medea . . .' (Εἰ δ' ἄγε νῦν Ἐρατώ, παρ' ἔμ' ἵστασο καί μοι ἔνισπε / ἔνθεν ὅπως ἐς Ἰωλκὸν ἀνήγαγε κῶας Ἰήσων / Μηδείης ὑπ' ἔρωτι . . ., 3. 1–3). This invocation, of course, looks as if it will stand for the whole second half of the poem, and the new invocation at the beginning of Book 4, with the new declaration of a *girl* as the epic subject, is by so much the more remarkable.[117] There, the Muse of both *Iliad* and *Odyssey*[118] is asked, not even to tell Apollonius the sequel to the action of Book 3, but to tell it *herself* (Αὐτή, the first word in the book). The poet cannot account for the motivations of his created character; he affects no longer to have control over the acute psychological realism he had created in Book 3—a realism which had itself been carefully kept, in the last resort, unemancipated from the epic norms of 'unreality'.

When the Muses are named for the last time, their relationship to the poet is the exact reverse of what it was on their first mention. There, 'let the Muses be the interpreters of the song' (1. 22); here, as Apollonius narrates the incredible prodigy of the heroes' twelve-day portage across the desert: 'This is the story of the Muses, while I sing in obedience to them, and I heard their voice telling this infallibly . . .' (Μουσάων ὅδε μῦθος, ἐγὼ δ' ὑπακουὸς ἀείδω / Πιερίδων, καὶ τήνδε πανατρεκὲς ἔκλυον ὀμφήν . . ., 4. 1381–2).[119] Not only is Apollonius now needing the authority of the Muses to make his narrative 'credible', they are actually taking over responsibility for the continuation of the story—a point which emerges all the more clearly if we consider these lines as a condensation of what is presented elliptically in the episode which prepares for the poet's abnegation. This is an episode which shows the Argonauts and the poem being rescued from a premature

---

[116] Campbell (1983), 1–7.
[117] Hunter (1987), 134 very clearly lays out the progression in the three different invocations.
[118] So Livrea (1973), 3.
[119] It is the story of Pindar, *Pyth.* 4. 25–7. On such phrases in Hellenistic poetry, see Bulloch (1985a), 161–2.

ending by the agency of creatures who resemble Muses in more ways than one.

The Argonauts have dispersed in the desert to die, their ship stranded (4. 1278–1304). They would all have died, says Apollonius, with their task unachieved, without a name, unknown by men—that is, without poetry (*this* poem) to preserve them (1305–7). But they are pitied by the Herossae, resident nymphs of Libya, who appear to Jason in an atmosphere which is and is not dream-like (1312–31). Livrea is right to refer the uncertainties here to the intense contemporary interest in the nature of Hesiod's experience with the Muses: was it a dream or not?[120] The Herossae, indeed, speak like Muses, and especially like Homer's Sirens, who are also by way of being Muses,[121] when they declare, with characteristic anaphora of ἴδμεν ('we know'), that they know the subject-matter of epic: 'We know that your ask is the golden fleece, we know every one of your toils . . .' (ἴδμεν ἐποιχομένους χρύσεον δέρος, ἴδμεν ἕκαστα / ὑμετέρων καμάτων, 1319–20).[122] It is *this* epic of which they know the subject-matter, and it is *this* epic which they restart with the portage, and preserve from oblivion.[123]

At the moment when he comes to transcribe the incredible tradition of the portage, the poet's only means of authenticating it is to attribute it to the all-knowing Muses. Yet in this poem, and after this poet's earlier self-generating authority, the attempt to authenticate the fiction by such means is a sure way of undermining it. The issues which bulked so large in the first chapter, of plausibility, fiction, poetic 'truth', and the narrator's status, are plainly of high importance for the *Argonautica*. It is this framework which accommodates many of the striking features we have

---

[120] Livrea (1973), 381; cf. Kambylis (1965), 55–9.

[121] Buschor (1944); Pucci (1979), 126–8; the mother of Apollonius' Sirens is 'Terpsichore, one of the Muses' (4. 896). A fragment survives of a contest between the Muses and the Sirens (Pack 1786). Eustathius has it that Homer is setting up correspondences between his craft and that of the Sirens (1708. 62–1709. 7): cf. Lamberton (1986), 7–8.

[122] Pucci (1979), 127 compares the Sirens' use of this anaphora to that of Hesiod's Muses at *Th.* 27–8. The force of the anaphora is clearly seen by the fact that it is reversed in Callimachus' *Aetia*, for there the poet uses repeated οἶδα of *himself* (in the singular, naturally)—in a conversation with the *Muses* (43. 46, 50).

[123] Compare the way in which Apollonius asks the Muse to restart the poem at the beginning of Book 4, after the emphatic τετελεσμένος ('finished') in the last line of Book 3.

been observing in Apollonius' treatment of the gods, for it is precisely with the divine realm, and its intersection with the human, that the problems of the epic fiction become most acute. Here belongs the fascination with questions of how to 'represent' the gods—now to be seen as the sharpest edge of the problem of how to represent anything; here belong the preoccupations with plausibility, and realism, and with the whole range of issues involved in creating and authenticating the fictive world of the epic.

From this perspective, the *Argonautica* is, among many other things, an exploration of various modes of narrative, with the gods, as epic fiction's most problematic element, at the forefront of the experiment. The interplay between the modes of fantasy and realism is at the heart of the problem, and it is at this interstitial point that the action of the gods often locates itself. The initial establishment of a high degree of realism is an important part of the design, for without it there would be no scope for hesitation over the status of the fantastic.[124] Apollonius from the outset, as the confident narrator, showers us with data about the actual world, including his own contemporary world—names, places, techniques, customs, peoples[125]—an entire apparatus of ephemeral cultural information, which critics, since Barthes's *S/Z*, have accustomed themselves to labelling as the 'referential code', the prime device for emphasizing the authority of the author.[126] Apollonius' frequent aetiologies have an interesting function in this regard, for they become more and more problematic, anchoring contemporary and real facts in a past which becomes less and less 'real' as the poem goes on; they start off as a way of ensuring the verisimilitude of the epic's action ('my story must be true because you can see its results all around you'), and they end up by undermining it. The poem ends in a spate of *aetia* (note even 4. 1770–2), with the *aetia* of Thera (4. 1732–64) and of the rites on

---

[124] Todorov (1973), 25, followed by Brooke-Rose (1981), 63, distinguishes between the 'fantastic' proper, where hesitation is maintained as to the status of the unnatural, and the 'marvellous' of epic and tragedy, where the unnatural is taken on its own terms. This is clearly a helpful distinction, but I do not use these terms rigorously, since Apollonius adheres sometimes to the acceptance characteristic of the marvellous, sometimes to the uncertainties of the fantastic.

[125] See the passages in the index of Fränkel (1968), 634–6.

[126] Barthes (1974), 18–20; cf. Brooke-Rose (1981), 42, on how the 'referential code falls to pieces' outside texts of realism, as it seems to me to do in the *Argonautica*.

Anaphe (4. 1701–30) as the most realistically portrayed fantastic origins of all.

It may now be seen what an appropriate emblem Phineus is for the narrator of the *Argonautica*, with his fragmentary imparting of knowledge, his refusal to narrate methodically, blow-by-blow, right up to the end, and his effectively misleading hints about the role of the gods: he will not tell the mind of Zeus, he misleads concerning Athene at the Symplegades, and Aphrodite at Colchis.[127] Altogether, Apollonius' technique may be thought to approximate to what modern criticism refers to as 'metafiction', 'a term given to fictional writing which self-consciously and systematically draws attention to its status as an artefact in order to pose questions about the relationship between fictions and reality'.[128] But then, such concerns had always been at the core of Greek poetics, while Apollonius' contemporaries were every bit as preoccupied with the dilemmas of poetic truth and fiction as he was.[129]

If the complex treatment of the gods has a cardinal role in the poetics of the *Argonautica*, it is also very important in establishing the currents of unease and pessimism which have long been acknowledged in the poem,[130] and which we have already encountered at more than one point. Many of the distinguishing features of the *Argonautica*'s created world owe their nature to the force of the divine action: the clouded, imperfect knowledge of motive, purpose, and even fact; the oppressive sensation of inextricable consequence, by which few actions have clean issue; and the failure of codes of practice, with norms of morality made difficult and obscure. Jason's dutiful rote acknowledgement of Zeus' role in the conventional pieties is only the most spectacular example of the failure of the religious norms to keep making sense.[131] It is a world where even the narrator finds it hard to discern a pattern.

One of the most striking features of the gods in the *Argonautica* is

---

[127] See, again, Margolies (1981), 46–7, 134–5, 141–3, 188.

[128] Waugh (1984), 2.

[129] Goldhill (1986).

[130] Visser (1938), 60–2 (an account handicapped by an inability to accept that a pessimistic picture of the world can be presented ironically); Herter (1944–55), 282; Bulloch (1985*b*), 596–7.

[131] Apollonius' showing up of the fissures in the inherited religious solutions is not as relentless and intense as in Callimachus, whose techniques have been splendidly analysed by Bulloch (1984); but Bulloch's discussion is indispensable reading for students of the *Argonautica*.

their otherness, their difference and distance from humans—the very qualities which make them so problematic as characters. Yet there is in the poem a character who crosses that extraordinary boundary, a man who becomes a god. We may finish our discussion of Apollonius' gods with this coda, a brief account of Heracles, whose transformations reveal so much about the nature of the divine and the mortal.[132]

Apollonius' treatment of Heracles was by no means preordained for him by tradition, for Heracles was the most protean and ambivalent creature in Greek myth. He was ambivalence itself: hero and god, receiving divine and heroic sacrifice in cult, lying, as Silk well puts it, 'on the margins between human and divine, [occupying] the no-man's-land that is also no-god's-land, . . . a marginal, transitional, or, better, *interstitial* figure'.[133] That is, he occupies the interstices, the zones of transition, potentially always one thing or the other. He may be the hero in epic, tragedy, or comedy. He is at home in the shared feast, sometimes as a glutton, and he is also famous for violating the holy laws of hospitality. He is the ultimate expression of Greek virility, and spends a year as the slave of a woman, the Asiatic Omphale. He is physical strength incarnate, and also a philosopher's paradigm of intellectual resource and self-control. He is the great civilizer, clearing the world of monsters to make it safe for humans, who wears the untanned skin of an animal. One of his stock weapons, the club, is the very emblem of pre-technological aggressive brutishness, while the other, the bow, is the embodiment of craft in war. His very name is a paradox: the glory of Hera, the glory of the goddess who persecuted him all his life.[134]

Apollonius maintains many of these ambiguities in the first part of the poem, when Heracles is still a character, playing especially on the antitheses involved in seeing Heracles as the archetype either of restrained wisdom or of physical violence. In particular, the issue of Heracles' immortality is made prominent, as Apollonius keeps open the question of whether he will follow Homer in having Heracles as a mortal, or else the later tradition,

---

[132] For a fuller discussion of Heracles in the poem, with bibliography of earlier studies, see Feeney (1986*a*).

[133] Silk (1985), 6.

[134] On these Heraclean paradoxes, see Galinsky (1972), 1–39; Burkert (1985), 208–11.

which had the hero elevated amongst the Olympians.[135] Only when Glaucus speaks to the Argonauts at the end of Book 1 do we learn that Heracles will become a god, *if* he accomplishes the full quota of labours assigned to him (1317–20). After his disappearance and Glaucus' pronouncement, it is natural for the Argonauts and the reader to assume that Heracles will not cross their paths again. Yet, in the last book, in Libya, when they are desperate with thirst, at the other end of the Mediterranean from where they had last seen Heracles, the Argonauts, to their great surprise and ours, only just miss Heracles, to find themselves literally in his footsteps—and in no other sense than literally.

They come tantalizingly close to meeting with him again, for only on the previous day he had passed through this very stretch of desert (1436). The Argonauts are in the Garden of the Hesperides: there is the dragon, killed only the day before by Heracles (1400); there is the tree, despoiled of its golden apples (1397); there are the Hesperides, bemoaning their loss (1406–7). One of the Hesperides tells them the story, bitter with anger against the bestial Heracles, whom she calls 'dog-like' (1433), and compares to a beast of the field, as he fills his great belly from the spring he has caused to flow by kicking a rock (1449). This spring is the salvation of the Argonauts, as one of them observes: 'Friends, even in his absence Heracles has saved his companions, afflicted with thirst' (῏Ω πόποι, ἦ καὶ νόσφιν ἐὼν ἐσάωσεν ἑταίρους / Ἡρακλέης δίψῃ κεκμηότας, 1458–9). The best-qualified of the Argonauts dash off to find him (1464–7): the sons of Boreas, who can fly;[136] Euphemus, the fastest runner; Lynceus, with the wondrous eyesight, who, as the story went, could see even under the earth (1. 153–5). One unmarvellous Argonaut also goes—Canthus, of whom more in a moment. All fail. 'Only Lynceus thought he could see Heracles, far off, on the limitless land, seeing him as you see the moon, or think you see the moon, on the first day of the month, all obscured' (ἀτὰρ τότε γ' Ἡρακλῆα / μοῦνος ἀπειρεσίης τηλοῦ χθονὸς εἴσατο Λυγκεύς / τὼς ἰδέειν, ὥς τίς τε νέῳ ἐνὶ ἤματι μήνην / ἢ ἴδεν ἢ ἐδόκησεν ἐπαχλύουσαν ἰδέσθαι, 4. 1477–80).[137] Lynceus rejoins his com-

---

[135] Feeney (1986a), 52–8.

[136] Little knowing, of course, that, according to Apollonius' new version (1. 1302–8), Heracles would have killed them if they had found him.

[137] Following the text and interpretation of Vian–Delage (1976–81), vol. 3 ad loc.

panions, swearing to them that none of the searchers would be able to catch up with Heracles on his route (1481–2).

What does all this mean? Above all, it means that Heracles has managed to fulfil the conditions stated by the sea-god Glaucus at the end of Book 1. He has completed his labours, he has taken the golden apples of eternal life, which represent his final labour, and won his prize of immortality.[138] He has gone virtually all the way down the path towards becoming a god, and that is the extraordinary interstitial point which Apollonius captures in that beautiful moment when Lynceus sees him in the far distance, or thinks he sees him. In this last mention of him in the poem, he is passing out of the world of men, and into the world of gods. In saving his companions, even in his absence, he has already begun to fulfil the functions of a god.[139]

Apollonius luxuriates here in the paradoxes at his command. Just when Heracles lays his hands on his guarantee of apotheosis, Apollonius casts him at his most brutish, a creature of violence, wearing the raw untanned hide of a beast (4. 1438–9). Heracles causes misery to the Hesperides, but as the 'averter of evil' (ἀλεξίκακος) he saves the Argonauts. Brutish and thirsty, he can still use his wit, or be thought capable of it (1445). If his paradoxical nature here corresponds to the bizarre nature of his particular divinity, he approximates also to more general notions of the divine, in his power, his invulnerability, his self-sufficiency, his otherness.[140] He may be beneficent, but he is so much 'himself' that he moves eventually into total isolation. In the course of the poem, he is separated from the Argonauts, from Hylas, from Polyphemus. In the second book, we see four of his companions from the Amazonian expedition, who were cut off from him in Asia Minor (957). As Heracles moves out of the poem for good, Canthus tries to follow him, but is prevented from doing so, for he is killed by a local shepherd (4. 1487–9). His death, by a ring-pattern, takes us back to the moment when Heracles first disappeared, at the end

---

[138] On the significance of the apples, see Bond (1981), 166.

[139] Cf. *Od.* 4. 444; and compare *Arg.* 4. 1436 with *Od.* 2. 262. The contemporary interest in deification of great men is clearly behind this talk of Heracles as a 'saviour': on such language, see Nock (1972), 78, 720–35. There is a very extended and striking reference to contemporary ruler cult in the cult offered to the Dioscuri by the Mariandyni, out of gratitude for Polydeuces' killing of their oppressor, Amycus (2. 756–8, 796–810).

[140] His apartness already stressed in the Homeric nekyuia, *Od.* 11. 601–27; see the acute comments of Galinsky (1972), 12–13.

of the first book, for Canthus is trying to find out where Heracles left Polyphemus, after the two had been stranded together. Heracles did not protect Polyphemus either; Polyphemus followed along the coast of Asia Minor looking for Argo, and died there (4. 1473–5).

A god, says Aristotle, is self-sufficient, and does not need friends; it is, indeed, not possible to be friends with a god.[141] Aristotle also sheds light on what lies behind Apollonius' dramatic polarities of Heracles as god and beast. 'Man is by nature', says Aristotle, 'an animal intended to live in a polis. He who is without a polis, by reason of his own nature and not of some accident, is either a poor sort of being, or a being higher than man.'[142] Heracles does not belong with the Argonauts, or with any human company: he has no fixed polis—does he belong to Tiryns, Argos, or Thebes?—; he cannot tie in successfully with a family, for he kills his children and is killed by his wife. Aristotle further says, 'The man who is isolated—who is unable to share in the benefits of political association, or has no need to share because he is already self-sufficient—is no part of the polis, and must therefore be either a beast or a god' (*Pol.* 1253 a 27–9). The *Argonautica* is not a commentary on Aristotle, but some such preconceptions lie behind Apollonius' paradoxes here, as he tells us of the bestial and god-like Heracles striding off alone across the desert, towards divinity, out of the poem.[143]

---

[141] *Eth. Eud.* 1244 b 8–10; *Eth. Nic.* 1158 b 35–1159 a 6.

[142] *Pol.* 1253 a 2–4; I give the translation of Barker (1946).

[143] We return to the boundaries around humans formed by gods and beasts in the discussion of Vergil and Ovid.

# 3

# From Greece to Rome: Naevius and Ennius

Μεγίστην δέ μοι δοκεῖ διαφορὰν ἔχειν τὸ Ῥωμαίων
πολίτευμα πρὸς βέλτιον ἐν τῇ περὶ θεῶν διαλήψει.

The greatest point of difference which counts in favour of the
Roman political system's superiority strikes me as being their
attitude concerning the gods.

Polybius 6. 56. 6

The Romans' creation of a national literary culture in response to
the literary culture of the Greeks is a phenomenon which fascin-
ates and baffles us as it fascinated and baffled them, a phenomenon which invites enquiry from many directions.[1] Here we have
no more than three aims: first (and most modestly), to give a
sketch of how the Romans took over Greek literature, together
with the apparatus of scholarship which had become an inextricable element of that literature; second, to mark out those key
differences between Greek and Roman attitudes to religion which
will be most important for an understanding of how Roman epic
treated the divine; finally, to investigate the role of the divine in
the epics of Naevius and Ennius, so as to set the scene for our enquiries into the *Aeneid*, and the subsequent tradition.

For the Greeks, Homer's inimitable pre-eminence was the primary
fact of their literature, and their evolution of systematized ways of
reading the epics was, as we have seen, a long process. Roman
literary history runs the reverse course. Whereas the Romans had
to wait long for their poetry to attain anything like the achieved
quality of the Greeks', writers in Latin experienced literature from
the start (literature being to them, of course, nothing but *Greek*

---

[1] Toynbee (1965), 2. 416–34; Petrochilos (1974); Momigliano (1975), 12–49;
Wardman (1976); Balsdon (1979), 30–58; Kaimio (1979); Rawson (1985). One
awaits with eagerness Andrew Wallace-Hadrill's work on the Hellenization of Roman culture; in the meantime, note the power of the aphorism of Cornell (1978),
110: 'an independent or autonomous Latin culture never had a chance to emerge'.

literature) through the medium of Greek literary scholarship.[2]
Thus it was that the first poets writing in Latin were also remembered as having been the first to 'interpret' Greek poetry (Suet.
*Gram.* 1). 'Half-Greeks' our source calls these men, Livius
Andronicus and Quintus Ennius; the Greek city of Tarentum in
Southern Italy was where the former was born and the latter, very
likely, educated.[3] The interdependence of poetry and scholarship
at Rome was to remain normative for the whole of our period,
and the scholarship itself bore a markedly Greek stamp. Literary
studies were the one area of Roman intellectual endeavour where
the Romans adhered to Greek paradigms with the utmost fidelity,
as Rawson observes: 'Only in one subject, but that the most basic
of all, *grammatica*, does it become hard to distinguish Greeks and
Greek scholarship clearly from Roman.'[4]

   Livius Andronicus in all probability came to Rome as a prisoner
of war, enslaved after the fall of his city to the Romans in 272 BCE.
Eventually he was manumitted, and hence became a Roman citizen, acquiring the Roman name of Livius to go with his native
Greek name 'Andronicus'.[5] When Suetonius says that he 'interpreted' Greek authors, no very high level of scholarship need be
implied.[6] He was presumably teaching the children of his patron
and of his patron's friends, and would have had no audience for
exposition at a higher level, even if he had had the capacity and
the will. Yet he certainly utilized at least the basic tools of Hellenistic scholarship when he turned Homer's *Odyssey* into Latin
Saturnians, for, as Fränkel has shown, in one observable instance
he translated the paraphrase of a Hellenistic glossary rather than
the Homeric text itself.[7]

   With Ennius (239–169 BCE) we are securely in the world of Hellenistic learning. Even before he composed his masterpiece, the
*Annales*, he had translated the work of Euhemerus.[8] In tackling
such a comparatively out-of-the-way author, Ennius showed considerable familiarity with the world of Greek scholarship—not to

[2] Russell (1981), 44–5; Kenney (1982a), 5; Fantham (1989), 220.
[3] Fraenkel (1931), 599 (Livius); Skutsch (1985), 1 (Ennius).
[4] Rawson (1985), 98; cf. 268–9.
[5] Leo (1913), 55; Fraenkel (1931), 599.
[6] Fraenkel (1931), 601.
[7] Fränkel (1932), 306–7; cf. Sheets (1981); wider claims made for Livius'
scholarship by Mariotti (1952); Ronconi (1973), 13–17.
[8] Skutsch (1985), 3; Garbarino (1973), 289–308.

mention a direct interest in problems of religion. When he wrote the *Annales*, the first Roman epic in the Greek metre of hexameters, he evidently considered his achievement a good notch above his predecessors in learning as well as everything else. Even allowing for the disparaging conventions of literary polemic, we must still recognize the force of Ennius' words when he asserts, in his important second proem, that he is the first poet of Rome to be *dicti studiosus*, 'devoted to the study of language' (fr. 209). The phrase is a Latinizing of the Greek φιλόλογος, 'philologist'; Ennius is claiming that he has the care for learning characteristic of the great Greek scholar-poets.[9] His poem bears out his claim, as much as one might expect for the time. He read his Homer with commentaries, and adapted Homer in the light of those commentaries.[10]

The Romans, so justly proud of their engineering achievements, remembered the cause of their first direct contact with the main course of Greek scholarship as being a cracked sewer on the Palatine hill. Here was broken the leg of Crates of Mallos, the Pergamene scholar, who was taking part in an embassy to Rome just after Ennius' death, probably in 168 BCE. Forced to extend his stay, he gave a series of display expositions and lectures, so impressing the Romans, says Suetonius, that they took to imitating him, studying Latin poems in his manner (*Gram.* 2). Scepticism is necessary here, but there is no doubt that the following years show evidence of a considerable amount of literary scholarship.[11] The poems of Naevius and Ennius were the object of study, even commentary, though it is impossible to know quite what sort of enterprise is at issue.[12] An important tragedian, Accius (170–c.87 BCE), took this emulation of the scholarly researches of the Greeks a stage further with a work in nine books on literary history, covering the entire period from Homer and Hesiod to his own time.[13] The claim implied even by the scope of this work is extraordinary, one which

---

[9] Skutsch (1968), 5–7: all fragments of the *Annales* are cited according to the edition of Skutsch (1985).
[10] Skutsch (1985), 392, 592, 629; Zetzel (1974). On the question of Ennius' knowledge of commentaries on the Greek tragic texts which he adapted, see Jocelyn (1967), 46, 308 n. 1.
[11] Christes (1979), 6–72; Zetzel (1981), 10–26.
[12] Rawson (1985), 269; Skutsch (1985), 9.
[13] The work concentrated on drama, as its title shows (*Didascalia*): Rawson (1985), 268.

could not possibly have been made by any other contemporary culture: Roman literature is a continuation of Greek literature, a part of the same phenomenon.[14] The clearest way to appreciate the diffusion of Greek literary and scholarly culture amongst the élite at Rome by the end of the second century BCE is to read the fragments of the ninth and tenth books of the *Satires* of Lucilius. Here one finds extended discussion of Accius' theories on orthography, together with accomplished treatment of many questions of Hellenistic literary theory.[15] It remains none the less true that the Mithridatic Wars in the East, from the 80s to the 60s BCE, had a decisive effect in accelerating the Hellenization of intellectual life at Rome, as displaced Greek scholars found their way to Italy in the retinue or slave-train of returning Roman grandees.[16] It was in this heightened atmosphere of direct contact with Greek scholarship that the learned 'new poets' were at work, and also their inheritor Vergil.[17] Modern scholarship's understandable concentration on the 'new poetry' of the late Republic should not, however, obscure the very considerable learning which is manifest in the poetry of Cicero or Varro of Atax.[18]

It was likewise in the intellectual revolution of the late Republic that systematic Roman analysis of Rome's own religion started to find its voice. Ennius may have translated out-of-the-way Greek works of speculation about the divine, but only in this second half of the first century BCE do we encounter a thorough attempt by Roman intellectuals to apply Greek techniques of enquiry to their own native religious institutions.[19] Cicero and then Varro are the dominating figures, and their combined efforts made the religion

---

[14] It remains true, none the less, as Professor Woodman reminds me, that Greek and Latin works were invariably stored and catalogued separately in Roman libraries: Kenney (1982*a*), 24.

[15] Krenkel (1970).

[16] Rawson (1985), 7–9.

[17] Parthenius is a particularly controversial figure here: Clausen (1964); Wiseman (1974*a*), 44–58; Crowther (1976). On Vergil's use of Homeric scholarship, see Schlunk (1974); Lausberg (1983); on his use of Homeric and Hesiodic scholarship, Hardie (1986), esp. 31–2, on the methodological implications.

[18] On Cicero's use of commentaries on Aratus, see Atzert (1908); Goetz (1918), 12–17; on Varro's use of Apollonian commentaries, see Hofmann (1928), 160–2.

[19] Jocelyn (1982); Momigliano (1984*b*); Beard (1986); North (1986), 253–4; Brunt (1989); cf. Attridge (1978), for the next generations.

of the city a topic, an intellectual concern, but also an issue, and a problem.[20]

After this background sketch, it is necessary to delineate some key areas of difference between the Greeks and Romans in their experience of the gods in epic. The first chapter demonstrated how central the epic tradition was to Greek religious and moral thinking. It is, of course, natural for modern philologists to exaggerate the impact of poetic forms of expression on actual Greek religious experience. A harmonious congruence between all forms of religious discourse in Greece is more often assumed than proven, and Mikalson's study of Athenian popular religion ends with a cautious statement of the disparity between the norms of everyday religion and the perspectives of poets, mythographers, and philosophers.[21] Still, the fact remains that the vision of the poets was an inescapable reference-point for Greek intellectuals who examined religion. In Rome, on the contrary, the productions of poets— Greek or native—were marginal not only for actual practice and belief but also for intellectual inquiry into religion.[22] The Romans had no feeling that their picture of the gods had been fixed for them by their first poets, and they had no feeling that even Homer had much to tell them about their relationship to the divine—this despite the more or less conscious assimilation of some aspects of their own religion to some aspects of Greek religion.[23] Cotta, one of Cicero's characters in his dialogue *De Natura Deorum* ('On the Nature of the Gods'), is able to represent the mythological stories about the gods as something wholly Greek, and wholly at odds with conventional Roman religion (*Nat. D.* 3. 60). It was quite normal for many Greek intellectuals to deride the theology of the poets, but the very tradition of derision had its origins in the habit of taking the poets seriously. When a character in one of Cicero's dialogues disparages the *fabulae* of the poets,[24] at one level he is talking like a Greek intellectual; but, more fundamentally, such talk from a Roman reflects the inveterate conviction of his society

[20] Rawson (1985), 298–316; on Varro in particular, Cardauns (1976) and (1978).
[21] Mikalson (1983), 117; above, p. 4.
[22] Wardman (1976), 73; Momigliano (1984a), 885–6.
[23] Wissowa (1912), 65–7; Latte (1960), 161–76.
[24] e. g. *Nat. D.* 1. 42; 2. 70.

that poetry and poets are peripheral to the issues. The distinctions
are clearly seen in Cicero's *De Natura Deorum*. The Epicurean
speaker makes much of the fact that the Greek Stoic, Chrysippus,
devoted the second book of his work *On the Gods* to a systematic
account of the theology to be found in the early poets (1. 41);
when Cicero's own Stoic character speaks, however, he is acting
like a Roman aristocrat when his references to Homer are incidental, not an organizing principle.[25]

The reasons behind the Romans' comparative disregard for the
theology of the poets are various, and there is more at issue than
the fact that written and preserved poetry was one of the late ar-
rivals in the life of the Roman people, rather than being, as for
classical Greek culture, at the beginning of what was known and
remembered. A prime explanation is to be found in the prime
force of Roman religion, which was located in the social and public areas of life.[26] Where the relationship of the state to the gods
was paramount, where religion's function was to maintain that
relationship in equilibrium, there was little place for narrative and
for the more speculative modes of myth. The major gods of the
Romans were persons, with attributes and powers;[27] none the less,
from the time we first encounter them, they are 'without kinship
and unmarried, without adventures or scandals, without connections of friendship or hostility, in short, without mythology'.[28] It
has, indeed, long been conventional to observe that such mythology as the Roman gods in time acquired was either borrowed
from the Greek stock of tales, or else formed by analogy.[29]

This commonplace, like so many others about Roman religion,
is now being challenged and revised, and we are having to accus-
tom ourselves to thinking of a much richer and older Roman
mythical imagination than had traditionally been taken for
granted.[30] Even if, however, most contemporary scholars would

[25] *Nat. D.* 2. 70–1, 166.
[26] Jocelyn (1966); Wardman (1982), esp. 1–22; Beard and Crawford (1985), 25–
39; Scheid (1985), esp. 12–13, 17–36.
[27] On the long controversy over this point, see Beard (1983).
[28] Dumézil (1970), 32; cf. 48–9; Muth (1978), 333–8; Radke (1987), 296–7;
Liebeschuetz (1979), 22: 'In Roman religion, as opposed to Greek-influenced literature, the personalities of even the great gods are of no practical consequence.'
[29] Dumézil (1970), 455–7; Brunt (1989), 178.
[30] See the important review of Bremmer and Horsfall (1987) by Wiseman
(1989), esp. 129. Conversely, it is important to remind ourselves that the personalities of the Greek gods were far more attenuated in cult and daily life than in the

cheerfully accept the indigenous character of such core Roman myths as Romulus and Remus,[31] we must acknowledge that the Romans of the historical period, together with Greek observers, regarded the Roman gods themselves as being qualitatively different from the Greek gods in their freedom from the apparatus of fable and story. Dumézil makes this point very forcefully by quoting the lengthy passage in which Dionysius of Halicarnassus, a Greek historian of Augustus' time, expresses his admiration for the absence of myth concerning the Romans' gods.[32] We have already referred to Cotta's declaration that the myths about the gods are Greek imports (*Nat. D.* 3. 60); earlier in the same dialogue Cotta reveals the startling lack of extra dimension to the Roman gods when he ridicules the notion that anyone would really apply the name Jupiter to heaven, rather than to Jupiter Optimus Maximus on the Capitoline Hill (3. 10–11).

As a result, there was no core of anecdote to make sense out of, no authority in poetic accounts of the divine. To the Romans, religion was an aspect of the life of the state, evolving with the life of the state, so that our natural modern antitheses between 'religion' and 'politics' have no reference in a Roman context.[33] A single sentence of Cicero's *De Natura Deorum* (3. 5) captures at once the public orientation of Roman cult and its emotional underpinning of security in past achievement:

cumque omnis populi Romani religio in sacra et in auspicia diuisa sit, tertium adiunctum sit si quid praedictionis causa ex portentis et monstris Sibyllae interpretes haruspicesue monuerunt, harum ego religionum nullam umquam contemnendam putaui mihique ita persuasi Romulum auspiciis, Numam sacris constitutis fundamenta iecisse nostrae ciuitatis, quae numquam profecto sine summa placatione deorum immortalium tanta esse potuisset.

Now, the whole of the religion of the Roman people comes under the

great events of drama or epic; see here the characteristically incisive remarks of Liebeschuetz (1979), 177 n. 5, referring to Vernant (1965), 267-8. The discrepancy between the personalities of the Greek and Roman gods which so strikes modern observers is, then, an aspect of literary, as well as religious, history.

[31] On Romulus and Remus, see Cornell (1975); Bremmer in Bremmer and Horsfall (1987), 25–48.

[32] Dumézil (1970), 49–50, quoting Dion. Hal. *Ant. Rom.* 2. 18. 3–19. 1, and 2. 20; Dionysius attributes this lack of fable to the wisdom and foresight of Romulus, who established Roman religion.

[33] The pithiest and most memorable expression of this matter is to be found in Weinstock (1971), 1-3; cf. Koch (1937), 128-9; Beard and North (1990), 7-9.

headings of ritual and auspices, with the third section of whatever prophetic warnings the interpreters of the Sibyl or the haruspices have given
on the basis of portents and omens. I have always thought that none of
these forms of religion should be looked down on, and I am quite convinced that Romulus with his auspices and Numa with his establishment
of ritual laid the foundations of our state, which would certainly never
have been able to be so great if the immortal gods had not been placated
to the utmost.[34]

It is highly significant that the greatest work of intellectual research on religion ever produced in Rome should be presented as
part of an antiquarian enquiry into the life of the city as a whole.
Such was the masterpiece of Cicero's contemporary, Varro, whose
*Antiquitates Rerum Humanarum et Diuinarum* arrived at the gods
of Rome last, on the grounds that divine cult was a product of the
human state: *sicut prior est pictor quam tabula picta, prior faber
quam aedificium, ita priores sunt ciuitates quam ea quae a
ciuitatibus instituta sunt* ('just as the painter comes before the
painting, and the builder before the building, so states come before things instituted by states').[35] The first book of the divine section will have made explicit the implications of this focus, for it
was probably here that Varro expounded the doctrine of the 'three
theologies', explaining why he was treating the 'civic' theology
only.[36] He was fully aware, then, that there were other ways of
writing about the gods: he says explicitly that if he had been writing a complete account of the human and the divine, instead of an
account of Rome, he would have begun with the gods instead of
beginning with humans.[37] The very concentration on Rome which
produces this arrangement, however, strikes one as the quintessentially Roman way of going about it. If one places Varro's work beside the greatest Hellenistic work on religion, Apollodorus' 'On
the Gods', one is impressed by the different priorities of the two
intellectual cultures, for Apollodorus' work was, as we saw above,
'essentially a work on Homer'.[38]

After laying such stress on the public nature of Roman religion, it

[34] Nothing illustrates the force of this Roman conviction more powerfully than
the efforts of the Christians to disprove it: Heck (1987).
[35] Fr. 5 Cardauns (1976); cf. Momigliano (1984*b*), 203–4.
[36] So Rawson (1985), 313: frr. 6–11 Cardauns (1976). See p. 47 above on the
three theologies of the poets, the state, and the philosophers.
[37] Fr. 5 Cardauns (1976).          [38] Pfeiffer (1968), 261; above, p. 33.

is important to state emphatically that the religion of each Greek state or city was itself, of course, a civic and political affair.[39] Further, religious manifestations of civic identity were very highly developed in Greece, as may readily be seen in the Athenian building programmes of the Periclean period, where a range of mythical paradigms was exploited on the great temples in order to articulate the city's view of itself, presenting to the city what was important and distinctive about its nature.[40] The Gigantomachy in particular was an abiding emblem of a Greek state's self-definition, reaching a climax at the Kingdom of Pergamum, especially with the Great Altar of Zeus.[41] Yet the Romans' public piety, a manifestation of a powerful social integration which religion helped to guarantee, was different in scale, and kind. The Romans were convinced of the superiority of their system of religion, as repeated testimony shows;[42] and the Greeks likewise recognized the unique relationship between the Romans' political practice and their state religion—even if, like Polybius, they sometimes needed to make sense of what they observed by putting the élite's behaviour into a Greek intellectual tradition, which allowed for the upper classes' manipulation of the mass's ignorance.[43]

The intimate connection between Roman religion and Roman public life makes its force felt in the picture of the divine which we may reconstruct from the remains of the first Roman epics. The tight bond between Roman epic and the Roman historical experience is well known, but it deserves to be registered here. Only fragments survive of Roman epic before the *Aeneid*, and we must assume that some pre-Vergilian epics have left no trace at all. Still, on the evidence we have, epic at Rome was 150 years old before anyone wrote an epic that was not historical epic.[44] And history at

---

[39] Nilsson (1951); Burkert (1985), 216–75; Atherton (1986), 314–15; Yunis (1988), 19–28.

[40] Herington (1955), 48–67; Thomas (1976), esp. 10–12; Stewart (1985); Boardman (1985), 38–46, 247–51.

[41] Pollitt (1986), 79–110.

[42] Collections of testimonia in Appel (1909), 54–5; Pease (1955–8), 566–7; cf. Liebeschuetz (1979), 1.

[43] Polyb. 6. 56. 6–15, with Walbank (1957) ad loc.; cf. Liebeschuetz (1979), 4–5. For a clearly nuanced account of the difference between the public nature of religion in Rome and the Greek states, see Atherton (1986), 333–4.

[44] Not counting translations such as that of the *Odyssey* by Livius Andronicus.

Rome meant the history of Rome,[45] so that these were poems telling of the deeds of the Roman people. The first non-historical epic
written in Latin was composed by a contemporary of Vergil,
Varro of Atax. Even this poem was an adaptation, verging on
translation, of a Greek original, Apollonius' *Argonautica*; and
even Varro also wrote an historical epic, on Caesar's Gallic campaign of 58 BCE.[46] The gods in historical epic present their own
theoretical problems, which will receive attention in Chapter 6,
yet some discussion of the earliest historical epics, the epics of
Naevius and Ennius, is necessary here, to chart some of the distinctive features of Roman epic which will occupy us in the rest of
the book.

The poet Naevius was himself a soldier in the war which he took
as the subject for his epic, Rome's first war against Carthage
(264–241 BCE).[47] The grandeur of the subject was self-evident—the
longest, most unbroken, and greatest war the Mediterranean
world had ever seen.[48] Making poetry out of it presented many
problems. As far as domesticating Greek poetic norms into Latin
was concerned, Naevius had a predecessor in Livius Andronicus,
but nobody had ever written a poem about Rome before. For all
its fragmentary nature, some of the poem's solutions are already
recognizable as utterly characteristic of Roman epic. The deeds of
the Roman armies were recounted, but took up no more than
some 60 per cent of the work. The balance was a panorama which
extended back to the ultimate origins of the people, showing that
the mighty climax of the war against Carthage was the long-
planned design of the gods acknowledged by the Roman state.[49]
    It will become clear that the details of Naevius' aetiology are a
matter of keen dispute, yet the basic elements are clearly recoverable from the fragments. Early on in the poem Naevius told of
how Aeneas left captured Troy and settled in Latium, where his
grandson Romulus founded the city of Rome (frr. 5, 6, 27). Beside

[45] Fornara (1983), 53: 'the Romans wrote the history of their city and only incidentally that of the world.'
[46] Schanz–Hosius 1. 312.
[47] Fr. 2 (Gell. 17. 21. 45, stating that Naevius himself mentioned this in his
poem). Fragments of Naevius and Livius Andronicus are cited according to the edition of Büchner (1982). Bibliography on Naevius' *Bellum Punicum* in Waszink
(1972), 902–21; Büchner (1982), 20–1.
[48] So Polybius, 1. 63. 4.
[49] Buchheit (1963), 53.

this foundation-legend for Rome, a blend of indigenous folk-tale and Greek antiquarianism,[50] we know that Naevius also mentioned the person who founded the rival city of Carthage—Dido (fr. 17). Beyond so much all is controversy.[51] It is an old and almost irresistible conclusion that Naevius' Trojans came to Africa, and that a quarrel at this point was given as the original cause of the war between their descendants.[52] It is virtually impossible to accept that Naevius described a failed love-affair between Aeneas and Dido, for the universal testimony to Vergil's invention of the story is hardly to be circumvented.[53] Mesmerized by the *Aeneid*, we may easily overlook the variety of possible ways in which trouble might have flared between the first Carthaginians and the refugee Trojans arriving suddenly on their shores. In the *Aeneid*, Jupiter takes special care that the Carthaginians do not simply attack the Trojans when they are driven by storm to Africa (1. 297-300): perhaps he is preventing a repetition of what happened in Naevius.

What counts amongst all this uncertainty is the prime importance for Naevius of òpening up a time-scale which can fix Rome's present achievement as the planned outcome of centuries of divine design.[54] Throughout the early portion of the poem, he was systematically using the conventions of epic prophecy to further this aim. The principal scene is from the first book, in a passage which was later extensively adapted by Vergil (*Aen.* 1. 223-96). From Naevius (according to Macrobius' discussion of the Vergilian passage), Vergil took the picture of Jupiter consoling his daughter Venus over the troubles of her son, Aeneas, and his people, cheering her with a prophecy.[55] In her concern for her son and her favoured Trojans, Naevius' Venus is following the motives of her Homeric prototype, Aphrodite. Naevius, however, must have given his character an extra motive for concern, one which led down in time to the contemporary world of the poet and his audience.[56] For it was in Naevius' own lifetime that it had become

---

[50] Cornell (1975).

[51] Waszink (1972), 911–15.

[52] Horsfall (1973–4), 12. Nilsson (1951), 13, and Richter (1960), 48, see here the influence of the mythical *aetia* given by Herodotus at the beginning of his history (1. 1–5).

[53] Horsfall (1973–4), 12.

[54] Richter (1960), 48–9; Buchheit (1963), 53.

[55] Macr. 6. 2. 31 (fr. 14).

[56] Here one is relying to some extent on the precise force of Macrobius' words

possible to speak of the goddess Venus as the ancestress of the Roman people. The Roman acknowledgement of Venus as their ancestress received its first impetus at the beginning of the war which was Naevius' subject, when the people of Segesta, home of the cult of Aphrodite of Eryx, sided with the Romans on the grounds that they were both descended from Venus.[57] The cult of Venus of Eryx was vowed in Rome in 217 BCE, the second year of the second Punic war (Liv. 22. 9. 10), and her temple was dedicated by Fabius Maximus in 215 (Liv. 23. 31. 9)—very likely before Naevius wrote his poem, in other words.[58] Much controversy surrounds the question of when, and how explicitly, Venus was imagined as the ancestress of the Roman race;[59] however she may have been apprehended in her cult manifestation, for a poet there was more than enough purchase in the connection with Aeneas. The goddess may be represented in Naevius' poem, then, as being concerned for her Trojans in the mythical past, and concerned for her Romans in the historical present. When Naevius' Venus addresses Jupiter, and asks him 'Why do you hate my offspring?' (*quianam genus odisti?*, fr. 16), the word 'offspring' covers both the Trojans of myth and their descendants, the Romans.[60] It is possible that the mythical conversation between Jupiter and Venus was anchored for Naevius' audience in the physical reality of their

(an uneasy position). He describes the range of the Vergilian and Naevian prophecies with virtually identical language (*de futurorum prosperitate solatur*, of Vergil's Jupiter; *consolantis spe futurorum*, of Naevius'); since Vergil's prophecy extends hundreds of years down to the time of the poet, it is hard to believe that Macrobius would have used such language if he had thought that Naevius' prophecy referred only to the immediate future. See the careful discussion of Koch (1955), 36.

[57] Zonaras 8. 9. 12; Weinstock (1971), 16.

[58] At *Sen.* 49–50, Cicero has Cato speak of the joys of remaining intellectually active into old age. He first gives the example of the astronomer Gaius Gallus, whom Cato saw working day and night. His next example is Naevius, who took great delight in his *Punic War*. Although Beare (1949) would have it that this is probably only a reference to his *reading* of his poem, I must agree with Mattingly (1960), 426 n. 56, that the context makes it virtually certain that Cicero is referring to his hard work at *composition*. Naevius is therefore to be imagined as working on the poem in his old age, which could well be after the end of the Second Punic War, as Mattingly argues.

[59] Schilling (1954), 239–66; Koch (1955), 35–44; Bömer (1958), 77–8; Latte (1960), 185–6; Galinsky (1969), 174–6, 185–6; Weinstock (1971), 16; *RE* 2R 15. 853–4 (Koch).

[60] For this interpretation (seeing *meum*, rather than *tuum*, understood with *genus*), see Bömer (1958), 78.

locations in Rome, for the temple of Venus Erycina was placed right on the Capitoline hill, close by the temple of Jupiter Optimus Maximus.[61]

For the mechanics of the prophecy-scene itself, Naevius has blended two scenes from the *Odyssey* where Athene complains to Zeus about the undeserved suffering of Odysseus (1. 44–79; 5. 7–42).[62] In both of these scenes we hear Zeus prophesying a favourable outcome for Odysseus (1. 76-9; 5. 22–4). In Naevius, however, this traditional epic device of prophecy has been vastly expanded. In Greek epic, so far as we can now tell, prophecies reach (like those of Zeus to Athene in the *Odyssey*) only to the time-span of the narrative, or, at least, not beyond the lifetimes of the human characters who are the subject of the prophecy.[63] Yet, if Macrobius' comparison with the *Aeneid* has any force, Naevius' Jupiter will have revealed historical events lying hundreds of years in the future, down to the time of the poet.[64] Vergil's climax is the end of discord with the reign of Augustus (*Aen.* 1. 291–6); where did Naevius' prophecy culminate? With the peace of Q. Lutatius at the end of the war (frr. 46–7)? The problem acquires a intriguing extra dimension when one reflects that Naevius was writing his poem on the first Punic war in his old age, during, or even after, the second war.[65] It is conceivable (though no more) that Jupiter's range carried him well beyond the action of the poem, to include even victory over Hannibal.

'Jupiter's revelations in this crucial early scene appear to have been communicated to human characters also. Venus gave to her lover Anchises, Aeneas' father, 'books containing the future' (*libros futura continentes*).[66] Apart from anything else, these books presumably contained the information—selected and ambiguous perhaps—which she had had from Jupiter.[67] Anchises'

---

[61] Liv. 23. 31. 9.

[62] These two Homeric scenes are themselves, of course, the 'same' incident, narrated sequentially instead of simultaneously.

[63] The Cyclic epics are full of prophecies with this sort of range: *Cypria*: p. 31. 12–16 *EGF*; *Ilias Parva*: p. 52. 6–8*EGF*; *Aethiopis*: p. 47. 15–16 *EGF*; *Nostoi*: p. 67. 15-17 *EGF*.

[64] See n. 56 above.

[65] See n. 58 above.

[66] Fr. 4: the quoted words are those of the scholion on Verg. *Aen.* 7. 123, our source for this information.

[67] Though Büchner (1982), in his comment on fr. 4, dates this action to a time before the Trojans leave Troy.

mantic gifts were evidently a feature of the early Latin tradition,[68] but the techniques which Naevius gives him are not to be found in Greek epic. Poetic seers in the Greek tradition do not consult books; Anchises, it appears, will have acted like one of Rome's *decemuiri* when he wanted to know the will of the gods.[69] Or else he followed the practices of the *auspices* or *augures*, marking out a *templum* in the sky and there 'seeing his bird' (*postquam auem aspexit in templo Anchisa*, fr. 25, with *auem aspexit* making a plain pun on *auspex*).

A final occasion for prophecy was provided by a Sibyl (fr. 11), whom the Campanian Naevius located in his own *patria*, calling her a 'Cimmerian', after the people who (by one reading of Homer) inhabited the borders of the Homeric underworld.[70] A prophecy to Aeneas is to be assumed; again, it is tempting to imagine a range of revelation far more extensive than that given to Odysseus by Teiresias.

The narrative device of epic prophecy, then, has been greatly extended to serve a consistent end: the foundation of Rome after Troy's fall, and her victory over Carthage, come to be the inevitable result of the gods' plan. The clearest demonstration of how fixed this conviction of their divinely guaranteed success came to be for the Romans is provided by the Stoic astrological poet Manilius, who chooses, as his first example of the inexorable working of fate, the rise of Rome after Troy's fall (*Astron.* 1. 511–12). Quite when the Romans first began to think in such terms, it is not possible to say with certainty.[71] Naevius is our first witness to a perspective which was to find its canonical expression in the *Aeneid*, and it may very well have been precisely the extraordinary experience of the Carthaginian wars themselves, Naevius' very subject, which generated this sense of divinely-guaranteed mission for dominion.[72]

Whether Greek aetiological epic controlled such perspectives it

---

[68] Cf. Enn. *Ann.* 1. xvii Skutsch (1985).

[69] The Sibylline books of the Roman Republic were, however, not used in the manner of epic prophecies, for predicting the future, but for prescribing cult acts of various sorts, particularly in response to prodigies and catastrophes: Wissowa (1912), 539–40; Parke (1988), 190–215, esp. 193, 195–6.

[70] See Colin Hardie's appendix in Austin (1977), 279–86.

[71] Dumézil (1970), 499–504.

[72] So Vogt (1943), 118–69. This use of epic prophecy is by no means 'original to Virgil', as claimed by Williams (1983), 5.

is impossible to determine, on the available evidence. Other poetic forms show gods or seers of the mythical past giving prophecies which are to be fulfilled in contemporary time, and this looks like an adaptation of epic practice for panegyric.[73] Yet what we see in Naevius is unique.[74] And it is unique not least because the god who guarantees Roman supremacy is Jupiter. This fact, and its implications, need to be registered in full.

Naevius identifies the national god of the Roman state, Jupiter Optimus Maximus, with the Greek supreme deity, Zeus. When he takes over the first scene of Homer's *Odyssey*, and has Venus address Jupiter, the blending of the Greek and the Roman gods is vividly shown with the collocation of two distinctive epithets: *patrem suum supremum optumum appellat* ('she addresses her father, highest, best', fr. 15). *supremum* is the Homeric epithet ὕπατε, as used by Athene to Zeus in the corresponding scene in the *Odyssey*.[75] *optumum*, however, is one half of the cult title of the god who sat enthroned on the Capitoline. The consequences of this identification of Jupiter and Zeus appear not to have been properly noted, perhaps because the identification is so familiar to us, but they are momentous. In superimposing their national deity on Zeus, the Romans were engaged in an enterprise which no Greek state could have contemplated.

One may easily imagine the Hera of Argos, for example, prophesying her people's future greatness in an Argive epic about the founder of the city; one may easily imagine Athene prophesying the future greatness of her city in an epic on Erichthonius. But what Greek city had Zeus as its own proper god, to enunciate his people's destiny? 'Zeus stands above all faction.'[76] There simply was no Greek city-state that was Zeus' city as Athens was Athene's, or Argos Hera's. It is impossible to imagine a Greek epic where Zeus represents an individual state, championing its interests, promoting the victory of its people on the grounds that they are peculiarly his own.[77] Kings, regarded since Homer as being

[73] Pind. *Pyth.* 4. 13–23; Call. *Del.* 162–90.
[74] Stressed by Snell (1967), 160–1.
[75] *Od.* 1. 45; Naevius follows Homer more closely in another fragment from this context, using a synonym in the vocative: *summe* (fr. 16).
[76] Burkert (1985), 130.
[77] Professor Burkert and Dr. Richardson both point out to me the Iliadic passage where Zeus claims that Troy is his favourite city (*Il.* 4. 44–9). Certainly this passage

under the protection of Zeus, vaunted their closeness to the supreme god, from Philip of Macedon down to the Hellenistic monarchs who were contemporary with Naevius;[78] yet Greek states and cities did not claim this personal relationship with Zeus, so that even the informal attempts of Corinth to tout itself as Zeus' city aroused derision and resentment.[79] The temples of Olympian Zeus were generally outside the city—even at Olympia.

Zeus was, of course, honoured in civic cults all over the Greek world, often as Zeus Polieus ('Zeus of the city').[80] Yet the meaning of such cult was not the same as in the case of each city's distinctive deity. Zeus was honoured whenever groups, of whatever size, acknowledged the subsuming of smaller identities in a larger, and this is the context within which to regard the honour which the polis pays to Zeus, without asserting him as the expression of the sense of identity felt by the polis: when Greeks think of groups submerging themselves in something higher they think of Zeus, but this is not the same as being a self-conscious way of giving an identity to the resultant unit—for that the polis will go to some other god.[81] Such a perspective explains also why Zeus is an ideal god for leagues and federations.[82] Accordingly, the coins of the Achaean League show Zeus Amarius; those of the Messenians, Zeus Ithomatas; and those of the Arcadian League show Zeus Lycaeus—while the Arcadian towns which stayed out of the League do not have Zeus on their coinage.[83]

A federal Jupiter did exist, not twenty miles from Rome, and every year Jupiter Latiaris was honoured on the Alban Mount by all the Latin states.[84] Yet this Jupiter, shared with the other Latins, was quite ousted in Roman esteem by their own Capitoline Jupiter, who was the pre-eminent god of the city, guarantor of Roman

must have impressed Roman poets, yet the *Iliad* in no sense shows Zeus as the partisan of the Trojans (let alone as their national god): his plan is for the destruction of the city.

[78] Gardner (1918), 423, 426; Seltman (1933), 229–41; Schwabl (1978), 1391–1405; Fears (1981a), 764–73. If Naevius' Jupiter had any precedent in Greek epic, it will have been in the lost Alexander-epics; for the powerful impact of the Alexander-ideology on third-century Rome, see Weinstock (1957); Burnett (1986).

[79] Pind. *Nem.* 7. 106, with schol. ad loc.

[80] Farnell (1896–1909), 1. 56–8, 64–75; Schwabl (1978), 1052–3.

[81] Schwabl (1978), 1335.

[82] Farnell (1896–1909), 1. 63.

[83] Seltman (1933), 165–7.

[84] Wissowa (1912), 40, 124–5.

victory, expression of the city's identity to the citizens and to the outside world.[85] It was in his temple every year that the consuls first sacrificed and the senate first met; it was here that the general sacrificed before going on campaign, and here that he returned in triumph after victory to discharge his vow. The relationship between Rome and Jupiter was unique.

The reason why Greek states avoided claiming Zeus as their proper god was that he was pan-Hellenic, supranational, 'the only god', in fact, 'who could become an all-embracing god of the universe'.[86] It was precisely this universality to which the god of the expanding Roman empire could aspire. It remains impossible to establish whether Naevius' careful identification of Rome's Jupiter and Homer's Zeus is the first sign of this aspiration. It may well be that Naevius is already making the shattering assertion which will be plain to see in Ennius and in Vergil: the god who ordains the destiny of the world, the guiding force in the universe, is the god of Rome and her empire.

The identification of Jupiter with Zeus is something of the highest potential, but it is only one example of the elaborate syncretism which the poets of Rome were establishing, building on the centuries-old symbiosis of Roman and Hellenic culture. Already by the time of Naevius, 'the men of letters had almost completed the great dictionary of equivalences'.[87] Greek Cronus has found a double in Saturnus, who is fashioned into the father of Jupiter and Juno; this pair are now husband and wife, brother and sister, like their Greek counterparts; and the other members of the family are likewise fitted into the scheme, acquiring a mythology and a character as they are mapped on to their Greek correspondents.[88] Some of the equivalences are by this time grounded in centuries of cult-practice. The worship of Ceres on the Aventine, for example, overtly modelled on the worship of Demeter, and practised with Greek ritual, had been flourishing for almost 300 years by the time Naevius began writing his poem.[89] Other ways of looking at long-established gods were more recent. Apollo had been honoured in Rome for centuries, pre-eminently as a god of healing,

[85] Bailey (1932), 168–72; Koch (1937), 122–6; Fears (1981b), esp. 17–40.
[86] Burkert (1985), 131.
[87] Dumézil (1970), 456.
[88] Wissowa (1912), 65–7; Dumézil (1970), 455–6.
[89] Wissowa (1912), 297–300; Latte (1960), 160–2.

but Naevius refers to him in his capacity as the oracular god at Delphi, calling him *Pythius* (fr. 24). Here Naevius is responding to events of his own lifetime, for it was the crises of the Hannibalic war which drove the Roman Senate to consult the oracle for the first time, giving the Apollo of Delphi his topical prestige.[90] Finally, some of the correspondences which the poets were establishing would have had minimal purchase in the lived experience of the Roman audience. A reader of Livius Andronicus' translation of the *Odyssey* would have seen, at the end of the poem, the familiar Mercury in the role of Hermes, the escorter of dead souls to the Underworld; but when he rolled up the volume, the Mercury he knew in the city remained none the less no more than the god of commerce.[91]

The custom of establishing correspondences between gods of different nations was not a game played by Romans deferring to Greeks, but a habit of thought diffused round the Mediterranean.[92] One would give a lot to know what Naevius made of one pervasive non-Greek syncretism—the identification of Juno with the chief goddess of Carthage, Tanit. This identification was no fiction of the poets. The Punic–Etruscan inscription found at Pyrgi, near Caere, which dates to around 500 BCE, appears to link Uni, the Etruscan Juno, with Astarte, who is one aspect of Tanit.[93] Hannibal himself, in honouring Juno Lacinia, linked the goddesses together,[94] as did the Roman government, who strenuously honoured Juno at various crises during the Hannibalic war, counteracting the Carthaginian's propaganda and calming the widespread fear that the goddess was disaffected.[95] Considering the time of writing, it is natural to suspect that Juno might have played a hostile role in Naevius' poem. In the crucial scene between Venus and Jupiter, as we have seen, Venus remonstrates with her father over the sufferings of the Trojans, as Athene remonstrates with Zeus over the sufferings of Odysseus. If the paradigm of the *Odyssey* is to hold, then there should be talk of

[90] Parke and Wormell (1956), 1. 271–2.
[91] Wissowa (1912), 305–6, on Mercury's mercantile character.
[92] Ferguson (1970), 211–23; MacMullen (1981), 90–4.
[93] On the inscription, see conveniently Dumézil (1970), 680–2; on Tanit, and her links with Astarte, see Warmington (1969), 145–6; on links between Tanit and Juno, see *RE* 2R 4. 2184; Pease (1935), 162–3; Picard (1954), 65, 109.
[94] Liv. 28. 46. 16; Cic. *Div.* 1. 48; Dumézil (1970), 464–5.
[95] Liv. 21. 62. 8, 22. 1. 17–18, 27. 37. 7–15; see Bloch (1972), 394.

the hostile will of an opposed deity, just as there is much talk of Poseidon in the first scene of the *Odyssey* (1. 68–79): who else but Juno–Hera, bitter antagonist, in the Homeric tradition, of everything Trojan, and now recently revealed in a newly significant role of hostility, as the principal goddess of the Carthaginians?[96] Both Venus and Juno, then, will have had two motives for their actions, corresponding to their two guises: a Homeric motive, reaching back to the *Iliad*, and a newly topical historical motive, grounded in contemporary cult and religious propaganda.

If it was vital for Naevius to devote over one third of his poem to the mythical aetiology, the question of how this mythical material was integrated remains the most vexed in Naevian scholarship. Did Naevius begin at the beginning, with the fall of Troy, or did he interrupt his narration of the war early on and introduce the aetiology in flashback?[97] At face value, the ancient assignments of book numbers indicate a poem opening with the start of the war, and soon moving back to the remotest origins.[98] Many have objected to this postulated insertion of mythical material into an historical narrative,[99] yet our easy and confident demarcations between myth and history run the risk of smothering the use made of myth by Naevius' historical protagonists. The cockpit for Rome and Carthage was Sicily, an island rich in the Aeneas-legend.[100] As we have seen, in the second year of the war the people of Segesta appealed to Rome on the basis of their shared divine kinship, while the response of the Romans to the cult of Aphrodite at Eryx was of the highest importance in establishing their own devotion to the new persona of Venus as ancestress of the Roman people. Further, the struggles between Greeks and Carthaginians in Sicily had been cast, just like the eastern struggles between Greeks and Persians, in terms of myth—specifically, in terms of the most

---

[96] Cf. Buchheit (1963), 54–5, although he does not bring Poseidon into the argument; Häussler (1978), 196–7.

[97] Bibliography in Waszink (1972), 905–10. The crucial contribution was that of Strzelecki (1935); see Rowell (1947).

[98] It is important to remember that the division of the poem into seven books was not the work of Naevius, but of the grammarian Octavius Lampadio (Suet. *Gram.* 2). With Rowell (1947), Mariotti (1955), and Büchner (1982), I am sure that Strzelecki's reconstruction is basically correct, in seeing the aetiology being introduced in flashback.

[99] Waszink (1972), 905–10.

[100] Galinsky (1969), 63–140.

durable and prevalent prototype of the fight between civilized
order and barbaric chaos, the Gigantomachy.[101]

Somewhere in his first book, Naevius described a Gigantomachy on an artefact:

> inerant signa expressa,    quomodo Titani,
> bicorpores Gigantes    magnique Athamantis
> Runcus ac Purpureus,    filii et Terras . . .

On it were moulded figures, representing how the Titans, two-bodied
Giants, and Runcus and Purpureus, the sons of great Athamas and of
Earth . . .[102]

It was long ago suggested that Naevius is here describing the
Gigantomachy displayed on the eastern pediment of the temple of
Zeus Olympius in the Sicilian city of Acragas.[103] It was then further noted that Acragas was attacked by the Romans early in the
war, and fascinating prospects opened up. The Gigantomachic
sculpture, a mythic reflection on the Sicilian Greeks' victory over
the Carthaginians in 480 BCE, had a counterpart on the western
pediment, where the sack of Troy was depicted.[104] To the Greek
designers, the defeat of Troy was a restatement in heroic time of
the victory for Greek values which the gods' triumph assured in
mythic time. To the Romans the end of Troy was the beginning of
Rome, and the suggestion has accordingly been made that it was
the Trojan scenes on the western pediment which provided
Naevius with the occasion for his shift to aetiology, as he described the legions coming to Acragas and viewing the vicissitudes
of their Trojan ancestors.[105]

The proposal is as unprovable as it is attractive, and debate on
the question of the switch to aetiology has, paradoxically, dis-
tracted attention from the significance of the Gigantomachy itself.

---

[101] The key text is Pindar's first *Pythian*, and the key monument is the temple of
Zeus Olympius at Acragas; cf. Thomas (1976), 26, 63.

[102] Fr. 8; I accept the emendation of Luck (1983), 272–3, giving *Athamantis* for
*Atlantis* in the second line of the fragment, and supplementing *et* before *Terras* in
the third.

[103] By Bergk in 1842, referred to by Fraenkel (1954), 15–16, who gives a history
of the debate. The notion was also suggested by Fränkel (1935), 59–61. Our source
for the programme on the temple is Diod. Sic. 13. 82. 4.

[104] Again, Diod. Sic. 13. 82. 4.

[105] Strzelecki (1935), 11; cf. Rowell (1947), 45; Mariotti (1955), 26 (cautious).
The other favoured departure point for the aetiological flashback is the appeal of
the people of Segesta: see Buchheit (1963), 52.

Whatever artefact Naevius may have chosen as the setting for his Gigantomachy,[106] we need to concentrate on the fact that his poem exhibited, early on, an example of the quintessential Greek paradigm of brutish revolt against the order of divine power. It is difficult to believe that his use of such a potent symbol was gratuitous. He may well have smuggled the 'barbarian' Romans into the Greek position in the paradigm, insinuating that the Romans were now taking up the burden of civilization against the Carthaginians. Certainly, by the time of the poem's composition, the Romans had been acquainted for almost a century with Gigantomachic representations of their chief god, Jupiter. It seems to have been the Celts who brought out such a response from the Romans.[107] The year before the crucial battle against the Celtic-Samnite coalition at Sentinum in 295 BCE, the brothers Ogulnii placed a statue of Jupiter, riding in a four-horse chariot, on top of the god's Capitoline temple: in the characteristic Gigantomachic pose of Zeus, he was brandishing the thunderbolt, with Victory (perhaps) driving his chariot.[108] It was entirely characteristic of the Romans that they chose to present, not, like the Greeks, a narrative, but an isolated emblem of power which focused on the city's god. Around the time of Sentinum there was a great flurry of cultic activity concentrating on Jupiter and his Victoria: the programme has powerful links with the perspectives of Gigantomachy.[109] When the Celts next massed in threat, in 225 BCE, the Romans responded in similar fashion, with a long run of 'quadrigati' coins, which show the statue of the brothers Ogulnii—Jupiter riding in his chariot to crush the wild enemy, thunderbolt in hand, Victory at the reins.[110]

However Naevius may have exploited the Gigantomachy, his poem will have asserted the divine sanction for Roman power, a sanction guaranteed by the victorious might of Jupiter. His

---

[106] According to Fraenkel (1954), 16, and earlier opinion cited there, a shield; according to Büchner (1982), on fr. 8, the ship of Aeneas.

[107] As they also did from the Greeks and Pergamese: Pollitt (1986), 79–101.

[108] Liv. 10. 23. 12; Fears (1981*b*), 38–9. For the Gigantomachic character of this pose, see Vian (1952), 129, and (1951), nos. 392–4; Fears (1981*a*), 817. For the problem of whether or not the original statue had a figure of Victory, see Hölscher (1967), 74–5.

[109] Fears (1981*b*), 34–6.

[110] Crawford (1974), nos. 29–34; 'the types were presumably chosen in response to the Gallic threat' (715).

approaches were developed and amplified by his successors, to the first of whom we now turn.

Quintus Ennius came to the writing of his *Annales* in his early to middle fifties, with many years of varied reading and creation behind him.[111] In his translations of Greek tragedies, and in his reading of the scholarship on those tragedies, he would have been exposed to refined opinions about the divine.[112] In particular, he had displayed sufficient interest in recherché Greek theories of divinity to produce two works, based on Greek originals, which treated the problem of the gods: the *Euhemerus* and the *Epicharmus*. The disparity between Roman state cult and the picture of the gods offered in these two books is quite remarkable.

The *Epicharmus* took as its base a body of writings attributed to the Sicilian comic poet Epicharmus, of the early fifth century.[113] What Ennius found here was a series of physical speculations, of the sort by now familiar to the reader, which purported to reveal the nature of the universe, conventionally clothed by the names of the principal gods. The longest surviving fragment speaks of Jupiter in terms of the phenomena of the atmosphere:

> istic est is Iuppiter quem dico, quem Graeci uocant
> aerem; qui uentus est et nubes, imber postea,
> atque ex imbre frigus, uentus post fit, aer denuo.
> haecce propter Iuppiter sunt ista quae dico tibi,
> quando mortales atque urbes beluasque omnis iuuat.

That is this Jupiter whom I mean, whom the Greeks call Aer ('air'); who is wind and clouds, and then moisture; and out of moisture he becomes cold, and afterwards wind, and air once more. That is the reason why those things which I mention to you are Jupiter, since he helps all men and cities and beasts. (*Var.* 54–8 Vahlen)[114]

In the last two lines, Ennius is clearly cutting loose from the details of his Greek model, and independently applying Greek etymological techniques to Latin, for Greek cannot connect 'Zeus'

---

[111] Skutsch (1985), 4–6.
[112] Jocelyn (1967), 371–4, 424.
[113] Garbarino (1973), 276-89.
[114] These trochaic septenarii could, of course, be from a tragedy: see Timpanaro (1948), 10 (a reference I owe to Professor Jocelyn). Jocelyn (1967) includes them amongst the *fragmenta incerta* of the tragedies (356–60). They are quoted by Varro (*Ling.* 5. 65), who does not assign them to any work.

with 'helping', as Ennius here connects 'Iuppiter/Iouis' with *iuuo*.[115] Another fragment shows him performing the same operation on the Latin name Ceres, the Romans' Demeter. The Greeks saw 'earth/mother' in their goddess's name, and Ennius searches for a like correspondence in Latin, to produce an etymology of fruitfulness for Ceres as mother earth: *quod gerit fruges, Ceres* ('called Ceres, because she bears—*gerit*—crops', *Var. 50* Vahlen).[116] If the true nature of the gods may be hidden in Greek names, they may also be hidden in Latin.

Such significant etymologies of the gods' names are a feature of the earliest Latin, as they had been of the earliest Greek, poetry and scholarship. Ennius' practice in the *Epicharmus* must have been fairly systematic, but his predecessors Livius and Naevius will have experimented here themselves. Certainly Naevius gives etymologies for place-names in the Greek manner.[117] In the fragments of these two earlier poets only one case survives where a deity's name is so treated. The Greek name for the mother of the Muses was Mnemosyne ('Memory'). When Livius chose 'Moneta' as his Latin equivalent, he seems to be suggesting *moneo* ('remind') as the significant root, and he reinforces the hint when he has her 'teaching': *nam diua Monetas filia docuit* ('for the divine daughter of Moneta taught', fr. 21). The surviving fragments of Ennius' *Annales* likewise offer only one case of the divine etymologizing he had absorbed and displayed in the *Epicharmus*. An address to Jupiter (444) sets *genitor* ('progenitor') against the epithet *Saturnie* ('son of Saturn'), as if to hint at the lurking presence there of another 'progenitor' word, *sator*.[118]

Later Latin poetry domesticated this type of learning so systematically that we now take it virtually for granted, and it requires an effort to remind ourselves of how bold and novel Ennius' procedure is in the *Epicharmus*. To those few of his contemporaries who read this book, accustomed as they were to thinking of their

[115] Ennius is presumably working off a Greek etymology which saw Zeus' beneficence in his being responsible for 'life' (ζῆν): Pease (1955–8), 712.

[116] On both the Greek and Latin etymologies, see Pease (1955–8), 722.

[117] fr. 28 says that the Palatine is really the 'Balatine', from the 'baa-ing' (*balare*) of sheep; fr. 29 says that the Aventine comes from 'birds' (*aues*). Ennius follows this second etymology in his account of Romulus' augury: *in alto . . . Auentino* he looks for the breed of *altiuolantum* (75–6).

[118] Cf. Jocelyn (1967), 331 (on fr. 192), for an analogous, but translingual, pun in a tragedy.

gods as cult figures with a life fixed in the life of the city, it will
have been a mental feat of considerable strain to accommodate
themselves to the task demanded of them by this new citizen.

Even more radical, to a Roman view, is the account of the gods
given in the *Euhemerus*. Ennius took over Euhemerus' presentation of the gods as great kings and statesmen of the past, who
were granted immortality by a grateful mankind.[119] As in the
*Epicharmus*, he Latinized the process, giving Caelus for Uranus,
Saturnus for Cronus, and Jupiter for Zeus. Ennius' audience
would have been surprised, at the very least, to hear of their
mighty Jupiter as a mere man, cunningly setting up divine worship
for himself (*Var.* 123–5 Vahlen). They would have been even
more taken aback at the picture of Venus, presented as nothing
but a slut, who set up the art of prostitution so that she would not
be the only woman who seemed loose and lustful (*Var.* 142–5
Vahlen). Such schemes are wholly at odds with the state cult—and
with the 'philosophy' of the *Epicharmus*.

These two little books display startlingly novel ways of looking at
the gods whose statues and temples Ennius' contemporaries encountered in their city. This novelty carries forward into the
*Annales*. At least one euhemerist story concerning the major gods
went into the *Annales*, namely, the story of Saturn's quarrel with
his brother Titan, his attempt to kill his son Jupiter, and his flight
to hiding in Latium.[120] There is room for doubt whether the version of this story in the *Annales* was euhemeristic in the strict
sense. In Vergil's version, Saturn is definitely a god who flees to
Latium, not a man who later becomes a god (*Aen.* 8. 319–20). It
is possible that in Ennius' version Saturn was likewise a god from
the beginning, and that the skeleton of the story was all that survived recasting from the treatise to the epic.

It is highly likely that the deification of Romulus, who performed the mighty benefaction of founding the city, was the innovation of Ennius.[121] Ennius here will have been placing Romulus
in the tradition of the great Hellenistic monarchs who won im-

---

[119] Above, p. 32.

[120] 25 (with Skutsch (1985) ad loc.).

[121] Skutsch (1985), 205; Jocelyn (1989), esp. 55. When Ennius asserted in the
*Annales* that Romulus had become a god, he did not do so by identifying him with
Quirinus, who was a god acknowledged by the Roman state: Skutsch (1968), 130–
7; Jocelyn (1989), 40, 55.

mortality by emulating Hercules.[122] The basic idea, thus baldly stated, has a clearly euhemerist cast, yet the colour of the application is now lost. The death of Romulus was the occasion for the announcement that he had become a god. The pained reaction of the bereaved people, with their mixed sense of loss and gratitude (105-9), gives a naturalistic preparation to the declaration that Romulus is now a god (110-11). Yet Romulus clearly was the son of Mars in the poem (54), and he was taken up to heaven in the chariot of his father, in fulfilment of Jupiter's promise.[123] With the loss of the narrative, we are unable to begin to determine whether the pomp of the heavenly ascent was conveyed, for example, as the actualization of a metaphor, to be read aright by the politically astute.

The sheer range of ways of looking at the fate of Romulus is striking, and it has recently been extended, by the arguments of Jocelyn concerning the language with which Ennius announces the apotheosis: *Romulus in caelo cum dis genitalibus aeuom degit* ('Romulus leads his life in the sky with the engendering gods', 110-11). If Jocelyn's approach to the problem is right, then these words are those of the poet himself, with an abstruse theological reference to the elaborately Pythagorean explanation of the nature of the universe which opened the work as a whole.[124] The poem began with a remarkable parade of Pythagoreanism, as the shade of Homer told Ennius that his soul had transmigrated into the body of the Latin poet (1. ii–x); Homer gave also the necessary background in physics for this phenomenon, with material from the *Epicharmus*.[125] Yet more variety of Greek learning is evident, then, and there was Empedoclean physics too, coming into the poem by some channel or other in Book 7 (220-1), where Ennius embodied Empedocles' cosmic principle of Strife as the creature from Hell, Discordia.[126]

The emphasis so far has been on the elements of Greek learning which were assimilated into the poem, and it is very important to stress how bizarre the doctrines of the poem would have seemed

---

[122] Fuller argument of this point in Feeney (1984), 187-8.

[123] Skutsch (1985), on 1. lxii.

[124] Jocelyn (1989), esp. 54–5.

[125] Skutsch (1985), 146, 160–1 (citing Epicharmus, 23 B 9 DK), 162 (citing Epicharmus, 23 B 4 DK).

[126] See Skutsch (1985), 394–5.

to the conventional thinking of its audience.[127] Yet the *Annales* contained a great deal of material which would have seemed more familiar. In particular, there was considerable detail bearing on Roman state cult, much of it presumably culled from the contemporaries of Ennius who were beginning the slow process of imitating Greek religious antiquarianism, inventing aetiologies for their institutions.[128] The beginning of the second book described King Numa's establishment of diverse religious institutions, with modes and instruments of worship (114–18). Cult activities of the state were described in action. We may have a fragment narrating the arrival of the Magna Mater in Rome towards the end of the Hannibalic War (dub. i). The great *lectisternium* of 217 BCE, when six couches were displayed, one for each pair of male and female gods, calls forth a bravura piece of metrics from the poet, who gets all twelve names into two lines (240–1):

> Iuno Vesta Minerua Ceres Diana Venus Mars
> Mercurius Iouis Neptunus Volcanus Apollo.

As the epic's operational norm, of course, we have the gods on the Homeric plane as characters: talking amongst themselves in council and in dialogue, interacting with each other and with humans, advising, marrying, and impregnating. In this guise the gods are indeed ἀνθρωποπαθεῖς, acting and feeling on analogy with human action, with partialities and designs like Homer's gods.[129]

Quite clearly, there is no one area of belief onto which the religion(s) of the poem can be mapped, and such a catalogue of variety may give an impression of hotch-potch: Jupiter, for example, is the son of a euhemeristic Saturn, a cosmic force of cohesion, something on a couch at a Roman *lectisternium*, a dedicatee for a Greek king, a Zeus-figure chairing a meeting of factious kin, a clap of thunder.[130] With the loss of the narrative itself, the possibility of a resolution is denied us. What personality the gods of Ennius may have achieved in the poem is therefore gone, but a divine plot of sorts may be recaptured, through which at least some pattern may be seen.

[127] On the incompatibility of important strains in the poem with conventional Roman attitudes on religion, see Jocelyn (1972), 1010–11, and (1989), 54–5.

[128] Rawson (1985), 298; Latte (1960), 4–5.

[129] Above, pp. 48–9.

[130] 444 (son of Saturn); 555–6, 446–7 (cohesion); 241 (*lectisternium*); 181 (Pyrrhus' dedication); 52–3, 444–5 (council of gods); 541 (thunder).

The densest cluster of divine action was in the first book, where the poet covered the aftermath of the Trojan war down to the foundation of the city and the apotheosis of its founder, Romulus. The epoch is Homeric, and the Homeric divine characters are on display to grace the beginning of the work and of the city with the highest possible grandeur.[131] If the poem is thus overtly a continuation of Homer, it is reasonable to assume that the gods continued their Homeric partialities. Certainly Venus is as solicitous for her son Aeneas as Aphrodite had been in the *Iliad*. She inspires his father Anchises with prophetic knowledge, meets Anchises and Aeneas, and protects Aeneas' daughter Ilia, the mother of Romulus, as she is about to be drowned in the Anio.[132] Just as in the case of Naevius, it is reasonable to assume that Venus is outstripping her Homeric allegiances, and fostering the family of Aeneas because of the status which she enjoyed amongst the Romans as the ancestress of their race.[133]

Again, by the Homeric model, where there are favourable gods there will be unfavourable ones, and a fine opportunity for the poet to allow the anti-Trojan, anti-Roman side its voice will have been provided by the set-piece Council of the Gods in the first book (51–5). On the agenda of this famous meeting was the apotheosis of Romulus, grandson of Trojan Aeneas.[134] Waszink has made a strong case for seeing Neptune as a speaker hostile to the Roman enterprise in this council, following up his Homeric role as an enemy of perfidious Troy, determined to stop the foundation of the new Troy in Latium.[135] Many diverse pieces of evidence converge to produce the impression that another of the speakers at the council was Juno, notorious from Homer's picture of Hera as the enemy of everything and everyone Trojan.[136]

Horace's third 'Roman Ode' reports a speech given by Juno at a council of the gods, on the subject of Romulus' apotheosis; Horace's last stanza virtually states outright that he has been recounting epic material (3. 3. 69–72), and it is in fact generally

---

[131] Cf. Liv. *Praef.* 6–7.

[132] 15–16, 19, 58–60.

[133] Above, pp. 109–11.

[134] The main sources for Ennius' council are Hor. *Carm.* 3. 3, and Ov. *Met.* 14. 806–15, *Fast.* 2. 485–8, together with Lucilius' parody, frr. 5–46 Warmington. For Romulus as the grandson of Aeneas in Ennius, see Serv. auct. on *Aen.* 1. 273.

[135] Waszink (1957), 324–5.

[136] Fuller argumentation of the following points in Feeney (1984).

reckoned that Ennius' council is somehow behind the ode.[137] The goddess speaks from the outset as the Homeric Hera, still bitter about her defeat in Paris' beauty-contest.[138] Now, however, the war is over, Troy is destroyed (18–30), and Juno is prepared to come to terms: she will give over her anger and allow Romulus to become a god (30–6). As we saw above, the fundamental model for Ennius' deification of Romulus is the apotheosis of Heracles, and it is highly significant that an indispensable element of the traditional accounts of Heracles' apotheosis resided in Hera's abandonment of the angry hatred which she had nurtured against the hero since his birth.[139] Horace's poem is strong evidence for the supposition that Ennius included this element of the Heracles-tradition along with the rest, by making Juno give over her hatred of the Trojans in order to allow the grandson of Aeneas to be enrolled among the gods.[140]

A great and proud goddess like Juno or Hera is not likely to make such concessions without exacting a recompense. In Horace's poem she demands the perpetual disappearance of Troy in exchange for her acquiescence (37–68). Vergil's Juno likewise, as we shall see, demands the end of Troy when she makes a deal,[141] and the congruence makes it likely that Ennius' Juno stipulated that there should be no more Troys. The final bargain may have looked something like this: let the new city be founded, on condition that it not be another Troy; Romulus and Remus will have a competition in augury to see which will be the founder, and the winner will become a god, giving his name to the city ('Rome' if Romulus wins, 'Remora' if Remus wins).[142]

One factor only has prevented scholars from readily using Horace's poem, in the way it has been used here, as evidence for

---

[137] Pasquali (1964), 687; Oksala (1973), 102, 156–7. It must be stressed that, for reasons which will soon emerge, very few scholars believe that the substance of Juno's speech in Horace is Ennian; the reconstruction offered here is highly controversial.

[138] NB *iudex* ('judge') in line 19.

[139] Feeney (1984), 187–8; note that Hercules, like Romulus, is present at the beginning of the ode as a model for Augustus (9).

[140] Note that Horace follows the Ennian version in making Romulus a grandson of Aeneas, the daughter of the Trojan priestess: *inuisum nepotem, / Troica quem peperit sacerdos* (31–2). In Ovid's picture of the council which decides on the apotheosis of Aeneas, we see Juno relenting: *Met.* 14. 592–3.

[141] Below, pp. 147–8.

[142] The key evidence for the competition and its terms comes from Enn. *Ann.* 54–5 and 77, with Ov. *Met.* 14. 806–15 and *Fast.* 2. 485–8; again, fuller argumentation in Feeney (1984), 190–1.

the words of Ennius' Juno in the Council of *Annales* 1, and that is the solid testimony of Servius that it was during the second Punic war that Ennius' Juno was placated and began to favour the Romans, having fought against them on the side of Carthage.[143] How can she have made any agreement favourable to the Romans at the very beginning of their history, if she was hostile during the Hannibalic war? Only when we come to Vergil's Juno in the next chapter will a full account be possible, for only in the fully preserved *Aeneid* is it possible to survey the whole range and variety of Juno's hostility. For now, it may be observed that Ennius' Juno is not only the Hera of Homer, but also (as she probably was in Naevius) the Tanit of the Carthaginians.[144] The assuaging of one element of her persona need not necessarily entail a full-scale capitulation. Her reconciliation in the council in Book 1 will have been a partial one, affecting only her Homeric nature, and leaving open the potential for a re-emergence as Rome's divine antagonist under another guise.[145] The ancients' ability to view a deity as a many-sided prism, at first sight an embarrassment to a poet's achievement of character, seems to have been turned by Ennius into a positive aid: two crises of the Roman state call forth two divine responses, which are yet one.

Hannibal's war will have been the climax of Juno's hate, as she struggled to ensure dominion over the world for her Carthaginians. In the course of the war, as Servius tells us, she was induced to abandon her hostility and to favour the Romans (*Aen.* 1. 281). Various occasions for her reconciliation have been suggested, of which perhaps the most attractive is the ceremony performed to appease Juno in 207 BCE, when twenty-seven virgins sang a hymn of expiation composed by Rome's first poet, Livius Andronicus (Liv. 27. 37. 7–15).[146] As far as Ennius' divine plot is concerned, it is especially important to note that Juno's husband and brother, Jupiter, almost certainly had a part to play in her capitulation, convincing her of the futility of further effort by prophesying Rome's inevitable victory.[147] Ennius was presumably the

---

[143] Serv. *Aen.* 1. 281 (Enn. *Ann.* 8. xvi); cf. Vahlen (1903), clix; Buchheit (1963), 146; Skutsch (1985), 204.     [144] Above, p. 116.

[145] Note the way in which Ovid's Juno turns up as an antagonist of the Romans, helping the Sabines, even after her acquiescence in the apotheosis of Aeneas (*Met.* 14. 592–3): *Met.* 14. 781–2 (cf. *Fast.* 1. 265–6).

[146] Feeney (1984), 193 n. 94; Skutsch (1985), 466.

[147] *Ann.* 8. xv, with Skutsch (1985) ad loc.

first to cast the Hannibalic war as a struggle between Rome and
Carthage for rule over the world,[148] and the scene between Jupiter
and Juno will have been the most powerful possible actualization
of this theme's resolution, as the Carthaginians' chief goddess
abandoned her people in order to become wholly Roman, recon-
ciled with Jupiter Optimus Maximus.

Jupiter's prophecy may well have owed much to the prophecy
of Naevius' Jupiter, foretelling the same result over the same enemy. Throughout, Jupiter will have shown the same concern for
the victory of Roman arms as he had in Naevius.[149] Whatever
other manifestations Jupiter may have had in the poem, as a god
of nature, or as Homer's Zeus, he was before all the Capitoline
god of the Roman people. When a goddess addressed Jupiter in
Naevius, he had been adorned both with Homeric epithets and
with one of his two Capitoline cult titles, *optumum*, 'Best' (fr. 15–
16). Ennius performs exactly the same operation, blending the
other cult title, *maximus*, 'Greatest', into an Homeric line of address.[150] The first half of the Homeric line (ὦ πάτερ ἡμέτερε,
Κρονίδη, 'O our father, son of Cronus', *Il.* 8. 31), goes directly
into Ennius' Latin as *o genitor noster Saturnie* ('O our father, son
of Saturn', 444). The second half (ὕπατε κρειόντων, 'highest of
the ruling gods') becomes *maxime diuom*, 'greatest of the gods'.
Zeus is now Jupiter Optimus Maximus, and the world he rules is
now a Roman world.

Many Roman epic poems intervene in the 150 years between
Ennius' *Annales* and Vergil's *Aeneid*, which was published after
the poet's death in 19 BCE. All are now lost, and since all but one
were historical poems, their fragments may be conveniently discussed in Chapter 6, where the problems of historical epic will
confront us directly. Now, after the survey of how Greek epic poetry and scholarship came to Rome, we may turn to the *Aeneid* itself, inheritor of these powerful traditions.

---

[148] The key passages are Lucr. 3. 833–7, with Liv. 29. 17. 6, 30. 32. 2, and Verg.
*Aen.* 1. 17–18, 4. 106; see Kenney (1971), on Lucr. 3. 832–42; Feeney (1984), 181.

[149] On his involvement even in the portions of the poem which covered the
events of the third century, see Wülfing-von Martitz (1972), 282–3, with the comments of Suerbaum, 287.

[150] The link with Naevius would be even tighter if we could be sure that the
speaker in Ennius is the same as in Naevius, namely, Venus: see Skutsch (1985), on
444.

# 4

## Vergil's *Aeneid*

### I

Τίνα, ἦν δ᾽ ἐγώ, δύναμιν ἔχον;
'Possessing what power?' I asked.

Plato, *Symposium* 202 e

Arma uirumque cano, Troiae qui primus ab oris
Italiam fato profugus Lauiniaque uenit
litora, multum ille et terris iactatus et alto
ui superum, saeuae memorem Iunonis ob iram,
multa quoque et bello passus, dum conderet urbem
inferretque deos Latio; genus unde Latinum
Albanique patres atque altae moenia Romae.
Musa, mihi causas memora, quo numine laeso
quidue dolens regina deum tot uoluere casus
insignem pietate uirum, tot adire labores
impulerit. tantae animis caelestibus irae?

I sing of arms and a man, who first from the shores of Troy, an exile by fate came to Italy, to Lavinium; and he was much buffetted both on land and sea by the violence of the gods above, because of the unforgetful anger of savage Juno; he suffered much in war as well, until he could found his city and bear his gods into Latium: from this origin come the Latin race, the Alban fathers, and the walls of high Rome. Muse, recount to me the reasons why, tell me what offence to her divinity it was, or what pain the queen of the gods had suffered, which made her force a man famous for his piety to go through such a cycle of disasters, to undergo so many ordeals. Do minds of the heavenly ones have such vast anger? (*Aen.* 1. 1–11)[1]

---

[1] Bibliography on the *Aeneid*'s gods, and related topics, in Suerbaum (1980–1), 62–70, 163–8; the most important general treatments are Heinze (1915), 291–318, indispensable here as elsewhere; Kühn (1971); Thornton (1976); Johnson (1976);

War, a man, then fate; and not fate alone, but the anger of a savage goddess, with the narrator compelled to ask the Muses for aid in explaining how a deity can persecute a man of such piety. Characters in tragedy had expressed the same resourceless shock;[2] here it is the poet who is at a loss. The question also has a purchase in centuries of philosophical debate concerned with denying the gods such motivations of anger.[3] In these opening lines the problem posed by the question, the problem of the goddess as a personality, is sharpened by the proximity of the general 'fate' of line 2, and the vague 'gods' carried by the hero. Is this a question which the poem can answer?

While the devastating question still resonates, the poet moves into the action with superbly economical power, expounding Juno's motives, introducing the goddess in speech and action, setting the narrative in train. Within three hundred lines we have experienced the great storm begun by Aeolus at Juno's instigation, seen it calmed by Neptune, and heard the conversation between Venus and Jupiter in which the eventual triumph of Aeneas and his descendants is prophesied. In sharp contrast to Apollonius, and adhering rather to the Odyssean model, Vergil begins with the gods dominating the frontispiece of the poem. These first three hundred lines provide, in fact, a rich display-case of the prime techniques which the poem will deploy in its treatment of the gods. We may begin by following through these opening sections, to pick out the themes which will principally concern us in this chapter.

*Urbs*, 'city', is the first word after the proem. Not Rome, nor even Troy, but Carthage, and Juno is its goddess. 'She is *said—fertur—*to have favoured this city above all others' (15). Such language of tradition and authority will engage us throughout this chapter; here, Ennius' *Annales* are being established as the source, for Vergil goes on to sketch Juno's Ennian partisan zeal for Carthage,

---

Pötscher (1977); Coleman (1982); Williams (1983); Lyne (1987), 61–99. Hardie (1986) is not overtly a book on the gods of the *Aeneid*, but it is a book of such huge importance for the ideology of the poem that it must be mentioned here.

[2] Segal (1981), 70, citing Soph. *OT* 895–910, Eur. *Hipp.* 1103–10. The end of Euripides' *Bacchae* (esp. 1348–9) is particularly pertinent.

[3] Coleman (1982), 143–4, citing Cic. *Off.* 3. 102, *at hoc quidem commune est omnium philosophorum . . . numquam nec irasci deum nec nocere* ('but it is common ground for all the philosophers . . . that god never feels anger and never inflicts harm').

and her fear of the rival city of Rome (16–22). As in Ennius (and possibly Naevius), Juno here is to be viewed under the aspect of the Carthaginian Tanit.[4] Besides making Ennius' narrative of the Carthaginian wars into the *Aeneid*'s sequel, and thereby at once establishing Ennius as a cardinal model for the poem, the identification taps into one of divinity's main ways of being a vehicle for meaning. Juno stands here for her people, a people more hated and feared by the Romans than any other they ever met. Her presence at once establishes the fact that the gods of this poem are going to be indispensable elements of whatever historical statements it has to make.

The goddess is more than this, however. Lines 23–4 show her animosity stretching back into the past as well as forward into the future: *ueterisque memor Saturnia belli, / prima quod ad Troiam pro caris gesserat Argis* ('and remembering the old war, the one which she first of all had fought at Troy on behalf of her dear Argos'). Now she is the Greek, Homeric Hera, remembering the Trojan war and the catalogue of affronts suffered in the Greek epic tradition (24–8). No derogation is made here from the harsh wilfulness of Homer's Hera. In the cluster of her grievances against the people of Troy, the climax is the honour paid to the abducted Ganymede (*rapti Ganymedis honores*, 28). This is the poem's first allusion to Juno's consort, Jupiter, who raped Ganymede and now honours him. It is an oblique touch, but no more is needed on such a hoary topic.[5]

The historical perspective of Ennius and the mythical perspective of Homer converge in this one character, heightening and extending her force, and making her traditional malevolence oppressively meaningful in a Roman context. At the same time, the twin motivation of Juno's hate fixes the time of the poem's action in its own limbo between myth and history, moving out of the one and into the other, partaking of both and not fully involved in either. The rest of the poem will exist in the penumbra of transition which this deftness has so elegantly created,[6] while Juno's twin motivations will provide the poem's main elements of structure, and its principal thematic centres of gravity. All done in

[4] Above, pp. 116, 127.
[5] See p. 66 above.
[6] On this transitional atmosphere of the *Aeneid*, see Pöschl (1962), 23–4; Greene (1982), 66–7.

twenty lines. And some would have it that Vergil's gods are dispensable.

The goddess has not yet been figured in the narrative, and she has yet more facets. She speaks a soliloquy: a tragic prologue, in fact, which harps on her slighted honour, τιμή, (*honorem*, 49). Homer's Poseidon had been concerned that he would lose τιμή if his enemy Odysseus came safely and richly home (*Od.* 13. 128–9). This hint Vergil magnifies and filters through the masks of such outraged tragic deities as Aphrodite and Dionysus, who justify the havoc they are about to let loose.[7] Juno's rage has now been actualized for us, and given a context in a tradition which is itself intensely preoccupied with the problems of divine anger. The *honos* of Juno will recur, and re-engage our attention, at the crucial plot-turns of Books 7 and 12.[8]

Her passion must have consequence, and she approaches the king of the winds, Aeolus. After Juno as the chief object of Carthaginian devotion, Juno as the Hera of Homer, and Juno as the outraged tragic divinity, we are introduced to another way of apprehending the goddess, now according to the systems which allegorized the gods as forces in the natural world. By this tradition of interpretation, Vergil's audience will have known Juno as *aer*, the lower air, the sphere for storms of wind and cloud.[9] The identification is reinforced by the fact that, in the Iliadic scene which is Vergil's model here, Hera's minion speaks of a great storm which Hera stirred up against another of her hated enemies, Heracles— as he sailed from Troy (*Il.* 14. 249–56).

The entire context of the storm, as Hardie's powerful arguments have now shown, is saturated with a complex series of allegories, which have their beginning in physical allegories.[10] Vergil is here manipulating certain scholarly interpretations of Hesiod's *Theogony*, which presented Hesiod's picture of the Titans, imprisoned after their defeat by Zeus, as an allegory of the destructive natural power of storm-winds, kept in precarious control by divine providence.[11] It is certainly Jupiter's divine providence which curbs these titanic forces in Aeolus' cave (60–2), and Juno's

---

[7] Eur. *Hipp.* 10–22; *Bacch.* 45–6; cf. *Tro.* 69–71; Soph. *Aj.* 127–30.

[8] Harrison (1976), 103; Lyne (1987), 94–5.

[9] Above, p. 9; on this interpretation of Vergil's Juno, see Heinze (1915), 299; Thornton (1976), 48–9; Murrin (1980), 3–23.

[10] Hardie (1986), 90–7.

[11] Ibid., 95–6.

attempt to disrupt the dispensations of that providence is the first act in a struggle which will persist until the end of the poem.

As with the gods of Homer and Apollonius, the naturalistic behaviour of Juno and Aeolus, with all its decorum of speech and convention, is accommodated to the norms of contemporary society. Aeolus is like some petty client king, placed in control of a circumscribed area, given strict limits to his authority, and allowed to exercise it only on command: *regemque dedit qui foedere certo / et premere et laxas sciret dare iussus habenas* ('Jupiter gave the winds a king who, under fixed terms, might know how to constrain them and how to loosen the reins and give them their head—when he was ordered', 1. 62–3).[12] When Juno talks him around, she is the gracious matchmaker, selecting a suitable wife from her entourage (71–5).

In this capacity she is, naturally, discharging the prime function of the Roman and Greek wife of Jupiter or Zeus, as the goddess of marriage. To the Greeks, this function gave Hera the epithet Ζυγίη, 'goddess of the marriage-yoke'.[13] The same metaphor of joining gave the Latin epithets *Iuga* and *Iugalis*: one ancient etymology explained *Iuno Iuga* by the fact that people thought she joined marriages together (*quam putabant matrimonia iungere*).[14] Vergil suggests such an etymology when he has Juno say that she will join her nymph to Aeolus in marriage (*conubio iungam stabili*, 73). Indeed, Vergil appears to be manufacturing a connection between 'joining' and 'Juno', between *iungo* and *Iuno*, the 'dear *coniunx* of Jupiter'.[15] At this stage in the poem, Juno's joining is confined to her marriage-function alone. In the light of her catastrophic disruptive force, any extension of the etymology

---

[12] Philips (1980), 23–4 thinks rather of a proconsul or propraetor; see Henry (1873–92), vol. 1. 286–9, on the court atmosphere of the whole interaction between Juno and Aeolus.

[13] See Roscher 2. 1. 588–92 on Juno as goddess of marriage; Roscher 1. 2098–104, on Hera in this role; 1. 2103–4 on Ζυγίη.

[14] Paul. *Fest.* p. 104 M; cf. Roscher 2. 1. 588–9. On the importance of the links between Juno and marriage customs in this scene, see Williams (1968), 373–4; Della Corte (1983), 24.

[15] 1. 73 is repeated in Book 4 (126), where Juno's second plan to foil Aeneas is worked, again, through a marriage (to Dido) and a storm. There may be another play on this etymology at 1. 252, where Venus complains that she and the Trojans are being 'disjoined' from Italy by Juno (*disiungimur oris*). Valerius Flaccus appears to pick up Vergil's etymology, when he says that Juno seeks to join Medea to Jason (*Iuno duci sociam coniungere quaerit*, 6. 450).

appears out of the question. Yet by the end of the poem her joining etymology will come into its own.

Such is the conversation of Juno and Aeolus. Without further
ado, Aeolus lets loose the winds (81-3).

The storm caused by Juno and Aeolus is no freak event, but a sign
of a fundamental dislocation in the providential natural order: one
of the world's constituent elements is running amok. This agent of
natural chaos has already been shown to us as the representative
of the greatest historical obstacle to Rome's hegemony, and also
as an Homeric creature endowed with an unassuaged venom,
whose vindictiveness we know and fear from the Greek tradition.[16] What threatens the Trojan and Vergilian enterprise from
the beginning is a multivalent frustrating negativity which finds
actualization in one character, Juno, whose words and actions are
powerfully represented through the medium of various authoritative reading conventions. Each manner of looking at 'Juno' gives
something hostile and destructive: chaos threatens from all directions, from history, myth, and nature.[17] Yet the power with which
Juno is figured in the narrative acts as a magnet for these potentially disparate viewpoints, so that her savage force is greater than
the sum of its parts. The intellectual exercise of readjusting to the
different things Juno 'is' might have been a frigid operation, but
her speech, her ethos, her anthropomorphism succeed in directing
our response in one channel of fearful anxiety: her realization as a
character is vital to the strategy of expounding the levels at which
this poem will find its ways of meaning.[18] The distinctive nature of
the epic fiction is no discardable superfluity. It makes possible the
economical marshalling of our understanding of what is being illustrated; it goes even further, to involve us emotionally in that
process of understanding, to make the issues vital and, within the
terms of the narrative, credible.

Yet it is often claimed that the vividly anthropomorphic characterization of the gods detracts from the *Aeneid*'s force. The most

---

[16] Philips (1980) picks out many of these constituent elements in the make-up of
Juno, though his comments on the physical allegory are very dismissive.

[17] Pöschl (1962), 13-24.

[18] The dramatically successful realization of the character is the only way of
combining the diverse elements which scholars have regarded as fragmenting the
poem's gods into their constituent pieces: Greene (1963), 88; Gellie (1972), 142-4.

consistent recent exponent of this view is Gordon Williams,[19] in whose book the gods' 'unreality' is systematically set against the 'real world' of the human action. Williams criticizes the scene with Juno and Aeolus, for example, as 'pure rococo', together with the Neptune-scene which follows: 'Not only are we not being asked to believe; we are being asked not to believe.'[20] 'Belief' and 'reality' are significant problems in the *Aeneid*, as we shall see. In this context, however, Williams's approach betrays the instinctive modern antipathy to the epic norms of divine action. To ancient readers of Homer, as we saw in the first chapter, such particularizing of the gods' action could have the primary force of contributing to the authentication of the poetic fiction, rather than detracting from it.[21] Williams's consistent literalism concerning the 'real world' in the poem is the reverse side of the same coin: 'Such passages establish a connection between the divine machinery and the real world in such a way as to subvert literal interpretation of the former.'[22] This sentence makes more cogent sense if 'latter' is substituted for 'former' as the last word. The poem is neither a real world nor a transcription of one, a fact which we may call Roman values to attest on grounds of historicity alone, without engaging in formalist polemic.[23]

When the sea-god Neptune interrupts to quell the storm, Vergil maintains the same stereoscopic focus, so that Neptune is at once anthropomorphic actor and sea-element. When Neptune feels the tempest he is, in both aspects, 'greatly disturbed' (*grauiter commotus*, 126); yet his divine head is serene as it looks over the scene (*placidum*, 127).[24] His speech to the winds is a fine piece of characterization, masterful in its authority, contemptuous of the petty king who has forgotten his place (132–41). The austere dignity of the speech does not close off the scene, for the god and his assistants proceed to aid the Trojans. Cymothoe and Triton lever ships off the rocks on which they have stuck, and Neptune himself (*ipse*) sets them afloat with his trident (144–5). As Neptune moves

[19] Williams (1983); cf. Coleman (1982), 162–4.

[20] Williams (1983), 28.

[21] Above, pp. 49–51.

[22] Williams (1983), 28.

[23] For Livy, the period before the foundation of the city is clearly in a different category of historicity: *Praef.* 6–7.

[24] *placidum* already worried Servius; see Austin (1971), on both lines; and Heinze (1915), 299.

over the sea in his chariot, accompanied by his traditional cortège,[25] the poet's audience are at home in the world of art which adorned their houses and villas.[26]

Once again, the beauty and self-sufficiency of Neptune's actions are entirely necessary energy to infuse his re-establishment of harmony against chaos. Juno's storm and Neptune's pacification represent in one sequence the altercations which will govern the entire epic,[27] yet it is precisely its fictive exuberance which rescues the passage from the bald schematizations (order/disorder, chaos/harmony) that inevitably overtake it in our paraphrases. Peremptory demythologizing of the divine action here robs the poem of more than beauty and colour (though that would be sacrifice enough to protest against). It strips away the poem's power to engage us in the sweep of fear and release which makes the critics' isolated 'themes' mean something. Proust's response to Giotto's allegorical frescoes may offer us some guide to reading such Vergilian passages:

The 'Invidia' ... should have had some look on her face of envy. But in this fresco ... the symbol occupies so large a place and is represented with such realism; the serpent hissing between the lips of Envy is so huge, and so completely fills her wide-opened mouth that the muscles of her face are strained and contorted, like a child's who is filling a balloon with his breath, and that Envy, and we ourselves for that matter, when we look at her, since all her attention and ours are concentrated on the action of her lips, have no time, almost, to spare for envious thoughts. . . . But in later years I understood that the arresting strangeness, the special beauty of these frescoes lay in the great part played in each of them by its symbols, while the fact that these were depicted, not as symbols (for the thought symbolized was nowhere expressed), but as real things, actually felt or materially handled, added something more concrete and more striking to the lesson they imparted.[28]

The gods of the *Aeneid* may be 'figures', 'tropes', 'symbols', but only as Aeneas is a figure or a trope. Neptune and Juno need the

[25] 1. 147, 154–6; on the sea-cortège accompanying the god, see Bühler (1960), on Mosch. *Eur.* 115.

[26] See, e.g. the mosaic represented in Strong (1988), 187. Some of the audience may also have been made to think of cameos of Octavian riding over the sea like Neptune, celebrating his naval victories over enemies such as Sextus Pompeius and Antony: Zanker (1988), 96–7.

[27] Pöschl (1962), 13–24; Otis (1963), 227–35.

[28] Proust (1922), 108. We return in Chapter 7, Section III, to the question of the fictive power of allegories.

same fictive energy to be creators and channellers of meaning as does Aeneas. If we accept that the gods are figural, symbolic, in that they refer to areas of meaning beyond themselves, we need not then feel baffled at their 'unnecessary' colour and force. It is not the case that the poem's gods have too much verisimilitudinous energy to be symbols. Rather, the nature of fictive narrative is such that this type of symbol absolutely requires abundant, even redundant, fictive energy and power, if it is to succeed.[29]

Nor can the poem's first simile achieve its affect if the reader refuses to accord Neptune his proper status. In a profound inversion of the *Iliad*'s first paradigmatic similes (*Il.* 2. 144–6, 209–10, 394–7), Vergil compares the god's action in calming the storm to a human statesman's action in quelling a riot (1. 148–54). In its correlation of divine power in the cosmos and human power in history, the simile establishes one of the *Aeneid*'s cardinal areas of ambition: an ideal synthesis of the natural order and of Rome's historical order is something which the poem strives to establish as attainable.[30] The main narrative of the poem, directly involved with the divine agents of the cosmos, and pregnant with Rome's future system, occupies the interstices between Neptune's action and the action of the anonymous Roman statesman.[31]

Of all this divine involvement the exhausted Aeneadae know nothing. They make landfall near Carthage, have a meal, mourn their dead (157–222), and it is time for Jupiter's first appearance.

*et iam finis erat, cum Iuppiter aethere summo / despiciens ...* ('and now it was the end, when Jupiter, looking down from the highest point of heaven, . . .', 223).[32] From the beginning Jupiter is associated with the end. Aeneas has just expressed the hope that god will put an end to their sufferings (*dabit deus his quoque finem*, 199). His mother Venus will soon ask what end Jupiter will give for the Trojans' toils (*quem das finem, rex magne, laborum?*, 241).[33] The poet is already looking forward to the eventual end which Jupiter will impose on the poem, and on the anarchy of

---

[29] The failure of the gods of Silius will demonstrate the point (Chapter 6, Section IV).

[30] Pöschl (1962), 23–4; Hardie (1986) *passim*.

[31] Again, Pöschl (1962), 24; Hardie (1986), 204–5.

[32] I give a literal translation, not knowing what 'the end' refers to.

[33] Cf. Wlosok (1967), 32. Generally on the Venus–Jupiter scene, Wlosok (1967), 11–73; Kühn (1971), 19–27.

Juno, who, as befits the deity of the Kalends, has dominated the beginning: her second word is 'beginning' (*incepto*, 1. 37).[34] In the *Argonautica*, Zeus' part in the τέλος ('end, fulfilment') had been a problem of the highest importance, precisely because Apollonius had been so reticent about it at the outset.[35] Here, by contrast, Jupiter's association with the *finis* is given immediate prominence (although what the *finis* will be remains, until we get there, unknown).

Jupiter looks down from the highest part of the *aether*, the pure expanse above Juno's *aer*. As in the case of Neptune and Juno, Jupiter will simultaneously be associated with one of the world-elements, and realized in anthropomorphic terms. From their origins, Zeus and Jupiter are gods of the sky and weather,[36] and, in Neptune's claim that the sea is his by lot (*sorte*, 139), Vergil has already alluded to the traditional schemata of world division.[37] A further step is being taken here, however, for, as Hardie remarks, Vergil's 'elevation of Jupiter to the aether is consonant with the philosophically-tinged piety of Hellenistic times'.[38] The imperturbability posited of God by the philosophers does not carry over into the *Aeneid*, however, for Jupiter is 'tossing cares in his heart' (*iactantem pectore curas*, 227); and we soon see him kissing his daughter, in full anthropomorphism (256). This initial picture remains quite deliberately unemancipated from the Homeric norms which the ancient commentators picked out. Together with the earlier allusion to Jupiter's rape of Ganymede (28), these touches alert the reader from the outset to the fact that Jupiter, too, is a character. As an actor in an epic, how can he not be?

The crucial divine scene from the first epic of Rome is now activated, as Vergil recasts Naevius' conversation between Venus and Jupiter.[39] In Naevius, Venus had been, like Homer's Aphrodite,

---

[34] On Juno's association with the Kalends, see Ov. *Fast.* 1. 55; Macr. *Sat.* 1. 15. 18–20; Wissowa (1912), 185, 187–8.

[35] Above, pp. 58–65.

[36] Nilsson (1967), 390–401, on Zeus; Bailey (1935), 132–5, and Latte (1960), 79–81, on Jupiter. However much Cotta may protest against the identification (Cic. *Nat. D.* 3. 10–11), Jupiter's celestial character is clear even from such epithets as *Fulgur, Tonans*. On the identification of Zeus with the *aether*, see Buffière (1956), 106.

[37] Hom. *Il.* 15. 187–93; famously doubted by Callimachus in his *Hymn to Zeus*, 60–5.

[38] Hardie (1986), 315; cf. Wlosok (1967), 28 n. 6, and (1983), esp. 188.

[39] Above, pp. 109–11; Buchheit (1963), 53–7.

the partisan of Aeneas and the Trojans, as well as (almost certainly) the ancestress of the Roman people. She is all these things here, but the intervening years have delivered a stupendous bonus into the hands of the later poet, for the ruler of Vergil's world was a Julius. Venus' son Aeneas is now not simply the ancestor of the Roman people, but the founder, through his son Iulus, of the family of Julius Caesar, and of his son, Augustus.[40] In Naevius and Ennius the gods had been concerned with their human offspring in mythical time, and with the Roman race as a whole in historical time. In the *Aeneid*, by virtue of a spectacular historical accident, the same divine concern for the same particular family can be made to extend from mythical time down into the very era of the poet and his audience. As Venus Genetrix, 'Venus the Ancestress', the goddess had become a primary element of Julius Caesar's religious programme, and Vergil looks here to a fruitful confusion over the question of whose ancestress she might be imagined to be: the Romans altogether (as in Lucretius' first line), or the family alone, or the emperor exclusively.[41]

Venus remonstrates with her father, reminding him of his promise that the descendants of the Trojans would rule the world (234–7). These words look like an echo of how Jupiter had spoken in Naevius and Ennius. We may, at any rate, detect a Homeric pattern for the deal to which Venus alludes, whereby Troy would fall, but the future glory of the survivors' heirs would be a compensation for Venus (238–9).[42] To console his daughter, Jupiter pronounces the future of Aeneas and his people. As he speaks, the time-perspective opens up, extending right down to the poet's day, so that a mere seven words concern the action of the poem: *bellum ingens geret Italia populosque ferocis / contundet* ('he will wage a huge war in Italy, and crush fierce peoples', 263–4). Jupiter's foresight appears to be not simply a matter of knowledge, for the fates (*fata*) which he reveals are his will: by a bald etymological play, Jupiter gives us to understand that the *fata* ('things

---

[40] Spelt out by Jupiter at 1. 286–90. On the power of this (pre-Vergilian) myth of the descent of the Julii, see Wlosok (1967), 62–3, 119–20; Weinstock (1971), 15–18, 80–90.

[41] On the usefully malleable epithet of the goddess, see Weinstock (1971), 85; Taylor (1931), 63–4; Schilling (1954), 316. We return to these issues in Section II of the next chapter.

[42] Harrison (1984a), 105, taking in *Aen.* 4. 227–31 as well.

said') are what *he* 'says' (*fabor*, 261).[43] His very first words, a promise that the fates of Venus' people remain unmoved (257–6), are a direct response to Venus' accusation that he has changed his mind, and gone back on his promise (234–7). That fate is what he promised, and Venus' aggrieved question, as Jupiter acknowledges (260), implies that fate would be different if he altered his mind.[44]

The question of the relationship between Jupiter and Fate will demand some discussion further on. Here, we may note only that the viewpoint of Jupiter is not that of a detached author of events, for he speaks, first as a father, but more significantly, as the national god of the Roman state. In his first sentence, the Aeneadae are Venus' people (*tuorum*, 257), but once his survey has reached the foundation of Rome the Romans become his.[45] He foretells Juno's eventual reconciliation: *consilia in melius referet, mecumque fouebit / Romanos* ('she will bring her policies around for the better, and will cherish the Romans along with me', 281–2). He will extract due payment of the promise his wife gave in the *Iliad*, and ensure that the Romans subdue her favoured cities as they conquer Greece.[46] From this partisan angle, the *imperium populi Romani* is, very remarkably, a slavery:

> ueniet lustris labentibus aetas
> cum domus Assaraci Pthiam clarasque Mycenas
> seruitio premet ac uictis dominabitur Argis.

With the gliding passage of lustral cycles, an age will come when the house of Assaracus will oppress Pthia and famous Mycenae with slavery, and be the slave-master over conquered Argos. (283–5)[47]

By this stage of his speech, the directing god of the universe is even dividing future time with the distinctive Roman measurement of the *lustrum*.[48]

[43] On the etymology, see Serv. *Aen.* 2. 54, and the material collected by Commager (1981), 102.

[44] So Henry (1873–92), vol. 1. 556–7; Lyne (1987), 73–4.

[45] Note the reversal of this pattern in the mirror scene at the end of the poem, where Juno, speaking to Jupiter, refers to the Romans as *tuorum* (12. 820).

[46] At *Il.* 4. 51–4 Hera says that she will sacrifice Argos, Sparta, and Mycenae if she can have the destruction of Troy; in 1. 284–5, Vergil mentions two of these three, and substitutes the home of Achilles for Sparta. Greeks could speak of, for example, the destruction of Corinth in 146 BCE as being the revenge of the Aeneadae for the sack of Troy: *Anth. Pal.* 7. 297; 9. 381. 6.

[47] On the empire of the *populus Romanus* as a slavery, see Weinstock (1971), 51–2.

[48] Conington–Nettleship–Haverfield (1858–98), ad loc.: 'It will be observed that "lustra" being a strictly Roman measure of time, Jupiter is thus made to speak the language of the great nation.'

The Roman domain is an empire without end (279): *his ego nec metas rerum nec tempora pono* (278). No limit in time or space: not an unrooted grandiloquence, but a precise reference to the origin of the cult of Jupiter Optimus Maximus, in whose precinct remained two gods when the site was being cleared for the great temple—Terminus and Iuuentas, Boundary and Youth, guarantors with Jupiter of Rome's limitless expanse and duration.[49] As Jupiter speaks, Rome does not yet exist, and his sacred hill, the Capitol, is covered in thickets. Yet he is there on the hill (8. 347–54), and his local manifestation will grow as the empire grows, so that the people and the god will together occupy all available space, assimilating everything.

Jupiter's national force as Rome's god is a mighty counterbalance to Juno's role as Carthage's chief deity, while his concern for the people as a unit is to be set against the personal concern for her son and family which is shown by Venus.[50] On his first appearance, like the Jupiter of Naevius and Ennius, Vergil's supreme god speaks, through one facet of his make-up, as the god of the Roman state; he does not here afford an impersonal vantage-point for the reader.

Immediately after Jupiter's awe-inspiring revelation, the gulf between the knowledge of men and gods establishes itself, as Jupiter sends Mercury to Libya, to ensure that Queen Dido does not, in her ignorance of fate, deny hospitality to Aeneas (297–300). *fati nescia Dido*, she is called: ignorant of *fate*, ignorant of what Jupiter has just said.[51]

These first 300 lines introduce half a dozen divine characters, and as many ways of regarding the gods, through different conventions of reading and understanding. They are inescapably the gods of Homer, set in the same fundamental laws of epic action; they are also the gods of Naevius and Ennius; the gods of various national cults, with the attendant historical force; the gods of

---

[49] On the stories, and especially on the apparently late addition of Iuuentas, see Ogilvie (1970), on Liv. 1. 55. 3, and 5. 54. 7. According to Ogilvie, the stress on Iuuentas may be owing to initiatives set in train by Augustus at the very time at which the *Aeneid* was being composed. In his discussion of the relationship of Terminus and Iuuentas with Jupiter, Dumézil (1970), 202 refers to these lines of the *Aeneid*.

[50] Wlosok (1971), 21–2, on the differing motivations of Jupiter and Venus.

[51] Commager (1981), 105–6. In a slip which reveals how instinctive it is for many scholars to exempt Jupiter from characterful machination, Bailey (1935), 215 attributes the sending of Mercury to Venus, not Jupiter.

specific family and personal allegiance; the gods of nature, the constructs of learned interpretation of the earliest poetry. Jupiter and Juno in particular partake of virtually all these elements, so that the reader has been alerted to the variety of ways in which the divine characters generate meaning. There is no one key, no great trope: even the nature-correspondences, which approximate most closely to allegory, are discontinuous, not operating throughout at consistent pressure.[52]

Along with these conventions, various significant preoccupations have emerged, many only tentatively: the problem of divine justice; the question of the poet's tradition and authority; the power-structure among the gods, with the related problem of Fate; the interplay of myth and history; the gap between human and divine perspectives. Many of these preoccupations impinge on one another, and the best way into exploring them will be by investigating the main lines of the gods' plot. Throughout, it will be necessary to be selective, even (at times) brusque, for the poem's divine elements are richly complex, and the bulk of scholarly discussion overwhelming.

How, then, do Jupiter and Juno act in the plot? Most importantly, how is the poem's initial stand-off between Juno and Jupiter resolved, to achieve the 'end', *finis*, which Juno's beginning had thrown up as a problem for Aeneas and Venus?

After his sending of Mercury, Jupiter fades out of the poem for some time, to reappear with terrifying force in Aeneas' account of the sack of Troy. Aeneas is standing on the roof of Priam's palace, when his mother Venus appears to him undisguised, and reveals that the gods are destroying his city.[53] She removes the mist that clogs all mortal vision, so that he may see the gods at their terrible work—the ancient city-dweller's final nightmare (2. 604–23). At the climax of the revelation, after Neptune, Juno, and Pallas, is Jupiter himself (617–18), urging on the gods in fulfilment of the promise which he had made to Hera/Juno in the *Iliad*, that he would accede to the destruction of the city after the death of Hector.[54]

---

[52] 'Discontinuous' is the word of Murrin (1980), 23; generally, on the 'discontinuous' and 'polysemous' nature of the gods' representation, Murrin (1980), 19–24.

[53] 2. 589–93. Venus never appears to her former lover, Anchises, although she certainly had done so in Naevius (fr. 4 Büchner) and almost certainly in Ennius (19 Skutsch (1985), with 15–16).

[54] *Il.* 15. 69–71; see here Harrison (1970), 320.

This is a vision of the highest horror, but Aeneas and his father Anchises soon experience a token of Jupiter's concern for the Aeneadae, as the god thunders in answer to Anchises' prayer, sanctioning the family's flight from the burning city (2. 692–3). Certainly the shift in perspective is dismaying,[55] yet the reader has already had assurances that the end of Troy is a beginning, and that the reborn Trojans will in their turn exact revenge for the sack of their city. Jupiter promised as much to Venus in Book 1 (283–5), and the deceitful Greek, Sinon, unwittingly confirms the prophecy, when he tells King Priam the 'lying' tale of the Trojans' future assault upon the cities of Greece (2. 192–4).[56] The *Aeneid* reflects the tragic insights into the guilt and suffering of victory which the sack of Troy is capable of representing in the *Odyssey*, and especially in Athenian tragedy:[57] besides the long-range fate of Greece, the poem points to the sufferings of Ulysses, Ajax, Diomedes, and Neoptolemus.[58]

Anchises believes that he and his family are entitled to survive because of their *pietas* (2. 690). Jupiter's own view is bluntly put when he next intervenes, in Book 4, sending Mercury to force Aeneas to leave Carthage, and Dido: Aeneas is important because his Roman descendants will rule the world (229–31). Here too, the reader encounters open use of the anthropomorphic conventions of epic. Until he is alerted to the liaison of Aeneas and Dido, the highest god appears (or is allowed) not to notice.[59] In one respect, Vergil's Jupiter here is distinct from Homer's Zeus, for he is not stirred to the passion of anger.[60] This apparent response to the purging demanded by the scholars and philosophers has, however, its own disconcerting implications. Jupiter's reaction is, strictly,

---

[55] Too dismaying for Austin (1964), xx–xxi.

[56] Block (1981), 272–3.

[57] *Od.* 1. 326–7; 8. 521–31. Aeschylus' *Agamemnon* is of course the major tragic exposition of this theme; it is constantly recurring in Euripides: *Troades*, *Hecuba*, *Orestes*, *Andromache*, even *Helen*. The painting of the fall of Troy in the Athenians' Stoa Poikile focused on the moment when the Greeks met to discuss the rape of Cassandra by Ajax (Paus. 1. 15. 2).

[58] Diomedes' speech in *Aeneid* 11 is Vergil's most extended treatment of this topic, where he goes through the vicissitudes of the Greek heroes (255–77); cf. 1. 39–41; 3. 330–2. This pervasive interpretation of the Greek victory over Troy explains much of the force behind Vergil's need to recast the Trojan victory over the Latins as a second version of the *Iliad* (Anderson (1957) ); it is his most economical way of associating Aeneas with the moral failures of victory.

[59] Lyne (1987), 78, 84–5; cf. Coleman (1982), 163–4, for some revealing misgivings about the anthropomorphism of Jupiter here.

[60] Kühn (1971), 66–7.

inhuman. A god who can feel anger can feel pity, and this god appears to feel neither. Even Juno can feel pity.[61]

Sexual passion, at least, is within the scope of Vergil's Jupiter.
The prayer which moves him to action is delivered by one Iarbas,
the son of Jupiter (in his African manifestation as Hammon) by a
raped African nymph (*rapta Garamantide nympha*, 4. 198). At the
moment when Aeneas is to be separated from Dido, Vergil activates the inveterate distinction between human responsibility and
divine imperviousness, by showing the inconsequentiality of the
god's sexual involvement beside the catastrophic repercussions of
the human's.[62] This is the second time that Jupiter has furthered
his ends by separating Aeneas from a woman he loves. As Aeneas
leaves burning Troy, he panics, and loses contact with his wife,
Creusa: *nescio quod trepido male numen amicum / confusam
eripuit mentem* ('some hostile divinity, I don't know which,
robbed me of my confused wits in my panic', 2. 735-6). He is un-
sure whether his wife's disappearance was the work of fate or
chance (2. 738-9), but is finally told by the very ghost of Creusa
that Jupiter's decision was responsible (778-9).

Once the Trojans have arrived in Latium, Jupiter's concern for
the Trojan enterprise displays itself again, for he sets up the table-
eating prodigy (7. 110), and marks Aeneas' favourable acknowledgement with a triple roll of thunder (141-3). The very next
time he acts, he is granting the same honour to Aeneas' son,
Ascanius, as a sign that Juno's hostility will prove futile (9. 630-
1).[63] For by this stage Jupiter's wife and sister is operating openly
against his concern, shattering the apparent accomplishment of
the arrival in Book 7. Under her instigation Turnus attacks the
Trojan camp while Aeneas is away. As the hero rages within the
Trojan walls, aided by the goddess, Jupiter intervenes to stop the
two of them (9. 803-5), and forthwith convenes a divine council
to resolve the catastrophe (10. 1).

For many years the council of the gods was read as a stirring vindication of the highest god's sublime authority, yet a number of
recent studies have concentrated on the equivocations of Jupiter's

---

[61] 4. 693; 10. 686. On the one occasion when Jupiter is spoken of as feeling pity,
it is the interpretation of the character Anchises (5. 727).

[62] Griffin (1986), 100-1.

[63] On the links between all these signs from Jupiter, see Harrison (1985), 144-5.

response to the contending claims of Venus and Juno.[64] At the very least we must take stock of the way in which Jupiter's incorporation as a character necessarily involves him in characterful reactions and assertions. He is engaged in a nexus with other characters from which he cannot be extricated. Simply stopping the war by *fiat* seems not to be an option, and his grand declaration of impartiality at the end of the council, with its vague gesture towards the fates, resists quasi-theological exegesis: *rex Iuppiter omnibus idem. / fata uiam inuenient* ('the kingship of Jupiter will be the same for all: the fates will find a way', 10. 112–13). Heinze would cut the knot with his blunt declaration that, if Jupiter had asserted himself, the poem would have been over and done with.[65] Yet Jupiter does not simply hold back for the moment from imposing his planned end, for the end, when it comes, is, as we shall see, a compromise. Venus wants Aeneas' foundation to be another Troy (10. 60–2), and it might appear from Jupiter's words in Book 1 that his aim accords with hers; yet the poem's solution shows Jupiter moving away from that position, towards Juno's.

Still, victory for Aeneas is indispensable for any resolution. It does seem mistaken to read Jupiter's last words in the council as promising abstention, since he works steadily to achieve Trojan victory, and his language of impartiality is revealed as a blind.[66] From three books out, for over two and a half thousand lines, the poem gathers to its end in a sustained crescendo of power which has no parallel in epic. Only Jupiter is powerful enough to achieve the poem's *finis*. He will intervene decisively at the climax, with his mighty question to Juno, his wife (*quae iam finis erit, coniunx?*, 'what now will the end be, wife?', 12. 793), but his increasingly oppressive direction is felt throughout this portion, as he gradually moves away the obstacles until Aeneas and Turnus can stand face to face and the poem can stop. We are to understand him watching events in Latium throughout (10. 473, 606–10, 758).

Jupiter first prevents the meeting of Pallas and Lausus (10. 436–

---

[64] Vindication: Klingner (1967), 566–8; Kühn (1971), 139–40; otherwise, Harrison (1980), 390; Block (1981), 86–92, Lyne (1987), 88–90.

[65] Heinze (1915), 297 n. 1.

[66] Harrison (1980), 389–90; my whole discussion of Jupiter's actions in these last three books is much indebted to Harrison's clear presentation.

8), since Pallas must fall to Turnus, to provide the spark for Aeneas' eventual killing of Turnus, and Lausus must fall to Aeneas, to trigger the duel between Mezentius and Aeneas. Pallas is duly dispatched by Turnus in the next episode, with Jupiter looking on and declining to intervene (10. 467–73). A deal with Juno preserves Turnus for the while, the first delay of many (*mora*, 10. 622). In Turnus' absence, the mighty Mezentius dominates the field, and his death at the hands of Aeneas is set in train by Jupiter: *Iouis interea monitis* . . . ('meanwhile, at the prompting of Jupiter', 689). In the next book, likewise, the main enemy of the Trojans, Camilla, is disposed of as the result of a roundabout chain of causality which can be traced back to Jupiter.[67] Her dying words abort the plan of Turnus to ambush Aeneas, and this too is what 'the savage will of Jupiter demanded' (*et saeua Iouis sic numina poscunt*, 11. 901). Jupiter's 'savagery', once activated, has doomed Camilla, protected Aeneas, and left the two antagonists to face each other at last. There is still one book of extraordinary tension to go, with delay after delay being contrived by Juno and her forced accomplice, Juturna, the sister of Turnus, herself a nymph who has been raped by Jupiter (12. 140–1). After diverse false starts and initial clashes, Aeneas and Turnus, one with a sword, one with a spear, charge against each other for the final moment of the duel (12. 788–90). And Jupiter speaks to Juno: *quae iam finis erit, coniunx?* ('what now will the end be, wife?', 12. 793).

What has brought Juno to this final moment? Since the poem's opening, her plans have received one set-back after another. In Book 4 she tries to detain Aeneas in Carthage by exploiting her status as the marriage-goddess, producing a marriage that is not a marriage (4. 90–172); the only result, by causing hostility between Aeneas and Dido, is to make inevitable the eventual destruction of Carthage which she is fighting to prevent. In Book 5 she tries to keep the Trojans in Sicily by having Iris burn their ships (5. 605–63); all she achieves is the foundation of the city of Segesta (5. 718), which will be Rome's staunch ally in the First Punic War. In Book 7 her actions reach a climax, as she unleashes the demon Allecto to destroy the pact between Trojans and Latins, and herself opens the gates of War (7. 286–622). The mirror-scene of

---

[67] Harrison (1980), 389–90.

Juno's discord in Book 1 gave way within two hundred lines to the reassurance of Jupiter's speech to Venus (1. 257–96), but in the second half of the poem, we must wait for six books to reach Jupiter's resolution.

As her husband and brother addresses her in the last book, she is passive in a cloud, still in her element,[68] looking at the duel. Jupiter's reproofs are stern, his prohibitions final: *uentum ad supremum est . . . ulterius temptare ueto* ('we have arrived at the final moment . . . I forbid you to make any further efforts', 12. 803, 806). Her frustration seems complete as she answers with a submissive expression (807), yet the conversation takes an unexpected turn. Juno's fight all along has been against the rebirth of Troy, and in this her last speech she bargains to win her point. Let the two peoples join, let there be a Latium, Alban kings, yes, even a Roman race—but Troy must go for ever: the hated name is Juno's last word in the poem:

> sit Latium, sint Albani per saecula reges,
> sit Romana potens Itala uirtute propago:
> occidit, occideritque sinas cum nomine Troia.

Let there be a Latium, let there be Alban kings through the centuries, let there be a Roman race, powerful with Italic virtue: Troy has fallen, allow it to stay fallen, name and all. (12. 826–8)[69]

This point she wins,[70] as Jupiter smilingly acknowledges that her vast anger is a true token of godhead, and of her kinship with himself:

> olli subridens hominum rerumque repertor:
> 'es germana Iouis Saturnique altera proles,
> irarum tantos uoluis sub pectore fluctus.
> uerum age et inceptum frustra summitte furorem:
> do quod uis, et me uictusque uolensque remitto . . .'

Smiling at her, the author of mankind and the world spoke: 'You *are* the sister of Jupiter, the other offspring of Saturn—so vast are the waves of anger which you roll beneath your breast. Come now, lay down the

---

[68] On 12. 792, *de nube tuentem*, Servius comments: *de aere, de elemento suo* ('from the *aer*, her own element').

[69] It will not do to quote the first two of these three lines only, and present them as some kind of celebration by Juno, as does Jenkyns (1985), 74 n. 60; the first two lines are, as it were, a μέν clause, with the third as a δέ clause.

[70] Though not as clearly as she thinks, if Lyne (1987), 81–3 is right in his interpretation of 12. 835–40.

madness which you began to no avail: I give what you want; overcome, willingly, I waive my claim . . .' (12. 829–33)

His words also betray, to the readers who know their Ennius, Jupiter's oblique recognition of her other unspoken grievance—Carthage. From the start, like the great goddesses of Naevius and Ennius, with their double motivations,[71] she has had two motives for her hostility to the Aeneadae, one mythological (the judgement of Paris and all the Homeric matter connected with the name of Troy), and one historical (her predilection for Carthage and fear of the fate that awaits the city at the hands of Aeneas' descendants). This second, historical, motive is the engine that supplies the momentum of the narrative of Books 1 and 4, which culminates in Dido's curse and the evocation of Hannibal, to engage Rome and Carthage irrevocably in future warfare (4. 622–9). In this final scene only Juno's mythological grievance is removed; the other remains potent, its consequences already irresistibly in train.[72] Juno knows it, and Jupiter knows it; hence his chillingly suave acknowledgement of the vast anger she still feels.[73]

The final scene does accomplish something which the momentum of the poem establishes as worth accomplishing. This much is guaranteed even by the elaborate formal correspondences between the Jupiter-scene in 12 and the Jupiter-scene in 1:[74] the relief which Jupiter promises Venus may not be unalloyed when it comes at the end of the poem, but, in some measure, it does come. What the scene between Juno and Jupiter resolves is the question of Aeneas' settlement in Latium, and the final passing away of Troy. It does not resolve any more of Juno's grudges. The divine reconciliation is qualified to the extent that it reflects only so much of the Roman endeavour as has been accomplished so far; it leaves open what historically remains open. Just as in the *Iliad*, where the last book re-establishes the relentless nature of the gods' animosities,[75] so in the *Aeneid* the immortal sphere remains unrecon-

---

[71] Above, pp. 116–17, 125.

[72] Note here the loaded 'meanwhile' which signals Juno's departure (*interea*, 12. 842).

[73] Other readings of this scene which stress the qualified nature of Juno's reconciliation: Conway (1935), on 1. 281; Büchner (1955–8), 1457; Harrison (1984*a*); Rudd (1986), 41–2; Lyne (1987), 94–8; above all, Johnson (1976), 123–7.

[74] On these correspondences, see Knauer (1964), 324–7; Kühn (1971), 164–5; Buchheit (1974), 499–501.

[75] Davies (1981).

ciled within itself at the close. Yet whereas in the *Iliad* mortals are permitted to achieve a reconciliation, in the *Aeneid* they are denied this much.[76] The end of the *Aeneid* establishes a powerful contrast between the deadly weakness of men's efforts and the ease with which the gods can make an arrangement while still unreconciled in full: this is their essential invulnerability, their power. Homer's gods reach a temporary accommodation without their grievances being abnegated; Juno does the same with Jupiter, winning a point, losing a point, and deferring a third.

Accommodations with Juno and Hera are fundamentally of this nature. The goddess is 'dangerous, malicious, and implacable in her rage',[77] so that her relentments are paradigms of tenuous reconciliation. In the *Iliad* her agreements with Zeus are conditional, and continually liable to fracture. In Greek cult, as Burkert says, 'wherever we learn any details about Hera festivals we discover that it is never simply a joyful wedding feast, but a deep crisis in which the established order breaks down and the goddess herself threatens to disappear.'[78] To the Romans Juno was particularly disquieting. The other Latins, and the Etruscans, honoured the goddess more than they did;[79] we may note here a parallel with Hera's unsympathetic representation in Athenian tragedy, for Hera 'had no special connection with Athens, which facilitated her acquisition of a malignant *persona*'.[80] As Tanit, she was the chief goddess of the Romans' chief enemy, Carthage, and their earliest poetry will have shown her in this role.[81] Ennius' *Annales* may well have shown Juno making a provisional agreement in the first book, as a model for Vergil's scene in his last book.[82] Horace's ode about the apotheosis of Romulus may also depend on the Ennian scene; there Juno's reconciliation is hedged about with conditions, her wrath provisionally given over.[83]

The physical allegory had its own ways of acknowledging the

[76] Davies (1981), 61.
[77] Burkert (1985), 134; cf. Bond (1981), xxiv–v.
[78] Burkert (1985), 134.
[79] Wissowa (1912), 187–9; cf. Feeney (1984), 193–4. She was, of course, part of the Capitoline triad from Etruscan times, but dramatically inferior to Jupiter in cult.
[80] Bond (1981), xxv n. 30.
[81] Above, pp. 116–17, 127.
[82] Above, pp. 125–7.
[83] 3. 3. 30–68; further, Feeney (1984), 193–4.

phenomenon which Greek cult presented as Hera's threatened disappearance, and which myth presented as tenuous agreements between Zeus and Hera, Jupiter and Juno. It saw a perpetual
alternation of antagonism and rapprochment between the elements of *aer* and *aether*, and of wet and heat.[84] When Plutarch
was confronted with the festival of the Daedala in Plataea, with its
enactment of a rupture between Zeus and Hera, followed by
reconciliation, it was natural for him to see the myth behind the
rite as a cover for the tussle between *aer* and *aether*: when Hera is
disaffected, then follow rain and storm, but when calm returns
after the flood, this is said to be the goddess's reconciliation with
Zeus.[85] Juno's chaos manifested itself in this same realm at the
very beginning, and it was in Jupiter's corresponding realm of
*aether* that the reader first encountered the supreme god (1. 223).
Now at the end Juno vacates her turbulent sphere as she moves
closer to Jupiter, towards provisional equilibrium. At the beginning of the scene Juno is looking down at the human action from
a cloud (12. 792), 'from her own element', as Servius comments;
at the end she leaves it (*nubemque relinquit*, 842).

Juno throughout has been the principal embodiment of the anarchy which threatens the progress of poem and empire, in opposition to the aspect of her *persona* and name which leads to
joining (*iungo*).[86] Yet this etymological force is not annulled, for
the disorderly goddess is the poem's principal force for structural
cohesion, initiating the two mighty storms which introduce the
poem's two halves, and returning now at the last, in the great
mirror-scene to the first divine action, to contribute to a pattern of
synthesis that is, for once, not only structural.[87] There is more
than a pleasing paradox here, for in her shifting relationship with
Jupiter we may catch a glimpse of the incomprehensible currents
of violence for order which are at the heart of the poem and its
empire. The poem can never forget, and can never let its readers
forget, that the Roman order is founded on institutionalized violence, and Juno's participation in the creation of Rome's essence is
one of the ways that the poem has of reflecting upon that inescap-

---

[84] Cornutus, *Theol. Graec.* 3; Ps.-Plut. *Vit. Hom.* 96; Serv. *Aen.* 1. 47; Macr.
*Comm. Somn. Scip.* 1. 6. 24–33 (*aer* and *ignis*); Buffière (1956), 106–10; Vernant
(1980), 103; Whitman (1987), 49.

[85] In Eusebius, *Prae. Ev.* 85 c–86 d.

[86] Above, nn. 13–14.

[87] Halter (1963), 78–93.

able truth.[88] Juno is not simply eclipsed, but remains an intractable emblem of the intractable and unpredictable lurchings of the historical process.[89] Without her, after all, there would not have been a Rome, but only another Troy.[90] The slow lapse of time might annul some of her aspects, and the poem can even allow for her eventual complete reconciliation in historical time; but at the end of the poem we have a moment of equilibrium in a shifting balance.

Her main antagonist is Jupiter, yet she is not simply defeated by him. Rather, he accommodates himself to her, as he realizes that her request for Troy's disappearance is not ruled out by fate (*nulla fati quod lege tenetur*, 12. 819).[91] *es germana Iouis* . . .; the kinship between them which Jupiter has acknowledged now comes into its own, as Jupiter moves forthwith to bring proceedings to a close, sending down from the highest point of heaven one of the twin Dirae, to force his former beloved, Juturna, to abandon her brother (12. 843–54). The phrase which describes his sending of the Dira from the highest point of heaven (*ab aethere summo*, 853) takes us back to Jupiter's first appearance, when he was looking down at the Aeneadae *ab aethere summo* (1. 223). The very first and the very last words in the first and last Jupiter-scenes are identical, so that we enter and leave Jupiter's realm with the same phrase, moving from a god tossing care in his chest for humans to a god paralysing his lover's brother, laying him open for the kill. The ghastly Dira is not the same creature as Juno's agent Allecto, but it is a close relative.[92] Juno's Allecto and Jupiter's Dira stand in polar relation to one another, for one brings disruption while the other imposes final order;[93] yet their similarities are not accidental. At Jupiter's moment of self-assertion he is *uictus* ('overcome', 833); when he acts, he employs an agent

---

[88] On the special character of the Roman state's use of violence, see the interesting discussion of Harris (1979), 50–3.

[89] Rudd (1986), 41–2, has some fine points on this matter.

[90] Indeed, as Professor Wills reminds me, without her Troy would never have fallen in the first place—so indispensable is Juno's (unwitting) contribution to the formation of the nature of Rome.

[91] Wilson (1979), 366.

[92] Hübner (1970), 12–34; Edgeworth (1986).

[93] Hübner (1970), 74–5. In a way, the Dira stands to Allecto as Jupiter stands to Juno: they are siblings, and share many qualities and effects, but have different functions.

whom we cannot but read as a creature of evil. Jupiter's force is Junoesque, not of a different essence from hers, as his acknowledgement of their kinship marks.[94]

For Jupiter is not beyond the world, or the poem. From the vantage-point of myth, we may regard this as a reflection of the fact that these gods are of the cosmos, not outside it. The gods (certainly not the Greek gods, and much less the Roman ones) did not create the world, but were born from its nature, so that Jupiter is an aspect of the way the world is. The generations of gods receive notice in the *Aeneid*, where we are regularly reminded that Jupiter supplanted his father, to rule in his stead.[95] Just as in the *Georgics*, then, in the *Aeneid* Jupiter is the emblem of the post-Saturnian age, an age where man must endure toil, disease, and misery.[96]

If Jupiter has his *imperium* from the supplanting of his father, the poem also follows the norms of the mythic and poetic tradition in asserting, at times, that he rules men and gods with might and fear, as his daughter declares at his first appearance: *o qui res hominumque deumque / aeternis regis imperiis et fulmine terres* ('Oh you who rule the affairs of men and gods with eternal commands, and terrify them with the thunderbolt', 1. 229–30). Power, with immortality, is the distinctive attribute of deity,[97] and Jupiter's power is supreme. His terrifying thunderbolts are the ultimate sanction, a blend of sound, fear, flame, and anger (*fulgores nunc terrificos sonitumque metumque / miscebant operi flammisque sequacibus iras*, 8. 431–2). The very core of his Roman manifestation is revealed in Book 8 to be based on the fear that the locals feel when storm and thunder surround the Capitoline hill.[98] The *Aeneid* is preoccupied with power before any other subject, and Vergil was not the first poet to be exercised by the problem of

---

[94] The chapter on *Aeneid* 12 by Putnam (1965), 151–201, stands at the source of any reading of the book which admits of anxieties over the figure of Jupiter; cf. Johnson (1976), 14–15.

[95] 8. 319–20; 9. 84.

[96] G. 1. 121 ff., with Ross (1987), 98, 142. Tibullus gives an endearingly pat thumbnail sketch of Jupiter's iron age: *nunc Ioue sub domino caedes et uulnera semper, / nunc mare, nunc leti mille repente uiae* (1. 3. 49–50). The *Aeneid*'s hopes for an Augustan restoration of the Golden Age are a notorious problem: for an interesting recent discussion, see Smolenaars (1987).

[97] Beller (1979); Armstrong (1986), 74–6.

[98] 8. 349–54; Hardie (1986), 218.

how the power of divine violence could be used for harmony.[99] The eventual order which Jupiter's power will enforce is one altogether congenial to the Roman state (1. 291–6); it is, indeed, an order guaranteed on earth by the power of the Roman state. The dilemmas involved in Rome's use of violence for order are a principal subject of the poem,[100] and they take their lead from the problems involved in the judgement of the state's patron god.

From the vantage-point of the poem's workings, seeing Jupiter as a character entails an analogous recognition of his ultimate accommodation—to the demands of the narrative system in which he figures.[101] Jupiter cannot be distilled out of the narrative, for he remains an agent, a character. He remains part of a nexus of relationships in which the apparently evil has its place; his area of operation includes (without sublimating) the realms of evil and death, as we see in his deal with Juno and his use of the Dira.

The Jupiter of the *Aeneid* has been considerably refined. It is, of course, clearly wrong to speak of him as free from Xenophanean moral lapses—the first allusion to Jupiter in the poem is a mention of the rape of Ganymede (1. 28), and he has raped females as well.[102] Still, he is not tricked, as Zeus so notoriously was in the *Iliad*, nor does the poem concentrate overtly on the physical basis of his supremacy over the gods in conflict.[103] More than one perspective is available on his control. In the scene where Venus appeals to Jupiter's rule of fear with the thunderbolt, we see him also as the beneficent controller of the elements, exercising a calming power by the force of his smile alone (*uultu, quo caelum tempestatesque serenat*, 1. 255).[104] Jupiter, to speak in social terms, is often seen in the poem presiding like a politic superior over an emerging consensus, preferring, if possible, not to force the issue.[105] Vergil's tactfulness in this matter creates many unresolved areas

[99] I am thinking especially of Aeschylus' *Oresteia*; on the frequently noted links between the end of that trilogy and the end of the *Aeneid*, see Harrison (1984*a*), 112.

[100] Lyne (1983); in the next Section we return to the problem of the exercise of power, in discussing the human characters who come closest to divine power.

[101] On 'accommodation', see p. 47 above.

[102] Lyne (1987), 85.

[103] *Il.* 14. 292–351 (tricked by Hera); *Il.* 1. 589–94; 8. 18–27; 15. 18–24 (physical supremacy).

[104] Cf. 10. 100–3; Hardie (1986), 328.

[105] Pötscher (1977), esp. 157, and (1978), 412–13.

of vagueness around Jupiter, Fate, and Providence, and this comparative reticence has opened the path to readings of Jupiter as an omniscient, omnipotent, and imperturbable—even impartial—Providence.[106] Some qualification of this traditional image has already emerged from discussion of the god as a character;[107] if it is difficult to glide over the implications of Jupiter's characterful participation, it is also difficult to accede to these attempts to find in Jupiter a vantage-point from which to dispel the problems created by the experience of reading the poem.

The Stoics are often called to account here, as the most prestigious advocates of the view that the problem of evil disappears if one takes up a perspective of sufficient detachment, regarding the world with the levelling gaze of the providential deity.[108] In fact, the Stoics themselves were mightily exercised by the problem of evil in the world, and their position on the theodicy question was not as monolithic as it is often pictured.[109] Still, it was possible to write an epic Jupiter who represented the providence of the world, the sum total of its parts. Cicero, for one, did exactly that.[110] The Aeneid, however, does not take this option.[111] Instead, it concentrates insistently on the problem of evil and divine (in)justice, refusing to embrace the solution of referring these dilemmas to a Jupiter who can provide a framework where they make sense. The poet's initial stance of incomprehension (tantaene animis caelestibus irae?, 'do minds of the heavenly ones have such vast anger?', 1. 11) carries through to the end: tanton placuit concurrere motu, / Iuppiter, aeterna gentis in pace futuras? ('did it

---

[106] Wlosok (1983) is the most extensive recent discussion along these lines; cf. Kühn (1971), esp. 139–40.

[107] Harrison (1980) and Lyne (1987) are of particular importance here; they concentrate on what sort of character he is, and not so much on the implications of the fact that he is a character at all.

[108] On this position, see Long (1968), 333. Cleanthes' Hymn to Zeus expresses it memorably (SVF 1. 537. 18–21). The Homeric scholia give expression to a kind of watered down Stoicism on this topic: bT 4. 4; 8. 429; 21. 465.

[109] Long (1968); Sandbach (1975), 101–8; Long and Sedley (1987), 1. 323–3.

[110] Div. 1. 17 (fr. 6. 1–10 Büchner); cf. the overtly allegorizing verses of Valerius Soranus (fr. 2 Büchner), and of the anonymous poet quoted by Servius on Aen. 4. 638, where the various gods are clearly referred to as aspects of Jupiter's essence.

[111] As the ancient commentators recognized, with their standard line being that Vergil, like all poets, uses the sects of the philosophers ad hoc, varying his pronouncements according to the particular needs of the poem: Serv. 1. 227; 6. 264; 10. 467; Ti. Donatus Prooemium (1. 6. 1–12 Geo). Against attempts to read Jupiter as a 'stoischer Allgott', see Pötscher (1978), 413.

please you, Jupiter, that peoples who would live together in eternal peace should collide with such vast upheaval?', 12. 503–4).[112] The fact that Jupiter is in the narrative and reacts for his own reasons (as god of Rome, husband of Juno, father of Venus), means that even his perspective is unavailable as a neutral, dispassionate vantage-point. There is no Archimedean hypothetical point in space from which to regard the action of the poem and evaluate it. Every vantage-point the poem offers is inextricable, part of a competition of views.

Jupiter's perspective is, naturally, a commanding one. It is the perspective of Fate, of Time, of history.[113] It cannot be unsaid, undone. He regards events from a height that shrinks human values. Yet it is not a perspective from which problems disappear. In this dismaying poem, most readers want to find a vantage point of comfort, and it is therefore tempting to construct a 'high' Stoic position in the portrayal of Jupiter, yet his participation in the narrative means that it is never easy, and it becomes finally impossible at the accommodation with Juno and the sending of the Dira. The narrator is ultimately unable to commit himself to Jupiter's perspective, as his helpless question in the last book shows: *tanton placuit concurrere motu, Iuppiter . . .?*

II

ὁ μὴ δυνάμενος κοινωνεῖν ἢ μηδὲν δεόμενος δι' αὐτάρκειαν οὐθὲν μέρος πόλεως, ὥστε ἢ θηρίον ἢ θεός.

The man who is unable to share in the benefits of political association, or has no need to share because he is already self-sufficient, is no part of the polis, and must therefore be either a beast or a god.

Aristotle, *Politics*[114]

---

[112] Henry (1873–92), vol. 1. 196–7; Johnson (1976), 14–15, 167; Veyne (1986), 265–6.

[113] Most forcefully put by Long (in Foster (1977), 135): 'We have . . . a viewpoint that cannot be denied, not one of approval and disapproval, because the concept of *fatum* has nothing to do with these two, what it has to do with is Time'. The bibliography on the problem of Jupiter and Fate is enormous: Neri (1986), 1978.

[114] 1253 a 27–9, trans. Barker (1946).

One character is privileged, if that is the word, to both human and divine perspectives, and the same character is also privileged to human and divine power. This is Hercules, whose function in the poem affords a focus for some of the poem's key conceptions about divinity. He may provide us, in a reverse route to the one he himself took, with a bridge from the world of gods to the world of the human characters.

Apollonius had taken the character of Heracles out of the body of the narrative, turning him into a figure of anecdote and report. Vergil reverses that direction, having him at first only spoken about,[115] and then actually introducing him into the narrative as a character in his own right. He traces Hercules down that path where even Lynceus could not see, and shows him to us at its far end, as a god.

In the great battle in Book 10, Jupiter keeps Pallas and Lausus apart, reserving each for a greater enemy (436–8). Immediately there follows the unequal combat between Pallas and Turnus, with Pallas praying to the recently deified Hercules for favour (460–1). The response is extraordinary: *audiit Alcides iuuenem* ('Hercules heard the young man', 464). Vergil introduces Hercules into the action itself, hearing Pallas, but unable to do anything but weep. He is unable even to speak, so that the poem goes by without our hearing a single word from him: *audiit Alcides iuuenem magnumque sub imo / corde premit gemitum lacrimasque effundit inanis* ('Hercules heard the young man, and quelled a mighty groan deep in his heart, and poured forth empty tears', 464–5). We actually encounter the god who was recently a man, and we see him powerless to honour the ties he established as a man, when he enjoyed the hospitality of Pallas' father, Evander. The closeness to humanity of the creature who was famous as the tearless one is marked by the fact of his weeping, for gods do not shed tears.[116]

---

[115] On these earlier passages, see Feeney (1986a), 66–74.

[116] As announced by Artemis, Eur. *Hipp.* 1396 (the same goddess who—uniquely—weeps in the *Iliad*, 21. 493); cf. Barchiesi (1984), 24–5, citing Soph. *Trach.* 1074 and Theoc. 24. 31 for Heracles' notorious imperviousness to tears; Bömer (1969–86) on Ov. *Met.* 10. 45 and (1958) on *Fast.* 4. 521–2. Note that when Bacchylides says that Heracles only ever wept once, he refers to the demigod at that moment as the son of a human father (Ἀμφιτρύωνος παῖδα, 5. 156). Elsewhere in the *Aeneid* the closest Vergil comes to having a god weep is when he introduces 'laughter-loving' Venus, describing her as *lacrimis oculos suffusa*

Jupiter, however, has never been anything but a god, and he tells the newcomer how a god regards these things:

> stat sua cuique dies, breue et inreparabile tempus
> omnibus est uitae; sed famam extendere factis,
> hoc uirtutis opus.

Each person has his own fixed day, and all have a brief and irretrievable span of time; but the task of virtue is to stretch fame out with great deeds. (10. 467–9)

A short life for all, but fame for the virtuous. Hercules should know, for he had been one of Anchises' models in Book 6, along with Bacchus (801–5), when Anchises urged Aeneas on to his mission: *et dubitamus adhuc uirtutem extendere factis?* ('and do we still hesitate to stretch virtue out with great deeds?', 806).

Vergil refers directly to the Homeric model for the scene in Book 10 when Jupiter goes on to mention Sarpedon, who was his son, and who nevertheless died at Troy (10. 470–1).[117] In the *Iliad*, however, when Sarpedon was about to die, it was not Zeus who insisted upon the inviolability of Fate, but Hera, acting as an inflexible foil to Zeus' pity and grief (16. 439–43). Now the tables are turned, as Hercules is overcome, and Jupiter enunciates—*dictis amicis* ('with friendly words', 466)—the lesson he has learnt from Hera.[118] These few lines represent a shattering collision of human and divine perspectives, as the most human of the gods is told by the father of the gods how to regard the action. Every reader has to try to be open to these two perspectives, to learn, like Hercules, to be able to see both at once.[119]

Vergil's manipulation of the conflicting perspectives of gods and men is vividly highlighted by the way in which he adapts the Homeric model for the immediately following scene. Turnus proceeds to strip Pallas of his baldric (10. 495–505), an act which will in the end bring about his own death. In the Homeric model, as Hector strips Patroclus of Achilles' armour, Zeus looks down and

*nitentis* ('with a film of tears over her gleaming eyes', 1. 228); Venus also mentions her own weeping, and that of Thetis and Eos, in her supplication to Vulcan, 8. 380–4.

[117] Knauer (1964), 299; esp. the valuable discussion of Barchiesi (1984), 16–24.

[118] The Iliadic scene is even more systematically reversed less than 150 lines later, when Jupiter tells Juno that she cannot, in the long run, save her favourite, Turnus (10. 621–7).

[119] On the disparity between the god's-eye and the human's-eye view, see especially Commager (1981), 112.

reflects on Hector's ignorance of the death which he now faces at the hands of Achilles (*Il.* 17. 198–206). In the *Aeneid*, the corresponding observation is not attributed to Jupiter, but pronounced by the poet himself (10. 501–5). In fact, Vergil's exclamation is virtually a translation, not of the Homeric text itself, but of the commentators' gloss, with its explicit spelling-out of the moral message, in terms of the commonplaces of Hellenistic philosophy.[120] And the same commentators remark on the fact that Homer has chosen to attribute his moral comment to Zeus, rather than voicing it himself, so that Vergil's change of speaker looks all the more deliberate. It is not for Vergil's chief god to provide moral comment on the action; the poet, the human artist, must provide it himself, for this god is above, or at least beyond, human categories of virtue.[121]

Vergil's Hercules wins godhead by the same means as Apollonius', by beneficently warding off evil. Book 8 presents Aeneas at the site of Rome, bringing aid to the people of Evander, and conforming to the Apollonian prototype which stamps him as being, like Polydeuces, an emulator of Hercules, winning immortality through being a saviour, an averter of evil.[122] Aeneas arrives as Evander's people are celebrating the feast day of Hercules, the day on which he had killed the monster Cacus, a feat which is presented as the crown of the achievements which entitle him to divinity. Evander relates the deed to Aeneas (8. 190–267), and his speech concentrates, as had the account of the nymph in Apollonius' fourth book, on the frenzy and power of Hercules, while maintaining an extreme distance from him, so that Hercules is as isolated as he had been in the desert of Libya.[123]

When Hercules hears the lowing of his cattle, stolen by Cacus, *Alcidae furiis exarserat atro / felle dolor* ('Hercules' atrabilious resentment flared up in frenzy', 219–20). He rushes to Cacus' lair: *ecce furens animis aderat Tirynthius ... / dentibus infrendens*

[120] Barchiesi (1984), 52, referring to bT 17. 201.

[121] We return to discuss the question of the gods' amoral nature in Section I of the next chapter.

[122] Binder (1971), 141–9; Galinsky (1972), 142–6; Feeney (1986a), 48–50.

[123] Propertius, indeed, in his treatment of the Hercules and Cacus story, blends the Apollonian and Vergilian stories together, giving us Hercules searching for water after his great feat, with local nymphs hostile to him (4. 9. 21–50; cf. Ap. Rhod. 4. 1441–3).

('look, in a spirit of frenzy Hercules was there, . . . gnashing his teeth', 228–30). He dashes around the hill: *ter totum feruidus ira / lustrat Auentini montem* ('three times, blazing with rage, he went round the Aventine hill', 230–1). The impression, even more strongly than in Apollonius, is one of terrific, manic violence. Even when saviour and candidate for apotheosis, Hercules is *uis, βία,* 'force' incarnate.[124] As we contemplate the picture of Aeneas listening to the exemplum spoken by Evander, we must wonder what it means for him, whether this is part of the paradigm which he will also emulate.

Hardie has demonstrated the way in which the fight between Hercules and Cacus is shot through with images of Gigantomachy.[125] The inherent complexity of the Gigantomachic paradigm, so well stressed by Hardie,[126] with its paradoxes of violence for order, and the common power of the antagonists, means that easy antitheses dissolve before inspection. Hercules' violent power is scarcely sublime; his mountain- and rock-throwing tactics are, in fact, very close to those of the Giants, especially of the gigantesque Polyphemus, whom in other respects Cacus resembles.[127] According to Evander, the monster Cacus is *semihominis* ('half man', 'semi-human', 194), and he means that the other half is beast, as he shows seventy lines later, when he calls him *semiferi* ('half beast', 267); yet the god Vulcan is this creature's father (198), so that he is half-god as well. Hercules' semi-divine parentage likewise places him beyond the normal categories of humanity. Bestial and divine both surround the human, and extreme behaviour on either fringe may meet, so as to be indistinguishable.[128] When Servius explains Hercules' difficult epithet of *communis* as meaning 'between gods and men' (8. 275), he may be mistaking the gist of that particular passage, but he is putting his finger on something determinative about the significance of Hercules.

The implications of the Herculean paradigm become clearer for

---

[124] Vergil's concentration on Hercules' manic violence emerges very strongly if one sets it beside Ovid's account in the *Fasti* (1. 561–79), where Hercules is, by comparison, a model of restrained discipline.

[125] Hardie (1986), 110–18.

[126] Ibid., 155–6.

[127] Ibid., 115–16.

[128] Vernant and Vidal-Naquet (1973), 128–9.

Aeneas later in the poem, when he himself starts exercising mas-
sive violence in battle, and is eventually compared in his berserk
battle-frenzy to the Hundred-hander Aegaeon, enemy of Jupiter
(10. 565–70). The use of such power and violence is in itself an
attempt to attain to the status of divinity, and any such attempt is
fraught with terrible moral hazard, always susceptible of being
represented as gigantesque.[129] Recent attempts to redeem Aeneas'
violence from any suspicion of anxiety miss the point of the identification with Hercules.[130] Hercules' outsize power and his
unassimilable nature are his hallmark from the very beginning of
the tradition, and these characteristics become a way of reflecting
upon the unassimilable nature of the divine, and the arbitrary
nature of divine power, which may always manifest itself to
humans as mere violence. The terrific energy of Hercules impels
him towards godhead, as he exercises power to aid humans, but it
is always bursting its banks and spilling over into misdirected violence.[131] This catastrophic and inexplicable violence is itself an aspect of being close to the divine. The starkest illustration of such a
mentality is perhaps to be found in the story of the boxer
Cleomedes, who killed his opponent in the Olympic Games, and,
mad with grief at being stripped of his prize, returned home to
Astypalaea, where he pulled down the roof of a school on top of
sixty children.[132] He hid in a chest in the temple of Athene, and
disappeared. The Delphic oracle ordered the people to honour him
as a hero, on the grounds that he was no longer mortal (ἅτε
μηκέτι θνητὸν ἐόντα). Spectacular and unaccountable violence

[129] Dauge (1981), 33.

[130] Cairns (1989), 82–4: 'So the *furiae* of Aeneas and Hercules are virtuous,
while the *furor* of Turnus is evil' (84). Cairns does not mention the comparison of
Aeneas to Aegaeon, and when he says that *tenet se* at 10. 802 'suggests that Aeneas
is not out of control' (83), we need to read ten more lines of text to find Aeneas
losing his control and killing Lausus (813–20). I find the reflections of Lyne (1983)
on the indivisible nature of violence in the poem more sympathetic. Boyle (1986),
93–111 has trenchant observations on the failure of Aeneas to exercise power with
restraint, but I find his position weakened by his vendetta against the character of
Aeneas, as he refuses to consider that Aeneas is a victim as well as Turnus and
Lausus, if a victim of a different sort.

[131] March (1987), 75 has some pithy observations on judging the tragic Heracles
by divine standards rather than human; cf. Silk (1985), on Heracles' participation
in the divine, and on tragic responses to his anomalous position. On the violence of
Heracles, see Galinsky (1972), 3–4, 10–12; Fitch (1987), 15–24, esp. 15: '. . .any
strength that goes so far beyond the human norm is potentially dangerous and unpredictable.'

[132] Paus. 6. 9. 6–8.

may be so inhuman that it can only be conceived of as being akin to the divine—or else (as one sees repeatedly with Hercules) to the bestial, and the gigantesque.

Models are there to be outstripped as well as matched. And, inasmuch as he is the embodiment of an historical force, Aeneas does indeed outstrip his model, and himself provides a model for his descendant Augustus, who has inherited control of the historical force first given expression by Aeneas.[133] As the poem progresses, Aeneas finds himself being increasingly absorbed into Herculean patterns of status and function. As an ἀλεξίκακος, a warder-off of evil, a victorious saviour, and a wielder of great power, he even outstrips Hercules, and will become, like him, a god. Yet, in adopting a Herculean status, and discharging Herculean functions, he also finds himself being assimilated to some of the more forbidding aspects of his paradigm. In his exercise of *uis* and *furor*, and in his frightful solitude, Aeneas comes all too close to another side of Hercules. Even here, there are marked differences between, on the one hand, the mythical Hercules and, on the other, the quasi-historical Aeneas, together with his successor Augustus, ruler of Vergil's own contemporary world. The isolation of Hercules and Aeneas is one of their most striking similarities, a function, partly, of their incipiently divine status, in that they are both moving out of human society without yet being members of divine society. Yet Hercules is ἄπολις, 'stateless', while Aeneas lives for the city; Hercules is alone because he cannot belong with any organization, while Aeneas is alone because he is wholly identified with an organization.[134] This historical dimension sets Aeneas and Augustus quite apart from the Greek god-hero; yet their power, function, and status place them, even on earth, as close to the boundary of the divine as it is possible to be. And some things about being on the boundary of the divine do not change.

In the Roman world Hercules had been the paradigm for apotheosis ever since Ennius' *Annales*, and the *Aeneid* is not the only work of the period to follow this path.[135] In Vergil's world,

[133] A large and contentious topic: see Camps (1969), 98–104; Binder (1971); Hardie (1986), 369–75.

[134] On the isolation of Aeneas which follows from his political status, see Stewart (1972–3).

[135] Hor. *Carm.* 3. 3. 9 makes Hercules one of the paradigms for the apotheosis of Augustus; see here Pietrusiński (1978).

Augustus occupied the same interstices between the human and the divine as his ancestor Aeneas occupies in the poem.[136] Quite how to categorize the quasi-divine power of the emperor was a problem for all those who were trying to regularize ways of defining the emperor's novel position. Price's invaluable recent studies of the ruler-cult have clearly laid out some of the techniques developed for making sense of the emperor's might by locating him 'at the focal point between human and divine'.[137] As an epic, the *Aeneid* has its own ways of concentrating on where this focal point might be, and what it might be like to occupy it.

### III

> Our patient is confronted with a power of will and suggestion more than equal to anything his consciousness can put against it. In this precarious situation it would be bad strategy to convince him that in some incomprehensible way he is at the back of his own symptom, secretly inventing and supporting it. . . . It is far better for him to understand that his complex is an autonomous power directed against his conscious personality. Moreover, such an explanation fits the actual facts much better than a reduction to personal motives. An apparently personal motivation does exist, but it is not made by his will, it just happens to him.
>
> C. G. Jung, *Psychology and Religion*[138]

Hercules and Aeneas are straining out of their human status, yet Aeneas remains a human for the poem, and like the other humans must live in a world occupied also by the gods. What do the humans know of the gods, and how do the two spheres interact? It is especially when the divine impinges upon the human that modern readers tend to feel most acutely their lack of sympathy with the conventions of epic. Having begun with Juno in Section I, we may now follow Vergil's symmetry by beginning this Section with her intervention in Book 7.

In Book 1 Juno had exploited the king of the winds. Here, con-

---

[136] On Aeneas' status as intermediate between gods and men, see Liebing (1953), 22; Highet (1972), 43.

[137] Price (1984a), 233; cf. Price (1980) and (1984b).

[138] Jung (1958), vol. 11. 16.

templating the imminent marriage of Aeneas and Lavinia, with a peaceful settlement for the Trojans, she descends to the agencies of Hell. On the level of earth, the boundary of air and underworld, she summons the Fury Allecto (323). This monster is described in six lines by the poet (324–9), and her attributes are further commemorated by Juno's ten-line address (331–40), so that we have some considerable preparation for her ensuing actions.

She is a creature who embodies and revels in all manner of evil, and is therefore at odds with conventional ancient pieties, which focused little on evil.[139] She need not necessarily have been so. Euripides' Lyssa is an interesting case of a divine agent of madness who remains rational, emancipated from her characteristic effect.[140] Allecto, on the other hand, *is* her essence. Above all, Vergil stresses how variable and multiple she is: *tot sese uertit in ora*, says the poet ('so many are the faces into which she turns herself', 328).[141] This warning of complexity is picked up by Juno's catalogue in her ghastly mock-hymn of address: *tibi nomina mille, / mille nocendi artes* ('a thousand names hast thou, a thousand artful ways of causing hurt', 337–8).[142] Her variety of action is something we will therefore concentrate on; note, for the moment, how her last plan is introduced with *arte noua* ('a new artful trick', 477). Her πολυωνυμία is captured in the following scenes: she is, or becomes, *Allecto* (324), *Erinys* (447), *Calybe* (419), *Cocytia uirgo* (479).

In pedigree she is likewise multifaceted. Most directly, she is one of the Greek Erinyes, or Eumenides, with their snaky attributes and infernal, nocturnal origin. Yet the Eumenides, for all their horror, at least have a function in the punishment of family crime, and in the preservation of natural order;[143] Allecto disrupts an almost consummated order and 'punishes' those who have committed no crime. In this regard she might be thought more like Euripides' Lyssa, who deranges Heracles although she knows and declares him to be guiltless (*HF* 849–54); yet Lyssa acts with

---

[139] On her evil, Buchheit (1963), 102; Johnson (1976), 144; on the normally attenuated interest in divine evil in the pre-Christian world, see Armstrong (1986), 79, 92–3.

[140] *HF* 843–58.

[141] The multifaceted nature of Allecto is stressed by Foster (1977), 120.

[142] On the prayer form of the address, see Fraenkel (1945), 4 n. 7.

[143] Dodds (1951), 7–8; Armstrong (1986), 92.

sympathetic reluctance, not with Allecto's glee.[144] The figure of discord best known to a Roman audience would be Ennius' Discordia, who was at once the emblem of historical discord and of disharmony in the natural world.[145] Allecto depends intimately on Ennius' Discordia, as has long been recognized,[146] but we must note that Discordia seems to have been only tangentially a psychological agent, and that Vergil's audience will not necessarily have been prepared to see Discordia's descendant manipulating the minds of humans.

Allecto is no simplex entity with one mode of acting, and her interventions in this section illustrate something of the variety of ways in which Vergil can depict the gods impinging on humans. Allecto acts three times, in three episodes of sixty-five, sixty-nine, and sixty-five lines—and in three very different ways.

The goddess of marriage has commissioned her to prevent a wedding, and she begins, naturally enough, with the girl's mother:

> tacitumque obsedit limen Amatae,
> quam super aduentu Teucrum Turnique hymenaeis
> femineae ardentem curaeque iraeque coquebant.

She besieged the silent threshold of Amata. Feminine anxiety and anger over the arrival of the Trojans and the wedding-ceremonies of Turnus were bringing the heated queen to the boil. (7. 343–5)[147]

Naturally enough . . . The queen has already been shown to us as being passionately committed to the suit of Turnus,[148] and Vergil's presentation here, with its artfully condescending *femineae*, and colloquial *coquebant*, caters to the culture's expectation of what is natural in a woman in such a circumstance. The reader is being inveigled into expecting a description of something humanly plausible. Allecto's method is to pluck a serpent from her snaky locks and throw it at Amata, to infect the queen with its and Allecto's venom (346–7). The reader may feel lulled

---

[144] Buchheit (1963), 101; on Allecto and Lyssa, see also Otis (1963), 324.

[145] Above, p. 123.

[146] Norden (1915), 1–40; Skutsch (1985), 392–3; reservations of various kinds expressed by Fraenkel (1945), 7, 12–14; Klingner (1967), 511–12, 523–6.

[147] No English can capture the sheer ugliness of the sound of the Latin of the last half-line.

[148] 7. 56–7; I keep changing my mind over the plausibility of Lyne's interesting reconstruction of Amata's incestuous passion for her prospective son-in-law: Lyne (1987), 13–19.

into gliding on, registering that Amata is now even more angry;
yet a block of eleven lines stands in the way (346–56):

> huic dea caeruleis unum de crinibus anguem
> conicit, inque sinum praecordia ad intima subdit,
> quo furibunda domum monstro permisceat omnem.
> ille inter uestis et leuia pectora lapsus
> uoluitur attactu nullo, fallitque furentem
> uiperam inspirans animam; fit tortile collo
> aurum ingens coluber, fit longae taenia uittae
> innectitque comas et membris lubricus errat.
> ac dum prima lues udo sublapsa ueneno
> pertemptat sensus atque ossibus implicat ignem
> necdum animus toto percepit pectore flammam, . . .

The goddess throws one of the snakes from her dark blue hair at her, and
slips it into her bosom, to the inmost areas of her vitals, so that, maddened by this unnatural horror, she might turn her whole household up-
side down. The snake glides between her clothes and her soft breasts, it
twists its way with no contact; as it breathes its viperous breath into her
the maddened queen does not realize what is happening. It becomes
twisted gold about her neck, the huge snake, it becomes the fine ends of
her long headband, it binds up her hair, and meanders, slippery, over her
limbs. And while the first stage of the contagion, infiltrating with its wet
poison, assails her senses and wraps fire round her bones, and her mind
has not yet fully and wholly taken in the flame . . .

What is happening in these lines? And why, beyond the evocation of horror and disgust, are we being told it? We are forced to
concentrate on the supernatural physicality of the snake, and on
the process it is performing, to the extent that it becomes
extremely difficult to gloss these lines as 'Amata went mad with
rage', and also extremely difficult to disentangle what is 'happening'. The lines present an irresolvable tension between the
minutely particularized description of the event and the impossibility of the event. The honest difficulties of the modern commentators are the clearest indicator of the irreconcilable plays
which Vergil is establishing. Does the snake touch Amata or
not?[149] Does the snake 'really' become a (substantial) necklace and

---

[149] Henry (1873–92), vol. 3. 545: 'If the snake does not touch her at all, how is
it possible for it to form itself into a necklace round her neck; . . . how is it possible
for it to glide over her limbs in every direction, slimy and slippery? There is so
downright an impossibility in all this, that ATTACTU NULLO must have some other
meaning than *not touching her*. What other meaning, then? Why, simply *not being
felt to touch her, conveying no impression to her sense of feeling* . . .'

a (fine) ribbon?[150] If Amata does not feel the snake, in what way is
it *lubricus* ('slippery')? The mention of the poison in 354 calls
forth disparate reactions. According to Fordyce, 'to modern ears
the "clammy poison", mysteriously conveyed without contact, en-
hances the incongruity of the physical description'; but according
to Conington, the adjective 'is another attempt to make the thing
physically credible'.[151] Far too ingenious, is Heyne's verdict on
351-3, the kind of thing that would be all right in Ovid—and
Fordyce is inclined to agree.[152] Quite unlike anything in Homer,
this surreal play with the integration of the supernatural into the
fiction is inspired, in the first instance, by Apollonius, and is one
of the very few passages where Vergil displays an Apollonian
interest in the problematic φύσις of the divine, the nature of its
nature.

The sheer effort of finally baffled comprehension demanded of
the reader in these eleven lines is immediately put to another test,
as Vergil nudges us back in the direction of a naturalistic reading.
The queen addresses her husband *mollius et solito matrum de
more* ('in quite a mild manner, and according to the normal way
in which mothers act', 357). Once more the reader is returned to
the familiar social judgements of female behaviour, watching
Amata, the match-maker, standing by her prerogatives as she
works on her husband. We stay in this register throughout her
speech (359-72), and for one and a half lines after it:

> his ubi nequiquam dictis experta Latinum
> contra stare uidet, *penitusque in uiscera lapsum
> serpentis furiale malum totamque pererrat* . . .

When she had sounded Latinus out with these words to no avail, and saw
that he was fixed in his opposition, *and when the maddening evil of the
serpent slipped deep into her insides and wandered around all over her
. . .* (373-5)

No sooner are we reassured that this is all very understandable
than we are returned to the incomprehensible action of the serpent. By concentrating on the weird supernatural physicality of
the possession, Vergil's technique here makes it difficult to gloss,
to skip, to be confident that we understand what is being

---

[150] See Henry (1873-92), vol. 3. 546, on how the transformations are not literal,
but a way of saying that the snake was 'like a gold necklace' etc.
[151] Fordyce (1977), and Conington–Nettleship–Haverfield (1858-98), ad loc.
[152] Heyne–Wagner (1830-41), and Fordyce (1977), ad loc.

described—what is 'happening'. In these thirty lines is concentrated the tension between naturalism and fantasy which Apollonius' account of Medea's motivation had teased out over two books.

The immediately following simile, which compares Amata to a spinning top, flying along as the boys whip it (378–84), is equally open to this double interpretation. To most readers it will appear to reinforce the picture of Amata's helplessness under the external influence of Allecto. A recent article, however, has pointed out that a Stoic reading of the simile yields the opposite conclusion.[153] The Stoic Chrysippus used the analogy of a cylinder or top in discussing human responsibility, arguing that 'the "complete" . . . causes of our actions are our moral qualities', just as with a cylinder or top 'it is ultimately the object's shape which bears the responsibility' for its moving in the way it does.[154] By this perspective, 'Allecto furnishes merely the "proximate and auxiliary" cause of the queen's anger, the beginning of motion . . . For the rest, she moves in accordance with the force of her own bitter and angry nature.'[155] Many readers will want to opt for one interpretation or the other, but the indeterminacy seems entirely in harmony with the technique we have been observing throughout the passage.

Again, at 385 Amata rushes to the woods, *simulato numine Bacchi* ('under the pretense of the inspirations of Bacchus'). Who is pretending, Amata or Allecto?[156] On a first reading, most will take this to be Amata's cunning, but at the end of the episode, we are told *reginam Allecto stimulis agit undique Bacchi* ('Allecto drives the queen everywhere with the goads of Bacchus', 405). Finally, at 376 Amata is described as *ingentibus excita monstris*, 'stirred up by huge unnatural horrors'. *Monstra* are portents which signal a supernatural involvement of some sort, but the epithet *ingens*, 'huge', points to Amata's own nature, by way of an etymological play on *ingenium* ('natural character').[157] Amata is presented in these three words as stirred up by something at once supernatural and innate.

[153] Babel (1981–2).
[154] Long–Sedley (1987), 1. 341.
[155] Babel (1981–2), 31.
[156] Foster (1977), 123; Fordyce (1977), ad loc.; Williams (1983), 63.
[157] I thank Professor Hinds for drawing my attention to this etymology, which was first proposed by Mackail (1912), and has recently been revived by Ross (1987), esp. 115.

From beginning to end, reading the Allecto–Amata episode is
like looking at an object through a pair of binoculars with incompatible lenses. If you close each eye in turn you can get the picture
into focus, but it is impossible to harmonize the image with both
open at once. What happens to Amata is understandable and it is
not understandable. She feels, she is, responsible; she does not feel,
is not, responsible. She at once seems and does not seem, to herself
and to the reader, to be acting 'normally'. The palpable images of
the slippery snake, oozing wet poison, are at odds with the calculated plausibility of the tête-à-tête with Latinus, yet this symbiosis
of the concrete and the hallucinatory fantastic catches at something central to the experience of madness. By laying bare the
impossibilities of adequately narrating such extremes of behaviour, this technique involves the reader in the recognition of our
inability to understand madness in others, or acknowledge it in
ourselves. And this recognition should be allowed to come home
with all the disgusted horror that Allecto's snake can evoke. It is
remarkable testimony to Vergil's confidence in his art that he can
enmesh us in such reflections on human behaviour even as his
technique flaunts the fictionality of the entire episode by continually unsettling us, keeping us dithering between two incompatible reading conventions.

Allecto now moves off to Ardea, where the Rutulian war-lord,
Turnus, is asleep, enjoying *quies* for the first and last time in the
poem (414). Whereas in the case of Amata we were twice given a
description of her pre-existing emotions, we are told nothing
whatever about Turnus' attitude to events before Allecto sets to
work on him. She disguises herself as Calybe, a priestess of Juno,
and speaks to Turnus, trying to rouse him to war by making him
feel resentment at the slight of his broken betrothal to the daughter of Amata and Latinus (415–34). Turnus' reply is brusque, even
scornful, as he tells the supposed priestess to leave matters of state
to him (436–44). Yet he is entirely in command of himself here,
quite rational, calm in his disdainful refusal to be lectured to by
Calybe; above all, he is wholly uncommitted as to whether or not
he will go to war. Incensed by his failure to respond, the Fury goes
berserk, throws off her disguise, and thrusts her torch, smoking
with black light, in his chest. He wakes up and is mad (456–60).
This episode is generally read, in accordance with modern con-

ventions for reading epic, as a piece of quasi-realism, or veiled
naturalism, with a 'realistic' narrative just beneath the allegorical
surface. In his commentary, for example, Williams claims that
Allecto 'does not create the passions which are let loose; the
causation is not imposed externally, but arises from the perversion
of existing human qualities'.[158] Again, Quinn will have it that 'the
irrational impulse is already there; all Allecto needs to do is to
touch it off (Heroic Impulse) by representing to Turnus that his
honour has been affected'.[159] Something is supposed to be happening which makes sense even if Allecto is spirited away, so that
Quinn even poses the question: 'How are we to explain this sudden reversal of attitude in Turnus from inactivity to belligerence
without Allecto?'[160] This insistence that the human narrative is
comprehensible on its own terms is variously labelled 'double motivation', 'parallel divine and human motivation', 'working
with'[161].

What happens to Turnus is almost invariably regarded as being
analogous to what happens to Amata.[162] Yet Allecto's diverse
modes of action must be allowed to register. Amata's initial state
of mind is clearly described according to expected norms of characterization before Allecto attacks her. In the case of Turnus,
Vergil tells us nothing whatever about Turnus' initial reactions to
the arrival of the Trojans, or Latinus' decision to marry his daughter to Aeneas. Indeed, he vouchsafes very little information
altogether about Turnus' nature.[163] It is often maintained that
Turnus is angry because of his broken betrothal to Lavinia,[164] but
for this the text gives no authority. Anger, indeed, is, literally, the
last thing Turnus feels: *saeuit amor ferri et scelerata insania belli, /
ira super* ('love of the sword rages in him, and the accursed madness of war—and, in addition, anger', 461-2). As Fordyce remarks, developing an observation of Conington's, 'the analysis of

---

[158] Williams (1973), on 7. 323 ff. discussing both Amata and Turnus; cf. Kühn
(1971), 111-13.
[159] Quinn (1968), 181.
[160] Ibid., 182 n. 1.
[161] The terminology of, respectively, Williams (1983), 22; Quinn (1968), 316-
20; Lyne (1987), 66-71. I by no means wish to imply that these critics are unanimous in their approaches.
[162] So Williams (1973), on 7. 323 ff.; Williams (1983), 23. Exceptions include
Thornton (1976), 111-12; Coleman (1982), 151.
[163] Rightly stressed by Thornton (1976), 111-12, and Coleman (1982), 151.
[164] e.g. Quinn (1968), 181-2.

feeling which represents personal resentment as supervening on an infatuate desire for fighting is hardly plausible'.[165] The whole encounter between Allecto and Turnus is 'hardly plausible', and it forces us to keep readjusting to the level of reality we need to inhabit. Most readers, I imagine, assume that Turnus has woken up when he speaks to the disguised Allecto (435–44), but we are then told that he wakes up after having the torch thrust into his chest (458), so that we must reread the conversation with Allecto–Calybe, and see it as a dream-experience.[166] Again, the simile at the end of the encounter likens Turnus to a simmering cauldron which is brought to the boil when a torch is placed beneath it (462–6). It is inevitable that we should wish to see here an image of Turnus' natural resentment being brought to a climax by the torch of Allecto.[167] The simile is, however, the first and only element in the passage which lends support to such an interpretation, and it seems to me that we see here a lesser example of the hovering between two types of reading which formed the backbone of the Amata episode.

This inherent lack of plausibility makes it very difficult to read Allecto here as a representation of some natural process in the character of Turnus. There is not enough realism in the scene for us to get a purchase—or at least, such realism as there is seems to be going in the wrong direction. What point would be served in a naturalistic narrative by stressing, as Vergil does, the contrast between Turnus' 'natural' reaction of calm self-control and his subsequent berserk madness, so that he now has an unendurable yearning (as the commentator Ti. Donatus puts it) for that which he had formerly dismissed out of hand?[168]

Let Allecto have her force on her own terms as a character in a narrative which has an intermittent and tangential relation to realism. The perplexing switch in Turnus' behaviour is allowed to become effective, to become the poet's principal device for arousing

---

[165] Fordyce (1977), ad loc. Note that Turnus says nothing whatever about Lavinia in his pronouncements to his men (469–70), so that his anger at 461–2 should not automatically be taken to refer to his feelings about her.

[166] The parallels with Agamemnon's dream in *Iliad* 2 (18–41), however, might alert a reader from the start to the possibility that Turnus is dreaming here: Knauer (1964), 236–7.

[167] Lyne (1987), 69.

[168] *ut impatienter cuperet quod ante contempserat*, 2. 68. 26–7 Geo; it is clear that Donatus sees a radical invasion of Turnus by Allecto.

our horrified pity and shock, as we apprehend the chasm between rationality and murderous mania, two extremes embodied in the same individual within a dozen lines. The essentially impressionistic nature of Vergil's technique in this area of his art was eloquently shown in Johnson's *Darkness Visible*,[169] yet his example has still to make its deserved impact on our readings of such scenes. Allecto is not being used here as a device of psychological revelation. Vergil is not interested as such in establishing the character of Turnus, but in conveying the impression of a mind possessed by an overpoweringly mad lust for killing; his concern for capturing that impression is so strong that he feels no compunction in jettisoning what might be necessary for us to establish a character for Turnus. The way in which he conveys this impression, indeed, makes it very hard for us to develop a picture of why or how it happened. I should say that his technique makes it impossible. Allecto's action does not illuminate the switch in Turnus, it obscures it; she is not there to make it easier for us to understand, but to make it harder, or impossible. The hypothesis that such madness should be understandable is ultimately behind the 'naturalistic' readings, yet it is worth canvassing the possibility that the poem suggests incomprehension as a more worthwhile response to the grotesque manifestations which it persists in creating.

A related consequence of the realistic readings—and a related reason for questioning them—is that they cannot help but end by fixing Turnus as responsible. At times this assignment of responsibility becomes more than a corollary of a reading method, as it serves a determination to ensure that Turnus is guilty and deserves his death.[170] Yet the approach sketched here allows Turnus to remain a victim, and declines to engage in confident attributions of guilt, acknowledging that throughout Book 7 Vergil is engaged in what Horsfall calls a 'studied refusal to assign individual human responsibility for the outbreak of hostilities'.[171]

This refusal is seen even more clearly in Allecto's next action, as she causes the first blood to be shed between Trojans and Latins (475–539). She spies out a place where Aeneas' son Iulus is hunting,

[169] Johnson (1976).
[170] Otis (1963), 325 ('no diminution of moral responsibility'); Klingner (1967), 513; esp. Renger (1985), 38–42.
[171] Horsfall (1987), 49; cf. Pöschl (1962), 92–5.

and sends a sudden madness amongst his dogs (477–80). Iulus ends by shooting—with Allecto guiding his arrow (498)—a pet stag which belongs to the family of a rustic Latin, Tyrrhus. The incident itself, with the confused melée which results, is at one level a means of bringing the two sides together in conflict without fixing blame on, or alienating the reader's sympathy from, either Trojans or Latins.[172] Readers since antiquity have reacted adversely to the wounded stag,[173] yet modern readers do not need to strain to find parallels for the wretched process by which a trivial incident generates its own momentum for war.

Allecto's devastating sweep of action by no means exhibits every Vergilian technique of divine manipulation of humans, but it has enough variety to provide an opportunity for some conclusions.

Most current ways of reading these and like scenes begin and end in naturalistic realism, with a token circuit en route through the divine agency, as if the divine element in the narrative is something to be read through, purged, in a reading which arrives at acute, novelistic insights. In fact, as the case of Turnus in particular shows, Vergil's techniques seldom focus on being revelatory of character-process, on representing symbolically what is 'really' happening. Partly this is a function of the generally low priority which the poem sets on characterization, but the principal explanation lies in the poem's (and the genre's) distinctive narrative level.[174]

The poem is not dealing with given facts which need a poetic colour, it is not located in a reality upon which has been superimposed a divine gloss for the reader to pare away. In the poem's terms, as Johnson has clearly demonstrated, Allecto and Juno are characters as much as Aeneas and Turnus.[175] Such a view has been strenuously challenged by Gordon Williams, who claims that 'the text of the *Aeneid* enjoins a reading that is entirely consistent with the theology of Epicurus'.[176] Behind this approach lies a fundamental unwillingness to come to terms with the genre, but even so, the urge to read an Epicurean *Aeneid* founders with Dido, who is

[172] Heinze (1915), 190–2.
[173] See, however, the valuable discussion of Griffin (1985), 170–2.
[174] On the poem's muted interest in the sort of characterization one looks for in Homer, see Kenney (1974), 276.
[175] Johnson (1976), 146.
[176] Williams (1983), 213.

herself a character with an Epicurean reading of the poem's action—a reading which is proved comprehensively wrong.[177] The question of how a supernatural creature should be represented as acting upon a human is an endlessly fascinating poetic challenge, given the endlessly debateable nature of the supernatural, yet the poem is intolerably impoverished if we regard the human action as the only real action, and gloss over the excess, if we, in effect, stop reading ('these eleven lines just mean that Amata got very angry'). The divine action, as we saw in the case of Amata, may be a way of making certain suggestions about observing and narrating human behaviour, but if we disregard the divine action's part in the poetry, we make it impossible for ourselves to glean those suggestions. What is being said or hinted at can only be listened to if we accord full narrative status to the divine actors and action, if we resist the temptation to glide over the supernatural contribution in our reading.

More is involved here than recognizing why such comments as the following, on Turnus, are beside the point: 'How are we to explain this sudden reversal of attitude in Turnus from inactivity to belligerence without Allecto? Presumably Turnus had relied on justice, and then on impulse decides to take justice into his own hands.'[178] The urge to read naturalistically again and again elides entire dimensions of meaning and effect. The same critic, following his declaration that sometimes 'an impulse to action has a divine origin ascribed to it in a way that strikes us as purely formal', gives the example of 'Aeneas' sudden realization (as we should put it) that he must leave Carthage before it is too late (ascribed to the message brought him by Mercury from Jove, 4. 265-82)'.[179] One can only say that it is not up to us how to put it. It has been 'put' by the poem as Mercury relaying to Aeneas the order which Jupiter utters after he has heard the prayer of Iarbas—a process which

---

[177] Her sister asks her at 4. 34, *id cinerem aut manis credis curare sepultos?* ('do you think that ash and buried shades care about this?'); here Servius comments, *dicit secundum Epicureos* ('she speaks according to the Epicureans'). Note especially 4. 379-80, *scilicet is superis labor est, ea cura quietos / sollicitat* ('Oh yes, of course, this is something the gods exert themselves about, this is an anxiety that disturbs their tranquillity'); see the note of Pease (1935), ad loc. Even when she prays to Jupiter at the end of Book 1, Dido says 'people *say* that you . . .', 1. 731.

[178] Quinn (1968), 182 n. 1. Such remarks are particularly odd coming from a critic who is one of the very few to recognize the poem's grounding in fantasy: 34-58, 305, 320.

[179] Ibid., 317-18.

takes eighty-two lines, some 11 per cent of the book (4. 196–278). It matters terribly for Aeneas' tragedy that an external constraint makes him leave. His conscience has surrendered. He cannot 'leave before it is too late'—it *is* too late.

It would have been perfectly feasible for Vergil to represent Aeneas deciding to leave under the influence of conscience, with no divine impetus. That is how Apollonius proceeded in the model scene, when he has Heracles shame his companions into leaving the women of Lemnos and resuming their mission (*Arg.* 1. 862–78). Vergil has quite deliberately not followed this obvious lead, although he does have Aeneas refer to the promptings of conscience when he speaks to Dido, mentioning his thoughts for his son, as well as apparitions of his father (4. 351–5).[180] The very elaboration of the divine element in Book 4 should make it impossible for us to sum it all up as a dramatic way of revealing Aeneas' conscience, or inner thoughts. At one level, Vergil's solution is an epically plausible way of resolving the impasse without destroying Aeneas' characterization, for he can show both a totally besotted Aeneas and a dutifully obeying Aeneas. More importantly, though, we must actually read what is described, and go to Olympus, and hear Jupiter's words.

There we are given the historical perspective enjoyed by the supreme god, with a vision that extends down to the establishment of Roman rule over the whole world (229–31). Aeneas' personal fate is only a particle in this sum, but that is obviously not how it feels to Aeneas, or to us. As we watch Aeneas' reaction to Mercury's message, with the words of Jupiter still in our ears, we are forced to see this in the perspective of twelve centuries of history even as the reading itself makes us feel that here and now, Aeneas and Dido, is all that counts. The reader's sense of disjunction, of trying to harmonize these two irreconcilable focuses, catches the bewilderment of the character, Aeneas, who is performing an analogous act of harmonization, juggling his priorities to restore them to their correct balance.[181] Only if we listen to

[180] This looks like a complication of an interesting moment in the *Odyssey*. After Athene appears to Telemachus to tell him to leave Sparta (15. 9–43), Telemachus describes his decision to Menelaus as being the work of his spirit (θυμός, 15. 66).

[181] It is not an identical act of harmonization, since the reader hears more from Jupiter about the future than does Aeneas from Mercury, who speaks only of Ascanius, and rule over Italy (274–6); on the interesting question of the differences between Jupiter's and Mercury's words, see Harrison (1984*b*), 18–23.

Jupiter and Mercury can we feel this disjunction fully, as we follow Aeneas in trying to inhabit two (mutually incompatible) worlds of significance simultaneously. It matters very much that it is Mercury who delivers the message of Jupiter, for Mercury/ Hermes was understood by the allegorists as the mediator, the interpreter (ἑρμηνεύς) of the divine word, the Logos which regulates the world.[182] It is, then, very precisely the word, the perspective of Jupiter, of history, of the inevitable, to which Aeneas is straining to attune himself. This is not a quasi-novelistic way of representing a decision made by Aeneas, a *faute de mieux* which we must tolerate in narrative until the invention of the realism of the developed novel. It is a stunning way of doing something which Vergil does in various ways throughout the poem, putting Aeneas into a vice between the two blocks of being his own person and being an embodiment of his people's aspirations, and then turning the handle as tightly as it will go. And we feel only a fraction of any of this if we brush aside Jupiter and Mercury as nothing more than Vergil's oddly roundabout way of revealing to us how Aeneas changed his mind and decided to leave Carthage.

More attractive, but sometimes equally misleading, is the approach which sees divine characters exploiting tendencies which are already present in the humans.[183] Certainly passages in Homer read in this way, and Vergil's reading here could have been guided by the explicit practice of the commentators.[184] At times Vergil comes very close to this technique. Amata is eminently predisposed to Allecto's workings; readers since Servius and Ti. Donatus have felt that Dido would have fallen in love with Aeneas 'anyway', without the work of Venus and Cupid;[185] the Trojan women in Book 5 are tinder for Juno's and Iris' spark (613–17). Even here, however, it is important for readers to be on their guard,

---

[182] Buffière (1956), 289–96. Heinze (1915), 307–8, first applied such readings of Hermes to the passage in *Aeneid* 4. Hardie (1986), 278–9 has some excellent remarks on this aspect of Mercury here; he cites the scholia on *Od.* 5. 45–8 and *Il.* 24. 343 (the Latin commentary tradition follows suit: Serv. auct. *Aen.* 8. 138). At *Od.* 1. 38, the scholion refers to the same interpretation of Hermes as Logos; the context may appear very apt, since Zeus is speaking of how he sent Hermes to persuade Aegisthus not to kill Agamemnon and marry Clytaemnestra.

[183] Most recently and compellingly in Lyne (1987), esp. 66–71.

[184] Above, p. 55.

[185] Serv. *Aen.* 1. 670; Donat. 1. 132. 30–133. 8 and 1. 354. 24–355. 17 (Dido); 2. 57. 17–19 (Amata).

since Vergil either does not allow the originally natural to remain in the naturalistically comprehensible mode,[186] or else he declines to resist inventive play with the conventions at his disposal.

The action of Iris at the end of Book 5 is a good example of this second tendency. Iris disguises herself as one of the Trojan women, Beroe, and passionately urges the women to burn the ships (620–40). The sweep of action is interrupted, however, when Pyrgo disconcertingly speaks up: 'This isn't Beroe, you know' (*non Beroe uobis*, 646). This looks like a god, says Pyrgo; besides, she has just seen Beroe herself (647–52). One might be tempted to label this deft exposure of the convention as 'Callimachean', were it not for the fact that Homer himself uses this quasi-comic device, when Noemon says that he had seen Mentor getting in a boat to leave Ithaca—'or else a god who looks just like him; that's what amazes me; I saw god-like Mentor here yesterday morning, but the other day he was getting on a ship to Pylos' (*Od.* 4. 653–6). And it is important to note that the women are still uncertain what to do, and are only impelled to action when the goddess reveals her divinity (5. 654–60).

Plausibility is often (whether explicitly voiced or not) the justification for the conventional ways of interpreting these scenes of divine intervention.[187] Yet, if the readings proposed here of the scenes with Amata and Turnus have any validity, Vergil's methods regularly appear to destabilize the prevailing criteria of plausibility, even as accepted by the poem itself. The authority of realistic norms in narrative is still so powerful for most modern readers that it is very difficult to adapt to the very different narrative techniques which may be encountered in epic generally, and in the *Aeneid* in particular. It demands a considerable effort on the part of classicists to remind ourselves of just how recent the dominance of realism is, yet the effort must be made if we are to do justice to the variety and strangeness of the gods' means of operation in the poem.[188]

Further, the adherents of plausibility almost inevitably find themselves arguing that Vergil presents the gods acting in the

---

[186] Johnson (1976), 43–5, on Dido.

[187] Especially, Lyne (1987), 67–8.

[188] Johnson (1976), 25–6, on the *Aeneid*; Frye (1976), 35–61, on the tyranny of realistic reading conventions.

poem in the way he does because that is how he conceived of them acting in the world; the success of the divine action is the token of the sincerity of the belief (and, with inevitable circularity, the sincerity of the belief is the guarantee of the success of the divine action).[189] The theoretical objections to such an approach have been rehearsed many times.[190] It is striking that such ways of reading epic persist among many classicists, when the mainstream of classical criticism has come around to questioning their usefulness in the reading of non-epic poetic forms. 'In fact these questions about truth and sincerity ought to be translated into questions of literary technique and imagination'—that remark of Gordon Williams on the Latin love-poets, highly controversial on first publication in 1968, would now command widespread assent; something like it should begin to inform the reading of epic also.[191] Certainly the ancient commentators on Vergil took it for granted that he exercised the poet's prerogative of eclecticism in matters of religion and philosophy, adapting what he said according to the demands of the poem.[192]

It must be stressed that our objection to the biographical approach is not based on any judgement of whether or not the historical Vergil might have been capable of seeing the gods at work in human emotion. There were available, in his culture, authoritative ways of talking about the gods as a direct influence on human beings. The most explicit such account surviving is that of Plutarch, whose dialogue on love purports to follow Plato's *Phaedrus*. The characters agree that it is impious simply to identify Eros or Ares as the names of human passions; there really are gods responsible for these passions in human beings.[193] The point is simply that the gods' mode of operation in the *Aeneid* cannot be validated by an appeal to the hypothetical religious sentiments of the poet.

All the *Aeneid* needs in order to achieve its effects is to create its own grounds of belief, or assent, such as may authenticate its fictions. Even if we had, therefore, independent evidence for Vergil's religious beliefs at the time when he was writing the

[189] Heinze (1915), 331; Boyancé (1963), esp. 37–8; Kühn (1971), esp. 176–8; Lyne (1987), esp. 65–8.
[190] Belsey (1980), 15–19.
[191] Williams (1968), 525.
[192] Serv. 1. 227; 6. 264; 10. 467; cf. Ti. Donatus *Prooemium*, 1. 6. 1–12 Geo.
[193] Plut. *Eroticus* 757 b–e.

*Aeneid*, we would not be any nearer to an account of what the gods contribute to his poem. To take another tack. Vergil clearly did not 'believe' that Aeneas met the founder of Carthage, since his account involves a glaring anachronism which would have been obvious to any Roman schoolboy. Yet his story of the love of Dido and Aeneas is one of the most powerful, memorable, and 'true' events in the poem, contributing to what the poem has to say in ways which are wholly independent of the reader's latent awareness of the actual unreality of the event. Ancient speculation about the nature of poetry had, as we saw in the first chapter, been preoccupied from the beginning with the power of poetry to create this kind of truth.[194]

It is, accordingly, too blunt to make the poem's success or failure in this sphere depend on a reconstruction of what the first audience 'believed about the gods'. The question of the religious beliefs of the Roman élite has become very controversial recently, after many years' confident assurance that an educated contemporary of Vergil must have been as sceptical and rational about 'Roman religion' as the modern observer.[195] The whole question of what such people believed is now open for discussion—indeed, the very terms of debate are being called into question, as classicists absorb the lessons of the anthropologists' consummate scepticism about transferring such culturally determined concepts as 'belief' from one society to another.[196]

The poem's first audience will have been accustomed to various different discourses about the divine, and accustomed to adjusting to the preconceptions required for being at home in each. Certainly, from the start, the Roman tradition had been much less inclined than the Greek to look for authority in poetic accounts of the divine. Poetic and dramatic representations of the gods must have had some kind of impact on the way in which Romans conceived of their gods, although it is exceedingly difficult to know what the nature and extent of that impact may have been.[197] None

---

[194] Cf. Daiches (1984), 214: 'The truth of poetry, as distinct from that of philosophy or theology, is self-authenticating. Other truths or alleged truths can be argued about, there can be proofs and disproofs, believers and unbelievers . . .; but poetry operates differently'.

[195] Jocelyn (1966) was a path-breaking study; cf. North (1986).

[196] Price (1984*a*), 10–11, referring to Needham (1972); cf. Geertz (1974).

[197] Momigliano (1984*a*), 886.

the less, the first readers of the *Aeneid* would have instinctively felt that the Homeric, mythic basis for the gods' actions in the poem was not something that applied with much power to other areas of their own lives: this is *fabulae*, how poets talk. Further, a reasonable amount of philosophical learning was demanded of the audience, before they could penetrate the varieties of allegory exploited by the poem. This, too, is a mode of thought which readers needed self-consciously to recover and apply, and which did not inform many (or any) other aspects of their lived experience.

Some features of the poem will have spoken more directly to the religious duties of the individual, and the religious ceremonies of the city. Most conspicuous here is the concern of Jupiter for the well-being of the Roman state, an image which chimed in with Romans' most fundamental assumptions about their world. The Penates, likewise, are very important to the poem, as an emblem of the religious city's links with the past, and of its permanence into the future.[198] The Roman reader will have taken for granted the centrality of their worship to the city's existence, and will have been used to connecting the cult of the Penates with the city's past, as a result of the careful maintenance of the custom whereby the consuls and praetors sacrificed every year to the Vesta and Penates of Lavinium.[199] Again, the poem's representations of the divine have many powerful points of contact with the cults being fostered or established by Augustus, and the contemporary audience will have responded to Cybele and Apollo through the medium, in part, of Augustus' constructions concerning those gods.[200] Romans must have responded favourably to the poem's picture of how the divine forces in the world are progressively won over to the Roman enterprise. The anti-Trojan deities, Minerva and Neptune, are no longer hostile, while Vulcan, the father of Cacus, and the maker of arms for Turnus' father (12. 90–1), is shown as relenting, and fabricating the arms of victory for his wife's child, Aeneas.[201]

It is not, however, a question of recapturing what is 'really' religious about the poem, and then discarding the rest as the fiction.

---

[198] On the Penates, Latte (1960), 108; in the poem, Heinze (1915), 34–5.

[199] Wissowa (1912), 164.

[200] Wiseman (1984); Paschalis (1986).

[201] 8. 370–453; the god of fire, then, joins the god of water in the Trojan–Roman camp, and only the god of air is missing, until the war against Hannibal.

Rather, we must recognise that there was no one homogeneous background of 'belief' for the poem to map itself onto in order to succeed. The variety of ways of talking about the divine which the poem assumes in its audience, and uses itself, is so diverse that it means virtually nothing to ask the question 'Did Vergil's audience believe in the gods of the *Aeneid*?' The poem has to authenticate its own fictions by exploiting the capacity for assent which is present in the society's range of discourses about religion and the divine.

## IV

I must Create a System, or be enslav'd by another Mans
I will not Reason & Compare: my business is to Create
William Blake, *Jerusalem*[202]

In the light of the discussion of Apollonius in Chapter 2, it might be questioned whether assent or authentication are really what the poem is after. In this connection, much might be made of the question which Nisus asks as he gazes out from the Trojan camp at the sleeping Latins, and feels the urge to fight: *dine hunc ardorem mentibus addunt, / Euryale, an sua cuique deus fit dira cupido?* ('do the gods add this zeal to our minds, Euryalus, or does each person's dire passion become a god for him?', 9. 184–5). Nisus asks here of himself a question which characters in the *Odyssey* (and not the *Iliad*) pose of others' actions: οὐκ οἶδ᾽ ἤ τίς μιν θεὸς ὦρορεν, ἦε καὶ αὐτοῦ / θυμὸς ἐφωρμήθη ἴμεν ἐς Πύλον ('I don't know whether some god stirred him, or his own spirit was stirred to go to Pylos', 4. 712–13).[203] To Vergil, these questions come in the train of a long intellectual history,[204] and they open the possibility of a consistently rationalized reading of the poem's divine action. In this instance, however, the issue is not, as it might so easily have been, and as it was in Apollonius, a

---

[202] Ch. 1, Plate 10, 20–1.
[203] Cf. 7. 263; 9. 339; 16. 356–7. The closest the *Iliad* comes to this form of expression is at 6. 438–9. This is not to say that every impulse in the *Iliad* is ascribed to a god (in the model for the Nisus and Euryalus scene, Diomedes says that his spirit urges him on to the night raid, 10. 220–2); it is just that no one in the *Iliad* wonders if someone is acting at the prompting of a god or of his or her own spirit.
[204] Schaerer (1944).

dilemma which calls into question the *modus operandi* of the epic. For there are three aspects to this problem of the awareness of the divine: what is the knowledge of the human characters, of the reader, and of the poet?

The human characters show a wide variance in their knowledge and ignorance of the divine processes at work in their world, but the norm is a dismaying failure of recognition or understanding (moments when humans recognize divine action clearly for what it is tend to be moments of final catastrophe).[205] At one extreme is Dido, marked out as *fati nescia*, 'ignorant of fate', at her first mention (1. 299), and doomed throughout to incomprehension of how two gods and two goddesses are making a wreck of her life. Aeneas, on the other hand, is the recipient of many prophecies, signs, and visitations, so that when he stands before the assembled hosts in Book 12 and says that he is confident of the gods' backing (188), he is entitled to be as close to certainty as any pagan could expect. And yet, of course, even Aeneas' perspective is at best imperfect. Even as late as the eighth book, even after his father has prophesied the glories of the line in Book 6, he is reduced to helpless anxiety at the unexpected collapse of his hopes in Latium (8. 18–25), while the consummation of his mission, as has been noted many times, is performed in ignorance (8. 729–31).

The gods themselves play upon human pious ignorance to achieve their ends, and the second book in particular shows them sending signs which deceive the credulous mortals.[206] It is inevitable that divine signs will mean different things to different people. A good example comes at 8. 524–9, where great claps of thunder, and flashing weapons in the sky, follow Evander's offer of alliance to Aeneas. Evander is terrified, especially since the name of his son was the last word he spoke. Eden quite rightly interprets the sign as favourable for Aeneas, and stresses the 'latent irony of the situation'.[207] A reference to Apollonius seals the irony, since after a similar portent in Book 4 of the *Argonautica*, the Argonauts drop

---

[205] Turnus at the end recognizes the hostility of Jupiter (12. 895); Panthus recognizes that Jupiter has marked Troy for destruction (2. 326–7).

[206] Block (1981), 255–94.

[207] Eden (1975), on 532 ff. On the conflicting meanings of the two signs here, see the excellent discussions of Grassmann-Fischer (1966), 29–38, and Barchiesi (1984), 74–90.

off the son of Lycus (4. 298), who is the model for Pallas.[208] If
Evander had made his interpretation the primary one, then Pallas
would not have gone on the expedition.

This gulf between human and divine understanding creates resources of irony which contribute powerfully to the tragic atmosphere of the poem. Again and again, trenchant juxtapositions cast
into relief the feebleness of human effort beside the gods' impervi-
ous self-sufficiency. When Juno, for example, realizes that Dido
has been captured by love for Aeneas, the goddess is described as
*cara Iouis coniunx* ('dear wife of Jupiter', 4. 91). When Venus has
arranged that Aeneas may go safely into Carthage to meet Dido,
she moves serenely off to her favoured Paphos, *laeta*, 'happy' (1.
416); less than a hundred lines later, Dido appears for the first
time, *laeta* (503). The 'happiness' of the gods is a constant feature
of their immortal nature, but whenever humans are 'happy' in this
poem, disaster is very near.[209] On their own plane, gods kiss, console, converse, and make love with one another in a manner consistently denied the human actors.[210] The poem has one beautiful
domestic simile, of a woman who rises early for the spinning, to
keep her husband's bed chaste and rear her small children (8.
407–13). This picture of the rhythm of human life is (mis-)applied
to mark the time when Vulcan leaves to work on the shield of his
adulterous wife's bastard; a god may accommodate himself even
to this much.

The poem's comparative paucity of divine intervention on the
human level is, in some regards, an aspect of the same phenomenon. This paucity can, in fact, be overstated.[211] Juno and Venus
deflect spears from Turnus and Aeneas, Jupiter stirs up Mezentius
and Tarchon to battle, and helps Ascanius to shoot Numanus
Remulus.[212] Still, there is a distinct lack of the Homeric patterns of
conversation, aid directly given, and even blows exchanged
between men and gods. Some of these passages had scandalized
generations of readers, and Vergil acknowledges this tradition

---

[208] Feeney (1986*a*), 49–50.
[209] Cf. 1. 35; 7. 288.
[210] 1. 227–9, 254–6; 4. 90–128; 12. 791–842; 8. 370–406.
[211] e.g. Boyancé (1963), 25–6.
[212] 9. 745–6 (Juno and Turnus); 10. 331–2 (Venus and Aeneas); 10. 689; 11.
725–8; 9. 630–1 (Jupiter).

when he makes the Greek hero Diomedes repent of his mad attack upon Aeneas' mother (11. 275–8). Yet modern critics are perhaps too ready to attribute Vergil's departure in technique entirely to decorum.[213] There is indecorous divine action enough in the *Aeneid*, after all, and such a response may obscure the fact that Vergil's norms also result in a shutting-out of the intimacy and co-operation between men and gods which is a corollary of Homer's technique.

Juno aids Turnus throughout Book 9, and rescues him from the rampaging Aeneas in Book 10, yet he remains always unaware of her presence, and attributes these actions to Jupiter and Venus, while a Homeric pattern would have allowed for the possibility of conversation and a sustaining partnership between man and patron goddess.[214] Turnus does speak with his sister Juturna when she acts to save him (12. 632–49, 676–80), but she is a minor goddess, an ex-mortal, who, in her eternal mourning for her brother, remains exempt from the divine prerogative of ultimate invulnerability (12. 872–86). Even Aeneas, the son of a goddess, does not converse with his mother as Achilles does with Thetis.[215] The first time they meet in the poem, she is in disguise, and runs away from him as he recognizes her (1. 314–409); when she gives him his shield, she speaks to him but receives no answer (8. 608–15). Only her epiphany at the sack of Troy remains in the memory of Aeneas and the reader as a moment of acknowledged salvation (2. 589–632).

If the human characters experience great difficulty in recognizing the divine at work in the poem, the reader is in a more privileged position—necessarily, for the poem's fundamental tragic irony depends precisely on the reader's knowledge. It by no means follows that the reader's role is problem-free. From the moment we are introduced to the perspectives of Juno and Jupiter in the first book, the difficulty involved in switching between the views of gods and humans becomes the poem's principal way of disturbing our judgements.

Even within this framework, however, Vergil at times manipulates our responses, and follows his master Apollonius in setting

---

[213] Heinze (1915), 309–10, 481–3; Schlunk (1974), esp. 8–35.
[214] 10. 668–9 (attribution to Jupiter); 12. 52–3 (Venus).
[215] Wlosok (1967), 110–11; Highet (1972), 37–8.

puzzles for the reader, even though he refrains from creating the
wide-ranging dilemmas of the *Argonautica*. He capitalizes on the
practices of Roman augury, in which the deity who sends a
prodigy is left unspecified, to leave open the question of whether
or not it is Venus who sends the doves to guide Aeneas to the
golden bough: they arrive by chance (6. 190), yet Aeneas recognizes them as his mother's birds (193).[216] Uncertainties may proceed from Vergil's technique of focalizing through a particular
character.[217] Aeneas, for example, is not sure whether the snake he
sees at his father's tomb is the *genius loci* or the *famulus parentis*
(5. 95), and Vergil leaves the reader uncertain also. Similarly, in
the same book, when Aeneas prays to Jupiter to save the ships
from fire, we see the colossal storm which follows through
Aeneas' eyes, without Vergil explicitly naming the god responsible
(687–99); it is only when Anchises' shade appears in a dream
twenty-five lines later that Aeneas and the reader learn for certain
that Jupiter was the saviour (726–7). This last example is more
characteristic, for Vergil normally resolves the reader's uncertainties after a space. After reading the opening storm caused by Juno,
we are bound to have our suspicions about the great storm that
Aeneas describes in Book 3 (192–204); two references much later
in the poem combine to confirm the supposition that Juno was indeed responsible.[218]

If we turn to consider the stance of the poet, especially with the
Apollonian model in mind, the reassertion of the poet's command
is very striking. Where there are gaps for the reader to fill, Vergil
creates the impression that it is not that he cannot tell, but that he
need not tell all he knows.[219] The poet's relationship with his
Muse, his authority and his source, is not the organizing principle
of uncertainty which it had become in Apollonius. The poem
begins and ends with the poet questioning the ways of the divine,
but even at these limits his pose is not Apollonian. He cannot account for the apparent evil that comes from the gods, but he can,
and does, vouch for his narration of it.

[216] On this aspect of Roman augury, see Grassmann-Fischer (1966), 117.

[217] On this useful concept, see Genette (1980), 189–94 and (1988), 72–8; Bal
(1985), 100–18. These issues have been made accessible for classicists by de Jong
(1987).

[218] 5. 801, with Williams (1960), ad loc.; 7. 300. See here Block (1981), 133.

[219] On the impression of power in Vergil's selection and knowledge, see Conte
(1986), 171–2; further, on Vergil's authority, Putnam (1987).

Vergil's reassertion of the epic narrator's control after Apollonius has its primary rationale in the aetiological force of the *Aeneid*. The poem, striving to establish itself as the myth which explains the nature of Rome, needs an authoritative, validating voice—and this voice the Augustan picture of the *uates* was ideally equipped to provide.[220] This is one of the ways in which the *Aeneid* is striving towards the status of genuine myth, which explains the present state by retelling the original determinative acts of mythical time. As Mircea Eliade puts it, 'certain decisive events took place during the mythical period, and it was after them that man became what he is at present'.[221] The twist of the *Aeneid* is to invest quasi-historical events with such a significance, for, as Eliade points out, as far as the mythical imagination is usually concerned, 'historical events proper have no significance since they carry no soteriological message'.[222] Kirk's description of the function of aetiological myths sounds uncannily like a description of the variety of critical responses which may be applied to the *Aeneid*'s meditations on the nature of the Roman experience:

the myth offers an apparent way out of the problem, either by simply obfuscating it, or making it appear abstract and unreal, or by stating in affective terms that it is insoluble or inevitable, part of the divine dispensation or natural order of things, or by offering some kind of palliation or apparent solution for it.[223]

The poet's voice is not, however, simply a return to Homer instead of Apollonius. Vergil is composing the *aetion* to end all *aetia*: everything in the world is the way it is because of this beginning. And it is the master-poet of *aetia* ('causes'), Callimachus, who provides the prime role-model for Vergil when he confronts the problems of inspiration, authority, and tradition.[224] Callimachus represents himself in the first two books of the *Aetia* in conversation with the Muses, guiding and directing the dialogue. He is, therefore, as E. V. George puts it, 'indispensable to his own scheme': 'he must have his dream; his audience must have him, to whom the Muses will talk, through whom others may gather the information given.'[225] He even goes so far as to banter

[220] Newman (1967), 30–42.
[221] Eliade (1963), 91.
[222] Ibid., 134; his first example is the Trojan war.
[223] Kirk (1970), 258.
[224] Klein (1974); George (1974), esp. 12–15.
[225] George (1974), 12.

with the Muses by arrogating to himself their characteristic
anaphoric claim to knowledge: 'I know', he says in fr. 43, 'I know'
(οἶδα, οἶδα, 43. 46, 50).[226] In the second half of the poem, when
the conversation with the Muses is dropped, Callimachus' own
status as authorizer necessarily heightens.[227]

Vergil announces his subject in his own voice (*cano*), and when
he first turns to the Muses it is in order to know causes (1. 8). This
unsubordinated stance is maintained in the second proem, which
introduces the second half of the poem. Here Vergil calls on the
Muse Erato in Apollonian fashion (*nunc age ... Erato*, 7. 37; Εἰ
δ' ἄγε νῦν Ἐρατώ, 3. 1). Yet Apollonius follows on with a command to the Muse to speak, whereas Vergil keeps the reader waiting for three lines of indirect questions before emphatically placing
his first person verb at the head of the line: *expediam* ('I shall ex-
pound', 7. 40). As in the first proem, the goddess's job is to remind (*mone*, 7. 41); and Vergil's pose as he lays out the facts is
Callimachean, as the consulter of authorities (*accipimus*, 7. 48).
The partnership of poet and Muse, the asserted harmony between
tradition and authority in the poet's own voice, is powerfully seen
in the invocation in Book 9, where Vergil asks the Muse to 'unroll
the huge boundaries of the war *along with me*' (*et mecum ingentis
oras euoluere belli*, 9. 528). The status of the Augustan poet
stands out in clear relief against the Ennian model for this line,
since Ennius asked 'Who is able to unroll the vast boundaries of
the war?' (*quis potis ingentis oras euoluere belli?*, 164), and probably went on to say, or imply by prayer: 'only the Muses'.[228]

The fiction of the *Aeneid* must be asserted with so much power
that it will itself become a tradition. The poem faces head-on the
fact that it is a fiction, yet one that has its own achieved power,
effect, and truth: it can make the invented characters of Nisus and
Euryalus live (9. 446–9); it can flaunt the implausibility of the
transformation of the ships (9. 77–122), knowingly conceding that
such things are no longer 'believed', but asserting that the *fama* of
the event has lasted, and will last, through the ages (9. 79). Other
versions become part of the new *fama* that is the *Aeneid*, while
Vergil can describe his own innovation as *incredibilis fama*, which
we must none the less accept.[229] In Book 4 Vergil shows us Fama

---

[226] Cf. Hes. *Th.* 27–8, ἴδμεν, ἴδμεν, 'we know, we know' (the Muses speaking).
[227] Fr. 75. 53–5, 75–7.
[228] Skutsch (1985), on 164.
[229] 3. 294 (bringing Andromache into the Aeneas-saga for the first time).

in action, working like the poet, singing a mixture of truth and falsehood (190), pouring, rather than flying, over the lips of men (195).[230] Yet his voice subsumes hers—is able, indeed, to give a report of the report-giver.[231] This is the most self-referential moment in the poem, for Vergil flaunts here, more dramatically than anywhere else, his awareness of the power of his fictive art to command credence even in the face of the audience's knowledge that the anachronistic affair between Aeneas and Dido is the poet's own created fiction. As soon as Fama has left the poem, Vergil gives the actions of Iarbas, who 'is said' to have prayed to Jupiter (*dicitur*, 204). By whom? By none other than the poet, the author of the new tradition which is evolving as we read.

The *Aeneid* is therefore the quintessential epic, in its sustained creation of a fiction which comprehends the true and the false, the real and the unreal, history and myth. It is in this achieved fiction that the gods belong, as real as Aeneas, as real as Dido.

[230] Hardie (1986), 275 n. 118.

[231] See the baffled comments of Servius on Vergil's use of the phrase *ut perhibent* ('so they say') to introduce the family connections of Fama (4. 179): *quotienscumque fabulosum aliquid dicit, solet inferre 'fama est'. mire ergo modo, cum de ipsa fama loqueretur, ait 'ut perhibent'* ('whenever he says something out of myth, he customarily says "the famed story is". So it's amazing that just now, when he's talking here about Fame herself, he says "so they say" ').

# 5

## Ovid's *Metamorphoses*

### I

For given Man, by birth, by education,
Imago Dei who forgot his station,
The self-made creature who himself unmakes,
The only creature ever made who fakes,
With no more nature in his loving smile
Than in his theories of a natural style,
What but tall tales, the luck of verbal playing,
Can trick his lying nature into saying
That love, or truth in any serious sense,
Like orthodoxy, is a reticence?

W. H. Auden, ' "The Truest Poetry is the
most Feigning" '

Ovid's *Metamorphoses* afford us something of an intermezzo. The
very appearance of a chapter on this poem in a book on epic is itself an issue—a fact which the poet would no doubt have found
highly diverting. From its first lines the poem continually confronts us with the problem of the extent to which, and the ways in
which, it is and is not epic.[1] There is no obligation here to enter
into a full account of the poem from the viewpoint of its continually destabilized generic norms, yet by taking this line as a first
thread into the poem it may be possible to discover a promising
starting-point for our investigation into what the poem has to say
about epic and its gods. As a commentary on the epic view of the
gods the poem is priceless, while it will prove to be of the highest
importance for the epics which follow it, especially the *Thebaid*
and *Argonautica*, where its influence on this aspect of epic form is,
if anything, greater even than that of the *Aeneid*.[2] It will emerge

[1] The entire debate over the epic nature of the *Metamorphoses*, a key issue since
Heinze (1919), has been set on a new footing by Hinds (1987); cf. the anticipations
of Nicoll (1980).
[2] Bibliography on the gods in the *Metamorphoses* in Hofmann (1981), 2188–9;
Elliott (1979–80).

that Ovid's emphases are markedly different from those of the poets we have been examining so far, for his range of mythological interest is vast, and his coverage eclectic in the extreme. For all that, his preoccupation with epic modes is pervasive, and highly enlightening.

Novelty is proclaimed in the poem's second word, and paradox follows straight after, as the proem's dense allusions, followed by the opening cosmogony, adumbrate the perspectives we will need in order to read this un-epic epic, an uncategorizable multi-form prodigy:

> In nova fert animus mutatas dicere formas
> corpora; di, coeptis (nam uos mutastis et illa)
> adspirate meis primaque ab origine mundi
> ad mea perpetuum deducite tempora carmen.

My spirit leads me to tell of shapes changed into new bodies; gods, breathe on my undertakings (for you have changed them as well), and, from the first origin of the world, spin out my poem unbroken down to my own time. (*Met.* 1. 1–4)

In the fourth line, *perpetuum* appears to distance the poet from the non-epic aesthetics of the master, Callimachus, while *deducite* draws him simultaneously nearer.[3] The ensuing cosmogony picks up this tergiversation. Certainly the cosmogony is not serious philosophy for its own sake, but it is concerned with mapping out the terrain of possibility for the poem. It is highly significant that there is a good measure of control and direction behind Ovid's evolving universe, as is very much not the case in, for example, the neoteric universe sung of by Silenus in Vergil's sixth *Eclogue*. Silenus' world is 'essentially fragmented, not ordered, fortuitous, not designed'.[4] Ovid's world, on the other hand, emerges from strife by the work of a god, or nature (21), who organizes the separate

---

[3] Hinds (1987), 19, with bibliography of the numerous discussions, esp. Kenney (1976): add Hofmann (1985). Such, at least, is the reading imposed by the blunt dichotomies which two generations of Latin poetry had read into the prologue to Callimachus' *Aetia*. A fascinating (as yet unpublished) interpretation by S. J. Heyworth blurs the apparent rigidity of the paradox, yielding a reading of the proem that sees it as true to the spirit of the *Aetia*; see, rather differently, Knox (1986), 9–10. For a restatement of the importance of epic to the definitions of Callimachus and Ovid, see Hinds (1989), Anderson (1988). For the latest and most thorough defence of the reading *illa* in line 2, see Kovacs (1987).

[4] Hubbard (1975), 61. Note, however, that the *Metamorphoses* begins as if it were an epic ecphrasis (compare Ap. Rhod. *Argon.* 1. 496 ff.).

locations of the constituent elements (22–31). This world is more epic than neoteric in the very fact of its controlled organization— although, as we shall see shortly, the *mundi fabricator* does not act in a very epic manner. The oddness of the control is caught in a moment of comparison with Vergil's universe: Vergil's Jupiter controls the winds by putting on top of them a mass of high mountains (*Aen.* 1. 61), while Ovid's *mundi fabricator* places above them the *aether*, explicitly 'liquid and lacking weight, containing nothing of earthly sediment' (*liquidum et grauitate carentem / aethera nec quicquam terrenae faecis habentem*, 1. 67–8).

In many important ways Ovid's cosmogony is redolent of anti-epic allegiances,[5] yet the element of control (however qualified) is indispensable to Ovid's conception of the nature of metamorphosis: as Barkan points out, 'for all its emphasis upon the blurring of clear categories, metamorphosis is as much concerned with reduction and fixity as with variability or complexity'.[6] There is more involved here than acknowledging that agreed categories are necessary for representation of transition. Aristotle's discussion of change, for example, 'insists that in every change (whether movement in space or alteration in quality or size) *something remains the same*'.[7]

The story which most dramatically illustrates the poles of fixity and flux is the weaving-contest between Minerva and Arachne. This story also affords key insights into the poem's conceptions of art, into its ways of talking about the gods and divine power, and will therefore repay some attention.[8] The Arachne story follows on from Book 5, whose last portion is concerned with genre, as Minerva listens to the Muses' account of their singing competition with the mortal Pierides (5. 251–end). Since the issues there have been fully discussed by Hinds (1987), let us analyse the sequel, and follow the goddess as she changes role, becoming herself a competitor in art with a mortal.

[5] Knox (1986), 10–13.
[6] Barkan (1986), 66; cf. Coleman (1971), 462, on the cosmogony as a necessary minimum backdrop of order for the metamorphoses to follow.
[7] Ackrill (1981), 31 (his italics); cf. Anderson (1963), 4–5; Solodow (1988), 183–6.
[8] The passage is much discussed. See, above all, the extremely valuable article of Leach (1974); also Lateiner (1984); von Albrecht (1984); Hofmann (1985), 230–4; Barkan (1986), 1–18; Brown (1987).

Arachne's superlative craftsmanship is described in terms which not only establish her credentials as a mistress of neoteric art, but also (at first) align her with the *mundi fabricator*, and hence with Ovid himself. She begins with rude, unwrought material, as does the demiurge (*rudem ... lanam*, 6. 19; cf. *rudis ... moles*, 1. 7); this she forms into a globe (*glomerabat in orbes*, 6. 19; cf. *magni speciem glomerabat in orbis*, 1. 35). From here on she becomes more and more neoteric. She sets to work the *opus*, making it *soft* by drawing it out to a length, turning the *smooth* spindle with a *light* thumb (*mollibat, leui teretem*, 21–2).[9]

Pallas' work, however, is described first, marked out as artistic-ally and morally weighty, symmetrical and accessible: 'the com-position of the goddess' work is flawlessly Classical, perfectly centered, balanced, and framed, highly moral and didactic in con-tent'.[10] Her competition with Neptune at Athens is the first ele-ment to be described, occupying the centre of the composition (6. 70–82): self-praise and self-vindication are therefore the sub-ject. The Olympian gods are all there, two times six—with Jupiter in the middle of the assemblage and the line—in all their august weightiness (*augusta grauitate*, 73).[11] Each deity is recognisable by his or her distinctive attributes (73–4); appearance corresponds with actuality.[12] When Pallas 'simulates' an event on her tapestry, it is no dissimulating lie, but the event itself (80–1). Around this satisfying centre are arranged in symmetry four neat scenes show-ing contests 'between a rash woman and a goddess, all resulting in the metamorphosis of the mortal (83–100)'.[13] The whole is framed by a border of Pallas' own tree, the olive: this is the *modus* (102), a terminus of artistic moderation. The composition is now finished, with the word 'end' at the end in a culminating gesture of decorum (*finem*, 102).

Arachne's work is, by contrast, a neoteric masterpiece,

---

[9] On the loaded import of such vocabulary, see Cairns (1979), 21; Hinds (1987), 21–2. Ovid also aligns the poetic craft of Orpheus with the action of the demiurge, as they each make a concord out of discordant elements (1. 25, 10. 146–7). On the correspondence between the power of the creator and of the poet, see Lieberg (1982) and (1985).

[10] Anderson (1972), 160.

[11] We will return to the resonance of the epithet: Augustus belongs here, if we take him and the gods on their own valuation.

[12] Barkan (1986), 90 acutely remarks that only the gods can have faith in their form (*fiducia formae*, 2. 731).

[13] Anderson (1972), 160.

asymmetrical and wilful.[14] The picture it gives of the gods is, correspondingly, far from Pallas' justified order: these gods are swept pell-mell through the currents of natural flux, not static and identifiable by attribute, but bewilderingly mutating in order to work their sexual will upon helpless humans. In the goddess's work, only humans were undergoing change; in the human's work, the humans are a given, while the gods mutate. Jupiter's characteristically regal *imago* on Pallas' tapestry is now the *imago* of a bull, or a satyr (103, 110), adopted for disguise. As the humans in the tapestry are tricked, cheated, duped (*elusam*, 103; *luserit*, 113, 124; *deceperit*, 125), so the spectator is gulled by Arachne's craft: *you* would be tricked, like Europa, into thinking Jupiter's *imago* was a real bull (103–4), even though you have read the story already in the poem and know that the bull is *fallax* and *falsus* (2. 871, 3. 1). The apparently true is an illusion. As Pallas' last lines had capped her stately, measured performance, so Arachne's border is graced with the programmatic *tenui* ('slight', 127).

Pallas and Envy could not pick Arachne's work to pieces (129–30, with yet another weaving/criticism play, on *carpere*). What are *we* to make of it, and of Pallas' own work? This is, after all, a competition, with judgement invited. Most modern readers will instinctively side with Arachne's neoteric vision, and most modern readings, accordingly, offer an Arachnaean version of the poem as a whole.[15] Other important modern readings, however, adopt a Minervan perspective. Otis sees the episode (and the poem) from Minerva's point of view, while Bömer's commentary gives here, as elsewhere, a consistently Minervan reading.[16] A path through these alternatives is offered by Leach, whose fine article demonstrates that if we adhere to one antithesis or the other we will fail to do what justice we can to the complexity of the poem's perspectives.[17] Ovid's pendulum never rests in its oscillation between the poles of Minerva and Arachne, epic and neoteric canons: 'As the creator of the poem, Ovid maintains a vision embracing both points of view.'[18] The episode is a lesson in perspective, with divine and human order and flux, fixity and instab-

---

[14] Anderson (1972), 164–5; Galinsky (1975), 82–3; Hofmann (1985), 230–4.

[15] e.g. Little (1970); Solodow (1988), 196–7.

[16] Otis (1970), 146; Bömer (1969–86), vol. 3. 35–6.

[17] Leach (1974); cf. Brown (1987).

[18] Leach (1974), 104. As Professor Hinds points out to me, the weaving of both contestants is described in markedly neoteric terms in 61–9 (note especially the key

ility—this is why it comes at a moment which has often been marked as the transition from a predominantly divine perspective to a predominantly human one.[19] Minerva's work is an exaggerated picture of divine epic decorum, Arachne's an exaggerated picture of neoteric divine abandonment. Yet Arachne depicts nothing about the gods that was not already present, however faintly, in epic tradition. Minerva's reading is *too* epic, glossing over the difficulties of divine action which had been present in epic from the beginning.[20]

This is not to say that Arachne's craft might not be, in the end, closer to the poem's dominant mode.[21] In the last resort, Ovid is a human artist, like Arachne, and not a god.[22] Arachne corresponds to one commonly available archetype of the artist: obsessive, naïve, destroyed (like Ovid) by direct encounter with the power of the world she is trying to describe. Her metamorphosis into a spider is a sickeningly appropriate punishment for Minerva to devise. The perpetual weaver of webs that are proverbially easy to destroy,[23] her qualities of fine grace are exaggerated into parody as she becomes simply small, tiny (142), her fingers programmatically *exiles*, embodying the stylistic thinness which is the fate of failed small-scale composition (143). The celebrator of beautiful disorder is now doomed to the spider's weaving of utter symmetry.[24] Worst of all, as Seneca tells us in a fascinating disquisition on animal instinct, a spider's work is not art. All spiders produce the same, none is more skilled than the next:

Nascitur ars ista, non discitur. itaque nullum est animal altero doctius: uidebis araneorum pares telas . . . incertum est et inaequabile quidquid ars tradit: ex aequo uenit quod natura distribuit.

*deducitur* of 69: cf. Hofmann (1985), 231. As he puts it, 'the two contestants have more in common than they are prepared to admit; neotericism depends on what it subverts'.

[19] Otis (1970), 166, 315; Wilkinson (1955), 148.

[20] Ovid delights in resensitizing us to epic's evasions. It has been objected, for example, that his battle descriptions are too distant: 'Urbane hexameters and pointed conceits adorn the violence and gore of the battle of the Lapiths and Centaurs' (Lyne (1984), 13). Yet these tactics may jolt us into seeing Homer and Vergil as being themselves merchants of beautiful descriptions of the horrific and macabre.

[21] So Brown (1987), 219–20, and (one suspects) Leach (1974).

[22] Leach's discussion is extremely valuable here as well.

[23] Otto (1890), 34.

[24] Plin. *HN* 11. 80–2; Philostr. *Imag.* 2. 28.3; Plut. *Mor.* 966 e–f.

That art is innate, not learnt. And so no animal is more learned than the next: you'll see that spiders' webs are all equal . . . Whatever art bestows is uncertain and uneven; what nature distributes issues from an even source. (Sen. *Ep.* 121. 23)

At the end, it really is true that you would know she was taught by Minerva (*scires a Pallade doctam*, 23).

It becomes necessary to enquire into what the boundaries and transgressions are which constitute the *Metamorphoses'* disorderly order, and where the divine belongs in them, especially in relation to the human. How much is stable, how much in flux? What are the rules for the categories of perspective across these divisions?

The cosmogony establishes the rules of the game, the fundamental boundaries whose limits the poem's transgressions will explore. Gods, humans, and animals belong each in their own sphere (1. 69–78). From the first, the relationship between the human and divine becomes an issue. It is left unclear whether the first humans were made by the creator-god, and hence had a share in his divine nature, or else were made from the earth's new mud, and thereby gained an element of the ethereal (1. 78–88). The picture is further complicated as we go on, as we learn of the offspring of the Giants' blood (151–62), and of Deucalion and Pyrrha (313–415).[25] Since the appearance of mankind is a metamorphosis of the earth (1. 87–8), a human's transformation into a rock or tree is a reversion to origins; yet, since there may have been divine elements at man's creation, and since the celestial element may have been lingering in the primeval mud (1. 79–81), a human's elevation to deity may also be seen as a return to something cognate.

Being human is living in suspension between the divine and the inanimate or animal.[26] As inhabitants of the iron age, humans demarcate themselves off from the categories on either side by laws and conventions, so that the question of how natural it is to be a human being becomes one of the poem's main preoccupations. The Greek explanatory myths of the Ages of Men allowed a large space for sacrifice, and its associated topic of diet, as a means of

---

[25] Not to mention mushrooms (7. 392). See Bömer (1969–86), vol. 1. 70, on the inconsistencies of Ovid's accounts of man's origins.

[26] Detienne (1972).

showing how men are distant from, and yet close to, the gods.[27] Ovid's poem follows up its initial interest in the divine element in man's origins by likewise concentrating on the dietary relations between gods and men. The very first metamorphosis in the poem after the cosmogony shows a man becoming an animal as a result of offending divinity by an abuse of the sacrifice, by violating the alimentary norms.[28] Lycaon offers Jupiter human sacrifice, part boiled, part roasted, to test his divinity, and becomes a wolf (1. 226–39). Yet dietary relations are not Ovid's principal means for charting what is human about being human, how near humans are to the divine, or how far from it. Perhaps unsurprisingly, for his most systematic charting of the main similarities and differences across these categories, Ovid uses sex.

Three tales of aberrant sexual impulse (two adjacent) cluster in Books 9 and 10: Byblis desires her brother (9. 454–665); Iphis is in love with one of her own sex (9. 666–797); and Myrrha sleeps with her father (10. 298–502). Each of these urges provides different ways of viewing what is natural for humans, using gods and animals as the demarcations.

Iphis cannot see her desire for another female as anything but unnatural: animals do not behave like this (9. 726–34).[29] Iphis' story ends happily, as Isis transforms her into a male so that her marriage may be performed, but the incestuous Byblis and Myrrha, on either side of her, flail about in their determination to undermine any natural basis for the sexual conventions which bar fulfilment of their desires. Myrrha, like Iphis, uses the example of animals, but this time she justifies her own licence by appealing to animals' promiscuity, exploiting a style of argument which was over 400 years old by the time Ovid put it in her head.[30] Her desire, sex with her father, is clearly 'natural', argues Myrrha, since animals do it; it is only human *cura* which has created *leges* and *iura* to prevent it (10. 324–31). In a sense, of course, Myrrha is right. Sexual perversion is a concept that relates only to humans: what is 'natural' for animals cannot be 'natural' for humans. It is

---

[27] Vernant (1980), 168–85.

[28] Barkan (1986), 27.

[29] See McKeown (1989), on *Am.* 1. 10. 25–8, for this style of argument in philosophy and oratory.

[30] A famous fragment of Philemon already encapsulates Myrrha's line of argument (fr. 93 *CAF*); see Heinimann (1945), 145–7.

'natural' (inevitable, part of the condition) for humans to be 'unnatural' (different from creatures in Nature).[31] Morality means nothing in relation to animals: 'the [incest] taboo does not alter the violence of sexual activity, but for disciplined mankind it opens a door closed to animal nature, namely, the transgression of the law'.[32]

If Myrrha and Iphis use animals as a reference point, in the first of these three tales Byblis uses the gods as her yardstick for human behaviour. She meanders into thinking of the divine in the course of the fluctuating soliloquy which follows her dream of making love with her brother. What does this dream mean?, she asks herself (9. 495). Dreams can't have any weight—can they? Gods forbid! This last phrase is a conventional translation of *di melius*—'gods better', literally, an elliptical way of saying 'may the gods bring about a better outcome'. The mention of the gods sends her veering to their sexual practice—at which point 'gods worse!' begins to look like a more appropriate exclamation:[33] *di nempe suas habuere sorores* ('certainly the gods have had their own sisters', 497). Appealing to divine licence to justify human licence is the sophistic obverse of Myrrha's appeal to animal behaviour.[34] The nurse in Euripides' *Hippolytus*, for example, urges Phaedra to indulge her passion by pointing to the gods' examples of sexual self-gratification: 'you ought', she says, 'to acquiesce in these norms, conventions' (νόμοι, 451–61).

What the nurse does not know is that in her play the νόμοι of gods are not commensurate with the νόμοι of humans. Ovid's afflicted Byblis does recognize this very fact: *sunt superis sua iura. quid ad caelestia ritus / exigere humanos diuersaque foedera tempto?* ('The gods have their own codes. Why am I trying to make human ways conform to divine laws, which are quite different?', 9. 500–1). Yet within fifty lines she is writing to her brother with the gods once more as her sanction. Laws, conventions, right and wrong are for the old; we are young: *quid liceat, nescimus*

---

[31] Dover (1974), 75. The classic Latin exploration of these dilemmas is Seneca's *Phaedra*; cf. Boyle (1987), 18–24. Bataille (1962), 214, goes so far as to claim that 'man is the animal that does not just accept the facts of nature, he contradicts them.'

[32] Bataille (1962), 219. For Lévi-Strauss, the incest taboo is the definitive transition from Nature to Culture: Lévi-Strauss (1947), 28–9.

[33] Doblhofer (1960), 230.

[34] Ar. *Nub.* 1080 ff.; Eur. *HF* 1314–22; Dover (1974), 76.

*adhuc, et cuncta licere / credimus, et sequimur magnorum exempla deorum* ('We don't yet know what is allowed, and we believe that everything is allowed, following the examples of the great gods', 9. 554–5). After rejection from her brother, the bewildered Byblis turns to the alternative world of demarcation. How could he spurn me?—*neque enim est de tigride natus / nec rigidas silices solidumue in pectore ferrum / aut adamanta gerit, nec lac bibit ille leaenae* ('For he wasn't born of a tigress, nor does he carry hard flint or solid iron or adamant in his breast, nor did he drink the milk of a lioness', 9. 613–15). Normally this topos leads to a climax of expected human behaviour: you are not an animal, or a rock, and should therefore feel compassion or pain as a human does.[35] The handle of Byblis' argument turns in her grasp. It is precisely because he is not an animal that he is reacting as he is, as a human: rejection is what she should expect.

We have already had cause to remark that there are centuries of tradition behind the categories of definition which Ovid is manipulating in order to test what constitutes the naturalness or conventionality of human *natura*. If we confine ourselves to the compatibility of human and divine, it is clear that the tradition offered various positions. It was, first of all, possible to claim that gods and humans were ruled by the same codes (natural or conventional).[36] From this starting-point, it was possible for a human such as Byblis, Phaedra's nurse, or Theseus (in Euripides' *Heracles*, 1314–21) to excuse human behaviour by referring it to divine. The validity of such reference could, on the other hand, be denied, by refusing to accept that the stories of the gods' behaviour were true, and hence available as a yardstick.[37] This is how Heracles responds to Theseus' attempts at consolation (*HF* 1341–6). The opposed responses to the basic dilemma which are offered by Theseus and Heracles in Euripides' play are a polarized way of getting at the problems scouted in *Bacchae* or *Hippolytus*, concerning how human the gods' ways of operation are, or ought to be, or ought to be represented as being (the *Aeneid* never succeeds in escaping from this area of difficulty, as established by its proem). Yet another response to the dilemma is that which modern

[35] Pease (1935), 314–19.
[36] Pind. fr. 169?; Thuc. 5. 105. 1–2; Eur. *Hec.* 799, *Hipp.* 98.
[37] So Xenophanes, Plato, and the other critics discussed in Chapter 1.

scholarship tends to espouse, especially in relation to the *Iliad*; namely, that the gods' norms are quite other than human ones.[38]

The *Metamorphoses'* relation to these issues is a complex one. From the viewpoint of the afflicted women in these three tales, it does appear that gods and animals can behave as they like, while intermediate humanity, hemmed about by civilization's laws and conventions, is cut off from *natura*. The gods are set off from humans by their immense *licentia*, their power for self-indulgence.[39] In this respect, Byblis' first reaction—that it is futile to use divine canons as a yardstick for human—is correct, and her subsequent impulse to follow the example of the gods is deluded.

If humans are defined by being neither gods nor animals, the problem of the compatibility of divine and human behaviour will not, however, go away. Gods may have their own *iura* ('codes'), which humans cannot claim for themselves, yet the poem does not calmly present this as an accepted fact, as we have already been warned by the Arachne episode, with Minerva's refined version of the gods' distinctive (estimable) *iura*, and Arachne's presentation of the gods acting just like, or worse than, human beings. Instead, from various angles, the poem worries away at the extent to which, and the ways in which, divine and human are compatible. As we saw above, the beginning of the poem sets up the problem of how divine humanity is; the corollary is the problem of how human divinity is. Are the gods like us, or not, and what are the implications of asking, and attempting to answer, such a question?

Ovid's exploration of these dilemmas is set by his form. It is typical of him that he should embrace the confinements of his conventions, and set about testing them to destruction. His starting-point is the starting-point of epic, that narrative representations of divinity must proceed by analogy. The poem's first episode of divine action establishes this inevitable point of departure; the first pattern of analogy suggested in the poem, and the first simile, together establish pervasive parallels between divine and human action.

The first emotion felt by a god in the poem is Jupiter's anger, a

---

[38] Otto (1954), 241–3; Reinhardt (1960a), 24–6; Kerényi (1975), 91–113 (on the marriage of Zeus and Hera); cf. the regular comments in the Iliadic scholia along these lines, a sort of watered down Stoicism (cf. Cleanthes' *Hymn, SVF* 1. 537. 18–21): bT 4. 4; 8. 429; 21. 465.

[39] Vernant and Vidal-Naquet (1973), 128; Little (1970), 92–6.

response to the outrage of Lycaon. Ovid's stance here is far from the questioning anxiety of Vergil's *tantaene animis caelestibus irae?* (*Aen.* 1. 11), for he introduces the sequence with the blandly unproblematic *ingentes animo et dignas Ioue concipit iras* ('he conceived in his heart vast anger, worthy of Jupiter', 1. 166). He next sets the scene for the divine council. The social organization of the gods, living in their various suburbs, is made analogous to the Roman orders: nobles, plebs, each have their own place (168–74). The climax is a bold inversion of the expected terms of comparison, as the seat of divine government is compared to the residence of Augustus: *hic locus est, quem, si uerbis audacia detur, / haud timeam magni dixisse Palatia caeli* ('this is the place, which, if I were bold enough to say it, I would not fear to call the Palatine of great heaven', 1. 175–6). The correspondence with Augustus is particularly tight at this point, since we know that Augustus held Senate meetings in the library attached to his temple of Apollo on the Palatine, which was itself intimately linked with his residence.[40]

The reaction of the assembled gods to Jupiter's story of Lycaon becomes the subject of the poem's first simile, comparing their reaction to that of the Roman Senate, hearing the news of a conspiracy against the life of Augustus:[41]

> confremuere omnes studiisque ardentibus ausum
> talia deposcunt: sic, cum manus impia saeuit
> sanguine Caesareo Romanum exstinguere nomen,
> attonitum tantae subito terrore ruinae
> humanum genus est totusque perhorruit orbis:
> nec tibi grata minus pietas, Auguste, tuorum
> quam fuit illa Ioui.

All made a noise together, and with burning zeal demanded the one who had dared to do such a thing, just as, when an impious band made their

---

[40] Suet. *Aug.* 29. 3; see the very interesting discussion of Thompson (1981).

[41] So first Due (1974), 71–2, against the interpretation which sees the assassination of Julius Caesar as the point of reference; Due's originality here is typical of his excellent, and oddly uninfluential, book. The correspondence of the simile is very close indeed if Thompson (1981), 339, is right in suggesting that Senate meetings in Apollo Palatinus began in 23 BCE, with Augustus' convalescence from his near-fatal illness; for it may then have been in the temple of Apollo that the news was announced of the attempt on Augustus' life by Caepio and Murena. But the whole dating of these events is most vexed: see Nisbet and Hubbard (1978), 151–7. The atmosphere of Senatorial procedure is well caught in the discussions of Wilkinson (1955), 195, and Ahl (1985), 79.

savage attempt to blot out the name of Rome with Caesar's blood, the human race was astonished with a sudden fear of complete disaster, and the whole world shuddered. Nor was the pious devotion of your people less pleasing to you, Augustus, than was this display of devotion to Jupiter. (1. 199–205)

Jupiter relates the atrocity and punishment of Lycaon, and announces his intention of destroying all mankind, ending his speech in a rant, *frementi* (209–44). As he concludes, the typically human behaviour of the gathering of gods is wittily highlighted by their reaction. Various reactions of dissent and agreement are the norm in divine councils;[42] times have changed, however, and Ovid holds back two key words to show that now the only competition is in degrees of acquiescence:

> Dicta Iouis pars uoce probant stimulosque frementi
> adiciunt, alii partes *adsensibus implent.*

One group declared their approval of Jupiter's words with speech, goading him on further as he ranted; others played their part with applause. (1. 244–5)

More deft humour follows, rerunning the old topic of the gods' anxiety over the deprivation of their sacrifice;[43] so that Jupiter promises a new race to succeed the doomed generation (246–52). His frantic mood is accentuated, however, as he vacillates over the means of destruction. He is about to throw his bolts, but is anxious over the possible celestial damage. No, flood is better: the fire next time (253–61).

The unabashedly human characterization of the whole episode is clear, and is presented by the comparison and simile as no oblique inevitability, but a prime focus of interest. The poet's bland acceptance of his convention is disconcerting: can he possibly be unaware of the fact that the divine anger which he depicts here had been a stumbling-block in epic for centuries?[44] In fact, as the poem proceeds, divine anger and its power become Ovid's principal medium for testing the donnée of epic's religion, the humanity of the divine.[45] A problem of judgement does emerge.

[42] Hom. *Il.* 4. 20–4; Verg. *Aen.* 10. 96–7; Ov. *Met.* 9. 418–21.

[43] Aristophanes' *Birds* is built around this joke; cf. Ar. *Plut.* 1113–14; Pl. *Symp.* 190 c; and Lucian's marvellous *Iuppiter Tragoedus.*

[44] According to Wilkinson (1955), 193, he is.

[45] Besides anger, his other main medium is love; cf. Wilkinson (1955), 196–9; Otis (1970), 122–4. Note that the epic theme of divine anger, in the stories of Lycaon and the flood, comes before the love theme of 1. 452 ff.

Two episodes of divine anger follow the opening tableau (2. 602, 659), before the reader encounters a case where judgement becomes overtly an issue.[46] Ovid introduces the story of Actaeon (changed to a stag by Diana after seeing her naked, and torn to death by his own dogs), with an explicit avowal that Actaeon had committed no crime, but had merely blundered through ill luck (*at bene si quaeras, Fortunae crimen in illo, / non scelus inuenies; quod enim scelus error habebat?*, 'but if you made a proper inquiry, you would find in this case the fault of Fortune, not a crime; for what was criminal about a mistake?', 3. 141–2). At the end of the episode, having announced that Diana's anger was sated only by Actaeon's death (3. 251–2), Ovid reports the varying responses to her act of vengeance:

> Rumor in ambiguo est; aliis uiolentior aequo
> uisa dea est, alii laudant dignamque seuera
> uirginitate uocant: pars inuenit utraque causas.

People's opinions went either way. To some the goddess appeared more violent than was fair; others praised her, and described her as acting in accordance with her stern virginity. Both sides found good grounds. (3. 253–5)

The only person who does not speak on one side or the other, but who feels mere joy at the disaster to the family of the hated Europa, is Juno (3. 256–9). Here at last, after the witty false start of an early reconciliation between Jupiter and Juno (1. 734–8), the Vergilian theme of Juno's vast anger is activated, with a reprise of Vergil's proem: she has here also a longer-standing and a more recent cause for her anger (3. 258–61), which now dominates until the end of Book Four. And we encounter a decided escalation: Diana can at least be sated by Actaeon's dogs being sated with their master's blood (3. 140, *canes satiatae sanguinis erili*; 252, *ira ... fertur satiata Dianae*), but *Saturnian* Juno cannot be sated (*nec sum Saturnia, si non ...*, 271).[47]

Within eighty lines we have heard the story of Juno's treatment of Teiresias. As the only person to have been both male and female, he is asked by Jupiter and Juno to give a verdict on a playful dispute (*lite iocosa*, 3. 332): does the male or the female have

[46] Glances at the problem, though, at 2. 435, 567–8.
[47] On this wordplay in the *Aeneid*, see Anderson (1958), 523–5. Ovid's clearest play is to be found in the mouth of the dying Hercules, who calls on *Saturnia* to 'sate her bestial heart' with looking at his death (*corque ferum satia*, 9. 176, 178).

more pleasure in sex? Teiresias takes Jupiter's side, declaring for greater female joy. The result:

> grauius Saturnia iusto
> nec pro materia fertur doluisse suique
> iudicis aeterna damnauit lumina nocte.

Juno is said to have felt more pain than was right—out of all proportion; she condemned the eyes of the arbitrator to eternal night. (3. 333–5)

The impersonal report leaves it unclear whether the poet is associating himself with the judgement. In the next book, the Theban women judge Juno 'insufficiently just and too savage' when she engineers revenge against Ino (*parum iustae nimiumque in paelice saeuae*, 4. 547).

The inevitability of judging divine characters in epic by human standards is, then, stressed again and again after the programmatic first simile. Yet, as we have already seen, many strands in the poem reflect on the gods as something wholly other, *sui iuris*— either as stable and consistent (as on Minerva's tapestry), or else unchallengeable in their *licentia*, the ability to indulge their mood in the self-gratifying exercise of power.[48] From here, gods are defined precisely by their incompatibility with humanity. The depth of the gap between the two species is shown in a flash by an Ovidian example of their different languages. One of the divine dream-creatures in the House of Sleep has the job of imitating wild beasts, birds, and snakes (11. 639). Humans, naturally, call him *Phobetor*, 'Terrifier'. To the gods, he is just something that looks like something else: they call him *Icelos*, 'Resembler' (640).

Gods are touched by 'human' emotions, but, in the end, they remain, as on Minerva's tapestry, for ever themselves, for ever exempt from the human standards of suffering, and the mutability of suffering. For the gods, in this most mutable of all environments, are exempt from ultimate change. They may metamorphose for the moment, but they always become again themselves. Only they, as Barkan insists, have *fiducia formae* ('reliance on, confidence in, their form', 2. 731).[49] The god Aesculapius, in one of the poem's most spectacular gestures, can even become a god

---

[48] See especially 6. 269–70 (Niobe, *mirantem potuisse irascentemque, quod ausi / hoc essent superi, quod tantum iuris haberent*); 5. 668, and 6. 2 (the Pierides).
[49] Barkan (1986), 90.

again after being a corpse (2. ˈ647–8). Note that when Ovid describes the subject of his poem from exile, he encapsulates it as *mutatas hominum . . . formas*, 'the changed forms of *humans*' (*Trist.* 1. 7. 13).

This *ultimate* invulnerability[50] is emblematized by the convention that gods cannot weep: *neque enim caelestia tingui / ora licet lacrimis* ('for the faces of the heavenly ones are not allowed to be wet by tears', 2. 621–2).[51] An apparent exception confirms the rule. As Juno beholds Ino, she reflects that Bacchus was able to punish his enemies: *nil poterit Iuno nisi inultos flere dolores?* ('will Juno be able to do nothing but weep over her unavenged grievances?', 4. 426). If Juno cannot achieve revenge as Bacchus does, the contemplated loss of status is so huge as to reduce her to the level of a human, powerless to do anything but weep. It appears that humans have to be superior to gods in morality—or rather, it appears that, with gods as the point of comparison just as with animals, morality is a term that only has meaning in relation to human beings.[52] Ovid's presentation is a restless and anxious version of an insight that could be, in other contexts, regarded as 'one of the strengths of ancient spirituality', namely, 'its instinctive recognition that there are other kinds of worshipful excellence in the universe than those that meet our moral concerns or our human self-interest.'[53] In Ovid's world, for 'worshipful excellence' one must substitute simply 'power'.

By calling such explicit attention in his first simile to epic's procedure of analogy, Ovid appears to promise that divine action will be at least systematic and comprehensible. Yet judgements prompted by the poem continually lead the reader towards seeing the gods as escaping beyond human categorization—only to defeat our attempts to conceptualize that escape in any other than human terms. Minerva's tapestry would show an idealized form of divine justice, a way of conceiving divine action that does fullest justice to epic's capacity to capture both the sublime, refined power of the divine, and the meaning of human action in the light

[50] 'Ultimate' must be stressed; cf. Otto (1954), 131; Vermeule (1979), 123–6.
[51] As announced by Artemis, Eur. *Hipp.* 1396; cf. Bömer (1969–86) on Ov. *Met.* 10. 45 and (1958) on *Fast.* 4. 521–2.
[52] Vernant and Vidal-Naquet (1973), 128–9; see above, pp. 68–9, on the amoral might of Zeus in Apollonius.
[53] Armstrong (1986), 76.

(or shadow) of that power. Yet her passionate response to Arachne's craft shows her being pulled down into acting. Her vengeance can only be conceived of, and represented, humanly, and in those terms can only strike most readers as unjust, disproportionate.[54] Such a complex of reactions is itself a comment on epic, as we have seen. Ovid's competition invites us to see Minerva's version as epic, and then destabilizes that easy judgement by showing that her anger is also epic.[55]

Are the gods like us or not?—an old question, and one which is capable of carrying a heavy religious weight.[56] In the *Metamorphoses*, the diverse responses become a way of questioning the extent to which the world accommodates itself to human understanding: the question transforms into, 'Does the world make sense in human terms?'[57] Ovid's manipulation of the gods of epic exploits the power they have to inform the meaning of human experience, by continually flaunting the possibility that such will be their function—only to deny it. A common response to this denial is to see the poem as an exercise in sardonic belittlement, but we may rather view these strategies as a comprehensive manner of reflecting upon the ways in which the workings of the world are not assimilable to human norms; and the resulting dismay is something which the experience of reading the poem (like the experience of being in the world) prompts the reader to challenge and resist—always to be defeated. Ovid's poem is unique amongst ancient writings in the ruthlessness of its refusal to provide an environment which shapes the meaning of human experience.[58]

[54] The familiar issue of accommodation thus returns: cf. pp. 47, 51.

[55] A splendid comic statement of these same issues comes in Plautus' *Amphitryo* (130–2). Sosia imagines that the night is prolonged because Sun is sleeping off a hangover, and the listening Mercury indignantly remarks *ain uero, uerbero? deos esse tui similis putas?* ('indeed, you punchbag? You think the gods are just like you?'). And the god who so objects to the human's measurement proceeds to thrash his inferior with physical violence.

[56] The Stoics, for example, for all their attempts to idealize the supreme divinity, could not help, in the end, attributing to it human characteristics; it was simply that they attributed only *good* human characteristics (Cic. *Nat. D.* 2. 78–9).

[57] See Gould's powerful analysis of Greek polytheism from this viewpoint: Gould (1985).

[58] Finely argued by Segal (1969), esp. 88. Indeed, in the light of the remarks of Daiches (1984), 24, on the Book of Job, one sees how rare such a vision is in European literature altogether: 'The mind of man and principles of Nature are not intimately fitted to each other, as Wordsworth believed. There are no moral principles to be deduced from Nature, and no comfort to be derived from it, apart from the dubious comfort of realizing its mysterious otherness. This sense of the otherness

The participation of the unaccountable gods is indispensable for Ovid's creation of this *paysage démoralisé*.[59]

Ovid's use of mythology is often portrayed as straightforwardly frivolous, unburdened by any concern beyond the discrete and immediate.[60] Yet patterns of complexity and import may emerge from the poem's endlessly entertaining gymnastics (although I am gloomily aware that the critic, in delineating them, cannot help but squeeze out the inexhaustible vital zest which sustains the poem). It should not surprise that Ovid's mythology comes to be a prime thematic centre of gravity. The gods of epic, participants in a widely shared and understood tradition of great intellectual and artistic richness, provide him with a series of extremely powerful and economical strategies for communicating his vision of human experience.[61] The alternative modes of explanation, after all, science and philosophy, meet with a dusty reception in this poem.[62] The most extended piece of overt philosophy in the poem, the rant of Pythagoras (15. 75–478), has sometimes been seized on as a unifying key, to lock the poem's bewildering variety of perspectives. Arriving here (be it confessed, a little exhausted), readers understandably want a synthesis. But Pythagoras' is only another voice.[63]

II

| τί θεός; τὸ κρατοῦν· | 'What is a god? Wielding of power. |
| τί βασιλεύς; ἰσόθεος. | What is a king? Like a god.' |

Anon.[64]

of the natural world appears intermittently in later European literature; it is given splendid expression in Hugh MacDiarmid's *On a Raised Beach*; but it can hardly be said to play a central part in the European literary imagination.'

[59] 'The Ovidian gods, or metaphors for causal principles, are neither a social class lampooned nor a superstition derided. Pictured or not, they are the carnival mirroring of a cosmic absurdity that, for the poet, is all too real', Skulsky (1981), 52; cf. Phillips (1983), 812.

[60] e.g. Solodow (1988), 108–9. An exception is the interesting discussion of Neschke (1986), who sees Ovid using the gods of myth to point to enduring realities of emotion. In general, I see Ovid as more precisely indebted to Greek mythical ways of ordering experience than she does.

[61] Skulsky (1981), 15: '... the virtue of fantasy is that some intimate features of the terrain of fact can be properly mapped only from the vantage point of the counter-factual.'

[62] Johnson (1970), 138–45; Coleman (1971), 473; Due (1974), 111–12, 162–3.

[63] Very good discussion in Solodow (1988), 162–8.

[64] Anonymous apophthegms on papyrus, quoted by Price (1984a), 234, as the motto for his final chapter (from Bilabel (1925), 339).

Of the many boundary crossings in the poem, the passage from humanity to divinity is the one which will best repay our pursuit, both for its insights into epic procedures of apotheosis, and for the light it sheds on what the poem has to say about the norms of Roman religion.

The poem's first case of a demigod undergoing apotheosis is Hercules. Already, in our discussions of Hercules in the *Aeneid* and *Argonautica*, we have seen the characteristic issues which his transgression brings into play. With his distinctive acuity, Ovid has penetrated to the kernel of the epic (and tragic)[65] picture of Hercules, and highlights his presentation of Hercules' monstrous essence by introducing him into the poem through the perspective of someone who lost a fight with him—Achelous, the river-god, contender for the hand of Deianira. The philosophers' model of self-control is dismissed at a stroke as Achelous reports Hercules' response to his taunts: *accensae non fortiter imperat irae* ('he does not exercise strong command over his kindled wrath', 9. 28). Ovid hastens on, via the story of Deianira and Nessus, to the hero's death, his apotheosis so dominating that the deeds which justify it are crowded out: *longa fuit medii mora temporis, actaque magni / Herculis implerant terras odiumque nouercae* ('the intervening period of time was a long one; the whole world, and the hatred of his stepmother, were replete with the deeds of great Hercules', 9. 134–5).[66] The deeds which filled the earth have not filled a line here; the hero himself will catalogue them as he dies, in less than twenty lines (9. 182–98). We hear more about the labours of Hercules' mother than we do about those of Hercules himself.[67]

As the fire plays around the recumbent hero, the key image of feasting is activated (9. 236–8).[68] Here Ovid introduces a second divine council, where the poem's first analogy is recapitulated. The

---

[65] Silk (1985); March (1987), 75.

[66] Hercules suffers the same fate from another narrator, Nestor, who leaves him out of the story of the Centaurs and Lapiths (*praeteriti Alcidae*, 12. 538).

[67] 9. 281–315. Note the plays on *labores* (289), and *laboriferi* (285).

[68] Hercules' feasting with the gods is the elevated counterpoint of his comic gluttony: Hom. *Od.* 11. 603; Theoc. 17. 22; Call. *Dian.* 144–61 (a highly comical passage, of course); Ap. Rhod. 1. 1319; Hor. *Carm.* 3. 3. 9–12. See *Lex. Icon. Myth.* 3. 1. 472, nos. 578–84, for Heracles in divine symposiastic settings with Dionysus. In many of these representations there is the same tinge of the ridiculous as in Ovid's.

new senatorial procedure of Augustan times surfaces once more, as Jupiter commends his son to the gathering, utilizing the jargon of imperial apotheosis:[69]

> nostra est timor iste uoluptas,
> o superi, totoque libens mihi pectore grator,
> quod memoris populi dicor rectorque paterque
> et mea progenies uestro quoque tuta fauore est.
> nam quamquam ipsius datis hoc immanibus actis,
> obligor ipse tamen.

This fear of yours is a pleasure to me, o gods; and I felicitate myself with all my heart that I am called ruler and father of a people who know their obligations, and that my offspring is safe under your favour as well. For although it is his own tremendous acts which you acknowledge in this way, I am beholden to you all the same. (9. 243–8)

The new member of the heavenly assembly begins to appear larger, and to become awesome in his august gravity (*maiorque uideri / coepit et augusta fieri grauitate uerendus*, 9. 269–70). He is moving into the sphere of Minerva's gods, who enjoy the same august gravity (6. 73). The divine–human analogies of both divine councils allow the adjective's force to spill over from the gods to Augustus, and back again.

The next two apotheoses, of Aeneas and Romulus, exhibit the same compound of epic action with the diction and procedures of genuine political transactions: in their case, we are explicitly in the world of Roman cult. The apotheosis of Aeneas (14. 581–608) has the trappings of epic, with due notice of the wrath and reconciliation of Juno (582, 592–3), and the supplication of Jupiter by Venus (585–95). Yet Venus 'canvasses' the gods, as does Hercules in the *Apocolocyntosis*:[70] the author of that skit knew exactly what he was about when he inserted his splendid joke on Claudius' apotheosis being added as a footnote to the *Metamorphoses*, for he thereby declares the basis of his and Ovid's procedure to be the same parody of senatorial procedure (*Apoc.* 9). The last lines of the episode show Aeneas receiving state cult, with altars and a temple (14. 607–8).

[69] See Bömer (1969–86) on 9. 247–8 for the prosaic quality of the diction, and especially on the quasi-technical force of *immanis* (cf. Vell. 2. 46. 1; Ov. *Tr.* 2. 335). Wilkinson (1955), 195 catches very well the atmosphere of the scene.
[70] After Diespiter's speech, *Apoc.* 9.

Romulus' apotheosis (14. 806–51) is similar, though linked even more closely to that of Hercules.[71] Again, there is the disconcerting eclipse of the actual deed which entitles the hero to divinity: Rome is founded in five words, in the passive, with no named agent (14. 774–5), so that we learn more about the foundation of Crotona at the beginning of the next book than we do about the foundation of the greatest city in the world (15. 9–59). In accordance with this weakness of the euhemeristic element, the epic colour is very strong, with direct quotation of father Ennius.[72] At the height of the epic moment, as Romulus is snatched heavenwards in his father's chariot, Ovid has an odd few lines which return us to the contemporary world of cult. A striking simile has Romulus' mortal body disappearing like a lead slingshot dissolving in midair (14. 824–6). Forthwith, after being invited to concentrate on the wondrous transformation from physical to non-physical, we read of the new god's *facies* and *forma*—in the guise which he will have at the gods' banquets, and at the *lectisternium* of Roman cult, in his role as Quirinus:

> pulchra subit facies et puluinaribus altis
> dignior, est qualis trabeati forma Quirini.

A beautiful appearance comes over him, one more worthy of the high couches, the form which Quirinus has, in his ceremonial dress. (14. 827–8)

Before we reach the climactic apotheoses which close the work, Ovid pursues the sustained interest in the state mechanisms for divinity by telling the story of how the god Aesculapius came to Rome in 292 BCE. It is the second of only two stories from the entire history of the Roman Republic which find their way into the *Metamorphoses*.[73] This tale of Republican forms for introducing new cults is the immediate precursor to the institution of the imperial ruler-cult, and occupies about the same amount of space;[74]

---

[71] Even to the extent that Ovid has Hercules' father snatch him away in his chariot (9. 271–2), instead of the canonical Minerva or Victory; this is done to match the traditional account of what happened to Romulus, who was taken to heaven in the chariot of *his* father, Mars (14. 819–24; cf. Skutsch (1985), 260).

[72] 14. 814; cf. Skutsch (1985), 205, and Conte (1986), 57–9, on the reminiscence of Ennius both here and at *Fast.* 2. 487.

[73] The other, immediately preceding Aesculapius, is the story of how Cipus refused to become the king of Rome (15. 565–621).

[74] Aesculapius takes 123 lines (622–744), Caesar and Augustus together 126 (745–870).

the contrast between the two forms is marked by Ovid at 15. 744–6, and the differences are indeed instructive.[75] The story of the importation of Aesculapius' cult is a piece of Roman history (most unfortunately, Livy's eleventh book, where we would have found the historian's version, does not survive); as such, it is almost inevitable that Ovid should introduce it with his only appeal to the Muses, slyly labelled as 'bards' *ever-present* divinities' (*praesentia numina uatum*, 15. 622).[76] He refers to Aesculapius as the son of Coronis, in order to send us back to Book 2, where we had read of Coronis' death and Aesculapius' birth, and heard a prophecy of his extraordinary oscillations from semi-divinity to divinity, then to death, and back once more to divinity (2. 600–648). His move to Rome is his last metamorphosis, a token of Rome's stupendous expansion. In Book 2 he is hailed as *toto* . . . *salutifer orbi* ('bringer of health to the whole world', 642). When he arrives at Rome, he comes as *salutifer urbi* ('bringer of health to the city', 15. 744). The apparent descent from 'world' to 'city' is recuperated by the familiar *urbs/orbis* play: the city *is* the world.[77]

The Republican modes of operation emerge clearly, to set up what will follow. When the decision to consult the Delphic oracle is taken, and when the Roman embassy arrives there, the third person plural verbs have no subject, so that the communal nature of the decision and mission receives the highest stress (*cernunt*, 628; *petunt*, 630; *adeunt*, 631; *orant*, 633). The Senate responds to the oracle's advice (641), and they send to Epidaurus a legation (643), whose actions are, likewise, reported in the anonymous third person plural (644–6). Even when the god appears to the leader of the embassy, no name disturbs the pattern of effacement. Ovid reports that the god appeared *ante tuum, Romane, torum* ('before your bed, Roman', 654). This man was Q. Ogulnius Gallus,[78] any of whose three names will fit into the hexameter, so that his anonymity is seen as part of a comprehensive strategy. From beginning to end, no individual is named.

When the embassy is referred to collectively, they are called

---

[75] Although the transition from Aesculapius is normally seen as void of significance; e.g. Solodow (1988), 26.

[76] The 'gods' of the poem's second line may conceivably include the Muses, but *di* does not mean them exclusively; at 10. 148–9, the poet is not Ovid, but Orpheus.

[77] Hardie (1986), 364–6, with bibliography cited there.

[78] Broughton (1951–60), 1. 182.

*Aeneadae*, the descendants of Aeneas (682, 695). Nowhere else in the poem is this lofty Lucretian and Vergilian title[79] applied to Romans; we shall shortly see a new appropriation of this corporate epithet. Finally, when the new god arrives in Rome, the whole people goes to meet him, together with the Vestal Virgins (729–31). The collective nature of the idealized Roman Republic could hardly have been more strenuously asserted; the elder Cato, who supposedly suppressed the names of all Roman commanders in his *Origines*, would have understood, and approved.[80]

Some three centuries now go by, and Ovid turns to the apotheoses which will close the poem. Aesculapius came to Rome as a foreigner, a new-comer, but Caesar is a god in his own city (*Caesar in urbe sua deus est*, 15. 746). As often in Roman literature, the question is posed: which Caesar, Julius or Augustus? An elaborate sentence keeps decision poised for four lines, with a reference to quickly-won glory perhaps tilting the balance to Augustus, before the question is resolved:

> Caesar in urbe sua deus est; quem Marte togaque
> praecipuum non bella magis finita triumphis
> resque domi gestae properataque gloria rerum
> in sidus uertere nouum stellamque comantem,
> quam sua progenies; neque enim de Caesaris actis
> ullum maius opus, quam quod pater exstitit huius.

Caesar is a god in his own city. He was outstanding in war and peace, but it was not so much his triumphantly concluded wars, or his achievements at home, or his rapidly-won glory, that turned him into a new heavenly body, a comet-star; no, it was his offspring. For out of Caesar's deeds no achievement is greater than the fact that he was the father of this person. (15. 746–51)

These disconcerting lines offer the blunt interpretation (corresponding to what actually happened) that what made Julius Caesar a god was his son: it was, indeed, his son who made him a

---

[79] Surely it was Ennius who domesticated this Greek form. Titus Flamininus described himself in the singular and the Romans in the plural as 'descendants of Aeneas' in the (Greek) epigrams which accompanied the offerings he made to Delphic Apollo after declaring the freedom of Greece in 196 BCE (Plut. *Flam.* 12. 5–6). An epigram in the *Palatine Anthology* concerning the sack of Corinth in 146 BCE describes the Romans thus (the sack is revenge for Troy; 7. 297. 6).

[80] Plin. *HN* 8. 5. 11. Griffin (1985), 178–80, has a useful collection of ancient and modern testimonia on 'Rome as a collective state'.

god.[81] This notion is still present in the next few lines, as we are invited to reflect on the paradox that all Caesar's mighty deeds shrink to insignificance beside the fact that he was Augustus' father (750–9). These are certainly lines which it is very tempting to read ironically.[82] Is it *really* the case that none of Caesar's acts was more important, more worthy of apotheosis, than the 'begetting' of Augustus (*genuisse*, 758, is a worrying word)? Great deeds ought to be the entitlement to heaven for Hercules and his successors; such is the entire point of the euhemeristic enterprise.[83] Even in the case of Hercules and Romulus, however, we saw the actual mighty feats being oddly muted, with apotheosis being presented as the result of divine power politics. Ovid's account of how Caesar became a god is always, as it were, stumbling against the mechanics of his elevation—through his heir.

Next, as with the previous apotheoses, we veer from constitutional procedure into the plane of epic myth, with an Ennian account of Venus' concern (761–80). Even here, of course, her actions are caught by analogy, for her concern manifests itself in 'canvassing' (*ambitus* is what she is up to at 15. 764, just as at the apotheosis of Aeneas, 14. 585). Eventually she is addressed by Jupiter, in the middle of whose speech the mythical and procedural perspectives are blended: *ut deus accedat caelo templisque colatur, / tu facies natusque suus* ('that he should come to heaven a god, *and* be worshipped in temples, this you will bring about, you *and* his son', 818–19).[84] Once more we are confronted with the fact that, 'in real terms', Caesar is a god because his adopted son made him one.

The realm which provides this language of sons making their fathers gods is that of imperial panegyric.[85] Panegyric being what it is, the focus is fixed on the *laudandus*, the son, and the role of the Senate and people in the process of deification is eclipsed.[86] At

---

[81] Though we will soon need to qualify this statement.

[82] Hinds (1988), 24–5.

[83] White (1988), 353: 'There was an essential connection in Roman thought between apotheosis and activity in public life.'

[84] In 15. 808–15, where Jupiter speaks of his celestial archives, it is tempting to see a glance at the *tabularium* housed in Augustus' Palatine complex: for the *tabularium*, see Millar (1977), 264.

[85] Vell. 2. 126. 1, with the parallels ad loc. of Woodman (1977), esp. [Sen.] *Oct.* 528–9; Plin. *Pan.* 11. 2–3.

[86] For the importance of the roles of Senate and people in the institution of Caesar's cult, see Weinstock (1971), 389–90; Wardman (1982), 51–2.

this climactic moment in the *Metamorphoses*, the eclipse of Senate and people is not idle. The wave of popular enthusiasm after the Ides of March, culminating in the response to the appearance of the comet in July 44; the debates in the Senate on 1 January 42, and the carrying of a law to institute the cult—all missing. And not simply absent, but conspicuously and meaningfully absent, since the introduction of Caesar's cult has been presented by Ovid directly after the Republican institution of a new cult, that of Aesculapius, which serves as an introduction, and a foil.

The disparities are instructive, and the concentration on the 'constitutional' element of Caesar's deification is sharpened, even more than in the apotheoses of the other demigods. The decision to introduce the cult of Aesculapius to Rome is, of course, taken by the Senate, and welcomed by the people. Caesar's cult, on the other hand, is presented as the sole responsibility of his son and his 'mother'. The most dramatic illustration of the switch from the communal to the individual is provided by Ovid's use of the powerful language which clusters around Venus and Aeneas.[87] When the Roman Republic invites Aesculapius to the city, the representatives of the people are twice called *Aeneadae*, 'descendants of Aeneas' (15. 682, 695). Perhaps since Naevius and Ennius, and certainly since the late Republic,[88] the ancestress of the Aeneadae, the Roman people as a whole, had been Venus, hailed by Lucretius in the first line of his poem as *Aeneadum genetrix*, 'mother of the descendants of Aeneas'. When Venus first appears in Ovid's narrative of Caesar's apotheosis, she is *Aeneae genetrix*, 'the mother of *Aeneas*' (15. 762), in a return to the original personal use of the word in Ennius.[89] The disturbance of the Lucretian tag has its tally forty lines later, when Venus prepares to spirit Caesar away from his fate (804): here the collective epithet is definitively displaced, for Caesar is *Aeneaden*, in the singular. [90]

[87] It is the vital thematic importance of this language which makes it necessary for Venus to be the one who rescues Caesar's soul in the *Metamorphoses*, whereas in the *Fasti* it is Vesta (3. 701–2).

[88] See p. 110.

[89] Aeneas' daughter describes Venus as *genetrix patris nostri* (58 Skutsch). See Weinstock (1971), 23, on the relationship between Lucretius and Ennius here. At *Aen.* 12. 554, Vergil hints at the sort of move we see in Ovid, by placing *Aeneae* beside *genetrix*; this is a trick, however, for *Aeneae* is dative, not genitive (*hic mentem Aeneae genetrix pulcherrima misit...*). Note also the beautifully suggestive language of *Aen.* 1. 589–90: *ipsa decoram / caesariem nato genetrix...*

[90] Bömer (1969–86) ad loc. doubts the text, but it is guaranteed by this movement.

Not simply '*a* descendant of Aeneas', but '*the* descendant of Acneas'. Venus Genetrix was Caesar's pre-eminent contribution to Roman cult, the objectification of claims which he had been asserting from his youth,[91] and the goddess was prominent in the funeral and cult which followed his death.[92] The title was now charged with a finely calculated ambiguity. Of whom was Venus Genetrix the ancestress? Of the gens Iulia? Of Caesar? Of the Roman people?[93] The run of Ovid's narrative splits the welding to reveal starkly the appropriation of the corporate by the individual. Ovid can even represent Venus describing Julius Caesar as 'the only thing left to me from Trojan Iulus' (*quod de Dardanio solum mihi restat Iulo,* 15. 767); the rest of the *populus Romanus* have vanished from her concern. The epic cast to the apotheosis, with the conversation between Venus and Jupiter, accentuates this privatization. When Venus spoke to Jupiter in Naevius, she was, beyond her care for her son Aeneas in mythical time, the future ancestress of the Roman race.[94] In the corresponding scene in the *Aeneid,* her familial concern returns as a motive even in historical time, by virtue of the stupendous accident which had delivered control of the world into the hands of one of the family of Aeneas' son Iulus.[95] Now the scene between Venus and Jupiter is played yet again, and the mythic concern for an individual and a family has become overwhelming, crowding out the Vergilian balance between communal and individual which emerges as one of the most striking features of the *Aeneid* scene when one returns to it after reading the *Metamorphoses.*

Ovid deftly turns the same Vergilian speech in other ways, furthering the concentration on one individual, who, as Caesar's heir, will bear the burden *alone* (15. 820). Vergil's Jupiter speaks to Venus of 'the fate of your people' (*fata tuorum,* Aen. 1. 257–8). Ovid's Jupiter speaks to Venus of 'the fate of your offspring' (*fata tui generis,* 15. 814), referring to Caesar alone, yet using a word for offspring which is cognate with Genetrix, and which usually

[91] Weinstock (1971), 17–18, 23–6; Horsfall in Bremmer and Horsfall (1987), 24.

[92] A model of his temple of Venus Genetrix contained his bier (Suet. *Iul.* 84. 1); in a reciprocal arrangement, Venus' temple housed a statue of Caesar while Caesar's temple housed a painting of Venus (Dio 45. 7. 1; Plin. *HN* 35. 91): Weinstock (1971), 361, 363, 393; Horsfall in Bremmer and Horsfall (1987), 24.

[93] Taylor (1931), 63; Schilling (1954), 316; Weinstock (1971), 85.

[94] Above, pp. 109–11.

[95] Above, p. 139.

refers to a race, not an individual. Vergil's Jupiter had described the Romans as *'masters* of the world' (*Aen.* 1. 282), with the subjugated Greeks held in 'slavery' (*seruitio*, 285). This startlingly blunt language is part of Republican panegyric, but Caesar first appears to have replaced the corporate *populus Romanus* with himself as lord of the earth.[96] In the mouth of Ovid's Jupiter, as he talks of Augustus, the supplanting accordingly follows: *quodcumque habitabile tellus / sustinet, huius erit: pontus quoque seruiet illi* ('the entire habitable portion of the world will be his: the sea also will be in his thrall', 15. 830–1).[97]

The climax of this process is the great prayer which closes the section on Augustus. He is compared to Jupiter (15. 857–60, lines to which we return shortly), and then the gods are asked to delay the moment when he will be called to join them (861–70). The prayer is worth setting out in full:

> Di, precor, Aeneae comites, quibus ensis et ignis
> cesserunt, dique Indigites genitorque Quirine
> urbis et inuicti genitor Gradiue Quirini
> Vestaque Caesareos inter sacrata Penates,
> et cum Caesarea tu, Phoebe domestice, Vesta,
> quique tenes altus Tarpeias Iuppiter arces,
> quosque alios uati fas appellare piumque est:
> tarda sit illa dies et nostro serior aeuo,
> qua caput Augustum, quem temperat, orbe relicto
> accedat caelo faueatque precantibus absens.

Gods, I pray—companions of Aeneas, for whom sword and fire gave way; our country's native gods; Quirinus, father of the city, and Mars, father of invincible Quirinus; Vesta, enshrined amongst Caesar's household gods, and along with Caesar's Vesta, you, Apollo, part of his household; Jupiter, you who occupy on high the Tarpeian citadel; and all the other gods whom it is allowable and pious for a bard to invoke: may that day be far removed, and later than my own time, when Augustus, leaving the

---

[96] Weinstock (1971), 52. Note that Vergil does apply this language of personal slavery to Octavian in the panegyric at the beginning of the *Georgics* (*seruiat*, 1. 30, referring to his domain after apotheosis); this is too strong for the balance between corporate and individual which the *Aeneid* strains to maintain.

[97] But it is possible that Ovid redresses the balance in his closing lines, where he talks of 'Roman power' extending over the world, not Augustus' (15. 877); it is tempting to see a rebuff to Augustus' flawed reading of Ovid's poetry in Ovid's claim there that he will be read by the lips of *the people* (*ore legar populi*, 15. 878).

world which he regulates, reaches heaven and listens to our prayers, no longer among us. (15. 861–70)

It is immediately obvious that the prayer is, so to speak, chronological, and that its focus moves from the communal to the individual. It begins with the fall of Troy, with the Lares and Penates whom Aeneas rescued and carried to Latium. Ovid knew as little as we do who the *di Indigetes* were, but he took them to be ancient, and ancestral, on the basis of Vergil's words at the end of the first *Georgic*, in the great prayer which is Ovid's model throughout (*di patrii Indigetes*, 1. 498). As in Vergil, Romulus/ Quirinus follows, the founder of the city; next his father Mars; then we reach Vesta, the third of the deities in Vergil's prayer, whom Vergil addressed as *Vesta . . . mater, / quae Tuscum Tiberim et Romana Palatia seruas* ('Mother Vesta, you who keep Etruscan Tiber and Roman Palatine', G. 1. 498–9). All of Vergil's three addressees are communal, with Vesta linked to the Palatine as the home of Rome's founder, Romulus.[98] But Ovid's Vesta is now among the gods of Augustus' household[99]—and along with her, with *Caesar's* Vesta, is placed Apollo, called *domesticus*, belonging to the household of Augustus.

After the death of Lepidus in 12 BCE, when Augustus was finally able to claim the last prize and become *pontifex maximus*, he did not move into the residence of the pontifex near the temple of Vesta, but made part of his private house public land, and instituted there a cult of Vesta, linked with the domestic worship of his own Lares and Penates: 'thus the hearth and home of the state religion was localized on imperial land'.[100] It was an extraordinary transformation for *Vesta publica populi Romani Quiritium*, the guarantor of the city's identity and continuity, whose whole raison d'être consisted in remaining fixed in her *sedes*.[101] The mighty temple of Apollo on the Palatine was, likewise, linked intimately with the ruler's private residence; it was, even physically, inextricable

---

[98] See Thomas (1988), on G. 1. 499.

[99] Contrast the language used of the cult of Vesta during the Aesculapius episode of the Republic (15. 730–1).

[100] Wardman (1982), 69; cf. Taylor (1931), 184; Latte (1960), 305–6; Liebeschuetz (1979), 70. Ovid links Vesta and Augustus intimately at *Fast.* 3. 415–28, on the anniversary of Augustus' assumption of the chief pontificate.

[101] Lacey (1986), 126, describes Vesta as 'the most basic of the city's gods, immovable'; his language highlights the extraordinary nature of Augustus' innovations.

from the residential complex.[102] The enmeshing of Vesta, Apollo,
and Augustus is caught by the intricate word order of 864–5:
*Vestaque Caesareos inter sacrata penates, / et cum Caesarea tu,
Phoebe domestice, Vesta.* The same phenomenon is caught in the
*Fasti*:

> Phoebus habet partem: Vestae pars altera cessit;
> quod superest illis, tertius ipse tenet.
> state Palatinae laurus, praetextaque quercu
> stet domus: aeternos tres habet una deos.

Phoebus has a part; another part has gone to Vesta; what is left over from
them, he himself holds as a third member. Live on, you laurels of the
Palatine, and may the house live on, bordered with its oak wreath: the
one house has three eternal gods. (*Fast.* 4. 951–4)

These phenomena put into question the very terms 'public' and
'private';[103] the privatization of communal cult and the commun-
alization of private cult are only one aspect of the evolution of the
principate from an individual household into the state government.[104] In Ovid's presentation, this vision is part of a pattern sustained over the entire closing portion of the poem. It
answers, in fact, the first divine action of the poem, which compared the gods' residence to the Palatine, and set up the poem's
main lines of analogy. Following that first divine episode, Apollo
came next; on rereading, we see that Apollo's first appearance in
the poem looks forward to his association with the Princeps, as he
predicts to the laurel (in the poem's first prophecy) that it will
adorn Augustus' residence (1. 562–3).

With Apollo and Vesta thus linked in Ovid's prayer with
Augustus, one may be prompted to find a more personal tie to the
princeps in the case of the two gods, Mars and Jupiter, who flank
the Palatine deities. Out of all Augustus' buildings, Suetonius
chooses Mars Ultor, Apollo Palatinus, and Jupiter Tonans for special mention (*Aug.* 29. 1). Is Ovid's *Gradiuus* then Augustus'
Mars Ultor? Is Jupiter on the Tarpeian citadel perhaps not
Optimus Maximus, but a competitor, Augustus' own Jupiter
Tonans?[105] A fascinating story in Suetonius reveals the extent to

---

[102] Zanker (1988), 51.
[103] Cf. Liebeschuetz (1979), 70, on how 'the domestic worship of Augustus'
household became a public cult and citizens in general could be asked to join in'.
[104] On this process, see, above all, Millar (1977), esp. 16, 189–201. On religion
in particular, the clear comments of Latte (1960), 305–6, are very valuable.
[105] It looks as if Lucan reads this Jupiter in his Ovid; cf. Caesar's appeal to

which Augustus' new Jupiter was regarded as a rival for the established Capitoline Jupiter.[106] There is no doubt that Iuppiter Optimus Maximus lost much ground in the reign of Augustus. The pre-eminent god of the Republic, whose temple was coextensive in time with the Republican constitution, saw the Sibylline books removed from his care and entrusted to Augustus' Apollo Palatinus, while the elaborate ceremonials which inaugurated and terminated the military expeditions of Rome were now staged before Augustus' Mars Ultor.[107]

The metamorphoses of Vesta and Apollo (and perhaps of Mars and Jupiter) are almost smuggled into the poem's close, to highlight the themes concerning Roman religion which have dominated since Ovid invoked the Muses, and told the tale of the introduction of Aesculapius' cult to Rome.[108] The increasing identification of Augustus with the *res publica* is nowhere more vividly highlighted than in Ovid's treatment of state cult against a backdrop of epic (particularly Vergilian) scenes. The power of the characteristic Roman way of looking at the gods comes through very strongly: they are part of the constitution, and evolve with it. Prepared for by the apotheoses of Aeneas and Romulus, the interest in the constitutional procedures of state religion dominates the poem's climax, from the importation of Aesculapius, to the deification of Caesar by his son, and finally to the roll-call of gods, once public (in the strict sense), and now—not private, exactly, but 'Caesarian', with all the blurring of public and private which that epithet connotes. The poem's gods, so vital and mesmerizing, have indeed now become 'august', a cluster around the Princeps. These enervated creatures group together at the poem's close, like the anonymous little idols who observe Aeneas at sacrifice on the Ara Pacis.

*Tonans* at *BC* 1. 195–200, a prayer modelled on both the *Georgics* and *Metamorphoses* prayers, anticipating Augustus' religious reforms: Grimal (1970), 56–7; see below, p. 293.

[106] *Aug.* 91. 2: Augustus dreamt that Jupiter Capitolinus complained to him that the new Jupiter Tonans was taking away his worshippers.

[107] On the identification of Iuppiter Optimus Maximus with the Republic, see Koch (1937), 121–6; Oliver (1960), 17–18; on the whittling away of his functions unde Augustus, see Latte (1960), 305–6; Zanker (1988), 108.

[108] The vital importance of having a truly Republican foil to the Principate explains why Ovid chooses Aesculapius as the deity to import rather than Apollo or Cybele, who are 'two of the most obvious migrating deities' (Coleman (1971), 473 n. 6). Apollo and Cybele are simply far too closely tied to Augustus: Wiseman (1984).

Ovid's treatment of Caesar and Augustus is usually handled as a matter of judging whether or not Ovid is sincere, whether he is praising or subverting, being enthusiastic or ironic.[109] Or else, it is claimed, this is only literature, we are dealing with topoi or adaptations, so that such questions are beside the point.[110] At its most extreme, this second view appears unconvincing. If one of Ovid's prime concerns in the last two hundred and fifty lines of the poem is precisely the state's religious ideology, it is difficult to see how the problem of praising Augustus in that context can be 'more of a literary problem than an ideological or political one'.[111] The terms of debate on the first count ('panegyric/subversion') are perhaps themselves too polarizing. It may be worth moving into the problem once again, keeping the divine theme to the forefront.

It is, at the outset, striking to observe the degree to which Ovid is concentrating on 'facts'. Otis is very precisely inaccurate when he says that 'the apotheoses—including that of Julius and prospectively that of Augustus—are all assimilated to the realm of amusing fantasy'.[112] Bömer's matter-of-fact observation is more to the point, when he remarks on Ovid's claim that Caesar was made a god by his son rather than by his mighty deeds (15. 746-50): 'sie entspricht den Tatsachen'. Of course, what Ovid gives us, in the case of Caesar as with Aeneas and Romulus, is a blend. Williams describes an antithesis between 'literature' and 'real life',[113] but both elements are present in Ovid's account, and in the context of this catalogue-poem of myth, the concentration on facts is startling and obtrusive. The concentration on Julius Caesar has itself traditionally been regarded as startling and obtrusive, in accordance with the conviction that Augustus played down the importance of his father,[114] but a new context for regarding Ovid's treatment of Julius has recently been provided by Peter White's in-

---

[109] See the bibliographical discussions of Bömer (1969–86) on 15. 1 ff., 871 f., 877 ff.

[110] Williams (1978), 93–5; Knox (1986), 77–80, inclines to this view.

[111] Galinsky (1975), 260–1.

[112] Otis (1970), 351; cf. Solodow (1988), 75: 'For [Ovid] all myths were the same. He does not distinguish between Greek and Roman and eastern, between historical myths and local legends and tall tales. For him myth is not related to cult, as it was still for Callimachus.'

[113] 'The apotheosis of Julius Caesar was a poetic concept, but that was literature; in real life, deification meant a temple and a ritual, not a belief or a legend,' Williams (1978), 93–4.

[114] Syme (1978), 190; Due (1974), 88.

cisive demonstration that the cult of Diuus Iulius was used by Augustus as an instructional device, a model for the honours he expected after his own demise.[115] The finale of Ovid's poem catches exactly this movement of expectation.

Outside the apotheosis, in Ovid's reflections on Augustus' religious practices, one is struck by the same revealing interest in the details of actual practice. Augustus' pre-eminent position, with the blurring of the boundaries between his *domus* and the *res publica*, is a notorious problem of definition; what is so striking about Ovid's treatment is the economical acuity with which he captures so much of what was novel about Augustus, what had changed even since Vergil's time. Again, Ovid enforces a rereading of the *Aeneid*, and makes one realize just how finely balanced that poem is between the private and the communal. In all these cases one is prompted to ask: is Ovid being too fulsome, or too frank? Readers ancient and modern have a variety of responses available to the transformations paraded here by Ovid, responses conditioned above all by their own judgement of those transformations.[116]

This emphasis on the constitutional facts of Roman cult has its corollary in the politically coloured anthropomorphism which infuses the epic descriptions of deities in action. From Hercules to Caesar, the celestial politicking which accompanies the apotheoses is drawn in terms of the power-structures which frame the world of the poet and his audience, power-structures in which the new cults of the gods participate. The preoccupation with such systems of analogy is something we have been familiar with since the actions centring on the poem's first simile, in which Jupiter was compared to Augustus, and Jupiter's council to Augustus' (1. 200–5). At the climax of the poem Ovid returns to this same analogy, now comparing Augustus to Jupiter, and he uses explicitly self-conscious language of comparison to highlight what he is doing. Popular fame, says Ovid, exalts Augustus over Caesar, his father:

> sic magnus cedit titulis Agamemnonis Atreus,
> Aegea sic Theseus, sic Pelea vincit Achilles;
> denique, ut exemplis ipsos aequantibus utar,
> sic et Saturnus minor est Ioue: Iuppiter arces

---

[115] White (1988), 355–6: 'a maquette which he had liberty and time to shape in preparation for his own apotheosis' (355).
[116] On the range of audience response, see Hinds (1988), 25–6; Phillips (1983), 806–7.

temperat aetherias et mundi regna triformis,
terra sub Augusto est; pater est et rector uterque.

Thus does great Atreus yield to the honours of his son, Agamemnon; thus does Theseus overcome Aegeus, and Achilles, Peleus; finally, to use an example which is equal to the stature of Caesar and Augustus, thus is Saturn less than Jupiter. Jupiter regulates the heights of heaven and the three kingdoms that make up the universe; the earth is under Augustus. Each is father and ruler. (15. 855–60)

Only before the settlement of 27 BCE do we find widespread advertisement of links between Jupiter and Octavian.[117] Thereafter, while the direct public identifications on the coinage ceased (at least until after his death), it is very striking that links between Jupiter and Augustus continued to be promulgated in a more restricted circle, including those, for example, who received cameos.[118] On the Strozzi-Blacas cameo, Augustus is shown wearing Jupiter's aegis, while on the famous Gemma Augustea he is clearly the god himself, with the eagle beneath his throne.[119] Horace had spoken of Augustus as Jupiter's vice-regent;[120] Ovid here establishes an analogy rather than an identification (in the exile poetry, as we shall see shortly, he needs a different tactic).

The climactic comparison of Jupiter and Augustus exemplifies the slippery terrain of such panegyric, for the gods are not (least of all in this poem) neutral ground of praise, nor can the terms of comparison be easily fixed or controlled. The young Octavian had encountered this problem directly during the triumvirate, when he participated with eleven others (so it was alleged) in a mock *lectisternium*, dressed as the god Apollo. Famine held Rome at the time, and the next day the cry went up that, yes, he was Apollo, but Apollo the Torturer (with reference to a cult-title held by the god in one region of the city).[121] Since nothing is known about this particular cult, any extra edge to the allusion is not securely to be recovered. Perhaps the people wished to label Octavian as the

[117] Wallace-Hadrill (1986), 71; Albert (1981). Generally, on links between Augustus and Jupiter, see Ward (1933); Schwabl (1978), 1406 (chiefly on associations between Augustus and Zeus in the Greek world); Fears (1981*b*), 56–60.

[118] Burnett (1983), 564.

[119] Fine illustrations in Hannestad (1986), 79, 81; cf. Zanker (1988), 230–4.

[120] *Carm.* 1. 12. 49–60; cf. Weinstock (1971), 304–5.

[121] Suet. *Aug.* 70. The historicity of the story is denied by Weinstock (1971), 15; Fishwick (1987), 81 locates the anecdote in the Hellenistic tradition of posing as one's favoured deity.

flayer of Marsyas, whose statue was a symbol of Libertas.[122] Perhaps the point lies in the location of the temple of Apollo Tortor, which, according to one suggestion, received its name from being located by the place where whips were sold for the chastisement of slaves.[123] A parallel case of the same difficulties comes from Plutarch's sardonic comment on the favoured identification of Octavian's rival, Antonius (*Ant.* 24. 4–5). When the people of Ephesus welcomed him in 41 BCE, they hailed him as Dionysus, using the cult epithets of Joygiver and Gentle One. So he was to some, says Plutarch, but to most (here using other Dionysian epithets) he was Eater of Raw Flesh, Savage.[124]

The comparison of man with god is subject to the same plasticity as any analogy, simile, or metaphor, for the boundaries of the analogy are malleable, and its applications cannot remain rigidly fixed. If Caesar, for example, is Saturn, and Augustus is Jupiter, then we must now be in the Iron, and not the Golden, Age.[125] Augustus is indeed a great lawgiver, as befits an inhabitant of the Iron Age (15. 833); we learnt early in the first book that in the Golden Age men lived without need of laws (1. 89–93). The current era is never labelled Golden in the *Metamorphoses*, although it is in other parts of Ovid's work.[126] Again, we are here invited to contemplate and admire the temperate regulation of the universe by the celestial Jupiter, with Augustus as his terrestrial equivalent. This is the Minervan perspective on the gods' behaviour, in all their *augusta grauitas* (6. 73). Yet the first time we met Jupiter in the poem, so far from ordering the cosmos, he was instigating cataclysm (1. 262–74). In the context of the poem as a whole, this Minervan picture stands as only one element of the whole. The Arachnean tally, the god's punishing wrath, is encountered in the epilogue:

> Iamque opus exegi, quod nec Iouis ira nec ignis
> nec poterit ferrum nec edax abolere uetustas.

---

[122] Platner-Ashby (1929), 449, with reference to Serv. *Aen.* 3. 20.

[123] Jordan (1870), 232.

[124] See Suet. *Nero* 39 for a similar quip against Nero's favoured identification with Apollo, in an epigram which says he should be Apollo the Archer against the Parthians, not just Apollo the Lyre-player at Rome.

[125] Johnson (1970), 146; Galinsky (1981), 199–200; Wallace-Hadrill (1982*a*), 27–8.

[126] *Ars* 2. 277; 3. 113. It need hardly be said that these references in the *Ars* are not straight-faced.

Now I have erected a work, which neither the anger of Jupiter, nor fire, nor sword, nor devouring time will be able to abolish. (15. 871–2)[127]

It is still sometimes denied that 'the anger of Jupiter' refers to the thunderbolt which descended on Ovid from the Palatine and drove him into exile.[128] Yet the pairing of Jupiter and Augustus is not simply *an* analogy available in the poem. It is the first analogy and the last.[129] Led by this circular movement, we are reminded that the very first mention of Jupiter in the poem, immediately before his residence is compared to the Palatine, shows him conceiving wrath (1. 166). The Jupiter-like status of Augustus, and especially his Jovian wrath, with full apparatus of bolt and fire, are insistent themes in the exile poetry.[130] From exile Ovid exploits the Alexandrian technique of remorselessly pursuing the implications of the claimed identification; he challenges the implacable Princeps to be like a god in more than anger, and relent by showing clemency.[131] *Clementia* is itself, naturally, a quasi-divine attribute, for it implies an untrammelled will, to be directed in favour of a person in the power of a superior. Seneca, in whose works this novel terrain, as so many others, is first explicitly charted, appeals to Nero via exactly this two-sidedness of the divine analogy; imitate the *clementia*, not the *fulmina*, of the gods.[132]

It is a god-like prerogative to be beyond the limits of human behaviour, an insight which the *Metamorphoses* explicates more systematically than any other ancient poem. Herculean demigod figures, as our analyses have repeatedly shown, share these prerogatives, in exposed and disquieting fashion. Augustus is the son of a god, and virtually a god himself, wielding divine power; the kindred nature of imperial and divine power is the entire point of

[127] Professor Wills points out to me that the architectural metaphor of *opus exegi* looks to Augustus' physical constructions, mentioned only five lines before; the reference is aided by the more explicit architectural comparisons in the Horace Ode which provides the verbal source: *exegi monumentum . . .* (*Carm.* 3. 30. 1).

[128] Bömer (1969–86), vol. 7. 489. In favour of seeing an allusion to Augustus here, Marg (1968), 511; Nisbet (1982), 54; Kovacs (1987), 463–4.

[129] Stressed by Buchheit (1966), 106–7 (though to very ameliorative ends); see rather Müller (1987).

[130] *Tr.* 1. 4. 26; 1. 5. 78, 84; 2. 179; 3. 5. 7; 3. 11. 62; 4. 3. 69; 5. 2. 46; 5. 14. 27; cf. Scott (1930), 53–6; Syme (1978), 223; Kenney (1982*b*), 444–5; Kovacs (1987), 463.

[131] Syme (1978), 223.

[132] In his *De Clementia*, 1. 7. 1–3, 26.5.

conceiving of humans as god-like. That power can be saving in epiphany, a source of manifest blessing for the threatened;[133] it can be arbitrarily and unpredictably devastating.

The overlap in attitude here towards Princeps and deity is astonishingly exact. Millar's study of imperial power stresses again and again its underlying arbitrariness, and the impossibility of predicting or averting the emperor's displeasure.[134] He cites poetic analogies between human and divine utterances, remarking that these passages 'embody literary affectations, ultimately for the purpose of flattery. But they also reflect real anxieties about the success of approaches to the emperor, and the realization that all would depend, like everything else, on his attitude at the time'.[135] One finds precisely the same apprehensive preoccupation with divine anger as a key element throughout ancient religious practice: 'Like an electric current, the power of the gods had great potential for helping and harming; unlike electricity, it was unpredictable and mortals could do no more than attempt to channel its force in advance. Any account of pagan worship which minimizes the gods' uncertain anger and mortals' fear of it is an empty account.'[136] The pages of the *Metamorphoses* contain one of the most extended encounters with this attitude that we possess.

Attempts have been made to remove the cloud of menace from Ovid's association of Jupiter and Augustus, by asserting that Roman social custom allowed for the wilful exercise of power by the mighty.[137] Yet it was precisely the conventional Roman resentment of such behaviour which put the relationship between the princeps and the higher orders under most strain, eliciting from the emperors a studied projection of their *ciuilitas*, their status as one

[133] The beneficent aspect of Augustus' power is nowhere more beautifully illustrated than in a story from his last days (Suet. *Aug.* 98. 2). As he sailed near Naples, the crew and passengers of an Alexandrian ship honoured him as a god, attributing to him the fact that they lived, sailed, and enjoyed their freedom and fortunes. Such a mentality is summed up by Pliny's aphorism, *deus est mortali iuuare mortalem* (*HN* 2. 18).

[134] Millar (1977), 9–10, 74, 112–13, 300; cf. esp. 527: 'Whatever its legal justification, if any, the emperor's power to inflict death, confiscation or exile was from the beginning an integral part of his role, an inheritance it seems from the summary hearings, punishments and confiscations of the civil war period. So was the informal and untrammelled procedure by which it was exercised, and ... the immediate and drastic cruelties which could accompany it ...'

[135] Millar (1977), 469, on Ov. *Pont.* 3. 1. 131–8 and Mart. 5. 6. 7–11.

[136] Lane Fox (1986), 38; cf. esp. 109–10.

[137] von Albrecht (1981), 2336–7, on the first divine council.

citizen among the many.[138] Ovid's Neptune attracts open censure
for offending against this code; his epic and unrelenting anger
against Achilles is described as going beyond the bounds of
*ciuilitas* (*exercet memores plus quam ciuiliter iras*, 12. 583). From
exile, Ovid can ironically refer to Augustus' decision to do no
more than exile him as a 'civil exercise of his resentment' (*est odio
ciuiliter usus, Tr.* 3. 8. 41).

With an apparent guilelessness that never entirely vanishes,
Augustus' repeated assertions of his quasi-divine status are taken
at face value by Ovid, and nobody—not Augustus, nor Ovid, nor
any reader—can circumscribe the limits at which the implications
of this status cease to register. Deeply engrained attitudes towards
the power of the gods are questioned and explored by the movement of the *Metamorphoses*. At the climax, the currents of this
questioning flow into the organization of the contemporary world,
to cap the poem's repeated confrontation of human and divine
power.[139] The princeps is as august, and as mighty, as the gods he
has made his own.[140]

### III

*di quoque carminibus, si fas est dicere, fiunt*

'Even the gods, if it is permissible to say it, are created by
poetry'.

Ovid, *Ex Ponto* 4. 8. 55

[138] Wallace-Hadrill (1982*b*). The same pressures could lead even to an actual
circumscribed reversal of the power relationship: see Suet. *Aug.* 91. 2 for the extraordinary story of Augustus' annual act of begging alms from the populace with
outstretched hand. For the extensive ancient literature on the controlling of anger,
see Rabbow (1914).

[139] One of the fundamental points of Price's indispensable book is that imperial
cult is a way of conceptualizing power: Price (1984*a*), esp. 234–48; cf. Armstrong
(1986), 74, on the analogous nature of divine and imperial power.

[140] In this respect, Ovid's treatment comes close to fulfilling the function of myth
described in the discussion of the Dionysus revenge-myths by McGinty (1978)
(although Ovid questions rather than justifies, as many would see the Dionysus
myths themselves doing): 'these myths are best understood as ideology, i.e. as representing narratives which define the Greek universe as hierarchical by nature and
by design and which thereby justify the asymmetrical allocation of power, privi-
lege, and status among gods and men. I argue, then, that the most central function
of the vengeance myth is as a mechanism for social control by reinforcing accepted
concepts of social stratification' (79). For divine power as an image of Augustus'
power in the *Metamorphoses*, see Segal (1969), 86; Otis (1970), 133, 145.

Ovid's clear vision of what the Principate was doing to Rome's religion heralds a preoccupation which will recur in our next author, Lucan. Before moving on to that topic, however, we may close the chapter on the *Metamorphoses* with a discussion of the perennial epic problems involved in the representation of the divine in narrative—problems which, as we have repeatedly seen, take the reader to the heart of any author's conception of fiction. Ovid's procedures here are not only worth investigating in their own right, but they provide illuminating commentary on the epic tradition, and themselves become normative for the following generations of Latin epicists, for whom the power of the *Metamorphoses* was to be as irresistible as that of the *Aeneid*.

Ovid's poem is a world in which anything—apart from the irreversible metamorphosis of a god—is possible. He presides over his cockpit with a mesmerizing assurance. As Solodow, who has most fully described this phenomenon, puts it, 'he calls attention to himself so that we are ever aware of his mediating presence. In the end it is he himself more than anything who holds together the world of the poem.'[141] His assurance is even more stunning for its self-sufficiency, since he does not need the Muses for aid or inspiration. His own mind leads him to undertake his task, and the undifferentiated gods are called on for favour alone (*fert animus . . .; di coeptis . . . adspirate meis*, 1. 1–3). Only once, as we saw in the previous section, does Ovid call on the Muses, when he treats the openly historical importation of Aesculapius' cult into Rome. Ovid's only acknowledged Muse, then, is Livy; otherwise he relies on his own resources. Accordingly, although his book is drenched with allusion to poetic predecessors, his attitude towards these forebears is, as we shall see with the house of Fama at the end of this section, remarkably unanxious.

As the (virtually) sole acknowledged originator of his fifteen-book world, Ovid sports ceaselessly with his power to command or suspend our credence in his fictions. No Latin poet shows such a systematic or inventive engagement with the issues of fiction and authentication which have preoccupied us throughout this book. Ovid had been obsessed with these issues since the start of his career. Towards the end of his *Amores*, for example, in 3. 12, Ovid had devoted a poem to the fictive power of poetry, explicitly

[141] Solodow (1988), 2; cf. 37–73 for his general discussion.

involving his audience in the problems of belief in the created world of his elegies.[142] The extreme complexity of this poem may be traced in McKeown's article.[143] The poet complains that he has created rivals for himself by making Corinna irresistibly attractive in his poems. His audience should never have believed him, he maintains. Using conventional metaphors from the lawcourt, Ovid asserts both the power of poets to invent, and the accepted lack of belief in their inventions: *nec tamen ut testes mos est audire poetas; / malueram uerbis pondus abesse meis* ('but it is not customary to listen to poets as if they were witnesses; I would have preferred that my words carried no authority', *Am.* 3. 12. 19–20).[144] He goes on to give a list of stock implausibilities from mythology, all created by 'us poets' (*per nos . . ., nos . . ., nos . . ., fecimus . . ., fecimus,* 21–31). Far from exploding the power of poetry to convince, however, his elegy ends up corroborating it. At the close of the mighty catalogue, he protests that his audience have been duped. They should have read Ovid's Corinna as another example of poetic licence, but they have been won into belief by his poetic power—with a final twist being provided by the 'fact' that Corinna actually is 'real':

> exit in immensum fecunda licentia uatum,
> obligat historica nec sua uerba fide;
> et mea debuerat falso laudata uideri
> femina; credulitas nunc mihi uestra nocet.

The fruitful licence of bards has no boundaries to its movements, and it does not bind its words by the belief that's appropriate in a work of history. My lady also should have looked as if she had been falsely praised; as it is, the credulity of all of you is doing me harm. (3. 12. 41–4)

The first example of poets' unbridled inventiveness in Ovid's catalogue is the myth of Scylla, and he highlights the licence by referring to a version which conflated two originally separate stories about two different Scyllas—the Homeric partner of Charybdis, and the daughter of Nisus, who stole her father's talismanic lock and became the bird Ciris: *per nos Scylla patri caros furata capillos / pube premit rabidos inguinibusque canes* ('we poets are responsible for Scylla robbing her father of his cherished hair, and

---

[142] McKeown (1979); Lieberg (1985), 26–9.
[143] One eagerly awaits the commentary.
[144] For the imagery of 'witnesses', cf. p. 40.

packing rabid dogs in her private parts and loins', 21–2).[145] Either story of Scylla is incredible enough on its own, and it is clearly even worse to be expected to believe in a composite tale which yokes together versions which any reader would have recognized as distinct.[146] These same Scyllas are in Ovid's mind when he comes to one of his most explicit treatments of these topics in the *Metamorphoses.*

The first Scylla we meet in the *Metamorphoses* is the daughter of Nisus, who transforms into Ciris according to the normal story (8. 1–151). It may appear that Ovid is muting the resonances of his elegy, until we reach the second, Homeric, Scylla, at which point the poet suddenly activates the complexity of his earlier poem:

> Scylla latus dextrum, laeuum irrequieta Charybdis
> infestat; uoràt haec raptas reuomitque carinas,
> illa feris atram canibus succingitur aluum,
> uirginis ora gerens, et, *si non omnia uates*
> *ficta reliquerunt,* aliquo quoque tempore uirgo.

Scylla infests the right side, tireless Charybdis the left. Charybdis snatches boats, swallows them, and vomits them back up again; Scylla's black womb is ringed with wild dogs. She has the face of a girl, and, *if the stories handed down by the bards are not all fictions,* at one time she was indeed a girl. (13. 730–4)[147]

As Galinsky well points out, Ovid himself is now one of these very 'bards', who proceeds forthwith to narrate his fiction.[148] Yet the ironies go further, for Ovid's aside on the fictions handed down by bards takes us back to his initial treatment in *Amores* 3. 12, where the conflated Scylla stories had headed off the list of obviously incredible fictions handed down by bards. By breaking up the conflation into its constituent parts in the *Metamorphoses,* Ovid is 'correcting' his version in the *Amores* (which he had then

---

[145] On the conflation, which we first encounter in Vergil's sixth *Eclogue* (74–5), see Coleman (1977) ad loc., and the lengthy expostulations of the author of the *Ciris* (54–91), with Lyne (1978) on line 54.

[146] So McKeown (1979), 169.

[147] Note that the existence of the monster Scylla is not put in jeopardy by Ovid's aside, but only the question of whether or not she had changed from a previous existence.

[148] Galinsky (1975), 176. On such expressions of disbelief and scepticism, see Stinton (1976); Bömer (1969–86), on this passage, and on 3. 106.

followed in his subsequent poetry),[149] and giving us—what? The truth? Of course not, for we cannot accept as 'truth' anything which this bard tells us, coming as it does with his health warning, 'if the stories handed down by the bards are not *all* fictions'.

Just as in the elegy, however, Ovid does not stop with a simple puncturing of the fictive illusion, but toys with our credulity. The testing-point for the fiction has been identified by Ovid as the transformation from girl to dog-infested freak, and when we reach that point, some four hundred lines later, he invites us to recognize that we have committed ourselves insensibly to his strategies of involvement.[150] As Scylla wades into the pool which has been doctored by the drugs of her rival Circe, and sees her loins being made foul by the barking dog-monsters, her first reaction is one of incredulity:

> ac primo credens non corporis illas
> esse sui partes, refugitque abigitque timetque
> ora proterua canum, sed, quos fugit, attrahit una ...

But at first, not believing that those can be parts of *her* body, she shuns, rejects, and fears the dogs' thrusting mouths; but in running away from them, she drags them along with her. (14. 61–3)

So comprehensively have we been won over by Ovid's narrative, so 'real' has the character become for us, that we can be invited to share in her human disbelief—a very different variety of disbelief from the one canvassed when she was first introduced. We are incredulous, but our incredulity is in sympathy with Scylla's own characterful incredulity, not directed against her existence. She remains, however, the thing whose very existence we were at first invited to doubt, as we are reminded within a dozen lines, when Ovid blandly alludes to the standard rationalizing explanation of Scylla, as a dangerous rock, 'which is still standing today' (*qui nunc quoque saxeus exstat*, 73).[151]

---

[149] *Ars* 1. 331–2; *Rem.* 737; *Her.* 12. 123–4; *Fast.* 4. 500. He has his tongue in his cheek when he treats his version as gospel: see Hinds (1984), on the *Fasti* passage.

[150] Not without playing in the interim on the fictive status of his Scylla. The created character whose status has been made so problematic is brought to listen to the speech of the sea-god Glaucus, who narrates his own miraculous transformation: *res similis fictae*, he says to her, *sed quid mihi fingere prodest?* ('the event is like a fiction, but what advantage is it to me to make a fiction?', 13. 935).

[151] On this rationalization, see Bömer (1969–86), ad loc. Other rationalizations describe Scylla as a fast ship, or courtesan: Festa (1902), 28. 1–29. 2; 73. 12–74. 3.

The *Metamorphoses'* challenges to our belief in its fictions are relentless, for Ovid continually confronts us with such reminders of his work's fictional status.[152] It is, however, too easy to conclude that 'he encourages our scepticism through the expression of his own'.[153] Rather, his techniques involve a preternaturally keen awareness of the suspension of disbelief and belief which constitutes fiction. In a superb discussion of Ovid's plays on the literarity of Ariadne in the *Fasti*, Conte has elucidated the key implications of Ovid's procedures:

Ovid is playing here with the relationship between poetry as an autonomous reality and the literary process which constructs that reality . . . Such a shattering of the artistic illusion does not imply that the poet does not believe in the power of art. On the contrary, it means that he claims to know it through and through . . .[154]

These problems receive their most explicit treatment in a discussion on belief and fiction in the context of divine action. This comes as no surprise, for, as we have repeatedly seen (most dramatically in the case of Apollonius), the gods are the hardest case for epic fiction, the sharp edge of the problem of how to represent and authenticate anything in the world of the narrative. In the very centre of his poem, Ovid removes the cover, to reveal the complicity between poet and audience which underpins his enterprise, as well as the fragile limits to that complicity. The mighty river Achelous has been telling his guests (Theseus and his companions) of wondrous transformations of local nymphs:

Amnis ab his tacuit. factum mirabile cunctos
mouerat: irridet credentes, utque deorum
spretor erat mentisque ferox, Ixione natus
'ficta refers nimiumque putas, Acheloe, potentes
esse deos,' dixit, 'si dant adimuntque figuras.'
obstipuere omnes nec talia dicta probarunt,
ante omnesque Lelex animo maturus et aeuo,
sic ait: 'immensa est finemque potentia caeli
non habet et, quidquid superi uoluere, peractum est ...'

---

[152] Doblhofer (1960), 223–7; Galinsky (1975), 173–9. Perhaps Ovid's most spectacular example comes at 10. 301–3, where we are invited by the poet Orpheus to pick and choose whether or not we will believe in the Myrrha story, or how much of the story we wish to believe.
[153] Solodow (1988), 71.
[154] Conte (1986), 63.

After this the river fell silent. The amazing event had moved all of them.
The son of Ixion [Pirithous], as someone of fierce mind, who scorned the
gods, laughed at them for believing: 'Your stories are fictions, Achelous,'
he said, 'and you take the gods to be too powerful if they bestow and remove forms.' Everyone was stunned, not approving such words; Lelex
above all, mature in mind and years, said: 'Boundless and without limit is
the power of heaven; whatever the gods wish comes to pass . . .' (8. 611–
19)

Two possible audience reactions to the divine stories of the
*Metamorphoses* are acted out for us here.[155] Everyone except
Pirithous is lulled by the persuasiveness of Achelous' speech into
believing his story (*credentes*, 612), mesmerized by its convincingness into the state of trance-like acceptance which poets and critics
since Homer had depicted as the ideal response to the magical
powers of the poet.[156] For them, as for an element of ourselves, an
Achelous' account becomes a *factum*, an event, however amazing
(*mirabile*). For Pirithous, however, these are *ficta*, and although an
element of ourselves will agree with him as well, we must recognize that we cannot identify wholly with him, for his response is
as much a critical solecism as a blasphemy. His companions may
be like the theatre-goer of critical legend, who would rush onto
the stage to stop Othello smothering Desdemona;[157] yet some suspension of disbelief is necessary for the narrative to proceed at all
(and readers who energetically agree with Pirithous will always
have to remind themselves that he too is a *fictum*). Ovid is not interested in irrevocably exploding our ability to give necessary credence to his fictions, nor is he interested in letting us forget that
fictions are indeed his subject. By splitting our response up into
these two polarized alternatives he is making us realize that to
swim successfully in the sea of the *Metamorphoses* we must be
both Lelex and Pirithous.

Readers tend to be either Lelex or Pirithous. If Solodow and
Otis concentrate on Ovid's explosion of the narrative illusion,[158]
Kenney necessarily and sympathetically insists on Ovid's astonish-

---

[155] Anticipated earlier, in the reaction of Leuconoe's sisters to her story (4. 271–
3).
[156] *Od.* 11. 333–4; 13. 1–2; Walsh (1984), 14–15, 22; Thalmann (1984), 129–
30. Ovid appears to be signalling a reaction to epic narrative in particular: see
Hinds (1988), 19, on the way Ovid builds Achelous as a grand epic narrator.
[157] Walton (1978), 12.
[158] Solodow (1988), 68–73; Otis (1970), 361–7.

ing conviction and credibility:[159] no matter how often Ovid reminds us, either through his own voice or by allusion, of the fictional status of his poem's events, we still give enough credence to these events to be impelled to keep reading, to discover what 'happened' next. The double vision that comes from being both Lelex and Pirithous may indeed be seen as a necessary condition for reading any fictions, as Newsom has recently claimed in the first systematic study of literary probability:

*in entertaining fictions . . . we divide our beliefs between real and fictional worlds. . . .* an essential part of reading stories or of entertaining any kind of make-believe is 'having it both ways'. It is insisting on our belief in the fictional world *even* as we insist also on our belief in the world in which the reading or make-believe takes place.[160]

This necessary knowing complicity between poet and audience is something which had exercised the first Greek theorists, and receives extended notice in Plutarch's essay 'On how the young man should study poetry':

For the element of deception in [poetry] does not gain any hold on utterly witless and foolish persons. This is the ground of Simonides' answer to the man who said to him, 'Why are the Thessalians the only people whom you do not deceive?' His answer was, 'Oh, they are too ignorant to be deceived by me'; and Gorgias called tragedy a deception wherein he who deceives is more honest than he who does not deceive, and he who is deceived is wiser than he who is not deceived. (Plut. *Quomodo Ad.* 15 c–d)[161]

What Lelex and Pirithous are talking about through their discussion of the power of the gods is the power of poets. When Pirithous accuses Achelous of 'taking the gods to be too powerful if they bestow and remove forms' (8. 614–15), he is actually opening up the possibility that we will not follow the poet in his bestowal and removal of forms. And when Lelex replies in defence of the gods, we may substitute the poet's own quasi-divine craft: 'Boundless and without limit is the power of poetry; whatever the

---

[159] Kenney (1973), 143; (1982), 436: 'probability, or at all events conviction, was paramount; all the poet's art was applied to achieve credibility (*fides*) . . .'; cf. the points made by Coleman (1973), 177, in his review of Otis (1970).

[160] Newsom (1988), 134–5 (his italics).

[161] Translation of Babbitt (1927).

poets wish comes to pass' (618–19).[162] Part of that power is the ability to make us 'believe' in the teeth of the poet's continual reminders of his poetic world's fictional status.

My interest in maintaining Ovid's interest in maintaining our belief may appear timid, especially against the background of the more radical destabilizations achieved by the master of fictional destabilization, Apollonius, and his Alexandrian colleagues.[163] There will always be readers who prefer to side with Pirithous throughout, and I am myself often one of those readers. The sense of reality in fiction is, after all, a two-edged business. While particularity of detail is vital to the authentication of any narrative,[164] there are many ways of resisting the ensuing impression of reality.[165] Readers who concentrate hard enough on the authorial manipulation involved in the provision of such particularity will always be able to talk themselves into a position of scepticism.[166]

The gods are the hardest case for Ovid's fictional power, as his character Hercules reminds us when he is (unbeknownst to himself) in the process of becoming a god, raging against the injustice of his torture: *et sunt qui credere possint / esse deos* ('and there are those who can believe that gods exist!', 9. 203–4).[167] Ovid is, of course, fully aware of the epic norms of analogy and authenticating detail in representing the divine, as he explicitly shows in his first set-piece divine scene, where he brings to the surface the inevitable narrative accommodation of divine to human action (1. 168–76).[168] Throughout the poem, the gods are given the characterful anthropomorphism which they need in order to be

---

[162] Cf. above, p. 191, on the 'god-like' craft of Arachne and Orpheus. On the divine creative powers of poets, see Lieberg (1982) and (1985): 'For Ovid, poets are completely free to create their own imaginary world' (1985), 27.

[163] Above, pp. 90–4; Goldhill (1986).

[164] Above, pp. 49–51.

[165] Belsey (1980), 1–36.

[166] Bayley (1987), 7–18, has a spirited attack on theories of reading which use authenticating detail as a way of undoing the illusion of authenticity. Few will follow him all the way, but his redressing of the balance is vital for understanding the polyvalent nature of fiction.

[167] An even bolder smashing of the fictive illusion than that which is sometimes read in Euripides, who notoriously attributes to Heracles the opinion that the gods' sins are 'the miserable stories of the bards' (*HF* 1346). On this very difficult passage, see now Yunis (1988), 155–66.

[168] Above, pp. 198–200; cf. Stirrup (1981), on Ovid's 'imagined reality' in depictions of the divine, building on the insights of David West in Parker (1977), 157.

able to participate. Jupiter wheedles, blusters, and rants, resembling Lucian's supreme deity more than Vergil's, or even Homer's.[169] The gods' general passions of love and hate are depicted with the minute details of expression, gait, and speech which allow these passions to make narrative sense for the reader.[170] Further, Ovid knows full well that epic moments of fantasy have a ground in verisimilitude, as is shown by the contemporary political atmosphere to his divine councils and deliberations. His Phaethon episode is a splendid example of how even the most bizarre moments can be given a colour of plausibility in this way.[171] The fantastic chariot ride across the firmament, a genuine flight of the imagination, begins like a chariot race in the circus, with the meticulously named horses beating their hooves on the starting gates (2. 153–5).

No one, however, would expect Ovid to rest at so much, and in fact he delights in driving his wedges into the lines of strain which crisscross the apparently perspicuous convention. Just as, in thematic terms, the gods' humanity is tested to the point where it breaks down as a conceptual model, so too, in representing the divine in action, Ovid pushes at epic's divine realism until it collapses: the more authenticating detail he gives, the more he undermines his fiction.

One of his favourite areas for such activity is the physicality of divinities who represent aspects of the natural world,[172] where the accumulation of authenticating detail ends in humour so marked that the aura of plausible fiction is entirely exploded. All readers of the *Metamorphoses* know and relish these marvellous moments; the best of them are collected by Galinsky.[173] Ovid particularly enjoys the tension between the anthropomorphic deity and its natural element when that element is water, so mutable and

[169] Esp. 1. 244–5, 2. 396–7. On the overtly human element in Ovid's divine characterization, see Bernbeck (1967), 80–94; Little (1970), 86–105; Otis (1970), esp. 145; Galinsky (1975), 162–73; Solodow (1988), 89–97; Kenney (1973), 145: 'what could be more human than the gods of the *Metamorphoses*?'

[170] e.g. 2. 601–2 (Apollo's aghast reaction to hearing the news of Coronis' unfaithfulness); 2. 752–5 (Pallas' anger at Aglauros). Examples are to be found throughout; cf., again, Solodow (1988), 89–97.

[171] Bernbeck (1967), 93–4.

[172] Wilkinson (1955), 201; Doblhofer (1960), 87–9; Solodow (1988), 95–6; above all, the careful study of Eggers (1984).

[173] Galinsky (1975), 171, citing 1. 583–4 (the river Inachus); 5. 574–5 (the spring Arethusa); 11. 125 (Bacchus); 2. 302–3 (Earth). The mountain Tmolus (11. 157–64) is another master-stroke, a hit at Vergil's Atlas (*Aen.* 4. 246–51).

resistant to shape. The disjuncture is already present in Homer, and is a basic habit of thought for both Greeks and Romans.[174] As Odysseus floats towards the island of Phaeacia and sees a river-mouth, he prays to the river-god, speaking as a suppliant, saying 'I come to your flow *and your knees*' (σόν τε ῥόον σά τε γούναθ' ἱκάνω, *Od.* 5. 449). When Achilles is killing the Trojans in the river Scamander, the 'deep-swirling river addressed him in anger, making himself like a man, and spoke out of the deep swirl' (χωσάμενος προσέφη ποταμὸς βαθυδίνης, / ἀνέρι εἰσάμενος, βαθέης δ' ἐκφθέγξατο δίνης, *Il.* 21. 212–13). The 'deep swirls' are first a characteristic of the river itself, and then a place from which the anthropomorphic deity of the river performs his man-like (and god-like) act of speech; the 'deep-swirling' epithet of the first line is, in the next line, split up into its constituent parts to provide an encircling bracket for the act of speech, so that we are left wondering exactly who or what the river 'is', and in what his (or its) nature consists.[175] Greek and Roman sculpture regularly represented rivers in anthropomorphic shape, with Hellenistic art in particular enjoying the challenge of having the anthropomorphic figure embody 'the property of the great river, with its cascading limbs and flowing beard'.[176] It is quite natural for Pliny, when he is describing the spring of Clitumnus, to give us half a page on the actual river, and then to mention the cult statue of the river-god with the words *stat Clitumnus ipse* ('there stands Clitumnus himself', *Ep.* 8. 8. 5).

There is precedent in Callimachus for Ovid's transformation of this double habit of mind into an arena for humour,[177] yet it is a field of display which Ovid makes all his own. His mighty river, Achelous, when he meets Theseus, 'is swollen with rain as a river, yet he talks as though he had nothing to do with the water and wished to protect Theseus from its danger'.[178] Even more elabo-

---

[174] Eggers (1984), 67–83; see *RE* 6. 2784–90 for representation of rivers in human (that is, divine) shape.

[175] Matters are not clarified later on, when the river is described as making a sound like a bull (21. 237): see *RE* 6. 2780–2 for the common representation of rivers as bulls.

[176] Onians (1979), 137.

[177] Hollis (1970), on *Met.* 8. 549 ff., quoting Call. *Del.* 77–8, where Asopus is described as moving slowly because of injuries sustained from Zeus' thunderbolt; 'βαρύγουνος suits the river-god, πεπάλακτο ("was sullied") the river-water'.

[178] Anderson (1972), on 8. 550; Anderson's points throughout this section catch Ovid's humour very acutely.

rately, when Achelous is telling the story of how he raged at the nymphs for neglecting him in sacrifice, Ovid produces a series of splits between entities and their embodiments:

> intumui, quantusque, feror cum plurimus umquam,
> tantus eram, pariterque animis immanis et undis
> a siluis siluas et ab aruis arua reuelli
> cumque loco nymphas, memores tum denique nostri,
> in freta prouolui.

I swelled up, and I was as big as I am at my greatest rush; equally terrible in feeling and flood, I tore up the woods from the woods, the fields from the fields, and I rolled the nymphs together with their locales into the sea—they finally thought of me *then*. (8. 583–7)

The river swells with water and with anthropomorphic rage.[179] The more Achelous concentrates on the harmony between his personality and his element, however, the more difficult it becomes for the reader to overlook the split. The disjuncture is further accentuated by the other divisions in the same lines. If the water and the person are presented as one and the same, how can the woods or the fields be separated from themselves? And if these material objects are separated from their material embodiments, what of the nymphs, who find themselves swept into the sea together with the physical environments which are their habitation, and simultaneously their 'selves'?[180] A final collapse of *numen* into physicality is acted out in Book 5, where the fountain-nymph Cyane breaks through the boundary between herself and her element, dissolving through grief into the very water itself (425–37).

When he engages with the difficulties of representing the Olympians themselves, Ovid concentrates not so much on their problematic φύσις ('nature') as on the threat which their action poses to the norms of his narrative mode. Here, as always, he is insisting on making dominant the inherent problems of the genre. As we have seen, he makes much of his adherence to epic's necessary

[179] Hollis (1970) and Anderson (1972) on 8. 583. Even a sceptical reader of Ahl (1985) may feel impelled to see the river (AMNIS) lurking in the most personal, anthropomorphic moment of these lines (ANIMIS IMMANIS); Achelous is called *amnis* at the opening and close of this speech (8. 577, 611).

[180] The most dramatic reflection of Ovid's techniques in later epic comes in the ninth book of Statius' *Thebaid*, where there is an extended play on the personality and physicality of the river Ismenus, as he reacts to the death of his grandson in battle (9. 404 ff.).

characterful anthropomorphism in representing the gods;[181] yet he uses this necessary norm as a backdrop for his preferred concentration on epic moments of φαντασία, in which the gods' stunning and unassimilable power strains to the limit the power of narrative to capture its operation, as the poet exploits to the full the characteristic *licentia* of epic.[182]

When Ovid describes Apollo's reaction to the news of Coronis' adultery, for example, he first follows the pattern of epic action established by Homer, in his description of Apollo's reaction to the prayer of Chryses in *Iliad* 1 (43–7).[183] The god's characterful gestures and emotions are minutely (and comically) captured: his wreath slips off, he loses his expression, plectrum, and facial colour all at once, he rages, he picks up his bow (2. 600–3). When he comes to Apollo's actual shooting of Coronis, however, Ovid cuts away from Homer's careful figuring of the god's movements and actions. The archery of Homer's Apollo at the Greek camp is described with meticulous detail (1. 48–52), yet Ovid capitalizes, as it were, on the eery underpinning to Apollo's involvement which is revealed by Homer's half-line in the middle of his fully-patterned action: 'and he went like night' (ὁ δ' ἤιε νυκτὶ ἐοικώς, 1. 47). For Ovid passes immediately from Apollo picking up his bow to the aim and the shot, with the intervening miles annihilated.[184] The deliberate eclipse of any attempt to accommodate the divine action to a human action transforms the god's peremptory deed into something unaccountable, all the more morally terrifying for being incommensurate with humanly imaginable action.

Ovid had precedent enough in Homer, let alone in Apollonius or Vergil, for his impressionistic capturing of such moments of *phantasia*; as we have seen, the monstrous and striking character of divine narrative was a constant feature of critical responses to epic.[185] The unprepared, stunning descent of Vergil's Juno to smash open the gates of war is as catastrophic a rupture of verisimilitude as anything in Ovid (*Aen.* 7. 620–2); it is itself indebted

---

[181] Above, p. 232.

[182] On such strands in epic divine action, see above, pp. 51–2. To some extent, of course, this is only one manifestation of the characteristically quirky and contrapuntal nature of Ovid's narrative in the *Metamorphoses*.

[183] Above, p. 50.

[184] *arma adsueta capit flexumque a cornibus arcum / tendit et illa suo totiens cum pectore iuncta / indeuitato traiecit pectora telo*, 2. 603–5.

[185] Above, pp. 51–2.

to the magnificent gesture of Apollonius' Athene, impelling Argo through the Clashing Rocks (*Arg.* 2. 588–9).[186] Ovid's use of this epic technique, however, is far more pervasive than in any of his predecessors.[187] The aberrations of his tradition become his norm; it is as if he is responding to the uneasiness of the critics, who often registered their anxiety about moments in epic where the gods' action appeared inchoate, unintegrated.[188]

In *Metamorphoses* 2, Juno notices the birth of a boy to one of Jupiter's mistresses, Callisto, and delivers a soliloquy (466–75). The reader imagines the goddess to be in heaven, or at least in a cloud, and it is a great shock to read immediately afterwards: *dixit et aduersam prensis a fronte capillis / strauit humi pronam* ('she spoke, and, facing her, took her hair by the front and laid her out flat face down on the ground', 2. 476–7). Earlier, when Callisto loses her maidenhead to Jupiter, the effortless act of rape itself is elided altogether, marked only by the epithet of *uictor* given to Jupiter as he returns to heaven (2. 437). Such ellipses become a general feature of the narrative of divine action. In Book 9, the miraculously rejuvenated Ioläus enters the room to interrupt Alcmena and Iole. In apparent parenthesis Ovid tells us the reason for Ioläus' youth, as a gift from Hebe (400–1); but the next lines verge into a narrative of the bestowal of the gift, with a prophetic speech from Themis (401–17). And at the end of this floating exchange between Hebe and Themis we find ourselves in the middle of a council of the gods, which we must now try to read back as the framework from the start: *haec ubi faticano uenturi praescia dixit / ore Themis, uario superi sermone fremebant...* ('when Themis, knowing the future, said this with her prophetic mouth, the gods made a hubbub, all speaking at cross purposes', 9. 418–19).

---

[186] Lloyd-Jones (1984), 68–9.

[187] Bernbeck (1967) is the fundamental discussion of this aspect of Ovid's technique: esp. 10–11, 17, 79.

[188] AbT *Il.* 15. 668; AT 16. 432; bT 16. 666; AT 18. 356. Such attitudes make their way into the Latin commentary tradition on the *Aeneid*: Serv. 1. 226 (congratulating Vergil on a deft introduction of divine action); 11. 532 (censuring him for an *ineptus... et uituperabilis transitus*). Heyne continues the tradition, with some very Servian comments on 9. 802 ff., and 9. 638 ff.: Heyne–Wagner (1830–41), ad locc. On the possibility of Ovid responding to criticisms of the *Aeneid*, see McKeown (1979), 172, with reference to Servius' comments on the metamorphosis of the ships at *Aen.* 9. 81 and 3. 46.

The Silver Latin epic poets followed Ovid's lead enthusiastically. Valerius Flaccus sets his Argonauts on their journey, and then begins his epic storm (1. 574–621). In the middle of the action, without any motivation or preparation, Neptune appears in a *cum*-clause: *undique feruent / aequora, cum subitus trifida Neptunus in hasta / caeruleum fundo caput extulit* ('everywhere the sea is raging, when all of a sudden Neptune, trident and all, bore his blue head out of the deep', 1. 640–2). The contrast with the Vergilian model scene (*Aen.* 1. 124–30) is very marked, for there Vergil had motivated Neptune's reaction as carefully as Homer had Apollo's.[189] Even more drastic is the dislocation in the story of Io. She is walking over the fields, when an *ecce* introduces from thin air Tisiphone: *ibat agris Io uictrix Iunonis, at ecce / cum facibus flagrisque et Tartareo ululatu / Tisiphonen uidet* ('Io was going over the fields, triumphant over Juno, when—look!—she sees Tisiphone with her torches, whips, and Hellish howling', 4. 392–4).[190]

Statius' splendidly precipitous narrative likewise capitalizes on Ovid's example, with a continual use of abrupt and jolting divine manifestations.[191] His goddess of war outdoes Vergil's Juno, by standing on the citadel of Argos at the beginning of *Thebaid* 4 and throwing her spear 120 kilometres to Thebes (4. 5–8). At another point, Statius shows us Jupiter sitting and watching events below, to all appearances alone (3. 218–19). Jupiter calls Mars, and in the middle of his orders to the war-god he breaks off with *uos, o superi . . .* ('you, o gods . . .', 239). Are we then in a council of the gods? It is not yet possible to be sure, for Statius' Jupiter can easily apostrophize absent personages while engaged in conversation.[192] Only at the end of his speech is the setting clarified, as the assembled gods react to his words (3. 253).

Incoherence and perfunctoriness are the main threats to poets who engage in such Ovidian practices. Statius and Valerius succeed in catching something of Ovid's drama, while Silius, as we shall see in the next chapter, demonstrates one aspect of his funda-

---

[189] Mehmel (1934), 68: 'Bei Valerius taucht Neptun unerwartet auf einmal auf. Man weiss nicht, woher und warum.'

[190] von Albrecht (1977), esp. 145; the pervasive importance of Ovid for such aspects of Silver Latin technique emerges very clearly from this valuable article; cf. Mehmel (1934), 67–72 ('Klarheit').

[191] On Statius' staccato narrative technique, see von Moisy (1971).

[192] Cf. 7. 20, where in a speech to Mercury he cries out to Mars.

mental incompetence by his systematic inability to make any sense of Ovid's innovations in divine narrative.[193]

Scarcely a single area of epic technique is left unscathed by Ovid's powerful experiments. Human emotion and divine possession, for example, become the object of Ovid's commentary. Apollonius' Medea, a victim of external and internal forces which resist being lumped together, becomes in Ovid a vehicle for extended self-analytical speech, where we can glimpse the fugitive tracks of a divine intervention without being granted the narrative means to stabilize a divine interpretation. Her falling in love is described as an act of 'conceiving powerful flames' (*concipit ... ualidos ... ignes*, 7. 9), yet we are shown no burning arrows. Some god or other, so she says, is making it impossible for her to resist (*nescio quis deus obstat*, 12). She speaks of herself as a victim of *cupido* (19); not only here, but also when Ovid closes her speech by saying that *cupido* was routed (73), and when she herself says to Jason that *amor* will lead her astray (92–3), there is a hesitation between seeing the name of a responsible god, or the name of a human passion.[194] Throughout, it is exceedingly difficult to know whether Ovid is forswearing, and correcting, the divine dimension of Apollonius' picture, or else inviting us to supplement his version (where Medea is the sole focalizer) with our knowledge of Apollonius' more panoramic presentation. This difficulty itself, of course, exploits the problems already present in Apollonius' own treatment.

A more direct engagement with a powerful prototype comes in Book 4, where Tisiphone's possession of Athamas and Ino takes up the challenge posed by Allecto's baffling possession of Amata in *Aeneid* 7 (346–56).[195] The indeterminate physicality of Allecto's weird snake is the strangest feature of that very strange scene, as it slides over Amata's clothes and breasts without any contact, breathing its spirit into her without her knowledge, turning itself into necklace and ribbon, still slippery. Ovid gives us four lines on Tisiphone's snakes (4. 491–4), and then blandly demolishes

[193] Below, Chapter 6, Section IV.

[194] Anderson (1972), 252: 'The "defeat" and "flight" of *cupido* can easily take place symbolically within the human soul.' Similarly Whitman (1987), 55.

[195] A very good discussion of the Ino and Athamas scene in Bernbeck (1967), 1–43; for Ovid's debts to Vergil's scene, see Bömer (1969–86), on 4. 473–511, and throughout.

Vergil's equivocations, taking us by the elbow and pointing out
what is 'really' going on:

> inde duos mediis abrumpit crinibus angues
> pestiferaque manu raptos immisit, at illi
> Inoosque sinus Athamanteosque pererrant
> inspirantque graues animas; *nec uulnera membris*
> *ulla ferunt: mens est quae diros sentiat ictus.*

Then she rips away two snakes from the middle of her hair; grabbing
them, she throws them with her pestilential hand. The snakes wander
over the breasts of Ino and Athamas, breathing into them their grievous
breaths. *Nor do they bear any wounds on their limbs; it is their minds*
*that feel the dread impact.* (4. 495-9)

Not content with this much, Tisiphone and Ovid go further.
The Fury had brought—*quoque* ('*in addition*')—a bucket of physical and metaphorical poisons, everything all ground up together
(*omnia trita simul*, 500-5). This is divine machinery with a vengeance, hyperbolical, redundant, and gratuitous.

It should be more than enough to do the job, and so it appears
at first, with Athamas' immediate frenzy (*protinus*, 512). Yet Ino
does not react until Athamas has smashed their son's head against
a rock: 'then *finally* she was roused, in her capacity as mother'
(*tum denique concita mater*, 519). And Ovid goes on to opine that
her madness may have been natural after all—or else the result of
the poison: *seu dolor hoc fecit, seu sparsum causa uenenum* (520).
In this one line, and in the larger contrast between Athamas and
Ino, Ovid is splitting up Vergil's two incommensurate ways of
reading Amata's madness. The hyperbolical barrage of supernatural equipment deranges Athamas, yet Ino is driven mad by the
natural frenzy she feels at seeing her son's brains dashed out (or
else, of course, says Ovid, by the poison . . .).[196] The zestful accumulation of Tartarean detail comes to appear more and more like
a way of exploding epic narrative's distinctive manner of describing human experience. As an image Ovid's divine scene is
magnificent; as a way of reflecting on human behaviour it has
been turned into nothing.

---

[196] The split between Athamas and Ino is seen even more clearly in the *Fasti* version of this story, where Athamas is driven mad by Furies and a false vision (6.
489), while Ino remains self-possessed until the moment of her son's funeral (491–
4): Bernbeck (1967), 32 n. 85.

It is in Ovid's poem that we see for the first time extended use of an alternative way of reflecting on human behaviour, one which was eventually to emerge triumphant in European verse narratives—personification allegory. We may postpone the main discussion of the problems of this mode until we reach Statius' *Thebaid*, where it attains its fullest manifestation in classical epic.[197] Here it will be enough to point to the main elements of Ovid's contribution.

First, some brief words of context. Personifications appear in classical literature from the very beginning, wholesale in Hesiod's *Theogony*, and commonly enough in Homer.[198] Yet if we concentrate on the allegorical use of personifications as we see them in Ovid, Statius, and the later medieval or Renaissance tradition, it is plain that Hesiod and Homer scarcely exploit personification allegory as such, in that their personifications are (crucially) not characterful agents who engage with human beings, occupying the same narrative space as the human characters, and interacting with them in the same way as do the gods themselves. Hesiod's personifications are ways of talking about the way the world is made; nowhere does he show us Strife, for example, or Deceit impinging on a human agent. In Homer, Phobos and Deimos are mentioned as companions of Ares (*Il.* 4. 440, 15. 119), and they appear on Agamemnon's shield (11. 37), yet the only personifications who have any mimetic character at all are Eris (*Il.* 4. 440–5) and the Litae (*Il.* 9. 502–12). Sleep and Death may carry off the corpse of Sarpedon (*Il.* 16. 681–3), but these verses, memorable as they are, do not tell us anything about the experience of being Sarpedon at that point; they form a remarkable emblem of Sarpedon's state, but reveal nothing about the man or his emotions. We are still very far from Ovid's Envy visiting Aglauros (*Met.* 2. 797–805), or Statius' Virtue visiting Menoeceus (*Theb.* 10. 632–782).

None the less, it is clear that allegorical treatment of moral issues was in large measure a response to moralizing interpretations of Homer, and narrative enactments of moral dramas may be traced back at least to Prodicus' *Choice of Heracles* in the

---

[197] Chapter 7, Section III.
[198] Generally, on Greek personifications: Deubner in Roscher, 2068–169; Petersen (1939); Reinhardt (1960*b*); Hamdorf (1964); Whitman (1987), 269–72 ('On the History of the Term "Personification"').

late fifth century, where we see the hero confronted with the competing appeals of personified Vice and Virtue.[199] It is impossible to establish with any certainty what sort of prototypes earlier epic may have provided to Ovid. The technique of using personifications as major actors in epic may well have been very early. The *Cypria* appears to have made extensive use of personifications.[200] We hear of Themis and Eris, Nemesis, and possibly Momus as characters,[201] and we can reconstruct the moment when 'Strife' spreads her own essence among the guests at the marriage-feast of Peleus and Thetis, but the fragmentary nature of the evidence makes it impossible for us to know what sort of characterful energy 'Strife' or her counterparts were given.[202] There are good grounds for assuming that Hellenistic literature made use of such scenes, but, again, we lack the actual texts we need for comparison.[203] Apollonius, of course, has Eros as a major character, but he does everything he can to make him a creature of epic mythology, rather than the personification which he could easily have been.[204] Vergil's techniques in the *Aeneid* are remarkably restrained in their classicism. His Fama (*Aen.* 4. 173–97) owes much to Homer's Eris;[205] his Underworld is home to a throng of Hesiodic monsters (Disease, Fear, etc.: *Aen.* 6. 273–9). Although his Fama is clearly very important for Ovid,[206] nothing in Vergil really prepares us for what we find in the *Metamorphoses*.

Ovid has four set-piece scenes in which personifications, and their

---

[199] Xen. *Mem.* 2. 1. 21–34; very good discussion in Whitman (1987), 20–31. Note Whitman's arguments against the eclipse of this earlier material in the important discussion of Lewis (1936): 'It is no longer possible to argue . . . that the divided will, or *bellum intestinum*, is effectively the discovery of the first century AD, or that from this division personification follows' (30). On Euripides' marvellous Lyssa in the *Hercules Furens*, see below, p. 370.

[200] Davies (1989), 35–6, 39.

[201] Themis and Eris (*EGF* p. 31. 5–8); Nemesis (*EGF* F 7–8); Momus (*EGF* F 1).

[202] Professor Powell points out to me that the story of Eris at the marriage-feast must be post-Homeric in the form we know, since its key element is the *written* inscription on the apple, 'To the most beautiful'.

[203] So Hollis (1970), 138–9, referring to the Nemesis-scene in Nonnus, *Dion.* 48. 370–470, which is very reminiscent of Ovid's Fames and Invidia in particular.

[204] In accordance with his general policy of maintaining the gods' names as titles of epic personalities, not as metonymic labels: above, p. 76.

[205] See now Hardie (1986), 273–8.

[206] Due (1974), 178–9; Braudy (1986), 140–1.

effects, are depicted at length: *Inuidia*, 'Envy' (2. 760–832); *Fames*, 'Hunger' (8. 799–822); *Somnus*, 'Sleep' (11. 592–649); and *Fama*, 'Rumour' or 'Fame' (12. 39–63).[207] Despite the alluring comprehensiveness of the term 'personification allegory', it is important to note the variety of technique which Ovid controls in these four scenes.[208] If the picture of Fama is concerned with elucidating the nature of both poetic and non-poetic reputation and authority in the world,[209] the remaining three personifications, on the other hand, involve us in what it is like to feel something— sleepy, famished, or envious. Even these three differ in the amount of mimetic character they have, in rough accordance with the differing degree to which the conditions of sleep, hunger, and envy involve interaction. Sleep is, as it were, a self-contained state, which is why the House of Sleep is a self-contained unit of narrative, with Sleep himself uninvolved in any direct engagement with the characters of the narrative; such action as he partakes in is indirect, mediated via his agent, Morpheus. In comparison, the ravening hunger which besets Erisychthon—however personal a phenomenon—is a social event, and one which mirrors the blind voraciousness of its victim's moral character; it is, therefore, fitting that he should be actually visited by the creature who embodies his affliction. The most complex case is that of the effect of Envy, for here we are dealing with a human emotion which issues from human interaction and manifests itself in human events. Ovid's use of personification is at its richest here, for he presents us with a scene in which characters act in the same realm of narrative as an entity who embodies the timeless characteristics of their particular moral failing: the characters and the personification perform together in a sequence which, taken as a whole, provides a complex set of ways of thinking about the emotion. This technique is the distinctive domain of personification allegory 'proper', as we shall see it fully realized in Statius, and as it was to rule in post-classical literature.

The possession of Aglauros by Invidia has a fairly involved context. We first meet Aglauros 200 lines earlier in Book 2 (552–61),

---

[207] Bömer (1969–86) has his main discussion of Ovid's personifications on 11. 592–673, with bibliography.
[208] Well marked by Zumwalt (1977), 210.
[209] Zumwalt (1977); we return to Fama at the close of this section.

when we hear the story of how Minerva entrusted the child Erichthonius, hidden in a wicker basket, to Cecrops' three daughters, Aglauros, Herse, and Pandrosos. She had told them not to look inside the basket, but Aglauros untied the bindings, and they saw the child with his snake companion. Ovid returns to the sisters when he describes Mercury falling in love with Herse, and attempting to visit her bedchamber (2. 708–39). Aglauros sees him first, and demands gold as the price for her complicity in his affair (740–51). At this juncture, Minerva looks at the girl, remembers her previous offence in uncovering Erichthonius, and visits Invidia in order to have her possess Aglauros (752–86). Invidia obeys, and infects Aglauros with bitter envy of her sister; finally, Aglauros is turned into a stone by Mercury, when, as a result of her envy of Herse, she refuses to aid him as she had promised (787–832).

The episode has attracted a certain amount of comment; the focus of attention has been the virtuoso description of the actual figure of Invidia, and of her House (760–82).[210] Important insights into Invidia's nature have emerged from these discussions,[211] but the episode as a whole needs to be the focus, with all its characterful interactions, if we are to allow Ovid's use of Invidia its full effect. The apparent plenitude of Ovid's painting of Invidia's appearance is clearly responsible for the feeling that we need look only at her in order to glean what Ovid has to say about the experience of envy—as Solodow explicitly declares: 'Ovid builds up his portraits almost solely through descriptions of appearance, that is to say, of surfaces. To understand Envy we need only to look at her. She simply is what she seems to be.'[212] One should react with caution to the suggestion that anything in the *Metamorphoses* simply is what it seems to be. 'Only looking' turns out to be an activity which is interestingly fraught with difficulty in Ovid's account of Invidia, an activity which goes via the name of the emotion to the heart of the experience.[213]

---

[210] Dickie (1975); Solodow (1988), 200–2; unfortunately, I have not seen the (as yet unpublished) 1988 Michigan dissertation of Alison Keith, in which Aglauros and Invidia are discussed.

[211] Dickie (1975) finds many ancient preconceptions about the nature of envy embodied in the figure and abode of Invidia.

[212] Solodow (1988), 202.

[213] Ovid's technique is striking confirmation of the power of the allegorical theory espoused by Quilligan (1979), summed up in her definition of the form as 'the generation of narrative out of wordplay' (22): 'out of a focus on the word as word, allegory generates narrative action' (33). Van Dyke (1985) has some cogent

Invidia's name, after all, refers to a flawed act of vision. The act of *in-uidere* is 'to look at askance',[214] as Ovid goes out of his way to remind us when he describes Invidia's appearance: *nusquam recta acies*, he says, 'the line of her vision is never straight' (776). When Invidia looks at Minerva departing, she does so *obliquo lumine*, 'with eye askance' (787). Aglauros will be a ready victim for this creature, for, from the first moment she appears, peering into the secret basket of Minerva, she is someone who has trouble controlling her vision.[215] Her eyes lead her astray again at the beginning of the Invidia-narrative, when she sees Mercury going to her sister's bedchamber (*uenientem prima notauit*, 740), and Ovid explicitly links her two dangerous acts of sight: *adspicit hunc oculis isdem, quibus abdita nuper / uiderat Aglauros flauae secreta Mineruae* ('Aglauros looks at the god with the same eyes with which she had recently seen the hidden secrets of blonde Minerva', 748-9).

Aglauros' vision, however flawed, is not yet envious when she looks at Erichthonius and Mercury, but her wayward looking sets her up for the act of wayward looking which Ovid presents as the essence of Invidia. Before Aglauros becomes the victim of Invidia, however, Ovid presents Invidia's first victim—Minerva:

> Vertit ad hanc torui dea bellica luminis orbem
> et tanto penitus traxit suspiria motu,
> ut pariter pectus positamque in pectore forti
> aegida concuteret: subit, hanc arcana profana
> detexisse manu, tum cum sine matre creatam
> Lemnicolae stirpem contra data foedera uidit,
> et gratamque deo fore iam gratamque sorori
> et ditem sumpto, quod auara poposcerat, auro.

The warrior-goddess turned towards her the orb of her angry eye, and drew deep sighs with such force that she shook both her chest and the aegis, positioned on her brave chest. She thought of how this was the one who had uncovered the secret objects with her profane hand, when, against the given agreement, she saw the offspring of Vulcan, born without

objections to accepting Quilligan's definition as a universal explanation of allegory, but the validity of Quilligan's approach in many areas of allegory is beyond dispute.

[214] *OLD* s.v. § 1a.
[215] Note how this theme of illicit looking is reinforced by the narrative frame for the first Aglauros story. It is related by the crow, who tells of how he spied on Aglauros' act of spying (2. 557-8), and was punished by Minerva.

a mother. Now she would be welcome to the god, and welcome to her sister too—and she would be rich, with the gold which she had greedily demanded. (2. 752-9)

The goddess's act of looking at Aglauros produces the peevish sense of begrudging someone something which is one of the manifestations of the act of *inuidere*.[216] Minerva's deep sigh at the sight of Aglauros is mirrored by the sigh which Invidia later gives, when she sees the magnificent form of the goddess (774).[217] The nagging sensation of envious resentment is caught with the repetition of the maddening *gratam* in line 758, and capped by the next line ('as if that isn't bad enough, she'll be rich as well'); when Invidia is described for us later, we learn that she too finds the success of others 'unwelcome' (*ingratos*, 780).[218] When the goddess visits Invidia, the difficulty she has in looking at Invidia mimics in reverse the very obliquity of vision which Invidia embodies, by capturing the shame which the dignified person feels at having succumbed to this base vice: *uidet intus edentem / uipereas carnes, uitiorum alimenta suorum, / Inuidiam uisaque oculos auertit* ('she sees, inside, eating vipers' flesh, the nourishment of her vice, Invidia—at the sight of her, she turns away her eyes', 768-70).[219] Invidia's reciprocal difficulty in looking at Minerva (*obliquo lumine*, 787) is the quintessence of her own affliction: she must look, she cannot bear to look.

When Invidia emerges from her house and looks at the goddess, we get our chance to look at her:

> pallor in ore sedet, macies in corpore toto,
> nusquam recta acies, liuent rubigine dentes,
> pectora felle uirent, lingua est suffusa ueneno;
> risus abest, nisi quem uisi mouere dolores;
> nec fruitur somno, uigilantibus excita curis,
> sed uidet ingratos intabescitque uidendo
> successus hominum carpitque et carpitur una
> suppliciumque suum est.

Pallor sits on her face, emaciation on her whole body, the line of her vision is never straight, her teeth are discoloured with tartar, her chest

---

[216] *OLD* s.v. § 2.

[217] So much is certain, whatever one decides about the text of line 774.

[218] It is difficult in English to catch the rather illogical way that *gratam* in 758 and *ingratos* in 780 look to each other.

[219] At *Pont.* 3. 3. 101-2 Ovid comments on the incompatibility of snake-like envy and high character.

thrives with poison, her tongue runs with venom. Laughter is absent, unless the sight of pain moves her; nor does she enjoy sleep, stirred by watchful anxieties; rather, looking at people's success is unwelcome to her, and she wastes away through looking at them; she gnaws and is gnawed simultaneously; she is her own punishment. (2. 775–82)

The dominance of sight in defining Invidia's manner of action is immediately apparent (*uisi*, 778; *uidet . . . uidendo*, 780). Yet only the first three of these eight lines are devoted to what Invidia looks like, as if Minerva, or Ovid, finds it easier to generalize about Invidia's manner of action than to gaze steadily upon her.[220] When Invidia visits Aglauros, she works through the girl's flawed sight, placing her sister, her marriage, and the god before her eyes (*ante oculos*, 803), and distorting her vision: *cunctaque magna facit*, 'she magnifies everything' (805). So successful is she that Aglauros often wishes to die in order to be able to avoid seeing such a sight (*ne quicquam tale uideret*, 812).

The basic word-play behind Ovid's Invidia-narrative may be rather pat, but it acquires depth and resilience in its acting-out. The essence of Ovid's envy is that it comes from and feeds on 'looking', but cannot bear to look, so that it must look askance, and therefore distorts everything in its field of vision. Simply looking at Invidia is not enough. If we look at what happens to Aglauros, we gain some notion of the stupefying pain of the experience. The most interesting light on the experience of envy is, however, shed obliquely (as is fitting), by the sensations of Minerva, who is ostensibly there only to instigate the 'real' story. It is Minerva's inability to watch Aglauros' success which makes her visit Invidia, and as we watch Minerva watching Invidia eating her snakes, we catch something of the nauseated shame which a proud person feels at condescending to begrudge a lesser person her success. When we look at Invidia, after all, we see her with Minerva's averted eyes.

A glance, in conclusion, at Ovid's last set-piece personification allegory, the House of Fame (12. 39–63), returns us to the issues of poetic authority which were the subject at the beginning of this

---

[220] Contrast the description of Fames, likewise eight lines long (8. 801–8), where nothing but the physical appearance of the creature is given. Even the physical details of Invidia's appearance, of course, contain moral generalization: see Hollis (1970), on 8. 802, for the 'backbiting' pun contained in *rubigine* (776), and Solodow (1988), 202, for the 'envious' metaphor of *liuent* (776).

Section. As a condensation of ancient attitudes towards the plasticity of tradition and the variable nature of poetic truth, Ovid's House of Fame has no parallel:

> atria turba tenet; ueniunt, leue uulgus, euntque
> mixtaque cum ueris passim commenta uagantur
> milia rumorum confusaque uerba uolutant;
> e quibus hi uacuas implent sermonibus aures,
> hi narrata ferunt alio, mensuraque ficti
> crescit, et auditis aliquid nouus adicit auctor.

A crowd occupies the entrance-halls; a fickle mob, they come and they go; thousands of rumours wander everywhere, lies mixed with truth, and jumbled words fly about. Some of these fill empty ears with their talk, some bear the stories elsewhere; the dimensions of the fiction grow, and each new author adds something to what he has heard. (12. 53–8)

As has been shown by the fine discussion of Zumwalt (1977), Ovid immediately goes on to demonstrate what he means with his own comprehensive rewriting of Homer, and with the portrayal of Nestor's partial and misleading paradigmatic act of epic narrative, which itself supplants the Trojan war as it smothers the mighty Hercules (12. 169–541). Other poets have been nearly paralysed by this heightened awareness of their position at the receiving end of a fluid tradition, but Ovid remains confident and alert in his energetic production of a new Fama. At the end of a poem in which he has incessantly been reminding us of his dependence on Fama as a source—*fama est, fertur, ferunt, memorant*[221]—Ovid presents himself as a new repository for the Fama which future generations will inherit. Some of the inhabitants of the House of Fama suffer oblivion;[222] but Ovid will live, as his last lines defiantly proclaim, with the final verse containing a last ironic explosion of the doubt over the truth of his words:

> Iamque opus exegi, quod nec Iouis ira nec ignis
> nec poterit ferrum nec edax abolere uetustas.
> cum uolet, illa dies, quae nil nisi corporis huius
> ius habet, incerti spatium mihi finiat aeui:

---

[221] Examples are legion; one each for the words given in the text: 2. 268; 3. 318; 4. 266; 7. 430. On Ovid's use of such expressions, see Bömer (1969–86), on 3. 106.

[222] Such is the force of 12. 46, *nocte dieque patet*, which aligns Fama's House with Vergil's underworld (*noctes atque dies patet atri ianua Ditis*, *Aen.* 6. 127). Vergil's underworld is easy to enter and difficult to leave; Ovid's House of Fama is easy to enter and fatally easy to leave.

parte tamen meliore mei super alta perennis
astra ferar, nomenque erit indelebile nostrum,
quaque patet domitis Romana potentia terris,
ore legar populi, perque omnia saecula fama,
siquid habent ueri uatum praesagia, uiuam.

Now I have erected a work, which neither the anger of Jupiter, nor fire, nor sword, nor devouring time will be able to abolish. When it wishes, let that day, which has power over nothing but this body, mark off the end of my uncertain span. Still, with the better part of my self I will be borne through the years above the high stars; my name will be indestructible; wherever Roman power extends over the conquered lands, I will be read by the lips of the people, and through all the centuries, in fame—if the prophecies of bards have any truth—will I live. (15. 871–9)

He will himself become one of the manufacturers of the slippery Fama which constructs our literary world: so he asserts, not only with the emphatic *fama* at the end of the penultimate line, but with the 'fame' word he uses to describe his astral progress, *ferar* (876).[223] Outdoing Julius Caesar, who went higher than the moon and became a star (15. 848–50), Ovid will go higher than the stars, and become a book.

[223] 'Carried', literally, but also 'borne in report, spoken of', punning on such phrases as *fertur*, *ferunt*, which he so commonly uses in the poem to describe rumour and report.

# 6

## Epic of History: Lucan's *Bellum Ciuile* and Silius' *Punica*

### I

'True history,' said Hearst, with a smile that was, for once, almost charming, 'is the final fiction. I thought even you knew that.'

Gore Vidal, Empire[1]

Already in Chapter 1, with the discussion of critical attitudes to the historical status of Homer's narrative, and in Chapter 3, with Naevius and Ennius, we have brushed against the problems which arise when the gods participate in the epic narrative of historical events.[2] Here, as we come to the two historical epics from our period which survive in non-fragmentary form, it becomes necessary to engage with these issues directly. An investigation into the theoretical background must stand as prelude, together with a discussion of the lost or fragmentary historical epics which preceded Lucan.

When the role of the gods in historical epic becomes the subject, there is more at issue than our common naturalistic prejudices. In considering the gods enmeshed in events of documented, even recent history, the instinctive modern antipathy to the convention as such is allowed full expression, for the modern reader automatically regards it as incongruous that any work which poses as 'historical' should involve the presence of supernatural beings participating in, and manipulating, the affairs of real people who really existed. The problem is compounded by the inevitable antithesis into which discussion is cast by the accidents of trans-

---

[1] Vidal (1987), 472.

[2] pp. 44–5. In general, on historical epic, see Kroll (1916); Ziegler (1966); Clinard (1967); Häussler (1976, 1978).

mission. Lucan, conventionally described as having abandoned the gods from his poem, has long been recognized as a powerful poet, and is currently being carried by one of Classics' periodic movements of reassessment towards the status of a genuinely fine one.[3] Silius, on the other hand, in whose poem on the Hannibalic war the gods take part as characters, is a quite remarkably bad poet, on virtually every count and according to virtually every authority.[4] It becomes irresistible to applaud Lucan for discarding the divine apparatus, and to blame Silius for retaining it against his example.

Still, whatever the supposed merits or failings of our authors, they only serve to corroborate the initial judgement, that the gods have no place in a narrative which describes historical events, even if they may be tolerated in a narrative of myth. Ahl's comment on Lucan and the civil war is representative: 'The facts, even the details, of what happened would have been well known to his readers. The literary and intellectual infancy of the Roman world was long past, and with its passing, the possibility of representing familiar, historical events in the extravagant manner of traditional epic faded.'[5] And yet one might reply with the battle of Actium on Aeneas' shield in *Aeneid* 8, not a passage composed in the literary and intellectual infancy'of the Roman world. Why is the *Aeneid*'s closest engagement with the contemporary world a theomachy? It is commonly objected against Silius' divine machinery that it necessarily strips historical events of their true grandeur.[6] Are Augustus and Agrippa then belittled by the fact that their great victory is encapsulated in Vergil's war of divinities?

---

[3] Johnson (1987), 1–2. The study by Ahl (1976) was, in the English-speaking world, the most important contribution to Lucan's return to favour; in Germany, a genuine revival of interest began much earlier, with the studies of Gundolf (1924) and Fraenkel (1927). Due (1962), 77–86, has a lively sketch of the ups and downs of Lucan's popularity since his death.

[4] Ahl is part of a recent corporate attempt to do for Silius something of what he helped to do for Lucan (Ahl–Davis–Pomeroy (1986)); he faces a qualitatively different problem.

[5] Ahl (1976), 69; cf. Burck and Rutz (1979), 187; Le Bonniec (1970), 166: 'Le sujet moderne, pleinement historique, dépourvu de toute "aura" légendaire, interdisait, sous peine de ridicule, toute participation directe des dieux à l'action'; Vessey (1982), 591, comparing Lucan and Silius: 'Lucan's excision of such machinery was poetically wise as well as Stoically orthodox. Juno, Venus and the Sibyl find an acceptable habitation in the world of Aeneas. In the era of Hannibal and Scipio their presence is obtrusive.'

[6] Miniconi–Devallet (1979), lxviii; cf. Duff (1964), 254, for the mirror-image comment on Lucan: 'Well aware of the intrinsic greatness of the figures in a colossal

It appears that we still have major difficulties in coming to terms with epic modes. If modern critics can scarcely help but praise Lucan the more closely he approximates to the office of historian, the reverse is true of the ancient critics. These folk are so unperturbed by the difficulties that beset us, so comfortable with their notion of what an historical epic should look like, that their automatic, pat response (to anticipate the argument for a moment) is to deny that Lucan is a poet at all.[7] A related aspect of this complex of problems is the (often unexamined) difficulty of the term 'history' in the confident antitheses which we set up between history and epic, or history and myth. Our own high valuation of historical discourse contributes to the enthusiasm which is accorded to Lucan: he comes to share in the approval which is naturally granted to veracity and pragmatic analysis.[8] Yet these are *our* qualities of historical writing, and if recent studies of ancient historiography have taught us anything, it is that we must be exceedingly cautious in assuming any congruence between what historians do now and what they did then.[9] As a first step through these problems, it is worth relocating 'history' in an ancient context. From there we will be involved in the background of epic theory and—for the sake of utility and completeness—of epic practice, and can then move on to the surviving poems themselves.

It is pointless to hope to encapsulate in a paragraph 'the ancients' attitude to history and myth, or history and epic': the time-span, the competition of theories defeat the attempt. Still, given the ancients' invincibly canonical turn of mind, enough measure of generalization may be achieved to set the scene for the discussion of our two epics. The task is made a good deal more accessible by

struggle, Lucan relied for his effects more on history than on romance.' As so often, one has the impression that the irritation felt by many critics over the divine machinery in historical epic is in fact the same impatience with which they respond to it in other epics.

[7] Here I mean not only Petronius' Eumolpus (to whom we return soon), but Martial (14. 194), Servius (*Aen.* 1. 382), Suetonius (Rostagni (1944), 13 f.)—anyone who has left an opinion.

[8] See Ebener (1984) for a strong statement of Lucan's poem's realistic nature. It will emerge that I see such values as radically out of place in reading Lucan: see, rather, Martindale (1976), 50–1; Conte (1985), 84–6; Johnson (1987); Henderson (1988).

[9] Wiseman (1979); Finley (1985); Woodman (1988).

the recent appearance of several important studies on ancient historiography, and on its relation with myth.[10] As we attempt to discover how the ancients distinguished between history and myth, the clearest and (to us) most disconcerting feature is the acceptance, by virtually all authors in virtually all circumstances, of the basic information in the inherited tradition.[11] We are not talking here about accepting the Trojan war as an event, but about, for example, regarding as an actual person such a minor player in Homer as Elpenor,[12] or estimating the number of Agamemnon's army from Homer's catalogue (Thuc. 1. 10. 3–5). Nor, as this last example shows, are we dealing with fools and hacks. Thucydides offers a very clear example of the standard mode of operation. It is not that he regards the epics as 'historical': that form of words, however natural for us, begs the question. He certainly does, however, take it quite for granted that Homer's narrative contains a great deal of genuine information about the first great war fought by Greeks. He is aware that Homer's technique leads him to embellish and exaggerate (1. 10. 3), but he does not call into question the essential veracity of the data. The general approach is that of the rationalizers discussed in the first chapter, paring away the obviously poetic to get at the facts.[13] Not only Homer is authoritative for Thucydides, for the historian applies the same technique to the non-Homeric epic tradition. Agamemnon, for example, according to Thucydides' interpretation of the myth, exercised enough authority to gather and lead the expedition because of his pre-eminent power, not because of any oaths administered at the wedding of Helen (1. 9. 1). The basic data of pan-Hellenic epic are accepted under this guise: the arrival of Pelops from Asia (1. 9. 2), the existence of Hellen, son of Deucalion (1. 3. 2), the return of the sons of Heracles (1. 12. 3).[14]

---

[10] Wiseman (1979), Veyne (1983), Woodman (1988); cf. Walbank (1960). As so often, one finds a lucid and economical anticipation of many of the issues in Kroll (1924): on this topic, 44–63.

[11] Gomme (1954), 3–4; Walbank (1960); Wardman (1960); Strasburger (1972), 16–17; Häussler (1978), 22–38.

[12] Strasburger (1972), 19–20.

[13] pp. 31–2.

[14] Gomme (1954), 117; cf. the interesting paper of Howie (1984), which tests the credulity of Thucydides by comparing it to the approach of Pindar.

Such an accepting attitude is wholly typical. In general, throughout antiquity, the process continued of redeeming for 'history' as much of tradition as possible by jettisoning only the clearly fantastic, fabulous, and poetic, all of which remained under the heading of 'myth' (μῦθος or *fabula*): 'it seems as though the ancient grammarians, Greek and Roman, reserved the name μῦθος or *fabula* for what was impossible κατὰ φύσιν ["by nature"], while all the subject matter of legend, as well as what we should call history, fell under ἱστορία ["history"], provided that it was physically possible'.[15] A clear and extended example is easily found in the discussion of Homer by Strabo, the Greek Augustan geographer. The first two sections of his work (some seventy or eighty modern pages) are entirely devoted to vindicating the historical and geographical authority of Homer: Hades, Cyclopes, the cattle of the sun, and so on are all obvious marvels, whose removal does not affect the credit of the rest of the picture.[16] Roman intellectuals were as much at home in this tradition as they were in the rest of Hellenistic criticism and literary culture.[17]

The question of belief is a notorious problem here.[18] We baulk at attributing the title of history to this process, whereby a kernel of 'truth' is redeemed, narrated, and handed down to the next historian in the chain to elaborate according to his own purposes. Belief in the fact behind the tradition appears to be of minor relevance; or at least, people appear to have been prepared to 'believe' almost anything. It is not a question, however, of redeeming 'facts' or 'truth', but of finding material which could be spoken about in a convincing and meaningful manner, which contributed to a sense of satisfaction in charting the past, filling the *horror uacui*, assimilating the past to the present.[19] An approachable parallel for us is perhaps pre-modern imaginary landscape painting. These are not representations of actual pieces of

---

[15] Walbank (1960), 226; cf. Kroll (1924), 59, 62; Wiseman (1979), 49, 145–9; Veyne (1983), 25–7, 69–80.

[16] 1. 2. 11; cf. above, pp. 44–5.

[17] Wiseman (1985), 196–7.

[18] Veyne (1983).

[19] This *horror uacui* explains the 'expansion of the past' (the phrase of Badian (1966), 11); cf. Wiseman (1979), esp. 21–6 (*horror uacui* is his phrase, 22). Did anyone 'believe' the manufactured genealogies of the late Republic (Wiseman (1974b)), with their links back to Aeneas, Hercules, or Odysseus? Regardless, these fakes certainly meant something; they mattered, and they counted, as Wiseman's excellent paper demonstrates beyond any doubt.

ground, but that would have struck a contemporary as an entirely irrelevant observation. We must remember that, by the grammarians' categories at least, the historicity of an event (whether it happened or not) was not at issue: 'the difference between *fabula* and *historia*,' according to Servius, 'is that *fabula* is the *narration* of something against nature, *whether it happened or not* (e.g. Pasiphae), while *historia* is whatever is *narrated* in accordance with nature, *whether it happened or not* (e.g. Phaedra)' (*historia est quicquid secundum naturam dicitur, siue factum siue non factum, Aen.* 1. 235). The state of affairs in the ancient world is remarkably similar to that described by Fleischman for the Middle Ages:

Were we to compile a medieval dictionary, history would no doubt have to be redefined as 'familiar', 'legendary', 'what was held to be true'. This definition might provoke discomfort in certain quarters inasmuch as legendary has since come to be synonymous with false. But the issue at the time was not objective truth as distinct from subjective belief. For the Middle Ages and even well beyond, historical truth was anything that belonged to a widely accepted tradition.[20]

There were, of course, sceptics. Those who were technically Sceptics were obliged to doubt the facts of tradition as they were obliged to doubt anything else. Sextus Empiricus is, accordingly, extremely hard-headed in his dismissal of the historians' pretensions to any science or knowledge (*Math.* 1. 248–69); much of the subject-matter treated by the historians, says Sextus, is wholly false and unverifiable (1. 265–8). At the very beginning of historiography, Herodotus demonstrates an unruffled acknowledgement of the fact that key components of the Homeric tradition are there because Homer freely exercised his poetic prerogatives, suppressing what really happened to Helen in favour of a version that better suited his poetic purposes.[21] It is, of course, crucial to note that Herodotus does, after all, claim to have recovered what really happened to Helen, from the Egyptian tradition.

As we saw in the first chapter, a powerful, but minority tradition of Hellenistic scientific scholarship vigorously denied that it was possible to recover worthwhile data from the poets.[22] According

---

[20] Fleischman (1983), 305.
[21] 2. 116. On Herodotus' scepticism about early tradition, see Gomme (1954), 117; Neville (1977).
[22] pp. 39–40.

to Eratosthenes, for example, there were no geographical facts to be retrieved from Homer's accounts of Odysseus' wanderings.[23] Such positions were distinctly unpopular and uninfluential.[24] Eratosthenes' claims provoked pages of polemic from Strabo; he restates the dominant ancient view of Homer's narrative as *fundamentally* accurate in fact. Even in the case of Eratosthenes, however, scepticism about the data of tradition was not truly radical. His *Chronography* gave dates for the fall of Troy, the return of the sons of Heracles, and the Ionian migration: 'For the Greek mind', as Pfeiffer puts it, 'the siege and taking of Troy was no legend, but a momentous fact of history for which any chronological system must provide a date.'[25]

This glance at the handful of sceptics serves only to reinforce the impression of an intellectual environment in which the overlap between 'history' and 'myth' was very extensive indeed. Yet the ancients insisted strenuously that there were divisions between the two,[26] and we must attempt to establish in detail what they considered those divisions to be.

It is sometimes claimed that the ancients used chronology to clear boundaries between myth and history, establishing a mythical period of time and an historical one.[27] Fornara fixes on the return of the sons of Heracles as the accepted dividing line: this is where Ephorus began his *History*.[28] The notion of such events being historical is bizarre to us, of course; but, leaving that aside, there was too much fluidity for any particular system to take hold. The chronological schemes of Erathosthenes and Apollodorus began with the fall of Troy,[29] while numerous historians, as Fornara himself shows, backtracked even beyond this point.[30] Diodorus Siculus has the Trojan war as a *de facto* division, explicitly follow-

---

[23] Eratosthenes' position is extrapolated from the early pages of Strabo; cf. Pfeiffer (1968), 166.

[24] The geographer Agatharcides followed Eratosthenes (*GGM* p. 117), as did the great Apollodorus in his geographical study of Homer's catalogue of ships: Pfeiffer (1968), 259.

[25] Pfeiffer (1968), 164.

[26] Above, pp. 42–5.

[27] Fornara (1983), 7–9.

[28] Ibid., 8–9.

[29] Pfeiffer (1968), 163, 255–6.

[30] Fornara (1983), 9.

ing Apollodorus (1. 5. 1); he none the less devotes six of the forty books of his *History* to events before that war.

Roman tradition was altogether more slippery, since no authoritative demarcations had established themselves.[31] Knowing that the declaration of such divisions contributed to an authoritative, 'historical' tone of voice, Roman writers could produce them at will. Cicero stresses at length the fact that belief in Romulus' apotheosis took root instantly, at a period of literacy and high culture, after the period when fables and lies were readily accepted (*Rep.* 2. 18). Livy is so alert to the prestige of these utterances that he produces two of them; of course, the implied division is different each time. In his Preface he appears to advance the foundation of the city as the boundary between *fabula* and *historia* (*Pr.* 6–7), and he accordingly speaks of the subject-matter of his history as going back over seven hundred years, that is, to the foundation of the city. Indeed, only three chapters are devoted to the material before the foundation (although the neatness of the pattern is artfully disrupted by the insertion of the Hercules and Cacus story as a digression in the section on Romulus, 1. 7. 3–14). After the first five books, however, Livy starts afresh, and the reader learns with a start that only now, at the beginning of Book 6, are we emerging into certainty and clarity from the obscurity of Rome's first 365 years (6. 1. 1–3); only now is real history possible.[32] The modern reader's surprise is the greater because there is absolutely no qualitative difference in narrative mode between, let us say, Book 3 and Book 23. It is all 'history': names, dates, reported speeches, detail, facts, elections, and so on—the whole paraphernalia of report as laid down by Herodotus.

Distinctions of chronology, in other words, are not in the end very helpful, since historians could, and did, write about anything from the creation of the world on, in the narrative mode appropriate to 'history'. There were no 'out-of-bounds' for history;[33] the same events could be, and were, treated by historian and poet alike.[34] Indeed, history and poetry (in particular, epic poetry) were

[31] Horsfall in Bremmer and Horsfall (1987), 5; see Wiseman (1979), 157–9, for the chronological schemes of Varro and Nepos.

[32] Note that one of Livy's predecessors, Claudius Quadrigarius, began his history with the sack of Rome by the Gauls, possibly mentioning the same factors as Livy: *RE* 3. 2859.

[33] It is Diodorus Siculus who begins with the creation of the world (1. 7).

[34] Cf. Else (1957) 315–16, on Aristotle's position: 'Aristotle makes no distinction

commonly regarded as having many points of kinship.[35] History is clearly a descendant of epic in many significant senses,[36] and certain types of history writing were self-consciously spectacular and 'poetic' in their effects.[37] The problem of discriminating between historical and poetic versions of the same events begins to look intractable. We are fortunate in having a discussion surviving from a practitioner.

The opening of Cicero's dialogue *De Legibus* ('Laws') shows the author at his villa in Arpinum, with his brother Quintus and friend Atticus. Prompted by the sight of an oak tree, which might be the very one described in Cicero's poem on his famous compatriot, C. Marius, they hold a brief discussion on epic and history. Atticus asks if the story involving the oak (a tale of a wondrous omen) was Cicero's own invention, or part of some tradition (1. 3).[38] Using standard examples, one Greek, one Roman, Cicero replies with the standard line, that earnest enquiry into traditionally accepted supernatural stories is pointless. Atticus presses him further: *atqui multa quaeruntur in Mario fictane an uera sint, et a nonnullis, quod et in recenti memoria et in Arpinati homine uersere, ueritas a te postulatur* ('But people are asking about many things in the *Marius*, whether they are made up or true; and certain people are demanding the truth from you, since you are dealing with recent events and a man from Arpinum', 1. 4). The ensuing exchange shows the reference of *ueritas* (translated above as 'truth') undergoing an almost insensible shift, as the discussion moves to genre:

*Marcus: Et mehercule ego me cupio non mendacem putari; sed tamen nonnulli isti, Tite noster, faciunt imperite, qui in isto periculo non ut a poeta, sed ut a teste ueritatem exigant; nec dubito quin idem et cum*

between "myth" and history as poetical subjects, but only between the ways in which the poet and historian . . . handle their material'; cf. pp. 44–5 above. We return shortly to the historical events treated by poets of epic, and to the problem of whether poets regarded certain periods as inappropriate for their treatment.

[35] Norden (1898), 1. 91–3, quoting such texts as Quintilian 10. 1. 31, *est enim proxima poetis, et quodam modo carmen solutum est* ('history is very close to the poets, and is a sort of poetry without metre'); Wiseman (1979), 143–53; Woodman (1988), 98–101.

[36] Strasburger (1972), 38–9; Fornara (1983), 31–2; Woodman (1988), 1–4.

[37] Walbank (1960) and (1972), 32–40. We return to this area below.

[38] This dichotomy will be familiar from the discussion concerning Homer as inventor or user of tradition: above, pp. 40–1.

Egeria conlocutum Numam et ab aquila Tarquinio apicem inpositum
putent.
*Quintus*: Intellego te, frater, alias in historia leges obseruandas putare,
alias in poemate.
*Marcus*: Quippe, cum in illa omnia ad ueritatem, Quinte, referantur, in
hoc ad delectationem pleraque; quamquam et apud Herodotum, patrem
historiae, et apud Theopompum sunt innumerabiles fabulae.

*Marcus*: And certainly I have no desire to be thought a liar; but still, my
dear Titus, those 'certain people' of yours act without any critical sense
when, in a case like this, they demand the sort of truth you get from a
witness, not from a poet. I suppose these same people think that Numa
had conversations with Egeria, and that Tarquin had his cap placed on
his head by the eagle.
*Quintus*: I understand then, brother, that you think that one set of laws
are to be observed in history, and another in poetry.
*Marcus*: Absolutely, since in history the yardstick for judging everything
is *ueritas*, while in poetry the yardstick is generally pleasure; in
Herodotus, though, the 'father of history', and in Theopompus, there are
any number of fables.

I have left Cicero's *ueritas* untranslated, since 'truth' is misleading to a modern reader, who will naturally take the word to refer
to the problem of finding out whether or not an event is (in our
sense) 'historical'. On the contrary, as Woodman has clearly
shown, Cicero is referring here to the concepts of verisimilitude
that were taken as normative for history writing: the yardstick for
history is first and foremost 'real life', and the probabilities of real
life, and only secondarily whether something happened or not.[39]
As soon as the type of narrative becomes the issue, the inter-
locutors move automatically into the familiar hierarchy of genres
discussed in the first chapter: the province of history is
probabilistic narrative, whereas epic contains much that is implausible and unnatural. The starting-point—whether or not
Marius actually saw an omen in this actual oak—fades into the
question of what you can narrate in a particular genre.[40]

[39] Woodman (1988), 114–15; cf., rather differently, Lieberg (1985), 23–5, on
this passage, discussing Cicero's conception of poetry's power to create a 'spiritual
reality', which 'is of a higher level than the physical reality of nature, and . . . is
strictly separated from historical reality' (25).
[40] The power of the generic framework of discussion reminds one of the way in
which Sextus Empiricus finds himself pulled towards demarcating between history
and myth in terms of mode even as he tries strenuously to determine a division in
terms of subject-matter (above, p. 44).

Even in discussing a recent poem about a man who had died not forty years earlier, the critical views formulated to discuss Homer are felt to be entirely appropriate. There is a substratum of fact to Cicero's poem, yet he is entirely within his rights (rather, the rights of the genre) when he covers the account with *fabulae* of the sort which would offend the probabilistic and verisimilitudinous needs of history. Exactly the same attitude is to be seen in another discussion between Cicero and his brother, with another of Cicero's poems at issue. In the *De Diuinatione*, Quintus attempts to prove the efficacy of divination by quoting a long passage from his brother's poem *De Consulatu suo*, in which all manner of divine portents concerning the Catilinarian conspiracy are narrated by the Muse, Urania (1. 17–22). In his reply, however, Marcus refuses to be held accountable for what he said in a poem (2. 45–7). With his scornful dismissal of the scientific validity of his own words, he reveals in the most dramatic fashion possible his understanding of the decorum that governs the various genres of which he is master.

In a fundamental sense, then, we are dealing with distinctions of mode and genre—not of subject-matter, nor chronology, nor even, as we would put it, 'historicity' (whether something really happened or not):[41] what counts is the appropriate treatment of the data of received tradition. Historical narrative aims to convince and persuade by keeping to what can be accepted as probable or likely[42]—and here 'probable' and 'likely' must be understood, in the light of the earlier part of our discussion, as one pole of an antithesis, with 'mythic', 'unnatural', and 'fabulous' at the other.[43] In other words, the 'likely' is what is left over when you have dis-

[41] Ligota (1982), 3–13, in an interesting but difficult discussion, attempts to prove that ancient historians had no concept as such of 'historical reality', of the past as 'something out there, existing in its own right' (3); cf. Martin and Woodman (1989), 19, on Tacitus' 'predisposition to see history as text, rather than as whatever reality lies behind the text'.

[42] Woodman (1988), esp. 87. One of the clearest proofs of how 'truth' could be looked on as a literary effect is to be found in the AbT scholion on *Il.* 2. 478–9: 'Historians aim at truth, tragedians at what is more grand than truth, and comedians at what is lesser.' History certainly does not persuade by documentation or minute analysis, as Quintilian acknowledges: *scribitur ad narrandum, non ad probandum* ('history is written with a view to furthering the narration of events, not with a view to proving a case', 10. 1. 31).

[43] The conventional distinctions are economically expressed by Fornara (1983), 10: 'Quite simply, a story was "mythical" if it was "contrary to nature," while a

qualified the 'fabulous', and is therefore a considerably more comprehensive category than we would allow under such a label. Ancient historians narrated many portentous events, though it was regular to signal such sections by remarking on their more mythic content.[44] They could, accordingly, even give two versions of a tradition, first the 'mythical' one, and then the rationalized, 'historical' one, as does Dionysius of Halicarnassus in his account of Heracles' visit to the site of Rome (*Ant. Rom.* 1. 39–40). It is clear that histories now lost to us indulged in pictures of extreme divine spectacle. Polybius, for example, criticizes historians who used the *deus ex machina* to get Hannibal over the Alps (3. 48. 8–9); one assumes that some epiphany of Hercules was described, as the Carthaginian followed in the footsteps of his protector over the roof of the world.[45]

Epic and history, then, could be very close; but, from Herodotus on, the historians were committed to celebrating 'human as opposed to divine . . . occurrences',[46] and therefore refrained from following Homer into the narration of divine action on its own plane. Even epiphanies in historians are, after all, accounts of human experience. An ancient historian will describe a report of a deity appearing in battle, for example, but he will not narrate the decision of the deity to appear, or transcribe the god's conversation before he sets off for the battle-site.[47] The more identity one sees between historical epic and history proper, the more clearly it emerges that the characterful narration of divine action is the irreducible line of demarcation between epic and history—in particular, the more flamboyant species of history. Epic narrative, by the conventional ancient assessment, is perfectly entitled to treat the same events as 'history', yet it does so in its own distinctive

"historical" narrative possessed verisimilitude and concerned actual events and people (including heroes recognized by the literary tradition).' One must bear in mind that practically anything could be (and was) considered an 'actual event'.

[44] Dion. Hal. *Ant. Rom.* 2. 68–9 is a fine example; see the pronouncement of Lucian *Hist. Conscr.* 60, with Avenarius (1956), citing, e.g. Hdt. 2. 173, Dion. Hal. *Ant. Rom.* 1. 48. 1.

[45] DeWitt (1941), 60–1.

[46] Ligota (1982), 2, stressing the exclusive force of Herodotus' declaration in the preface that his subject is 'the things done by human beings'.

[47] Note how Herodotus does not say, for example, that Philippides saw Pan, but that he told the Athenians that he did (6. 105. 1; cf. 6. 117. 3, on the apparition which blinded Epizelos at Marathon). On epiphanies, see further below, pp. 266–7.

fashion: it is not necessarily verisimilitudinous, it has a tangential relationship with 'reality', it achieves its characteristic effects principally through stunning and extraordinary displays of power, to which the gods above all contribute.[48] Epic stripped of all this becomes sub-epic, as the epic cycle becomes in the bald and godless prose of Dictys and Dares.[49]

Such is the background for the conventional critical judgements delivered on Lucan's epic by the ranting poetaster Eumolpus, in Chapter 118 of Petronius' *Satyricon*.[50] It is important to realize that Eumolpus is not denying that history is a proper subject for epic, as many take him to be saying, when he declares *non enim res gestae uersibus comprehendendae sunt, quod longe melius historici faciunt* ('events are not to be packaged up in verses—historians do that much better', 118. 6).[51] If he had thought so, he would not have produced his own version of how to do it. He means that the writing of epic based on history is entirely feasible, but that it is not just a matter of cramming historical events into verse form. His objection is precisely that made by Aristotle, when he declared that the difference between historian and poet was nothing to do with whether or not they wrote in verse, and that the work of Herodotus would be just as much history if it were put into metre (*Poet.* 1451 b 1–4). This, rather, is the way to do it, says Eumolpus:

---

[48] Above, pp. 42–3.

[49] The absence of the gods in these little books is also a factor of the point of view. Dictys' *Ephemeris Belli Troiani* openly purports to be the journal of an eyewitness, while Dares' *De Excidio Troiae Historia* is the report of an eyewitness report. Note, in this connection, the remarkable *Iliad*-hypothesis which omits all mention of the divine action: O'Hara (1984). As O'Hara says, philosophical or religious motives are possible.

[50] The debate about whether or not Lucan is at issue in this passage seems to me to have been settled by the fine dissertation of Connors (1989), to which I refer the reader for a stimulating reassessment of this extremely puzzling piece. As Connors demonstrates, it is vital to see that that the sum effect of the entire episode (criticism plus sample poem) is by no means straightforward in its attitudes to Lucan. For bibliography on the episode, see Connors, 4–22; Häussler (1978), 112–3 nn. 14–17; Soverini (1985), esp. 1754–9. Despite the value of many contributions, before Connors it is only Koster (1970), 139–41, who attempts to put Eumolpus' pronouncements into the context of the critical tradition that formed them, so as to show what preconceptions he brought to his reading of Lucan.

[51] Häussler (1978), 242: 'Von Eumolp war Lucan abgelehnt worden, weil er *res gestae* in Versen, statt *fabulosa* gab'.

sed per ambages deorumque ministeria et fabulosum sententiarum
†tormentum† praecipitandus est liber spiritus, ut potius furentis animi
uaticinatio appareat quam religiosae orationis sub testibus fides.

but the free spirit of the poet must charge headlong through oblique representations, through agencies of the gods and ideas from myth, so that
the result looks more like the oracular utterances of a mind possessed
than sworn testimony under oath before witnesses. (118. 6)[52]

There is nothing terribly novel in the critical attitudes behind
the prescription. The antithesis between the licence of the poet and
the self-control of the historian is traditional, as is the image of the
witnesses.[53] The point is the same as in discussions of Homer, or
of Cicero's *Marius*; the data only become poetry with the application of the transfiguring power of myth (which means, above all,
the divine). This reaction to Lucan becomes canonical in the Latin
critical tradition.[54] Servius congratulates Vergil on an oblique use
of myth to convey an historical fact (*per transitum*),[55] and goes on
to censure Lucan by comparison: *Lucanus namque ideo in numero
poetarum esse non meruit, quia uidetur historiam composuisse,
non poema* ('so Lucan hasn't been thought worthy of being
counted as one of the poets, because he is regarded as having composed a history, not a poem'). A passage which has been plausibly
attributed to Suetonius spells the matter out:

officium autem poetae in eo est ut ea, quae uere gesta sunt, in alias species
obliquis figurationibus cum decore aliquo conuersa transducat.[56] unde et
Lucanus ideo in numero poetarum non ponitur, quia uidetur historias
composuisse, non poema.

The job of the poet is to convert actual events, with indirect and oblique
forms of expression, into something that looks quite different, by trans-
forming them through the right embellishment. For this reason Lucan is

---

[52] I follow the great majority in thinking that *tormentum* must be corrupt; I give
a gesture towards a translation for the sake of continuity. But *fabulosum* looks
absolutely in place, since the whole point of the passage is the difference between
history and fable (i.e. myth or epic).

[53] Licence: Luc. *Hist. Conscr.* 8, with Avenarius (1956), 18. Witnesses: Cic. *Leg.*
1. 4; Ov. *Am.* 3. 12. 19; Lucian, *Iupp. Trag.* 39.

[54] Sanford (1931).

[55] *hoc loco per transitum tangit historiam, quam per legem artis poeticae aperte
non potest ponere* ('here he touches in passing on historical matter, which by the
rules of the art of poetry he cannot openly set down', *Aen.* 1. 382). For similar
comments, cf. 1. 443; 2. 636; 3. 256; 5. 45; 7. 170; 10. 91.

[56] Rather than the transmitted *transducant*: Häussler (1978), 239.

not counted as one of the poets, because he is regarded as having composed a history, not a poem.[57]

These passages illuminate one of the key words of Eumolpus' criticism: *ambages*. The word has been variously interpreted;[58] the expressions used by Servius and Suetonius indicate that the sense is akin to that of *OLD* s.v. §2: 'applied to behaviour which indicates something obliquely' (hence my translation, 'oblique representations').[59] Epic's relationship to reality had been regarded from the beginning of criticism as something tangential, oblique, and the testimony of these critics demonstrates that what they missed in Lucan's poem was epic's distinctive mythic transfiguration. His example no doubt focused the minds of the critics, but they criticized him from the perspective of a long tradition which took for granted the presence of divine elements in historical epic, regarding them as one of the key indispensable components that differentiated history from poetry.

We have left entirely open the question of how adequate such critical responses are to Lucan's practice. So far all that has been established is the basic attitude, the overwhelming weight of the critical consensus, which saw nothing odd in the presence of gods in epic of history, and everything odd in their absence. A brief survey of the lost and fragmentary epics of history will confirm this picture, before we arrive at the poems themselves, and address the question of what Lucan and Silius accomplished.

We must register at the outset the vast bulk of what has been lost.[60] Epics treating the deeds of kings and peoples, contemporary, recent, or remote, were composed all over the Mediterranean, and at every period, from the late fifth century BCE to the age of the Byzantine emperors.[61] No literary form was more durable or more persistent (except, *si parua licet componere magnis*, the

[57] These lines, given by Isidore (*Etym.* 7. 7) and Lactantius (*Inst.* 1. 11. 25), are attributed to Suetonius by Rostagni (1944), 13–14.

[58] 'Oracles', Häussler (1978), 217; 'digressions or side issues', Grube (1965), 266 n. 2; 'episodes', Koster (1970), 139.

[59] Grimal (1977), 28 adduces an apposite parallel for the meaning 'symbole': at Liv. 1. 56. 9, Brutus carries a staff which is *per ambages effigiem ingenii sui*, 'an expression, by oblique representation, of his character'.

[60] Stressed by Ziegler (1966), 16–18.

[61] Wiseman (1979), 146, rather undoes the power of his own arguments when he says that 'Greek epic poets hardly ever dealt with contemporary themes'; in fact, as we shall see, contemporary historical epics were extremely common.

epigram). Of this huge output, the poems of Lucan and Silius alone survive intact—besides them, nothing but fragments and testimonia.[62]

The role of the gods in Greek historical epic is more controversial than in Roman, where the evidence for their presence is, as we shall see, more clear-cut. It is often claimed that there can have been no divine participation in the epic on the Persian Wars composed by the genre's founder, Choerilus of Samos, towards the end of the fifth century, and that, further, Choerilus' example was normative for his followers.[63] Choerilus had a vivid notion of the novelty of his enterprise,[64] yet there is room for doubt over whether his innovations were so radical. We must take account of the fact that divine action in any of these poems might have taken a variety of forms. The full Homeric panoply (councils, divine interventions, interactions between humans and gods) is one possibility. More attenuated forms (gods conversing amongst each other, without directly affecting humans) are imaginable. The picture of the battle of Actium on Vergil's shield in *Aeneid* 8 reveals yet another possibility, where human action is provided with a context of divine action of which the human actors are not necessarily aware. Once one entertains such a range of options, and once one takes stock of Greek painting and sculptural programmes, it becomes virtually inconceivable that epic narratives of history would have presented themselves nude of any divine dimension to their meaning and effect.[65]

The painting of the battle of Marathon in the Stoa Poikile at Athens depicted Athenians, Plataeans, and Persians, to be sure, yet a context for the feat was provided by the appearance of two heroes (Marathon and Theseus) and two gods (Athene and Heracles);[66] this painting was executed some thirty years after the battle, when many of the veterans will have been still alive. The sculptures of the Parthenon itself, and of Athene Nike, show the city's achievement of asserting civilization against barbarism being

---

[62] Until the Byzantine age, beyond the scope of this book.

[63] Ziegler (1966), 24–8, 67; Clinard (1967), 19; Misgeld (1968), 29–30. Ziegler sees the gods' role in historical epic as coming in during the Hellenistic age, while Clinard maintains the ban (with a few exceptions) for the whole of our period.

[64] Huxley (1969b), 12–16.

[65] This is essentially the argument of Häussler (1976), 65–6, building on Koepp (1898).

[66] Paus. 1. 15. 3–4.

given shape and meaning by the interrelated levels of human, heroic, and divine.[67] Did poets refrain? When the Spartan Lysander finished off the Peloponnesian War with his victory at Aegospotami, some said that the special gods of his city, Castor and Polydeuces, appeared as stars beside his ship as he set out for battle (Plut. *Lys.* 12. 1), and Lysander himself dedicated twin stars at Delphi to mark his victory (18. 1). We are told that the inventor of historical epic, Choerilus of Samos, was maintained by Lysander in order to celebrate his deeds (18. 7); if he sang of the battle of Aegospotami, can he possibly have suppressed mention of the divine aid which his patron acknowledged in public dedication?

Choerilus' two areas of work show how closely linked historical epic and panegyric were from the beginning,[68] and in the explosion of panegyrical historical epics on Alexander and the Hellenistic kings, the probability of divine reference becomes quite overwhelming. This was the starting-point for Kroll's seminal article on historical epic, in which he quoted Curtius Rufus' testimony to the fact that epics on Alexander compared him to Heracles, Dionysus, and the Dioscuri, and deduced that such poems must have had a powerful mythical colour.[69] We know of epics on Alexander and on his father, on Antigonus One-Eye, Antiochus I, Eumenes II, and Attalus I.[70] Such monarchs lived in a blaze of divine aura,[71] and epics dealing with them must have engaged with their divine pretensions, and its repercussions. One gets some notion of the atmosphere from a work like Theocritus 17, with its fantasies of Ptolemy's dining with Alexander and Heracles amongst the gods (16–33).[72] Again, the famous epiphanies which saved Delphi from the Celts in 279 BCE were recorded in inscrip-

---

[67] Thomas (1976), esp. 10–12; Stewart (1985); Boardman (1985), 38–46, 247–51.

[68] Feeney (1986*b*), 146–7.

[69] Kroll (1916), 3–4, referring to Curtius 8. 5. 8. This tradition of divine comparison persists into the Roman Empire: see *GLP* p. 544, for fragments of a Greek historical epic in which Diocletian and Galerius are compared to Zeus and Apollo.

[70] Alexander: *SH* 17, 45, 207–9, 333; Philip II: *SH* 913–21; Antigonus: *SH* 491; Antiochus: *SH* 723; Eumenes and Attalus: *SH* 561. Not to mention Marcus Antonius (*SH* 230) and Cleopatra (*SH* 752).

[71] Habicht (1970); Préaux (1978), 1. 258–71; Fishwick (1987), 8–20.

[72] Some lines of Rhianus appear to be a reaction against such forms of praise (fr. 1 Powell). Compare the splendid riposte of Antigonus One-Eye to being described by the poet Hermodotus as 'the son of Helios': 'That's not the way the man who empties my chamber-pot looks at it!' (Plut. *Mor.* 182 c).

tions and histories.[73] Ptolemy II's poet Callimachus touched on this glorious event, and tried to associate it with his king's eradication of some mutinous Celts in Egypt (*Del.* 171–87); it seems to me wholly incredible to suppose that an epic on these crises would have assumed speech no grander than that of a town council.

The strategies of representation used by the Kings of Pergamum provide a good context for speculation.[74] The sculptural monuments for their various victories over the Galatians depend intimately on the Gigantomachic programmes of the Athenian Parthenon, with the Great Altar in particular placing 'the Attalid achievement in a very broad setting—theological, cosmological, legendary, and historical'.[75] Ziegler first suggested that epics on these victories must have shared in the monuments' allegorical thrust.[76] Now, we know that Musaeus wrote epics on the victories of Attalus I and Eumenes II over the Galatians.[77] When we read a Pergamene inscription of that era describing the Galatians as 'acting impiously against the gods and committing crimes against the Greeks',[78] and when we read another Pergamene inscription commemorating an epiphany of Athene in a battle against the Galatians,[79] is it imaginable that the encomiastic poet restrained himself to language more cautious, and eschewed a divine dimension to the conflict?

The way is clearer when we turn to Rome, where, from the beginning, the national epic was historical epic, and contemporary historical epic at that. As we have already seen in Chapter 4, the divine backdrop for Naevius' *Bellum Punicum* is wholly indispensable for the poem's meaning, while Ennius' *Annales* display the gods at work in their planning and intervention at least as far down as the Hannibalic War (which was already the subject of history books, Greek and Latin, in the poet's lifetime).[80] Such facts are in themselves virtual proof of divine participation in Hellen-

---

[73] Pritchett (1976), 30–2; see 11–46, 'Military Ephiphanies', for a highly interesting collection; cf. Pfister (1924), 293–4.

[74] Fascinating and powerful discussion in Hardie (1986), 123–43.

[75] Hardie (1986), 142.

[76] Ziegler (1966), 48, concentrating on the Gigantomachic level exclusively.

[77] *SH* 561.

[78] Cited by Hardie (1986), 129 n. 28.

[79] Pritchett (1976), 36; cf. 36–7, on other, later, inscriptions at Pergamum which refer to epiphanies of Zeus on behalf of the armies of the king.

[80] Above, p.128.

istic historical epic, for contemporary Greek epic is the obvious model for these 'half-Greeks'; it defies all probability that the Roman poets should be the first to transgress a self-denying ordinance of two hundred years' standing.[81]

Cicero has already engaged our attention with his *Marius*. He wrote, besides, two epics on himself, one with the self-explanatory title of *De Consulatu Suo*, the other dealing with his exile and return, entitled *De Temporibus Suis*. In the first, if we are to believe Ps. Sall. *Cic.* 2. 3, Cicero displayed himself being admitted to the council of the gods and being taught by Minerva how to fend off the danger to Rome, while in the second there appears to have been another council, this time not graced with the statesman's presence.[82] However much one may admire Cicero, it remains fair to observe that he is more likely to have been following than resisting the norm in making the gods participants in these stirring events.

The megalomaniacal zeal of the Roman dynasts, pursuing divine associations by any means possible,[83] makes the presence of a divine lustre in poems celebrating their deeds all the more plausible an assumption. Yet nothing is recoverable. We are quite in the dark as to whether the gods figured in Varro Atacinus' *Bellum Sequanicum*, on Caesar's Gallic campaign of 58 BCE, or in Furius' *Annales Belli Gallici*, or Cornelius Severus' *Bellum Siculum*, or Rabirius' poem on the war between Octavian and Antony, or Albinovanus Pedo's poem, from which we have twenty-three lines on Germanicus' sea-voyage in 16 CE.[84] We have clipped and enigmatic fragments, recovered from Herculaneum, of an epic on the war between Octavian and Antony and Cleopatra.[85] A fragment describes Atropos, one of the three Parcae, laughing at Cleopatra as she looks at her from a distance, in hiding (*procul hanc occulta uidebat / Atropos inridens*, col. VII. 3–4). This looks like more

---

[81] Wülfing-von Martitz (1972), 282–3; Häussler (1976), 69.

[82] See Häussler (1976), 281; note also the lengthy account of the omens presaging Catilina's conspiracy given by the Muse Urania at *Div.* 1. 17–22. Urania is addressing Cicero here.

[83] Weinstock (1971); Zanker (1988), 33–65; Fishwick (1987), 46–82.

[84] On these works, see Schanz–Hosius 1. 312 (Varro); 1. 163 (Furius; note the interesting speculation of DuQuesnay (1984), 54–5, who suggests that this work was a parodying lampoon); 2. 268–9 (Cornelius Severus); 2. 267 (Rabirius); 2. 266 (Albinovanus Pedo).

[85] The so-called *Bellum Actiacum*: Benario (1983); Zecchini (1987)—highly speculative, but interesting. Even the scope of the poem is problematic (Zecchini, 31): did it even describe Actium before moving to Egypt?

than a *façon de parler*, but one cannot be sure, and a larger divine context is beyond us.

The obscurity is even denser in the Neronian and Flavian periods. We know nothing of the type or nature of the epics of Saleius Bassus, for example, or Serranus, mentioned by Quintilian (10. 1. 90), or Statius' eminent friend Manilius Vopsicus (*Silv.* 1. 3. 102), or Carus, victor at the Alban contest (Mart. 9. 23, 24). But we do know of two epics written on the fighting on the Capitol in 69 CE, one by the emperor Domitian himself,[86] one by the father of Statius. In the lament which the son wrote for the father, there are clear signs of the mythic content which must have formed part of the poem (*Silv.* 5. 3. 195–204). If the schoolmaster wrote in these terms, the son of the princeps may well have done likewise. In a later period, one thinks of how Trajan associates the gods with his mission on the arch at Beneventum, or on the column, where Jupiter guarantees Roman victory with his thunderbolt.[87] Poetry on such topics will naturally have moved in the same areas.

With such great gaps in our knowledge, there is no room for dogmatism. But what we know of the tradition inclines us to regard as most likely the hypothesis that divine participation in Roman historical epic (in whatever guise) was the norm rather than the exception. John Bramble has recently made a spirited and interesting claim for Severus and Pedo as precursors of Lucan.[88] As he himself acknowledges, one's reaction will in the end largely depend on how much weight one gives to the ancient critics' impression of Lucan's incomprehensible originality. While not feeling able to rule out his approach, then, we may leave this section with the observation that the ancient debate about Lucan appears to make more sense if he was swimming against, rather than with, the tide.

II

'Is there any point to which you would wish to draw my attention?'
'To the curious incident of the dog in the night-time.'

---

[86] Bardon (1940), 282–3.
[87] Scene no. XXIV, Cichorius (1896–1900).
[88] *CHCL* 2. 485–91.

'The dog did nothing in the night-time.'
'That was the curious incident,' remarked Sherlock Holmes.

A. Conan Doyle, *Silver Blaze*

The gods do not act in Lucan's poem, for he abandoned the divine machinery, jettisoned the 'Götterapparat'. Such descriptions of the poem's treatment are virtually unanimous, though not the ensuing judgements, nor the explanations.[89] Before attempting to judge or explain, we may pause to establish what exactly is absent, or present. A number of protests have in fact been made against the consensus at its bluntest, noting that this supposedly godless poem is actually obsessed with the gods, crammed with references to their plans and deeds, with prophetic scenes, with the poet's addresses to the ones above.[90] As has been noted many times,[91] it is specifically the mimesis of divine characters in action which is missing, thus amputating one half of the pair desiderated by tradition and the critics (epic is made up, as Servius puts it, of 'divine and human *characters*', *ex diuinis humanisque personis*[92]). Petronius' creature Eumolpus highlights Lucan's departure, for his offering displays precisely the representation of divinity in speech and action which is missing from Lucan.[93]

Yet some qualification of this sure finding is necessary. At times, particularly in the first book, before his norms have had space to delineate themselves, Lucan flirts with the possibility that supernatural characters will play a role in the narrative. When the Homeland (*Patria*) appears before the invading army of Caesar at the Rubicon (1. 185–90), the apparition is described in language which is equally appropriate for a dream or for an actual waking vision: either ὄναρ or ὕπαρ, as the Greek distinction had it.[94] The

---

[89] For bibliography on the divine in Lucan, see, most conveniently, Haüssler (1978), 96–7; also the bibliographies of Rutz (1964), 271–83, 292–4; (1965), 249; (1984), 186–91; (1985b).

[90] Thierfelder (1934), 4–5; Schönberger (1958), 235–8; Jal (1962), 179–80; Johnson (1987), 4–11.

[91] Rutz (1984), 187.

[92] *Aen.* Pr. 1. 4 Thilo–Hagen.

[93] Though his technique, as Connors (1989), 92 shows, is very interestingly complicated by the fact that one of these divine characters is Fortuna, an abstract deity who is here made a character for the first time; an entity, moreover, whom Lucan mentions again and again in *Bellum Ciuile*, without ever actualizing.

[94] Pfister (1924), 281–2; Lane Fox (1986), 150–67. Compare the closely similar

apparition, on either interpretation, is just within the bounds of what one might find in a history book; indeed, it appears that Lucan did find it in a history book.[95]

The extraordinary series of portents that introduces the climax of the first book has roots in traditions of both history and poetry.[96] It has been noted that many of the prodigies used by Lucan to mark Caesar's aggression are taken from the prodigies that marked his assassination;[97] his attack on Rome, not his murder, is now viewed as the great outrage that disturbs Nature, and it will lead inevitably to his death—and apotheosis. As Lucan's catalogue progresses, his portents become increasingly actualized, and supernatural. With an artfully postponed *accipimus* ('our sources tell us', 1. 559), he carefully gives authority for the more standard manifestations, such as might be found in the historians (weeping and sweating statues, ill-omened birds, and so forth, 556-60), while the more bizarre and poetical prodigies are not given as a report, but described as events.[98] When savage Vulcan is said to loosen the jaws of Aetna (545-7), most readers will take this as *façon de parler* and carry on; Charybdis in the next line is harder, and the mournful barking of the savage dogs of Scylla is a genuine shock (*flebile saeui / latrauere canes*, 548-9).[99] The climax comes with the perambulation of the city by a text-book tragic or epic Fury, who is signalled as such, for the benefit of the sluggish

language at 3. 9-12, when Julia appears to Pompey while he is asleep; our initial assurance that the experience was a dream (Rutz (1963), 340) is disturbed by the sequel, when Julia's shade slips away from his embrace, acting like a true shade, not a dream-figure (3. 34-5). (Very similar difficulties over, e.g. Anchises' appearance in *Aen.* 5. 722-42: Steiner (1952), 57). For the crossing of the Rubicon, the tradition appears to have split, with the more sober relating a dream of Caesar's (Plut. *Caes.* 32. 6), the more indulgent an apparition that manifested itself in daylight (Suet. *Iul.* 32, a transformation from the world of pastoral to the world of war).

[95] That is, if Narducci (1980) is right to see as the source here a story about the elder Germanicus which later recurs in Dio Cassius (55. 1. 3-5, where Dio animadverts on the extraordinary nature of the story, but confesses that he must believe it).

[96] Verg. *G.* 1. 464-88; Cic. *Div.* 1. 17-22 = *poet.* fr. 6 Büchner (Narducci (1980) ); Ov. *Met.* 15. 783-98; Dio 41. 14.

[97] Connors (1989), 100.

[98] For the historians' reports, see the diverting and still useful collection of Krauss (1930).

[99] Typically, Scylla is not named, and one might think of the more mundane howling dogs listed in Obsequens' prodigies after the death of Caesar (68); yet editors and commentators have good grounds for feeling impelled towards Scylla by the vicinity of Charybdis.

reader, by explicit similes which spell out the literary prototypes:

> ingens urbem cingebat Erinys
> excutiens pronam flagranti uertice pinum
> stridentisque comas, Thebanam qualis Agauen
> inpulit aut saeui contorsit tela Lycurgi
> Eumenis, aut qualem iussu Iunonis iniquae
> horruit Alcides uiso iam Dite Megaeram.

A vast Fury was ringing the city, shaking a pine torch with blazing top, holding it turned down—shaking out her hissing hair too; like the Fury that attacked Theban Agave, or shot off the weapons of savage Lycurgus; or like Megaera, at whom Hercules shuddered in fear by order of unjust Juno, although he had already seen the God of Death. (1. 572–7)

Next follow ghosts, of Sulla and his victims (580–1), and, at the cap, dead Marius himself, rising from his shattered tomb (582–3). Lucan then shifts abruptly into the curt style of historical discourse at its most terse, highlighting by juxtaposition the twin extremes at his command: *haec propter placuit Tuscos de more uetusto / acciri uates* ('on account of these things it was decided that, according to ancient custom, Etruscan seers should be summoned', 584–5).[100]

In this atmosphere the words that Lucan gives to Caesar early on in the poem look like more than simply a good joke, and hint at a possibility that is more nearly realized than readers usually allow: *nec numina derunt*, says Caesar to his troops, 'nor will the gods be missing' (1. 349). Still, these passages are as close as Lucan comes to the depiction of supernatural characters. With the exception of the Fury and (possibly) Patria, no supernatural beings (and certainly no Olympians) are, so to speak, on stage, figured as actors in word or deed.[101] In retrospect (and even at first reading, to one expecting the traditional), the very opening of the poem, with its silence on divine causes, is a clear early sign of the poem's new emphases.[102] Unlike the poems of Homer, Vergil, even

---

[100] Vergil is the immediate model for such language in epic (*Aen.* 3. 58–9 is the best example); Ennius must have led the way. It is interesting to note that Lucan goes directly against the historical tradition at this point; according to Dio, no expiation was performed in response to the prodigies of 50–49, since each side hoped and thought that the prodigies were directed at their opponents (41. 14. 2–6).

[101] I give here other main passages where gods (singular or plural) are spoken of as acting: 1. 677; 3. 36; 5. 165–74, 625–6, 814; 6.3, 443–4, 464–5; 10. 336–7.

[102] Piacentini (1963), 22–3; Conte (1966).

Apollonius, this epic has nothing to say about the wishes or designs of any deity in its proem.[103] The divine causes are shifted, under a novel guise, to the end of the first book and beginning of the second. At this point, as we have just seen, the gods' anger is revealed, and it appears that divine anger, in good epic tradition, will be a prime causal force in the poem. Yet, crucially, there is no explanation or description of the divine anger, only a picture of its manifestations, and of attempts by characters and poet to understand those manifestations. Hence the finely judged anti-climax that opens the second book: *iamque irae patuere deum* ('And now the anger of the gods was obvious to see', 2. 1). 'Obvious' is the last thing the anger of the gods is here.[104]

Statements on the absence of the gods from the poem need, then, to be cautious, and exact; the secondary literature can sometimes give the impression that we are dealing with a rationalist text. Once again we observe the tendency to praise Lucan for the virtues of an historian, in the frequent assumption that he has written in the way he has in order to make his poem look like a history book. Granted that Lucan does, as we have just seen, manufacture historical atmosphere at will for various purposes; granted that much of Lucan's historical tradition was sensational in the extreme; granted that Lucan's statements about the gods are often no more than a Roman historian could have said;[105] we must nevertheless resist the notion that Lucan's poem consistently hits the tone and voice of history: his outrageous procedures and spectacular poetics place him in a totally different dimension from even the most colourful historian.[106] If he wanted his poem to occupy a prudential and plausible register, he needed to do a good deal more than remove the gods as characters. The metempsychosis

---

[103] Johnson (1987), 9.

[104] The point is reinforced by the adjective used to describe the portents in the first line: *manifesta*.

[105] For Lucan's distinctively prosaic feel, see Bramble (1982), 539–42; for his exploitation of the historical tradition, Syndikus (1958), 1–16; Lintott (1971); Burck and Rutz (1979), 171–6. On the sensational nature of much of Lucan's historical tradition, Lintott (1971), 489; Marti (1964). For historians using similar language to Lucan in, e.g. his denunciation of the gods' vindictiveness (2. 1–4, etc.), see Tac. *Hist.* 1. 3. 2; *Ann.* 4. 1. 2, 16. 16. 2; further, Jal (1962).

[106] Nothing written on Lucan conveys the extraordinary audacity of his techniques and achievement as powerfully as the electrifying study of Henderson (1988)—a paper which indeed deserves the overworked epithet of 'brilliant'.

of Pompey at the beginning of Book 9 and the necromancy of Erictho in Book 6 enter realms of fantasy barred to the most 'tragic' historian. So far from being written like a history book, Lucan's work is written in direct antithesis to a history book—namely, Caesar's own *Commentarii de Bello Ciuili.*[107]

If the gods' absence is not to be ascribed to the historical nature of the poem, it is sometimes claimed that Lucan dispensed with the gods as characters because belief in their participation was not (or, was no longer) sustainable.[108] Such language of 'belief' has been put in jeopardy by the progression of our study. In earlier chapters we saw how inadequate the concept of belief proved to be in the context of the operations performed by Ennius' and Vergil's readers. Lucan's strategies are often (usually implicitly) set against a supposed earlier time when there was no difficulty in representing the gods; yet the question of the sort of belief demanded by poetry had always been intensely problematical. Besides, belief in the gods is something that much of the poem takes for granted, in the sense that the poet commonly addresses the gods, and affects to attribute to them motives and will. The only thing that the poet will not do is figure them as characters in his narrative. We will see that the issue of belief in the gods is something of tremendous importance in the poem, yet not simply in these terms of what poet and audience were prepared to tolerate in epic poetry.

From the outset, the gods in our study have been inextricably involved with the dilemmas of fiction, and of the poet's authority and voice. Let us see if an enquiry into these aspects of Lucan's poem will shed any light on the manifold problems of the divine with which it engages.

It was remarked above that Lucan breaks radically with epic tradition in recounting no divine, but only natural, *causae* for the

---

[107] Henderson (1988), 132–3. In stressing Lucan's spectacular and hyperbolic procedures, I do not wish to deny the poem's basic fidelity to what we can reconstruct of Lucan's historical tradition, a fidelity established by Grimal (1970); cf. Ahl (1976), 70–1. Grimal has some highly judicious comments on the discrepancy between the impact made by the poem as one reads it, and the scrupulosity revealed by analysis (115). Besides, when Lucan does depart from the historical record (taking Cicero to Pharsalia, Cato to Siwa, and Caesar to Troy), we are not dealing with *blunders*: cf. Marti (1964), 190–8.

[108] Tremoli (1968), 6–7; Le Bonniec (1970), 166; Ahl (1976), 69–70; Burck and Rutz (1979), 187.

war. His proem is immediately startling for the comprehensiveness of its disavowal of inspiration, and hence of superhuman knowledge and insight.[109] There is no Muse in the first lines (not even, as in Apollonius, by way of afterthought), and Lucan explicitly forswears divine inspiration at the end of the proem: no Bacchus or Apollo will be troubled by this poet (1. 63–5).[110] The omission is thrust dramatically before us in the eighth line: *quis furor, o ciues, quae tanta licentia ferri?* ('What madness is / was this, o citizens, this vast indulgence in violence?').[111] In the eighth line of the *Iliad* and *Aeneid* the poet questions the Muse about the starting-point of the poem's action.[112] Here the outward energy of epic is redirected back inwards, to the citizens who are the subject (and the audience) of the poem. What answer can the question expect if it is addressed to those who are responsible for its being asked? The closing scene of the book offers a counterpoint, to remind us of what the poet's tradition dictated he should do (1. 674–7). There we meet a divinely-inspired poet-figure, a matron who is possessed by Apollo and compared to someone possessed by Bacchus—the very deities, in other words, whom Lucan had forsworn at the beginning of the book. The matron speaks in language that recalls Lucan's own, yet she addresses, as is 'proper', the god: *quis furor hic, o Phoebe, doce* ('what madness this is, o Apollo, teach me . . .', 681).

Lucan's inspiration for his poem of despotism's triumph is not Apollo, Bacchus, or the Muse, but another figure, virtually divine—Nero:

> sed mihi iam numen; nec, si te pectore uates
> accipio, Cirrhaea uelim secreta mouentem
> sollicitare deum Bacchumque auertere Nysa;
> tu satis ad uires Romana in carmina dandas.

But to me you are already a god, an inspiration. If I as bard receive you in my chest, I would not wish to trouble the god who brings to light the

---

[109] Conte (1966); in general on these issues, Henderson (1988), 135–6; O'Higgins (1988), an excellent paper. An extremely valuable discussion of Lucan's poetic stance is to be found in the dissertation of Masters (1989), which will shortly be published.

[110] The association of Apollo with the Muses and inspiration goes back to Hesiod (*Th.* 94) and the *Homeric Hymns* (25); for Bacchus in this connection, see Nisbet and Hubbard (1978), 316–17.

[111] On this point, see Conte (1966), 45–6.

[112] In the *Aeneid*, we get an indirect question at first, until the direct question at line 11.

hidden truths of Delphi, or to make Bacchus move away from Nysa; you are enough to give strength for the composition of poetry by a Roman about Rome. (1. 63–6)

Griffin remarks on these lines that 'Lucan hails Nero as a suitable divinity to inspire a Roman poem';[113] just how suitable will emerge in our discussion. The discordant spurning of divine inspiration and epic insight, together with the selection of Nero as substitute, combine to create an epic voice without precedent.

Lucan must speak as he does, and not as his character of the matron speaks, because his knowledge is not that of the Roman epic poet. He is doing the opposite of what an epic poet must do; *his* Roman poetry (what *Romana carmina* have now become) involves narrating the destruction of a universe, not its creation.[114] Since Naevius, the Roman epic task had been the narration of *Fata*, the divine plan of the gods for the Roman mission; Lucan, however, must sing of *nefas*, the unspeakable. This is what he announces in his first sentence, proclaiming as his subject 'the struggle to produce unspeakable wrong on all sides, implicating everybody' (*certatum . . . in commune nefas*, 1. 5–6). At the beginning of the second book, convulsed nature 'declares the unspeakable' (*indixitque nefas*, 2. 4), a play on the language of declaring war,[115] where *nefas* stands precisely for *bellum*, and has become the impossible subject of the poem: how can you 'declare' something which is —the pun is even more obvious in Latin—'unspeakable'?[116] The climax to this movement comes at the height of the battle of Pharsalia, the irrevocable centre of gravity of the epic:

> hanc fuge, mens, partem belli tenebrisque relinque,

[113] Griffin (1984), 153. We shall return to the notorious problem of the address to Nero; for the moment, a reference to Johnson's superb hits on Nero as Lucan's Muse: Johnson (1987), 118, 121–3.

[114] Hardie (1986), 381: 'whereas the *Aeneid* is a poem about the creation of a universe, the *Bellum ciuile* is about the destruction of a universe'; von Albrecht (1970), 286, 299–300; Henderson (1988), 142–3. Lucan's poem is very precisely the destruction of Vergil's universe: Narducci (1979).

[115] For *indicere bellum* as the set phrase for 'declaring war', see TLL 2. 1837. 50–62; for the links between *fari* and *fas/nefas*, see above, p. 140. Cf. Thomas (1988), on Verg. G. 1. 478–9, remarking on the 'artful juxtaposition of the virtual opposites, *locutae / (infandum!)*, "they spoke (unspeakable!)"'.

[116] Cf. 1. 21 (*belli nefandi*), 325 (*bella nefanda*); O'Higgins (1988), 217; Masters (1989), 143–50. Masters (1989), 130, has an excellent discussion of another of the poet-figures at the end of Book I, the seer Arruns, who responds to the *nefas* he sees in extispicy (626) by declaring that it is not *fas* for him to speak (631–2); he ends by doing the logical thing, and saying (in effect) nothing.

nullaque tantorum discat me uate malorum,
quam multum bellis liceat ciuilibus, aetas.
a potius pereant lacrimae pereantque querellae:
quidquid in hac acie gessisti, Roma, tacebo.

Flee this part of the war, my mind, and leave it to darkness; may no age learn how much indulgence is allowed to civil wars from listening to my account of such great evils. Rather let these tears be wasted, these complaints be wasted; whatever you performed in this battle-line, Rome, I shall be silent about. (7. 552–6)

Faced with civil war, not foreign wars rich in triumphs, he abnegates his epic task.[117] Only the bards of the barbarians can discharge the epic role any more (1. 447–9, a wicked parody of Vergilian language).[118] Instead of perpetuating and commemorating glory as do Homer and Vergil,[119] he tries, at the moment of climax, to consign his subject to darkness by being silent; in apostrophizing his own mind, he highlights his un-epic divorce from the Muses, who aid the poet in preservation.[120] The celebration of Pompey's obscure burial is the inverse of this stance (8. 815–22). The victor whom he must acclaim, the victor whose name will live for ever, is evil and unworthy of eternity,[121] and Lucan cannot escape being implicated, because he has chosen to sing this tale, to speak what should not be spoken. Therefore he resists, by delaying and delaying, and by 'refusing to narrate' when delay becomes finally impossible.[122] Hence the refusal to give us, for example, the spear-throw which begins the battle of Pharsalia, or the actual moment of Pompey's death.[123]

The poem can barely be told, then, against the will of the reluctant singer, whose unspeakable subject cuts him off from the resources

[117] Narducci (1979), 33, on how Lucan is 'praticamente defraudato della sua materia'; cf. O'Higgins (1988), 215–16; Masters (1989), 106.

[118] By making the barbarian bards into epic eulogists, Lucan appears to be 'correcting' Caesar, who had described the Druids as composers of learned, scientific, cosmological poetry (*B Gall.* 6. 14. 6).

[119] On Homer, Nagy (1979); Thalmann (1984), 131–3, 153; Lynn-George (1988), 153–229; key passages in Vergil are *Aen.* 9. 446–9 and 10. 793, *tua . . . optima facta . . . / non equidem nec te, iuuenis memorande, silebo.*

[120] Narducci (1979), 78.

[121] Zwierlein (1982), 98–9, and (1986), on the tremendous section, 9. 980–6.

[122] Grimal (1980); Bramble (1982), 540; Henderson (1988), 133–4, 136: 'Lucan hates, spurns, defers, resists his projected narrative' (134).

[123] On the spear-throw, Bramble (1982), 539–40; on Pompey's death, Mayer (1981), 162.

of the more fortunate celebrators of fated achievement. This poet is all too often helpless, as powerless to ward off the future as are the very institutions of the doomed Republic (1. 592–604). His attempts to influence the events of history are futile; the war will run its course however he may try to stop it, whether he prays for cataclysm (4. 110–20), for concord (4. 189–92), or for discord (5. 297–9).[124] Further, from the very beginning of the poem, as we have seen, this poet insists, obliquely or directly, on his ignorance, on his ' "failure" of vatic powers'.[125] The omniscient, divinely-guaranteed perspective of the archetypal epic poet has disappeared with Lucan's commitment to Nero as the appropriate inspiration for this work. He does not know whether a dark dawn is caused by the gods' will or by the springing up of the South wind (1. 234–5). He cannot tell why Libya is so rich in snakes: *non cura laborque / noster scire ualet* ('my care and hard work are not powerful enough to know', 9. 621–2). He forswears knowledge of the operation of the tides:

> quaerite, quos agitat mundi labor; at mihi semper
> tu, quaecumque moues tam crebros causa meatus,
> ut superi uoluere, late.

Enquire away, you who are engaged by the hard study of the universe. But you, whatever cause you are who effect these constant movements, remain hidden from me, as the gods have wished. (1. 417–19)

Above all, the operation of the divine remains consistently beyond the knowledge of the poet—as is inevitable, given the nature of the conventions, once he is severed from the Muses, from Apollo, and Bacchus. The gods' failure to participate as characters must be approached from here, within the context of Lucan's shocking disavowal of the poet's 'patrimony of knowledge'.[126] He cannot represent the gods in action because he is radically uncertain on everything to do with their motives and meaning. The destruction of the Republic is a catastrophe of cosmic proportions,[127] and the poem embodies Lucan's enraged bafflement at the defeat

---

[124] Marti (1975), 86.

[125] Henderson (1988), 124. It need scarcely be said that Lucan's stress, and mine, on his stance of ignorance should not be mistaken for a claim that he is unlearned. Any doubt on that score will be dispelled by a reading of Lausberg (1985).

[126] Henderson (1988), 136.

[127] On this topic see Lapidge (1979); the programmatic first simile (1. 72–80) establishes the correspondence between cosmic and political dissolution.

of the party with all right on its side; how could the gods possibly have willed such a result?[128] This rage at times carries the poet into denouncing the gods for their complicity in the victory of evil: *uictrix causa deis placuit, sed uicta Catoni* ('the gods backed the side that won, Cato the side that lost', 1. 128).[129]

More striking than this stance, however, is the spring of anxiety which uncoils from the apprehension that a worse alternative exists than divine malevolence: it may be that there is no plan behind this disaster, merely randomness. One of Lucan's poet-figures at the end of Book 1, Nigidius Figulus, is the first to voice this possibility, and to articulate the opposition between the extremes of planned Fate or chaos:

> 'aut hic errat' ait 'nulla cum lege per aeuum
> mundus et incerto discurrunt sidera motu,
> aut, si fata mouent, urbi generique paratur
> humano matura lues . . .'

'Either,' he said, 'this universe wanders through time without any governing law, and the stars go in different directions with random motion, or else, if the fates do control these movements, then imminent destruction is in store for the city and for the human race . . .' (1. 642–5)

Shortly afterwards, at the opening of the second book, Lucan himself voices the same hesitation between these two alternatives, in an address to Jupiter:

> siue parens rerum, cum primum informia regna
> materiamque rudem flamma cedente recepit,
> fixit in aeternum causas, qua cuncta coercet
> se quoque lege tenens, et saecula iussa ferentem
> fatorum immoto diuisit limite mundum,
> siue nihil positum est, sed fors incerta uagatur
> fertque refertque uices et habet mortalia casus,
> sit subitum quodcumque paras.

[128] Jal (1962); Le Bonniec (1970), 168–9, 179–80; Liebeschuetz (1979), 147–8. Pompey, deluded as normal, expects that the gods will favour the better side: *causa iubet melior superos sperare secundos*, 7. 349.

[129] There are many other such passages imputing malevolence to the gods: 1. 522–5; 4. 807–9; 7. 647; 8. 597, 800: Syndikus (1958), 93. For characters expressing similar views, cf. 2. 44; 7. 58–9, 85–6, 725; 9. 143–4. This is an attitude widely spread through Roman literature on civil war: Jal (1962). The best-known expression of this attitude outside Lucan is Tacitus' aphorism at the beginning of the *Histories*: . . . *non esse curae deis securitatem nostram, esse ultionem* ('the gods were not concerned to conserve us, but to punish us', 1. 3. 2).

Whether the father of all, when he first took over his shapeless domain
with its raw matter after the departure of the fire, then established causes
for ever, and divided up the universe, along with its apportioned eras,
according to immovable boundary-lines of the fates; or whether nothing
is fixed, but chance wanders uncertainly, turning the circle again and
again, and accident rules human affairs: may whatever you have in store
be sudden. (2. 7–14)[130]

This uncertainty persists through the poem, a confrontation between the Stoic dispensation and a non-teleological randomness
which it does no harm to associate with the Epicureans. One aspect of the dilemma dominates the poem's scenes of prophecy,
which we discuss further on. A token of the pervasiveness of the
uncertainty is the way in which Lucan uses language of destiny
and randomness more or less interchangeably: *fatum/fata, fortuna/
fors, dei/superi* are explanatory terms which jostle beside
each other in every imaginable context.[131] Much, perhaps too
much, has been written about these terms in Lucan;[132] here we
may note only that a term from either category is virtually never
mentioned without a term from the other in very close proximity,
as if to destabilize any assurance for reader or author.[133]

The ignorant narrator, then, whose belligerently fallible voice
has been so elaborately established, is necessarily a victim of the
ignorance and uncertainty which plagues his characters when they
try to penetrate the divine dimension to the meaning of events, to
understand whether the catastrophe of the poem is the will of the
gods or simply haphazard accident. Lucan's exploitation of the
uncertain narrator's voice can look rather like an extreme de-

---

[130] Johnson (1987), 5–8, acutely discusses this passage, and its implications.

[131] That is, 'fate' or 'fates', 'fortune' or 'chance', 'the gods' or 'the gods above'.

[132] Friedrich (1938) is still basic; see Rutz (1984), 187–90, for bibliography of
recent discussions.

[133] 1. 226–7 (though here one should accept Housman's emendation *satis his*,
which removes *fatis*), 264, 309–10, 393–4; 2. 68–72, 91–3, 240, 699–701, 726–8,
732–5; 3. 21–2, 392–4, 510–17, 752–3; 4. 255–6, 342–4, 496–7, 661–2, 737–8; 5.
41–2, 57–9, 239–40, 301–2, 325–7, 352–4, 482, 581–2, 695–7, 730; 6. 7, 590–2,
611–15; 7. 88–9, 205–6, 504–5, 646–7; 8. 21–3, 31–2, 206–7, 486, 701; 9. 212–
13, 550–2, 1046; 10. 23–4, 339–41, 384–5, 485. A Stoic such as Seneca could
explicitly use nature, fate, and fortune as synonomous names of god in his various
operations (*Ben.* 4. 8. 3), but that does not mean that Lucan is following him, as
first claimed by Pichon (1912), 175; fate and fortune are natural opposites (cf. Tac.
*Hist.* 4. 26. 2: *quod in pace fors seu natura, tunc fatum et ira dei uocabatur*); and
Lucan's theological remarks do everything they can to keep the opposition to the
fore.

velopment of Apollonius' position. I do not claim that Lucan is following Apollonius as such (though I am not concerned to deny it); rather, this is a possibility inherent in the form, which Lucan, of all our poets, most systematically develops. A first conclusion on the absence of the gods as characters naturally follows. A narrated divine presence, with the gods represented in speech and act, would necessarily have involved the poet committing himself on this point at least. As it is, the poet enmeshes himself in the same difficulties as his characters and audience, deliberately refusing to stand outside his creation to provide a focus; this is, as it were, the strong side of his often denounced declamatory pose.[134] A divine apparatus is capable of sustaining many ambiguities, but not this fundamental inability to decide whether the action of the poem is design or happenstance. By being absent, the gods are robbed of any opportunity to follow their epic predecessors in sanctioning or validating the outcome of the poem; if they did plan the end of liberty, they will at least not have the chance to impose their own meaning and value upon the conclusion.[135]

At the climactic battle of Pharsalia, a hundred lines before Lucan abnegates his task of narration, he appears to achieve a definitive insight. After spending some sixty lines itemizing the catastrophic repercussions of the imminent battle, he breaks off in mid-line with a devastating pronouncement, which tips the scale towards accepting the alternative of chaos:

> sunt nobis nulla profecto
> numina: cum caeco rapiantur saecula casu,
> mentimur regnare Iouem. spectabit ab alto
> aethere Thessalicas, teneat cum fulmina, caedes?
> . . . mortalia nulli
> sunt curata deo.

There are indeed no governing deities for us Romans;[136] while the ages are whirled along by blind chance, we lie in saying that Jupiter rules. Will Jupiter look on at the slaughter in Thessaly and hold back his thunderbolts? . . . The affairs of men are of no concern to any god. (7. 445–55)

[134] Marti (1975).

[135] Ahl (1976), 68.

[136] Following the interpretation of Haskins (1887), ad loc., for *nobis*. Lucan has just been comparing the Romans' lot to that of eastern peoples, who have never known slavery, and he appears to use that observation as a springboard into his outburst against the chief Roman divinity.

The concern of Jupiter Optimus Maximus for the Roman state, the bedrock of Roman epic and Roman public life, is here exploded,[137] as the poet abandons design and embraces a position that is scarcely to be distinguished from the teachings of Epicurus: the gods exist, but have no care for human affairs, and events in the world are therefore random chance.[138]

It is extremely tempting to take these lines as Lucan's final word on the matter.[139] There is indeed a sense in which a current of energy in the poem runs to this climactic point;[140] yet some key passages subsequent to Lucan's outburst are at odds with its apparent finality of judgement. Only 150 lines later, as Brutus rushes towards Caesar in the battle-line, Lucan tells him not to anticipate Philippi, which is fated (*nec tibi fatales admoueris ante Philippos*, 7. 591). More elaborately, as Pompey goes to his death, Lucan comments on how he is being dragged to the shore by the laws of fate, and by the close proximity of death directed by the command of the eternal order (*quod nisi fatorum leges intentaque iussu / ordinis aeterni miserae uicinia mortis / damnatum leto traherent ad litora Magnum*, 8. 568–70). Nothing fortuitous about Pompey's death, it appears.

This fractured voice, unsystematic and at odds with itself, is what one must expect in an epic told by one who forswears true knowledge and insight, committed to the untellable and unknowable; this is indeed a demented form of uncertainty, in which the poet as often proclaims his fixed and sure resentment as his lack of understanding. His strategies here achieve diverse ends which it is more profitable to see as overlapping than as self-contradictory.[141] If a recurrent and prominent possibility in the

[137] With the help of a demolition of Horace's confidence in the reign of Jupiter, *caelo tonantem credidimus Iouem / regnare*, *Carm.* 3. 5. 1–2: Zetzel (1980).

[138] It has been claimed that Lucan at first denies the existence of god outright: Due (1962), 101–2, (1970), 213–14. This seems to me mistaken, as my translation attempts to show. Both of Due's above-mentioned discussions, however, are extremely valuable and challenging.

[139] Due (cited in previous note); Ahl (1976), 280–1; Liebeschuetz (1979), 148–9.

[140] Narducci (1979), 68–9, on a process of disillusionment in the poem.

[141] Many scholars take it for granted that Lucan is confused and undecided on these matters: Dilke (1960), 40–1; Le Bonniec (1970), 178; even (though rather differently) Johnson (1987), 3, 123 n. 19. Lucan's carefully created narrative voice has, it appears, been all too successful. His extreme youth is often the explicit justification for his supposed inability to know what he was doing from one month to the next: Dilke (1972), 62 ('we are dealing with a young man...'). Syndikus (1958) establishes beyond doubt the assured and intricate cohesion of this masterpiece, without pressing spurious 'unities' upon it.

poem is a despairing anarchism, the poet still cannot abandon altogether the compulsion to blame the guilty gods, nor can he deprive himself of the claustrophobic sense of trapped inevitability which is provided by the language of Fate. The complex of views in Lucan is very reminiscent of the variety of views in Tacitus (as is the scholarly discussion of the issues). The similarity to an historian's pose is, indeed, part of the point. 'Certitude is not given to mortals', observes Syme in his parting apophthegm on Tacitus' opinions in this area;[142] but a certitude of a sort is given to epic poets, and Lucan does not have it.

The certainty of philosophy is, however, regularly posited for this poem. The doctrines of the inexorable Stoa saturate the work, in ethics, cosmology, and physics.[143] The political resonance of the Stoicism of the Republican hero, Cato, is very important to the poem,[144] while the Stoic apparatus of cataclysm, ecpyrosis, and sympatheia provides a compelling cosmic setting for the political catastrophe[145]—though setting is actually too weak a term for Lucan's effects of excess, as he asserts the end of liberty to be worse than the end of the world, not simply comparable with it.[146] Here above all may be seen the primary influence of his uncle Seneca's brilliant writings, and of his equally (we may readily conjecture) brilliant conversation. In the light of the passages we have been considering, however, a clear stumbling-block presents itself in the matter of Stoic Providence, one of the school's best-known and most characteristic tenets, which identified god and fate, attributed to them supreme justice and benevolence, and eliminated chance.[147] Lucan's attribution of malevolence to the gods is an affront to this elevated theodicy; his canvassing of the possibility

---

[142] Syme (1958), 527; see 521–7 for discussion of Tacitus' pronouncements, with references to accounts of *fatum* and *fortuna*; cf. Liebeschuetz (1979), 192–4. See Jal (1962), esp. 177, for discussion of the historians' attitudes to the gods' role in the civil wars.

[143] Pichon (1912), 165–216; Schotes (1969); Lapidge (1979), 344–5; Billerbeck (1986), 3121–6; Most (1989), 2053–7.

[144] On Cato's philosophical and political reputation, most clearly seen as paradigm in the younger Seneca, see Wünsch (1949); MacMullen (1966), 1–45; on this tradition in the poem, Lintott (1971), 499; for reservations about seeing a wholly Senecan, Stoic, Cato in Lucan, Syndikus (1958), 98–101.

[145] Schotes (1969), 18–25; Lapidge (1979).

[146] 1. 651–60; 4. 110–20.

[147] See the collected passages and discussion of Long–Sedley (1987), 1. 326–33. Seneca's *De Prouidentia* is of course the key text, especially for Lucan.

that the world operates by chance, and that the gods are indifferent to man, is even worse.

A surprising number of scholars still rack Lucan on the Procrustean bed of Stoic divine Providence; if his poem fits some aspects of the school's teachings, it must be made to fit them all.[148] Yet the more one documents the Stoic atmosphere of the poem in other departments, the more obvious, purposeful, and shocking the elimination of Providence appears to be. Indeed, the elimination is most precise, for it is very specifically Providence in relation to mankind that Lucan denies. As emerges clearly from Schotes' careful study, Lucan maintains Stoicism's belief in providential government of the natural world; the absence of divine regulation of human affairs is an exposed exception to a comprehensive system.[149] Lucan has contrived to place himself more or less in the position of Lucilius, the addressee of Seneca's *De Prouidentia* (1. 1–5): he can accept a belief in providential nature, but not in providence towards men.

Lucan adheres to a system of philosophy in order to depart from it—and in one of its most vital areas. None of the poem's options for the action of the gods is accommodating to the security offered by the Stoa. Ultimately, the poem has no philosophical scheme for understanding or explaining the gods' role in the destruction of the Republic, for the poet is trapped, as we have seen, by a paralysing collapse of authorial power, which bars him from enlightenment.

If the philosophical failure is striking enough on its own, it is complemented and compounded by the poetic failure, for Lucan likewise adheres to a system of poetry in order to depart from it— and in one of its most vital areas. Lucan is most emphatically not writing a history book, and his uncertainties are not those of the historian, no matter how much they may resemble them. He is not

---

[148] Marti (1945); Le Bonniec (1970), 179–82; Häussler (1978), 96–7; Neri (1986), 1981–99 (bibliography of the issue, 1981); most recently, explicitly, and astonishingly, Newman (1986), 208–11: 'Lucan's epic is guided by a basic religious theme, that *fatum* or *Fortuna* was at work in all the carnage, and for this attempt at philosophical/religious explanation, far more plausible and convincing in that time and in that place, even the most disaffected Romans could feel grateful' (208); '. . . secure in his faith that the divine purpose will ultimately triumph in history' (211). For a typically precise and compelling answer to such approaches, see Syndikus (1958), 82–4.

[149] Schotes (1969), 105–10, 116–29. Scholars who acknowledge Lucan's aban-

operating confidently within a tradition, but cutting himself off from one; he is straining to an epic status and power which he can never attain, and is therefore for ever falling short of something he ought to be hitting. The absence of the gods is a means of creating a pervasive and terrifying incomprehension, but it is far more than that. Lucan's epic tradition held as its ideal the creation by a Homer or a Vergil of a world of interlocking meaning: at its highest form, with the apotheosis of Homer, such poetry had the keys to the cosmos.[150] Lucan's renunciation of this tradition involves him in the surrendering of entire dimensions of meaning and effect. Narrating the actions of the gods is not, of course, a perfect key to easy understanding, nor are those narrated actions *per se* comprehensible. Yet a poet who claims to have access to them has at his disposal capacities of tremendous power. Vergil, for example, cannot explain the divine anger he narrates; but by representing Juno's anger and its interaction with Jupiter, he gives his readers more supple and resourceful ways of approaching the problem of Rome than we would otherwise have commanded. This is an oblique representation of the sort posited by the ancient critics, moving in illuminating parallel to the events on earth, providing structures for apprehending them which are indirect, mysterious, and tangential, yet unfailingly significant.

Although it is commonly assumed that Lucan kept the gods as characters out of his poem because he wanted, by refusing to distract from exposition of the human issues, to give more explanatory power to his work, he has in fact engineered their absence into being the poem's principal device for obfuscation and aporia. We instinctively assume that the removal of what we call the divine apparatus must be an aid to understanding, clearing out clutter which stands in the way of meaning; yet Lucan was clearly capitalizing on his audience's assumption that the gods were epic poetry's most powerful and economical frame of reference. His failure to represent the gods is testimony to their poetic power, not their weakness. He has not abandoned the gods, they have abandoned him.

---

doning of Providence include Due (1962), 86, and (1970), 213–4: 'Le masque que porte Lucain dans la *Pharsale* est celui d'un stoïcien qui a perdu la foi'; Ahl (1976), 281; Liebeschuetz (1979), 147–9; Johnson (1987), 5–11; Most (1989), 2054–5.

[150] Hardie (1986), 5–31 ('Poetry and Cosmology in Antiquity').

III

res est publica Caesar
'Caesar is public property, the state, the republic . . .'
Ovid, *Tristia* 4. 4. 15

It was noted above that the theme of uncertainty dominates the poem's scenes of prophecy.[151] As a coda to the previous Section, we may briefly examine those scenes, and move through them to other cardinal areas of interest: the poem's treatment of the uses to which religion is put, and its judgement on religion's response to the impact of Caesarism.

The prodigies at the end of Book 1 elicit futile efforts at propitiation from the state, together with three prophecies of widely varying nature. The prophecy of the matron in particular sheds light on some important departures from normal epic practice. She ends her speech with repetition, seeing the new round of civil war, the same as the first, which follows the assassination of Caesar: Pharsalia and Philippi are the same battle. Although her words refer to the familiarity of the second round after her vision of the first, they have an easily available reference to the position of the poet and his audience, facing familiar material which is fixed in history:

> consurgunt partes iterum, totumque per orbem
> rursus eo. noua da mihi cernere litora ponti
> telluremque nouam: uidi iam, Phoebe, Philippos.

The opposing sides rise up again, and I travel once more through the whole world. Give me new sea-shores and a new land to scry; I have already, Phoebus, seen Philippi. (1. 692–4)

Lucan and his audience have indeed already seen Philippi/ Pharsalia—in Caesar, Pollio, Livy, Cremutius Cordus, and Aufidius Bassus. A prophecy in epic, like that of Apollonius' Phineus (*Arg.* 2. 311–407), or Vergil's Helenus (*Aen.* 3. 374–462), normally reads like a mirror of the poet's task. The prophet in epic feels his way forward through alternative futures just as the composing poet moves backwards, sifting alternative and variant traditions from the past in order to establish his unique path. Lucan has no variant traditions, for the facts are fixed, and he is

[151] p. 280.

trapped. His characters are even more trapped than he is, but from their perspective, as the involved and undetached narrator, he can share in the anxiety as to how much of the action of the poem is predetermined.[152]

After the first book, the poem has two major scenes of prophecy, before the ninth book's climactic scene of prophecy denied. In Book 5 (67–236), Appius Claudius consults the Delphic oracle, a revered and defunct public institution, in order to discover the fate of the world, and is given no more than a highly misleading glimpse of his own fate. In Book 6 (413–830), Pompey's son, Sextus, consults an outsider and a criminal, the witch Erictho, and succeeds in receiving a large picture of the implications of the war, although the elements of prophecy (especially those relating to Sextus himself) are few and vague. Finally, in Book 9 (511–86), Cato refuses to consult the shrine of Jupiter Hammon in the Libyan desert, and delivers his own oracle instead.[153]

Appius is going to get more than he bargained for, so we are led to believe. He wants to pester the gods into telling him the *finem rerum* (5. 68): 'how events will end up', as it looks at first; but 'end of the universe' is actually what the future (and the phrase) holds. (The oracle once used to poi···ut a different, beneficent, sort of 'end' for mankind, a 'soluti· *monstrato fine*, 110.) The beginning of this book has already ··ncentrated on the end of senatorial and consular pow·r, as ··reshadowing the end of *libertas* (26, 44–5); the point is follow···l up at 181 and 200, and reinforced by Lucan's insistence on ··· fact that this is the last pronouncement the oracle will ever make.[154] Yet it is doubtful

---

[152] For Lucan's involved narrative pose, see Marti (1975), 86–9; anticipated in brief by Syndikus (1958), 39–40. Even the historical prophecies of the *Aeneid* are rather different in this regard; reaching as they do beyond the action of the poem, they do not trap the characters, who are unaffected by what will happen to their descendants.

[153] On the Delphic scene, see Dick (1965); Morford (1967), 65–6; Ahl (1976), 121–30; O'Higgins (1988); Masters (1989), 66–107; on Erictho, Paoletti (1963); Morford (1967), 66–73; Fauth (1975); Ahl (1976), 130–49; Martindale (1977) and (1980); Gordon (1987); Johnson (1987), 19–33; Masters (1989), 126–50; on Cato, Wünsch (1949), 86–108; Ahl (1976), 261–8; Johnson (1987), 61–2. Makowski (1977) is a very valuable discussion of our three passages; cf. Dick (1963), Schrempp (1964), and Morford (1967), 59–74, on prophecy in general in the poem.

[154] The 'last day of the universe' is part of the prophetic vision (181); cf. *suprema ruentis imperii*, 200–1. These are *extremae uoces* ('final utterances', 193);

from the start that this oracle will provide what Appius, and the audience, and the poet, expect: a full-scale epic prophecy. By Lucan's ways of proceeding, it is unlikely that an oracle sited in the centre of the world is going to be expert on extremity (71). Worse, the ruling spirits are the very ones denied by Lucan in his proem, Apollo and Bacchus (73).[155] A simile comparing Phemonoe to Vergil's Sibyl works in reverse: the public role of the Sibyl and her oracles, working their way into Roman destiny and state cult, gives way to an attempt to pick out the insignificant Appius (183–9). A confident barrage of scientific speculation, with pronouncements on the certainty (*fixa*, 105) and openness of the oracle (86–111), sets up the anti-climax into which we fall when the god actually speaks through the mouth of Phemonoe, using three lines to tell Appius that he will find peace and quiet in Euboea (194–6).

At this point Lucan steps back in astonishment, and asks why the god has not played his part and revealed all the events which are common knowledge to the poet and his contemporaries (198–203).[156] He is impelled, in a tone by now familiar, to question whether or not his past, the poem's future, was preordained (203–8). In this way the passage discharges its function in leading to the catastrophic denial of theodicy at the moment of the battle of Pharsalia (7. 445–55); for the Delphi scene is the narrator's first major crisis of disillusionment. All we have learnt is that Appius will die, but the emphasis on this solitary fact develops more power as we continue through the other scenes of prophecy.[157] Appius' reaction to the announcement of his death is a superbly ironic anticipation of the attitude towards death which will mark the wisdom of Cato. 'Nor did the closeness of death frighten you,' says Lucan: and then—'since you were tricked by the ambiguous

---

the priestess, Phemonoe, is given the same name as the very first priestess (Paus. 10. 5. 7). The very name of the consulter, Claudius, is ill-omened ('closer', as if from *claudo*). The same play is evident at the beginning of the book, when one of the consuls, L. Lentulus Crus, refers to the 'closing' of the two consuls' jurisdiction by the ending of the year (*nostrum exhausto ius clauditur anno*, 5. 44): the other consul is C. Claudius Marcellus.

[155] And the verb used of Appius' consultation (*sollicitat*, 69) is the same used by Lucan to describe what he will not do (1. 65).

[156] Makowski (1977), 195, a very acute section. Note how Lucan himself uses the prophetic future to spell out for Appius what will happen to him (230–6).

[157] Dick (1963), 49, and Makowski (1977) stress the centrality of death to the three scenes we are discussing.

response' (*nec te uicinia leti / territat ambiguis frustratum sortibus, Appi*, 224–5).

The venerable Delphic oracle, once so effective and open to all (103–111), has failed; in this connection it is very important to follow Ahl in noting that Appius is a notorious aficionado of the religious forms which are evanescing as we read.[158] The next attempt to gain insight into the future involves the effective exploitation of a creature who is outside society, the antithesis of Roman epic's normal area of operation—the witch Erictho.[159] The breathtakingly repulsive necromancy scene, Lucan's most intense imagining of order's collapse into evil and pain, has alienated many readers; those who find its horror too powerful should take every step they can to avoid living under a dictatorship. The passage affronts scholars' canons of plausibility, but it is meant to challenge and smash belief, as Lucan declares in language that assimilates the witches' action to his own, speaking of 'these witches, who couldn't be outdone by any poetic licence with its fictional monstrosities; the province of their skilled art is everything that is incredible' (*ficti quas nulla licentia monstri / transierit, quarum quidquid non creditur ars est*, 6. 436–7).[160]

The enquirer, Sextus Pompey, will have nothing to do with any of the legitimate, state-sanctioned organs of prophecy, Greek or Roman (6. 425–9). Nothing will do that is 'secret/silent but allowable/speakable', says Lucan, in a return to the language of 'speakable' and 'unspeakable': *aut siquid tacitum sed fas erat* (430). The organs that are *fas* cannot speak, and only the *nefas* has the power of utterance; it is, after all, the unspeakable which is Lucan's subject too. Sextus wants to know the same as Appius, the *certum finem*: 'definite outcome', as he thinks, but 'certain end', as it appears to the reader (592). This familiar language of (un)certainty pervades the passage. The poet is characteristically at a loss when it comes to explaining whether or not magic alters a

---

[158] Ahl (1976), 124–5.

[159] Gordon (1987) quite supersedes all earlier studies of magic in this scene. For official attitudes to magic practices in the early Empire, see Liebeschuetz (1979), 126–39.

[160] On the links between the art of Erictho and Lucan, see Masters (1989), 144–50. Like Lucan, Erictho 'moulds her spell/song/epic to new uses' (*carmenque nouos fingebat in usus*, 578); she 'had led her polluted art into new rites' (*inque nouos ritus pollutam duxerat artem*, 509); she 'does not call on the gods above, or ask for the aid of the divine with suppliant song' (*nec superos orat nec cantu supplice numen / auxiliare uocat*, 523–4).

fixed and certain order (492–9). The witch boasts that her clients are more certain when they leave than those who consult the Delphic oracle (770–3). She is right to an extent, for Appius was cheated by Delphic ambiguity, yet Sextus is essentially in the same position as Appius, for the entire point of the prophecy is death. The prophetic cadaver can be vague as to how, when, and where death will come to Sextus himself, his father, his brother, Scipio, Cato, and Caesar—but come it will (788–820).[161] The language of uncertainty carries over into a prophecy within the prophecy, as the corpse foretells a more certain prophecy for Sextus, from his father (813); but even Pompey will be uncertain as to how to protect his son (815). The only certainty which the individual enquirer can establish is the fact of death itself.

The threads are gathered together when Cato is given the opportunity to consult an oracle, at the temple of Jupiter Hammon in the Libyan desert. Poor and uncorrupt (9. 515–21), this shrine looks like one that will appeal to the hirsute hero. Urged to consult the god by Labienus, Cato replaces him, in effect, and utters an oracle of his own:

> ille deo plenus tacita quem mente gerebat
> effudit dignas adytis e pectore uoces:
> 'quid quaeri, Labiene, iubes? an liber in armis
> occubuisse uelim potius quam regna uidere? . . .
> an noceat uis nulla bono . . .?
> scimus, et hoc nobis non altius inseret Hammon.
> haeremus cuncti superis, temploque tacente
> nil facimus non sponte dei; nec uocibus ullis
> numen eget, dixitque semel nascentibus auctor
> quidquid scire licet. . . .
> Iuppiter est quodcumque uides, quodcumque moueris.
> sortilegis egeant dubii semperque futuris
> casibus ancipites: me non oracula certum
> sed mors certa facit. pauido fortique cadendum est:
> hoc satis est dixisse Iouem.'

Cato, possessed by the god whom he carried silently in his mind, poured out from his breast utterances worthy of the shrine. 'What enquiry do you order to be put, Labienus? Whether or not I prefer to die as a free man in battle rather than witness despotism? . . . Whether it is the case that no violence can harm the good man? . . . I know the answers, and Hammon

---

[161] Makowski (1977), 200.

would not implant this knowledge more deeply. We are all attached to the gods, and even without the temple saying a word we do not do anything unless god wills it. Nor does the deity need to speak; at the moment of our birth our maker told us once and for all what it is permitted to know. . . . Jupiter is everything you see, every move you make. Let the doubtful feel the need for soothsayers, those who are always dithering over future disasters; what makes me certain is not oracles but the certainty of death. Coward and hero both must fall; this is pronouncement enough for Jupiter.' (9. 564–84)

These are very difficult lines. We may note at first how this scene answers a movement in the poem: the futile public divination of Book 1 is followed by the collapse of the universal institution of Delphi, and by recourse to the forbidden and underground Erictho. Here we are given the private and self-sufficient response of Cato. This movement corresponds to the way in which all public institutions in the poem become irrelevant, leaving the solitary individual as the focus, living on posthumously, surviving the death of the *res publica*.[162] Again, the obsession with death as the only knowable thing in the future, together with the recurrent anxieties about the (un)certainty and futility of prophecy or divination, seem to be capped here, as Cato pronounces his Stoic certainty. Other forms of scrutiny are exposed as irrelevant. In the new circumstances, the private response of Cato appears to be setting itself up as the oracle which Lucan and his audience must follow.

Yet, after all we have seen in this poem, we are bound to have reservations about a culminating declaration of certainty from someone who says he has the answers. What is certain in this poem, and how can the poet guarantee it? We may readily agree with Due and Johnson that Cato is not simply a mouthpiece for the opinions of his author;[163] yet much of the poem's pressure still appears to want release at this point. The acceptance of death as the only worthwhile wisdom looks like a hard-won gain, one not to be surrendered, even if it is announced by a figure who is one of the poem's most bizarre creations. None the less, the cautious reader will perhaps feel justified in only reluctantly giving full assent to the words of Cato.

---

[162] Lintott (1971), 503; cf. Schotes (1969), 126.
[163] Due (1970), 223; Johnson (1987), 35–66, esp. 60–2.

If one movement in the poem shows religious forms sliding from public desuetude into the diverse privacies of Erictho and Cato, there is a corresponding current which carries along the religious system of the future: Caesarism. It is time to investigate what Caesar's catastrophic energy means for the realm of the divine, in the poem, and in Lucan's world. Many of the themes explored by Ovid, in response to Vergil, will find their fulfilment here.

Caesar bursts into the poem with an 'already' (1. 183); he comes to the tiny Rubicon, and sees there an image of Patria, the Homeland, and hears her speak (185-92). Caesar's magnetism is so stupendous that readers fall in with his egotism here, and assume that Patria is talking to him—Lucan himself says that Patria appears 'to the general' (186). But she is the (still only just) free *res publica*, and she addresses, not Caesar, but the whole army, using the collective plurals of the corporate state: *tenditis, fertis, uiri, uenitis, ciues* (190-2). Caesar, of course, uses only the first person singular in reply, with the first verb enjambed to drive the point home (*non te furialibus armis / persequor: en, adsum uictor terraque marique / Caesar, ubique tuus . . . miles*, 'I am not after you . . .; here *I* am, . . . Caesar', 1. 200-3). His speech as a whole prosecutes this split between the corporate and the individual, and within a religious context, for Caesar's first words in the poem are a prayer: after the last chapter's discussion of Ovid's address to Augustus,[164] the prayer will occupy an immediately familiar context:

> o magnae qui moenia prospicis urbis
> Tarpeia de rupe Tonans Phrygiique penates
> gentis Iuleae et rapti secreta Quirini
> et residens celsa Latiaris Iuppiter Alba
> Vestalesque foci summique o numinis instar
> Roma, faue coeptis.

O you who look out at the walls of the great city from the Tarpeian rock, Jupiter the Thunderer; and the Phrygian penates of the Julian family; and the mysterious rites of Quirinus, who was snatched away; and Jupiter Latiaris, sitting on high Mount Alba; and the hearths of the Vestals; and Roma, tantamount to a first-rank god—be favourable to my undertaking. (1. 195-200)

These lines, puzzling for many years, have been strikingly illu-

---

[164] pp. 214-17.

minated by the superb discussion of Pierre Grimal.[165] As he points out, the prayer's apparent anachronisms dissolve once one sees the prayer as a systematic anticipatory sketch of the imperial religious system of Augustus and the Julio-Claudian house.[166] It is, moreover, a sketch which meticulously footnotes Ovid's prayer at the end of the *Metamorphoses*, for the action of Lucan's poem is the beginning of the process whose perfection is marked by Ovid. Jupiter Tonans, then, is indeed the special rival of Optimus Maximus, established by Caesar's son in 22 BCE, more than a quarter of a century after the dramatic date of Caesar's speech.[167] The public cult of the Penates is already transformed by Caesar into a family affair (*gentis Iuleae*, 197). The mention of Quirinus is a token of Caesar's later cultivation of that god as a blueprint for his own apotheosis; in 45 BCE, four years after the dramatic date of this prayer, the Senate voted to place a statue of Caesar, with the inscription 'to the unconquered god', in Quirinus' temple (Dio 43. 45. 3).[168] Lucan is going even further than Ovid here, for Ovid seems to follow Vergil in keeping Quirinus as a communal figure.[169] Jupiter Latiaris is likewise brought into the Julian fold.[170] The hearths of the Vestals, as we saw in discussing Ovid's prayer, are the most dramatic example of the régime's transformations of public cult.[171] Finally, the cult of Roma, taken over from Greek practice to be linked with the cult of the emperor, is one of Augustus' most distinctive innovations, continued by his successors.[172] *Roma*,

[165] Grimal (1970), 56–9. My own discussion is only a supplement to his, adding a portion of detail, and relating the prayer to the context of Ovid's *Metamorphoses*.

[166] 'Elle comprend les divinités protectrices de Rome, mais dans la perspective de la théologie dynastique julio-claudienne' (57); 'Il est évident que Lucain a fait esquisser par César ... les grandes lignes de la religion impériale, telle qu'elle apparaît après Auguste' (ibid.); Caesar is 'la préfiguration du système politique et théologique qui, finalement, triomphera' (59). On Lucan's manipulation of time in this way, see Henderson (1988), 133.

[167] *Met.* 15. 866; Grimal (1970), 57; above, p. 216.

[168] Weinstock (1971), 175–88, esp. 186–8.

[169] Though one's confidence is, as usual, destabilized by rereading the model in the light of the adaptation. Ovid labels Quirinus 'unconquered' (15. 863); is it only Lucan's power of suggestion which makes one now detect in that epithet a reference to the inscription on Caesar's statue in the temple of Quirinus?

[170] Grimal (1970), 57: 'Le Jupiter Latin est le grand dieu de la Confédération albaine, et son culte, aux Féries latines, avait pour but de pérenniser la suprématie religieuse d'Albe, la ville fondée par Iule, l'ancêtre des Iulii.'

[171] *Met.* 15. 864–5; above, p. 215.

[172] Latte (1960), 306; Mellor (1981), 977–1004. Weinstock (1971), 297, 403, in

of course, is a perfectly good Latin word, but Republican usage avoided using *Roma* as a way of talking about the state, preferring *res publica* or *populus Romanus*—an attitude which is testimony, perhaps, to the Republican sense that 'Roma' was a cult invented and maintained by Greeks.[173] It is the Patria of the Republic who speaks to the invading army, but it is his own Imperial Roma whom Caesar addresses in reply.

This opening prayer of Caesar's is answered by another which he makes at the site of Troy, a prayer which lays bare his megalomaniacal determination to see the Roman enterprise as his story alone. The Lares of Troy, the embodiment of Vergil's vision of corporate continuity, are now, shockingly, 'the Lares of *my* Aeneas' (9. 991-2).[174] After a roll-call of the main Roman cults with Trojan connections (991-4), he calls himself 'the most famous descendant of the family of Aeneas' son, Iulus' (*gentis Iuleae . . . clarissimus . . . nepos*, 995-6). As far as Caesar is concerned, the effort of Aeneas was only for him and his family; they are the sole inheritors. To Lucan, the whole thing, the whole story of the descent, the *Aeneid*, is a fairy-story, a *fabula* (3. 212-13; cf. 6. 48-9, on the *Iliad* as *fabula*).[175]

In this context there emerges another vantage-point for considering Lucan's disavowal of the gods of his epic tradition. As Ovid had already seen, from any viewpoint which was unsympathetic to what the emperors had done to the *res publica*, the divine characters of Naevius, Ennius, and Vergil were no longer available as a vehicle for communal meaning, since they had become the creatures of the *princeps*. They are the gods of the victor, of course, and hence repulsive to Lucan's representation.[176] Worse, by Lucan's reckoning, the whole system, claimed by the emperors and made their own, stands (proleptically, in the poem's time-

accordance with his general thesis, sees tentative evidence for Julius' associations with Dea Roma during his lifetime. A final tribute to the acuity of Grimal and Lucan: note how the divinization of Rome (*numinis instar*, 199) is 'présentée par le poète avec quelque prudence', Grimal (1970), 57.

[173] Note Mellor (1981), 973, on the Republican choice of diction: 'There was still great reluctance to allow *Roma* to be used for the collective *patria*.'
[174] Of course Caesar is the opposite of Aeneas, as is obvious throughout: less than seventy lines later, Lucan censures Caesar for lacking true *pietas* (9. 1056).
[175] Cf. Tacitus' fine lines on the young Nero's speech on behalf of the people of Ilium, where he declaimed on *Romanum Troia demissum et Iuliae stirpis auctorem Aeneam aliaque haud procul fabulis*, *Ann.* 12. 58. 1.
[176] Cf. Ahl (1976), 68.

frame) rotten. As a result of this appropriation of public religious meaning, as we have seen, the individual's attempts to find meaning are marginalized, towards Erictho, or Cato. At the centre, monopolizing all religious meaning along with everything else, is Caesar: *omnia Caesar erat* ('Caesar was everything, everything was Caesar', 3. 108).[177]

An indispensable part of the system is the quasi-divine status of the tyrant. The gods favour Caesar because he is going to be one of them.[178] In our analysis of what the poem has to say on this topic, the central importance of Ovid's example will once more be plain.

When Caesar arrives at Rome for the first time, the people fear that he will scatter the gods and burn their temples (3. 98–100). We already know, however, that he and his successors will appropriate them instead. He calls a meeting of the Senate—in, of all places, the temple of Apollo on the Palatine (103). There was, of course, no temple of Apollo on the Palatine until Caesar's son built one there twenty years later. The commentator Haskins is driven to invent a temple which was 'afterwards rebuilt by Augustus',[179] but it is clear that Lucan is anticipating the Senate meetings held by Augustus in the temple of his favourite god, and it is clear that he is doing so by referring to the great opening scene of the *Metamorphoses*, which compared the Princeps with Jupiter, and the Palatine with Olympus (1. 163–76).[180] In Lucan's text, Caesar has in fact been compared to Jupiter just fifteen lines before, when he approaches Rome, and 'from a high cliff spies the city from a distance' (*excelsa de rupe procul iam conspicit urbem*, 3. 88). As Henderson points out, Caesar acts like an epic god here, and in language which takes us back to his own address to Jupiter Tonans and Jupiter Latiaris.[181] The sleight-of-hand in referring

---

[177] This movement in religion has a striking parallel in art: cf. Zanker (1988), 278: 'owing to the dominance of official imagery, it became impossible to find a means of individual expression'.

[178] Liebeschuetz (1979), 147.

[179] Haskins (1887), ad loc.

[180] Note in particular the self-conscious language of analogy used by Ovid: *hic locus est, quem, si uerbis audacia detur, / haud timeam magni dixisse Palatia caeli* ('this is the place, which, if I were bold enough to say it, I would not fear to call the Palatine of great heaven', *Met.* 1. 175–6).

[181] Henderson (1988), 146. On Caesar as god-like in the poem, see also Ahl (1976), 284–5.

'anachronistically' to Ovid's *concilium* is given a firm context; Caesar is already acting like a divine figure before he arrives at Rome.

Indeed, at his very first appearance Caesar is acting like Ovid's Jupiter. Here is Ovid's description of the divine anger which Jupiter conceives at the beginning of the *Metamorphoses*, the necessary divine impetus for the poem's epic action: *ingentes animo et dignas Ioue concipit iras* ('he conceived in his heart vast anger, worthy of Jupiter', 1. 166). And here is Lucan introducing Caesar into the action, providing the motive force for his poem: *iam gelidas Caesar cursu superauerat Alpes / ingentisque animo motus bellumque futurum / ceperat* ('Already Caesar had overcome the frozen Alps in his rush, and had conceived in his heart vast movements, the war to come', 1. 183–5). The simile which characterises Caesar in the introduction, accordingly, is that of Jupiter's thunderbolt, destructive and terrifying (1. 151–7). His quasi-divine anger receives mention (it is *even more* to be feared than divine anger), as does his quasi-divine (and equally unrepublican) *clementia*.[182] The climax is reached, as with so many of the poem's movements, at the battle of Pharsalia. Here Caesar acts exactly as an epic god acts, supplying the necessary inspiration and equipment, with a directing simile to ram the point home:

> hic Caesar, rabies populis stimulusque furorum,
> nequa parte sui pereat scelus, agmina circum
> it uagus atque ignes animis flagrantibus addit.
>                     . . . quacumque uagatur,
> sanguineum ueluti quatiens Bellona flagellum
> Bistonas aut Mauors agitans si uerbere saeuo
> Palladia stimulet turbatos aegide currus,
> nox ingens scelerum est . . .
> ipse manu subicit gladios ac tela ministrat . . .

Here Caesar, a source of madness for the nations, a stimulus to furious frenzy, in order to make sure that the crime of civil war should flourish in every area of its operation, goes wandering all around the columns and adds fire to their burning spirits. . . . Wherever he wanders, like Bellona shaking her bloody whip, or like Mars stirring up the Bistones, when he drives on with savage blow the horses which have been panicked by Pallas' aegis, there is a vast night of crime . . . He himself, with his own hand, provides swords and supplies weapons. (7. 557–74)[183]

[182] Anger, 3. 136; more fearsome than divine, 3. 439; *clementia*, 4. 363–4.
[183] For *ipse manu* of a deity's intervention or action, note *Aen.* 7. 143 and 621

Caesar acts like a god because his monstrous deeds will elevate him to divine status, in a perversion of the inheritance of Hercules, Aeneas, and Romulus. The civil war is consistently represented under the guise of Gigantomachy, as is natural given the impiety of the enterprise.[184] Yet it is a very odd sort of Gigantomachy, since the giant succeeds. The point of the Gigantomachic myth is to show the failure of the impious to disrupt divine order and take over the place of the gods, yet in Lucan Caesar does storm Olympus and gain the company of the gods.[185] The most extended comment on this bizarre result occurs, again, at the battle of Pharsalia, where it is given a yet more bizarre twist, as Lucan reflects on the gods' unconcern for the destruction of liberty:

> cladis tamen huius habemus
> uindictam, quantam terris dare numina fas est:
> bella pares superis facient ciuilia diuos,
> fulminibus manes radiisque ornabit et astris
> inque deum templis iurabit Roma per umbras.

Still, we have a way of avenging ourselves for this disaster, as much as may be extracted by mortals from gods: the civil wars will make the deified emperors the equals of the gods above, and Rome will adorn the spirits of the dead with thunderbolts, and rays of the sun, and stars, and in the gods' temples will swear by shades. (7. 455-9)

*Par/pares* ('equal') is one of the poem's key words,[186] and its civil war resonances work here also. Caesars and gods are 'well-matched' gladiatorial pairs, so that this is a violent competition with the state's gods; Caesars and gods are 'mutually suited', they deserve each other; Caesars are equal to the gods ('situated on a level' with those *above*?), indistinguishable from them, of the same

---

(*ipsa*). A passage in the *Thebaid* is very close to Lucan's language: *ipse* is used four times in twenty-two lines of Apollo helping Amphiaraus (7. 738, 752, 753, 759: note especially 752, *ipse . . . telis . . . ministrat*).

[184] 1. 34-6; 3. 315-20; 6. 347-8, 389-90, 410-12 (the setting for Pharsalia); 7. 144-50 (with a superb Ovidian *si liceat superis hominum conferre labores*); 9. 655-8.

[185] Henderson (1988), 145.

[186] On the basis of the logic so splendidly put by Caesar's mutinous soldiers: *facinus quos inquinat aequat* (5. 290). See Henderson (1988), 150; more generally, on the Romans' obsession with the sameness of the two sides in civil war, Jal (1963), 322-6, 415-16. We may note in passing that this complex of ideas guarantees the text at 7. 453, where *similis* is doubted by Shackleton Bailey (1987), 86 (and obelized in his 1988 Teubner text). The importance of the gladiatorial games to the poem was first brought out by Ahl (1976), 82-115.

essence, as bad as them, as callous and indifferent as they are.[187]
Here is the full development of Ovid's perspectives, expressed
with a despairing bitterness which Ovid never felt, or never cared
to express.

Caesar-cult is damned and scorned.[188] Its converse is found in
Lucan's opinion that Pompey was more deserving of state worship
after death;[189] and in the declaration that Cato is most worthy of
altars, and will perhaps receive cult if the state is ever free again.[190]
The reader first encounters Caesar-cult very early on in the poem,
when Lucan addresses the reigning emperor, and offers speculation on his fate after death (1. 33–66).[191] Our discussion so far
provides a context for a passage which is too often studied in isolation; only readers who do not read poems more than once need
be perturbed by the procedure of using the whole work as context
for the first occurrence of a motif.[192] Lucan's address belongs in
the tradition of imperial panegyric, with particular debts to the
opening of Vergil's *Georgics* (1. 24–32), and the finale of Ovid's
*Metamorphoses*;[193] if Ovid subverts Vergil's procedures, Lucan
even outdoes Ovid, following his lead here as he does throughout
his treatment of the Caesars' religious practice.

Gigantomachy is immediately provided as the context for
Nero's present position:

[187] The quoted phrases are from the *OLD* entries s.v., §13a, §3a, §6a.

[188] Cf. 6. 807–9.

[189] 8. 835–6, 846–50. Lucan does what he can for Pompey in this regard, at the
beginning of the ninth book: Le Bonniec (1970), 163. Commemorated in Lucan's
poem, Pompey will live more surely than if he had a lofty marble monument (8.
865–6, with much play on Horace's *Carm.* 3. 30).

[190] 9. 601–4; cf. Syndikus (1958), 41; Le Bonniec (1970), 163; Ahl (1976), 284–
5, 305.

[191] The passage is much discussed: Rutz (1964), 298–302, (1965) 249–50,
(1985a), 149–52. Note, especially, Due (1962), 93–102; Ahl (1976), 47–9. Since
then, Dumont (1986); and the valuable points of Johnson (1987), 121–2, and
Hinds (1988), 26–9.

[192] 'This very *detachable* section', according to Sullivan (1985), 145. The story
of the ban after three books' appearance (Ahl (1976), 333–53) has bedevilled
investigation, providing a purchase for those who see Lucan changing his mind
about what Nero meant after falling out with him. Even if the debate is conducted
in terms of reconstructed biography, Griset (1955) has exploded the idea that the
passage is an early position, later disavowed: if Lucan had time to write seven more
books after the ban, he had time to go back and rewrite thirty lines in his first
book.

[193] On Lucan's debts to Vergil and Ovid here, see the diametrically opposed discussions of Williams (1978), 163–5, and Hinds (1988), 26–9.

> quod si non aliam uenturo fata Neroni
> inuenere uiam magnoque aeterna parantur
> regna deis caelumque suo seruire Tonanti
> non nisi saeuorum potuit post bella gigantum,
> iam nihil, o superi, querimur; scelera ipsa nefasque
> hac mercede placent.

But if the fates found no other route for the approach of Nero; if eternal rule costs the gods a good amount, and heaven could not bow the knee to the Thunderer except after wars against the savage giants—then we make no complaint, o gods; the very crimes and unspeakable wrong [which are the subject of my poem] are acceptable at this price. (1. 33–8)

These staggering lines are remarkable enough for their equation of Nero's reign and the tyranny of Jupiter, with all the powerful Ovidian implications of that equation;[194] they are followed up, as we have seen, in the developed identification of Caesar and Jupiter, which serves as historical prototype for Nero. Lucan uses degrading mercantile metaphor to claim that he is pleased at the result; irony is too weak a term for this warped praise, since the sub-text is virtually on the surface. Further, in this poem the Gigantomachic motif is itself subverted, as we have seen, for the Caesars are intruders. Accordingly, a few lines later, when positions for Nero's apotheosis are being canvassed, Nero is a bullying usurper, before whom each deity will retire in turn, beginning with Jupiter:

> seu sceptra tenere
> seu te flammigeros Phoebi conscendere currus
> telluremque nihil mutato sole timentem
> igne uago lustrare iuuet, tibi numine ab omni
> cedetur . . .

Whether it be your pleasure to hold Jupiter's sceptre, or to mount the flame-bearing chariot of Phoebus and, with a wandering fire, circle the earth—an earth unafraid at the change of the sun-god; each deity will yield to you . . . (1. 47–51)

The emperor's elevation disturbs order, even if the poet claims the earth will feel no fear: such is the powerful reading given by Hinds, who demonstrates that the Ovidian Phaethon is behind this

---

[194] Above, pp. 221–4. Lucan here is taking up Nero's particular championing of Jupiter: 'The reign of Nero . . . was central in the re-establishment of Jupiter as the dominant divine figure in official imperial ideology', Fears (1981*b*), 71; see 69–71 for general discussion.

'wandering fire', in anticipation of the Ovidian primeval chaos which shortly follows, in the poem's first simile (1. 72–80).[195] Ovid's techniques are also evident in the lines which come between the two sections quoted here, when Lucan gives a long list of disasters from the civil wars, and says that they were all worth it if Nero was the result (1. 38–45). One is reminded of Ovid's list of Caesar's achievements at *Met.* 15. 752–7, which culminates in the bare-faced declaration that they were all nothing compared with the begetting of Augustus.[196] The invitation to agree is equally easy to refuse. Even after only thirty-three lines of introduction, let alone after ten books of bombardment, the catastrophe of the civil wars is not so easily to be sponged clean. The human and divine systems of Lucan's world are a cognate monstrosity, and every particle of energy in the poem, from the first line on, is directed to proving it.[197]

At this moment in the poem, Lucan is acting out the imperial appropriation of public language. Nero quite literally is the product of the civil war, as Lucan declares, and the poet, with mock dutifulness, shows his language being caught up in the resultant nexus of power, which binds subject and *princeps* together.[198] Hence the tremendous climax to the entire passage, the familiar lines in which Lucan accepts Nero as his inspiring divinity, preferable to Apollo or Dionysus, the ideal god to 'give strength for the composition of poetry by a Roman about Rome' (*tu satis ad uires Romana in carmina dandas*, 63–6). And so he is, the perfect presiding deity for the new, quintessential Roman poetry, which must

---

[195] Hinds (1988), 26–9. For Nero's associations with Apollo and the Sun (especially as charioteer and artist), see Sen. *Apoc.* 4; Suet. *Nero* 53; Griffin (1984), 120–1, 163, 216–17. Note that in Ovid's description of Phaethon there is already a glance at imperial apotheosis: the moment when Phaethon abandons control comes when he drives past Scorpio (*Met.* 1. 195–200), the location canvassed by Vergil for the catasterism of Octavian (*G.* 1. 32–5).

[196] Above, p. 211.

[197] See Ahl (1976), 42–6, for a trenchant dismissal of attempts to find portions of the poem which are less condemnatory of the post-Republican world than others.

[198] Cf. Grimal (1970), 117, on this passage: 'Lucain souligne—et c'est un mérite, qui annonce les conceptions modernes de cette période—que le principat est en fait la continuation de la révolution césarienne'; for a characteristic modern account of the process to which Grimal refers, see Millar (1977), esp. 527. Grimal's remarks were prompted by von Albrecht's alert invitation to place the Nero passage in the context of Caesar's prayer at the Rubicon (p. 116)—an invitation which I have attempted to take up here.

narrate the destruction of liberty and the erection of Caesarism in its place.[199]

The paralysis of the ancient critics is testimony to the unique nature of this extraordinary poem. They called it a history. It actually expends much energy in breaking down barriers between history and poetry. The *Aeneid* and *Iliad* are *fabulae* to Lucan, but so is (once) his own poem's subject-matter.[200] Herodotus' story of Xerxes bridging the Hellespont is *fama* (2. 672), as is the accepted tradition about the origin of the alphabet (3. 220); even the battle of Salamis is hard to credit, so changed is the world (3. 183); and Livy's direct personal testimony is not necessarily to be believed (7. 192, with Plut. *Caes.* 47). Yet old tradition is not idle in remembering Antaeus, who fought Hercules (4. 590).

Still, the ancient critics were half right. The poem's disavowal of characterized divine action does make it look at first more like an ancient history book than an epic. But they stopped there, the confident victims of their discipline's categories. They did not see that the gods' failure to participate is a vacuum which sucks the poem into active discontinuity with its tradition, exposing the abyss which had opened up since the *Aeneid*. The gods have not been blandly discarded, jettisoned as self-evidently irrelevant or out-of-date. As is the case with all epics, this poem's effects are inconceivable without the gods. Their presence is always being registered as absent, their absence as present; between these fractures the poem must find its unparalleled ways of speaking.

IV

> Approachable as you seem,
> I dare not ask you if you bless the poets,

---

[199] Johnson (1987), 122, is excellent here. For descriptions of the two-edged writing and reading practices necessary in this environment, see Due (1962), 93–102; Ahl (1976), 25–35, and (1984); Hinds (1988), 25–7. It is sometimes advanced as an argument against readings of the sort given here that Lucan would not have dared write anything that might upset Nero. This raises extremely difficult questions over what was tolerated (Ahl's discussion is good on this matter); we may note merely that, after Lucan fell out with Nero, he used one of Nero's verses to adorn his performance in the public privy, and attacked Nero and his friends in a scandalous poem (so says Suetonius in his life of the poet). The epic's address must have looked tame in comparison.

[200] 3. 212–13; 6. 48–9; 8. 606.

For you do not look as if you ever read them,
Nor can I see a reason why you should.

W. H. Auden, 'Homage to Clio'

A capricious Fortune has seen fit to spare only one other historical epic from the wreckage of Roman literature. Some thirty-five years after Lucan was forced to open his veins by his involvement in Piso's conspiracy (65 CE), Silius Italicus, Nero's last consul, abstained from food until he died, to terminate an unendurable illness.[201] Not before he had completed some 12,200 verses on the Second Punic War, an event three centuries distant from his own time, hallowed in the seventh and eighth books of Ennius' *Annales*, and in numerous books of history, especially in the third decade of Livy. The work is in many ways a vast exercise in nostalgia, grounded in a melancholy apprehension of contemporary decline, taking as its subject an era in which the seeds of that decline were being sown.[202]

In this poem, the *Punica*, we find the full epic panoply of divine action on display, and the judgement of modern scholars is virtually unanimous in denouncing Silius for the supposed folly of mingling the gods in historical events.[203] Although my own judgement of the success of the divine action in the *Punica* will prove to be as severe as that of any other critic, the argument so far shows that my starting-point will not be the usual modern assumption that divine action in historical epic is self-evidently ridiculous. Silius' gods are a failure, and a strikingly comprehensive and depressing failure; but they fail on their and his own terms, not ours, victims of the large-scale enervation which dooms the work as a whole. Silius' competence in many of ancient poetry's necessary skills is beyond dispute. He is well-read, learned, intelligent in

---

[201] Plin. *Ep.* 3. 7. 1–2. Extremely useful bibliography on Silius in the indispensable book of von Albrecht (1964), 215–37; add *CHCL* 2. 879–80; Ahl–Davis–Pomeroy (1986), 2558–61. On the gods and related issues in the *Punica*, see Schönberger (1965), 137–45; Delz (1969); Häussler (1978), 187–211; Liebeschuetz (1979), 167–80; Miniconi–Devallet (1979), lxv–lxx; Burck (1979), 286–90; Reitz (1982); Schubert (1984); Küppers (1986), 61–92.

[202] 'Nostalgia': Liebeschuetz (1979), 169. The key passages are 3. 573–81; 9. 346–53; 10. 657–8; 13. 850–67; 15. 125–7. On this theme, see Ahl–Davis–Pomeroy (1986), 2519, 2553, 2557–8.

[203] Gossage (1969), 77; Miniconi–Devallet (1979), lxviii; Vessey (1982), 591. Exceptions to this prevailing judgement are Mendell (1924), 105, and the sympathetic article of Matier (1981), 142.

organizing his vast material into shape, meticulous in his diction, even (at times) witty.[204] Further, he has certain well-formulated ethical concerns as the thematic skeleton for his work.[205] Yet pervasive narrative weaknesses, which will emerge as we investigate his poem's treatment of the divine, rob his creations of the power to move or convince.

The very spring of the *Punica*'s action, human and divine, lies in the *Aeneid*, where Dido's curse, conjuring up Hannibal, commits the two nations to eventual war (*Aen.* 4. 622–9), and where Jupiter prophesies the time when Carthage will attack Rome and the gods will have their battles to fight again (*Aen.* 10. 11–14).[206] As far as the divine plot is concerned, then, Silius' poem is a sequel to Vergil's, capitalizing on Ennius' picture of a pro-Carthaginian, anti-Roman Juno in order to represent the goddess's unassuaged wrath still active after the close of the *Aeneid*.[207] Silius, indeed, responds so strongly to the qualified nature of Juno's reconciliations that his last picture of the goddess in the poem shows her *still* disturbed, even after Jupiter has forced her to abandon Hannibal: *tunc superas Iuno sedes turbata reuisit* ('then Juno returned to her heavenly abode, in a state of disturbance', 17. 604); compare Vergil's last image of Juno, *laetata*, 'rejoicing' over the bargain she has made with Jupiter (*Aen.* 12. 841).[208]

The poem begins, as does the *Aeneid*, with Juno's fondness for Carthage, and with a soliloquy from the goddess, cataloguing the

---

[204] Silius' basic competence is established by von Albrecht (1964), his learning by Nicol (1936) and Juhnke (1972). For his organizational skills, see esp. Ahl–Davis–Pomeroy (1986), 2505–11. Those who have not read Silius may find themselves surprised at the pointed percipience of many of his similes: Hannibal's ambush for Flaminius at Trasimene is compared to a fisherman's construction of a wide-mouthed and tapering trap (5. 47–52); when Marcellus plans secret devices during the siege of Syracuse, he is compared to a swan which appears motionless, but whose feet are busy beneath the water (14. 189–91); see Sturt (1978).

[205] Bassett (1955) and (1966); von Albrecht (1964), esp. 55–89; Liebeschuetz (1979), 167–80.

[206] von Albrecht (1964), 167–8; Lorenz (1968), 4–67; Delz (1969), 89; Ahl–Davis–Pomeroy (1986), 2495–6.

[207] On the debts of Silius' Juno to Vergil's, see Ramaglia (1952–3); von Albrecht (1964), 167–8; Delz (1969), 88–9; Häussler (1978), 198–206; Küppers (1986), 61–92. On the probability that Juno was already hostile to Rome in Naevius, see Buchheit (1963), 54–5; Häussler (1978), 196–7; above, pp. 116–17.

[208] Silius' Juno is, at the end, still in the same state as she had been in Books 10 and 12: *turbata* (10. 337, 12. 701).

slights she has suffered.[209] The poem's divine action ends, as does that of the *Aeneid*, with Jupiter addressing Juno as she sits in a cloud, before the final combat, rebuking her for her mischief-making, and declaring an end to her activities.[210] The goddess meekly concedes,[211] making one request only.[212] Between these two extremes, Silius gestures towards Vergil's exploitation of Juno as the main organizing principle of his poem. The centre-piece of the *Punica* is the battle of Cannae,[213] and it is Juno who sets in train the events which lead up to this climax, by sending the nymph Anna to urge Hannibal on towards the battlefield (8. 25–38); then it is Juno who completes the action of the central portion by despatching another minor divinity, Somnus, to lay Hannibal to sleep and dissuade him from overreaching himself with a march against Rome (10. 337–50). She fulfils a similar structural function in Book 12, in an exchange with Jupiter which anticipates that of Book 17.[214] As Hannibal approaches the walls of Rome for the third time, Jupiter warns Juno to stop him (12. 691–700). Her intervention at this juncture is a counterpoint to her initial intervention in Book 1, and marks off as finished the run of success which Hannibal has had so far.

If Silius' Juno has many affinities with Vergil's, the same is true of his Jupiter.[215] Most clearly, he is shown, like Vergil's Jupiter, comforting his daughter Venus over the toils of her people, foretelling the eventual triumph of the Roman cause and praising the contemporary princeps.[216] Although this is the first appearance of Vergil's Jupiter, however, it is not the first appearance of Silius'.

The supreme gods of Homer and Vergil affirm a favourable outcome for the human protagonists when they first appear in the

---

[209] *Pun.* 1. 26–54, *Aen.* 1. 12–49.

[210] *Pun.* 17. 341–84, *Aen.* 12. 791–842; see the fine discussion of von Albrecht (1964), 168–71. Note esp. *Pun.* 17. 352 (*turbasti maria ac terras*), *Aen.* 12. 803–4 (*terris agitare uel undis / Troianos potuisti*); *Pun.* 17. 356 (*ad finem uentum est*), *Aen.* 12. 803 (*uentum ad supremum est*).

[211] *Pun.* 17. 357 (*supplex*), *Aen.* 12. 807 (*summisso . . . uultu*).

[212] *illud te . . .*: *Pun.* 17. 364, *Aen.* 12. 819.

[213] Ahl–Davis–Pomeroy (1986), 2505–11.

[214] Just as Juno's exchange with Jupiter in *Aeneid* 10 (606–32) anticipates her final meeting with him in Book 12.

[215] On Silius' Jupiter, see the extremely thorough and valuable work of Schubert (1984).

[216] *Pun.* 3. 557–629, *Aen.* 1. 223–96.

opening books of their respective epics,[217] yet Silius' Jupiter first appears earlier in the third book, and in very remarkable guise, as the instigator of Hannibal's attack upon Italy. He sends Mercury down to the sleeping Hannibal, to whom Mercury reveals an extraordinary vision of a snake on the rampage, portending the devastation of Italy (3. 163–214). The story of this vision comes originally from Hannibal's historian Silenus, and was available to Silius from the versions of Coelius Antipater and Livy.[218] In many respects, Silius' adaptation of the historians' versions to the conventions of epic has been skilful. Livy says that the guide in Hannibal's dream was 'a young man of divine appearance who said that he had been sent by Jupiter to guide Hannibal into Italy' (21. 22. 6); and, according to Cicero's report of Coelius, Hannibal spoke to Jupiter in a Council of the Gods, and was then allotted 'one of the members of the council' as a guide (*Div.* 1. 49). Mercury was the obvious choice for a poet remodelling such tales in epic form, and Silius could have done a lot worse than to choose as his exemplar Jupiter's dispatching of Mercury to Aeneas in *Aeneid* 4 (219–78).

Silius' sources had Jupiter as the prime mover in the story of Hannibal's vision. In following suit when he took over the famous story, rather than attributing the vision to another deity, Silius for the first of many times strays on to difficult ground. In the original story, the god in question must have been the Carthaginian equivalent of Jupiter, Ba'al Hammon.[219] Silius' Jupiter, however, is more closely and exclusively linked with the supreme god of the Roman state than any other epic Jupiter: in the poem as a whole, 'the core of the old religion, the providential care of Jupiter Optimus Maximus for Rome, is proclaimed with greater assurance than ever'.[220] Further, upon his first appearance, at the beginning of this scene, Jupiter is introduced as being omnipotent (*pater omnipotens*, 3. 163).[221] Why, then, should he permit his people to suffer the great disasters which it is within his power to avert? Worse, why should he actually incite his people's enemy to the

[217] Cf. *Od.* 1. 64–79 (promising Athene that Odysseus will return home). The corresponding scene in the *Iliad* (1. 518–27) is much more clouded; Zeus promises Thetis that her prayer will be answered, but the consequences are catastrophic for her.

[218] Cic. *Div.* 1. 49; Liv. 21. 22. 6–9.

[219] Walsh (1973), on Liv. 21. 22. 6.

[220] Liebeschuetz (1979), 173; cf. Schubert (1984), 123–4, 226–8.

[221] On the question of Jupiter's relationship with Fate in the *Punica*, see the highly judicious discussion of Schubert (1984), 159–66, esp. 164–6.

task of inflicting those disasters? Silius' solution is that the degenerate Romans need reinvigoration, and must be tested in order to raise their fame to heaven (3. 163–5, 573–5).[222] To any reader who has absorbed Silius' earlier traditional praise of the pristine hardihood of the Romans (1. 609–16), this information comes as a considerable surprise. Jupiter's motive may appear to be in some sort of rough agreement with the poem's thematic interest in Roman decline, but Silius' expedient here is a makeshift, a poetic saving of the phenomena.

In an epic filled with the military disasters of the *populus Romanus*, the role of Jupiter, ordaining the fate not only of Rome but of the world, was bound to be a severe test of the poet's tact and control. Perhaps his only hope of rising to the test lay in the creation of a genuinely resilient and energetic divine plot, but it is precisely this depth and force in the divine action which is missing from the poem, so that we have instead a series of confrontations with the basic dilemma represented by the failure of Roman epic's supreme deity to live up to his double inheritance.

Silius' expedients vary. Before the ambush at Trasimene, a series of ineffectual portents marks the Roman army's advance to destruction. The prodigies culminate in five lines of thundering and bolt-hurling from Jupiter (5. 70–4), after which the poet exclaims: *heu uani monitus frustraque morantia Parcas / prodigia! heu fatis superi certare minores!* ('Alas, futile warnings, prodigies vainly delaying Destiny! Alas, the gods, not equal to struggling against the Fates!', 5. 75–6). It appears here that Jupiter would have prevented the disaster to the arms of his people if he had had the power; have they then been cleansed and purified enough by the defeats at Trebia and Ticinus? At Cannae, the crowning catastrophe, Jupiter's uneasy relationship with the Fates is laid bare in a series of exchanges with lesser deities. He forbids Pallas to aid Hannibal against Scipio (9. 470–8); although she complies, she consoles herself with the thought that he cannot avert Fate, or avoid seeing the plain of Cannae steaming with slaughter (9. 481–3). Shortly thereafter, Jupiter intervenes to stop Mars helping the Romans, having just prophesied in minutest detail the eventual triumph of Scipio (9. 542–55). At other points in the poem, however, Jupiter takes specific steps to aid the Roman cause, sending

---

[222] On this theme in the poem, see von Albrecht (1964), 17–18; Ahl–Davis–Pomeroy (1986), 2504.

Mars to rescue Scipio the Elder at the battle of Ticinus (4. 417–30), or thundering to stop Hannibal's march on Rome, and inspiring the Senate to appoint Fabius Maximus to the dictatorship (6. 595–618).

Throughout the poem, Jupiter's motives oscillate meaninglessly between purgative zeal and protective concern. The divine power politics which might have given some texture to his relationship with Fate are consistently so inert that the problems involved in this oscillation are nakedly exposed. Only a rash person would claim to 'understand' the relationship between Jupiter and Fate in the *Aeneid*, where many of the difficulties which trip up Silius are, at times, very close to the surface. Yet Jupiter's intricately characterized relationship with his stupendous sister and wife is so engrossing, so richly significant in the tangential view it offers on the emergence of Roman *mores*, that very few readers feel compelled to descend to the banality of asking why Jupiter does not just stop Juno acting in the way she does. In Silius, the utter sterility of the interaction of the gods as characters is so pervasive that such bald objections obtrude themselves at every juncture.

If the large-scale conception of the gods' modes of action is faulty, the divine dimension of the poem is further handicapped by the perfunctoriness with which it is narrated. The exhilaratingly brusque ellipses of Ovid, his refusal to play the expected narrative games, here become incoherence.[223] The progress of the *Punica* is a relentlessly *ad hoc* business, successful enough on the tactical level, impressively well-organized on the strategic level, but irredeemably lame on the intermediate, operational, level.

Since the comment from here on will be negative, it is worth acknowledging that there are indeed occasional moments where Silius employs his gods in effective and interesting ways. His use of allegorical figures is especially rewarding.[224] The end of Saguntum shows the people of the doomed town being driven on to suicide by the odd co-operation of two opposed pairs, Hercules and Fides, Juno and Tisiphone (2. 475–707).[225] The collective suicide is certainly a noble deed, as Silius shows with his apostrophe

---

[223] On Ovid, see above, pp. 235–7.

[224] von Albrecht (1964), 82–3, on the 'Choice of Prodicus' scene (15. 18–130); Häussler (1978), 209–10.

[225] On this episode, see Vessey (1974); esp. Küppers (1986), 164–70, an interesting and penetrating discussion.

to the martyred allies at 2. 696–8, yet Juno also approves of their death, and it is her creature Tisiphone who actually brings about the deed (2. 543–613).[226] In effect, Fides and Tisiphone are collaborators. The divine figures have enabled Silius economically to encapsulate the paradoxical nature of the act, at once glorious and repellent, noble and bestial, by juxtaposing two diametrically opposed creatures as the jointly responsible agents.[227]

It is significant that the most successful of Silius' divine characters are allegorical figures, who may appear for the moment of need only, then vanish. He shows himself unable to sustain the commitment to a series of characters and interactions which is necessary for a divine plot. It is here that his shaky grip becomes most apparent—and from the very first appearance of a god. The first divine creature to figure in the *Punica* is Juno. Hannibal clothes himself with the anger of the goddess, so we are told (1. 37–8), and the delighted goddess delivers a soliloquy (1. 42–54). At the end of her speech, *haec ait ac iuuenem facta ad Mauortia flammat* ('she said this and fired the young man for deeds of war', 1. 55). Unlike the soliloquy of Juno which begins the action of the *Aeneid*, this is not an event which issues from a cause, and results in an action; it is a floating piece of colour, generating nothing. Why, when, and where did it happen? The extremely dependable Loeb editor betrays his unhappiness with Silius' lame manner here, for he ever so slightly miscues the last line quoted so as to give at least some context for the utterance of the goddess ('*With these words* she fired the youthful warrior . . .').[228]

The divine action in the battle of the Trebia, modelled closely on the divine action in Homer's River-battle (*Il.* 21. 211–382), affords a more sustained opportunity for comparison.[229] Homer puts the action on earth in the foreground, with an ever-present divine audience, whose marshalling and taking up of positions he reports, and to whom he often returns. There is nothing of this in Silius. In the middle of the human battle we suddenly read:

> Tum Trebia infausto noua proelia gurgite fessis

[226] Vessey (1974), 34.

[227] Livy's ghoulish account of another such incident in Scipio's Spanish campaign exhibits a similar mixture of abhorrence and grudging awe (28. 22. 5–23. 5); Silius' account owes much to Livy here.

[228] Duff (1934), trans. of 1. 55.

[229] On the debts to Homer here, see Juhnke (1972), 13–24.

inchoat ac *precibus Iunonis* suscitat undas.

Then Trebia, with its unlucky flood, began new attacks on the exhausted Romans, and, *in answer to the prayers of Juno*, stirred up his waves. (4. 573–4)

Well and good, except that this is the first mention of Juno since Book 2 (694), some 1,300 lines earlier. Here she flits in for a moment in the genitive, non-existent as a character.[230] The river rages on, and addresses the struggling Scipio in angry tones (4. 660–6). At this point, to rescue the hero, Silius blends two Homeric episodes, Achilles' cry for help to Zeus (*Il*. 21. 273–83), and the intervention of Hera and Hephaestus some sixty lines later (21. 331–41). In Homer, of course, the gods are there watching, we learn why and how they react to the human action, and why and how they interact with each other. But in Silius there has been no mention whatever of the presence of any such audience of gods; hence, to motivate Vulcan's intervention in favour of Scipio, he is reduced to perfunctory makeshift, and shoves his gods into the action in a garrulous aside before the prayer:

> Haec, Venere adiuncta, tumulo spectabat ab alto
> Mulciber, obscurae tectus caligine nubis.
> ingrauat ad caelum sublatis Scipio palmis:
> 'di patrii, quorum auspiciis stat Dardana Roma, . . .'

Vulcan, with Venus beside him, was looking at this from a high mound, covered by the murk of a dark cloud. Scipio uttered a reproachful speech, raising his hands up to heaven: 'Gods of my fatherland, by whose auspices stands Dardan Rome, . . .' (4. 667–70)

These conveniently inserted deities are not self-sufficient enough even to have a conversation: the groaning Venus turns her mute husband's fiery essence against the river as if he were a flame-thrower (675–7). The sketchiness of the episode's resolution follows suit. In Homer the river pleads first with Hephaestus, then with Hera, arguing with them, giving reasons why they should spare him; Hera is won over and tells her son to stop (21. 356–82). In Silius, no speech, no motivation, but a rush to finish the job off: *tum demum admissae uoces et uota precantis, / orantique datum ripas seruare priores* ('at last the begging river's words and

---

[230] A very similar, scarcely less perfunctory line occurs in the battle of Cannae, when Aeolus unleashes his winds 'through the prayers of Juno, offering him no small promises' (*Iunonis precibus, promissa haud parua ferentis*, 9. 494).

prayers were heard, and his plea—to be able to keep to his earlier
banks—was granted', 4. 696–7). In other words: here see Homer.

When the great Marcellus is about to die, the event is marked
by a similarly perfunctory Homerism. Marcellus embraces his son,
and prays to Jupiter for success: *nec plura, sereno / sanguineos
fudit cum Iuppiter aethere rores / atque atris arma aspersit non
prospera guttis* ('no sooner had he finished, than Jupiter poured
bloody dew from a clear heaven, and sprinkled their doomed
weapons with black drops', 15. 363–5). In Homer, Zeus sends
such a sign to honour his dear son Sarpedon, whom he is unable
to save from Patroclus (*Il.* 16. 458–61). But in Homer Zeus is
there before us; he has just had a conversation with Hera about
the death of his son (16. 433–57), he is watching and taking an
interest; this token is only part of an organized movement over
hundreds of lines, which culminates in the removal of Sarpedon's
corpse to Lycia (16. 666–83). In Silius, Jupiter's response is his
first action in the narrative for over 1,600 lines;[231] the blood-
shower has become simply an automatic piece of hoped-for sublimity, an isolated and floating motif.

It is important to recognise that it is not only the divine narrative which exhibits such piecemeal use of models, and such a radical inability to actualize what is being told. A striking example of
the same fumbling is to be found in the tale of Scipio at Canusium
(Liv. 22. 52. 7–53. 13; *Pun.* 10. 415–48). In Livy we see the fugi-
tives from Cannae gather at Canusium, and Scipio, with Ap.
Claudius Pulcher, is made their leader. As Scipio and his companions confer, P. Furius Philus comes to tell them of the planned
desertion of a group of young nobles, led by L. Caecilius Metellus.
Scipio leads a group to the tent of Metellus and administers an
oath of allegiance to the traitors. Silius likewise describes the
gathering of the army's remnants at Canusium (10. 387–414),
then begins with Metellus, and describes his treasonable activities
(415–25). A sudden switch follows: *quae postquam accepit
flammata Scipio mente . . .* ('after Scipio's inflamed mind heard of
this . . .', 426). The suppression of Furius, the omission of precise
detail is defensible, even praiseworthy. The problem is that this is
the first mention of Scipio since 9. 549, in the middle of the battle
of Cannae. Silius has one eye on Livy and one on his own work,

---

[231] One has to go back to 13. 326, *Pan Ioue missus erat.*

and does not perform the simple but necessary task of mentioning Scipio's presence at Canusium: he lets (insensibly or not) Livy do the job for him.

The success or failure of divine action in epic is commonly regarded as a function of the poet's own religious beliefs or sensibilities. At one extreme, the success of the divinities in the *Aeneid* is represented as being the result of Vergil's own religious outlook.[232] By analogy, Silius' failure is described as the result of some shortcomings in his own religious or emotional makeup: 'gli manca l'ἐνθουσιασμός che aveva dettato i versi di Virgilio, perché il suo spirito non aderisce alla materia trattata'.[233] Yet the failures we have been pursuing here have been failures of poetic imagination and technique, operative in narration of the human sphere as well as the divine. If Silius' divine action is a perfunctory and *ad hoc* matter, then so is his human action; in the end, we cannot accept Silius' divine apparatus for the same reasons that we cannot accept his human apparatus. So far from taking the divine action in his poem too far, he does not take it seriously enough as an integral part of the meaning-systems of his poem. There is nothing enthralling or compelling anywhere in the poem, whether on earth or heaven. The gods are only notions and tags, without the mimetic energy, the characterful gaps and ellipses which might make those tags mean something—and the same is true of the humans. Silius' gods come very close to being the tropes or figures which modern critics often take the gods of Vergil or Apollonius to be, and nothing can demonstrate the inadequacy of such readings of Vergil or Apollonius more powerfully than the experience of reading, and rereading, the seventeen books of the *Punica*.

More disconcerting than these shortcomings, because less expected, is Silius' failure to evoke the potency of Rome's antique cult and ritual. As Liebeschuetz says, 'compared with Virgil, or

---

[232] The most consistent exponent of such a view is Boyancé, who ends up by asserting that Vergil was a traditional polytheist: Boyancé (1963), esp. 37–8. Even the more representative work of Kühn (1971) betrays the presupposition that the power of Vergil's representations of divinity must correspond to what the man actually believed: Kühn (1971), esp. 39, 140.

[233] Ramaglia (1952–3), 35; cf. Schönberger (1965), 140; Häussler (1978), 210; Burck (1979), 287, on how, in comparison with Vergil's gods, Silius' lack 'eine vergleichbare innere Erfüllung'.

Livy, Silius Italicus seems to be less interested in the rich variety of traditional religious and political institutions of Rome'.[234] Liebeschuetz very appositely contrasts Livy's account of Fabius' religious measures after Trasimene (22. 9–10) with Silius' (7. 74–89), remarking that 'Silius' account is simplified and less specifically Roman'. Even in comparison with Livy, let alone Vergil, it is striking how feeble an impression one derives from reading the *Punica* of any grandeur, power, or vitality in connection with religious matters. Such a disparity is all the more striking (and all the more disconcerting for the advocates of a 'biographical' approach to these works) when one considers that Livy was—notoriously— a chair-bound *priuatus* all his life, while Silius, out of all the surviving Roman epicists, was the only one who had actually stood in the shoes of Marcellus and the Cunctator, performing public sacrifice as consul on behalf of the *populus Romanus*.

[234] Liebeschuetz (1979), 173.

# 7

# Epic of Myth: Valerius Flaccus' *Argonautica* and Statius' *Thebaid*

The last two epics of our study treat subjects from the time before the heroes of Homer. The voyage of the Argonauts is already a famous topic of poetry in the *Odyssey*. Circe speaks to Odysseus of 'Argo, which is in the minds of all' (*Od.* 12. 70). On our present evidence, this was the myth that first broke history's grip on Roman epic after one hundred and fifty years, when Vergil's contemporary, Varro of Atax, adapted Apollonius' *Argonautica* into Latin hexameters.[1] The subject of Statius' epic, the expedition of the Seven against Thebes, was likewise a long-standing favourite in the Greek world, which had also been treated by at least one earlier Roman epic poet.[2] It remains to see if these topics still have life in them, and if the gods are a part of that life.

The two poems benefit from being considered together. Their authors were very probably close in age, and the works have an interrelationship which looks like a matter of reciprocal influence over a number of years rather than a one-way dependence.[3] We begin with the *Argonautica*, but the main focus in this chapter will be on the *Thebaid*. It is the more influential and compelling work (though still woefully unappreciated), while some aspects of Valerius' technique may usefully be discussed in the same context as Statius'. Statius will be a real presence to many readers of this book, with Valerius being no more than a name to the majority, and not even that to some.[4] Yet Valerius has suffered long enough

[1] Livius Andronicus' translation of the *Odyssey* was into Latin Saturnians, not the hexameters of genuine epic.

[2] On the early Greek epics on Thebes, see Huxley (1969*a*), 39–50; for Antimachus' epic, see Wyss (1936); for Ponticus' effort, see Prop. 1. 7. 1–2.

[3] Steele (1930). For a highly sceptical discussion of the data of Valerius' life, see Cambier (1969), 223–8; on Statius, see, conveniently, Coleman (1988), 15–20.

[4] There is still lacking the book in English which would help put Valerius on the map, as Morford (1967) and Ahl (1976) did for Lucan, and Vessey (1973) for Statius. The work of Summers (1894) is, however, valuable. In Germany, Mehmel

from being patronised; let there be no prejudgements at the beginning of the investigation.

I

πολλὰ τὰ δεινὰ κοὐδὲν ἀν-
θρώπου δεινότερον πέλει·
τοῦτο καὶ πολιοῦ πέραν
πόντου χειμερίῳ νότῳ
χωρεῖ, περιβρυχίοισιν
περῶν ὑπ᾽ οἴδμασιν.

Wonders are many and none is more wonderful than man;
that marvel proceeds over the grey sea with the wintry south
wind, passing under swells which make troughs all round.

Sophocles, *Antigone* 332–7

As we shall see, one of the points about this poem is its apparent perspicuity. The first lines sketch the dominant preoccupations of the poem with an explicitness which has no parallel:

Prima deum magnis canimus freta peruia natis
fatidicamque ratem, Scythici quae Phasidis oras
ausa sequi mediosque inter iuga concita cursus
rumpere flammifero tandem consedit Olympo.
    Phoebe, mone, si Cumaeae mihi conscia uatis
stat casta cortina domo, si laurea digna
fronte uiret.

I sing of straits first traversed by great sons of gods, and of the oracular ship, which, having dared to pursue the shores of Scythian Phasis and to smash its course through the middle of the clashing rocks, finally came to rest in fiery Olympus.

Phoebus, prompt me, if my house is pure, where stands your cauldron,[5] which shares the knowledge of the Cumaean seer, if your laurel thrives green on a worthy forehead. (1. 1–7)

(1934) was the first of a number of fine book-length studies. Bibliography on Valerius in Helm (1956), 236–55; Ehlers (1971–2); Scaffai (1986); none of these has a separate section on the gods. Good discussions of the gods in Valerius in Schönberger (1965), 124–31; Schubert (1984).

[5] This cauldron was placed upon the sacred tripod from which the Delphic priestess prophesied; it figured prominently on the reliefs and actual dedicatory tripods which adorned the temple of Apollo Palatinus: Zanker (1988), 86–7, 247, 268.

Here stand already most of the motifs which will command our attention in this section. 'First' is the poem's first word;[6] Argo as the first ship is one of the work's richest veins. The catasterism of Argo, together with the description of the Argonauts as 'great sons of gods', signal the centrality of apotheosis. Yet the poet's relation to Apollo provides the best starting-point.

To anyone coming to Valerius from Apollonius, and especially to anyone coming to him from Lucan, the reassertion of the poet's control and inspiration in the first lines is immediately arresting. Apollonius had begun with Apollo, but only as the origin of the oracle which begins the poem's action, not as the poet's source of inspiration. Valerius, on the other hand, is claiming a doubly effective relationship between himself and the god. Not only is Apollo here the god of poetry (the capacity in which he was renounced by Lucan, 1. 64–5); he is also the god of prophecy, the mouthpiece of Fate. Such is the import of Valerius' reference to his official status as one of the Board of Fifteen in charge of the Sibylline Books, which since the reign of Augustus had been kept in the temple of Apollo Palatinus.[7] His vatic stance as the poet of epic is explicitly asserted here, for he may share the knowledge of the Cumaean Sibyl, the knowledge of Apollo. In harmony with this pose, Valerius repeatedly stresses his access to the knowledge which the Muses possess as original witnesses;[8] at one point he spells out the rationale by which he may know even the minds of the gods, so that he may narrate their doings without anxious qualm: *tibi enim superum data, uirgo, facultas / nosse animos rerumque uias* ('for you, virgin Muse, have been given the power to know the minds of the gods, and the pathways of events', 3. 15–16).

A number of characters in the poem embody this prophetic-poetic stance. Phineus (it comes as no surprise to readers of Apollonius) is a figure for the poet in the Latin *Argonautica* as well. Yet the prophet's voice is stronger in this poem (as is the poet's), and we do not find here the murkiness which made Phineus

---

[6] If I point out that 'third' is the first word of the third book, I run the risk of confirming some prejudices; but bear with the poet.

[7] As one of the *quindecimuiri* he keeps a model of the god's tripod in his house.

[8] 5. 217–18 (*uisa ... uobis ... bella*, 'the wars you saw'); 6. 33 (*quos uideris ... furores*, 'the madness which you saw'); cf. 6. 516.

such an ideal mask for Apollonius' poetics.[9] Valerius tries as hard as possible to assuage Phineus' uncertainty: he is 'fate-speaking Phineus' (*fatidici ... Phinei*, 4. 425). The prophet does mention that he was punished for revealing fate, as in Apollonius,[10] but he immediately goes on to soften the impact by revealing that the anger has passed, claiming to know that Jupiter, not chance, is behind the arrival of the Argonauts (4. 483–4). So certain is Phineus that he even speaks like Jupiter, the Jupiter of Vergil, pronouncing to the Argonauts *fabor enim* (4. 578), using the very words which Jupiter had used to Venus (*Aen.* 1. 261: 'I shall speak fate'). 'Jupiter himself,' declares Phineus, 'is the author of my fated utterance' (*ipse ... fandi mihi Iuppiter auctor*, 4. 559–60); and Phineus, accordingly, has the same insight into the 'pathways of events' which Valerius attributes to the Muses (*rerum ... uias*, 4. 558; cf. 3. 16). His prophecy is clearer and more explicit than it had been in Apollonius (it is, of course, a prophecy which he 'sings', *canit*, 4. 553). He declares that the gods themselves will perhaps give aid and inspiration at the Clashing Rocks (4. 567–8), whereas in Apollonius he had misleadingly given the impression that the crew's own strength would be sufficient (2. 332–6). Unlike his counterpart in Apollonius, he foretells the deaths of Idmon and Tiphys (though without naming them, 4. 591–8). Only at the end does he assert that he cannot tell the very last fated action, and he begs to be allowed to fall silent (4. 623–5). By this stage of his speech, these words have largely had their sting drawn, and we understand Phineus to be informing us that he will not retell Euripides', Seneca's, and Ovid's (now lost) *Medea*.

In a sense, Phineus is also refusing to repeat what Valerius' first prophet has already virtually told us. Early in Book 1 we are given a doublet-scene of epic prophecy, two forecasts delivered by the expedition's seers, Mopsus and Idmon, characters who are, like Valerius himself, men of Apollo.[11] Both are inspired by the prophetic god (1. 207, 230), yet Valerius, by a fine and unique stroke, uses them to give two quite different visions, which correspond to two visions of the epic experience. Mopsus speaks first. He is agitated and involved, a Cassandra, a frenzied Sibyl, foreseeing

[9] pp. 60–1.
[10] 4. 479–82; cf. Ap. Rhod. 2. 179–84.
[11] *Phoebeius Idmon*, 1. 228; *Phoebeum ... Mopsum*, 3. 372. Note, in the Book 3 passage, how assured is the knowledge of Mopsus: he will teach *causae* (377); his *cura* will find a solution (396–7).

what appear as sorrowful troubles: storm, the loss of Hylas, wounds of Pollux, the fire-breathing bulls, the serpent, the deaths of Jason's children, and the incineration of Creusa (1. 211–26). Idmon, on the other hand, although himself inspired, and possessed of the 'knowledge' signified in his Greek name (1. 231, *praenoscere*), is not in a frenzy, but 'full of the fates and a quiet Apollo' (*plenus fatis Phoeboque quieto*, 1. 230). Even though he can foresee his own death, he does not speak of it, but instead gives five lines of temperate, almost bland, preview: the Argonauts will suffer, but conquer; they must bear up and strive for their return home (1. 234–8). Nowhere in ancient epic do we have such a clear figuring of the competition between the form's distant and near perspectives. Valerius has captured here the two poles around which, for example, discussions of the *Aeneid* continue to revolve; and he has deftly (too deftly, perhaps) warned his readers that he is already ahead of the difficulties they will experience later in the poem, when they try to balance the grand achieved action against the characters' failures and disappointments.

A remarkably assured act of reassertion confronts us here. The first sections of the poem show Valerius' command of fated knowledge in operation, as he swerves away from Apollonius' uncertainties and silences. Through the voice of Pelias addressing Jason, he fills in the background to the epic with details about the story of Phrixus and Helle (1. 41–50; supplemented later by Orpheus, 1. 278–82). Pelias falls silent, and does not speak of the clashing rocks, the king's daughter, and the great serpent (1. 58–62). But in cataloguing Pelias' omissions the poet has made up for them, and besides, Pelias immediately fails, as his silent deceits come out into the open (*mox taciti patuere doli*, 1. 63). So much is out in the open in this opening portion. Jason prays to Juno and Pallas for aid, and is immediately answered with their concrete participation (1. 80–99). The country-dwelling heroes are told of the expedition by Fauns, nymphs, and River-gods, who are visible, singing, 'in the open light of day' (*manifesto in lumine*, 1. 103–6).

All this may strike some readers as mere doggedness, or as a disappointing lapse from the scintillating deviousness of Apollonius' poetics. Yet Valerius knows exactly what he is doing, and nothing could be more mistaken than to see him as the prisoner of an unthinking classicism. His use of Apollo and the Muses to reassert his epic knowledge and power is part of a comprehensive strategy for the poem; we may best find our way into this strategy from the perspective of the source of Fate, the supreme god, Jupiter, from whom Apollo himself derives his knowledge.[12]

Valerius' very subject is a 'fate-speaking ship' (1. 2), and Argo speaks Fate because her keel is oak of Dodona, from Jupiter's prophetic grove: she is the servant of the god (*famulam Iouis*, 1. 308). There exists an extraordinarily tight link between Jupiter, his fate-speaking ship, and his fate-speaking poet. Three forms of prophecy sent the Argonauts out, says Jupiter: 'my oaks, the tripods, and the shades of their relatives' (*meae quercus tripodesque animaeque parentum*, 1. 544).[13] One of the prophetic oaks is the ship itself, both instigator and performer of the heroic deed. The great expedition is Jupiter's doing, as we learn explicitly at the first divine council.[14] Here it emerges that Valerius' *opus* is Jupiter's *opus*; in an ultimate version of the hoary motif which equates poetry with a sea-voyage, the fated voyage and the fated poem are coextensive.[15] This is how Jupiter is introduced:

> siderea tunc arce pater pulcherrima Graium
> coepta tuens tantamque operis consurgere molem
> laetatur.

Then the father rejoices, seeing from his starry citadel the magnificent beginnings of the Greeks' enterprise, and seeing how the mighty mass of the work/task is surging upwards. (1. 498–500)

The English is inevitably laboured, but in Latin this identity of vocabulary for heroic and poetic achievement is entirely natural.[16]

[12] Aesch. *Eum.* 19; Verg. *Aen.* 3. 251.

[13] That is, the shrines of Dodona and of Delphi, and the apparitions of Phrixus and Helle (1. 47–50).

[14] After a teasing false phrase of introduction at 1. 350, where Valerius uses Vergil's portentous words of introduction for Jupiter, *et iam finis erat* (*Aen.* 1. 223); we have to wait another 150 lines. As we shall see, the speciality of Valerius' Jupiter is beginnings, not endings.

[15] Some famous passages include Verg. *G.* 2. 41, 4. 116–17; Prop. 3. 3. 22–4; Ov. *Ars* 326, *Fast.* 1. 4 (with Bömer (1958) ad loc.); cf. Curtius (1953), 128–30; Wimmel (1960), 227–30; Kenney (1958), 205–6, citing as Greek precedent Pind. *Ol.* 13. 49, *Pyth.* 2. 62.

[16] The words in the first instance refer to Vergil's *tantae molis, Aen.* 1. 33 (cf. *Arg.* 1. 75–6, *operis tanti . . . fama*). For *coepta* as referring to literary work, cf. Verg. *G.* 1. 40; Ov. *Ars* 1. 30, 771, *Met.* 1. 2; referring to great deeds, Liv. 42. 59. 7; Curt. 8. 6. 20; referring to both simultaneously, Luc. 1. 200; Sil. 1. 342. For *opus* as referring to literary work, cf. Cic. *Inv.* 2. 5; Hor. *Ep.* 2. 2. 92; *TLL* s.v.

The voyage of Argo is, as it were, one volume of Jupiter's larger story of the universe, the eternal *opus* whose scroll he unrolls (*aeternum uoluens opus*, 2. 358).[17] Jupiter's interest in this heroic performance is intense. His basic motivation is to end the Golden Age and inaugurate the Iron, as we are told by the words which immediately follow the lines quoted in the previous paragraph: *patrii neque enim probat otia regni* ('for he does not approve of the leisure of his father's reign', 1. 500).[18] Hereby he may open heaven to his sons (1. 563-7), and oversee the disruption of inertia which will lead to the testing of nations and the establishment of Roman dominion (1. 542-60).[19] The Argonauts will be the first to attain true fame by deeds of war (1. 539-41, 545-6, 563-6); in the Golden Age, after all, there was no warfare.[20] As a chronicle of the first heroic action of all, with a cast of demigods straining to apotheosis, this poem is being impelled towards true epic greatness by its pair of divine and human creators.

And yet, impatient readers will have been saying, remembering their Apollonius, and thinking ahead to the climax of Valerius' work, and yet the expedition of Argo is a love story. Indeed it is, and no one is more aware of the fact than Valerius himself. Early on in the first book, in a moment of transparent self-referential humour of the sort that no Roman poet ever cared to deny himself, he has Jason address the following words to Acastus, as he tries to persuade him to join the expedition: *nunc forsan graue reris opus* ('at this stage perhaps you consider this to be a grievous/weighty task/work', 1. 170).[21] At the climactic moment when

849. 66–850. 20; referring to great deeds, Cic. *Marc.* 12; Liv. 1. 21. 5; Sen. *Suas.* 2. 5; TLL s.v. 840. 76–841. 84; referring to both simultaneously, Verg. *Aen.* 10. 792; Stat. *Theb.* 1. 504, 6. 359, 11. 100.

[17] For *uoluo* as a word for unrolling a scroll, cf. Cic. *Brut.* 298, and the other passages cited at OLD s.v. §9. Valerius is taking up Vergilian language again, from the passage where Jupiter says *uoluens fatorum arcana mouebo*, *Aen.* 1. 262 (though some readers will react as does Henry (1873–92) ad loc., on the possibility of such a meaning in Vergil: 'I need hardly add that I cannot see even so much as the shadow of a ground for the opinion').

[18] We return below to this vital theme.

[19] Whether the Roman Empire is in fact the fated end of Jupiter's preview is much debated: Burck (1979), 232; Barnes (1981), 361; Schubert (1984), 38–9.

[20] See the passages referred to by Gatz (1967), 229, in his 'conspectus locorum', 4 b), *absentia belli*.

[21] Again, the language is equally appropriate to the journey or the poem: for the reference of *grauis* to the weightiness of the higher genres, especially epic, see Brink (1971), on Hor. *Ars* 14; McKeown (1989), on Ov. *Am.* 1. 1. 1.

Medea meets Jason to give him her indispensable help, she asks him, in effect, why he has not delivered conventional epic action:

> unde mei spes ulla tibi, tantosque petisti
> cur non ipse tua fretus uirtute labores?

Where did you get any expectation of depending on me? And why didn't you rely on your own valour when you sought out such vast labours? (7. 438-9)

The pervasive generic tussle created here, as the *Argonautica* strains to remain an epic of martial endeavour in the face of the threat of the love theme, is one of the poem's most diverting features. We will devote some discussion to it, before returning to the question of Jupiter's Iron Age, for it is in this context that some of Valerius' insights into the gods of epic emerge most clearly.

Very few formal aspects of Roman literature are more striking than the rigidity with which it defined epic. Epic is *reges et proelia*, as Vergil put it (*Ecl.* 6. 3): 'kings and battles'. Roman poets embraced this starkness under the powerful influence of Callimachean poetics, and in revolt against the same panegyrical epic tradition which itself produced Callimachus' reaction. Roman poets' formal pronouncements on epic lull one into forgetting that there had ever been an *Odyssey*, with a number of love themes at its core, with swineherds, oxherds, beggars as characters, and lumps of meat as victory trophies.[22] Yet this bluffness is a façade. As the work of Hinds, above all, has recently been demonstrating for us, Roman generic practice needs these apparently trenchant demarcations in order to achieve its effects of complication and disturbance: the confines of a genre can be established only by testing them, sometimes, it appears, almost to destruction.[23]

---

[22] Horace, for example, is really only describing half of Homer when he says *res gestae regumque ducumque et tristia bella / quo scribi possent numero, monstrauit Homerus* (*Ars* 73-4).

[23] Hinds (1987), (1989). Readers of Hinds's work will recognize how much I owe to his stimulating insights. Nicoll (1980) has an acute analysis of the tension between epic and elegy in the opening portions of Ovid's *Metamorphoses*. Cairns (1972), 127-31, has a valuable discussion of 'alterations of primary elements'. Cairns's approach is more authoritarian than that of Hinds, for he is more interested in how genres assert and maintain themselves than in how they constantly redefine themselves under pressure (especially clear in his discussion of 'inclusion', 158); cf. Cairns (1989), on Vergil and elegy, where the key language is 'harmonise' (137), 'reabsorb' (150). Still, I feel that Cairns's rather less nuanced approach is, in

Changing only the last word, we may adapt one of Hinds's sentences (describing Ovid's *Fasti*) to Valerius: 'the poem's generic self-consciousness is expressed not just in observance but also in creative transgression of the expected bounds of *epic*'.[24]

It is perhaps worth saying that this feature of Roman poetry is, of course, an exaggeration of Greek preoccupations, not something utterly novel. In our context, the most pertinent example is Apollonius, and especially his 'contamination' of epic with tragedy.[25] The meeting of Medea and Jason in Book 3 (948–1147), for example, is a tragic scene, with a chorus of twelve dancing maidens 'on stage', and with exchanged speeches between two 'actors'. Yet the key point is the way in which Apollonius maintains his focus on generic difference even as he blends another form into his work. Medea, for example, stops speaking at 3. 1062, and thinks gloomily of the future, before resuming her speech six lines later. Ancient tragedy, without stage-directions, was incapable of writing in a gap in one of a pair of speeches—let alone telling its audience the content of unspoken thoughts. After the scene closes, when Medea meets her sister, we are told that Chalciope asked her a question which Medea did not hear (1155–8). Again, in a tragedy it is not possible to have a question which is not heard; Apollonius is once more highlighting the uniqueness of his own form.[26]

Valerius is, however, qualitatively different from Apollonius in his treatment of the epic problem. His inherited attitudes to epic posited a far more fixed notion of the form ('kings and battles'); his epic predecessors (amongst whom, for this purpose, we include Ovid) had themselves used those fixed notions as a challenge to definition; and his tradition also gave him a powerful alternative genre which might be his natural (almost inevitable) counterpart— love elegy. Apollonius did not have this rigid pre-existing dichotomy, and his undermining of epic, fascinating and remorseless

the end, closer to what is achieved by the less nuanced Valerius. Finally, one is, as always, struck by Kroll's characteristic insight and clarity: 'die Kreuzung der Gattungen', Kroll (1924), 202–24.

[24] Hinds (1987), 117.

[25] Fränkel (1968), 399; Hunter (1989), 18.

[26] The matter is complicated yet further by the fact that it is radically un-Homeric of Apollonius not to report the words of Chalciope's question (since Medea did not hear it?). Apollonius has violated epic convention in order to make his point as starkly as possible: he finds himself compelled to move away from epic in order to demonstrate that he is returning to it after his tragic interlude.

though it may be, is consequently carried on in a less starkly demarcated arena: one sees what Hügi means when he says that Apollonius' third book is 'stark lyrisch-elegisch gefarbt', but one must acknowledge that his language is, strictly, anachronistic.[27] Valerius will have seen even in Vergil the confrontation of the two genres of epic and elegy. As a coda to his discussion of Ovid, Hinds touches on the destabilizations which come upon the *Aeneid* when it runs into Dido, and Cairns' recent book treats the subject of Dido as an elegiac heroine in detail.[28] An epic of grand achievement which relies on a love-affair for its consummation is going to confront these dilemmas in their most naked form.

The problems begin for Valerius and his heroes even before they get to Colchis. The first challenge to the crews' manhood comes at Lemnos, where the women have killed all their menfolk.[29] The episode is introduced with almost enough grandeur and background for a separate epic (2. 82–106);[30] Valerius has the full apparatus of Venus and Fama to activate the women's massacre (2. 101–34), on the model of Juno and Allecto in *Aeneid* 7; and at the end a divine reconciliation provides the resolution (315). The massacre-narrative is striving for greatness throughout, as Venus declares early on: *non . . . magnum aliquid spirabit amor?* ('will love not inspire some great deed?', 182–4).[31] Venus arrives to supervise the slaughter of the sleeping and helpless men 'girded for battle' (197); she is 'the wife of Mars' as she gives the signal (208). Valerius addresses Hypsipyle in grandiose terms, praising her for alone sparing her father, and promising her immortality in his poetry for as

[27] Hügi (1952), 80. Here is the weak link in Margolies' excellent treatment of Apollonius' generic play with Medea's effect on the *Argonautica*: all her evidence for seeing Callimachus as a love-poet is Roman (Margolies (1981), 158, n. 5), as she admits (168). Stimulating and compelling as her discussion is, it is painted in stronger colours than Apollonius' comparatively more fluid tradition ultimately allows. Of course Apollonius looks as if he is using an elegy-epic dichotomy to organize his effects, but he looks that way because we have read Propertius and Ovid and Vergil.

[28] Hinds (1987), 133–4; Cairns (1989), 135–50; see Cairns 135–6 for earlier discussions.

[29] Here I am indebted to the commentary on Book 2 by Harper-Smith (1988); she points out clearly the significance of the language used at 197 and 237.

[30] Mehmel (1934), 13–14; cf. Bahrenfuss (1951), 101–2, on the high epic colour of Venus' actions here.

[31] Cf. Hypsipyle's description of their deed, in Apollonius, as a μέγα ἔργον ('great deed', 1. 662).

long as the Roman Empire lasts (242–6). Jupiter himself co-
operates at the beginning and centre of the episode (199, 356).[32]
Yet all the while the epic poet is being exercised by the desperate difficulty of keeping this narrative 'straight'. Venus' very question (*non . . . magnum aliquid spirabit amor?*) is an oxymoron.
The poet finds himself, after all, obliged to give the full epic treatment to wives killing husbands under the direction of Venus, and
he protests at the difficulty of the task (216–19). A series of inversions springs from this basic inversion. Venus lashes the women
into the marriage-chamber (215)—but to murder, not sleep with,
their men. As some of the husbands try to flee from their burning
houses, they are confronted with a grisly inverse *paraclausithyron*:
*sed dura in limine coniunx / obsidet* ('but their hard wife is
planted there on the threshold, in siege position', 237–8). The
bluntest signs of the generic strain come once the Argonauts arrive
and become lovers. At the end of the episode, the archetypal epic
hero, Hercules, calls the men back to their epic task from dalliance
with the Lemnian women: 'It was love only of deeds that dragged
me out to sea with you,' he says to Jason, and the Latin word
order impels the supplement, 'not love of *women*' (*me tecum solus
in aequor / rerum traxit amor*, 380–1). As the expedition is saved
from elegiac sloth, the helmsman seeks 'tackle and crew' to restart
the great enterprise: enjambed, as object, are the first words of the
*Aeneid* (*arma uiros*, 392). Two physical descriptions of the island
frame the episode and show the two extremes it has been made to
encompass. At the epic beginning, 'and now Vulcan's Lemnos
rises up, on the very peak of the waves' (*et iam summis Vulcania
surgit / Lemnos aquis*, 78–9).[33] As the Argonauts sail away,
'Lemnos becomes fine' (*tunc tenuis Lemnos*, 431).[34] From beginning

---

[32] In the second passage, Jupiter appears to be allowing time for the Argonauts'
love because he is heeding Astraea and providing grief for the humans (361–4): this
stopover is a *dolor* (393).

[33] *surgere* is the verb which Ovid uses of his epic attempts in *Am.* 1. 1. 27 (see
McKeown (1989) ad loc. for further examples of the verb's grand register).

[34] 'Fine' is a makeshift, for I cannot think of an English word that will capture at
once the physical sense (Lemnos becomes a faint sight in the distance), and the
neoteric, Callimachean register of the word ('fine', 'slender': on this register see
Nisbet and Hubbard (1970), on Hor. *Carm.* 1. 6. 9; Ross (1975), index s.v.). This
neoteric language is already utterly hackneyed by the end of Horace's career; at *Ep.*
2. 1. 224–5 he makes fun of the way poets moan about how their fine neoteric
effects go unnoticed (*cum lamentamur non apparere labores / nostros et tenui
deducta poemata filo*; the last phrase is, as it were, in inverted commas).

to end, the sense of generic strain is placed in the foreground in a manner which is quite un-Apollonian.[35]

It is, in fact, Hercules' separation from the expedition in the next book which tips the balance. Jupiter rounds on Juno, who was responsible for making sure that Hercules would not participate any more; the burden of his words is nothing but 'So this is your idea of how to run an epic': *sic Iuno ducem fouet anxia curis / Aesonium, sic arma uiro sociosque ministrat* ('. . . this is how Juno provides *arms for a man*, and allies', 4. 7–8). Robbing Jason of Hercules means that the gaining of the fleece cannot remain a martial endeavour: now, says Jupiter, Juno will have to fall back on the Furies, and Venus, and Medea (*i, Furias Veneremque moue; dabit improba poenas / uirgo*, 13–14).[36]

Our expectation of some interesting complications in Colchis is reinforced *en route*, when Valerius presents us with a literal *praeteritio*, as the Argonauts sail by the Amazons' territory, sacred to the war-god Mars, without stopping and fighting (5. 120–39). This piece of drollery at the Argonauts' expense is already in Apollonius, who says that the heroes would have fought with the Amazons, and taken casualties, if winds from Zeus had not sped them past the danger (2. 985–95). Again, however, the generic implications are so much more to the foreground in the Latin poet. As he sails past, inactive, Jason asks some former comrades of Hercules to tell him of their mighty deeds against the Amazons; his command is crammed with programmatic language of epic,[37] yet he can only listen in silence to the lofty theme (5. 131–3). Immediately thereafter, the Argonauts pass by the Chalybes, the famous metallurgists, the inventors of weapons (5. 140–6). Valerius appears to be turning these creatures into the Telchines of Callimachus' *Aetia* prologue (1. 1), who were likewise spoken of

---

[35] Though I by no means wish to imply that Apollonius' Lemnian episode is generically flat; the parody of the agora-scene, in particular, is marvellously done (1. 653–708); cf. Margolies (1981), 45, on the Aristophanic colour to Apollonius' Lemnian women. It is simply that Apollonius' tradition had not undergone the same remarkable polarizations as Valerius'.

[36] It was Venus, assimilated to the condition of a Fury, who was responsible for the Lemnian episode (2. 101–6).

[37] *'uos mihi nunc pugnas' ait 'et uictricia' ductor / 'Herculis arma mei uestrasque in litore Martis / interea memorate manus'*, 5. 129–31. For the programmatic force of such language, see McKeown (1989) on Ov. *Am.* 1. 1. 1; Hinds (1987), 133–4. As Professor Hinds points out to me, the war Jason hears about is itself decidedly odd, a *belli uirginei* ('a war fought against *virgins*', 5. 132–3).

as the first metallurgists (though normally situated in Rhodes, not Asia Minor). The activity of the Chalybes is described in terms which make them sound like industrious epic poets, working hard all night, exhausting themselves in the production of *arma*.[38]

When he arrives at Colchis itself, the poet does not invoke the Muse and theme of love, as had Apollonius (3. 1–5). He still hopes to have a martial narrative, even if Medea will figure:[39]

> Incipe nunc cantus alios, dea, uisaque uobis
> Thessalici da bella ducis. non mens mihi, non haec
> ora satis. uentum ad furias infandaque natae
> foedera et horrenda trepidam sub uirgine puppem;
> impia monstriferis surgunt iam proelia campis.

Now begin other songs, goddess, and tell me the wars of the Thessalian chief [Jason] which you saw. My mind, my mouth are not enough. We have come to the madness and the unspeakable compacts of the princess, and the ship quaking beneath the dread virgin; now impious battles rise up from the plains with their crop of monsters. (5. 217–21)

He does indeed engineer an entire book of mighty war-narrative, as the Argonauts fight on King Aeetes' side in a Colchian civil war (Book 6).[40] All is organized on the grand epic plane, with a council of the gods to introduce the action (5. 618–95), with two invocations of the Muse (6. 33–41, 515–16), with interventions from Mars (6. 1–9, 279–80), Pallas (6. 173–81, 396–8, 739–51), and Juno (6. 650–1), and even an Iliadic address from Jupiter as he sees one of his sons coming to his death (621–30; cf. *Il.* 16. 431–8).

In the middle of the battle, however, Juno realises it is all futile:

> Talia certatim Minyae sparsique Cytaei
> funera miscebant campis Scythiamque premebant,
> cum Iuno Aesonidae non hanc ad uellera cernens

---

[38] *peruigil auditur Chalybum labor: arma fatigant / ruricolae, Gradiue, tui*, 5. 141–2.

[39] Wetzel (1957), 39–45, has good comments on the difference between Valerius and Apollonius here, and on the effects Valerius gains by postponing the love theme until after the announcement of war.

[40] Thus taking up a hint of declined epic action in Apollonius, who mentions the possibility of the Argonauts performing a great martial feat in order to induce Aeetes to give them the fleece (3. 351–3). It may be that Valerius here is following an alternative tradition in which the Argonauts did fight a great battle for Aeetes; see Hunter (1989) on the Apollonius passage.

esse uiam nec sic reditus regina parandos
extremam molitur opem . . .
sola animo Medea subit, mens omnis in una
uirgine, nocturnis qua nulla potentior aris.

Such were the deaths that the Minyae and scattered Cytaei, in competition with each other, were strewing over the plain, overwhelming Scythia,
when Juno, seeing that this is not the way for Jason to get the fleece, and
that this is not how to achieve his return home, sets in train her final
resource . . . Medea alone comes to her thoughts, her whole mind is on
this one girl, who is more powerful than anyone in the altars of the night.
(6. 427–40)

The confrontation between the irrelevant grandiosity of martial
epic and the present needs of this poem could not be more starkly
engineered. In order to ensnare her victim, Juno borrows Venus'
girdle, the 'arms' of Venus' children (*natorum . . . arma meorum*,
6. 475), and brings the helpless Medea to the walls, so that she
may see Jason in action (455–91); in the next book, the goddess of
love will herself take part in the seducing of Medea's mind (7.
153–399). The poem's great set-piece battle book is undermined,
to become only an occasion for the girl to fall in love with her
future husband; Jason's greatest moment of heroic action is engineered by Juno in order to impress Medea (6. 600–20). The hypertrophy of epic apparatus in the book of warfare (indeed, the
hypertrophy of epic apparatus from the beginning of the poem)
begins to look like an effect of polarization, a desperate reaction
against the collapse that will come when Medea takes over.

Yet it is, after all, only his own straw man whom the poet topples
here. Valerius' rigid dichotomy between grave martial epic and
lesser forms emerges as, in one aspect, a way of sharpening our
apprehension of the true power and compass of epic. For it will
not have escaped readers' notice that when Valerius turns from his
grand epic theme to introduce Medea, he does so by way of the
goddesses of the *Iliad*. He goes beyond even Apollonius to the
scene in *Iliad* 14 (188–223), where Hera borrows the girdle of
Aphrodite in order to seduce Zeus.[41] Again, the very fine scene in
which Medea is led to the walls by Juno is modelled, in reverse, on
the magnificent moment in the *Iliad* when Aphrodite meets Helen

---

[41] Valerius' Juno pretends to Venus that she needs the girdle for the same reason
as she had (or, strictly, will) in the *Iliad* (6. 462–6).

on the walls of Troy, and compels her to return to the bed-chamber of Paris (3. 383–420).[42] Valerius deliberately forswears the Cupid of Apollonius, adhering to the great goddesses, and maintaining a sombre and oppressive atmosphere throughout their scenes.[43] He also forswears Ovid's forswearing of the divine machinery, reinstating an explicit divine dimension to the passion of Medea, which Ovid had kept within the circuit of the heroine's consciousness.[44]

The generic fixation on martial achievement as such turns out to be something of a false lead, for, once this option for the poem has been exploded, Valerius does not move to the apparently necessary polar alternative of slight, frivolous, or godless narration.[45] We remember that when Jupiter had to give up on his great martial *opus* with the abandonment of Hercules, the inevitable alternatives were 'the Furies and Venus' (*Furias Veneremque*, 4. 13)—who are themselves creatures of epic.[46] The poem becomes a radically different sort of epic from the one which it had been trying to be at the outset, but it remains an epic, as Valerius' careful acknowledgements of his tradition continually remind us: it remains a poem committed to the narration of human action

[42] Vergil, too, is inextricable from these scenes. The colloquy of Juno and Venus in *Aeneid* 4 is behind the former (cf. esp. *Arg.* 6. 467 and *Aen.* 4. 127–8). Dido is behind the latter: the description of Medea as *futuri nescia* (*Arg.* 6. 490–1) goes back to the description of Dido as *fati nescia* (*Aen.* 1. 299), and Valerius uses Vergil's key phrase *at regina* of Medea (*Arg.* 6. 657; cf. *Aen.* 4. 1, 296, 504); see here Wetzel (1957), 69.

[43] Even darker and more claustrophobic is the prolonged scene in which Venus visits Medea, disguised as Circe, and guides her to meet Jason (7. 193–399).

[44] *Met.* 7. 9–99 (above, p. 239). Professor Hinds draws my attention to the way in which Valerius restores the action of Juno in beautifying Jason, elided by Ovid: in *Met.* 7. 84, when Medea sees him for the first time, Jason is '*by chance* more beautiful than normal', whereas in Valerius Juno is explicitly responsible (5. 363–5; cf. Ap. Rhod. 3. 919–23, Hera beautifying Jason).

[45] Although he flirts with the possibility when Jason and Medea meet for the first time (5. 350–98). Here there is no mention of Cupid or Venus; only the action of Juno restoring Jason's beauty, worn by his journey (5. 363–5; cf. Hom. *Od.* 6. 229–35).

[46] Despite the fact that Jason compares himself to Hercules (5. 487–8), his deed is actually performed for him by a woman, and therefore does not resemble Hercules' labours at all. This point is stressed again when Jason actually has possession of the fleece, a moment described as his 'last labour' (8. 117); again he is compared to Hercules (8. 125–6), and again the simile points up the vast gulf between their deeds. At the corresponding place in Apollonius, as Professor Hinds reminds me, Jason is compared to a young girl (4. 167–71); Valerius undoes Jason's heroic status by the opposite route. On Jason and Hercules, see, further, Adamietz (1970), esp. 36–8.

through the divine. Certainly, it has become a very Ovidian epic, and Medea is a very Ovidian creature, with many of the features of an elegiac heroine,[47] but the confrontation of the elegiac and epic world is seen through a new filter by the continual references to Homer, which remind us that the first epic poet claimed the right to illuminate any aspect of human life by using the gods. These Homeric references, as we have seen, crowd in at the moment when Juno leads Medea to the wall, but they begin when Medea and Jason first meet (5. 363–5). We do not hear there of Cupid or Venus, but of Juno, and she is acting as Athene had acted when Odysseus met Nausicaa (*Od.* 6. 229–35).

Valerius is engineering the wreckage of his grandiose epic gestures in order to show that the collapse reveals a more humane and comprehensive epic tradition still standing behind the rubble. To arrive at the position where this collapse can be most effective, he needs to establish an exaggeratedly epic manner in advance. Thus his copy-book rewriting of the Hylas episode into the modes of grand epic, with a colloquy between two goddesses to start it off, and a visit from a grand deity to an underling to engineer the human's doom; thus his provision of divine motive and participation for the story of Cyzicus.[48] He needs to establish a yardstick within his own poem with which to measure his responses to the intrusive presence of Medea. There, his modes will be Homeric, and epic, but turned to novel and un-Homeric ends: not only the awakening of a frenzied and obsessive sexual passion, but the gradual and Ovidian awakening of this passion.[49]

Jupiter is cheated, then, of the mighty conventional epic which he had expected at the beginning, the kind of epic which his taste in poetry would lead him to appreciate.[50] The actions of Valerius' heroes and heroines none the less take place within an organized epic world, whose order is maintained by Jupiter. Valerius gives an unusually explicit allegory of this world order at the beginning of the Lemnos episode (2. 82–6); cosmological lore is appropri-

---

[47] Wetzel (1957), 104–7; cf. Summers (1894), 24–5.

[48] 3. 487–564 (Hylas); 3. 14–331 (Cyzicus). Neither of these stories has any divine dimension to it in Apollonius: see Garson (1963), 266, on Valerius' innovations here.

[49] On the novelty and skill with which Valerius reveals the gradual process of Medea's infatuation, see Summers (1894), 24–5; Wetzel (1957), 96.

[50] Jupiter likes listening to Gigantomachies (5. 692–3).

ately out of place at this bizarre moment, as part of the tremendous tension between high and low which we have seen governing the entire episode. Valerius activates here possibly the most famous Homeric allegory of all, the golden chain by which Zeus held Hera suspended from heaven, with two anvils around her ankles (*Il.* 15. 18–24). The outrage to decorum was alleviated by the ancient allegorists, who discovered a physical allegory in the passage, an emblem of the four elements which made up the cosmic order: Zeus is the *aether* at the top, Hera the next element down, the *aer*, and the two anvils represent the two heavier elements beneath, earth and water.[51] It is plain that Valerius refers to the allegorical interpretation at this point, for he has placed his suspension of Juno in a context of cosmic organization. In Homer, Zeus' motive is to punish Hera for her persecution of Heracles (15. 24–8), whereas Valerius has Jupiter acting to preserve his new order (the order of his realm, the *aether*) against the grumblings of the other gods; and he shows Juno the alternative to his reign, dread chaos (thus importing the second main passage in Homer which was analysed for its picture of the universe's organization):[52]

> Tempore quo primum fremitus insurgere opertos
> caelicolum et regni sensit nouitate tumentes
> Iuppiter aetheriae nec stare silentia pacis,
> Iunonem uolucri primam suspendit Olympo
> horrendum chaos ostendens poenasque barathri.

At the time when Jupiter first noticed that the gods' open rumblings were mounting, as they swelled with resentment at the new dominion, and when he saw that the calm of aetherial peace was disturbed, he suspended Juno first of all from flying Olympus, showing her dread chaos and the punishments of the abyss. (2. 82–6)[53]

The poem makes mention (once at considerable length) of the victory over the Giants and Typhon by which Jupiter established his supremacy.[54] Indeed, as befits Jupiter's taste in high epic

[51] Schol. A *Il.* 15. 18; b 15. 21; Heraclit. *All.* 40; cf. Buffière (1956), 115–17; Lévêque (1959), 27–8 (the bulk of Lévêque's work treats the other 'golden chain' passage, *Il.* 8. 18–27).

[52] That is, *Il.* 8. 13–16; see schol. A on line 16, and cf. Buffière (1956), 213–14.

[53] For other passages where Juno is assimilated to the *aer*, cf. 5. 400–1; 8. 322–3. Jupiter elsewhere is normally associated with the realm of the stars, from his first appearance: 1. 498; 2. 357; 6. 622; *caelum* at 4. 415.

[54] 1. 563–5; 2. 16–33.

poetry, he listens on Olympus to Apollo and the Muses singing the tale of the battles against the Giants at Phlegra (5. 692–3; this is immediately before the humans begin their great epic battle, in Book 6).[55] If he has defeated the threats of chaos, and organized his ordered cosmos, there is still another stage to go for his dispensation to be complete, and it is this stage, as we have seen, which the poem enacts: the inauguration of Jupiter's own Iron Age with the sailing of the first ship.

Valerius uses Vergil's *Georgics* in particular to signal the fact that we are witnessing the end of the Golden Age, and the beginning of Jupiter's kingdom for mankind, the civilization of the Iron Age.[56] We are told that Jupiter 'does not approve of the leisure of his father's reign' (*patrii neque enim probat otia regni*, 1. 500), just as Vergil had said that Jupiter 'did not allow his reign to be slothful in heavy lassitude' (*nec torpere graui passus sua regna ueterno*, G. 1. 124). Jason announces to the crew that 'Jupiter *himself wanted* this interchange between the parts of his universe, and he *wanted* to mingle together the great *labours of mankind*' (*ipse suo uoluit commercia mundo / Iuppiter et tantos hominum miscere labores*,  . 1. 246–7); we are reminded of Vergil's Jupiter, who is responsible for *hominumque boumque labores* ('the labours of mankind and oxen', G. 1. 118), since, as Vergil puts it, 'the father *himself* did not *want* the path of cultivation to be easy' (*pater ipse colendi / haud facilem esse uiam uoluit*, G. 1. 121–2).[57] It is, further, a feature of the Iron Age that it accelerates human mortality;[58] accordingly, as the Iron Age begins in Valerius, we see Jupiter, the other gods, and the Fates rejoicing that new ways of death are opening up (1. 501–2; cf. 1. 648–9).

Valerius, obviously, concentrates on the aspect of the tradition

---

[55] Cf. Hes. *Th.* 71–5, where it appears that the subject-matter of the Muses' song for Zeus is his victory over the Titans, and his organization of the world; cf. Stat. *Theb.* 6. 358, where Apollo sings to the Muses of the Gigantomachy, and *Silv.* 4. 2. 55–6. For Latin poetry's treatment of Gigantomachy as the ultimate high epic topic, see Innes (1979).

[56] Schubert (1984), 24.

[57] On these themes in the *Georgics*, see Thomas (1988), vol. 1. 17, 87, 92–3. A further sign of Valerius' deep equation of his Iron Age with Vergil's is the simile after the first great storm of Book 1, when the Argonauts' propitiation of the sea-gods is compared to farmers' propitiation of the gods during plague and drought (1. 682–5).

[58] Hes. *Op.* 90–2, 116; Hor. *Carm.* 1. 3. 32–3; Sen. *Med.* 338–9.

which saw the invention of navigation and the sailing of the first ship as the vital rupture between the Golden and Iron Ages.[59] From the poem's first word and first line, the emphasis on Argo as the world's first ship is something of overpowering importance for the work as a whole, crowding out even mention of the golden fleece from the proem.[60] Catullus 64 will have been important to Valerius, together with Horace's *Carm.* 1. 3, and Ovid's account of the Ages in *Metamorphoses* 1 (94–5, 132–4); but the key background text is clearly Seneca's magnificent *Medea*, in which the sailing of Argo is insistently represented as the catastrophic harbinger of the violent civilization which we now inhabit.[61] Many of Valerius' turns come principally from Seneca, in particular the use of Argo to emblematize 'civilization's paradoxical dislocation of the world to produce order'.[62] Particularly Senecan, for example, is the force behind the highly pointed use of *discrimina*, a word which appears to be 'dangers' only, but also means 'demarcations', 'ways of keeping things separated'. The Argonauts are going to produce the civilized world of Jupiter's new order by travelling right through *discrimina rerum* (1. 217)—right through the sea, in other words, the thing that keeps the parts of the world separate.[63] Hence Jason's language, quoted in the previous paragraph, of 'interchange' and 'mingling'.[64] It is one of the basic inversions of the Iron Age that its agriculture imposes divisions upon the land while its navigation removes them from the sea.[65]

---

[59] This receives mention in Vergil, of course: *G.* 1. 137–8 (cf. *Ecl.* 4. 32–3, where we see sailing, war, and agriculture as the key differences between the Golden and Iron Ages). See the passages referred to by Gatz (1967), 229, in his 'conspectus locorum', 4 a), *absentia nauium*; and Bömer (1969–86) on Ov. *Met.* 1. 94.

[60] Burck (1979), 233–4; cf. Adamietz (1976), 21; cf. Getty (1940), 261 n. 7, for Valerius' rationale here.

[61] Two choral odes are especially important (301–79 and 579–669). See Preiswerk (1934), 435–41, on the relationship between the *Medea* and Valerius; on these themes in Seneca, see Fyfe (1983). Ovid's lost *Medea* must also have been important.

[62] Fyfe (1983), 87.

[63] Cf. 1. 37, *discrimina ponti*; in Seneca, Argo annulled boundaries by dragging everything together (335–6; cf. 364–5); on this theme in the *Medea*, Fyfe (1983), 86–7.

[64] Cf. Lucan's use of *miscuit* and *composuit* to describe Argo's actions (3. 193, 196).

[65] Verg. *G.* 1. 126–7; Ov. *Met.* 1. 135–6 (note what a marvellously demarcated and organized line Ovid uses for the demarcation of the land: *cautus humum longo signauit limite mensor*).

The task of the Argonauts, then, is to break down boundaries, and the sailing of their ship is comparable to other great breakings of boundaries. First of all, sailing is like flying, a connection hinted at when Argo disappears from the sight of those on shore: *donec iam celsior arbore pontus / immensusque ratem spectantibus abstulit aer* ('until the sea, now higher than the mast, and the immense air took the ship away from their sight', 1. 496–7).[66] More explicit is the simile used to describe Pelias' reaction when he sees Argo disappearing, utterly beyond his power:

> haud secus, aerisona uolucer cum Daedalus Ida
> prosiluit iuxtaque comes breuioribus alis,
> nube noua linquente domos Minoia frustra
> infremuit manus . . .

Just as, when winged Daedalus leapt off Ida as it rang with weapons, his companion on shorter wings beside him, the troops of Minos raged in vain as the novel cloud left the houses of Crete . . . (1. 704–7)

If, in its violation of boundaries, sailing is like flying, it is also very like the assault on heaven performed by the Giants: in the same way, in the second half of his Iron Age poem, *Carm.* 1. 3, Horace links the sailing of the first ship with the flight of Daedalus and the Gigantomachy (21–40). It is here that the complexity of the motif becomes most apparent, for the daring assault of the Argonauts upon the sea is sometimes presented in the poem as a piece of wantonness which is parallel to that of the Giants, and sometimes as a display of daring which entitles them to apotheosis.[67] Attempting to gain admission to heaven, as we have seen repeatedly, is something magnificent or outrageous, but it is in either case the product of excessive, superhuman behaviour—the path of the demi-gods or the path of the Giants.[68]

The gods of the sea obviously regard Argo's sailing as an outrage: it is wrong, mad, and a threat (*nefas*, 1. 598; *insanam . . . ratem*,

---

[66] Note how Apollo appears to equate the sailing of Argo with the temerity of his son, Phaethon, who disturbed cosmic order by riding through heaven (1. 525–7).

[67] Strand (1972), 8–9, sees only the optimistic side of the paradigm as operative. See, rather, Adamietz (1976), 25, on the difference in attitude between the sea-gods and Jupiter, and, especially, the judicious discussion of Schubert (1984), 24–5: 'Von vorherein erscheint hier die Beurteilung der Schiffahrt ambivalent' (25).

[68] pp. 160, 297.

605; *hominum . . . minas*, 606). The parallel with the effrontery of the Giants is so obvious that Jason does all he can to disavow it before they sail, in his prayer to Neptune:

> scio me cunctis e gentibus unum
> inlicitas temptare uias hiememque mereri:
> sed non sponte feror, nec nunc mihi iungere montes
> mens tamen aut summo deposcere fulmen Olympo.

I know that I alone out of all the nations am trying out forbidden paths, and deserve to meet a storm. But I am being borne along against my will, and it is not my intention to put one mountain on another, or call down the thunderbolt from the peak of Olympus. (1. 196–9)

After the great storm has been stilled by Neptune, Jason once again prays to him, and the other sea-gods. He pours libations from a dish which he has inherited from his great-grandfather, Salmoneus, famous for the fantastic impiety of imitating Jupiter, and for calling down upon himself the real thunderbolt (1. 660–5). The impious, transgressive character of the expedition cannot easily be talked away.[69]

Jupiter himself compares the expedition to the Gigantomachy, but in accordance with his determination to see the ameliorative aspect of the paradigm, he appropriates the Argonauts to his side in the combat, and concentrates on their claim to apotheosis:

> tendite in astra, uiri: me primum regia mundo
> Iapeti post bella trucis Phlegraeque labores
> imposuit; durum uobis iter et graue caeli
> institui.

Strive on to the stars, men: royal power placed me in control of the universe only after the war against fierce Iapetus, and the labours of Phlegra; for you I have instituted a hard and grievous route to heaven. (1. 563–6)

He is addressing his sons in particular here, the Dioscuri and Hercules (561–2), and only these three have explicit similes linking their deeds to deeds performed against Giants or Titans.[70] But there is no doubt that the programme is more comprehensive,

---

[69] Shelton (1974–5), 18, notes the links between the two passages of prayer, but attempts to gloss over the problematic implications of the second: 'By observing that this *patera* was owned by Salmoneus before, and not after, his great act of impiety, the poet suggests that the Argonauts are not guilty of a similar offense.' In *Aeneid* 6 (585–94), Salmoneus is Vergil's great counter-example to Augustus, embodying the mad risks of a mortal claiming divine honours for himself.

[70] 3. 130–4; 4. 236–8.

referring to the Argonauts as a whole, and to all subsequent mankind.[71] In Jupiter's new world, tremendous acts of power may indeed, for all their danger of impious madness, elevate to godhead. Even Jason is surrounded by hints of this attainment. At the moment of his arrival in Aeetes' palace, Jason is described as having 'the face of a star' (*sideris ora ferens*, 5. 466). As in the model scene, when Aeneas arrives at the palace of Dido (*Aen.* 1. 588–93), the appearance of the hero has clear tokens of apotheosis.[72] Further, the phrase reminds the reader of the future god Pollux, with his *sidereo ore* (4. 190), and *siderea fronte* (4. 331). Similarly, Jason is compared to the great prototype of apotheosis, Hercules, the model even for the Dioscuri.[73] Yet we know that Jason will fail; only poetry, this poem and others, will elevate him to the stars (4. 555).

The proem itself presents this two-sidedness, with its address to the emperor Vespasian, who, like Jupiter, rules the world after a mighty war.[74] Here the sailing of Ocean is the path to the stars in the case of Vespasian, but something resented by Ocean in the case of Julius Caesar and Claudius, members of the recently supplanted and discredited house of the Julio-Claudians:

> tuque o pelagi cui maior aperti
> fama, Caledonius postquam tua carbasa uexit
> Oceanus, Phrygios prius indignatus Iulos,
> eripe me populis et habenti nubila terrae.

And you, who have the greater glory of having opened up the sea, after the Caledonian Ocean carried your sails, while it had earlier felt indignation at the Phrygian Iuli, deliver me from the nations, and from the earth with its clouds. (1. 7–10)[75]

---

[71] Lüthje (1971), 39–40; Schubert (1984), 40. All humans, according to Mopsus, have a share of the Olympian divine fire (3. 380).

[72] See now Nicoll (1988), 469–70. The fact that Valerius has his eye on the Vergilian scene is shown even by the way in which he 'tidies up' Vergil's mysterious treatment of the cloud's disappearance (*Aen.* 1. 586–7); Valerius' Jason definitely takes the initiative and bursts out of the cloud (5. 465).

[73] 5. 486–7; 8. 125–6; cf. Adamietz (1970), 36–8.

[74] That Vespasian is the emperor addressed in the proem seems to me to have been established by the arguments of Strand (1972), 23–38; Ehlers (1971–2), 113–15.

[75] The reference to the Iulii applies in the first instance to the abortive expeditions of Julius Caesar in 55 and 54 BCE; if pressed, it will yield allusion to the farcical campaigns of Caligula as well (Suet. *Cal.* 46–7).

Crossing the Ocean is the natural development of the temerity of sailing motif: in a fragment of the historical epic of Albinovanus Pedo, describing the journey of Germanicus over Ocean in 16 CE, we see the very concentration on the impiety of the attempt which we have been observing as one of Valerius' perspectives:[76]

> di reuocant rerumque uetant cognoscere finem
> mortales oculos: aliena quid aequora remis
> et sacras uiolamus aquas diuumque quietas
> turbamus sedes?

The gods call us back, and forbid mortal eyes to know the end of the universe. Why do we violate with our oars seas that do not belong to us, holy waters? Why do we disturb the quiet abode of the gods?

The crossing of Ocean, then, is a fretful topic in Imperial literature. Valerius, however, appears to be diverting as much of the anxiety as possible away from Vespasian and onto the Julio-Claudians (just as, with his stress on the harmonious links between Vespasian, Titus, and Domitian (12–16), he appears to be celebrating right family relations after the recent chaos of Nero). Indeed, for all his immersion in the tradition's inescapably anxious treatment of human daring, Valerius' entire treatment of this range of ideas tends powerfully towards the ameliorative. Self-conscious he certainly is, even humorous, in his epic plotting of striving after greatness; yet he somehow refrains from the final ironies which mark the work of his predecessor, Apollonius.[77]

This attempt to salvage an area of achieved dignity has its place in a general tendency in the poem. As far as the gods are concerned, the markedly humane colour of the *Argonautica* manifests itself in a caring and sustaining relation between men and gods, of a sort not seen in extant epic since Homer, and in vignettes of an optimistic vision of humanity's place in the divine order. Certainly there are hideous and frightening encounters between gods and

---

[76] See the Elder Seneca's first *Suasoria* ('Alexander deliberates whether to sail the Ocean') for the topics. It is in this piece that Seneca quotes the twenty-three lines that are all we have of Albinovanus Pedo (15). Winterbottom (1974), 2. 505 n. 2, appositely cites Tac. *Germ.* 34. 2 as another example of the divine barriers to such expeditions. Summers (1894), 7 well speculates on the effects Valerius might have achieved, if he had finished his poem, by bringing the Argonauts through the North Sea (a route which, as he points out, they take in the *Orphic Argonautica*).

[77] Vessey (1982), 582–3.

humans; Medea's manipulation by Juno and Venus is highly repellent, as are Venus' antics at Lemnos.[78] Yet these scenes have more than a counterbalance. The open aid given to Jason when he first prays to Juno and Pallas is remarkable for its alacrity and solicitude (1. 91–9). Pallas listens to him when he prays to her, saying *eripe me* ('deliver me', 1. 88), speaking in the very words used by the poet himself to Vespasian (1. 10), the same words which the captive Hesione will use to Hercules (2. 489–90). Jason is protected throughout by 'gods who are allies and leaders, and by the kind art of Pallas' (*sociis ducibusque deis atque arte benigna / Pallados*, 4. 554–5). Valerius entirely removes the ghastly foresight of Apollonius' Hera, so that his Juno's concern for Jason may be unsullied. When Juno has Venus go to operate against Medea, we are told that she was anxious about the outcome, since she was 'still ignorant of the future' (*adhuc ignara futuri*, 7. 192).[79] Juno's traditional malevolence manifests itself only in her rage against Hercules, and Valerius contrives to put even this aspect of her persona in as good a light as possible when he introduces it, by having Juno herself contrast her hatred of Hercules with her benevolent concern for the rest of the company (1. 111–19).

Even the remote father is moved in un-Vergilian (though not altogether un-Homeric) fashion. When Hercules is left behind as he searches for Hylas, Jupiter first expresses Homeric anger against his wife (4. 1–14), but then manifests his concern for his son in an unprecedented manner, by himself anointing Hercules' temples with nectary dew (15–17).[80] The ensuing address by the deified Hylas to the sleeping Hercules veers uncertainly between grandiloquence and sentimentality; unmistakable, at least, is the poet's concern to present a shared and continuing affection (4. 24–37).

Most remarkable of all is the scene which closes the first book. After some hundred lines of blood-curdling necromancy and horror (1. 730–826), Valerius gives us the procession of Jason's dead parents and brother to the Elysian fields (1. 827–50). Here is a sure reward for the virtuous and philosophical (835–9), here is an immediately narrated alleviation of misery. This direct attempt to

---

[78] Burck (1979), 249–51, on Lemnos.
[79] In this respect no better off than the human Medea, who is described as *futuri nescia* (*Arg.* 6. 490–1), like Vergil's Dido, who is *fati nescia* (*Aen.* 1. 299).
[80] Schubert (1984), 201; cf. Jupiter's *cura* for Io (4. 415).

outweigh the earthly suffering is designed to have a solace which cannot be achieved by Vergil's more diffuse images of the Elysian fields (themselves, to some extent, counterbalanced by the numerous scenes of futility which introduce them). It is a tepid and unmoving moment, perhaps, but one which coheres with the poet's general attempts to recover some solace from the dismaying bleakness which the main elements of his tradition had to offer him in its picture of the human place in the scheme of things.

This is a poet whose self-awareness impresses one at every turn. He controls a massively overpowering tradition with insight and poise, and wittily demonstrates his understanding of the false polarities which that tradition threatens to press upon his own responses. If, in the end, this is not enough to make his work one that imperiously claims our attention, we may temper any disappointment by recalling the words of Helen Vendler:[81]

> But when one remembers how many separate talents go to make a formidable poet—talents musical, imaginative, psychological, visual, intellectual, metaphysical, temperamental—one wonders that the thing is done at all. Poets who lack one or more of these talents remind us why we so much admire the few who possessed them all.

## II

Thou art the thing itself; unaccommodated man . . .

Shakespeare, *King Lear,* Act 3, Scene 4

Statius today is perhaps not 'buried in the graveyard of literary history', as was said of him in 1932, nor is he 'in almost total eclipse', as was claimed in 1972, but devotees of his *Thebaid* are still entitled to be baffled at the condescension which smothers appreciation of this gorgeous poem.[82] To some degree, no doubt, this demeaning judgement is the result of the general prejudice against what we are pleased to call 'Silver Latin Literature': the poem is seldom read at all, let alone with the intent care and interest

---

[81] Vendler (1989), 30.

[82] Friedländer (1932), 215; Dudley (1972), xii. Burck (1979), 300–51, and Gossage (1972) may be recommended as sympathetic introductions. For an account of the poem's neglect, and a protest against it, see Ahl (1986), 2804–8.

it deserves. The critical attitudes which scholars have honed for the study of the great classical monuments prove to be worse than useless in reading Silver epic, and it is no surprise that many readers come away disappointed. Even Statius' advocates sometimes help put the halter around their client's neck. If open-minded novices go to Vessey, for example, in order to discover why the *Thebaid* is worth reading, they are likely to receive the impression of an earnest, dogmatic, and sclerotic work—an impression that stifles the sensational flamboyance of a poem which seduced not only its first audience, but audiences up to the Renaissance.[83] Readers who come to the *Thebaid* from Ariosto or Tasso seem to be in a better position to appreciate its power and beauty than readers who come to it from Vergil, so that one finds more sympathetic insight in Lewis's nine pages on the poem, written over fifty years ago, than in anything produced since.[84] Lewis's pages remain even now the most stimulating discussion of the aspect of the poem which engages us here, its treatment of the divine.[85]

Statius' use of the gods in the *Thebaid* is an astonishing exercise of resilient originality in the face of a tradition which must have threatened any sense of adequacy he possessed. Some will find this claim preposterous, and I shall do what I can to convince them of its worth. Conventional criticisms of Statius' divine machinery are extremely fragile, for they labour under the misapprehension that the poet is some sort of victim of his inherited matter. It has been my invariable experience in reading the *Thebaid* that, if you take

[83] 'Seduce' is my ameliorative gloss on Juvenal's picture of the *Thebaid* as a delectable prostitute, captivating the city, with Statius as her pimp (7. 82–6); for the impact of Statius on the Middle Ages and Renaissance, see Venini (1970), vii (though even this sympathetic critic must speak of the poem's 'larga, per non dire eccessiva, fortuna durante il Medioevo e il Rinascimento'). Vessey (1973) and (1982) are very important studies, to which all students of Statius are indebted, but I share the misgivings of Burck (1979), 306 n. 19, 338 n. 86, and Ahl (1986), 2810–11, concerning Vessey's overly rigid Stoic interpretations. There must be something wrong with a reading technique which can obliterate even something as clear as the difference between Polynices and Eteocles: Vessey (1973), 65–7, 78–81.

[84] Lewis (1936), 48–56; note especially 56 on the poem's 'charm', its 'graceful and romantic variation', its inspiration of 'so many willful beauties' in later literature.

[85] Other treatments of the gods: Legras (1905), 157–205; Schetter (1960), 5–29; Schönberger (1965), 132–7; Vessey (1973), 82–91, 230–69; Burck (1979), 334–43; Schubert (1984); Neri (1986), 2006–26. There are bibliographies in Venini (1970), xxxi–xl; Frassinetti (1973); Vessey (1973), 329–41; *CHCL* 2. 876–7; Ahl (1986), 2905–12.

the criticisms normally made against it and put them to the poem for answer, the poet is already there ahead of you. By way of example, before coming to grips with the gods, let us pause here for a moment, and deal with the charge that the poem is episodic.[86]

As soon as discord has been sown between the brothers, and we have been told of the plan of alternate kingship, Statius introduces his principal motif of divagation: *haec mora pugnae / sola* ('this was the only thing that delayed their fight', 1. 142–3). This delay, compounded with any number of others, puts off the necessary climax for another ten and a half books; it represents a bloated and highly self-conscious adaptation of Vergil's delaying tactics in the last three books of the *Aeneid*, and of Lucan's in the first seven books of the *Bellum Ciuile*.[87] Tydeus' embassy to Thebes in Book 2 is another retardation of the inevitable, as Tydeus declares with his last words to Eteocles: *sed moror* ('but I am causing a delay', 2. 467). At the end of the first three books, when the expedition has yet to start, and after Jupiter has ordered Mars to stop the dallying (3. 233), Adrastus gives us to understand that everything so far has been delay (3. 718–19). When they at last set off, the heroes are unable to progress even so far as a book before they are enmeshed in the narrative of Hypsipyle and the funeral games of Archemorus. The deceased infant's significant name spells out 'Beginner of Doom' (Μόρος, *moros*),[88] but it clearly also denotes 'Originator of Delay' (*mora*), as Statius shows with his references to *morae* at the beginning of the episode (4. 650, 677), and at the end, when the prophet Amphiaraus prays for yet more delays, so that they may never arrive at Thebes (5. 743–5).[89] One half of the poem has gone by, and Jupiter is still angry at the delay to the start of the war (*Atque ea cunctantes Tyrii primordia belli . . .*, 7. 1). In Book 11, the final duel itself is approached through one obstacle after another, as if the poet can hardly bring himself to narrate it.[90]

If a poet expends this much effort on calling attention to the

---

[86] Legras (1905), 152, 277; Williams (1978), 250–2.

[87] Very good discussion in Vessey (1973), 165–7. On Vergil's delays, see Semple (1959–60) (the subject would repay fuller treatment); on Lucan's, above, p. 277.

[88] Mozley (1928), on 4. 718; 5. 647, 738.

[89] Note the frame around the episode formed by *nectam . . . moras* (4. 677), and *innectere . . . moras* (5. 743–4).

[90] 11. 80, 169, 201, 268, 347, 447–8.

eddies and drifts of his narrative, it seems churlish to reproach him
for not proceeding briskly to the point. There seems no good reason why we should not allow ourselves to enjoy the sheer poise of
this procedure, while appreciating its enactment of the expedition's continually threatened collapse into dissolution. Fragmenta-
tion of authority is, as we shall see, one of the poem's main
preoccupations. The organizational powers of the princes are
barely sufficient to keep the expedition, and its poem, on the road;
and the war itself is without order or customary norms: *nullo
uenit ordine bellum, / confusique duces uulgo, et neglecta regen-
tum / imperia* ('the war comes in no order; the leaders are mixed
up with the people, and the commands of the generals are paid no
heed', 7. 616–18).[91] Such is the preparation for the tremendous climax of the brothers' duel, as they meet like two colliding ships at
night, rushing together haphazardly, without skill (*sine more, sine
arte*, 11. 524). Criticism of the poem's episodic progress evaporates before the evidence that the poet calls our attention again
and again to his dilatory manner of narrating—a manner which is
not only diverting but purposeful, as it helps create an environment for the poem's capturing of confusion.

As one of antiquity's most self-consciously professional poets, heir
to an oppressively rich inheritance, Statius confronts his be-
latedness head-on.[92] His explicit addresses to the *Aeneid* and its
characters are only the most overt demonstrations of his awareness that his tradition may suffocate him if he allows it to.[93] It is as
if he disarms his readers' expectation of jadedness by showing that
he has anticipated their worst fears. The tradition crowds around
the poet and his characters at every point, and Statius adopts the
risky strategy of declaring his debts in order for his departures to
stand forth—one thinks of the example of Ovid, who is at his
most original when most sedulously acknowledging allegiance.[94]

---

[91] The passage carries on with more disorder (618–21); related passages include
5. 7–9; 8. 323; 10. 12, 274; 11. 758–9. Dante's sense of justice sets the dead Statius
in a place where nothing happens that is 'sanza ordine' or 'fuor d'usanza' (*Purg.*
21. 40–2).
[92] Hardie (1983) is a splendid introduction to the world of learning and performance which Statius inhabited from childhood.
[93] 10. 445–8; 12. 816–17. Dante is even more overt in displaying his dependence
on the resources of his poetic inheritance, for he makes Vergil and Statius his
actual guides on the journey.
[94] Hinds (1988), 13–19. Vergil, too, is at his most original when he comes

We may see this atmosphere in many incidental moments. Burial, for example, will be a key concern at the poem's close, as was laid down by earlier treatments of the Theban story.[95] To Tydeus, fighting in Book 8, the question of Theban attitude to burial is already an issue (472–3); the character is proleptically aware of the problems which the tradition will force to emerge more than two books after he himself passes out of the poem. Similarly, the horses of Amphiaraus are already afraid of the ground beneath their feet a hundred lines before it will open up to swallow them and their master into Hell (7. 690–1). One book earlier, during the horse-race at the funeral games, as Amphiaraus' horses head for the finish, 'the earth gives a groan, and even then savagely threatens' (*dat gemitum tellus et iam tunc saeua minatur*, 6. 527). Again, Statius follows the basic tradition in having Oedipus' curse on his sons begin the poem's action (1. 56–87).[96] Now, this curse was delivered in a secret recess (1. 49–50), yet Iocasta and Polynices know all about it in Book 11 (344–5, 504–5).[97] In all these cases, the self-sufficiency of the tradition is such that characters and poet appear to have equal access to it. A very remarkable example of the acknowledged weight of the poem's inheritance is seen when Oedipus is made to speak of himself as a canonical character, performing canonical actions:

> o si fodienda redirent
> lumina et in uultus saeuire *ex more* potestas.

Oh if only my eyes could come back so that I could dig them out again, and I had the power to savage my face *according to my normal custom*. (11. 614–15)

The most overt recognition of these dilemmas comes as a stroke of genuine self-referential humour, in the episode where Tiresias and Manto organize a necromancy at Thebes (4. 406–645). No subject was more vulnerable to the charge of being hackneyed; not

---

closest to his models, as has been most conclusively shown by Thomas (1986); the impression of self-sufficiency which he none the less generates is, in contrast with Ovid and Statius, even more astonishing.

[95] Aeschylus' *Septem*, Sophocles' *Antigone*, Euripides' *Phoenissae*. Propertius (1. 7) implies that his friend's poem on the story will have burial as a theme, as appears from the antithesis between lines 18 and 23.

[96] *Thebais* F 2–3 EGF.

[97] Cf. Venini (1970), on 11. 504, pointing out how Statius departs from the Greek tragedians in having the curse of Oedipus unknown to the other characters—except here.

only did such scenes go back to the origins of the epic tradition, in the *Odyssey*, but they enjoyed a particular vogue in Statius' immediate predecessors and contemporaries.[98] Tiresias' daughter and helper, Manto, is describing the vision of the Underworld to the blind seer: she gives us thirteen lines of scenery before she breaks off:

> quid tibi monstra Erebi, Scyllas et inane furentis
> Centauros solidoque intorta adamante Gigantum
> uincula et angustam centeni Aegaeonis umbram?

Why should I to you of Erebus' monsters, the Scyllas, and the futile ravings of the Centaurs, of the chains of the Giants, twisted from solid adamant, and of the thin shade of the Hundred-hander Aegaeon? (4. 533–5)

This *praeteritio*-topos is well-known.[99] Here, in a move arresting even for Statius, whose liberties with language are notorious, Manto leaves out her verb, and there is none to be understood from the context (the effect in Latin is scarcely less odd than in the English of my translation).[100] Mozley is quite right to translate 'Why should I tell thee . . .?'; but Statius' ellipse jolts us into thinking that these things are so much spoken of that a verb of speech is redundant. Tiresias' reply consists of a well-timed double-take— and he, too, leaves out his verb of speech, in a usage which is even more bizarre than Manto's:[101]

> 'Immo' ait, 'o nostrae regimen uiresque senectae,
> ne uulgata mihi. quis enim remeabile saxum
> fallentesque lacus Tityonque alimenta uolucrum
> et caligantem longis Ixiona gyris
> nesciat? . . .'

'Indeed,' he said, 'O guide and strength of my old age, do not [tell] me things that even all the common people know about. For who does not

---

[98] Vessey (1973), 237–53; cf. his fine comments on Statius' 'search for variation and brilliance within a valued and coercive tradition' (258).

[99] Martin (1974), 289–90. Here the particular models appear to be Verg. *G.* 2. 118–21 (*quid tibi . . . referam?*); 3. 339–40 (*quid tibi . . . prosequar?*).

[100] On Statius' liberties with Latin, see Legras (1905), 312, 320–3; Williams (1978), 225–31. Ellipses of verbs of speech are fairly common in Latin (H.–Sz. 2. 424), but I find nothing that quite parallels this.

[101] The great difficulty of the expression is shown by the fact that the manuscripts show three different attempts (one of them unmetrical) to come up with an imperative. The omission of an imperative after *ne* is most odd in Latin, but Greek commonly omits the imperative after μή, especially with verbs of speech: Ar. *Vesp.* 1179, 1400; *Nub.* 84; *Ach.* 345; Soph. *OC* 1441 (with Jebb's examples ad loc.).

know the returning rock, the deceitful lakes, Tityos, the food of birds, and Ixion, dizzy from his long spinning circuits? . . .' (4. 536–40)[102]

If all these characters intermittently share their creator's heightened awareness of the history which they inhabit, the gods too show themselves to be conscious of the traditional parameters for their behaviour. Jupiter is tired of behaving like Jupiter, so he announces to the assembled gods, speaking of his thunderbolt with ornamental epithet, with the result that we seem to hear him referring to himself as a character: *taedet saeuire corusco / fulmine* ('I am tired of raging with flashing thunderbolt', 1. 216–17).[103] We will observe the gods in this poem departing from many of their canonical ways of behaving; hence, as a necessary preliminary, the common insistence on the gods as canonical objects, frozen in their familiar poses: Venus is seen in the embrace of Mars (9. 822), Bacchus is droopy in his vine-covered chariot (4. 652–7); Mars is blood-drenched in his chariot, with Bellona as his charioteer (7. 69–74).

Juno, for example, will prove in this poem to be very different from her normal self. At the end of the poem, therefore, Statius has her dwell for a moment on the traditional malevolence which she has not embodied here, as she refuses to follow up her resentment against the moon-goddess for her actions on the night of Hercules' conception: *ueteres sed mitto querellas* ('but I leave out my old grudges', 12. 301).[104] Again, the action of the Furies will be an arena for some of Statius' most stunning inventiveness:[105] hence the initial description of Tisiphone travelling 'the familiar

---

[102] Tiresias refers in the first instance to Ovid's picture of the Underworld (*Met.* 4. 457–63). The prophet denounces the use of well-known themes by copying Vergil's well-known denunciation of the use of well-known themes (*G.* 3. 4–5: *omnia iam uulgata: quis . . . nescit?*'); this joke is almost as good as Sterne's plagiarism of Burton's *Anatomy of Melancholy* in his denunciation of plagiarism at the beginning of Volume Five of *Tristram Shandy*.

[103] Schubert (1984), 80, comments on the oddness of this epithet in Jupiter's mouth.

[104] Compare the misleading Vergilian allusion in the proem (1. 12) to *saeuae Iunonis opus* (*Aen.* 1. 4, *saeuae . . . Iunonis*), and the way in which Mars, rather than Juno, imitates Homer's Hera in a vindictive scene modelled on the *Iliad* (*Theb.* 9. 834–40, *Il.* 21. 479–96). Valerius similarly signals his departures at 1. 112, *solitosque nouat Saturnia questus* ('Juno gives a new version of her customary complaints').

[105] On the importance of the Furies in all treatments of the Theban story, see Venini (1970) on 11. 58.

road to Thebes' (*notum iter ad Thebas*, 1. 101);[106] or her infection of the royal house 'with her usual cloud' (*adsueta ... nube*, 1. 124); or Jupiter's question to the assembled gods, *quis funera Cadmi / nesciat et totiens excitam a sedibus imis / Eumenidum bellasse aciem?* ('who wouldn't know about the death dealt by Cadmus, and the wars fought by ranks of Furies, summoned up *so often* from the depths?', 1. 227–9). As a final anticipatory example, we may point to the intervention of Virtus in Book 10. As we shall see, Statius is at his most original here, yet he introduces the episode with words which imply that we will be given the normal and expected epic treatment of the divine machinery, as he calls on the Muse to tell him who inspired Menoeceus: *neque enim haec absentibus umquam / mens homini transmissa deis* ('for this state of mind is never communicated to man without the presence of the gods', 10. 629–30).

This confiding in his audience, as he charts the straitened arena in which he must perform, is a most remarkable gesture of tact on Statius' part. We abuse his politeness if we come to the abrupt conclusion that these preparatory statements are a sign of resignation, rather than being an invitation to join him in testing the confines of his 'coercive tradition'.[107] Those who expect Statius to be nothing but derivative, paralysed by his mighty predecessors, should pause before his wry affirmations that no one is more aware of the risks than he is himself.

The way in which the *Thebaid* organizes its cosmos is the best guide for our enquiry into the divine action in the poem. The various spheres of action and motivation are clearly demarcated in the early stages, and the rest of the poem may, for our purposes,

---

[106] 'Familiar' to readers in the first instance from Ovid (*Met.* 4. 481–8). Statius' entire subject may be seen as supplementing Ovid's treatment of the house of Cadmus in *Met.* 2–4; in his proem (1. 4–14) he rejects those areas dealt with by Ovid, and devotes twelve books to the mighty topic skipped over by Ovid in five lines of prophecy (*Met.* 9. 403–7). The poem is an epic exaggeration of Ovid's technique of expanding on a model's brevity and abbreviating a model's expansion.

[107] Again, the phrase of Vessey (1973), 258. At this point a reference to Bloom's 'anxiety of influence' seems inevitable: Bloom (1973). Statius has two mighty progenitors, Vergil and Ovid, together with two godfathers, Seneca and Lucan, and a grandfather, Homer. Amongst classicists (and I am no exception), Bloom has suffered the fate of the archetypal 'strong' critic, and has become softened into what he would describe as 'weak' readings.

profitably be viewed as an exploration of what follows from this demarcation.

The obvious basis of the structure of the *Thebaid*'s universe is its arrangement in a vertical scheme, on three levels, with the world of the Olympians at the top, the Underworld at the bottom, and the human world in between. The scheme, clearly, is sanctioned by long custom, although different emphases were possible in epic (in the *Odyssey* Hades is 'down', but, more importantly, off to the far West, on the bounds of Ocean).[108] This is not simply a description of the geography of the epic. The action of the poem is split up amongst these levels in a very systematic manner.[109] The motivation of the action flows from these three spheres, and, as the narrative unfolds, there is continual movement from each sphere to the others, so that there comes to be an anxious tension as to where the centre of gravity of the poem resides.[110]

The first 300 lines deploy each of the three realms in turn. Oedipus is the first character we meet, a human being, whose relation to the realms above and below him is caught with expert economy. Self-blinded, hiding from the light in the inmost recesses of the house, closeted with the ancestral household gods whom he has only just discovered to be his own, he is living a species of death (46–52).[111] He is intimately linked with the Underworld, as is first marked by the fact that his self-blinding has cut him off from the light of the sky (50): Jupiter soon after says of him that he 'no longer enjoys my heaven' (*nec iam amplius aethere nostro / uescitur*, 1. 237–8).[112] Oedipus begins the action of the poem by turning his empty sockets to heaven and beating upon the ground, the partition between his level and the infernal level (53–5); his abjuration of both of the non-infernal realms will be made explicit in Book 11, where he declares that he abandoned sky and earth when he dug out his eyes (*caelum terramque reliqui*, 11. 692). His prayer, though it starts with a ringing 'Gods', is addressed not to

---

[108] *Od.* 11. 12–13; Vermeule (1979), 34–5.

[109] See, especially, Burck (1979), 338.

[110] Though scholars normally talk of the poem's 'double', rather than 'triple', motivation: discussion in Gossage (1972), 192–6.

[111] Vessey (1973), 72–4; cf. 11. 581–2, *profert / mortem imperfectam.*

[112] Blindness need not lead to divorce from the gods: light moved from Tiresias' eyes to his chest (4. 542); Oedipus' chest has Dirae (1. 52), and what he sees is Styx (57–8).

the celestial gods, but to those below—in particular, to the Furies. His appeal is a perversion of normal prayer, as he himself asserts, referring to his words as *peruersa uota* (59). His wish for his sons' destruction is addressed to the Fury Tisiphone because Jupiter is doing nothing:

> et uidet ista deorum
> ignauus genitor? tu saltem debita uindex
> huc ades et totos in poenam ordire nepotes.

And does the father of the gods see this and not stir himself? Do you at least be present here, the due avenger, and line all the descendants up for punishment. (1. 79–81)

The problem of Jupiter's involvement or inaction will prove to be one of the poem's greatest areas of anxiety. Apollonius and Lucan are the two predecessors who make most of this uncertainty over how, or whether, the supreme god will act, and Statius sounds a typically Lucanesque note in order to introduce the theme.[113] Tisiphone has 'avenger' emblazoned in her name,[114] and is therefore the ideal instrument for Oedipus' purposes; yet Oedipus' scepticism about Jupiter's involvement will soon be revealed as misplaced, when we hear Jupiter declaring that he wishes to be involved in this task of vengeance as well (*ultorem . . . Iouem*, 1. 241). If Oedipus regards Jupiter as unresponsive, he need have no concern about Tisiphone. Throughout the poem, the channels of communication between humans and the Underworld are a good deal more effective than those between humans and the upper world: Tisiphone responds instantly:

> talia dicenti crudelis diua seueros
> aduertit uultus. inamoenum forte sedebat
> Cocyton iuxta, resolutaque uertice crines
> lambere sulpureas permiserat anguibus undas.
> ilicet igne Iouis lapsisque citatior astris
> tristibus exiluit ripis.

The cruel divinity turned her grim face to his address. She happened to be sitting next to unlovely Cocytus; with her hair let down, she had given her

---

[113] Cf. *BC* 7. 447–8 (above, pp. 281–2; cf. pp. 65–9, on Apollonius); for a collection of expressions like that used by Oedipus here, see Pease (1935), on *Aen.* 4. 208. On Statius and Lucan, see Venini (1970), xv–xvii, with works cited there; Ahl (1982).

[114] In Greek, her name is 'avenger of murder': cf. Verg. *Aen.* 6. 570–1, *ultrix Tisiphone*, a phrase repeated by Statius (8. 757–8).

snakes the opportunity to sip the sulphurous water. Straight away, quicker than the fire of Jupiter and falling stars, she leapt up from the gloomy banks. (1. 88–93)

At face value, the last sentence is doing no more than telling us what we know already: she is indeed quicker to act than Jupiter, who has yet to appear.[115] Worse, however, than the fact itself is the disquieting arrogation of celestial language which conveys Tisiphone's destabilizing rush to action—a destabilization promoted by the perverted way in which her ascent is described in terms of a celestial descent. The end of this chain of action is eleven and a half books away, when she will swoop on Pietas at the climax of the brothers' duel, *caelesti . . . ocior igni* ('faster than heaven's fire', 11. 483)—and when Polynices, at last coming to grips with Eteocles, will call on the same infernal gods as had his father at the outset (11. 504–8). The comprehensiveness of Tisiphone's appropriation of this Jovian language is revealed in Book 3, when Statius says of Mars' speed that 'the anger of high Jupiter does not fall more quickly on the earth' (*non ocius alti / in terras cadit ira Iouis*, 3. 317–18). Since the Fury first claimed this pattern, Mars' impact is now, oddly, 'like' Tisiphone's, as well as Jupiter's.

When Tisiphone crosses the boundary from her sphere to the upper sphere, the organization of the cosmos is breached, and the world reacts with disarray:

> Taenariae limen petit irremeabile portae.
> sensit adesse Dies, piceo Nox obuia nimbo
> lucentes turbauit equos; procul arduus Atlas
> horruit et dubia caelum ceruice remisit.

She makes for the threshold of the Taenarian gate, which may only be crossed once. Day felt her presence, as Night blocked his path with pitchy cloud and threw his shining horses into confusion; far off, steep Atlas shuddered and let go of the sky on his teetering neck. (1. 96–9; cf. 118–22)

As the Fury appears and the cohesion of the universe buckles, we are in the world so unforgettably created by Senecan tragedy, a world where evil comprehensively deranges natural order.[116] The

---

[115] The germ of Statius' idea may be Lucan's description of Caesar's *celeritas*, *ocior et caeli flammis* ('faster than the flames of heaven', 5. 405).

[116] On this feature of Senecan tragedy, see Herington (1966), 433–5;

universal scope of her threat is highlighted by Statius' choice of an Ovidian scene as model. In *Metamorphoses* 4, Tisiphone likewise goes up to earth to punish members of the house of Cadmus:

> limine constiterat: postes tremuisse feruntur
> Aeolii pallorque fores infecit acernas
> solque locum fugit.

There she was on the threshold. The door-posts of Aeolus are said to have trembled; the maple doors lost their colour, and the sun fled from his proper position. (4. 486–8)

Ovid has a perfunctory disturbance of the sun, but by contrast with Statius his derangements of order are localized: the threshold is only that of the house, not the boundary between one world and another, as is the threshold crossed by Statius' creature.

In four words within a subordinate clause Tisiphone infects the house, to begin the falling-out of Polynices and Eteocles (1. 124). At this point Statius veers into a naturalistic account of the brothers' discord, with much sententious matter from Lucan's first book.[117] The brothers' differences are here explained in terms of the accepted clichés of political behaviour, with a soliloquy from an unnamed ordinary citizen to help marshal the observations (1. 173–96). Within this speech, we hear another baffled question to Jupiter: *tibi, summe deorum / terrarumque sator, sociis hanc addere mentem / sedit?* ('highest progenitor of gods and earth, was it you who resolved to make these men, who should be natural allies, decide on this course of action?', 1. 178–80).[118] This time there is an answer, for as soon as the citizen has finished speaking, the scene is transported to the last remaining sphere, the Olympian, as Jupiter calls a council of the gods (197–9), and we are allowed to see the celestial motivation for the action. The characterful action of this council will demand our attention further on; for now, we need only note that Jupiter announces his

Rosenmeyer (1989). Seneca's *Thyestes* is the clearest prototype for Statius here, having as it does in its first scene a magnificent Fury, who gloats over the world's disruption as she shepherds the shade of Thyestes around the stage (48–51, 106–21); the *Thyestes* is activated again at the beginning of Statius' second book, when Mercury leads the shade of Laius up from Hell. For Seneca's influence on Statius, see Venini (1970), xix–xxi, and literature there cited; Vessey (1973), 59, 72–3, 76–8, 251–3.

[117] Note esp. 1. 144–64 and Luc. 1. 87–97; Venini (1961), 68–83.

[118] Following (though not with much confidence) the interpretation of *sociis* given by Heuvel (1932), ad loc.

intention of punishing the royal houses of both Thebes and Argos, and overrides Juno when she attempts to turn aside the anger which he feels against Argos (214–302).[119]

The triple motivation provides the environment for a tussle over authority which carries through to the end of the poem, so that the arena for the warring brothers' struggle over dominion becomes itself a power-struggle.[120] The characters, and their creator, are caught up in an uncertainty over which of the poem's three spheres will predominate. Statius' most explicit deployment of this uncertainty comes, naturally enough, immediately after the introductory exposition of the triple motivation, when Polynices goes into exile, and decides to make for Argos:[121]

> tunc sedet, Inachias urbes Danaeiaque arua
> et caligantes abrupto sole Mycenas
> ferre iter impauidum, seu praeuia ducit Erinys,
> seu fors illa uiae, siue hac immota uocabat
> Atropos.

Then he decides to beat his undaunted path to the cities of Inachus, the lands of Danae, and to Mycenae, murky with the interruption of the sun—whether the escorting Fury led him there, or the chance of the road, or whether immovable Atropos called him by this route. (1. 324–7)

Here one of the Parcae stands for the will of Jupiter, and 'chance' for the human realm. In yet another interesting ellipse, Statius conveys the indirection felt in the human action by leaving out a verb for this one of the three alternatives; 'leading' or 'calling' is readily supplied from the context, but it remains significant that the human alternative, sandwiched in the middle, should lack the verb which the other two command. Again, at the beginning of the second book, as Mercury leads the shade of Laius up out of the Underworld to infect Eteocles, one of the watching shades addresses Laius, and speculates whether it is Jupiter, a Fury, or human witchcraft which is the explanation for his departure (2. 19–22). A similar concatenation of alternatives is given as Capaneus rises to attack heaven: he was impelled by the Furies, or by his own warrior's lust for glory and fame, or by the gods above

---

[119] Fine discussion of the first council in Schubert (1984), 71–105.

[120] Schubert (1984), 128: 'In diesem Epos wird das Problem der Abgrenzung einzelner Machtbereiche oft zum Thema.'

[121] Cf. Ahl (1986), 2851–2.

(10. 831–6).[122] Finally, when Polynices' wife and sister need a funeral pyre for his corpse, the glowing pyre of Eteocles is nearby—whether by chance or the will of the gods, as a result of the action of Fortune, or of the Eumenides (12. 420–3).

These realms interact in complex ways. The most starkly delineated tussle in the poem is the antithesis between heaven and hell, an adversity so marked that J. Kroll, in his *Gott und Hölle*, was able to speak of the 'dualism' of the *Thebaid*.[123] Polynices and Eteocles are not the poem's only pair of contending brothers, for their conflict is framed by the adversity between Jupiter and his brother Dis, king of the Underworld. Although Manichaeist dualism as such is not to be sought in the *Thebaid*, there is no doubt that, of all our poets, Statius comes closest to depicting a world where Good and Evil divine principles struggle for mastery (the markedly allegorical character of the poem contributes to this tendency[124]). Even the *Aeneid*, for all its obsession with evil, is not as dualistic in atmosphere as the *Thebaid*. Vergil's Juno exploits the powers of hell, but she is not one herself. She is part of a rhythm which involves Jupiter as well, and she is susceptible to change: Statius' Dis and Tisiphone will never change. In Statius, the polarization between Jupiter and Dis is thrown into relief by the absence of the third brother, Neptune, and also by the fact that Olympus is not common to all three brothers, as it is in the *Iliad* (15. 187–93): Dis' descent to Hades is a comprehensive defeat in the *Thebaid*, an irrevocable deprivation of the sky (8. 38–40, 11. 446).[125]

The rivalry between the two brothers is played down by some commentators, who describe Dis as furthering the design of Jupi-

---

[122] For this purpose it does not matter whether we read *fata* or *fama* in 10. 835. If *magnae data fata neci* (or *necis*) could be made to yield sense, we would have two different expressions in each of the three alternatives; but I am not sure that *fama* can be resisted: cf. Williams (1972), ad loc.

[123] Kroll (1932), 450, 453. On this antithesis, see Schetter (1960), 29; Schubert (1984), 128–30. Reservations from Burck (1979), 338; Ahl (1986), 2861.

[124] On the naturally dualistic cast of allegory, see Fletcher (1964), 222–4; Clifford (1974), 34. As Ahl (1986), 2861, points out, the biggest objection to seeing the poem as dualistic in a strict sense is the fact that only blind faith will see Jupiter as embodying absolute Good. There are, however, other celestials who come closer to doing so.

[125] Neptune acts only once in the poem, without any characterization whatever, in a few vague words which describe his refusal to see his horse-offspring, Arion, defeated in the chariot-race (6. 529, *sed uetat aequoreus uinci pater*).

ter. This is not how the outraged King of the Underworld sees the matter at the beginning of Book 8, and even Vessey characterizes the results of Dis' intervention as being 'truly the work of hell and of the powers of hell', and going 'beyond what Jupiter had planned and even Oedipus willed'.[126] One may as readily speak of Heaven doing Hell's work in the poem as of Hell doing Heaven's. As in the case of Tisiphone's arrogation of celestial language, we are dealing with a zealous rivalry in inflicting punishment which can have the effect, and appearance, of a co-operation.[127] Dis in fact emerges as a kind of anti-Jupiter, with his kingdom as an anti-Heaven. When Mercury wings his way through the Underworld, the atmosphere is a sickly inverse of the atmosphere of the upper world:

> undique pigrae
> ire uetant nubes et turbidus implicat aer,
> nec zephyri rapuere gradum, sed foeda silentis
> aura poli....
> hac et tunc fusca uolucer deus obsitus umbra
> exilit ad superos, infernaque nubila uultu
> discutit et uiuis afflatibus ora serenat.

On all sides the inert clouds blocked him, the roiling air clogged his progress; nor was it zephyrs which snatched him along, but the foul breeze of the silent realm.... By this route then the winged god, smothered by sombre shadow, leapt out to the world of the upper gods; he scattered the infernal clouds from his face and cleared his countenance with currents of air that were alive. (2. 2–5, 55–7)[128]

The climax of this conceit will come at the moment when Megaera arrives on earth to help Tisiphone arrange the brothers' final combat; her advent is accompanied by a ghastly blending of the upper and lower atmospheres: *exultant manes, quantumque profundae / rarescunt tenebrae, tantum de luce recessit* ('the shades of the dead rejoice; the darkness of the deep is diluted by as much as is lost from the light of day', 11. 73–4).

Dis himself, from Book 8 on, comes into his own as an anti-Jupiter,

---

[126] Vessey (1973), 264: on the same page, Vessey would have it that Dis' 'will, in essence, is identical with that of his Olympian counterpart, for both are executors of Fate'.

[127] Burck (1979), 338; Schubert (1984), 73: 'Jupiter und Tisiphone—eine interessante Kombination!'

[128] These last lines are imitated by Dante (*Inf.* 9. 82): Mozley (1928), vol. 2. 250.

instigating the horrors of the latter part of the war in revenge for having to tolerate the irruption of the still-living Amphiaraus into the Underworld at the end of Book 7. This breaching of boundaries is a moment of potential chaos, as Statius notes with an echo of Lucan's first programmatic simile of cosmic dissolution.[129] 'I will fight,' says Dis, 'let the boundaries of the universe pass away!' (*congredior, pereant agedum discrimina rerum*, 8. 37). He organises a reciprocal breach, by causing Capaneus to invade heaven, as Amphiaraus has invaded hell (8. 75–7). He orders Tisiphone to her ultimate horrors, and the Jovian nod at the end of his speech is marked by language that makes his power equal to Jupiter's: *non fortius aethera uultu / torquet et astriferos inclinat Iuppiter axes* ('Jupiter is not more powerful when he turns the aether with his nod, and tilts the star-bearing axes of heaven', 8. 82–3). If Dis nods like Jupiter, he even usurps his brother's most characteristic prerogative, and thunders from beneath the earth (11. 410–11); he is Jupiter of the lower realm, black Jupiter, the infernal Thunderer.[130]

The power of the Underworld increases as the duel between Eteocles and Polynices comes closer, and this increase is accompanied by a corresponding recession in the influence of the celestial sphere. Dis' supreme moment of rivalry with his brother comes as Creon prays to Jupiter. Tisiphone twists his words, so that the highest god becomes the lowest, and the lowest the highest:

> nec pater aetherius diuumque has ullus ad aras,
> sed mala Tisiphone trepidis inserta ministris
> adstat et inferno praeuertit uota Tonanti.
> 'summe deum, . . .'

The etherial father was not present at these altars, nor any of the gods; evil Tisiphone stood there, mingling with the quaking attendants, and twisted the prayers to the Thunderer down below: 'Highest of the Gods, . . .' (11. 207–10)

The climax of the Underworld's success, and the nadir of celestial power, is the duel between the sons of Oedipus, a combat engineered by twin Furies, against the futile opposition of the goddess Pietas. And at this climactic moment, in a typically self-

---

[129] *supera conpage soluta*, 8. 31 (and 144, *ruptaque soli conpage*); cf. *BC* 1. 72 ff., *sic, cum conpage soluta . . .*
[130] 1. 615–16; 2. 49; 11. 209.

referential gesture, Statius announces the end of the Underworld action, as the humans take over:

> nec iam opus est Furiis; tantum mirantur et adstant
> laudantes, hominumque dolent plus posse furores.

Now there is no need for the Furies; all they do is look on in astonishment, and stand by with words of praise; they grieve that men's fury can outdo them. (11. 537–8)

This is, in simple fact, just as Statius announces, the last appearance of the Furies, or any other infernal creature, in the poem's action.[131] The humans are left to themselves—as they are, likewise, by the celestial gods, to whom we now turn, before examining the human isolation at the poem's end.

The first celestial action in the poem, the council of the gods, is a magnificently Ovidian moment, especially in its capturing of a political atmosphere, for Statius' council develops the Ovidian picture of the contemporary world's political realities.[132] Just as Ovid had discarded Vergil's picture of a Jupiter who acts like an Octavian amongst the other gods, a tactful operator who veils his violence unless absolutely forced to act, so Statius follows the development of power into his own generation, and gives us a Jupiter whose autocracy is even more naked than Ovid's. His Jupiter enters with a placid expression, but he makes everything quake none the less (*placido quatiens tamen omnia uultu*, 1. 202), and it is quite clear that the gods are terrified of him;[133] at his last appearance, and introducing his last utterance, when we have got to know him better, he will have a savage face (*toruo . . . ore*, 11. 121). The gods do not dare to sit until he gives his gracious permission; as Williams points out, this touch recalls Statius' own reference to etiquette in the emperor's presence.[134] While Ovid spells out his analogies between human and divine power-politics with his very first comparisons (*Met.* 1. 175–6, 200–5), Statius keeps us waiting until the end of Jupiter's fulminations in the second divine

---

[131] At 12. 696 the Eumenides are part of a vision seen by Creon.

[132] Excellent discussion in Schubert (1984), 76–7, 99, 102–3, 296–7; cf. Williams (1978), 251.

[133] See Schubert (1984), 77–8, on the oxymoronic power of the quoted expression, and its implications.

[134] Williams (1978), 251, citing *Silv.* 4. 2. 17. Williams also refers to the similarities between the epic's description of Jupiter and the description of Domitian in *Silv.* 1. 1 (one might add 4. 2).

council, in which the god asserts his mastery, and mocks Juno's helplessness:

> dixit, et attoniti iussi. mortalia credas
> pectora, sic cuncti uocemque animosque tenebant.

> He spoke, and they were stunned by his commands. You would think they had the minds of mortals, such was the restraint which they ex ercised over what they felt and what they wanted to say. (3. 253–4)[135]

In the Homeric model, the gods are at first silent after Zeus' self-assertion, until Athene eventually speaks up (*Il.* 8. 28–30); here there is total and lasting silence. So also in the first council, where, apart from Juno, no god reacts: 'Die versammelten Götter schweigen von Anfang an'.[136]

In the first council, Jupiter's apparent geniality soon evaporates, as he reveals his wrathful, Ovidian, urge to punish the sins of human beings (1. 214–47). The bluster and rage of his speech is eminently Ovidian, and radically un-Vergilian. The more than Ovidian harshness of Jupiter is highlighted by the fact that Statius characterizes him with traits taken from Vergil's savage Juno, while simultaneously ameliorating his own Juno in order to accentuate the departure. Like Vergil's Juno, Statius' Jupiter dwells on his abiding memory of the human offences which caused his rage;[137] like Vergil's Juno, he turns to the Underworld to achieve his ends, sending Mercury to fetch the shade of Laius up from Hell.[138] Statius' Juno, on the other hand, is astonishingly mild in speech and action, considering her epic heritage. She pleads on behalf of Argos, although Jupiter takes no notice whatever of her intervention (1. 250–82), and she participates, as we shall see, in the human reconciliation at the end of the poem.

The passionately human characterization of Jupiter has been

---

[135] In Eteocles' *concilium*, only 250 lines earlier, there is at least some muttering (3. 92–3).

[136] Schubert (1984), 99; his whole treatment of the *Thebaid*'s divine power-structure is most valuable (cf. 102–5, 133–4). Williams's comments on this scene are, unfortunately, characteristic of the prejudices which dog criticism of this poetry: 'When Ovid painted the same scene (*Met.* 1. 163–252), he used the gods to punctuate Juppiter's speech with roars of applause and questions. But Statius completely forgets the other gods . . .' (1978), 251. See, rather, Schubert (1984), 99: 'Das Schweigen ist die Haupteigenschaft der Götter und nicht nur ein vorübergehendes Phänomen bei der Ankunft Jupiters.'

[137] 1. 246–7; cf. *Aen.* 1. 25–7.

[138] 1. 292–311; cf. *Aen.* 7. 324–5.

often documented.[139] Although he professes to be outraged at the crimes committed against the gods by Thebans, his very language reveals that the traffic in crime is a two-way affair. His term is *reticenda deorum crimina*, 'crimes committed against the gods, which must not be spoken of' (1. 230–1); yet the genitive is two-sided, and Juno is quite entitled to interpret the words as 'crimes committed *by* the gods'—and she *will* speak of them, as she resists Jupiter's attempt at hypocritical decorum by cataloguing his rapes of Semele and Danae (253–69).[140] The distinction between divine and human sin is collapsed by Jupiter's unwittingly self-incriminating phrase.

The cumulative effect of this human characterization of Jupiter is so relentless that it becomes exceedingly difficult to have any confidence either in Jupiter's worth as a moral adjudicator for the poem, or in interpretations which cast him in this role.[141] Even more pernicious to such a reading is Jupiter's dismaying abdication at the climactic moment of the brothers' duel—an act which caps the anxieties sounded at the very beginning of the poem, when Oedipus and the anonymous citizen each questioned whether Jupiter was directing, or even observing, the action. This washing of hands is itself part of a broader movement (corresponding to the disappearance of the infernal powers), by which the celestial realm evanesces from the close of the poem, leaving the humans isolated.[142] The preparation of the Furies for the brothers' duel sets the wider scene for the disappearance of Jupiter and the eclipse of the Olympians. When Tisiphone speaks to her sister Megaera, she anticipates no interference from the conventional gods: the only obstacles she fears are Fides and Pietas, and the human mother, sister, and father (11. 98–108). She aims to

[139] Gossage (1969), 81; Burck (1979), 334–5; Schubert (1984), 133.

[140] So, rightly, Schubert (1984), 84. We are sent back to the area of difficulty charted by Euripides' exchange between Dionysus and Cadmus at the end of the *Bacchae* (1346–9). This is not the only time that Jupiter's sexual derelictions will be commemorated in the poem; Eteocles and the river-god Ismenos give lists of his rapes (11. 212–16, 9. 421–6).

[141] Vessey (1973) is the most systematic exponent of the view that Jupiter, as the Stoic Providence, guarantees the moral meaning of the poem. See, rather, Burck (1979), 335–6, and Schubert (1984), 102–3, on how Jupiter's characterization is a stumbling-block to this interpretation.

[142] Schetter (1960), 26–9, has some excellent points on this feature of the poem; cf. Newman (1986), 239–40, on Jupiter's withdrawal, and Schönberger (1965), 136–7. Section III of this chapter will examine the gods' eclipse in more detail.

supplant the gods above: according to her, the ordinary horrors so far are the province of ordinary celestials, Mars and Enyo (11. 84, 97). Sure enough, when the brothers approach each other, the celestial gods of war are put to rout, and the Furies take their place (11. 409–15).[143] Shortly afterwards, there is Adrastus, pleading with the brothers, asking the pertinent question, *ubi iura deique?* ('where are ordinary codes of conduct, where are the gods?', 11. 430).

Between the address of Tisiphone to Megaera and the question of Adrastus, Jupiter has retired from the action. At the moment when the Furies Tisiphone and Megaera end their conversation, and move to commit the brothers to combat, Statius gives us an image of chaotic storm (11. 114–18). Jupiter is immediately introduced, but he refrains from quelling the chaos, and instead makes his last speech in the poem before absenting himself from the action for good. He forbids his fellow-celestials to play their traditional part of divine audience (*auferte oculos!*), and then declares that he will in fact act out the obliviousness which human characters have from the start feared, or suspected, of him: *absentibus ausint / ista deis lateantque Iouem* ('let the absent gods not be present at these events, may they escape the notice of Jupiter', 11. 126–7; from 9. 520–1, it appears that it is the norm for this Jupiter not to be watching the action). A few lines later (133–4), in a definitive gesture of dissociation, he turns his own eyes away from the human action—and unlike his Homeric model, Zeus, who averts his eyes from the plain of Troy at the beginning of *Iliad* 13, he will never look back to help guide the poem to its conclusion. Jupiter's abdication from his epic task of responsibility is castigated by Pietas, who laments the indifference or hostility of the gods, and of 'savage Jupiter' in particular, as she sits apart from their company, watching the brothers advance to combat (11. 457–64). The words of Pietas mark the evanescence of the celestials' influence, just as the catastrophe of the duel, when it finally comes, marks the disappearance of the infernal agents.

Not only the climactic horror, but the reconciliation which can recuperate it, are the work of humans operating with their own resources, in the absence of the gods. The climax to all the anxious

---

[143] Bentley's *subiere* at 415 is clearly right. See Schetter (1960), 26, on the Furies' taking over at this point.

questions about Jupiter's involvement comes in the final book, with the question asked by Capaneus' widow, Evadne, as she tells Theseus of the unburied Argive corpses polluting the Theban plain: *ubi numina, ubi illest / fulminis iniusti iaculator?* ('where are the gods, where is that hurler of the unjust thunderbolt?', 12. 561–2). Jupiter is associated only with punishment, not with return to order. The final book, with its concern over reconciliation and proper treatment of the dead, is very much an *Iliad* 24;[144] with its quickened tempo, and carefully systematic resolution, it is also an *Odyssey* 24.[145] Statius' radical departure from both Homeric poems (and from the *Aeneid*) lies in his removal of the gods, and especially of the supreme god, from the resolution of the poem's action—Jupiter's place is taken by the human Theseus, who is compared to Jupiter in a simile, as he marches against Thebes (12. 650–5).[146] The one exception to this comprehensive absence is the help given by Juno to the Argive women's supplication at Athens (12. 464–70). The goddess who was so vindictive in the *Iliad* and *Aeneid*, so resistant to any reconciliation, here takes on a kindly role, and does so secretly, to deceive Jupiter.[147] Her participation, so much at odds with her traditional persona, is made part of the resolution in order to highlight the fact that Jupiter and the other gods persist in their absence.[148]

With as much force as his tradition allows him to command, Statius makes it impossible for us to refer to the gods for help when we try to find a vantage-point, at the poem's end, from which to make some sense of the resolution. After the three realms' long tussle, it emerges at the end that the Olympians must surrender their claims to moral authority. Already at the end of the first book, with the story of Apollo and Coroebus (1. 557–668), Statius had prepared this theme. The god's traditional self-indulgence and savagery are put to shame by the noble self-sacrifice of the human. In a quite extraordinary moment, after

---

[144] Turolla (1956), 136; Schetter (1960), 77–8; Juhnke (1972), 158–9.

[145] Juhnke (1972), 162.

[146] The absence of Jupiter is well stressed by Burck (1979), 335–6; Schubert (1984), 299.

[147] At 12. 292 she slips away from Jupiter's bed; the *discordia thalami* of 1. 260 remains unhealed.

[148] The only other reference to the action of a god after Jupiter's withdrawal follows Theseus' declaration of war, when Pallas strikes her shield and shakes the aegis (12. 606–9).

the human offers to die for his community, the god feels awe, yields, and is astonished (1. 662–5). The same god, when he disappears from the action in Book 9, confesses to his sister that his failure to save Amphiaraus makes him unfit to be honoured: *saeuus ego immeritusque coli* ('I am savage and unworthy to be worshipped', 9. 657). In epic, the necessary humanity of divine characterization is always the fault-line on which the gods' claims to moral value are perched, ready for collapse. Statius follows Ovid in bringing so much pressure to bear at this point that the gods' claims do indeed become wreckage, but he goes beyond Ovid, and ends up in Lucan's camp, by eventually removing the gods from the scene altogether.

The human sphere, where the action will come to rest, is defined from the beginning by boundaries above and below, as we saw earlier with the first human character, Oedipus. The prophet Thiodamas tells us in his great prayer to Earth that the human domain is the centre of affairs, the cockpit, open to the influence of all realms: *o rerum media indiuisaque magnis / fratribus!* ('O centre of everything, not divided up amongst the great brothers', 8. 312–13).[149] The *Thebaid*'s elaborate cosmology, the setting of the poem and the world, is there for the human dimension. So we are obliquely informed by the former human, Hercules, who has become a god, when he reminds Pallas that she could not accompany him to the Underworld (8. 512–13). Only human characters may move in all of the poem's three realms.

When the living Amphiaraus pierces the lower boundary, and the living Capaneus attempts to pierce the upper, these are gross violations of the human norm, and each act provokes catastrophic retaliation from the lower and upper Jupiters. In sharp distinction to Valerius, Statius maintains a consistently pessimistic attitude to the ambivalent paradigm of humans bursting into heaven. The topic of the apotheosis of Domitian in the proem is cast in markedly guarded terms, for it is seen as a competition with Jupiter for divine prerogatives: the emperor should remain content with his regulation of the human realm, since elevation to heaven would require yielding on the part of Jupiter (1. 29–31).[150] In a sense,

---

[149] Note here how Statius does not say '*three* brothers', in accordance with his shifting of the Homeric division towards a bi-partite split between Jupiter and Dis.

[150] Schubert (1984), 129–31; Ahl (1986), 2820.

such language expresses the wish that the emperor's mortal life should continue for a long time, but the anxiety about attempts to leave the human realm is entirely in harmony with the poem's consistent position. In an epic context, as a disciple of Ovid and Lucan, Statius finds it quite impossible to restrain his anxiety when he faces his master's systematic cultivation of analogies with Jupiter.[151]

The spectacular fates of Amphiaraus and Capaneus are aberrations which help to demarcate the human norm. The problem of this human norm, poised between the upper and lower limits, becomes increasingly important as the poem proceeds, as the upper and lower spheres, which form its bounds, retreat and disappear. The last one and a half books come to be focused exclusively on the problem of human nature, viewed in the context of burial, an issue which comes to the fore when Creon will not allow the Argive corpses to receive their proper honours. Burial is a human duty, owed by humans to humans, but a duty which also involves responsibility to the powers above and the powers below, so that a resolution of this crisis is capable of being treated as a resolution of the discord among the poem's three realms of action.

The poem's movement towards some kind of reintegration begins as soon as the two brothers have killed each other. The human realm is now isolated, as Jupiter and the Furies end their participation. Just as Oedipus began the main action, so now he begins the dénouement by coming into daylight and the presence of his dead sons (11. 580–604). On his knees beside their corpses, he prays:

'tarda meam, Pietas, longo post tempore mentem
percutis? estne sub hoc hominis clementia corde?
uincis io miserum, uincis, Natura, parentem! ...'

'Now, when you are too late, Pietas, after long space of time do you smite my heart? Is there clemency in this human breast? You conquer, ah you conquer, Nature, this unhappy parent. ...' (11. 605–7)

---

[151] In the *Silvae*, he tries as hard as possible to annul the anxiety. In describing Domitian's new palace, for example, Statius reveals that it is in competition with the gods' residences, but asserts that the gods are pleased at Domitian's equation of his status with theirs (4. 2. 18–22). On Domitian and Jupiter, see Sauter (1934), 54–78; Fears (1981*b*), 77–80; Coleman (1988), on *Silv.* 4. 1. 17; 2. 11, 14, 52; 7. 49–50 (note Coleman's marvellously revealing, solitary, index entry under *Jupiter*: 'see *Domitian*').

These are lines to which we must return in the next Section, when discussing the poem's allegories. For now, we may note that Pietas appears to be still effective, despite her rout by Tisiphone shortly before (11. 482–95), and that Clementia and Natura will be key concepts in the human healing of the final book. Oedipus is made a human being again by the power of Pietas, Clementia, and Natura, rescued from his half-life, half-death on the brink of the Underworld.

Book 12 displays the development of these concerns, as the widows of the Argive host go to Athens and supplicate at the altar of Clementia, in order to prevail upon Theseus to march on Thebes and force Creon to allow the burial of their menfolk. Trapped by Creon's inhumane edict, the dead men are hovering in a no-man's land, and Creon has removed himself from human status by his cruelty, as an Argive remarks early in Book 12: *bello cogendus et armis / in mores hominemque Creon* ('Creon must be forced by war and battle into behaving as he should, into being a human', 165–6).[152] Here we may note that, in a manner familiar from Ovid, Statius also uses the animal realm to serve as a lower demarcation for defining the human. The Creon who is described here as having lost his human status was revealed only seventy lines earlier as one who wished to follow the wild beasts, and the hooked beaks of vultures, and show them the limbs of the dead kings: the word for 'show' is held back until the sentence is almost over, so that one is expecting *lacerare*, 'rend' (*utinam . . . fas ipsum . . . feras, ipsum unca uolucrum / ora sequi atque artus regum monstrare nefandos!*, 12. 95–8). The bestial act of Tydeus, who forfeits immortality by gnawing at the head of the man who has mortally wounded him, is the poem's clearest example of the Ovidian bounds of definition. Tydeus goes full circle from almost-god to almost-beast, demonstrating the linked outer limits of human excess.[153] In the context of mighty human achievement, as we have seen repeatedly, bestiality is next to godliness.[154] Bestial Tydeus, Creon, and bestial Jupiter are linked by Dis when

---

[152] Rieks (1967), 221–2; Rieks's whole discussion of Statius' *humanitas* is very valuable.

[153] Ibid., 214–15.

[154] The twin poles are automatic reference points for the elder Pliny, for example: *nec ideo proximum illi [deo] genitum hominem ut uilitate iuxta beluas esset* ('man was not born one step down from god in order to rank next to the beasts in vileness', *HN* 2. 5. 26).

he prophesies the escalation of horror at the beginning of Book 8:

> sit, qui rabidarum more ferarum
> mandat atrox hostile caput, quique igne supremo
> arceat exanimis et manibus aethera nudis
> commaculet: iuuet ista ferum spectare Tonantem.

Let there be one who savagely chews the head of his enemy, acting like the rabid beasts; let there be one who keeps the dead from their funeral pyre, polluting the aether with naked spirits: may it give pleasure to bestial Jupiter to look at that! (8. 71–4)

The scene for the Argive widows' supplication is the altar of Clementia, the human emotion to which Oedipus appealed when his humanity returned to him beside his sons' corpses.[155] Again, this is a passage to which we will return when discussing the poem's allegories in the next Section. Here we may observe only that Clementia is distinguished as being different in every way from the main gods who dominated the first ten and a half books, as Statius takes even further the Ovidian insight that the power of conventional divinity is incompatible with genuine kindliness:

> urbe fuit media nulli concessa potentum
> ara deum; mitis posuit Clementia sedem,
> et miseri fecere sacram.

In the middle of the city was an altar, assigned to none of the gods with power. Gentle Clementia made her seat here, and the unhappy made her sacred. (12. 481–3)

At this juncture Statius presents us with a major speech on human duties, and he puts it, with characteristic point, in the mouth of the widow of Capaneus, the most inhuman of the heroes (12. 546–86).[156] Evadne asserts that Theseus will satisfy the demands of all three spheres by ensuring burial of the Argives (*da terris unum caeloque Ereboque laborem*, 12. 580); and she bases her plea on the humanity which Theseus has in common with the dead men:

> hominum, inclyte Theseu,
> sanguis erant, homines, eademque in sidera, eosdem

---

[155] On the altar of Clementia, see Burgess (1972); Vessey (1973), 308–12; Ahl (1986), 2890–2.

[156] Vessey (1973), 312. Note especially the lines which introduce the extract quoted in the text, where Evadne is on thin ice in her claim that the Argives were not gigantesque monsters (12. 553–4); her husband was doing his best to break into this category (10. 849–52).

> sortitus animarum alimentaque uestra creati,
> quos uetat igne Creon . . .
> . . . heu princeps Natura! ubi numina, ubi illest
> fulminis iniusti iaculator? ubi estis, Athenae?

They were the offspring of humans, famous Theseus, and themselves humans, born to the same stars, the same mortal fate, the same sustenance as you, and now Creon bars them from fire . . . Alas, Nature, mother of all! Where are the gods, where is that hurler of the unjust thunderbolt? Where are you, Athens? (12. 555–62)

The gods, and Jupiter in particular, are not responsive. But Evadne and her companions do succeed in this appeal to Nature and to Athens, the home of Clementia—and we remember that Oedipus acknowledged Nature and Clementia, together with Pietas, when he accepted human status again (11. 605–7), while Pietas herself is the offspring of the same *princeps Natura* addressed by Evadne here (11. 465–6). When Theseus sets off for battle, the self-sufficiency of the human action is dramatically highlighted by the simile which compares him to Jupiter (12. 650–5). A man must, and can, take the place of the deity in asserting the rights and duties of man to man.

The movement of the last part of the poem appears to define itself readily. After the miasma of the first ten and a half books there is a purification, a victory for the weak forces of humanity, which had appeared to be no more than the cat's-paw of the mightier powers above and below.[157] Yet the reaction of many readers seems to show that the felt force of the poem is not necessarily congruent with this statement of its direction.[158] Theseus' intervention has a rushed, even perfunctory air.[159] In an epic which has been densely populated by participants from so many realms of poetry and experience, the absence of any divine dimension from the resolution generates a barren sense of anticlimax: the human agents appear to be operating in a vacuum rather than standing proudly alone.[160] Statius will not follow the natural impetus of the

---

[157] Kytzler (1955), 176–7; Rieks (1967), 221–5; most strongly, Vessey (1982), 575, and (1973), 307–16: 'The *Thebaid* is an epic not of sin but of redemption, a chronicle not of evil but of triumphant good' (316).

[158] Burck (1979), 339–43, esp. 343; Schubert (1984), 278; Ahl (1986), 2894–8.

[159] Those who wish to avoid such a reading will find the rapidity of the closing narrative best defended in Lewis (1936), 55.

[160] Schubert (1984), 278. Right to within 110 lines of the end of the *Iliad*, a sense of divine guidance persists.

poem, or the prompting of his own creation, Evadne, and present the act of burial as a resolution of the discord between the three spheres of the poem's action. It is not a comprehensive triumph. The brothers' hate persists unassuaged even in death, as we learn in the marvellous moment when the flame on their joint pyre divides in two (12. 429–41).[161] Evadne persuades Theseus to bring about the dénouement, and her speech is the clearest expression of the justice of humanity's claims to vindication, yet she commits suttee on the pyre of Capaneus, and has no part in the resolution which she helped to instigate (12. 800–2). The end of the *Seven Against Thebes* is the beginning of the story of the *Epigoni*.[162]

The narrative finishes with a declaration of incapacity from the poet. At the end of a poem which has been saturated with formal lament, he announces that he does not have the resources to present the laments for Tydeus, Polynices, and Parthenopaeus (12. 797–809). With the aid of all the Muses he could tell of the super-human insanity of Capaneus (10. 831), but not even if Apollo comes out of retirement can he tell how the widows attempted to express, or heal, their misery. If he refuses in this way to follow Homer's solutions at the end of the *Iliad*, he also refuses to follow the divine oversight which governs the resolution of the *Odyssey*. The gods' participation in the poem gives Statius weighty re-sources for his narration of human madness, but their withdrawal from the finale enables him to go one step further, as he suggests the weakness of human attempts to make sense of their cata-strophes.

The isolation of the (finally untellable) human action at the end corresponds to the poem's general refusal to construct a cosmic frame of reference into which human action may be plotted. Epic's distinctive metaphors for such frames of reference are often to be found emblematically caught in a cosmic icon, a material object (the shield of Achilles, or of Aeneas): 'such images contain the cos-mos of those works where they appear'.[163] Early on, the *Thebaid* has such an object, or a candidate for such an object, on display— the necklace of Argia (2. 265–305). This ornament was once the property of Harmonia, the daughter of Mars and Venus, and it

---

[161] Stressed by Burck (1979), 343.
[162] Well noted by Ahl (1986), 2897.
[163] Fletcher (1964), 219.

too is the work of Vulcan and the Cyclopes (2. 269–74).[164] In Statius' icon, however, we see no comprehensive vision of empire or of the rhythms of human life, but an internally bound miniature of pettiness and vice, a catalogue of lust and madness, deliberately set against its mighty predecessors by Statius' remark that the Cyclopes who made it were trained for bigger projects (*docti quamquam maiora*, 2. 273).

III

The germ of all the allegorical poetry.

C. S. Lewis, *The Allegory of Love*[165]

We have already discussed the gods' withdrawal from the end of the poem, and it is time to put that withdrawal in a larger, and different, context. The gods of the *Thebaid* yield to many pressures. Their claims to authority exploded, they surrender the moral stage, as we have seen, to the human actors. Further, the poet deprives them of the right to fulfil their proper epic modes of action, as they succumb to a double threat from allegory. The first threat is the long-standing one to their own epic natures and personalities, for in this poem we see the gods shedding their multiple ways of generating meaning, in the process of becoming the allegorical agents which many readers had seen in them for centuries.[166] The second threat is yet more radical, for the gods must yield not only to the Furies, who usurp their epic patterns of behaviour, but also to an array of personifications and allegorical constructs, who come into their own as alternative vehicles for the depiction of human action. Lewis puts it thus: 'On the one hand, the gods are becoming more and more like mere personifications; on the other, the personifications are beginning to trespass farther and farther beyond the boundaries which Johnson assigns them.'[167] The manifold power-struggles which make up the

---

[164] And, amazingly enough, of the Telchines (274–5).

[165] Lewis (1936), 54.

[166] As Lamberton (1986), 147, succinctly puts it: 'allegorical literature . . . is the outgrowth of a tradition of interpretation impinging on a tradition of creative literature'.

[167] Lewis (1936), 50 (his Johnson reference comes two pages earlier). Even from my introductory paragraph, it will be plain how much my whole approach owes to Lewis's splendidly provocative discussion.

*Thebaid* acquire another dimension, as the poem becomes a power-struggle among alternative narrative modes.

In Lewis's analysis, the gods' allegorical way of acting appears to be something which Statius deploys almost insensibly, as if it were the inevitable thing to do.[168] Yet, here as elsewhere, Statius exhibits a remarkable self-awareness at every stage of his operation, as he shifts certain of his gods from being personalities, with cult interests and a mythological history, into being allegorical emblems of human phenomena. The first key passage comes at the end of Book 2, with the first impact by an Olympian on a human personality, when Statius shows us Minerva hovering precisely on this boundary. Tydeus has slaughtered all but one of the Thebans sent to ambush him on his way back to Argos, and, says the poet, he would have marched on Thebes itself, were it not for Minerva:

> . . . ni tu, Tritonia uirgo,
> flagrantem multaque operis caligine plenum
> consilio dignata uirum: 'sate gente superbi
> Oeneos, absentis cui dudum uincere Thebas
> adnuimus, iam pone modum nimiumque secundis
> parce deis: huic una fides optanda labori.
> fortuna satis usus abi.'

. . . if you, Tritonian virgin, had not thought the man worthy of your counsel, in his heated passion, all in a fog as a result of his performance: 'Descendant of the race of proud Oeneus, whom I have just now allowed to conquer Thebes at a distance, now set a limit, and do not presume upon the over-favourable gods: you must hope for only this exploit to be believed. You have taken your luck far enough: depart.' (2. 684–90)

Minerva here is human wisdom, given a voice, and a compelling philosophical rhetoric—'undisguisedly a state of Tydeus' mind', as Lewis puts it.[169] The care which Statius lavishes on this effect begins with his refusal even to figure Minerva in the action. Lewis refers to her 'astonishing appearance', but Statius is in fact so far from having her appear that he contrives to introduce her words without using an actual verb of speech. He activates the tradition of reading Homer by which Athene represents Wisdom

---

[168] Most explicitly on p. 52: '. . . when the poet gives us a full-length description of Bacchus *he seems to forget* both his own romance and the materials with which Greek mythology would so readily have supplied him' (my italics).
[169] Lewis (1936), 52; cf. Vessey (1973), 147.

(φρόνησις, σύνεσις), while the fog surrounding the hero represents the fog of ignorance, which clouds the vision of the soul, and
which wisdom alone may penetrate.[170] It is, further, possible that
he labels the goddess 'Tritonian' in order to refer to one of the
oldest allegorical etymologies, by which Athene's Homeric epithet
of 'Tritogeneia' is taken to refer to the 'threefold' nature of wisdom's manifestation, in deliberation, speech, and action.[171] The
appearance of Athene to Achilles in *Iliad* 1 (188–222) is the obvious model for Statius' scene, yet the departure from Homer's
procedure is radical. However much sympathy one may feel for
the common interpretation which sees Athene as embodying
Achilles' rational power in the Iliadic scene, Homer's technique
resists us if we try to read the confrontation between goddess and
mortal as nothing more than an articulation of an inner human
process—if we try to read it, in other words, as some sort of
anticipation of what Statius is doing here.[172] The attenuation of
the goddess's personality in Statius, the absence of any narrative
dynamic or interchange, are astonishing if one reads his scene
immediately after reading Homer's, in which Athene is a character
with no less mimetic intensity than Achilles himself.

   To stop here, however, when the episode still has more than
fifty lines to run, is to do less than justice to the self-consciousness
of Statius' art. If we read on, we observe Tydeus following the
goddess's advice by sparing the sole survivor, Maeon; he proceeds
to mark his victory by constructing a trophy to Minerva (2. 690–
712). In this cult act, and especially in the elaborate prayer which
the hero then addresses to his protecting deity, we see full recognition of the goddess's cultic and mythic personality. Statius

---

[170] Athene as wisdom is the commonest allegorical identification of the Homeric
commentators: above, p. 37. Athene's action in *Il.* 5. 127, when she dispels the fog
around Diomedes, gave rise to readings of the sort given in the text: bT. 5. 127;
*Excerpta Vaticana* 20 (Festa (1902), 98); Buffière (1956), 284; cf. Heraclit. *All.* 34,
for a rather similar treatment of ἀήρ in Homer. Vergil appears to be relying on
such a tradition in *Aeneid* 2, when he refers to the mist which clogs Aeneas' mortal
understanding (604–6). This mist makes it impossible for Aeneas to see the divine
dimension to Troy's fall, but it also makes him unable to think; he is restored to
rationality by his mother, Venus.
[171] Democritus fr. 68 B 2 DK; bT *Il.* 8. 39.
[172] Roemer (1914), 177–9; especially, Whitman (1987), 14–19: 'The fact . . . is
that Athena is too literal a goddess too often to be consistently "something else,"
the something else of allegory. Any sustained correspondence we try to establish
between her and Wisdom must fail' (16). Of course, as Whitman stresses, 'the
allegorical potential of Homer's work remains striking' (19).

presents us with a fully developed cult hymn, replete with allusions to a variety of Minerva's exploits and manifestations (2. 715–42). Further, to Tydeus, the deity appears as no personification of wisdom, but in her other dominant guise, as the martial goddess who guarantees victory to her devotee: she is 'fierce goddess, powerful in war' (*diua ferox, . . . bellipotens*, 715–16).[173] Tydeus' reaction, in other words, preserves the goddess from being relegated to her purely allegorical function as a figure for wisdom. His initial address to her may be seen as catching the two alternatives which the episode sets up. 'Adornment and wisdom of her great parent', he calls her (*magni decus ingeniumque parentis*, 715): if 'wisdom' is her allegorical persona, she still claims the 'adornment' to which she is entitled in prayer and cult.

Lewis's clearest case of how the gods shift into allegory—the onrush of Mars in Book 3—provides us with the poem's most spectacular example of Statius' revelling in his innovation. With his customary lucidity, Lewis shows the force of Statius' departure from epic norms. This Mars is a genuinely allegorical creation, ' "an accident occurring in a substance", the martial or pugnacious spirit as it exists in the mind now of one nation, and now of another, at the bidding of Fate'.[174] Unlike Juno in the *Aeneid*, Mars has no mythological motivation for his onslaught; sent by Jupiter to incite war-lust in the Argives so that they will attack Thebes (3. 218–61), he rages because 'it is his *esse* to rage'.[175] This Mars is not a divine character who participates for characterful reasons, but an embodiment of the madness which is activating the human characters, and he does not possess any self-awareness beyond that function.

Of all the great gods, Ares had been, from the beginning, the deity most prone to such an allegorical identification with his clearly demarcated province.[176] None the less, in Homer he is still a partisan character, identified with the Trojan side, so that even the scholiasts, who wish to see Ares as nothing but 'War' wherever

---

[173] It is possible to see a unity of a kind in Pallas' twin realms of wisdom and warfare: Burkert (1985), 140–1. The point is that Statius, for his own purposes, is denying such a unity by creating the split in attitude which we see in this scene.

[174] Lewis (1936), 50–1.

[175] Ibid., referring also to the other great allegorical scene involving Mars, 7. 40–84; cf. Vessey (1973), 86–7.

[176] Burkert (1985), 169.

possible, can hesitate over his status: ἡ προθυμία τοῦ πολέμου. ἢ ὁ σωματοειδὴς θεός ('he is the urge for war. Or else the god in bodily form', D *Il.* 4. 439). In Vergil, while appearing as an emblem of mutual war-lust, and as a metonymy for war, Mars also has his tales of myth, and, in particular, carries a heavy load of significance as a national Roman god, father of Romulus and Remus.[177] Even in Valerius, who comes closest to Statius' usage, Mars has identifiable mythological grounds for his participation. At the beginning of Book 6, Valerius shows Mars uncertain over which of the two sides to back in the imminent battle. This looks very much like Statius' picture of Mars as the urge for war, yet Valerius' Mars is undecided for sound, characterful motives: he wishes to protect the fleece in his holy grove, and knows that there are persons in both camps who wish to plunder it.[178] Valerius' Mars is hovering over the choice of becoming no more than an allegorical agent, but he remains a god.

Statius' Mars is something new, then, in his allegorically obsessive patterns of behaviour, in his lack of affiliation or epic personality; and the allegorical tenor of the episode continues in the sequel, as Whitman shows, with the help later given Mars by the personified Fama (3. 420–30): god and personified agent now occupy the same space.[179] Any notion, however, that Statius is proceeding unawares is shattered when Venus steps into the path of Mars' rampaging chariot, and activates her sexual charge by leaning her breasts against the top of the chariot (3. 263–6). Her words of reproach and appeal show up Mars' novelty in the most astonishing manner. When she alludes to the fact that their own offspring, Harmonia, was married to the father of the Theban race, Cadmus, she is asking him, in effect, 'Have you quite forgotten your mythological personality and allegiances? Are you now nothing more than an allegory?':

---

[177] As war-lust or war: *Aen.* 6. 165; 7. 582; 8. 700; 10. 755–6. In myth: 7. 304–5. As national god: 6. 872 (with the note of Austin (1977), ad loc.); 8. 630; 12.

[179.] 

[178] So Lüthje (1971), 270. Statius' difference from Valerius could be conclusively shown if one could be confident that *Theb.* 6. 227–32 were genuine lines. In a simile, 6. 232–3 show Mars uncertain which side to back in a conflict, and the only reason for his uncertainty is precisely that the decision is immaterial to him, so long as blood is shed. The lines, however, are almost certainly spurious.

[179] Whitman (1987), 56: 'the allegorization of a god is converging with the amplification of a passion by the dynamic motion of an abstract agent'.

> bella etiam in Thebas, socer o pulcherrime, bella
> ipse paras ferroque tuos abolere nepotes?
> nec genus Harmoniae nec te conubia caelo
> festa nec hae quicquam lacrimae, furibunde, morantur?

War even against Thebes, o choice father-in-law, are *you* preparing war, preparing to destroy your descendants with the sword? You aren't slowed down at all, mad one, by the thought of the people of Harmonia, or the wedding [of Harmonia and Cadmus] celebrated in heaven, or these tears? (3. 269–72)

Venus' attempt to recall Mars to his epic inheritance is a bold one. It even has a limited success, for Mars promises that, when the war actually begins, he will help the side to which he is allied (3. 312–15)—and so he does (once).[180] More noteworthy than Venus' small gain, however, is the fact that the goddess is herself swept up into the narrative mode which she is attempting to resist. Her very attempt to remind Mars of his proper allegiances becomes itself an allegorical enactment.[181] Her sexual overtures to Mars, and her pleas that he should not harm the cause of Harmonia, are transformed into a figural acting out of one of the poem's key concerns, the powerlessness of love in the face of madness: as Whitman well puts it, the 'fable of love seeking to prevent discord from disturbing the effects of harmony is a shift from mythology toward argumentation that almost reminds us of Heraclitus' exegesis'.[182] The failure of Venus' appeal is shown immediately she has finished speaking, with Mars' failure to fit into the canonical, especially Lucretian, pose of disarmament:

> lacrimas non pertulit ultra
> Bellipotens, hastam laeua transumit et alto,
> haud mora, desiluit curru, clipeoque receptam

[180] 9. 821–40; cf. Snijder (1968), 144–5. Note, however, that Mars continues to embody war none the less: at 8. 383–5 he is in the middle of the battlefield, inspiring war in both sides.

[181] Though not, of course, without precedent. Allegorical interpretation of Demodocus' song of Ares and Aphrodite in *Odyssey* 8 was early and pervasive (Buffière (1956), 168–72); in Latin epic, Lucretius and Vergil exploited such interpretations extensively: Hardie (1985), 90–5, and (1986), 360.

[182] Whitman (1987), 56, referring to his earlier discussion (38–41) of the treatment of Demodocus' song in *Homeric Problems* 69. 1–11, where 'Heraclitus' brings in Empedocles to explain the relationship between Ares and Aphrodite, and the birth of their daughter, Harmonia. Cf. Vessey (1973), 86, with his fine point on the metamorphosis of Harmonia into a snake (3. 289–90): 'Harmony . . . is humiliated and debased in the world of man, just as Harmonia became a snake.'

laedit in amplectu dictisque ita mulcet amicis:
'o mihi bellorum requies et sacra uoluptas
unaque pax animo! . . .'

The God of War did not endure her tears any longer; he switched his spear to his left hand, and, without delay, jumped down from the high chariot; clutching her to himself within his shield, he hurt her in his embrace, and soothed her thus with friendly words: 'O, my rest from war, my sacred pleasure, the only peace my mind knows! . . .' (3. 291–6)[183]

The comedy here is rough, as Mars' gesture is rough. With his indecorous bluster, and his inflicting of pain even in solicitude, Mars is unable to cut away from his persona even for a moment. We may observe of Mars, as Reinhardt observed of Themis, in his classic discussion of personification, that he cannot disavow his essence.[184] Mars' identification with his *esse* represents allegory at its tightest, with the closest possible fit between the affect and its characterized embodiment. Allegory can, of course, exploit disjunctions between affect and embodiment, as may be clearly seen in one of classical literature's first fully achieved allegorical figures, Euripides' Lyssa ('Madness').[185] Lyssa's task is to drive Heracles mad, but her initial stance is one of reasonableness, and reluctance to fulfil her allotted task: 'I do not enjoy visitations against the mortals that I like,' she says, as she attempts to plead for the character she is supposed to victimize (*HF* 846). After being reminded by Iris that she was not sent by Hera in order to exercise rational self-control, she declares emphatically that she is acting against her will (857–8). Only then does she stir herself up to picture the frenzied catastrophe which she will inflict on the house of Heracles (859–72). In the scene as a whole, the reluctance of personified Madness to act, to fulfil what her nature dictates, catches the reluctance of those who are going mad to surrender to their madness, just as Madness's rational conversation with Iris acts out the last seconds of self-control's resistance. Statius never goes quite as far as Euripides in this separation of the allegorical character from its *esse*, though we will observe him

---

[183] One thinks immediately of Lucretius' proem, where the poet addresses Venus as *hominum diuumque uoluptas* ('pleasure of men and gods', 1. 1), and prays that Venus will disarm Mars (31–40). Also important is the scene in *Iliad* 15, where Athene disarms Ares (125–7).

[184] Reinhardt (1960*b*), 32: 'Themis kann ihr Wesen nicht verleugnen.'

[185] Cf. Petersen (1939), 42, on how different Lyssa is from the allegorical figures of Hesiod; 43–5, on the remarkable nature of Euripides' procedure in this scene.

opening up some rather similar lines of fracture, in our discussion of his allegorical personifications. Before examining those personifications, however, we must complete our investigation of what happens to the gods.

If some cardinal deities find themselves being subsumed into allegorical patterns, what becomes of the gods' traditional ways of acting? Of all the poem's gods, the chief one, Jupiter, remains most true to his traditional nature, becoming a kind of exaggeration of his epic self. In his violence, self-indulgence, and final indifference, he pushes to the limit the menacing side of his epic personality.[186] The poem's pessimism positively demands such a glowering and inflexible backdrop to the human action. The other gods also will inevitably strike any reader as canonical in their attributes and characteristics, yet their behaviour is in fact extremely circumscribed.[187] The new constraints upon them are concentrated especially in the one area of their traditional operation where they are most exposed to the new threats from the allegories—that is, in their influence on human characters. Such scenes are not only comparatively rare in the *Thebaid*, they are also very different from anything which had gone before. We have already seen the novelty of the first scene in which an Olympian impinges on a human character, with Pallas and Tydeus at the end of Book 2.[188] If we turn to Apollo and Amphiaraus at the end of Book 7, we see a novelty of a very different kind.

The prophet Amphiaraus is riding over the plain in his chariot, his horses already afraid of the ground beneath their feet (7. 690–2). At this point, his own special god, Apollo, enters the action:

> famulo decus addit inane
> maestus et extremos obitus illustrat Apollo.
> ille etiam clipeum galeamque incendit honoro
> sidere; nec tarde fratri, Gradiue, dedisti,
> ne qua manus uatem, ne quid mortalia bello

[186] The discussion of Schubert (1984) is fundamental here; cf. Burck (1979), 334–7.

[187] Canonical: above, p. 343. Circumscribed: Schetter (1960), 26–7, a most valuable discussion: 'Ein bedeutsames Charakteristikum der Thebais besteht darin, dass die traditionellen Göttergestalten in den Hintergrund treten. . . . Jedoch spielen diese Götter in dem grossen Weltdrama keine entscheidenden, vielmehr untergeordnete Rollen' (26); cf. Schönberger (1965), 136–7.

[188] Above, pp. 365–7.

laedere tela queant: sanctum et uenerabile Diti
funus eat. talis medios aufertur in hostes
certus et ipse necis, uires fiducia leti
suggerit; inde uiro maioraque membra diesque
laetior et numquam tanta experientia caeli,
si uacet: auertit morti contermina Virtus.
ardet inexpleto saeui Mauortis amore.

Sad Apollo adds empty adornment to his servant, and lights up his dying
moments. He makes his shield and helmet glow with a star-like fire, to
honour him. Mars, you were not slow to grant to your brother that no
hand or mortal weapon could harm the prophet in the fray, but that he
could go to Dis as a sacred and venerable death. This is how he is borne
into the thick of the enemy, himself certain of his death; his confidence
that he is about to die supplies him with strength; so the hero seems to
feel his limbs grow, the day become more favourable, never has his skill
at reading the sky seemed so great—if he were free to read it: but Virtue,
death's neighbour, distracts him. He burns with unassuaged passion for
savage Mars. (7. 692–703)

The Homeric model is very clear. At the beginning of *Iliad* 5
Athene aids Diomedes, giving him strength and courage, so that
he might win excellent glory, and causing a star-like fire to blaze
over his helmet and shield (5. 1–8).[189] Likewise very clear are
Statius' departures. Apollo does not give Amphiaraus strength and
courage, and he bestows, not excellent glory, but an adornment
that is empty, futile—*decus inane* (7. 692). At this point, it
appears, Apollo even has to rely on Mars to protect Amphiaraus
for him.[190] In Statius, as in Homer, the god's favourite receives
strength and inspiration, but in Statius he does not receive them
from the god. Instead, the hero is affected, in various ways, by
Mars (703), by Virtus (702), and by his confidence that he is
about to die (699–700)—that is, by an allegorized deity, by a personification, and by one of his own emotions.

The key phrase at the beginning of the scene is *decus inane*,

---

[189] Juhnke (1972), 121–2. Note how closely Statius annotates the Homeric text
further on, when Apollo, like Athene in Homer, takes over as charioteer. In
Homer, the chariot groans under the weight of the mighty goddess and outstanding
hero (*Il.* 5. 838–9). Statius imitates the Homeric phraseology of 'great hero, great
god together on the chariot' (7. 750), but postpones the mention of the groan till
the god gets off, and the sound becomes a lament: 'it was *then* that the chariot
groaned' (*tunc uero ingemuit currus*, 790).

[190] Later, however, Apollo does deflect weapons from Amphiaraus, and instruct
him in his shooting (7. 753–4).

'empty adornment'. One's suspicion that this phrase cannot be idle, and that the radical departures from Homer cannot be accidental, is confirmed by an extensive sequence which this scene of futile glorification anticipates. After the weeping Apollo jumps off the chariot of the doomed prophet (7. 789), he vanishes from the action for almost two books, to reappear two-thirds of the way into Book 9. Here his sister, Diana, encounters him, as she is moving to the battle-field out of concern for *her* favourite, Parthenopaeus:

> iamque fere medium Parnassi frondea praeter
> colla tenebat iter, cum fratrem in nube corusca
> aspicit haud solito uisu: remeabat ab armis
> maestus Echioniis, demersi funera lugens
> auguris. inrubuit caeli plaga sidere mixto,
> occursuque sacro pariter iubar arsit utrimque,
> et coiere arcus et respondere pharetrae.

And now she was at the half-way point of her journey, passing the leafy ridges of Parnassus, when she caught sight of her brother in a shimmery cloud—not at all looking the way he normally looked. He was returning in sadness from the Theban war, mourning the burial of the engulfed prophet. The section of the sky glowed at the mingling of the heavenly body; at the holy conjunction, a radiance shone out from each of them, their bows met, and the quivers reacted in response to each other.[191] (9. 643–9)

As the dejected brother goes on to castigate himself, saying that he is unworthy of worship, and that his oracle is now silent (657–8), it becomes irresistible (to me at least) to see in these lines an image of the sun-god going into eclipse.[192] And it is indeed the case that Apollo never figures in the action of the poem after this, apart from a glimpse at the end of Book 10, where we see him in the company of the other gods, as Capaneus mounts his assault on

---

[191] See Cornutus, *Theol. Graec.* 32, for a comparison of Apollo to the sun and Artemis to the moon, with the comment that the gods are represented as archers as an allegorical hint at their rays.

[192] Greek, like English, can use 'eclipse' metaphorically in this way (Polyb. 29. 16. 1; Plut. *Aem.* 17. 8; both passages mention an actual eclipse as a portent of the 'eclipse' of King Perseus in defeat at Pydna). The native Latin word for eclipse (*deficio*) may also be used of 'fading away', 'failing' (*OLD* s.v. §5, §6), though I do not find examples of punning on the astronomical usage. Statius' description of Apollo here is very reminiscent of Ovid's picture of the self-chastising Phoebus in *Met.* 2 (381–3), after the death of his son, Phaethon: Phoebus is stripped of his *decus*, just as he is when in eclipse.

heaven (889–90).[193] His direct contact with humans is severed, as that glimpse in Book 10 itself helps to show. The ghost of his prophet, Amphiaraus, when it appears to Thiodamas early in Book 10, cries out 'Give me back my gods!' (*meos . . . redde deos*, 207–8); and Statius himself, when he announces his final incapacity at the end of the poem, declares that not even Apollo would be powerful enough to inspire him to transcribe the laments for the Argive dead (12. 808).

Apollo tells Diana not to waste her time trying to help Parthenopaeus (9. 659–62). She replies with the key word which had introduced Apollo's futile glorification of Amphiaraus: 'But a final adornment I may certainly seek . . .' (*sed decus extremum certe . . . licet . . . quaerere*, 663–5). Some fifty lines later her participation in the last moments of Parthenopaeus' life begins, and we see a series of striking departures from epic norms. In order to make sure that her presence is not pointless, she replaces Parthenopaeus' arrows with her own, sprinkles the hero and his horse with ambrosial liquid, so that they may not be harmed before it is fated, and adds magical chants and spells (9. 726–35). The deliberately exaggerated magical atmosphere is very far removed from epic procedure. It is accepted epic practice for a god to honour and preserve a corpse with ambrosia;[194] it is accepted epic practice for a god to heal an afflicted warrior;[195] but this deity is acting like a witch in order to preserve a mortal from harm. Even if we allow for the *Thebaid*'s characteristically precious and unrigorous modes, this action of Diana remains unique. Statius has made it unique in order to deny Diana her epic function.

Less than a hundred lines later he denies the goddess her epic function even more comprehensively, when she is shunted out of the action by the new allegorical vigour of Mars. First we see her snubbed by her own protégé, when she advises him to withdraw from the combat (9. 812–20). Thereupon Venus, who has been viewing the action from the embrace of Mars, urges him to re-

---

[193] We are told that he also inspires the oracular pronouncement which leads to Menoeceus' self-sacrifice (10. 624, 667, 762–3); yet he does not appear as a character.

[194] *Il.* 16. 680 (Apollo and Sarpedon); 19. 38–9 (Thetis and Patroclus); 23. 186–7 (Aphrodite and Hector); see Griffin (1980), 165–7, for the *Iliad*'s avoidance of such motifs as magical invulnerability. Statius' Parthenopaeus, by being associated with this tradition, is marked as already virtually dead.

[195] *Il.* 15. 239–62 (Apollo and Hector); 16. 527–9 (Apollo and Glaucus); *Aen.* 12. 411–24 (Venus and Aeneas).

move Diana from the field (821–30). At this point, to prepare for the victory of Mars over Diana, Statius fabricates what is perhaps the bluntest allegorical moment of the poem. Instead of saying that Mars was angry, Statius gives us this:

> desiluit iustis commotus in arma querellis
> Bellipotens, cui sola uagum per inane ruenti
> Ira comes, reliqui sudant ad bella Furores.

The God of War leapt down, stirred by her just complaints; his only companion as he rushed through the shifting void was Anger—the rest of the Madnesses were toiling away at the war. (9. 831–3)

Before the new narrative threat of Mars, and the inexorable face of Jupiter, Diana is powerless (9. 838–40). Even her promised revenge for the death of Parthenopaeus is, in a sense, robbed from her, for when Parthenopaeus' killer falls, Diana is not given explicit credit for the deed, and the origin of the fatal blow is deliberately kept mysterious (876). As Diana herself had admitted to Apollo when they met at Parnassus (9. 663), her sphere of action has become exactly what the gods' sphere of action in epic had always threatened to become—*decus extremum*, an adornment at the end; or *decus inane*, empty, futile adornment, as the poet had said of Apollo's presence at the death of Amphiaraus (7. 692).[196]

Schetter, who first commented on the striking circumscription of the gods' action in the *Thebaid*, points to one exception. In only one place, says Schetter, does Statius give one of the traditional deities a decisively guiding role in the action: that is, to Venus, in Hypsipyle's narrative of the Lemnian massacre.[197] According to Schetter, Statius here is following the canonical version, yet it may be more attractive to see Statius deliberately isolating his one example of more traditional narrative within a parenthesis, marking Hypsipyle as the old-fashioned narrator, so as to allow his overall originality to stand out in more vivid relief. Indeed, when one

---

[196] At 8. 759 Pallas attempts to do better than this, and obtain *decus immortale* for her favourite, Tydeus. She fails.

[197] Schetter (1960), 27. One could add another apparent exception, the chain of events at 8. 456–518, where Hercules aids Haemon while Pallas aids Tydeus. Yet it is novel for the *arriviste* Hercules to be acting like a fully-fledged god at all (he is rigorously forbidden even so much as speech in his only appearance as a god in the *Aeneid*, 10. 463–4); and when he does come face to face with Pallas he bows out of the action, refusing to sustain the epic momentum (502–18).

thinks of the other surviving mythological epic of the time, with its vigorous, but none the less quite un-iconoclastic employment of the tradition's gods, and with its prominent use of Venus in its own Lemnian episode, one may be tempted to go further, and see Valerius being marked as the old-fashioned narrator, left behind in parenthesis by Statius' innovations.[198]

Tydeus' address to Minerva in Book 2, in the episode with which we began this Section, appears in hindsight to offer a blunt but serviceable formula for the polarization of the gods' action. 'Adornment and wisdom of her great parent', he called her there (*magni decus ingeniumque parentis*, 2. 715). Although it does violence to the poem's richness of action to press these alternatives too rigorously upon the divine narrative, it is not misleading to see in these words an early hint at the choices facing the gods of the *Thebaid*: ineffectual adornment, or allegorical affect.[199]

The space vacated by the gods is occupied by the allegorical personifications, and by the forces of the underworld, who are themselves markedly allegorical in nature. If the conventional deities have great difficulty in acting (especially when they try to influence humans in their customary manner), their competitors impinge at will upon the human characters, producing new and compelling ways of capturing human experience. The Furies' usurpation is more direct, in that, together with their master Dis, as we saw above,[200] they revel in supplanting the celestials, and in taking over their manner of acting. At the climactic moment of the brothers' duel, Tisiphone and Megaera oust Virtus, Mars, Bellona, and Minerva (11. 412–15). Vergil's Fury, Allecto, had been responsible for the war in Latium, but Statius employs Mars for the

---

[198] On the epic character of Venus' organization of events in Valerius' Lemnian episode, see Bahrenfuss (1951), 101–2.

[199] If I may be permitted to confine my sole discussion of the unfinished *Achilleid* to a footnote, then it is worth pointing out that divine action is remarkably scarce in that charming, almost novelistic, fragment. To be sure, Achilles' mother, Thetis, is a goddess, and the early part of the poem shows her in extensive patterns of action, planning, travelling, conferring with Neptune, removing Achilles from Pelion to Scyros (1. 25–396). Yet divine intervention is conspicuously missing, for example, from the scene where Thetis watches while Achilles falls in love with Deidamia (1. 283–37); and it is an absence highlighted by Statius' initial question, which is never answered: 'Which god bestowed deceit and cunning on the stunned mother?' (1. 283–4).

[200] pp. 350–2.

average misery of warfare, and reserves the Furies for the particular evil of the brothers' mutual madness.[201] Again, although the gods themselves find it difficult to move in their traditional patterns to inspire or aid human beings, the Furies astutely ape these patterns of behaviour, to infect and affect the human characters with unnerving efficiency. Tisiphone stirs up initial discord between Eteocles and Polynices (1. 124–30); she saves each brother from death at different times (6. 513–14, 8. 686–8); she ensures that Tydeus will eat his enemy's brains and lose immortality (8. 757–8); she tricks Hippomedon into abandoning the corpse of Tydeus (9. 148–74); she acts like Vergil's Juno, in summoning up a creature from the underworld in order to achieve her aims (11. 59–61); she impersonates an Argive in order to force Polynices to resist the mild counsel of Adrastus (11. 197–204). Tisiphone becomes one of the poem's most palpably realized creations, acquiring a repulsive tactile dynamism in passages such as this:

> centum illi stantes umbrabant ora cerastae,
> turba minor diri capitis; sedet intus abactis
> ferrea lux oculis, qualis per nubila Phoebes
> Atracia rubet arte labor; suffusa ueneno
> tenditur ac sanie gliscit cutis; igneus atro
> ore uapor . . .

A hundred horned asps, standing on end, shaded her face, the lesser of her dread head's twin troupes. An iron light sits in her deep-set eyes, like an eclipse of the moon, brought on by Thessalian witches' art, glowing red through the clouds. Her skin is stretched tight by the pressure of the venom welling up from within, it is distended with discharge of pus. From her black mouth, a fiery exhalation . . . (1. 103–8)

Tisiphone and her sister Megaera are far more than avengers of blood-guilt, as they were originally in Greek thought, and in the early versions of the Theban myth.[202] Under the pressure of Vergil's, Ovid's, and Seneca's creations, Statius' Furies represent every evil of which human beings are capable. As narrative embodiments of attributes of human nature which are regarded as timeless, they demand to be read allegorically.[203] Statius had

---

[201] Schetter (1960), 24, 26. Even Tisiphone's instigation of the actual fighting in Book 7 belongs here, since she is acting to thwart the appeals addressed to Polynices by his mother and sisters (534–81). The Fury is concerned to counteract the impact of humanity.
[202] Venini (1970), 20.
[203] So (rather differently), Vessey (1973), 75.

considerable background for such a treatment, since Tisiphone and her ilk had been candidates for allegorical treatment of various kinds for centuries. Already in Euripides' *Orestes*, by one kind of allegory, the Furies are, quite explicitly, Orestes' way of objectifying the guilt he feels over his act of matricide;[204] it became a commonplace to speak of the Furies of tragedy as the conscience of a guilty man, or his evil desires.[205] In a larger sense, a powerful impetus for Statius' creation of an epic world of moral allegory will have been the pervasive moral allegorical readings of Homer.[206] Homer was read as a teacher of universal ethical truths, as is seen very clearly from Horace's second *Epistle*, where (if we may adapt Lewis's adaptation of Dante's expression), Horace reads the *Iliad* as *literaliter bellum Troianum, allegorice homo.*[207] A brief glance at the problem of allegorical reading is in order at this point, as we move from the Furies to the personifications themselves.

The problem of reading such allegorical figures in Statius is, in some regards, the problem of reading epic divine action writ large. In reading allegory we seem to be given a positive sanction to gloss over the narrative itself as briskly as possible, for is not allegory mere 'other-saying', and is it not therefore our task merely to enucleate that 'other'? The name, and commonly accepted nature of the mode, lead naturally to the conclusion that we are dealing with a 'reality' and its 'disguise'; even more than when reading the actions of the gods themselves, we can find ourselves invited to believe that we have nothing more to do than penetrate the cover, and discard it.[208] It is not surprising, then, that the scholar who uses such language of 'reality' and 'disguise' ends by claiming that, in epic, 'the effect of the device is . . . purely intellectual and neutral emotionally'.[209] If the reader will look

---

[204] *Or.* 257–61, 395–400; cf. Jocelyn (1967), 192–3.

[205] Jocelyn (1967), 193, citing, e.g. Aeschines *In Tim.* 190–1; Cic. *Q Rosc.* 67; *Pis.* 46—where see also the note of Nisbet (1961).

[206] On which see Buffière (1956), 249–391; above, pp. 36–7.

[207] Lewis (1936), 56, takes over a phrase from Dante's letter to Can Grande and applies it to the *Thebaid*. On Horace's poem, see now Cairns (1989), 85–8.

[208] 'Reality' and 'disguise' are the terms used by Gordon Williams in his discussion of the allegory of the Silver period, and particularly of Statius: Williams (1978), 266. From here it is a straight line to his readings of the divine action of the *Aeneid*, five years later (above, pp. 134–5).

[209] Williams (1978), 265. Williams is setting Statius' use of personifications in epic against his personification of Sleep in *Silv.* 4. 5, which he regards as a success.

back a page and re-read the description of Tisiphone quoted there, trying to react with emotional neutrality, it will appear that something has gone badly wrong.

The first cogent objections to the reductionist readings of allegory were put forward (it comes as no surprise) by C. S. Lewis: 'When we have seen what an allegory signifies, we are always tempted to attend to the signification in the abstract and to throw aside the allegorical imagery as something which has now done its work. But this is not the way to read an allegory.'[210] Such insights have received extensive amplification in more recent work on allegory.[211] Even an appreciation of the New Criticism's vaunted 'heresy of paraphrase' should commit one to abandoning the notion that the vehicle is dispensable.[212] There is a deep flaw in any theory of reading which holds that meaning is independent of its expression, which is what conventional theories of allegory inevitably end up implying, in their assumption that allegorical texts are saying something which may be extracted and reformulated in other terms without loss or damage—'the premise,' as Van Dyke calls it, 'that texts are not important in allegory—that they are merely vehicles for pre-existing ideas'.[213] Whatever ideas are present in Statius' allegories, we may be confident that our apprehension of them is going to be inextricably involved with the experience of reading the allegories themselves, and that the fictional energy lavished on these creations is not going to be otiose.[214] Stated thus, the notion sounds so self-evident as to be

---

[210] Lewis (1936), 125; cf. 166, 269, 289.

[211] Especially Fletcher (1964); Clifford (1974); Quilligan (1979); Van Dyke (1985). All these works, naturally, have their own emphases, and their own reasons for refusing to gloss over the text of allegory: Quilligan, in particular, builds her own theory of allegory out of the 'literalness' (64–79) which she sees as constituting the mode. As a practical demonstration of how to read allegory most fruitfully, I have found Van Dyke's stimulating book particularly illuminating and helpful—witness my frequent references.

[212] Van Dyke (1985), 36–7; cf. the trenchant declaration of Clifford (1974), 53: 'The allegorical action is not a paraphrase of something capable of alternative expression.'

[213] Van Dyke (1985), 45. She continues: 'Against such a premise the objections are well known. Modern criticism takes it as axiomatic that whatever truths literature conveys are essentially literary truths, inseparable from their vehicles.' These words should not be misread as a claim that literature is a self-sufficient system.

[214] Van Dyke (1985), 45: 'To read an allegory properly is neither to extract a moral nor to construct a geometry of its referents but to follow what Roland Barthes calls "the very movement of meaning" ' (the reference is to Barthes (1974), 92); cf. the concise conclusion to the fine study of Prudentius' allegory in Nugent

hardly worth asserting, yet the actual experience of reading is given no prominence at all in discussions of Statius' allegorical composition, as if the ideas expressed were so obvious that lingering over their presentation is redundant.[215]

For the poem's purposes, the Furies, together with the personifications proper, such as Virtus and Pietas, are conceived of as being existing realities, abstracts which occupy their own conceptual sphere, and which must become embodied in the time, space, and conventions of the narrative's mundane reality in order to become accessible to our senses.[216] So Virtus, for example, is said to live next to Jupiter, and from there to have a contingent effect upon the earth (*unde per orbem / rara dari terrisque solet contingere*, 10. 632–3). This is not to say that Statius is committing himself or his readers to belief in the real existence of these Ideals—indeed, as we shall see, the poem eventually abandons this mode of narration altogether, so that it is difficult to see the poem sanctioning such a philosophical view in itself. Still, even a debased Platonism is background enough for the audience to be prepared to see Virtus and Pietas as Ideals, and to appreciate the challenge posed by the urge to represent their implication in the human world, the narrative world.[217] It is important to see Statius' allegorical creations as exterior entities in this way, for otherwise one is bound to regard them as being no more than vivid realizations, or distracting obfuscations, of what the individual characters are feeling 'anyway'. Statius' allegorical technique, in other words, is not a way of making the characters of the poem more interesting or accessible, a way of helping us think more clearly or more richly about Eteocles, or Polynices, or any other character; rather, it is an experiment in universalizing the moral experiences

(1985): 'in the process of reflection or representation, the medium itself (the mirror, the allegory) does not in fact self-destruct or disappear, however much it may lay claim to self-effacement' (100).

[215] The analysis of Ovid's Invidia-narrative revealed similar conclusions: above, pp. 243–7.

[216] Lewis (1936), 289: 'the concrete experience of a universal' (though Lewis sees the personifications of the *Thebaid* itself as 'belonging to the inner world', 56); Van Dyke (1985), 66 (on the technique of precursors to Prudentius' *Psychomachia*, including the *Thebaid*): 'such allegorical events proceed as does the *Psychomachia*—through the interconversion of static ideas and their temporal embodiments'; cf. 37–46, 65–7.

[217] It is interesting, in this regard, to read the *Thebaid* against the background of the Neoplatonists' obsession with the failure of language to catch the true forms of reality: Wallis (1986); Lamberton (1986), 85–90, 164–73.

described in the action. What makes Statius' allegorical action so rewarding (and so difficult) to read is the continual reshuffling of positions demanded of the reader, who is tracing the tussle between the action of the human characters and the action of the allegorical figures who impinge upon them.

The climax of this type of narrative in the poem is the duel of Eteocles and Polynices, where the Furies and Pietas clash. Before that episode arrives, Statius deploys a variety of personification allegories. Even the most apparently perfunctory becomes a challenge to our temptation to gloss. The appearance of Mors ('Death') on the battlefield, for example, 'means' that 'men died', if one wishes to put it like that:

> Stygiisque emissa tenebris
> Mors fruitur caelo bellatoremque uolando
> campum operit nigroque uiros inuitat hiatu,
> nil uulgare legens, sed quae dignissima uita
> funera, praecipuos annis animisque cruento
> ungue notat.

Let out from the Stygian darkness, Mors enjoys possession of the sky, and flies above the battlefield, covering it over. She invites men with her black gaping mouth, picking nothing common, but those deaths most worthy of life she marks with her bloody nail, those men outstanding in youth and courage. (8. 376–81)

The developed tactile sense will be familiar to amateurs of Statius. More noteworthy is the care with which these lines relate to the moral architecture of the poem, as we see Jupiter's sky appropriated by the polluting invasion of Death's disruptive force. Thirty lines later the allegorical event is actualized by description of the men's missiles, which do the killing 'in reality', yet the 'literal' description has become contaminated by the moral force of the allegory: *exclusere diem telis, stant ferrea caelo / nubila, nec iaculis artatus sufficit aer* ('they shut out the day with their javelins, clouds of iron stand in the sky, the crammed air has not space enough for the missiles', 8. 412–13). The humans co-operate with Mors in turning the battlefield cliché to the needs of Statius' universe, as they shut out air and sky, replacing the natural world with their own tools of madness, creating a suffocating claustrophobia in which it appears that nothing can move or live.[218]

---

[218] One wonders what Statius' rhetoric might have made of the transformations

The impact of personifications upon human characters is, however, the most original of Statius' usages. An extended example presents itself towards the end of Book 10, when a divine power descends to earth, puts on the disguise of Tiresias' daughter, Manto, and inspires Menoeceus to save the city of Thebes by offering himself in suicide as a sacrificial victim (10. 628–782). Lewis is absolutely right to stress the remarkable surprise which Statius creates here by his original choice of agent: 'who that knows only his Virgil and his Homer would have expected this part to be played, not by Pallas or Mercury or Apollo, but by the personification Virtus?'[219] Yet again, however, as we saw with Minerva, Mars, and Venus, Statius is not proceeding unawares. He flaunts his innovation in a richly ironic four-line address to the Muse, after which he keeps us waiting for two more lines before naming the entity at the exposed end of a verse:

> nunc age, quis stimulos et pulchrae gaudia mortis
> addiderit iuueni—*neque enim haec absentibus umquam*
> *mens homini transmissa deis*—, memor incipe Clio,
> saecula te quoniam penes et digesta uetustas.
> diua Iouis solio iuxta comes, unde per orbem
> rara dari terrisque solet contingere, *Virtus . . .*

Come now, who spurred the youth on to a beautiful death and made him rejoice in it—*for this state of mind is never communicated to man without the presence of the gods*—, begin to tell, commemorative Clio, since the centuries are in your power, and the distant past, all organized. A deity, a near companion of Jupiter's throne, from where she is wont to be rarely granted through the world, or to impinge upon the earth, *Virtus, . . .* (10. 628–33)

---

of modern weaponry, most movingly presented by Keegan (1976), 306: 'The long-bows of the Agincourt archers, the muskets of the Waterloo infantrymen were very effective agents for the temporary transformation of an airspace of modest dimensions into an atmosphere of high lethality. . . . By the beginning of the First World War, soldiers possessed the means to maintain a lethal environment over wide areas for sustained periods. Hence the titles of some of the war's most deeply felt novels, *Le Feu (Under Fire)* by Henri Barbusse, *A Man Could Stand Up* by Ford Madox Ford and *In Stahlgewittern (Storm of Steel)* by Ernst Jünger, through which each of these soldier-authors sought to convey in a phrase to their readers what it was about the new warfare which made it different from all other warfare men had hitherto experienced: that it marooned them, as it were, on an undiscovered continent, where one layer of the air on which they depended for life was charged with lethal metallic particles . . .'

[219] Lewis (1936), 53.

The reader has already encountered Virtus earlier in the poem, and in company which should be unsettling for those who wish to see her inspiration of Menoeceus as a moment of unalloyed sublimity. She follows Bacchus in 4. 661-2, along with Ira, Furor, Metus, Ardor (Anger, Madness, Fear, Passion). In Book 7 she is glumly in the House of Mars (51), once again with Ira, Metus, and Furor, and now also with Impetus, Nefas, Discordia, Minae, and Mors (Attack, Wrong, Discord, Threats, Death, 47-53). Her kinship with Death has been stressed in action, in her first narrative moment, when she turns Amphiaraus away from sky-gazing as he rides to his death (*auertit morti contermina Virtus* ('Virtue, death's neighbour, distracts him', 7. 702). The description of her abode near Jupiter's throne will make many readers associate Virtus with the Dira sent by Jupiter to destroy Turnus at the end of the *Aeneid* (12. 845-55). Statius adheres to the Roman preconceptions of the nature of Virtus: 'As a state deity, Virtus was not a goddess of virtue in general, but of courage in battle.'[220] Although Virtus is about to inspire Menoeceus to an act of self-sacrifice which will call forth Statius' high enthusiasm, the company she keeps should alert us to expect that neither the manner of her action, nor our reaction to it, will be straightforward.

As she arrives at Thebes, her feet are touching the earth, and her face is near the sky (10. 638). Not just a description of her size, this image aligns Virtus simultaneously with Vergil's Fama and Homer's Eris ('Strife').[221] As an economical snapshot of what produces manly virtue in the world of the poem, this literary parentage could scarcely be bettered: fame is certainly what Menoeceus desires, and wins (10. 790-1); rivalry with his brother has a role also, for Virtus tells him to hasten to suicide, lest Haemon do it first (10. 671). Virtus disguises herself as Manto, the daughter of Tiresias, a process which Statius describes as deceit (*fraus*, 640); deceit is precisely what the inspired Menoeceus will practise upon his father, not eighty lines later (720-34).[222] As

---

[220] Axtell (1907), 25.

[221] *Il.* 4. 442-3; *Aen.* 4. 176-7. As Statius' Virtus is the companion of Jupiter, so Homer's Eris is very closely linked with Zeus (*Il.* 11. 3, 73-81).

[222] Note how Statius stresses there the *fraus* inspired in the hero by the gods (720-1); and note how Menoeceus' first word to his father is *falleris* (720): 'you are mistaken (to assume what you assume)', and also, clearly, 'you are being deceived (by me as I speak to you)'. Menoeceus practices similar deceit in Euripides' *Phoenissae* (977-92). On Statius' relationship with Euripides here, see Legras (1905), 120-1.

she assumes the appearance and dress of the prophetess, Virtus softens, losing her awe-inspiring qualities to some extent (641–2). In a phrase with many resonances to come, we are told that 'little of her distinction remained' (_paulum decoris permansit_, 642). _decus_, translated here as 'distinction', may also mean 'seemly behaviour, decorum',[223] and it is this quality which is put into jeopardy by the goddess' assumption of pacific female guise:

> tamen aspera produnt
> ora deam nimiique gradus. sic Lydia coniunx
> Amphitryoniaden exutum horrentia terga
> perdere Sidonios umeris ridebat amictus
> et turbare colus et tympana rumpere dextra.

None the less, her fierce face and excessively grand strides betray the goddess. Thus his Lydian spouse [Omphale] laughed to see the son of Amphitryon [Hercules] take off his shaggy lion-hide and ruin the Sidonian garments with his shoulders, messing up the distaffs, smashing the timbrels with his right hand. (10. 645–9)

In his commentary, R. D. Williams records the reaction which will be felt by many at a first reading: 'This simile, which is brilliantly pictorial in itself . . ., is wholly inappropriate in the context of the transformation of the majestic goddess Virtus: Hercules' plight is comical and ridiculous.'[224] Yet readers who have come this far will be reluctant to assume blundering, and will rather seek some explanation for Statius' remarkable procedure here—especially since it is Statius himself who has made 'appropriateness' an issue, with his highlighting, before the simile, of Virtus' loss of 'seemliness' as she takes on her disguise (_paulum decoris permansit_ . . .), and with his description, immediately after the simile, of Menoeceus as 'not an unseemly object for the sacrifice' (_neque . . . indecorem sacris_, 650).

The first level of inappropriateness asserts itself readily enough, in the fact that Virtus is disguised as a pacific creature, just as Hercules is disguised as a woman (indeed, the womanly disguise of Virtus and Hercules may prompt one to reflect upon the distinct oddity of Virtus being figured as feminine in the first place, inasmuch as _uir-tus_ denotes 'the qualities typical of a true man'[225]). This fundamental inappropriateness leaks out into the

[223] _OLD_ s.v. §4.

[224] Williams (1972), on 10. 646 f.

[225] _OLD_ s.v. §1; _appellata est enim a uiro uirtus_, Cic. _Tusc._ 2. 43; _uirtus . . . a uirilitate_, Varro _Ling._ 5. 73.

entire context. Statius' death-besotted and reckless Valour is radically incongruous in any other than a martial setting (though she
may slip into Bacchus' train as a symptom of drunkenness, the
Dutch courage which adds strength and horns even to the poor
man[226]). The job of this Virtus is not to incite Menoeceus to
mighty deeds of war, but to remove the great hero from his orthodox martial arena, where he is already performing splendidly,
hacking away without respite—all in the *absence* of Virtus
(*necdum aderat Virtus*, 657); only before Virtus arrives is
Menoeceus 'not unseemly' (650). The potentially indecorous ba-
thos of the suicide itself is caught with the confrontation of the
obsessed hero and the outsize, underdressed female figure of
Virtus, with her wild eyes and bulging shoulders. As Menoeceus
flings himself from the walls, trying to land on top of his enemies,
it is difficult to feel altogether solemn: *seque super medias acies,
nondum ense remisso, / iecit et in saeuos cadere est conatus
Achiuos* ('he threw himself over the middle of the battle-lines,
without letting go of his sword, and tried to fall on top of the savage Achaeans', 10. 778–9). His mad urge to turn his violence
against himself as well as his enemies is going to save the city, and
it is, in the abstract, a pious and valorous act, as is shown when
the abstract figures of Pietas and Virtus honour his falling body by
bringing it gently to the ground (780–1). Yet the actualization of
his decision by means of the indecorous and inappropriate figure
of Virtus colours the entire action, if we allow the characterful intervention of the personification to register on our reading.

It is astonishing how Statius contrives to channel so many of the
poem's currents of energy together into the climactic moment of
the brothers' duel. His lavish experimentation with personification
and allegory is no exception. The duel displays the crescendo and
termination of the Furies' action, the abnegation of Jupiter and the
celestial powers, the rout of Pietas—and it prepares for the disappearance of the allegorical narrative mode itself. The sense of esca-
lating competition over the brothers' fate becomes quite
overwhelming, making this one of the greatest moments in the
poem.[227]

---

[226] *tu ... uiris ... et addis cornua pauperi / post te neque iratos trementi / regum
apices neque militum arma*, Hor. *Carm.* 3. 21. 17–20.

[227] To Williams (1978), 174, this is an example of Statius' over-use of the divine

The ever-inventive malignity of Tisiphone begins the 500 lines of action which will culminate in the death of both brothers. One Fury has sufficed so far, but she now needs her 'great' sister, Megaera, for the '*great* [literary] work' (*grande opus*, 11. 100) of the climax.[228] Tisiphone delivers herself of a 35-line speech to her sister, gloating over the carnage so far, and making the arrangements for the final duel (11. 76–112). Her loquacity meets with a rather odd silence. The second Fury speaks precisely eight words during her time on earth (11. 201–2), and that solitary speech is designed to stop delay and speed up the action (*abrumpe moras, celeremus!*). Megaera's evil appears to be of a less histrionic, more business-like variety than Tisiphone's. It is all the same to the professional Megaera which brother she infects: she seems sluggish to her excited sister Tisiphone (*quid lenta uenis?*, 11. 101), and does not respond when offered the choice, so that Tisiphone herself allots the victims (101–9). This contrast should make us concentrate on how Tisiphone lingers on her achievements and her plans. It is open to us to put the Fury's words to one side as we read on to the 'real' matter of the brothers themselves, yet we are going to miss much of what Statius is saying about the experience of evil if we do not absorb Tisiphone's infinite capacity for taking pains in the infliction of pain, and contrast her glee with the equally repellent torturer's matter-of-factness embodied by Megaera.

Tisiphone is confident of success, but she anticipates some resistance. 'Let kindly faith,' she says, 'and piety fight back, they will be beaten' (*licet alma fides pietasque repugnent / uincentur*, 11. 98–9). She goes on to explain that, whereas the brothers themselves are easy meat, she is anxious about the influence of the Theban populace, of the brothers' mother, sister, and father, and

machinery: 'the single combat of the two brothers in book 11 is very elaborately arranged by Tisiphone and Megaera. A more disappointing instance of this form of overkill occurs in book 1 . . .' A remark more beside the point can scarcely be imagined. Schetter (1960), 26, has some very fine observations on the escalation and outdoing of the whole episode.

[228] The same translingual pun appears to be operating in Sen. *Thy.* 252–4, where Thyestes wishes for Megaera to come, and then says that his heart is burning with a madness which is *not great enough*, and that he wants to be filled with a *greater* monstrousness. The obvious Greek etymology from μεγαίρω ('to grudge one a thing as too great for him', *LSJ* s.v.) is attested in Cornutus (*Theol. Graec.* 10, 11). Statius appears not to play on this etymology explicitly, but he may hint at it when Polynices (who is under the influence of Megaera) sees his brother's splendid entourage and accoutrements, and feels precisely this emotion (11. 396–9).

of Adrastus and the Argive people (102–11). Sure enough, the next 350 lines show the failure of faith and piety to sway the brothers, as these groups and individuals successively attempt to reason with them, or simply manifest misery at their intentions.[229] Polynices' essential superiority to Eteocles is shown by the fact that he is brought to the verge of acknowledging faith and piety three times, before capitulating for good (139–50, 193–7, 382–7). After all these delays, when the brothers finally charge at each other in combat, Statius pauses on the brink for yet more postponement, as their horses swerve, and the actual clash is put off yet again (447–56). At this point, when we must expect all resources of delay to have been exhausted, Statius begins afresh with an astonishing switch of direction, in which he actualizes Tisiphone's talk of the resistance of faith and piety by showing us the very personification of Pietas, as she observes the combat, decides to intervene, and is put to total rout by Tisiphone (457–96).[230]

Let us look again at Tisiphone's mention of Pietas in her initial speech to Megaera. 'Let kindly faith and piety fight back,' she had said there, 'they will be beaten' (*licet alma fides pietasque repugnent, / uincentur*, 11. 98–9). Modern editors must decide whether to print the two substantives with or without initial capitals, and they decide to print capitals because they know that personified Pietas will appear in the action some 350 lines later. In the ancient context, such a decision is not at issue. Statius' original audience could not, of course, hear any difference, any more than we can, but nor could they see one, for the printing conventions which force editors to choose between *pietas* and *Pietas* are postclassical (indeed, post-medieval). Statius perhaps marginally inclines his audience to think of personalities here, rather than mere qualities, by using a significant epithet (*alma*, 'kindly, nourishing'), which is a characteristic epithet of female deities, and of Fides in particular.[231] None the less, by the time the horses of Eteocles and Polynices are swerving away from each other 450 lines later, we think we have seen the defeat of Faith and Piety

---

[229] Venini (1970), on 11. 102, 110. Oedipus will appear only after the brothers are dead (11. 580–5). Otherwise, Thebans: 257–62, 416–19, 475–6; mother: 315–53; sister: 354–82; Adrastus: 196–7, 424–46; Argives: 246–7, 475–6.

[230] The surprise of the introduction of Pietas is well brought out by Lewis (1936), 54.

[231] Enn. *Trag.* 350 Jocelyn (1967), *o Fides alma*; OLD s.v. §b.

definitively enacted in the defeat of the human characters who have attempted to represent these qualities to the antagonists: Megaera puts a helmet on Polynices' head to block out Adrastus' 'words of faith' (*fidas exclusit casside uoces*, 11. 200), while Antigone is explicitly 'pious' (11. 321).[232] The reader's experience of the earlier parts of the poem reinforces the sense of surprise when Pietas appears, for in Book 7 a very similar scene of confrontation had enacted itself without any appearance of a personification, when Iocasta and her two daughters had attempted to stop the invading army of Polynices with appeals to piety (506, 529). With a very striking simile, Statius reveals that Pietas is indeed reduplicating the action of the human characters: *fraternaque bella, / ceu soror infelix pugnantum aut anxia mater, / deflebat* ('Pietas was bewailing the brothers' war, like an unhappy sister of the fighters, or an anxious mother', 11. 460–2).

The defeat of Pietas happens many times, in other words. We see Adrastus, Iocasta, and Antigone fail to make the brothers listen to the claims of faith and piety, and then, when we expect finally to see the combat which must follow as a consequence, Statius encapsulates that failure once and for all with the abortive intervention of Pietas herself.[233] The poet enables us to experience the defeat of piety and the defeat of Piety, by narrating first the interaction of pious advisors with the doomed princes, and then the interaction of Pietas and Tisiphone themselves. He gives us a (comparatively) naturalistic narrative, and then follows it by uncovering the urge to universalise the experience which has been latent in our reading of the human interchanges. The intervention of Pietas is fixed in a time subsequent to the human interventions, since narrative can do no other; yet it is not a subsequent event, but rather a retelling, in an entirely different mode, of the previous

---

[232] Statius responds a number of times to epic's use of the helmet as an emblem of the barrier placed between the hero and his humanity. Hector removes his helmet in order to be human enough to pick up his son (*Il.* 6. 472–3); on the only occasion in the *Aeneid* when Aeneas talks to his son, he kisses him through his helmet, in an almost exaggeratedly metaphorical gesture (12. 433–4). Polynices, whose humanity is closer to the surface than his brother's, responds to Antigone's plea: 'his helmet allows tears to appear' (*lacrimasque fatetur / cassis*, 11. 385–6). When Iocasta confronts the faceless mass of the invading army as she looks for Polynices, she asks: 'Tell me, under which helmet am I to find my son?' (*quanam inueniam, mihi dicite, natum / sub galea?*, 7. 491–2).

[233] Cf. Vessey (1973), 276–7 on how Pietas' 'descent to the battlefield is an allegorical repetition of the earlier attempts at peace-making'.

300 lines. The experimental nature of Statius' work must be allowed to register, as well as its marked originality. He is testing alternative modes for catching experience, and, at moments like this, appears almost to be leaving it up to the reader to decide which is more adequate or compelling.

For modern readers, with our knowledge of the subsequent development of allegory, the confrontation of Pietas and Tisiphone is a numinous moment. One has the sensation of being present at the birth of an entire tradition of composition, and the tingle in one's spine is increased by the realization that Statius is utterly—arrogantly—in command of this manner of composition. Yet, for all its posthumous influence, the *Thebaid* does not act out the triumph of personification allegory. The abstracts do not take over from the gods of epic, as is implied by Lewis, with his aphorism on the twilight of the gods being the mid-morning of the personifications.[234] For this narrative mode, which asserts itself against the background of the supersession of the epic gods, is itself superseded. Just as the brothers' duel shows the withdrawal of Jupiter and the end of the action of the underworld, it is likewise the cap for the action of the personifications: Pietas is the last such creation on view in the poem. Statius' acknowledging of his procedure will be plainly seen if we turn, in conclusion, to Clementia.

When Oedipus finally speaks over his sons' corpses, he addresses Pietas and Natura, and refers to the *clementia* of his human heart:

> tarda meam, Pietas, longo post tempore mentem
> percutis? estne sub hoc hominis clementia corde?
> uincis io miserum, uincis, Natura, parentem!

'Now, when you are too late, Pietas, after long space of time do you smite my heart? Is there clemency in this human breast? You conquer, ah you conquer, Nature, this unhappy parent.' (11. 605–7)

This mention of clemency anticipates the lengthy treatment of the Altar of Clemency to come in the next book (12. 481–511). Since Oedipus has appealed to Pietas, we may be led to expect that this anticipation of clemency will work in the same way as had the anticipation of Pietas, so that reference to the quality will be followed by the appearance of the personification in the narrative. This sense of expectation is reinforced early on in Book 12,

[234] Lewis (1936), 52.

when we are told that some of the Argive widows will go to Athens, to see if the clemency of the Attic people will be favourable to them (12. 175–6). Yet when we arrive with the Argive widows at the Altar of Clementia, we receive an ostentatious declaration from the poet that he is going to stay in the human mode, and refrain from picturing Clementia in the action: she is going to be an altar, a name, a quality of human nature, but not a character:

> nulla autem effigies, nulli commissa metallo
> forma dei, mentes habitare et pectora gaudet.

There is no image, the form of the deity is entrusted to no metal, she rejoices to inhabit minds and hearts. (12. 493–4)

Statius refers to the hoary Varronian notion that the earliest and purest form of worship was aniconic,[235] yet more than one form of representation is being forsworn here. Clementia is not going to be entrusted to paper any more than to metal. She will remain a human emotion in a human heart, as she had been described by Oedipus (*sub hoc hominis clementia corde*, 11. 606), and she will not follow Virtus and Pietas into characterful action in the narrative.[236]

Such an emphasis is in harmony with the poem's final concentration on the human dimension, which we discussed at the end of the previous Section. Indeed, this very concentration on humanity provides us with another way of looking at the role played by the personifications in the closing stages of the poem. As the gods themselves begin to fade out of the action, the personifications do, fleetingly, come into their own. Even they, however, cease to act as characters, and they come to be used, so to speak, without initial capital letters, as ways of speaking generally of human conditions. It is possible to see in this movement an image of the historical process of personification itself, as first reconstructed by Reinhardt, who saw the personifications of Greek religion emerging from the need to associate the Olympians with human emo-

---

[235] Fr. 18 Cardauns (1976). Statius' stress on the mildness of Clementia is also in harmony with Varro's contention, in the same context, that the iconic representation of the gods was the factor which spread fear amongst the worshippers.

[236] The fact that Clementia is a human emotion is stressed by Lewis (1936), 53; Vessey (1973), 309–11. Statius' unique conception of Clementia is brought out in the valuable article of Burgess (1972), which stresses the way in which Clementia is set apart from the gods' traditional power to pardon (344).

tions and conditions.[237] The personifications may be seen as a way of mediating between the gods and humans, of associating qualities and emotions both with gods and with humans: 'they emerge from an emphasis on *human* conditions'.[238] In a very short space, Statius acts out this process. The gods become unapproachable and ineffectual; the qualities which are associated with them and with humans are allowed to act for a while, with success, as in the case of Virtus, or without, as in the case of Pietas; finally, the poet's focus confines itself entirely to human emotions and exchanges. Clementia had been left among humans by the gods, so Statius tells us (12. 499–505); with the gods' disappearance, and with the abandonment of narrative through personification, this human realm is the only one in which she can now exist.

None of the poets discussed in this book is as innovative as Statius in the treatment of the gods. He possessed an extraordinarily acute sense of the nature and limits of this type of narrative, and was able to demarcate its possibilities by setting it beside other, more novel, narrative modes. Repeatedly chastised for being derivative, this exuberant, accomplished, and original artist deserves better of modern readers.

[237] Reinhardt (1960*b*), 18–32; cf. already Petersen (1939), 29, on the fifth century: 'Immer bilden die vergöttlichten Mächte des Lebens und Normen des Staates einen Weg der Menschen zu den Göttern, sie stehen zwischen ihrer ewigen Welt und dem menschlichen Dasein, für beide gültig.'
[238] Whitman (1987), 272 (his emphasis). Whitman's appendix 'On the History of the Term "Personification" ' is most valuable (269–72); cf. Burkert (1985), 185: 'the Archaic Greek personifications come to assume their distinctive character in that they mediate between the individual gods and the spheres of reality; they receive mythical and personal elements from the gods and in turn give the gods part in the conceptual order of things'.

# Epilogue

Roges me quid aut quale sit deus, auctore utar Simonide, de quo cum quaesiuisset hoc idem tyrannus Hiero, deliberandi sibi unum diem postulauit; cum idem ex eo postridie quaereret, biduum petiuit; cum saepius duplicaret numerum dierum admiransque Hiero requireret cur ita faceret, 'Quia quanto diutius considero,' inquit, 'tanto mihi res uidetur obscurior.'

Ask me what god is or what he is like, and I shall bring in Simonides as my authority. When the tyrant Hieron asked him this question, he asked for a day to think it over; when, on the next day, Hieron put it to him again, he asked for two days; and after repeatedly doubling the number of days, when Hieron in amazement asked him the reason why, he said: 'Because the more time I spend thinking about it, the more obscure the subject appears to me.'

Cicero, *De Natura Deorum* 1. 60

Anyone who spends any time on the issues involved in this study will end up sympathizing whole-heartedly with Simonides. I could go on doubling, and redoubling, the total of years expended on writing this book, but I would only become increasingly impressed with the obscurity of the subject, and with the variety and complexity of the gods' epic ways of being.

The gods continued to flourish in the Roman world for centuries beyond the chronological boundary of our study. Even after the triumph of Christianity, they lived on—and not only in poetry, but as acknowledged parts of the theological apparatus of the new dispensation, only demoted from their supreme status to the role of 'demons', δαίμονες.[1] This is a process which we may glimpse already in one of the last of our poets, Valerius, who represents Fama as a deity not of Hell or Heaven, but of the intermediate

---

[1] MacMullen (1984), 18; Lane Fox (1986), 137.

clouds, who visits earth as occasion demands.[2] Related to this movement is the attenuation of the gods' cultic personalities. Granted that Valerius' and Statius' poems have mythical subjects, the disappearance of this dimension of meaning from the gods is none the less very striking; it is a shock to realize that Valerius' Jupiter is only once given a cult epithet, and Statius' never.[3]

The scope of the present book, then, could be expanded, continuing to the Latin epics of Claudian, written 300 years after the death of Silius, or the Greek epics of Tryphiodorus, Quintus Smyrnaeus, or Nonnus, from the third to the fifth centuries CE; a case could be made for establishing *Paradise Lost* as the first really secure finishing-point. But an individual author's limits of competence establish a limit for the study. The chronological starting-point of C. S. Lewis's *Allegory of Love* is Statius' *Thebaid*. That masterpiece, confident inheritor of centuries of tradition, harbinger of medieval and Renaissance technique, is a fitting place to finish the enquiry.

[2] *Arg.* 2. 119–21. On the intermediate status of the δαίμονες, between gods and humans, see Pl. *Symp.* 202 e–203 a; Burkert (1985), 331–2.

[3] *Arg.* 5. 147; see Schubert (1984), 226.

# Bibliography

Ackrill, J. L. (1981). *Aristotle the Philosopher* (Oxford).

Adamietz, J. (1970). 'Jason und Hercules in den Epen des Apollonios Rhodios und Valerius Flaccus', *A&A* 16. 29–38.

——(1976). *Zur Komposition der Argonautica des Valerius Flaccus* (Munich).

Ahl, F. M. (1976). *Lucan: An Introduction* (Ithaca, N.Y.).

——(1982). 'Lucan and Statius', in J. Luce (ed.), *Ancient Writers. Greece and Rome II. Lucretius to Ammianus Marcellinus* (New York). 914–41.

——(1984). 'The Art of Safe Criticism in Greece and Rome', *AJPh* 105. 174–208.

——(1985). *Metaformations: Soundplay and Wordplay in Ovid and Other Classical Poets* (Ithaca, N.Y.).

——(1986). 'Statius' "Thebaid": A Reconsideration', *ANRW* 2. 32. 5. 2803–912.

——Davis, M. A., and Pomeroy, A. (1986). 'Silius Italicus', *ANRW* 2. 32. 4. 2492–561.

Albert, R. (1981). *Das Bild des Augustus auf den frühen Reichsprägungen: Studien zur Vergöttlichung des ersten Prinzeps* (Speyer).

Albrecht, M. von (1964). *Silius Italicus: Freiheit und Gebundenheit römischer Epik* (Amsterdam).

——(1970). 'Der Dichter Lucan und die epische Tradition', in *Lucain*, Fondation Hardt, *Entretiens* 15. 267–308.

——(1977). 'Die Erzählung von Io bei Ovid und Valerius Flaccus', *WJA* N.F. 3. 139–48.

——(1981). 'Mythos und römische Realität in Ovids "Metamorphosen" ', *ANRW* 2. 31. 4. 2328–42.

——(1984). 'Ovids Arachne-Erzählung', in Harmatta (1984). 1. 457–64.

Anderson, W. S. (1957). 'Vergil's Second *Iliad*', *TAPhA* 88. 17–30.

# Bibliography 395

——(1958). 'Juno and Saturn in the *Aeneid*', *SPhNC* 55. 519–32.

——(1963). 'Multiple Change in the *Metamorphoses*', *TAPhA* 94. 1–27.

——(ed.) (1972). *Ovid's Metamorphoses: Books 6–10* (Norman, Okla.).

——(1988). Review of Knox (1986), *AJPh* 109. 459–61.

Annas, J. (1982). 'Plato on the Triviality of Literature', in Moravcsik and Temko (1982). 1–28.

Appel, G. (1909). *De Romanorum Precationibus* (Giessen).

Armstrong, A. H. (ed.) (1986). *Classical Mediterranean Spirituality: Egyptian, Greek, Roman* (New York).

Atherton, P. (1986). 'The City in Ancient Religious Experience', in Armstrong (1986). 314–36.

Attridge, H. W. (1978). 'The Philosophical Critique of Religion under the Early Empire', *ANRW* 2. 16. 1. 45–78.

Atzert, C. (1908). *De Cicerone Interprete Graecorum* (Göttingen).

Austin, R. G. (ed.) (1971). *P. Vergili Maronis Aeneidos Liber Primus* (Oxford).

——(ed.) (1977). *P. Vergili Maronis Aeneidos Liber Sextus* (Oxford).

Avenarius, G. (1956). *Lukians Schrift zur Geschichtsschreibung* (Meisenheim am Glan).

Axtell, H. L. (1907). *The Deification of Abstract Ideas in Roman Literature and Inscriptions* (Chicago).

Babbitt, F. C. (ed.) (1927). *Plutarch's Moralia* 1 (Cambridge, Mass.).

Babel, R. J. (1981–2). 'Vergil, Tops, and the Stoic View of Fate', *CJ* 77. 27–31.

Bachmann, W. (1902). *Die ästhetischen Anschauungen Aristarchs in der Exegese und Kritik der homerischen Gedichte* 1 (Erlangen).

Badian, E. (1966). 'The Early Historians', in T. A. Dorey (ed.), *Latin Historians* (London). 1–38.

Bahrenfuss, W. (1951). *Die Abenteuer der Argonauten auf Lemnos bei Apollonios Rhodios (Arg. 1. 601–915), Valerius Flaccus (Arg. 2. 72–427), Papinius Statius (Theb. 4. 746–5. 498)* (Diss., Kiel).

Bailey, C. (1932). *Phases in the Religion of Ancient Rome* (Oxford).

——(1935). *Religion in Virgil* (Oxford).

Bal, M. (1985). *Narratology: Introduction to the Theory of Literature*, tr. C. van Boheemen (Toronto).

Balsdon, J. P. V. D. (1979). *Romans and Aliens* (London).

Barchiesi, A. (1984). *La traccia del modello: effetti omerici nella narrazione virgiliana* (Pisa).

Bardon, H. (1940). *Les Empereurs et les lettres latines d'Auguste à Hadrien* (Paris).

Barkan, L. (1986). *The Gods Made Flesh: Metamorphosis and the Pursuit of Paganism* (New Haven).

Barker, E. (ed.) (1946). *The Politics of Aristotle* (Oxford).

Barnes, W. R. (1981). 'The Trojan War in Valerius Flaccus' *Argonautica*', *Hermes* 109. 360–70.

Barthes, R. (1968). 'L'Effet de réel', *Communications* 11. 84–9.

——(1974). *S/Z*, tr. R. Miller (New York).

Barwick, K. (1928). 'Die Gliederung der Narratio in der rhetorischen Theorie und ihre Bedeutung für die Geschichte des antiken Romans', *Hermes* 63. 261–88.

Bassett, E. L. (1955). 'Regulus and the Serpent in the *Punica*', *CPh* 50. 1–20.

——(1966). 'Hercules and the Hero of the *Punica*', in L. Wallach (ed.), *The Classical Tradition: Literary and Historical Studies in Honor of H. Caplan* (Ithaca, N.Y.). 258–73.

Bataille, G. (1962). *Death and Sensuality: A Study of Eroticism and the Taboo* (New York).

Bayley, J. (1987). *The Order of Battle at Trafalgar, and Other Essays* (New York).

Beard, M. (1983). Review of Wagenvoort (1980), *JRS* 73. 215.

——(1986). 'Cicero and Divination: The Formation of a Latin Discourse', *JRS* 76. 33–46.

——and Crawford, M. (1985). *Rome in the Late Republic: Problems and Interpretations* (London).

——and North, J. (edd.) (1990). *Pagan Priests: Religion and Power in the Ancient World* (Ithaca, N.Y.).

Beare, W. (1949). 'The Date of the *Bellum Punicum*', *CR* 63. 48.

Bekker, I. (ed.) (1825). *Scholia in Homeri Iliadem* (Berlin).

Beller, M. (1979). *Jupiter Tonans: Studien zur Darstellung der Macht in der Poesie* (Heidelberg).

Belsey, C. (1980). *Critical Practice* (London).

Benario, H. W. (1983). 'The "Carmen de Bello Actiaco" and Early Imperial Epic', *ANRW* 2. 30. 3. 1656–62.

Bernbeck, E. J. (1967). *Beobachtungen zur Darstellungsart in Ovids Metamorphosen* (Munich).

Beye, C. R. (1982). *Epic and Romance in the* Argonautica *of Apollonius* (Carbondale, Ill.).

Bilabel, F. (1925). 'Fragmente aus der Heidelberger Papyrussammlung', *Philologus* 80. 331–41.

Billerbeck, M. (1986). 'Stoizismus in der römischen Epik neronischer und flavischer Zeit', *ANRW* 2. 32. 5. 3116–51.

Binder, G. (1971). *Aeneas und Augustus: Interpretationen zum 8. Buch der Aeneis* (Meisenheim am Glan).

Biraschi, A. (1984). 'Strabone e la difesa di Omero nei Prolegomena', in F. Prontera (ed.), *Strabone: Contributi allo studio della personalità e dell'opera* 1 (Perugia). 127–53.

Bloch, R. (1972). 'Héra, Uni, Junon en Italie centrale', *CRAI*. 384–96.

Block, E. (1981). *The Effects of Divine Manifestation on the Reader's Perspective in Vergil's* Aeneid (New York).

Bloom, H. (1973). *The Anxiety of Influence: A Theory of Poetry* (New York and London).

——(1989). *Ruin the Sacred Truths: Poetry and Belief from the Bible to the Present* (Cambridge, Mass.).

Boardman, J. (1985). *The Parthenon and its Sculptures* (Austin).

Bömer, F. (ed.) (1958). *P. Ovidius Naso: Die Fasten* (Heidelberg).

——(ed.) (1969–86). *P. Ovidius Naso: Metamorphosen* (Heidelberg).

Bond, G. W. (ed.) (1981). *Euripides: Heracles* (Oxford).

Bowra, C. M. (1963). 'The Two Palinodes of Stesichorus', *CR*, NS 13. 245–52.

Boyancé, P. (1963). *La Religion de Virgile* (Paris).

Boyle, A. J. (1986). *The Chaonian Dove: Studies in the Eclogues, Georgics, and Aeneid of Virgil* (Leiden).

——(ed.) (1987). *Seneca's Phaedra* (Liverpool and Wolfeboro).

——(ed.) (1988). *The Imperial Muse: Ramus Essays on Roman Literature of the Empire, I. To Juvenal through Ovid* (Berwick, Victoria).

Bramble, J. C. (1982). 'Lucan', *CHCL* 2. 533–557.

Brasewell, B. K. (1971). 'Mythological Innovation in the *Iliad*', *CQ*, NS 21. 16–26.

Braudy, L. (1986). *The Frenzy of Renown: Fame and its History* (Oxford).

Bremmer, J. N., and Horsfall, N. M. (1987). *Roman Myth and Mythography* (London).

Brink, C. O. (1960). 'Tragic History and Aristotle's School', *PCPhS*, NS 6. 14–19.

——(1963). *Horace on Poetry 1: Prolegomena to the Literary Epistles* (Cambridge).

——(ed.) (1971). *Horace on Poetry 2: The 'Ars Poetica'* (Cambridge).

Brooke-Rose, C. (1981). *A Rhetoric of the Unreal: Studies in Narrative and Structure, Especially of the Fantastic* (Cambridge).

Broughton, T. R. S. (1951–60). *The Magistrates of the Roman Republic* (New York).

Brown, R. (1987). 'The Palace of the Sun in Ovid's *Metamorphoses*', in Whitby–Hardie–Whitby (1987). 211–20.

Bruner, J. (1986). *Actual Minds, Possible Worlds* (Cambridge, Mass.).

Brunt, P. A. (1989). 'Philosophy and Religion in the Late Republic', in M. Griffin and J. Barnes (edd.), *Philosophia Togata: Essays on Philosophy and Roman Society* (Oxford).

Buchheit, V. (1963). *Vergil über die Sendung Roms: Untersuchungen zum Bellum Poenicum und zur Aeneis* (Heidelberg).

——(1966). 'Mythos und Geschichte in Ovids Metamorphosen I', *Hermes* 94. 80–108.

——(1974). 'Junos Wandel zum Guten: Verg. *Aen.* 1, 279–82', *Gymnasium* 81. 499–503.

Büchner, K. (1955–8). 'P. Vergilius Maro, der Dichter der Römer', *RE* 2R 15. 1022–16. 1486.

——(ed.) (1982). *Fragmenta Poetarum Latinorum Epicorum et Lyricorum Praeter Ennium et Lucilium* (Leipzig).

Buffière, F. (1956). *Les Mythes d'Homère et la pensée grecque* (Paris).

——(ed.) (1962). *Héraclite: Allégories d' Homère* (Paris).

Bühler, W. (ed.) (1960). *Die Europa des Moschos* (Wiesbaden).

Bulloch, A. W. (1984). 'The Future of a Hellenistic Illusion: Some Observations on Callimachus and Religion', *MH* 41. 209–30.

——(ed.) (1985*a*). *Callimachus: The Fifth Hymn* (Cambridge).

——(1985*b*). 'Hellenistic Poetry', *CHCL* 1. 541–621.

Burck, E. (ed.)(1979). *Das römische Epos* (Darmstadt).

——and Rutz, W. (1979). 'Die *Pharsalia* Lucans', in Burck (1979). 154–99.

Burgess, J. F. (1972). 'Statius' Altar of Mercy', *CQ*, NS 22. 339–49.

Burkert, W. (1985). *Greek Religion: Archaic and Classical*, tr. J. Raffan (Oxford).

——(1986). 'Der Autor von Derveni: Stesimbrotos Περὶ Τελετῶν?', *ZPE* 62. 1–5.

Burnett, A. M. (1983). Review of Albert (1981), *Gnomon* 55. 563–5.

——(1986). 'The Iconography of Roman Coin Types in the Third Century B.C.', *NC* 146. 67–75.

Buschor, E. (1944). *Die Musen des Jenseits* (Munich).

Buxton, R. G. A. (1982). *Persuasion in Greek Tragedy: A Study of Peitho* (Cambridge).

Cairns, F. (1972). *Generic Composition in Greek and Roman Poetry* (Edinburgh).

——(1979). *Tibullus: A Hellenistic Poet at Rome* (Cambridge).

——(1989). *Virgil's Augustan Epic* (Cambridge).

Cambier, G. (1969). 'Recherches chronologiques sur l'œuvre et la vie de Valerius Flaccus', in J. Bibauw (ed.), *Hommages à M. Renard* 1 (Brussels). 191–228.

Campbell, M. (1981). *Echoes and Imitations of Early Epic in Apollonius Rhodius* (Leiden).

——(1983). *Studies in the Third Book of Apollonius Rhodius' Argonautica* (Hildesheim).

Camps, W. A. (1969). *An Introduction to Virgil's Aeneid* (Oxford).

Cardauns, B. (ed.) (1976). *M. Terentius Varro: Antiquitates Rerum Divinarum* (Wiesbaden).

——(1978). 'Varro und die römische Religion. Zur Theologie, Wirkungsgeschichte und Leistung der "Antiquitates Rerum Divinarum" ', *ANRW* 2. 16. 1. 80–103.

Carroll, M. (1895). *Aristotle's Poetics, c. XXV, in the Light of the Homeric Scholia* (Baltimore).

Christes, J. (1979). *Sklaven und Freigelassenen als Grammatiker und Philologen im antiken Rom* (Wiesbaden).

Cichorius, C. (1896–1900). *Die Reliefs der Trajanssäule* (Berlin).

Classen, C. J. (ed.) (1976). *Sophistik* (Darmstadt).

Clausen, W. V. (1964). 'Callimachus and Roman Poetry', *GRBS* 5. 181–96.

Clifford, G. (1974). *The Transformations of Allegory* (London).

Clinard, J. B. (1967). 'A Study of the Historical Epic at Rome from the Early Republic to the Neronian Period', Ph.D. thesis (University of North Carolina, Chapel Hill).

Coleman, K. M. (ed.)(1988). *Statius: Silvae IV* (Oxford).

Coleman, R. G. (1971). 'Structure and Intention in the *Metamorphoses*', *CQ*, NS 21. 461–77.

——(1973). Review of Otis (1970), *CR*, NS 23. 177–9.

——(ed.) (1977). *Vergil: Eclogues* (Cambridge).

——(1982). 'The Gods in the *Aeneid*', *G&R*, NS 29. 143–68.

Combellack, F. M. (1987). 'The λύσις ἐκ τῆς λέξεως', *AJPh* 108. 202–19.

Commager, S. (1981). 'Fateful Words: Some Conversations in *Aeneid* 4', *Arethusa* 14. 101–14.

Conacher, D. J. (1980). *Aeschylus' Prometheus Bound: A Literary Commentary* (Toronto).

Conington, J., Nettleship, H., and Haverfield, F. (edd.) (1858–98). *P. Vergili Maronis Opera* (London).

Connors, C. M. (1989). 'Petronius' *Bellum Civile* and the Poetics of Discord', Ph.D. thesis (University of Michigan).

Conte, G. B. (1966). 'Il proemio della *Pharsalia*', *Maia*, NS 18. 42–53 = Rutz (1970), 339–53.

——(1985). *Memoria dei poeti e sistema letterario: Catullo, Virgilio, Ovidio, Lucano*² (Turin).

——(1986). *The Rhetoric of Imitation: Genre and Poetic Memory in Virgil and Other Latin Poets*, ed. C. P. Segal (Ithaca, N.Y.).

Conway, R. S. (ed.) (1935). *P. Vergili Maronis Aeneidos Liber Primus* (Cambridge).

Cornell, T. J. (1975). 'Aeneas and the Twins', *PCPhS*, NS 21. 1–32.

——(1978). Review of Wardman (1976), *CR*, NS 28. 110–12.

Crawford, M. H. (1974). *Roman Republican Coinage* (Cambridge).

Crowther, N. B. (1976). 'Parthenius and Roman Poetry', *Mnemosyne* ser. 4. 29. 65–71.

Culler, J. (1981). *The Pursuit of Signs: Semiotics, Literature, Deconstruction* (London).

Curtius, E. R. (1953). *European Literature and the Latin Middle Ages*, tr. W. R. Trask (London).

Daiches, D. (1984). *God and the Poets: The Gifford Lectures, 1983* (Oxford).

Damrosch, L. (1985). *God's Plot and Man's Stories: Studies in the Fictional Imagination from Milton to Fielding* (Chicago).

Dauge, Y. A. (1981). *Le Barbare: Recherches sur la conception romaine de la barbarie et de la civilisation* (Brussels).

Davies, M. (1979). 'A Commentary on Stesichorus' , D. Phil. thesis (Oxford).

——(1981). 'The Judgement of Paris and *Iliad* xxiv', *JHS* 101. 56–62.

——(1989). *The Epic Cycle* (Bristol).

Davison, J. A. (1966). 'De Helena Stesichori', *QUCC* 1. 2. 80–90.

De Lacy, Ph. (1948). 'Stoic Views of Poetry', *AJPh* 69. 241–71.

Decharme, P. (1904). *La Critique des traditions religieuses chez les Grecques* (Paris).

Della Corte, F. (1983). 'Giunone, come personaggio e come dea, in Virgilio', *A&R*, NS 28. 21–30.

Delz, J. (1969). 'Die erste Junoszene in den Punica des Silius Italicus', *MH* 26. 88–100.

Denniston, J. D. (1954). *The Greek Particles*[2] (Oxford).

Detienne, M. (1962). *Homère, Hésiode et Pythagore: poésie et philosophie dans le pythagorisme ancien* (Brussels).

——(1967). *Les Maîtres de la vérité dans la Grèce archaïque* (Brussels).

——(1972). 'Entre bêtes et dieux', *Nouvelle revue de psychanalyse* 6. 231–46 = Gordon (1981), 215–28.

——and Vernant, J.-P. (1974). *Les Ruses de l'intelligence: La Mètis des Grecs* (Paris).

DeWitt, N. J. (1941). 'Rome and the "Road of Hercules" ', *TAPhA* 72. 59–69.

Dick, B. F. (1963). 'The Technique of Prophecy in Lucan', *TAPhA* 94. 37–49.

——(1965). 'The Role of the Oracle in Lucan's *De Bello Civili*', *Hermes* 93. 460–6.

Dickie, M. W. (1975). 'Ovid, *Metamorphoses* 2. 760–64', *AJPh* 96. 378–90.

Dietrich, B. C. (1983). 'Divine Epiphanies in Homer', *Numen* 30. 53–79.

——(1985–6). 'Divine Concept and Iconography in Greek Religion', *GB* 12/13. 171–92.

Dilke, O. A. W. (1960). (revision of J. P. Postgate, ed.) *M. Annaei Lucani De Bello Civili Liber VII* (Cambridge).

Dilke, O. A. W. (1972). 'Lucan's Political Views and the Caesars', in Dudley (1972). 62–82.

Dindorf, C. (ed.)(1855). *Scholia Graeca in Homeri Odysseam* (Oxford).

Doblhofer, E. (1960). 'Ovidius urbanus: eine Studie zum Humor in Ovids Metamorphosen', *Philologus* 104. 63–91, 223–35.

Dodds, E. R. (1951). *The Greeks and the Irrational* (Berkeley and Los Angeles).

——(ed.) (1960). *Euripides: Bacchae*² (Oxford).

Dover, K. J. (1974). *Greek Popular Morality in the Time of Plato and Aristotle* (Oxford).

——(1978). *Greek Homosexuality* (London).

Duchemin, J. (1955). *Pindare: Poète et prophète* (Paris).

Dudley, D. R. (ed.) (1972). *Neronians and Flavians: Silver Latin 1* (London).

Due, O. S. (1962). 'An Essay on Lucan', *C&M* 23. 68–132.

——(1970). 'Lucain et la philosophie', in *Lucain*, Fondation Hardt, *Entretiens* 15. 201–32.

——(1974). *Changing Forms: Studies in the Metamorphoses of Ovid* (Copenhagen).

Duff, J. D. (ed.) (1934). *Silius Italicus: Punica* (Cambridge, Mass.).

Duff, J. W. (1964). *A Literary History of Rome in the Silver Age: From Tiberius to Hadrian*³, ed. A. M. Duff (London).

Dumézil, G. (1970). *Archaic Roman Religion*, tr. P. Krapp (Chicago).

Dumont, A. M. (1986). 'L'Éloge de Néron', *BAGB*. 22–40.

Du Quesnay, I. M. LeM. (1984). 'Horace and Maecenas: The Propaganda Value of *Sermones* I', in Woodman and West (1984). 19–58.

Ebener, D. (1984). 'Lucans Bürgerkriegsepos als Beispiel poetischer Gestaltung eines historischen Stoffes', *Klio* 66. 581–9.

Edelstein, L., and Kidd, I. G. (edd.) (1972–88). *Posidonius* (Cambridge).

Eden, P. T. (ed.) (1975). *A Commentary on Virgil: Aeneid VIII* (Leiden).

Edgeworth, R. J. (1986). 'The Dirae of Aeneid XII', *Eranos* 84. 133–43.

Eggers, T. (1984). *Die Darstellung von Naturgottheiten bei Ovid und früheren Dichtern* (Paderborn and Munich).

Ehlers, W. W. (1971–2). 'Valerius Flaccus 1940 bis 1971', *Lustrum* 16. 105–42.

Eichgrün, E. (1961). *Kallimachos und Apollonios Rhodios* (Diss., Berlin).

Eliade, M. (1963). *Myth and Reality*, tr. W. Trask (New York).

Elliott, A. G. (1979–80). 'Ovid's *Metamorphoses*: A Bibliography 1968–1978', *CW* 73. 385–412.

Else, G. F. (1957). *Aristotle's Poetics: The Argument* (Cambridge, Mass.).

——(1986). *Plato and Aristotle on Poetry* (Chapel Hill, N.C.).

Erbse, H. (1953). 'Homerscholien und hellenistische Glossare bei Apollonios Rhodios', *Hermes* 81. 163–96.

——(1960). *Beiträge zur Überlieferung der Iliasscholie* (Munich).

——(1964). Review of van der Valk (1963–4), *Gnomon* 36. 549–57.

——(ed.) (1969–88). *Scholia Graeca in Homeri Iliadem* (Berlin).

——(1986). *Untersuchungen zur Funktion der Götter im homerischen Epos* (Berlin and New York).

Faerber, H. (1932). *Zur dichterischen Kunst in Apollonius Rhodios' Argonautika (Die Gleichnisse)* (Berlin).

Fantham, E. (1989). 'The Growth of Literature and Criticism at Rome', in Kennedy (1989). 220–44.

Farnell, L. R. (1896–1909). *The Cults of the Greek States* I–V (Oxford).

Fauth, W. (1975). 'Die Bedeutung der Nekromantie-Szene in Lucans *Pharsalia*', *RhM* 118. 325–44.

Fears, J. R. (1981*a*). 'The Theology of Victory at Rome: Approaches and Problems', *ANRW* 2. 17. 2. 736–826.

——(1981*b*). 'The Cult of Jupiter and Roman Imperial Ideology', *ANRW* 2. 17. 1. 3–141.

Feeney, D. C. (1984). 'The Reconciliations of Juno', *CQ*, NS 34. 179–94.

——(1986*a*). 'Following after Hercules, in Apollonius and Vergil', *PVS* 18. 47–83.

——(1986*b*). 'Epic Hero and Epic Fable', *Comparative Literature* 38. 137–58.

Ferguson, J. (1970). *The Religions of the Roman Empire* (London).

Ferrari, G. R. F. (1989). 'Plato and Poetry', in Kennedy (1989). 92–148.

Festa, N. (ed.) (1902). *Mythographi Graeci*, vol. 3. 2 (Leipzig).

Finley, M. I. (1985). *Ancient History: Evidence and Models* (London).

Fishwick, D. (1987). *The Imperial Cult in the Latin West: Studies in the Ruler Cult of the Western Provinces of the Roman Empire* I. 1 (Leiden).

Fitch, J. G. (ed.) (1987). *Seneca's Hercules Furens* (Ithaca, N.Y.).

Fleischmann, S. (1983). 'On the Representation of History and Fiction in the Middle Ages', *History and Theory* 22. 278–310.

Fletcher, A. (1964). *Allegory: The Theory of a Symbolic Mode* (Ithaca, N.Y.).

Fontenrose, J. (1959). *Python: A Study of Delphic Myth and its Origins* (Berkeley and Los Angeles).

Fordyce, C. J. (ed.) (1977). *P. Vergili Maronis Aeneidos Libri VII–VIII* (Oxford).

Fornara, C. W. (1983). *The Nature of History in Ancient Greece and Rome* (Berkeley and Los Angeles).

Foster, J. C. B. (1977). 'Divine and Demonic Possession in the *Aeneid*', *LCM* 2. 117–28.

Fraenkel, E. (1927). 'Lucan als Mittler des antiken Pathos', *Vorträge der Bibliothek Warburg* 4. 229–57 = Rutz (1970), 15–49.

——(1931). 'Livius Andronicus', *RE* Suppl. 5. 598–607.

——(1945). 'Some Aspects of the Structure of *Aeneid* VII', *JRS* 35. 1–14.

——(ed.) (1950). *Aeschylus: Agamemnon* (Oxford).

——(1954). 'The Giants in the Poem of Naevius', *JRS* 44. 14–17.

——(1964). *Kleine Beiträge zur klassischen Philologie* (Rome).

Fränkel, H. (1932). 'Griechische Bildung in altrömischen Epen', *Hermes* 67. 303–11.

——(1935). 'Griechische Bildung in altrömischen Epen II', *Hermes* 70. 59–72.

——(ed.) (1964a). *Apollonii Rhodii Argonautica²* (Oxford).

——(1964b). *Einleitung zur kritischen Ausgabe der Argonautika des Apollonios* (Göttingen).

——(1968). *Noten zu den Argonautika des Apollonios* (Munich).

——(1975). *Early Greek Poetry and Philosophy*, tr. M. Hadas and J. Willis (Oxford).

Franz, M. L. von (1943). *Die ästhetischen Anschauungen der Iliasscholien im Cod. Ven. B und im Townleianus* (Zurich).

Fraser, P. M. (1972). *Ptolemaic Alexandria* (Oxford).

Frassinetti, P. (1973). 'Stazio epico e la critica recente', *RIL* 107. 243–58.

Friedländer, P. (1932). 'Statius an den Schlaf', *Ant* 8. 215–28.

Friedländer, U. (1895). *De Zoilo Aliisque Homeri Obtrectatoribus* (Königsberg).

Friedrich, R. (1987). 'Thrinakia and Zeus' Ways to Men in the *Odyssey*', *GRBS* 28. 375–400.

Friedrich, W.-H. (1938). 'Cato, Caesar und Fortuna bei Lucan', *Hermes* 73. 391–421 = Rutz (1970), 70–102 (abridged).

Frye, N. (1976). *The Secular Scripture: A Study of the Structure of Romance* (Cambridge, Mass.).

Fusillo, M. (1985). *Il tempo delle Argonautiche* (Rome).

Fyfe, H. (1983). 'An Analysis of Seneca's *Medea*', in A. J. Boyle (ed.), *Seneca Tragicus: Ramus Essays on Senecan Drama* (Victoria, Australia). 77–93.

Galinsky, G. K. (1969). *Aeneas, Sicily, and Rome* (Princeton).

——(1972). *The Herakles Theme: The Adaptations of the Hero in Literature from Homer to the Twentieth Century* (Oxford).

——(1975). *Ovid's* Metamorphoses: *An Introduction to the Basic Aspects* (Berkeley and Los Angeles).

——(1981). 'Some Aspects of Ovid's Golden Age', *GB* 10. 193–205.

Gallavotti, C. (1969). 'Tracce della Poetica di Aristotele negli scolii omerici', *Maia* 21. 203–14.

Garbarino, G. (1973). *Roma e la filosofia greca dalle origini alla fine del II secolo A. C.* (Turin).

Gardner, P. (1918). *A History of Ancient Coinage* (Oxford).

Garson, R. W. (1963). 'The Hylas Episode in Valerius' *Argonautica*', *CQ*, NS 13. 260–7.

Gatz, B. (1967). *Weltalter, goldene Zeit und sinnverwandte Vorstellungen* (Hildesheim).

Gaunt, D. M. (1972). 'Argo and the Gods in Apollonius Rhodius', *G&R*, NS 19. 117–26.

Geertz, C. (1974). 'From the Native's Point of View: On the Nature of Anthropological Understanding', *Bulletin of the Academy of Arts and Sciences* 28. 26–45.

Gellie, G. H. (1972). 'Juno and Venus in *Aeneid* IV', in J. R. C. Martyn (ed.), *Cicero and Virgil: Studies in Honour of Harold Hunt* (Amsterdam). 138–48.

Genette, G. (1980). *Narrative Discourse,* tr. J. E. Lewin (Ithaca, N.Y.).

——(1988). *Narrative Discourse Revisited,* tr. J. E. Lewin (Ithaca, N.Y.).

George, E. V. (1974). *Aeneid VIII and the Aitia of Callimachus* (Leiden).

Gerber, D. E. (1982). *Pindar's 'Olympian One': A Commentary* (Toronto).

Getty, R. J. (1940). 'The Introduction to the *Argonautica* of Valerius Flaccus', *CPh* 35. 259–73.

Giangrande, G. (1973). *Zu Sprachgebrauch, Technik und Text des Apollonios Rhodios* (Amsterdam).

——(1980). *Scripta Minora Alexandrina* 1 (Amsterdam).

Gianotti, G. F. (1975). *Per una poetica pindarico* (Turin).

Goetz, M. (1918). *De Scholiastis Graecis Poetarum Romanorum Auctoribus Quaestiones Selectae* (Diss., Jena).

Goldhill, S. (1986). 'Framing and Polyphony: Readings in Hellenistic Poetry', *PCPhS,* NS 32. 25–52.

Gomme, A. W. (1954). *The Greek Attitude to Poetry and History* (Berkeley and Los Angeles).

Gordon, R. L. (1979). 'The Real and the Imaginary: Production and Religion in the Greco-Roman World', *Art History* 2. 5–34.

——(ed.) (1981). *Myth, Religion, and Society: Structuralist Essays by M. Detienne, L. Gernet, J.-P. Vernant, and P. Vidal-Naquet* (Cambridge and Paris).

——(1987). 'Lucan's Erictho', in Whitby–Hardie–Whitby (1987). 231–41.

Gossage, A. J. (1969). 'Virgil and the Flavian Epic', in D. R. Dudley (ed.), *Virgil* (London). 67–93.

——(1972). 'Statius', in Dudley (1972). 184–235.

Gottschalk, H. B. (1980). *Heraclides of Pontus* (Oxford).

Gould, J. (1985). 'On Making Sense of Greek Religion', in P. E. Easterling and J. V. Muir (edd.), *Greek Religion and Society* (Cambridge). 1–33.

Grassmann-Fischer, B. (1966). *Die Prodigien in Vergils Aeneis* (Munich).

Greene, T. M. (1963). *The Descent from Heaven: A Study in Epic Continuity* (New Haven).

——(1982). *The Light in Troy: Imitation and Discovery in Renaissance Poetry* (New Haven).

Griesinger, R. (1907). *Die ästhetischen Anschauungen der alten Homererklärer, dargestellt nach den Homerscholien* (Diss., Tübingen).

Griffin, J. (1980). *Homer on Life and Death* (Oxford).

——(1985). *Latin Poets and Roman Life* (London).

——(1986). *Virgil* (Oxford).

Griffin, M. T. (1984). *Nero: The End of a Dynasty* (New Haven).

Griffiths, J. G. (1967). 'Allegory in Greece and Egypt', *JEA* 53. 79–102.

Grimal, P. (1970). 'Le Poète et l'histoire', in *Lucain*, Fondation Hardt, *Entretiens* 15. 51–117.

——(1977). *La Guerre Civile de Pétrone dans ses rapports avec la Pharsale* (Paris).

——(1980). 'En attendant Pharsale, Lucain poète de l'attente', *VL* 77. 2–11.

Griset, E. (1955). 'L'elogio Neroniano', *RSC* 3. 134–8 = Rutz (1970), 318–25.

Grube, G. M. A. (1965). *The Greek and Roman Critics* (Toronto).

Gundolf, F. (1924). *Caesar: Geschichte seines Ruhms* (Berlin). 32–6 = Rutz (1970), 10–14.

Habicht, C. (1970). *Gottmenschentum und griechische Städte*[2] (Munich).

Halliwell, S. (1986). *Aristotle's Poetics* (London and Chapel Hill, N.C.).

——(ed.) (1987). *The* Poetics *of Aristotle: Translation and Commentary* (London).

——(1989). 'Aristotle's Poetics', in Kennedy (1989). 149–83.

Halter, T. (1963). *Form und Gehalt in Vergils Aeneis* (Munich).

Hamdorf, F. W. (1964). *Griechische Kultpersonifikation der vorhellenistischen Zeit* (Mainz).

Händel, P. (1954). *Beobachtungen zur epischen Technik des Apollonios Rhodios* (Munich).

Hannestad, N. (1986). *Roman Art and Imperial Policy* (Aarhus).

Hardie, A. (1983). *Statius and the Silvae: Poets, Patrons and Epideixis in the Graeco-Roman World* (Liverpool).

Hardie, P. R. (1985). 'Cosmological Patterns in the *Aeneid*', *PLLS* 5. 85–97.

——(1986). *Virgil's* Aeneid: Cosmos *and* Imperium (Oxford).

Harmatta, J. (ed.) (1984). *Actes du VII*[e] *Congrès de la Fédération Internationale des Associations d'Études Classiques* (Budapest).

408      *Bibliography*

Harper-Smith, A. (1988). 'A Commentary on Valerius Flaccus Argonauticon 2', D. Phil. thesis (Oxford).

Harriott, R. (1969). *Poetry and Criticism Before Plato* (London).

Harris, W. V. (1979). *War and Imperialism in Republican Rome, 327–70 B.C.* (Oxford).

Harrison, E. L. (1970). 'Divine Action in *Aeneid* Book Two', *Phoenix* 24. 320–32.

——(1976). 'Structure and Meaning in Vergil's *Aeneid*', *PLLS* 1. 101–12.

——(1980). 'The Structure of the *Aeneid*: Observations on the Links between the Books', *ANRW* 2. 31. 1. 359–93.

——(1984*a*). 'The *Aeneid* and Carthage', in Woodman and West (1984). 95–115.

——(1984*b*). 'Vergil's Mercury', in A. G. M<sup>c</sup>Kay (ed.), *Vergilian Bimillenary Lectures 1982. Vergilius* Suppl. Vol. 2. 1–47.

——(1985). 'Foundation Prodigies in the *Aeneid*', *PLLS* 5. 131–64.

Haskins, C. E. (1887). (ed., with Introduction by W. E. Heitland) *M. Annaei Lucani Pharsalia* (London).

Haüssler, R. (1976). *Das historische Epos der Griechen und Römer bis Vergil: Studien zum historischen Epos der Antike. I. Teil: Von Homer zu Vergil* (Heidelberg).

——(1978). *Das historische Epos von Lucan bis Silius und seine Theorie: Studien zum historischen Epos der Antike. II. Teil: Geschichtliche Epik nach Vergil* (Heidelberg).

Havelock, E. A. (1966). 'Preliteracy and the Presocratics', *BICS* 13. 44–67.

Haywood, M. S. (1983). 'Word Play Between ΘΕΩ/ΘΟΟΣ and ΘΕΟΣ in Homer', *PLLS* 4. 215–18.

Heck, E. (1987). *MH ΘΕΟΜΑΧΕΙΝ, oder die Bestrafung des Gottesverächters. Untersuchungen zur Bekämpfung und Aneignung römischer religio bei Tertullian, Cyprian und Laktanz* (Frankfurt).

Heinimann, F. (1945). *Nomos und Physis. Herkunft und Bedeutung einer Antithese im griechischen Denken des 5. Jahrhunderts* (Basel).

Heinze, R. (1915). *Virgils epische Technik*³ (Leipzig and Berlin).

——(1919). *Ovids elegische Erzählung* (Leipzig).

Helm, R. (1956). 'Nachaugusteische nichtchristliche Dichter I', *Lustrum* 1. 236–99.

Hémardinquer, M. (1872). *De Apollonii Rhodii Argonauticis* (Paris).

Henderson, J. (1988). 'Lucan/The Word at War', in Boyle (1988). 122–64.

Henrichs, A. (1971). 'Scholia Minora zu Homer, I', *ZPE* 7. 97–149.

——(1975). 'Two Doxographical Notes: Democritus and Prodicus on Religion', *HSCPh* 79. 93–123.

——(1976). 'The Atheism of Prodicus', *BCPE* 6. 15–21.

——(1984). 'The Sophists and Hellenistic Religion: Prodicus as the Spiritual Father of the Isis Aretalogies', in Harmatta (1984). 1. 339–53.

Henry, J. (1873–92). *Aeneidea* (London and Dublin).

Herington, C. J. (1955). *Athena Parthenos and Athena Polias: A Study in the Religion of Periclean Athens* (Manchester).

——(1966). 'Senecan Tragedy', *Arion* 5. 422–71.

Hersman, A. (1906). *Studies in Greek Allegorical Interpretation* (Chicago).

Herter, H. (1944–55). 'Bericht über die Literatur zur hellenistischen Dichtung seit dem Jahre 1921, II. Teil: Apollonios von Rhodos', *JAW* 285. 213–410.

——(1973). 'Apollonios', *RE* Suppl. 13. 15–56.

Heuvel, H. (1932). (ed.) *P. Papini Statii Thebaidos Liber Primus Versione Batava Commentarioque Exegetico Instructus* (Zutphen).

Heyne, C. G., and Wagner, G. P. E. (edd.) (1830–41). *Virgilii Opera*⁴ (Leipzig).

Highet, G. (1972). *The Speeches in Vergil's Aeneid* (Princeton).

Hinds, S. E. (1984). '*Cave Canem*: Ovid *Fasti* 4. 500', *LCM* 9. 79.

——(1987). *The Metamorphosis of Persephone: Ovid and the Self-Conscious Muse* (Cambridge).

——(1988). 'Generalizing about Ovid', in Boyle (1988). 4–31.

——(1989). Review of Knox (1986), *CPh* 84. 266–71.

Hintenlang, H. (1961). *Untersuchungen zu den Homer-Aporien des Aristoteles* (Diss., Heidelberg).

Hofmann, E. (1928). 'Die literarische Persönlichkeit des P. Terentius Varro Atacinus', *WS* 46. 159–76.

Hofmann, H. (1981). 'Ovids "Metamorphosen" in der Forschung der letzten 30 Jahre (1950–1979)', *ANRW* 2. 31. 4. 2161–273.

410        Bibliography

Hofmann, H. (1985). 'Ovid's *Metamorphoses: carmen perpetuum, carmen deductum*', *PLLS* 5. 223–41.

Hollis, A. (ed.)(1970). *Ovid: Metamorphoses Book VIII* (Oxford).

Hölscher, T. (1967). *Victoria Romana. Archäologische Untersuchungen zur Geschichte und Wesensart der römischen Siegesgöttin von den Anfängen bis zum Ende des 3. Jhs. n. Chr.* (Mainz).

Horsfall, N. M. (1973–4). 'Dido in the Light of History', *PVS* 12. 1–13.

——(1987). '*Non Viribus Aequis*: Some Problems in Virgil's Battle-Scenes', *G&R*, ns 34. 48–55.

Howie, J. G. (1984). 'Thukydides' Einstellung zur Vergangenheit: Zuhörerschaft und Wissenschaft in der *Archäologie*', *Klio* 66. 502–32.

Hubbard, M. (1975). 'The Capture of Silenus', *PCPhS*, ns 21. 53–62.

Hübner, W. (1970). *Dirae im römischen Epos: Über das Verhältnis von Vogeldämonen und Prodigien* (Hildesheim).

Hügi, M. (1952). *Vergils Aeneis und die hellenistische Dichtung* (Bern).

Hunter, R. L. (1986). 'Apollo and the Argonauts: Two Notes on Ap. Rhod. 2, 669–719', *MH* 43. 50–60.

——(1987). 'Medea's Flight: the Fourth Book of the *Argonautica*', *CQ*, ns 37. 129–39.

——(ed.) (1989). *Apollonius of Rhodes: Argonautica Book III* (Cambridge).

Hussey, E. (1972). *The Presocratics* (London).

Huxley, G. L. (1969a). *Greek Epic Poetry: From Eumelos to Panyassis* (London).

——(1969b). 'Choerilus of Samos', *GRBS* 10. 12–29.

Ibscher, R. (1939). *Gestalt der Szene und Form der Rede in den Argonautika des Apollonios Rhodios* (Munich).

Innes, D. C. (1979). 'Gigantomachy and Natural Philosophy', *CQ*, ns 29. 165–71.

Jaeger, W. (1939). *Paideia: The Ideals of Greek Culture*, tr. G. Highet (Oxford).

——(1947). *The Theology of the Early Greek Philosophers*, tr. E. S. Robinson (Oxford).

Jal, P. (1962). 'Les Dieux et les guerres civiles dans la Rome de la fin de la République', *REL* 40. 170–200.

——(1963). *La Guerre civile à Rome: Étude littéraire et morale* (Paris).

Jenkyns, R. (1985). 'Pathos, Tragedy and Hope in the *Aeneid*', *JRS* 75. 60–77.

Jocelyn, H. D. (1966). 'The Roman Nobility and the Religion of the Republican State', *JRH* 4. 89–104.

——(ed.) (1967). *The Tragedies of Ennius* (Cambridge).

——(1972). 'The Poems of Quintus Ennius', *ANRW* 1. 2. 987–1026.

——(1982). 'Varro's *Antiquitates Rerum Diuinarum* and Religious Affairs in the Late Roman Republic', *BRL* 65. 148–205.

——(1989). 'Romulus and the *di genitales* (Ennius, *Annales* 110–11 Skutsch)', in J. Diggle, J. B. Hall, and H. D. Jocelyn (edd.), *Studies in Latin Literature and its Tradition in Honour of C. O. Brink* (Cambridge). 39–65.

Jong, I. J. F. de (1987). *Narrators and Focalizers: The Presentation of the Story in the* Iliad (Amsterdam).

Johnson, W. R. (1970). 'The Problem of the Counter-Classical Sensibility and its Critics', *CSCA* 3. 123–51.

——(1976). *Darkness Visible: A Study of Vergil's* Aeneid (Berkeley and Los Angeles).

——(1987). *Momentary Monsters: Lucan and his Heroes* (Ithaca, N.Y.).

Jordan, H. (1870). 'Zur römischen Topographie', *Hermes* 4. 228–65.

Jörgensen, O. (1904). 'Das Auftreten der Götter in den Büchern ι–μ der Odyssee', *Hermes* 39. 357–82.

Juhnke, H. (1972). *Homerisches in römischer Epik flavischer Zeit: Untersuchungen zu Szenennachbildungen und Strukturentsprechungen in Statius' Thebais und Achilleis und in Silius' Punica* (Munich).

Jung, C. G. (1958). *The Collected Works of C. G. Jung*, ed. H. Read, M. Fordham, and G. Adler (London).

Kahn, L. (1978). *Hermès passe, ou les ambiguïtés de la communication* (Paris).

Kaimio, J. (1979). *The Romans and the Greek Language* (Helsinki).

Kambylis, A. (1965). *Die Dichterweihe und ihre Symbolik* (Heidelberg).

Keegan, J. (1976). *The Face of Battle* (London).

412     *Bibliography*

Kennedy, G. A. (ed.) (1989). *The Cambridge History of Literary Criticism. Volume 1. Classical Criticism* (Cambridge).

Kenney, E. J. (1958). 'Nequitiae Poeta', in N. I. Herescu (ed.), *Ovidiana: Recherches sur Ovide publiées à l'occasion du bimillénaire de la naissance du poète* (Paris). 201–9.

——(ed.) (1971). *Lucretius: De Rerum Natura Book III* (Cambridge).

——(1973). 'The Style of the *Metamorphoses*', in J. W. Binns (ed.), *Ovid* (London). 116–53.

——(1974). Review of Highet (1972), *JRS* 64. 276–7.

——(1976). 'Ovidius Prooemians', *PCPhS*, NS 22. 46–53.

——(1982*a*). 'Books and Readers in the Roman World', *CHCL* 2. 3–32.

——(1982*b*). 'Ovid', *CHCL* 2. 420–57.

Kerényi, C. (1975). *Zeus and Hera: Archetypal Image of Father, Husband, and Wife*, tr. C. Holme (London).

Kerferd, G. B. (1981). *The Sophistic Movement* (Cambridge).

Kermode, F. (1971). *Shakespeare, Spenser, Donne: Renaissance Essays* (London and New York).

Kirk, G. S. (1970). *Myth: Its Meaning and Function in Ancient and Other Cultures* (Berkeley and Los Angeles).

——(1985). *The Iliad: A Commentary. Volume I: Books 1–4* (Cambridge).

Kirk, G. S., Raven, J. E., and Schofield, M. (1983). *The Presocratic Philosophers*² (Cambridge).

Kirkwood, G. (1982). *Selections from Pindar: Edited with an Introduction and Commentary* (Chico, Calif.).

Klein, L. (1931). 'Die Göttertechnik in den Argonautika des Apollonius Rhodius', *Philologus* 86. 18–51, 215–57.

Klein, T. M. (1974). 'The Role of Callimachus in the Development of the Concept of the Counter-Genre', *Latomus* 33. 217–31.

Klingner, F. (1967). *Virgil: Bucolica, Georgica, Aeneis* (Zurich and Stuttgart).

Knauer, G. N. (1964). *Die Aeneis und Homer: Studien zur poetischen Technik Vergils mit Listen der Homerzitate in der Aeneis* (Göttingen).

Knox, P. E. (1986). *Ovid's* Metamorphoses *and the Traditions of Augustan Poetry* (Cambridge).

Koch, C. (1937). *Der römische Juppiter* (Frankfurt).

——(1955). 'Untersuchungen zur Geschichte der römischen Venus-Verehrung', *Hermes* 83. 1–51.

Köhnken, A. (1974). 'Pindar as Innovator: Poseidon Hippios and the Relevance of the Pelops Story in Olympian I', *CQ*, NS 24. 199–206.

Koepp, F. (1898). *Sage und Geschichte in der griechischen Kunst* (Berlin).

Koster, S. (1970). *Antike Epostherien* (Wiesbaden).

Kovacs, D. (1987). 'Ovid, *Metamorphoses* 1. 2', *CQ*, NS 37. 458–65.

Kranz, W. (1933). *Stasimon: Untersuchung zu Form und Gehalt der griechischen Tragödie* (Berlin).

Krauss, F. B. (1930). 'An Interpretation of the Omens, Portents and Prodigies recorded by Livy, Tacitus and Suetonius', Ph.D. thesis (University of Pennsylvania).

Krenkel, W. (1970). 'Zur literarischen Kritik bei Lucilius', in D. Korzeniewski (ed.), *Die römische Satire* (Darmstadt). 161–266.

Kroll, J. (1932). *Gott und Hölle. Der Mythos vom Descensuskampfe* (Leipzig).

Kroll, W. (1916). 'Das historische Epos', *Sokrates* N.F. 4. 1–14.

——(1924). *Studien zur Verständnis der römischen Literatur* (Stuttgart).

Kühn, W. (1971). *Götterszenen bei Vergil* (Heidelberg).

Kullman, W. (1956). *Das Wirken der Götter in der Ilias* (Berlin).

Küppers, J. (1986). *Tantarum Causas Irarum. Untersuchungen zur einleitenden Bücherdyade der Punica des Silius Italicus* (Berlin).

Kytzler, B. (1955). *Statius-Studien. Beiträge zum Verständnis der Thebais* (Diss., Berlin).

Lacey, W. K. (1986). '*Patria Potestas*', in B. Rawson (ed.), *The Family in Ancient Rome: New Perspectives* (Ithaca, N.Y.). 121–44.

Lamberton, R. (1986). *Homer the Theologian: Neoplatonist Allegorical Reading and the Growth of the Epic Tradition* (Berkeley and Los Angeles).

Lanata, G. (ed.) (1963). *Poetica pre-platonica: Testimonianze e frammenti* (Florence).

Lane Fox, R. (1986). *Pagans and Christians* (Harmondsworth and New York).

414          Bibliography

Lang, C. (ed.) (1881). *Cornuti Theologiae Graecae Compendium* (Leipzig).

Lapidge, M. (1979). 'Lucan's Imagery of Cosmic Dissolution', *Hermes* 107. 344–70.

Lascaris, J. (ed.) (1517). *Scholia in Homeri Iliadem quae vocantur Didymi* (Rome).

Lasserre, F. (1946). *La Figure d'Éros dans la poésie grecque* (Paris).

Lateiner, D. (1984). 'Mythic and Non-mythic Artists in Ovid's *Metamorphoses*', *Ramus* 13. 1–30.

Latte, K. (1925). 'Glossographika', *Philologus* 80. 136–75.

——(1960). *Römische Religionsgeschichte* (Munich).

Lausberg, M. (1983). 'Iliadisches im ersten Buch der Aeneis', *Gymnasium* 90. 203–39.

——(1985). 'Lucan und Homer', *ANRW* 2. 32. 3. 1565–622.

Lazzarini, C. (1984). 'Historia/fabula. Forme della costruzione poetica virgiliana nel commento di Servio all'Eneide', *MD* 12. 117–44.

Le Bonniec, H. (1970). 'Lucain et la religion', in *Lucain*, Fondation Hardt, *Entretiens* 15. 159–200.

Leach, E. W. (1974). 'Ekphrasis and the Theme of Artistic Failure in Ovid's *Metamorphoses*', *Ramus* 3. 102–42.

Lefkowitz, M. R. (1989). 'Impiety and Atheism in Euripides', *CQ*, NS 39. 70–82.

Legras, L. (1905). *Étude sur la Thébaïde de Stace* (Paris).

Lehrs, K. (1882). *De Aristarchi Studiis Homericis³* (Leipzig).

Lennox, P. G. (1980). 'Apollonius, Argonautica 3, 1 ff., and Homer', *Hermes* 108. 45–73.

Leo, F. (1913). *Geschichte der römischen Literatur* I: *Die archaische Literatur* (Berlin).

Lesky, A. (1961). *Göttliche und menschliche Motivation im homerischen Epos* (Heidelberg).

Levin, D. N. (1971). *Apollonius' Argonautica Re-examined. I: The Neglected First and Second Books* (Leiden).

Lewis, C. S. (1936). *The Allegory of Love: A Study in Medieval Tradition* (Oxford).

Lévêque, P. (1959). *Aurea Catena Homeri: Une Étude sur l'allégorie grecque* (Paris).

Lévi-Strauss, C. (1947). *Les Structures élémentaires de la parenté* (Paris).

Lieberg, G. (1973). 'Die Theologia tripertita in Forschung und Bezeugung', *ANRW* 1. 4. 63–115.

——(1982). *Poeta Creator: Studien zu einer Figur der antiken Dichtung* (Amsterdam).

——(1985). '*Poeta Creator*: Some "Religious" Aspects', *PLLS* 5. 23–32.

Liebeschuetz, J. H. W. G. (1979). *Continuity and Change in Roman Religion* (Oxford).

Liebing, H. (1953). *Die Aeneasgestalt bei Vergil* (Diss., Kiel).

Ligota, C. R. (1982). 'This Story is not True: Fact and Fiction in Antiquity', *JWI* 45. 1–13.

Lintott, A. W. (1971). 'Lucan and the History of the Civil War', *CQ* 65. 488–505.

Little, D. A. (1970). 'Richard Heinze: Ovids elegische Erzählung', in E. Zinn (ed.), *Ovids Ars amatoria und Remedia amoris: Untersuchungen zum Aufbau* (Stuttgart). 64–105.

Livrea, E. (ed.) (1973). *Apollonii Rhodii Argonauticon Liber Quartus* (Florence).

Lloyd-Jones, H. (1971). *The Justice of Zeus* (Berkeley and Los Angeles).

——(1984). 'A Hellenistic Miscellany', *SIFC* ser. 3. 2. 52–72.

Long, A. A. (1968). 'The Stoic Concept of Evil', *PhilosQ* 18. 329–43.

——and Sedley, D. N. (1987). *The Hellenistic Philosophers* (Cambridge).

Lorenz, G. (1968). *Vergleichende Interpretationen zu Silius Italicus und Statius* (Diss., Kiel).

Lucas, D. W. (ed.) (1968). *Aristotle: Poetics* (Oxford).

Luck, G. (1983). 'Naevius and Virgil', *ICS* 8. 267–75.

Lüthje, E. (1971). *Gehalt und Aufriss der Argonautica des Valerius Flaccus* (Diss., Kiel).

Lyne, R. O. A. M. (ed.) (1978). *Ciris* (Cambridge).

——(1983). 'Vergil and the Politics of War', *CQ*, NS 33. 188–203.

——(1984). 'Ovid's Metamorphoses, Callimachus, and l'art pour l'art', *MD* 12. 9–34.

——(1987). *Further Voices in Vergil's* Aeneid (Oxford).

Lynn-George, M. (1982). Review of Griffin (1980), *JHS* 102. 239–45.

——(1988). *Epos: Word, Narrative, and the* Iliad (Atlantic Highlands, N.J.).

MacDowell, D. M. (ed.) (1982). _Gorgias: Encomium of Helen_ (Bristol).

McGinty, P. (1978). 'Dionysos's Revenge and the Validation of the Hellenic World-View', _HThR_ 71. 77–94.

Mackail, J. W. (1912). 'Virgil's Use of the Word _Ingens_', _CR_ 26. 251–5.

McKeown, J. C. (1979). 'Ovid, _Amores_ 3. 12', _PLLS_ 2. 163–77.

——(ed.) (1989). _Ovid: Amores. Volume II. A Commentary on Book One_ (Leeds).

MacMullen, R. (1966). _Enemies of the Roman Order: Treason, Unrest, and Alienation in the Empire_ (Cambridge, Mass.).

——(1981). _Paganism in the Roman Empire_ (New Haven).

——(1984). _Christianizing the Roman Empire, A.D. 100–400_ (New Haven).

Maehler, H. (1963). _Die Auffassung des Dichterberufs im frühen Griechentum bis zur Zeit Pindars_ (Göttingen).

Makowski, J. F. (1977). '_Oracula Mortis_ in the _Pharsalia_', _CPh_ 72. 193–202.

March, J. R. (1987). _The Creative Poet: Studies on the Treatment of Myths in Greek Poetry_ (London).

Marg, W. (1968). 'Zur Behandlung des Augustus in den "Tristien" Ovids', in M. von Albrecht and E. Zinn (edd.), _Ovid_ (Darmstadt). 502–12.

Margolies, M. J. M. (1981). 'Apollonius' _Argonautica_: A Callimachean Epic', Ph. D. thesis (University of Colorado).

Mariotti, S. (1952). _Livio Andronico e la traduzione artistica_ (Milan).

——(1955). _Il Bellum Poenicum e l'arte di Nevio. Saggio con edizione dei frammenti del Bellum Poenicum_ (Rome).

Marrou, H.-I. (1948). _Histoire de l'éducation dans l'antiquité_ (Paris).

Marti, B. (1945). 'The Meaning of the Pharsalia', _AJPh_ 66. 352–76 = Rutz (1970), 103–32.

——(1964). 'Tragic History and Lucan's _Pharsalia_', in C. Henderson (ed.), _Classical, Medieval and Renaissance Studies in Honor of B. L. Ullman_ (Rome). 1. 165–204.

——(1975). 'Lucan's Narrative Techniques', _Parola del Passato_ 30. 74–90.

Martin, J. (1974). _Antike Rhetorik: Technik und Methode_ (Munich).

Martin, R. H., and Woodman, A. J. (edd.) (1989). *Tacitus: Annals Book 4* (Cambridge).

Martin, W. (1986). *Recent Theories of Narrative* (Ithaca, N.Y.).

Martindale, C. A. (1976). 'Paradox, Hyperbole and Literary Novelty in Lucan's *De Bello Civili*', *BICS* 23. 45–54.

——(1977). 'Three Notes on Lucan VI', *Mnemosyne* 30. 375–87.

——(1980). 'Lucan's *Nekuia*', in C. Deroux (ed.), *Studies in Latin Literature and Roman History* (Brussels). 367–77.

Masters, J. M. (1989). 'Poetry and Civil War in Lucan's *Bellum Civile*', Ph.D. thesis (Cambridge).

Matier, K. O. (1981). 'Prejudice and the *Punica*: Silius Italicus—A Reassessment', *AClass* 24. 141–51.

Mattingly, H. B. (1960). 'Naevius and the Metelli', *Historia* 9. 414–39.

Mayer, R. (ed.) (1981). *Lucan: Civil War VIII* (Warminster).

Mehmel, F. (1934). *Valerius Flaccus* (Diss., Hamburg).

Mellor, R. (1981). 'The Goddess Roma', *ANRW* 2. 17. 2. 950–1030.

Mendell, C. W. (1924). 'Silius the Reactionary', *PhQ* 3. 92–106.

Michaelis, J. (1875). *De Apollonii Rhodii Fragmentis* (Halle).

Mikalson, J. D. (1983). *Athenian Popular Religion* (Chapel Hill, N. C.).

Millar, F. (1977). *The Emperor and the Roman World (31 BC–AD 337)* (London).

Miniconi, P., and Devallet, G. (edd.) (1979). *Silius Italicus: La Guerre punique. I. Livres I–IV* (Paris).

Misgeld, W. (1968). *Rhianos von Bene und das historische Epos im Hellenismus* (Diss., Cologne).

Moisy, S. von (1971). *Untersuchungen zur Erzählweise in Statius' Thebais* (Bonn).

Momigliano, A. (1975). *Alien Wisdom: The Limits of Hellenization* (Cambridge).

——(1984a). 'Religion in Athens, Rome and Jerusalem in the first century B.C.', *ASNP* 3. 14. 873–92.

——(1984b). 'The Theological Efforts of the Roman Upper Classes in the First Century B.C.', *CPh* 79. 199–211.

Montanari, F. (1979). *Studi di filologia omerica antica* 1 (Pisa).

Moravcsik, J., and Temko, P. (edd.) (1982). *Plato on Beauty, Wisdom and the Arts* (Totowa, N.J.).

Morford, M. (1967). *The Poet Lucan: Studies in Rhetorical Epic* (Oxford).

Mosino, F. (1961). 'Teagenes di Regio', *Klearchos* 3. 75–80.

Most, G. W. (1989). 'Cornutus and Stoic Allegoresis: A Prelimary Report', *ANRW* 2. 36. 3. 2014–65.

Mozley, J. H. (ed.) (1928). *Statius* (Cambridge, Mass.).

Mühmelt, M. M. (1965). *Griechische Grammatik in der Vergilerklärung* (Munich).

Müller, D. (1987). 'Ovid, Iuppiter und Augustus. Gedanken zur Götterversammlung im ersten Buch der Metamorphosen', *Philologus* 131. 270–88.

Münzel, R. (1883). *De Apollodori περὶ θεῶν Libris* (Bonn).

Murrin, M. (1969). *The Veil of Allegory: Some Notes Towards a Theory of Allegorical Rhetoric in the English Renaissance* (Chicago).

——(1980). *The Allegorical Epic: Essays in its Rise and Decline* (Chicago).

Muth, R. (1978). 'Vom Wesen römischer "Religio" ', *ANRW* 2. 16. 1. 290–354.

Nadjo, L. (1987). 'Les Noms de l'épopée en latin et en français', in *Études de linguistique générale et de linguistique latine offertes en hommage à Guy Serbat* (Paris). 195–205.

Nagy, G. (1979). *The Best of the Achaeans: Concepts of the Hero in Archaic Greek Poetry* (Baltimore and London).

——(1989). 'Early Greek Views of Poets and Poetry', in Kennedy (1989). 1–77.

Narducci, E. (1979). *La Provvidenza crudele: Lucano e la distruzione dei miti augustei* (Pisa).

——(1980). 'Cesare e la patria (Ipotesi su *Phars.* 1. 185–92)', *Maia*, NS 32. 175–8.

——(1982). 'Cicerone poeta in Lucano', *MD* 7. 177–84.

Needham, R. (1972). *Belief, Language and Experience* (Oxford).

Neri, V. (1986). 'Dei, Fato e divinazione nella letteratura latina del I sec. d. C.', *ANRW* 2. 16. 3. 1974–2051.

Neschke, A. (1986). 'Erzählte und erlebte Götter. Zum Funktionswandel des griechischen Mythos in Ovids "Metamorphosen" ', in R. Faber and R. Schlesier (edd.), *Die Restauration der Götter: Antike Religion und Neo-Paganismus* (Würzburg). 133–52.

Nestle, W. (1942). *Vom Mythos zum Logos*² (Stuttgart).

Neville, J. W. (1977). 'Herodotus on the Trojan War', *G&R*, NS 24. 3–12.

Newman, K. J. (1967). *The Concept of Vates in Augustan Poetry* (Brussels).

——(1986). *The Classical Epic Tradition* (Madison, Wisc.).

Newsom, R. (1988). *A Likely Story: Probability and Play in Fiction* (New Brunswick, N.J.).

Nicol, J. (1936). *The Historical and Geographical Sources Used by Silius Italicus* (Oxford).

Nicoll, W. S. M. (1980). 'Cupid, Apollo, and Daphne (Ovid, *Met.* 1. 452 ff.)', *CQ*, NS 30. 174–82.

——(1988). 'The Sacrifice of Palinurus', *CQ*, NS 38. 459–72.

Nilsson, M. P. (1951). *Cults, Myths, Oracles and Politics in Ancient Greece* (Lund).

——(1967). *Geschichte der griechischen Religion* I³ (Munich).

Nisbet, R. G. M. (ed.) (1961). *M. Tulli Ciceronis In L. Calpurnium Pisonem* (Oxford).

——(1982). ' "Great and Lesser Bear" (Ovid, *Tristia* 4. 3)', *JRS* 72. 49–56.

——and Hubbard, M. (1970). *A Commentary on Horace: Odes Book I* (Oxford).

————(1978). *A Commentary on Horace Odes Book II* (Oxford).

Nock, A. D. (1972). *Essays on Religion and the Ancient World*, ed. Z. Stewart (Oxford).

Norden, E. (1898). *Die antike Kunstprosa* (Stuttgart).

——(1915). *Ennius und Vergilius. Kriegsbilder aus Roms grosser Zeit* (Leipzig and Berlin).

North, J. (1986). 'Religion and Politics, from Republic to Principate', *JRS* 76. 251–8.

Nugent, S. G. (1985). *Allegory and Poetics: The Structure and Imagery of Prudentius' 'Psychomachia'* (Frankfurt).

Ogilvie, R. M. (1970). *A Commentary on Livy Books 1–5*² (Oxford).

O'Hara, J. J. (1984). 'Fragment of a Homer-Hypothesis with No Gods', *ZPE* 56. 1–9.

O'Higgins, D. (1988). 'Lucan as *Vates*', *ClAnt* 7. 208–26.

Oksala, T. (1973). *Religion und Mythologie bei Horaz: Eine literarhistorische Untersuchung* (Helsinki).

Oliver, J. H. (1960). *Demokratia, the Gods, and the Free World* (Baltimore).

420    *Bibliography*

Onians, J. (1979). *Art and Thought in the Hellenistic Age: The Greek World View 350–50* BC (London).

Otis, B. (1963). *Virgil: A Study in Civilized Poetry* (Oxford).

——(1970). *Ovid as an Epic Poet*[2] (Cambridge).

Otto, A. (1890). *Die Sprichwörter und sprichwörtlichen Redensarten der Römer* (Leipzig).

Otto, W. F. (1954). *The Homeric Gods: The Spiritual Significance of Greek Religion*, tr. M. Hadas (London).

Paduano Faedo, L. (1970). 'L'inversione del rapporto Poeta-Musa nella cultura ellenistica', *ASNP* 39. 377–86.

Paoletti, L. (1963). 'Lucano magico e Virgilio', *A&R* 8. 11–26.

Parke, H. W. (1988). *Sibyls and Sibylline Prophecy in Classical Antiquity*, ed. B. C. McGing (London and New York).

——and Wormell, D. E. W. (1956). *The Delphic Oracle* (Oxford).

Parker, A. A. (1977). *Luis de Góngora: Polyphemus and Galatea. A Study in the Interpretation of a Baroque Poem* (Edinburgh).

Paschalis, M. (1986). 'Virgil and the Delphic Oracle', *Philologus* 130. 44–68.

Pasquali, G. (1964). *Orazio lirico*[2] (Florence).

Pavel, T. G. (1986). *Fictional Worlds* (Cambridge, Mass.).

Pease, A. S. (ed.) (1935). *P. Vergili Maronis Aeneidos Liber Quartus* (Cambridge, Mass.).

——(ed.) (1955–8). *M. Tulli Ciceronis De Natura Deorum* (Cambridge, Mass.).

Pépin, J. (1958). *Mythe et Allégorie: Les Origines grecques et les contestations judéo-chrétiennes* (Paris).

Petersen, L. (1939). *Zur Geschichte der Personifikation in griechischer Dichtung und bildender Kunst* (Würzburg).

Petrochilos, N. (1974). *Roman Attitudes to the Greeks* (Athens).

Pfeiffer, R. (1968). *History of Classical Scholarship from the Beginnings to the End of the Hellenistic Age* (Oxford).

Pfister, F. (1924). 'Epiphanie', *RE Supplb.* 4. 277–323.

Phillips, C. R. (1983). 'Rethinking Augustan Poetry', *Latomus* 42. 780–818.

Phillips, O. (1980). '*Aeole, namque tibi*', *Vergilius* 26. 18–26.

Piacentini, U. (1963). *Osservazioni sulla tecnica epica di Lucano* (Berlin).

Picard, G. Ch. (1954). *Les Religions de l'Afrique antique* (Paris).

Pichon, R. (1912). *Les Sources de Lucain* (Paris).

Pietrusiński, D. (1978). 'Apothéose d'Auguste par la comparaison avec les héros grecs chez Horace et Virgile', *Eos* 66. 249–66.

Platner, S. B., and Ashby, T. (1929). *Topographical Dictionary of Ancient Rome* (Oxford).

Podlecki, A. J. (1969). 'The Peripatetics as Literary Critics', *Phoenix* 23. 114–37.

Pohlenz, M. (1920). 'Die Anfänge der griechischen Poetik', *NGG*. 142–78.

——(1933). '*Tò πρέπον*. Ein Beitrag zur Geschichte des griechischen Geistes', *NGG*. 53–92.

——(1948). *Die Stoa. Geschichte einer geistiger Bewegung* (Göttingen).

Pollitt, J. J. (1986). *Art in the Hellenistic Age* (Cambridge).

Pöschl, V. (1962). *The Art of Vergil: Image and Symbol in the Aeneid*, tr. G. Seligson (Ann Arbor).

Pötscher, W. (1977). *Vergil und die göttlichen Mächte: Aspekte seiner Weltanschauung* (Hildesheim).

——(1978). 'Das römische Fatum — Begriff und Verwendung', *ANRW* 2. 16. 1. 393–424.

Préaux, C. (1978). *Le Monde hellenistique: la Grèce et l'Orient de la mort d'Alexandre à la conquête romaine de la Grèce (323–146 av. J. C.)* (Paris).

Preiswerk, R. (1934). 'Zeitgeschichtliches bei Valerius Flaccus', *Philologus* 89. 433–42.

Price, S. R. F. (1980). 'Between Man and God: Sacrifice in the Roman Imperial Cult', *JRS* 70. 28–43.

——(1984a). *Rituals and Power: The Roman Imperial Cult in Asia Minor* (Cambridge).

——(1984b). 'Gods and Emperors: The Greek Language of the Roman Imperial Cult', *JHS* 104. 79–95.

Pritchett, W. K. (1976). *The Greek State at War. Part III: Religion* (Berkeley and Los Angeles).

Proust, M. (1922). *Swann's Way. Part One*, tr. C. K. Scott Moncrieff (London).

Pucci, P. (1977). *Hesiod and the Language of Poetry* (Baltimore).

——(1979). 'The Song of the Sirens', *Arethusa* 12. 121–32.

Puglisi, G. (1985). '*Πλάσμα*: num *ψεῦδος* an *ἀπάτη*?', *Philologus* 129. 39–53.

Putnam, M. C. J. (1965). *The Poetry of the* Aeneid: *Four Studies in Imaginative Unity and Design* (Cambridge, Mass.).

Putnam, M. C. J. (1987). 'Daedalus, Virgil and the End of Art', *AJPh* 108. 173–98.

Quilligan, M. (1979). *The Language of Allegory: Defining the Genre* (Ithaca, N.Y.).

Quinn, K. (1968). *Virgil's Aeneid: A Critical Description* (London).

Rabbow, P. (1914). *Antike Schriften über Seelenheilung und Seelenleitung auf ihre Quellen untersucht, I. Die Therapie des Zorns* (Leipzig).

Radke, G. (1987). *Zur Entwicklung der Gottesvorstellung und der Gottesverehrung in Rom* (Darmstadt).

Ramaglia, L. (1952–3). 'La figura di Giunone nelle Puniche di Silio Italico', *RSC* 1. 35–43.

Rawson, E. (1985). *Intellectual Life in the Late Roman Republic* (London).

Reichenberger, S. (1891). *Die Entwicklung des metonymischen Gebrauchs von Götternamen in der griechischen Poesie bis zum Ende des alexandrinischen Zeitalters* (Karlsruhe).

Reinhardt, K. (1960a). *Tradition und Geist: Gesammelte Essays zur Dichtung*, ed. C. Becker (Göttingen).

——(1960b). 'Personifikation und Allegorie', in C. Becker (ed.), *Vermächtnis der Antike: Gesammelte Essays zur Philosophie und Geschichtsschreibung* (Göttingen). 7–40.

Reitz, C. (1982). *Die Nekyia in den Punica des Silius Italicus* (Frankfurt).

Renger, C. (1985). *Aeneas und Turnus: Analyse einer Feindschaft* (Frankfurt am Main).

Richardson, N. J. (ed.) (1974). *The Homeric Hymn to Demeter* (Oxford).

——(1975). 'Homeric Professors in the Age of the Sophists', *PCPhS*, NS 21. 65–81.

——(1980). 'Literary Criticism in the Exegetical Scholia to the *Iliad*: A Sketch', *CQ*, NS 30. 265–87.

——(1985). 'Pindar and Later Literary Criticism in Antiquity', *PLLS* 5. 383–401.

Richter, W. (1960). 'Das Epos des Gnaeus Naevius. Probleme der dichterischen Form', *NGG*. 40–66.

Rieks, R. (1967). *Homo, Humanus, Humanitas: Zur Humanität in der lateinischen Literatur des ersten nachchristlichen Jahrhunderts* (Munich).

Robinson, T. M. (ed.) (1979). *Contrasting Arguments: An Edition of the Dissoi Logoi* (New York).

Roemer, A. (1879). *Die exegetischen Scholien der Ilias im Codex Venetus B* (Munich).

——(1914). *Homerische Aufsätze* (Leipzig and Berlin).

——(1924). *Die Homerexegese Aristarchs in ihren Grundzügen dargestellt*, ed. E. Belzner (Paderborn).

Rollinson, P. (1981). *Classical Theories of Allegory and Christian Culture* (Pittsburgh).

Romilly, J. de (1973). 'Gorgias et le pouvoir de la poésie', *JHS* 93. 155–62.

Ronconi, A. (1973). *Interpreti latini di Omero* (Turin).

Rose, A. (1985). 'Clothing Imagery in Apollonius' *Argonautika*', *QUCC*, NS 21. 29–44.

Rosenmeyer, T. G. (1955). 'Gorgias, Aeschylus, and "Apate"', *AJPh* 76. 225–60.

——(1973). 'Design and Execution in Aristotle, *Poetics* ch. XXV', *CSCA* 6. 231–52.

——(1989). *Senecan Drama and Stoic Cosmology* (Berkeley and Los Angeles).

Rösler, W. (1980). 'Die Entdeckung der Fiktionalität in der Antike', *Poetica* 12. 283–319.

Ross, D. O. (1975). *Backgrounds to Augustan Poetry: Gallus, Elegy and Rome* (Cambridge).

——(1987). *Virgil's Elements: Physics and Poetry in the* Georgics (Princeton).

Rostagni, A. (1944). *Suetonio De Poetis e biografi minori* (Turin).

——(1955). *Scritti minori 1. Aesthetica* (Turin).

Rowell, H. T. (1947). 'The Original Form of Naevius' "Bellum Punicum"', *AJPh* 68. 21–46.

Rudd, W. J. N. (1986). 'The Idea of Empire in the *Aeneid*', in R. A. Cardwell and J. Hamilton (edd.), *Virgil in a Cultural Tradition: Essays to Celebrate the Bimillenium* (Nottingham). 28–42.

Russell, D. A. (1964). *'Longinus': On the Sublime* (Oxford).

——(1981). *Criticism in Antiquity* (London).

——and Winterbottom, M. (1972). *Ancient Literary Criticism: The Principal Texts in New Translations* (London).

Ruthrof, H. (1981). *The Reader's Construction of Narrative* (London).

Ruthven, K. K. (1979). *Critical Assumptions* (Cambridge).

Rutz, W. (1963). 'Die Träume des Pompeius in Lucans Pharsalia', *Hermes* 91. 334–45 = Rutz (1970), 509–24.

——(1964–5). 'Lucan 1943–1963', *Lustrum* 9. 243–334, 10. 246–56.

——(ed.) (1970). *Lucan* (Darmstadt).

——(1984–5*a*). 'Lucan 1964–1983', *Lustrum* 26. 105–203, 27. 149–66.

——(1985*b*). 'Lucans *Pharsalia* im Lichte der neuesten Forschung (mit einem bibliographischen Nachtrag 1980 bis 1985 von H. Tuitje)', *ANRW* 2. 32. 3. 1457–537.

Sandbach, F. H. (1975). *The Stoics* (London).

Sanford, E. M. (1931). 'Lucan and his Roman Critics', *CPh* 26. 233–57.

Sauter, F. (1934). *Der römische Kaiserkult bei Martial und Statius* (Stuttgart).

Scaffai, M. (1986). 'Rassegno di studi su Valerio Flacco (1938–1982)', *ANRW* 2. 32. 4. 2359–447.

Schaerer, R. (1944). 'Sur deux vers de Virgile: Dieu sujet et dieu attribut', in *Mélanges offerts à M. Niedermann à l'occasion de son soixante-dixième anniversaire* (Neuchâtel).

Schefold, K. (1966). *Myth and Legend in Early Greek Art*, tr. A. Hicks (London).

——(1975). *Wort und Bild: Studien zur Gegenwart der Antike*, ed. E. Berger and H. C. Ackermann (Basel).

Scheid, J. (1985). *Religion et piété à Rome* (Paris).

Schenkeveld, D. M. (1976). 'Strabo on Homer', *Mnemosyne* 29. 52–64.

Schetter, W. (1960). *Untersuchungen zur epischen Kunst des Statius* (Wiesbaden).

Schilling, R. (1954). *La Religion romaine de Vénus depuis les origines jusqu'au temps d'Auguste* (Paris).

Schlunk, R. R. (1974). *The Homeric Scholia and the* Aeneid: *A Study of the Influence of Ancient Literary Criticism on Vergil* (Ann Arbor).

Schmid, G. B. (1982). *Die Beurteilung der Helena in der frühgriechischen Literatur* (Freiburg).

Schmidt, M. (1976). *Die Erklärung zum Weltbild Homers und zur Kultur der Heroenzeit in den bT-Scholien zur Ilias* (Munich).

Schönberger, O. (1958). 'Zu Lucan. Ein Nachtrag', *Hermes* 86. 230–9 = Rutz (1970), 486–97.

——(1965). 'Zum Weltbild der drei Epiker nach Lucan', *Helikon* 5. 123–45.

Schotes, H. A. (1969). *Stoische Physik, Psychologie und Theologie bei Lucan* (Bonn).

Schrader, H. (ed.) (1880–2). *Porphyrii Quaestionum Homericarum ad Iliadem Pertinentium Reliquiae* (Leipzig).

——(ed.) (1890). *Porphyrii Quaestionum Homericarum ad Odysseam Pertinentium Reliquiae* (Leipzig).

Schrader, J. (1893). *Palaephatea* (Berlin).

Schrempp, O. (1964). *Prophezeiung und Rückschau in Lucans Bellum Civile* (Diss., Winterthur).

Schubert, W. (1984). *Jupiter in den Epen der Flavierzeit* (Frankfurt).

Schwabl, H. (1962). 'Weltschöpfung', *RE* Suppl. 9. 1433–589.

——(1978). 'Zeus', *RE* Suppl. 15. 993–1481, with J. Schindler (999–1001) and S. Hiller (1001–9).

Scott, K. (1930). 'Emperor Worship in Ovid', *TAPhA* 61. 43–69.

Segal, C. P. (1969). *Landscape in Ovid's Metamorphoses: A Study in the Transformations of a Literary Symbol* (Wiesbaden).

——(1981). 'Art and the Hero: Participation, Detachment, and Narrative Point of View in *Aeneid* 1', *Arethusa* 14. 67–83.

——(1985). 'Archaic Choral Lyric', *CHCL* 1. 165–201.

——(1986). *Pindar's Mythmaking: The Fourth Pythian Ode* (Princeton).

Seltman, C. (1933). *Greek Coins. A History of Metallic Currency and Coinage down to the Fall of the Hellenistic Kingdoms* (London).

Semple, W. H. (1959–60). 'The Conclusion of Virgil's *Aeneid*: A Study of the War in Latium, with Special Reference to Books XI and XII', *BRL* 42. 175–93.

Shackleton Bailey, D. R. (1987). 'Lucan Revisited', *PCPhS*, NS 33. 74–91.

Shapiro, H. A. (1980). 'Jason's Cloak', *TAPhA* 110. 263–86.

Sheets, G. A. (1981). 'The Dialect Gloss, Hellenistic Poetics and Livius Andronicus', *AJPh* 102. 58–78.

Shelton, J. E. (1974–5). 'The Storm Scene in Valerius Flaccus', *CJ* 70. 14–22.

Silk, M. S. (1985). 'Heracles and Greek Tragedy', *G&R*, NS 32. 1–22.

Skulsky, H. (1981). *Metamorphosis: The Mind in Exile* (Cambridge, Mass.).

Skutsch, O. (1968). *Studia Enniana* (London).

——(1985). (ed.) *The Annals of Quintus Ennius* (Oxford).

Smolenaars, J. J. L. (1987). 'Labour in the Golden Age: A Unifying Theme in Vergil's Poems', *Mnemosyne* 40. 391–405.

Snell, B. (1967). 'Ezechiels Moses-Drama', *A&A* 13. 150–64.

Snijder, H. (ed.) (1968). P. *Papinius Statius, Thebaid: A Commentary on Book III* (Amsterdam).

Solodow, J. B. (1988). *The World of Ovid's* Metamorphoses (Chapel Hill, N.C.).

Soverini, P. (1985). 'Il problema delle teorie retoriche e poetiche di Petronio', *ANRW* 2. 32. 3. 1706–79.

Stallbaum, G. (ed.) (1825–6). *Eustathii Commentarii ad Homeri Odysseam* (Leipzig).

Steadman, J. M. (1985). *The Wall of Paradise: Essays on Milton's Poetics* (Baton Rouge).

Steele, R. B. (1930). 'The Interrelation of Latin Poets under Domitian', *CPh* 25. 328–42.

Steiner, H. R. (1952). *Der Traum in der Aeneis* (Bern).

Steinmetz, P. (1966). 'Xenophanesstudien', *RhM* 109. 13–73.

Stewart, A. F. (1985). 'History, Myth, and Allegory in the Program of the Temple of Athena Nike, Athens', in H. L. Kessler and M. S. Simpson (edd.), *Pictorial Narrative in Antiquity and the Middle Ages: Studies in the History of Art* 16 (Hanover and London). 53–73.

Stewart, D. J. (1972–3). 'Mortality, Morality and the Public Life. Aeneas the Politician', *Antioch Review* 32. 649–64.

Stinton, T. C. W. (1976). ' "Si credere dignum est": Some Expressions of Disbelief in Euripides and Others', *PCPhS*, NS 22. 60–89.

Stirrup, B. C. (1981). 'Ovid: Poet of Imagined Reality', *Latomus* 40. 88–104.

Strand, J. (1972). *Notes on Valerius Flaccus' Argonautica* (Göteborg).

Strasburger, H. (1972). *Homer und die Geschichtsschreibung* (Heidelberg).

Stroh, W. (1971). *Die römische Liebeselegie als werbende Dichtung* (Amsterdam).

Strong, D. (1988). *Roman Art*[2], ed. R. Ling, prepared for press by J. M. C. Toynbee (Harmondsworth).

Strzelecki, L. (1935). *De Naeviano Belli Punici Carmine Quaestiones Selectae* (Cracow).

Sturt, N. J. H. (1978). 'The Simile of *Punica* 14. 189–91', *CJ* 74. 19–21.

Suerbaum, W. (1980–1). 'Hundert Jahre Vergil-Forschung: Eine systematische Arbeitsbibliographie mit besonderer Berücksichtigung der Aeneis', *ANRW* 2. 31. 1. 3–358, 2. 31. 2. 1359–99.

Sullivan, J. P. (1985). *Literature and Politics in the Age of Nero* (Ithaca, N.Y.).

Summers, W. C. (1894). *A Study of the Argonautica of Valerius Flaccus* (Cambridge).

Syme, R. (1958). *Tacitus* (Oxford).

——(1978). *History in Ovid* (Oxford).

Syndikus, H. P. (1958). *Lucans Gedicht vom Bürgerkrieg: Untersuchungen zur epischen Technik und zu den Grundlagen des Werkes* (Diss., Munich).

Tate, J. (1927). 'The Beginnings of Greek Allegory', *CR* 41. 214–15.

——(1929). 'Cornutus and the Poets', *CQ* 23. 41–5.

——(1930). 'Plato and Allegorical Interpretation', *CQ* 24. 1–10.

——(1934). 'On the History of Allegorism', *CQ* 28. 105–14.

Taylor, L. R. (1931). *The Divinity of the Roman Emperor* (Middletown).

Thalmann, W. G. (1984). *Conventions of Form and Thought in Early Greek Epic Poetry* (Baltimore).

Thierfelder, A. (1934). 'Der Dichter Lucan', *Archiv für Kulturgeschichte* 25. 1–20 = Rutz (1970), 50–69.

Thomas, E. (1976). *Mythos und Geschichte: Untersuchungen zum historischen Gehalt griechischer Mythendarstellungen* (Diss., Cologne).

Thomas, R. F. (1986). 'Virgil's *Georgics* and the Art of Reference', *HSCPh* 90. 171–98.

——(ed.) (1988). *Virgil: Georgics* (Cambridge).

Thompson, D. L. (1981). 'The Meetings of the Roman Senate on the Palatine', *AJA* 85. 335–9.

Thornton, A. (1976). *The Living Universe: Gods and Men in Vergil's Aeneid* (Leiden).

Timpanaro, S. (1948). 'Per una nuova edizione critica di Ennio: 7–11', *SIFC*, NS 23. 5–58.

Todorov, T. (1973). *The Fantastic: A Structural Approach to a Literary Genre*, tr. R. Howard (Cleveland).

Toynbee, A. J. (1965). *Hannibal's Legacy: The Hannibalic War's Effects on Roman Life* (Oxford).

Tremoli, P. (1968). *Religiosità e irreligiosità nel Bellum Civile di Lucano* (Trieste).

Tsirimbas, B. (1936). *Die Stellung der Sophistik zur Poesie im V. und IV. Jahrhundert bis zu Isokrates* (Munich).

Turolla, E. (1956). 'La poesia epica di Papinio Stazio', *Orpheus* 3. 134–51.

Untersteiner, M. (1955). *Senofane: Testimonianze e frammenti* (Florence).

Vahlen, I. (ed.) (1903). *Ennianae Poesis Reliquiae*[2] (Leipzig).

Valk, H. M. H. A. van der (1963–4). *Researches on the Text and Scholia of the Iliad* (Leiden).

——(ed.) (1971–87). *Eustathii Commentarii ad Homeri Iliadem Pertinentes* (Leiden).

Vallauri, G. (ed.). (1956) *Euemero di Messene. Testimonianze e frammenti con introduzione e commento* (Turin).

Van Dyke, C. (1985). *The Fiction of Truth: Structures of Meaning in Narrative and Dramatic Allegory* (Ithaca, N.Y.).

Vendler, H. (1989). 'Four prized poets', *New York Review of Books* 36 no. 13 (17 August). 26–30.

Venini, P. (1961). 'Studi sulla Tebaide di Stazio. La composizione', *RIL* 95. 55–88, 96–109.

——(ed.) (1970). *P. Papini Stati Thebaidos Liber Undecimus* (Florence).

Verdenius, W. J. (1981). 'Gorgias' Doctrine of Deception', in G. B. Kerferd (ed.), *The Sophists and Their Legacy* (Wiesbaden). 116–28.

Vermeule, E. (1979). *Aspects of Death in Early Greek Art and Poetry* (Berkeley and Los Angeles).

Vernant, J.-P. (1965). *Mythe et pensée chez les grecs* (Paris).

——(1980). *Myth and Society in Ancient Greece*, tr. J. Lloyd (London).

——and Vidal-Naquet, P. (1973). *Mythe et tragédie en Grèce ancienne* (Paris).

Vessey, D. W. T. C. (1973). *Statius and the Thebaid* (Cambridge).

——(1974). 'Silius Italicus on the Fall of Saguntum', *CPh* 69. 28–36.

——(1982). 'Flavian Epic', *CHCL* 2. 558–96.

Veyne, P. (1983). *Les Grecs ont-ils cru à leurs mythes? Essai sur l'imagination constituante* (Paris).

——(1986). 'Une évolution du paganisme gréco-romain: injustice et piété des dieux, leurs ordres ou "oracles" ', *Latomus* 45. 259–83.

Vian, F. (1951). *Répertoire des gigantomachies figurées dans l'art grec et romain* (Paris).

——(1952). *La Guerre des géants: le mythe avant l'époque hellénistique* (Paris).

——(1973). 'Notes critiques au chant II des *Argonautiques* d' Apollonios de Rhodes', *REA* 75. 82–110.

——and Delage, E. (edd.) (1976–81). *Apollonios de Rhodes: Argonautiques* (Paris).

Vidal, G. (1987). *Empire* (Ballantine Books, New York).

Visser, C. E. (1938). *Götter und Kulte in Ptolemäischen Alexandrien* (Amsterdam).

Vogt, J. (1943). *Vom Reichsgedanken der Römer* (Leipzig).

Wagenvoort, H. (1980). *Pietas: Selected Studies in Roman Religion* (Leiden).

Walbank, F. W. (1957). *A Historical Commentary on Polybius: I–VI* (Oxford).

——(1960). 'History and Tragedy', *Historia* 9. 216–34.

——(1972). *Polybius* (Berkeley and Los Angeles).

——(1981). *The Hellenistic World* (Glasgow).

Wallace-Hadrill, A. (1982*a*). 'The Golden Age and Sin in Augustan Ideology', *Past and Present* 95. 19–36.

——(1982*b*). 'Civilis Princeps: Between Citizen and King', *JRS* 72. 32–48.

——(1986). 'Image and Authority in the Coinage of Augustus', *JRS* 76. 66–87.

Wallis, R. T. (1986). 'The Spiritual Importance of Not Knowing', in Armstrong (1986). 460–80.

Walsh, G. B. (1984). *The Varieties of Enchantment: Early Greek Views of the Nature and Function of Poetry* (Chapel Hill, N.C.).

Walsh, P. G. (ed.) (1973). *Titi Livi Ab Urbe Condita, Liber XXI* (London).

Walton, K. (1978). 'How Remote are Fictional Worlds from the Real World?', *The Journal of Aesthetics and Criticism* 37. 11–23.

Ward, M. M. (1933). 'The Association of Augustus with Jupiter', *SMSR* 9. 203–24.

Wardman, A. E. (1960). 'Myth in Greek Historiography', *Historia* 9. 403–13.

430    Bibliography

Wardman, A. E. (1976). *Rome's Debt to Greece* (London).
——(1982). *Religion and Statecraft among the Romans* (London).
Warmington, B. H. (1969). *Carthage*[2] (London).
Waszink, J. H. (1957). 'Zur ersten Satire des Lucilius', *WS* 70. 323–8.
——(1972). 'Anfangsstadium der römischen Literatur', *ANRW* 1. 2. 869–927.
Waugh, P. (1984). *Metafiction: The Theory and Practice of Self-Conscious Fiction* (London).
Wehrli, F. (1928). *Zur Geschichte der allegorischen Deutung Homers im Altertum* (Zurich).
Weinstock, S. (1927). 'Die platonische Homerkritik und ihre Nachwirkung', *Philologus* 82. 121–53.
——(1957). 'Victor and Invictus', *HThR* 50. 211–47.
——(1971). *Divus Julius* (Oxford).
Wendel, C. (ed.) (1935). *Scholia in Apollonium Rhodium Vetera* (Berlin).
West, M. L. (ed.) (1966). *Hesiod: Theogony* (Oxford).
——(ed.) (1978). *Hesiod: Works and Days* (Oxford).
——(1983). *The Orphic Poems* (Oxford).
Wetzel, S. (1957). *Die Gestalt der Medea bei Valerius Flaccus* (Diss., Kiel).
Whitby, M., Hardie, P., and Whitby, M. (edd.) (1987). *Homo Viator: Classical Essays for John Bramble* (Bristol).
White, P. (1988). 'Julius Caesar in Augustan Rome', *Phoenix* 42. 334–56.
Whitman, J. (1987). *Allegory: The Dynamics of an Ancient and Medieval Technique* (Oxford).
Wilkinson, L. P. (1955). *Ovid Recalled* (Cambridge).
Willcock, M. M. (1964). 'Mythological Paradeigma in the *Iliad*', *CQ*, NS 14. 141–54.
Williams, G. W. (1968). *Tradition and Originality in Roman Poetry* (Oxford).
——(1978). *Change and Decline: Roman Literature in the Early Empire* (Berkeley and Los Angeles).
——(1983). *Technique and Ideas in the* Aeneid (New Haven).
Williams, R. D. (ed.) (1960). *P. Vergili Maronis Aeneidos Liber Quintus* (Oxford).
——(ed.) (1972). *P. Papini Statii Thebaidos Liber Decimus* (Leiden).

——(ed.) (1973). *The Aeneid of Virgil* (London).

Wilson, C. H. (1979). 'Jupiter and the Fates in the *Aeneid*', *CQ*, NS 29. 361–71.

Wilson, N. G. (1969). Review of Pfeiffer (1968), *CR*, NS 19. 366–72.

Wimmel, W. (1960). *Kallimachos in Rom: Die Nachfolge seines apologetischen Dichtens in der Augusteerzeit* (Wiesbaden).

Winterbottom, M. (ed.) (1974). *The Elder Seneca: Declamations* (Cambridge, Mass.).

Wipprecht, F. (1892). *Quaestiones Palaephateae* (Heidelberg).

——(1902). *Zur Entwicklung der rationalistischen Mythendeutung bei den Griechen* 1 (Tübingen).

Wiseman, T. P. (1974*a*). *Cinna the Poet and Other Roman Essays* (Leicester).

——(1974*b*). 'Legendary Genealogies in Late-Republican Rome', *G&R*, NS 21. 153–64.

——(1979). *Clio's Cosmetics: Three Studies in Greco-Roman Literature* (Leicester).

——(1984). 'Cybele, Virgil and Augustus', in Woodman and West (1984). 117–28.

——(1985). *Catullus and His World: A Reappraisal* (Cambridge).

——(1989). 'Roman Legend and Oral Tradition', review of Bremmer and Horsfall (1987), *JRS* 79. 129–37.

Wissowa, G. (1912). *Religion und Kultus der Römer*[2] (Munich).

Wlosok, A. (1967). *Die Göttin Venus in Vergils Aeneis* (Heidelberg).

——(1983). 'Vergil als Theologe: Iuppiter-pater omnipotens', *Gymnasium* 90. 187–202.

Woodman, A. J. (ed.) (1977). *Velleius Paterculus: The Tiberian Narrative* (Cambridge).

——(1988). *Rhetoric in Classical Historiography: Four Studies* (London and Sydney).

——and West, D. (edd.) (1984). *Poetry and Politics in the Age of Augustus* (Cambridge).

Wülfing-von Martitz, P. (1972). 'Ennius als hellenistischer Dichter', in *Ennius*, Fondation Hardt, *Entretiens* 17. 252–89.

Wünsch, W. (1949). *Das Bild des Cato von Utica in der Literatur der neronischen Zeit* (Diss., Warburg).

Wüst, E. (1958). 'Von den Anfängen des Problems der Willensfreiheit', *RhM* 101. 75–91.

Wyss, B. (ed.) (1936). *Antimachi Colophonii Reliquiae* (Berlin).

Young, D. C. (1983). 'Pindar, Aristotle, and Homer: A Study in Ancient Criticism', *ClAnt* 2. 156–70.

Yunis, H. (1988). *A New Creed: Fundamental Religious Beliefs in the Athenian Polis and Euripidean Drama* (Göttingen).

Zagagi, N. (1985). 'Helen of Troy: Encomium and Apology', *WS* N.F. 19. 63–88.

Zanker, G. (1987). *Realism in Alexandrian Poetry: A Literature and its Audience* (London and Sydney).

Zanker, P. (1988). *The Power of Images in the Age of Augustus* (Ann Arbor).

Zecchini, G. (1987). *Il Carmen de Bello Actiaco: storiografia e lotta politica in età augustea* (Stuttgart).

Zetzel, J. E. G. (1974). 'Ennian Experiments', *AJPh* 95. 137–40.

——(1980). 'Two Imitations in Lucan', *CQ*, NS 30. 257.

——(1981). *Latin Textual Criticism in Antiquity* (New York).

Ziegler, K. (1966). *Das hellenistische Epos*[2] (Leipzig).

Zumwalt, N. (1977). 'Fama Subversa: Theme and Structure in Ovid *Metamorphoses* 12', *CSCA* 10. 209–22.

Zwierlein, O. (1982). 'Der Ruhm der Dichtung bei Ennius und seinen Nachfolgern', *Hermes* 110. 84–102.

——(1986). 'Lucans Caesar in Troja', *Hermes* 114. 460–78.

# Index of Passages and Works Discussed

# General Index

CPSIA information can be obtained
at www.ICGtesting.com
Printed in the USA
BVHW08s2025100818
524210BV00001B/9/P